Learning and Memory

Learning and Memory

William C. Gordon
University of New Mexico

Brooks/Cole Publishing Company
Pacific Grove, California

Brooks/Cole Publishing Company
A Division of Wadsworth, Inc.

Printed in the United States of America

10 9 8 7 6 5 4 3 2

Library of Congress Cataloging in Publication Data
Gordon, William C.
Learning and memory / William C. Gordon.
p. cm.
Bibliography: p.
Includes index.
ISBN 0-534-09498-8
1. Learning, Psychology of. 2. Memory. 3. Conditioned response.
I. Title.
BF318.G67 1988
153.1—dc19 88-23229
CIP

Sponsoring Editor: *Phil Curson*
Marketing Representative: *Tamy Stenquist*
Editorial Assistant: *Amy Mayfield*
Production Editor: *Penelope Sky*
Production Assistant: *Dorothy Bell*
Manuscript Editor: *Brenda Griffing*
Permissions Editor: *Carline Haga*
Interior and Cover Design: *Roy R. Neuhaus*
Cover Illustration: *Roy R. Neuhaus*
Art Coordinator: *Lisa Torri*
Interior Illustration: *Precision Graphics*
Typesetting: *Kachina Typesetting, Inc., Tempe, Arizona*
Printing and Binding: *The Maple–Vail Book Manufacturing Group, Binghampton, New York*

Credits continue on p. 341

To Kathy, Jason, and Scott, with great affection

Preface

During the last twenty years there have been dramatic changes in the field of learning and memory. First, empirical research has resulted in a greatly enlarged common pool of information. Second, there has been a decided change in the dominant kinds of theoretical approaches and even in the philosophies that guide research in this area. We have thus seen changes in the types of questions researchers ask, in the kinds of paradigms they use, and even in the language experimenters use to characterize their findings.

There is little doubt that many of these developments enhance our understanding of learning and memory processes. Still, these advances have not come without some cost. As our field has grown and become more diverse, it is increasingly difficult simply to keep abreast of our expanding research literature. It is also more challenging to integrate the topics in our field into a meaningful course of study for our students.

In response to these difficulties, some psychology programs no longer offer a unified learning and memory course to beginning undergraduate students, providing two separate courses instead. One of these courses typically focuses on basic learning processes in non-human species, while the other tends to concentrate on memory and cognition in humans. Often, in such courses the issues and theoretical approaches that are described overlap very little. In such programs, the study of learning and the study of memory are in effect treated as very separate areas of inquiry.

My own belief is that this approach is unfortunate for students who are just beginning their study of learning and memory. Students exposed to this approach sometimes fail to understand that basic conditioning processes play a critical role in the life and behavior of a human being. They can also form the misconception that complex memory processes are important for humans, but not for other species. Similarly, the divided approach can foster the idea that learning may be studied only within a behavioral framework, and that memory can be conceptualized only from a cognitive perspective. Finally, when students are introduced to learning and memory separately, they often fail to see how research in one area has an effect on research in the other.

Because of these potential difficulties, I have always believed that students should be exposed to an integrated learning and memory course at the beginning undergraduate level. This book was written with just such a course in mind. The first six chapters are about basic learning processes. Except for Chapter 6, on verbal list learning, this section is based on data gathered primarily from non-human subjects. Still, I have included numerous examples of how conditioning influences the behaviors of humans, and I show how our ideas about learning have evolved from a confluence of behavioral and cognitive approaches. The concept of memory, which is discussed at length later in the book, is introduced in these chapters in the context of contemporary conditioning models.

With basic learning processes well established, in Chapter 7 I discuss generalization, discrimination, and concept learning. These topics are covered in one chapter because I wished to demonstrate that data and theory in one area can contribute to the evolution of ideas in another. In this chapter I examine generalization and discrimination learning data gathered primarily from non-human organisms, and then show how theories about these data have influenced our thinking about concept learning in humans. The chapter ends with a discussion of contemporary human concept learning theories that have generated interest in the ways non-human species learn natural concepts.

Chapters 8–11 are concerned with different aspects of memory research. Chapter 8 is about the processes that are involved in the formation of a memory, and in Chapter 9 we ask questions about memory codes and organization of memory. In Chapter 10 we take an in-depth look at the retrieval process, and in Chapter 11 I offer an analysis of forgetting theories. Much of the material discussed in the memory chapters is necessarily based on research with human subjects. However, each of these chapters concludes by examining related kinds of memory studies that have been carried out with non-human organisms.

This book offers undergraduate students a clear and comprehensible integration of varied achievements in the field of learning and memory. Both classic and contemporary studies are cited throughout the text. Ample illustrations enable students to see how certain paradigms or findings actually look.

Acknowledgments

In developing this book I owed a great deal to a number of individuals. First and foremost, I note the contributions of students who have taken my own learning and memory course.

Several of them used earlier versions of this text and their comments, suggestions, and even demands contributed greatly to the readability of the final version. Their suggestions also helped me refine my discussion of certain concepts.

I have also benefited greatly from discussing various topics with my colleagues. I especially thank Michael Dougher, Henry Ellis, Robert Grice, Robin Jacobvitz, Peder Johnson, Frank Logan, and Ralph Miller, who were invaluable in helping clarify issues and in pointing out pertinent research literature.

I also appreciate those specialists who were kind enough to review earlier versions of this manuscript. They offered sound suggestions and constructive criticisms without destroying my confidence altogether. For their patience and their efforts I thank John Anson, Stephen F. Austin State University; John Capaldi, Purdue University; Stephen Davis, Emporia State University; Steven D. Falkenberg, Eastern Kentucky University; John Jahnke, Miami University; Henry Loess, College of Wooster; John Mueller, University of Missouri; Charles Richman, Wake Forest University; Michael Scavio, California State University, Fullerton; and Robert Schneider, Metro State College.

Finally, I would like to thank C. Deborah Laughton, Phil Curson, Penelope Sky, and the entire Brooks/Cole staff for their encouragement and guidance throughout the planning and development of the book. Only my wife Kathryn, who read every page, decoded my garbled sentences, and helped me type the manuscript, was more instrumental than they in bringing this project to fruition.

William C. Gordon

Brief Contents

1 Learning and Memory: An Introduction 1

2 Classical Conditioning: Learning About Stimuli as Signals 13

3 Classical Conditioning: Theoretical Issues 47

4 Instrumental/Operant Conditioning: Learning About the Consequences of Responding 71

5 Instrumental and Operant Conditioning: Theoretical Issues 103

6 Verbal Learning and Transfer 135

7 Generalization, Discrimination and Concept Learning 167

8 Memory Processes: The Formation of a Representation 195

9 Memory Codes and Organization 229

10 Memory Processes: Retrieval 261

11 Forgetting 289

Contents

1 Learning and Memory: An Introduction 1

Learning as an Adaptive Mechanism 2
Defining the Term "Learning" 5
Types of Learning Situations 7
The Concept of Memory 8
Topics Studied by Memory Researchers 10
Philosophical Differences in the Study of Learning and Memory 11

2 Classical Conditioning: Learning About Stimuli as Signals 13

The Concept of Contingency 14

Methods for Studying Classical Excitatory Conditioning 16
Pavlov's Original Experiments 16
Other Classical Conditioning Paradigms 17
Variables That Affect Excitatory Conditioning 22
The Physical Relationship between the CS and US 22
Characteristics of the CS and the US 27
The Presence of Other Stimuli during Conditioning 32
Conditioning without an Explicit US 36
Classical Inhibitory Conditioning 38
Problems in Measuring the Inhibitory CR 39
Conditions That Promote Inhibitory Conditioning 40
Extinction 43
Summary Statements 44

3 Classical Conditioning: Theoretical Issues 47

The Necessary and Sufficient Conditions for CR Development 49
Contiguity Theory: Basic Assumptions 49
Contiguity Theory: The Evidence 50
Contingency Theory: Basic Assumptions 51
The Formal Expression of the Rescorla-Wagner Model 53
Contingency Theory: The Evidence 55
What is Associated in Classical Conditioning? 62
Stimulus-Response or Stimulus-Stimulus Associations? 62
Evidence concerning the Elements in an Association 63
The Role of Context in Conditioning 66
Contextual Stimuli as CSs 67
Evidence for Contextual Stimuli as CSs 68
Contextual Stimuli as Cues for the CS-US Relationship 69
Evidence That Context May Serve as a Cue for a Specific CS-US Relationship 69
Conclusions about Contextual Stimuli 70
Summary Statements 70

4 Instrumental/Operant Conditioning: Learning about the Consequences of Responding 71

Consequences of Responding 72

Paradigms for Studying Instrumental/Operant Conditioning 73
The Instrumental-Operant Distinction 73
Instrumental Conditioning Paradigms 74
Escape and Avoidance Paradigms 76
Operant Conditioning Paradigms 78
Measuring Instrumental and Operant Responses in Humans 79
The Shaping Procedure 79
The Development of Superstitious Behavior 80
Variables That Affect Instrumental Responding 81
Positive Reinforcement Situations 81
Negative Reinforcement Situations: Escape Learning 85
Negative Reinforcement Situations: Avoidance Learning 85
Punishment Situations 88
Variables That Affect Operant Responding 91
Schedules of Reinforcement 92
Extinction 96
Variables That Affect Extinction of Positively Reinforced Responses 97
Variables That Affect Extinction of Negatively Reinforced Responses 99
Summary Statements 101

5 Instrumental/Operant Conditioning: Theoretical Issues 103

The Nature of Reinforcement 104
Primary and Secondary Reinforcers 104
Theories of Primary Reinforcement 105
Conclusions about Primary Reinforcement Theories 112
The Role of Reinforcement in Instrumental and Operant Conditioning 112
Reinforcement as a Necessary Condition for Stimulus-Response Associations 112
Reinforcement as a Motivator for Responding 115
Reinforcement as an Element in the Instrumental Association 119
Theories of Extinction 120
Amsel's Frustration Theory: A Competing Response Hypothesis 121
Capaldi's Sequential Theory: A Generalization Decrement Hypothesis 122

Reinforcement in Avoidance Learning 126
The Two-Factor Theory 127
A Cognitive Theory of Avoidance Learning 131
Summary Statements 133

6 Verbal Learning and Transfer 135
Methods for Studying Verbal Learning 136
The Paradigms 136
The Verbal Items 138
Tests for Learning 139
Variables That Influence Verbal Learning 140
Procedural Variables 140
Characteristics of the Verbal Items 146
Subject Strategies 150
Transfer Effects in Verbal Learning 158
Non-Specific Transfer 159
Specific Transfer 160
Summary Statements 165

7 Generalization, Discrimination, and Concept Learning 167
Stimulus Generalization 169
Methods for Studying Generalization in the Laboratory 169
Variables That Affect Stimulus Generalization 171
The Basis for Generalization Gradients 177
Discrimination Learning 180
Spence: A Continuity Theory of Discrimination Learning 181
Noncontinuity Theories: The Concept of Attention in Discrimination Learning 182
Two Tests of the Noncontinuity Position 183
Conclusions 185
Concept Learning 185
Associations as the Basis for Concept Learning 187
Natural versus Laboratory Concepts 190
Prototype or Exemplar Theories of Concept Formation 191
Natural Concepts in Nonhuman Species 193
Summary Statements 193

8 Memory Processes: The Formation of a Representation 195

Information Processing: The Computer Analogy 196

The Atkinson-Shiffrin Model 198

Evidence Supporting the Atkinson-Shiffrin Model 201

- Evidence for the Existence of Sensory Memory 201
- Evidence for Selection by Attentional Mechanisms 206
- Evidence for a Separate Short-Term Memory Store 211

The Levels of Processing Approach 216

- Evidence Supporting the Levels of Processing Approach 220
- Current Status of the Levels of Processing Approach 220

Models of Memory Formation in Nonhuman Species 223

- Consolidation Theory 224
- Active and Inactive Memories 225

Summary Statements 227

9 Memory Codes and Organization 229

Memory Codes 230

- Codes Used in Short-Term Memory 230
- Codes Used in Long-Term, Permanent Memory 236

The Organization of Long-Term Memory 247

- Tulving's Episodic-Semantic Distinction 248
- The Organization of Semantic Memory 250

Memory Representation in Nonhuman Species 257

Summary Statements 259

10 Memory Processes: Retrieval 261

Retrieval of Short-Term Memories 262

- Sternberg's Memory Search Experiments 262

Retrieval of Long-term Memories 266

- Theories of Retrieval 267
- The Tip-of-the-Tongue (TOT) Phenomenon 274
- The Encoding Specificity Hypothesis 275

Memory Construction at the Time of Retrieval 278

Studies of Retrieval in Nonhuman Species 281
Retrieval of Spatial Memories 281
Encoding Specificity in Animals 284
Retrieval and Memory Construction in Animals 286
Summary Statements 287

11 Forgetting 289

Forgetting and Retention 290
Theories of Short-Term Forgetting 291
The Peterson-Peterson Experiment 292
The Decay Theory and Its Interpretation 292
The Interference Theory and Its Interpretation 293
Evidence Pertinent to the Decay and Interference Theories 293
Theories of Long-Term Forgetting 298
The Role of Interference in Long-Term Forgetting 298
Contemporary Views of Forgetting 307
Forgetting in Nonhuman Species 309
Short-Term Forgetting in Animals 309
Long-Term Forgetting in Animals 311
Summary Statements 314

References 315
Author Index 345
Subject Index 353

Learning and Memory

1

Learning and Memory: An Introduction

The study of learning and memory has always been crucial to the more general study of behavior. The reason for this is clear. Humans and all other species are born with particular physical frameworks and features. These genetically determined characteristics give us the potential for sensing the world and for making responses or movements. In some cases, we even come preprogrammed to make specific responses in particular situations. Still, beyond these genetically preset capacities, most of what we are, who we are, and how we behave is learned.

When most of us think about learning, we tend to picture ourselves in a classroom or at a desk reading about new concepts or events. When we consider learning in other species, what we often think about are pets we have taught to perform tricks on command. Certainly, these are situations in which learning is occurring or has already taken place. However, these examples do not begin to capture the scope of learned behavior or the critical role learning plays in the lives of most species. In the truest sense, for most organisms the ability to learn and remember carries with it the ability to survive.

To truly appreciate the importance of learning, it is helpful to consider why the ability to learn may have evolved in so many species. If we assume that a process evolves because it provides an organism with some survival advantage, then what is the advantage that learning offers? We can answer this question rather simply. Learning is the most effective mechanism most organisms possess for adapting to environmental change.

Learning as an Adaptive Mechanism

Consider for a moment that your environment constantly changes. This constant variation occurs not only in your external world, but also within your own body. This means that you and all other organisms are continually being confronted with stimuli that require some adjustment or adaptation. Some of these adjustments are necessary simply for you to remain comfortable as the world around you changes. In other cases, however, survival itself depends on reacting appropriately to the stimuli you sense. How is it possible for organisms to react in an adaptive manner when so many different changes occur?

Fortunately, all animal species have evolved certain mechanisms for reacting appropriately to environmental events. One such mechanism is the simple reflex that involves making a specific, automatic reaction to a particular stimulus. A number of these reflexive reactions occur in a human being's behaviorial repertoire. When food touches your tongue, you automatically salivate. When your fingers touch a hot object, you immediately jerk your hand away. Your eyelids snap shut whenever a foreign object approaches your eye. Even the changes in heart rate and glandular secretion that occur when you experience pain qualify as reflexive responses.

These reactions and others found in other species are automatic, relatively rigid responses that allow organisms to deal with a specific set of important stimuli. We often say that such responses are "prewired" in the nervous system. This means that our nervous systems contain certain pathways that automatically produce given responses when we sense certain stimuli. These pathways, called *reflex arcs,* consist of nerve fibers that connect sense organs on the surface of the body to either the spinal cord or the lower stem of the brain. They also contain fibers that connect the spinal cord or brain stem to muscles, glands, and organs we call *effectors.* Thus, when a particular sense receptor such as the patellar tendon is stimulated, a nerve impulse travels directly to the spinal cord signaling the event. The impulse then moves directly to an effector (in this case the muscles in the leg) signaling the effector to make a specific response. Because of such nerve pathways, reflexive reactions can occur rapidly without an organism having to consider what response it should make.

Aside from reflexes, many species have at their disposal a second set of adaptive responses that also may be at least partially prewired. These responses, called *instinctive* behaviors, are similar to reflexes except that they are somewhat more complex. In his influential writings concerning instinctive behaviors, Tinbergen (1951) characterized the kinds of behaviors that should be labeled instinctive. According to Tinbergen, for a behavior to be classified as instinctive it must consist of a stereotyped sequence of responses that is characteristic of a particular species. In addition, such behaviors should arise from an organism's genetic makeup, not from an individual's environmental experiences. Finally, Tinbergen presumed that instinctive behaviors, like reflexes, were capable of being triggered automatically by specific stimuli.

Tinbergen (1952) and several others (Ardrey, 1966; Lorenz, 1965) have provided numerous examples of behaviors that appear to fit this characterization. Most of these behaviors are, in fact, rather complex mating or maternal rituals that some species exhibit in response to specific environmental cues. For example, it is well known that in an effort to entice a female that is ready to lay her eggs, the male stickleback fish sometimes performs an elaborate "dance" involving zigzag movements in the water. The movements function to lure the female to a nest that the male has already prepared. Once the female has been coaxed to the nest and induced to deposit her eggs, the male fertilizes the eggs and then cares for and protects his prospective offspring.

This sequence of behaviors is often termed instinctive because the ritual is virtually unchanged regardless of the number of times the male has performed it. The sequence also appears to occur in this manner only in sticklebacks, not in fish in general. Finally, the entire response chain is most often triggered by a particular set of environmental cues—specifically, the sight of the female stickleback swollen around the midsection by her soon to-be-released eggs.

It is evident that many species exhibit response sequences of this type, which appear to run off in a stereotyped manner. It is also apparent that many of these behaviors seem to be triggered by specific stimuli. What is not clear is the degree to which such behaviors depend on genetic programming as opposed to being shaped by environmental experiences.

Questions about the innate character of instinctive reactions have been raised by many researchers. For example, it is known that shortly after hatching, chicks will peck at grain-shaped objects on the ground. The appearance of this behavior so soon after hatching suggests that the response is genetically programmed in the chick's nervous system. However, in one very early study, Kuo (1932) observed embryonic chicks by inserting clear "windows" in their eggshells. What Kuo found is that early in the embryo's life the chick's own heartbeat forces its head to move in a way that is reminiscent of pecking. He also found that the opening and closing of the chick's beak accompanied these head movements. Such observations raise the question of whether it is genetic programming or prenatal experience that is responsible for pecking in the newborn chick.

Other research indicates even stronger links between what have been called innate behaviors and environmental influences. For example, certain male swallows (*Zonotrichia leucophrys*) invariably develop adult song patterns when they are approximately 8 months old. Since all these birds develop this capacity at the same stage of maturation, it had been widely assumed that the capacity itself was genetically preset to appear at a given age. This does not, however, appear to be the entire story. Researchers studying these birds have found that unless they are exposed to the adult songs of other birds during a critical period of development (10–90 days of age), they never develop the capacity for producing adult song (Marler & Mundinger, 1971).

Thus, the occurrence of adult singing patterns appears to depend on both maturational and experiential factors. Similarly, many other behaviors once thought to be genetically determined are now known to depend at least partially on environmental stimulation. For this reason, the current thinking is that many instinctive behaviors probably arise through a combination of genetic and environmental influences.

It is apparent, then, that most organisms are born with a set of prewired reflexive reactions that allow them to adjust to particular kinds of stimulus input. It is also reasonable to conclude that at least some species possess more complex, instinctlike behaviors that arise from some interaction of genetic and environmental factors. These instinctlike behaviors also qualify as mechanisms for adapting to environmental change. Still, for most organisms, these inborn tendencies to react in certain ways are inadequate for coping with a constantly changing environment. If organisms were limited solely to reflexive and instinctlike behaviors, many would simply fail to survive.

Such genetically determined behaviors are inadequate for purposes of adjustment for at least two reasons. First, most such behaviors are relatively stereotyped or inflexible. Once they have been triggered by some environmental event, they tend to run to completion even when the environmental requirements change. One example of this inflexibility can be seen in the behavior of the female greylag goose when she is incubating her eggs. If an egg appears outside her nest, the goose leaves the nest and approaches the egg. She then begins to roll the egg toward her nest with an up-and-down movement of her bill. Finally, she guides the maverick egg back into the nest and retakes her position over her brood.

Clearly, this behavior is an adaptive response, since it allows the female to retrieve any eggs that inadvertently roll from the nest. However, this egg-rolling response is so inflexible that it can be maladaptive. Once the egg-rolling response has begun, the goose will continue to move its bill in an up-and-down manner even if the egg is removed. In other words, if the egg disappears, the goose will continue to roll a "phantom egg" back toward the nest (Hess, 1965). This means that while the goose persists in trying to retrieve an egg that is no longer there, she is leaving the other eggs unguarded. There are numerous examples of this kind of rigidity in a variety of species. In effect, once genetically determined behaviors have been initiated, they tend not to change even when the environmental requirements do.

A second reason for the inadequacy of reflexive and instinctlike behaviors in coping with change is that such behaviors occur in response to only a limited number of stimuli. Certainly, the reflexive eye blink response is an adequate mechanism for adjusting to foreign objects that approach the eye. However, there are numerous important stimuli in the environment that require some adjustment but do not naturally elicit any response. Let's consider one example.

Assume that you are on a transcontinental airliner. About an hour into the flight you hear the pilot's voice over the intercom. Speaking calmly, the pilot informs the passengers that one of the engines has malfunctioned and he is *attempting* to return to the airport. Based on this stimulus input, your response and the responses of the other passengers would be reasonably predictable. Most probably you would experience a "rush" of adrenalin. Your heart would begin to race and your palms would begin to sweat. You might well look around for the nearest emergency exit and might even begin to read the emergency instructions you had earlier ignored. Almost certainly you would become quiet and would begin to listen carefully to the sounds of the aircraft.

Now, consider these reactions to the pilot's message. Not one of these responses is a natural or automatic reaction to hearing someone speak in a calm voice. None of these responses occurs reflexively when you hear someone's voice over an intercom. There is nothing in the stimulus input you have received that would automatically trigger any of the reactions you have made. Yet, all your reactions are clearly attempts to adjust to the changing of the environment.

Examples of response adjustments of these kinds are numerous. If you are driving a car and you see a stop sign, you apply the brakes. You do this even though your nervous system is not prewired to move your leg in response to visual inputs from a stop sign. A cat will often run into the kitchen when it hears the sound of a can opener because the sound usually signals the availability of food. The cat makes this response even though the sound, itself, produces no natural running reaction. If you hear a question in a classroom, you may raise your hand in the air. Yet, there is no arm-raising reflex that is produced by the sound of a question. In all these cases we make important adjustments to environmental changes that naturally elicit no adjustment responses. In all these cases we come to respond appropriately because of our prior experiences. In other words, many of our most important behavioral adjustments are not innate or prewired—they are learned through experience.

In a very real sense, learning is the ultimate mechanism that organisms have evolved for coping with environmental change. Our ability to learn, first and foremost, allows us to react in a flexible manner. We are not necessarily caught, as the goose is caught, in a series of automatic, rigid behavior patterns. Through its experiences an organism can learn that retrieving a lost egg may be worth while. However, it also might learn to respond differently if the egg vanishes. Through learning we can react adaptively and flexibly even when the world around us changes rapidly.

Aside from giving us flexibility, learning also provides us with a way of reacting to all those stimuli that do not naturally elicit adaptive responses. Through learning we are able to react appropriately to spoken words, to written symbols, and even to facial expressions. Everything from a road sign to a change in temperature requires some response, and learning provides the mechanism for making these responses in an adaptive manner. Clearly, the ability to learn has evolved in all organisms because it enables an organism to survive and prosper as the world around it changes.

Defining the Term "Learning"

"Learning" is a word that we all use in our daily conversations and when we do, everyone seems to know what it means. Still, "learning" is one of those common terms that most of us would have difficulty defining precisely. Part of this difficulty arises because we use the term to describe at least two different kinds of activity.

First, we use "learning" to describe the mental activities that are involved when we acquire new meanings for stimuli. For example, we say that we are "learning about psychology" or "learning the rules to a game" or "learning the names of the people in our class." In each of these cases we are talking about acquiring new information. We are saying that through our experiences with a set of stimuli, we are acquiring new meanings for these stimuli. When we "learn about psychology" what we are doing is attaching new meanings to certain words or concepts that had little or no meaning before. When we learn a person's name, we are actually giving the name greater significance by associating it with a person's face. Thus, we commonly use the term "learning" whenever we refer to the activity of attaching new meaning or significance to stimuli.

We also use the term "learning" to refer to situations in which we develop some new response. We talk, for example, about a child "learning to walk" or about a person "learning to drive a car." Here we use the term to describe the acquisition or modification of some behavior. The notion here is that by practicing or experiencing a response over and over, one becomes capable of refining or changing the response being made. We assume that learning is the process responsible for this change.

Since both the foregoing uses for the term "learning" are so common, is one technically more correct than the other? Probably not. Both these uses seem to capture at least part of what psychologists mean when they use the term. According to most psychologists, learning is primarily a process by which organisms form associations between stimuli and other events. In other words, by experiencing different stimulus situations, we discover that some stimuli are linked or related to other events in the environment. This linking or associating of stimuli to other things is what we do when we learn.

As a result of forming associations, we are really gaining new information about the stimuli in our environment. Stimuli that originally may have had little significance now acquire meaning because we discover that they are related to other events that are already meaningful. For example, when we learn the definition for an unfamiliar word, we associate or link the word to other words we already know. This imparts to the novel word a new meaning or significance. In a like manner, a cat may discover that the sound of a can opener is related to the availability of food. By associating the sound with food, the meaning of the sound changes. Finally, when you learn to drive a car, you associate the sensation of pushing the brake pedal with the slowing of the vehicle. From that point on, the sensation of reaching out for the brake pedal takes on a new significance. Clearly, the associations we form when we learn result in the acquisition of new meanings for stimuli.

Likewise, learned associations result in changes in our responses. When stimuli acquire new meanings through their associations, we usually begin to respond differently to these stimuli. When you learn what a word means, you usually increase your usage of the word in your written and verbal communications. Once a cat learns that a given sound is associated with food, it normally approaches the location of the sound in anticipation of being fed. Once you have associated a particular leg movement with the slowing of the car, you begin to perform that movement whenever you want the car to stop. Thus, the new meanings given to stimuli via their associations often result in new responses to those stimuli.

Now you should have a clearer notion of what we mean when we use the term "learning." We can think of learning as a process by which we discover associations between stimuli and other events. By forming these associations, we acquire new meanings for stimuli and we begin to respond to these stimuli differently. This characterization of learning is useful, especially when we are simply talking or thinking about the process. However, this way of defining learning is not as useful to researchers who study the process in the laboratory. These investigators must have a definition that allows them to recognize when learning has occurred and when it has not. Such a definition should also enable researchers to differentiate between learning and other processes that affect behavior. For this reason, learning is defined somewhat differently for purposes of experimental study. There is, however, a clear relationship between the formal definition of learning used by researchers and the more general definition we have discussed.

The formal characterization used by most experimenters is that *learning is reflected by a relatively permanent change in an organism's potential for responding that results from prior experience or practice.* As we have said, the use of such a definition is based on practical considerations. Although most researchers do view learning as a process by which associations are formed, it is impossible for the researcher to see or measure these associations directly. Presumably, such associations occur in an organism's brain, and we have few techniques for looking at brain changes that reflect the learning process.

Since researchers cannot measure associations or changes in meaning directly, they use an organism's behavior as an indicator of whether an association has been formed. It is assumed that when associations are formed and stimuli acquire new meanings, organisms will come to respond to those stimuli in a different manner. Thus, the definition of learning used in the laboratory specifies the kind of behavior that is presumed to reflect the learning process.

By defining learning in this way, it becomes possible to study the variables that affect the way we learn. In using this definition, however, at least three points must be kept in mind. First, according to this definition, learning is reflected by a change in the *potential for respond-*

ing. This phrase is important because it recognizes that learning does not always result in a change of responding. Learning only provides the potential or makes it possible for a new response to occur when the circumstances are appropriate. For example, when we say that a cat has learned that a sound is associated with food, this means that under appropriate circumstances (such as when the cat is hungry), the cat is capable of approaching the sound in order to obtain food. However, the mere fact that the cat has learned about the sound does not guarantee an approach response if the circumstances are not appropriate.

Second, this definition states that for a change in responding to be accepted as evidence for learning, the tendency to perform the new response must be *relatively permanent*. This provision is included to separate learned response changes from temporary behavior changes that are due to other factors. We know, for example, that once a response has been learned, the performance of that response can vary depending on an organism's motivational state, its degree of fatigue, or its interest in performing other responses. These variations in responding are, however, only temporary. A fatigued organism may stop making a learned response, but it will usually resume responding as soon as it is rested. Researchers differentiate between such short-term changes in responding and the more durable changes that result from learning.

The third point we should note is that only those response changes that *result from practice or experience* with the stimuli in question are assumed to reflect learning. There are several factors that can produce long-lasting changes in an organism's behavior. Toxic drugs and debilitating injuries are but two examples of factors that can change responding permanently. Thus, researchers make certain that only behavior changes that result from appropriate experiences are taken as evidence that learning has occurred.

Types of Learning Situations

The goals in the study of learning have been to determine the variables that affect the learning process, to formulate laws of learning based on these effects, and to devise theories of learning that can accommodate these laws. This has been a monumental task, given that learning occurs in so many species and in so many different situations. For this reason, researchers have found it helpful to categorize learning situations into different types and to study each type of situation separately. In the present section we will look at the three types of learning situations that have received the most attention. These three do not exhaust the types of situations in which learning may occur, but they are the categories that have been studied most extensively.

The first situation is labeled *Classical* or *Pavlovian conditioning*. In Classical conditioning, organisms learn to make reflexive or involuntary responses to stimuli that do not naturally produce such responses. As we have mentioned before, only a restricted set of stimuli naturally triggers reflexlike reactions. We know, for example, that painful stimuli naturally elicit a range of internal reactions that collectively are called fear responses. We also know that direct physical stimulation of a certain type will naturally produce sexual arousal. Still, it is obvious that reactions such as fear and sexual arousal can be elicited by any number of stimuli that do not produce these responses reflexively. For some people, fear reactions occur whenever they enter a physician's office. Others exhibit fear in elevators, on airplanes, and in classrooms. The same is true of sexual arousal. It can occur in response to a photograph or to the smell of perfume. It can be elicited by words, thoughts, or sometimes even by articles of clothing.

The importance of Classical conditioning should be evident. Through this type of learning we are able to make appropriate responses to important stimuli even though the stimuli do not produce these responses naturally. Through this type of learning we can also come to respond maladaptively if our reflexive responses become attached to inappropriate stimuli. Research into Classical conditioning has focused on the conditions that are necessary for this type of learning to occur. It has also centered on the variables that affect the rate and strength of this kind of conditioning.

A second learning situation that has been studied extensively is called *Instrumental* or *Operant conditioning*. For the most part, this type of conditioning involves the modification of emitted or voluntary responses through rewards, punishments, and consequences of other kinds. In other words, in Instrumental conditioning situations, organisms learn to alter their behaviors depending on what the consequences of those behaviors are.

We see examples of this type of learning every day. Children learn appropriate social behaviors through trial and error. When they behave correctly they are often praised. Inappropriate behaviors are often punished. By learning which behaviors lead to which consequences, children begin to exhibit more and more responses that adults deem appropriate. We learn to perform a variety of motor skills in the same way. Whether we are learning to swing a golf club, to ride a bicycle, or to write our names, we begin by making responses and then we alter those responses depending on the consequences we observe. Daily we provide consequences of different types to modify the behaviors of our friends, pets, spouses, and even strangers. Research into this type of learning has looked at how response consequences of certain kinds alter behaviors. It has also been concerned with how these consequences can best be arranged to promote the most efficient learning.

A final type of learning is simply labeled *Verbal learning*. This type of learning is concerned with how we go about linking together or associating verbal symbols. How, for example, do we learn sets of words such as a grocery list so that we can recall the words at a later time? How do children learn the alphabet or a poem so that they can recite the letters or words in order? What is involved in learning that certain verbal symbols go together while others do not? All these are questions that have been studied in the Verbal learning area.

Obviously, this type of learning is particularly relevant to many of the learning activities of humans. Much of the learning we do in the academic setting and much of what we learn through what we read and hear falls into this category. Most of the research into this type of learning has focused on the conditions that either facilitate or retard our ability to learn and remember verbal symbols.

In the chapters that follow we will discuss each of these categories or types of learning in much greater detail. In each case we will begin by looking at how that type of learning is studied and which variables most often influence learning of that kind. Then in each case we will look at the theoretical issues and questions that have arisen from the research that has been done in the area. Before doing this, however, we need to introduce the topic of memory, our second major concern in the coming chapters.

The Concept of Memory

We seldom give our memories much thought until we misplace one. Regardless of how remarkable the process of remembering might be, most of us take our memory systems for granted until we forget. In a sense this is unfortunate. There is probably no other topic in psychology that is more fascinating and mysterious than the subject of how we form memories of our experiences and how we are able to call up these memories when we need them. Why do we remember some events and not others? How can some individuals look once at a printed page and recall the entire text, while most of us could not remember the text verbatim if we studied it for hours? How can a group of individuals have the same experience and yet form such different memories of what transpired? After weeks of trying to remember some event, why does the simplest hint or cue cause the entire memory to come rushing back in vivid detail? These are but a few of the questions that have puzzled philosophers for centuries and are still being studied by psychologists today.

It is interesting that our most common and current definitions for the term "memory" differ very little from the kind of definition used by the earliest philosophers. To Plato, for example, who conceptualized the mind as being similar to a wax tablet, memory was like an etching or picture drawn on this tablet by experience. Although present-day psychologists might be more comfortable substituting "brain" for "mind" in this characterization, most would adhere at least generally to this view. Today, the term "memory" is most often defined as *an internal record or representation of some prior event or experience.*

Although such definitions of memory are common, they can be misleading in one respect. When most people hear this definition, there is a tendency to begin thinking of a memory as an exact replica or picture of some event. It is as if the brain functioned like a camera taking snapshots of events and then filing away the finished pictures. Almost certainly, this is not the case. As we will see in later chapters, our memories are seldom faithful replicas of any experience we have had. In some cases our memories contain less detail, or at least less vivid detail, than did our actual experiences when they occurred. In still other cases, our memories appear to differ from the original experiences by containing more or even different details. In effect, memories are probably best conceptualized as fabrications that are based on real events, not as actual pictures of the events as they happened.

From the definitions we have discussed, it should be obvious that the process of learning and the entity we call memory are closely related. One way to conceptualize this relationship is to think of learning as a process that triggers memory formation. Clearly, we form memories for what we have learned, so in this sense, we can think of a memory as being dependent on learning. At the same time, however, it is possible to think of learning as being dependent on memory. When we learn, we often associate events that are separated in time. Such associations could not be formed unless we were able to retain a representation of one event until the other occurred. If we had no memory for events, each event would be viewed in isolation, and relationships among events would not be recognizable. Thus, it is fair to say that without learning we would have little to remember, and without memory we would be unable to learn.

Even though learning and memory are closely related, we must be cautious about equating the terms "learning" and "memory formation." When we do this we run the risk of suggesting that the content of a memory and the ease with which a memory can be recalled depend entirely on factors present at the time of learning. Clearly, learning factors often influence both memory content and recall. However, this is not the entire story. Substantial evidence suggests that there are factors that affect learning but have little or no influence on our ability to remember. One variable that clearly fits this description is the meaningfulness of verbal materials. Likewise, it is known that numerous treatments and variables can affect recall of a memory even though they occur after learning has ended. For example, even if two individuals have learned a task in the same way and are tested under identical circumstances, their recall still may vary considerably depending on their experiences between the times of learning and testing.

Not only do different variables sometimes control learning and remembering, there is evidence that the content of a memory may be influenced by factors other than those present during learning. For example, some studies suggest that memory content may be altered at the time of recall, as well as at the time of original memory formation (see, for example, Loftus, 1979). Such studies suggest that it is probably impossible to predict what the content of a memory may be or how easily a memory will be recalled simply by understanding the learning process that triggers memory formation.

Topics Studied by Memory Researchers

In categorizing types of memory research, we cannot simply look at memory situations of different types, as we did when we discussed learning. We can say, however, that most memory studies have dealt with one of three aspects of memory. First, a large number of experiments have focused on what are called *memory processes.* These are the operations a memory goes through from the time an experience is perceived until the memory for that experience becomes permanently stored.

For example, some researchers have been concerned with the role of the rehearsal process in memory formation. We know that when we are learning verbal materials we often rehearse or repeat these materials to ourselves, to remember more effectively. The question of interest, however, has been how rehearsal affects a memory so that it is easier to recall. Some theorists have suggested that processes such as rehearsal are necessary for permanent storage of a memory, while others have proposed that rehearsal enables us to better organize or encode a memory. According to some, processes such as rehearsal appear to occur automatically or involuntarily, while others have viewed rehearsal as a process we can utilize differently depending on what we plan on doing with the memory later. Research in this area looks at these and numerous other issues. The concern has been to describe the processes a memory goes through, to delineate the effects of these processes on the content and structure of a memory, and to discover how these processes influence our ability to remember.

A second aspect of memory that has caught the interest of researchers has been the nature of memory content and structure. If we were to draw a picture of a memory, what would it look like? First of all, what are the elements contained in a memory? Does a memory include a representation of every stimulus we notice during an experience, or does it contain only a subset? Regardless of how many elements there are, how are the elements represented? Do we store visual or imaginal representations, or are they auditory, or symbolic in some form? Aside from these questions about memory content, researchers have dealt with the way these elements are structured. They have inquired whether all related elements appear to be linked together or whether elements seem to be arranged in some logical hierarchy. Obviously, the answers to such questions are difficult to uncover with any confidence, because memories cannot be seen directly. Still, the research techniques used in this area have suggested a number of interesting speculations concerning what memories consist of and how they are organized.

The final aspect of memory that has received extensive study concerns memory retrieval or recall. Basically, the work in this area has centered on the factors that cause us to remember and forget. For example, later we will discuss treatments that have been used to produce enhanced recall performance. We will also look at research into the factors that result in poor recall and we will discuss what this work tells us about theories of forgetting. In addition to this kind of research, experimenters have been concerned with the mechanisms that underlie the retrieval of memories. In later chapters we will describe in some detail this research on retrieval as well as the other kinds of memory research we have mentioned above.

Philosophical Differences in the Study of Learning and Memory

When students begin their first study of learning and memory, they are often surprised by how divergent the work on these two topics is. As we have seen, learning and memory are about as closely related as any two topics can be. Yet, the research on these topics appears to be guided by different philosophies, the language used to describe the topics is often very different, and the research in the two fields is often published in scientific journals of different kinds. What is even more disquieting is the apparent lack of communication between researchers interested in learning and those who concentrate on aspects of memory. It is legitimate to ask how the differences developed and how these developments have affected our knowledge of these two areas.

To answer these questions we can begin by saying that the study of learning and the study of memory developed out of very different philosophical traditions. First, learning as a research enterprise grew mainly out of the behavioristic tradition in psychology. Although we need not present the behavioral view in depth, a few points are worth noting. According to this view, the goal of research in psychology was to discover the lawful relationships between environmental events and an organism's behavior. Following this tradition, early learning researchers set out to find the variables that would produce enduring behavior changes. The term "learning" was used primarily as a label to describe these stimulus–response relationships. Few of the early learning researchers talked about the nature of the learning process as it actually occurred *inside* the organism. Thus, the emphasis was clearly on observable events and how they are related, not on describing processes taking place within an organism.

Another characteristic of learning research that developed from the behavioristic tradition was the frequent use of animals as experimental subjects. The early behaviorists viewed living organisms from a Darwinian perspective, seeing mankind as part of a continuum of species, not as a species somehow separate from all others. From this perspective the use of animal subjects became natural. The basic idea was that the rules of learning that governed the behaviors of animals should be similar in many respects to the rules governing learned behaviors in humans. An added advantage to using animals in experiments was that researchers could control the histories and current environments of their subjects. This made it easier to look at how novel experiences resulted in enduring behavior changes.

While behaviorism promulgated research in learning, interest in memory grew primarily from what is now called the "cognitive orientation." This general view had many early adherents in psychology, but its impact has been heaviest in the past two decades. The term "cognition" refers to the act of knowing or acquiring knowledge. This is an important point. Knowledge is never present in the environment itself. An organism can, however, derive knowledge from observing environmental events. For example, two stimuli can occur simultaneously in the environment. This occurrence is an observable event. However, an organism's knowledge about the relationship between these stimuli cannot be observed. This knowledge is formed and kept within the organism itself. Thus, the study of cognition is, by definition, a study of the internal processes that result in knowledge and a study of how this knowledge is structured. For this reason, researchers working within the cognitive tradition have emphasized the study of attentional, perceptual, and memory processes, as well as the organization of the memory itself.

Whereas early behaviorists believed that the subject matter of psychology should be behavior and its relationship to observable events, the cognitive tradition also emphasized behavior but not as the primary subject to be studied. Within the latter tradition, behavior usually has been viewed as an index or indicator for what goes on inside the organism. In other words, the cognitive psychologist does not study behavior in and of itself, but instead uses behavior as a tool for studying internal entities and processes. For example, the cognitive researcher may use the speed with which a person recognizes a word as an indication of whether the word is represented in the person's memory. Here, speed of responding itself is not being studied. Instead, this variable is being used to help illuminate a memory the experimenter cannot see directly.

We should make one final point about the cognitive orientation. The vast majority of studies on cognitive processes such as memory have been done with human subjects. Most probably this strategy developed for a number of reasons. First, many philosophers and psychologists have viewed humans as differing from other organisms primarily on the basis of their cognitive abilities. This is not to say that other organisms have no cognitive abilities, but simply that these abilities are more refined, more complex, and more numerous in humans than in other species. It follows naturally from this view that if we are to study cognitive processes, the subject of choice would be the human.

A related reason for studying memory in humans rather than other organisms is the absence of verbal behavior among nonhuman species. This means that whereas humans are able to report with some clarity what they recall, animals must be trained to make a response that will indicate what they recall. This also means that humans are able to speculate about how they may have processed some bit of information (speculations that may lead to testable hypotheses), but animals cannot make such suggestions.

Obviously, the behavioral and cognitive approaches are of great historical significance because of their impacts on early learning and memory research. Just as clearly, these approaches remain important today. Numerous learning experiments are still conducted within a behavioral framework, and the cognitive approach forms the basis for the great majority of contemporary memory experiments. Still, in recent years there has been an increasing tendency for aspects of these two approaches to merge.

For example, one of the most active research areas recently has been the field of memory and cognitive processes in animals. This is a clear step away from the notion that cognitive processes may be studied only in human subjects. Likewise, recently there has been an increase in the application of basic learning principles to humans in applied medical, psychotherapeutic, and educational settings. Such applications have been successful even though the principles were originally developed through laboratory experiments using animal subjects. Finally, as we will see, contemporary theories of learning are often theories based on how cognitive processes bridge the gap between stimulus events and an organism's behavior. In effect, many learning researchers have now begun to "look inside" the organisms they are studying.

These examples of cross-fertilization between the areas of learning and memory are healthy signs. In many cases they have opened up avenues of research that might otherwise have gone unexplored. Just as importantly, this trend suggests that researchers have finally realized what most beginning students have suspected all along: namely, that it makes little sense to talk about either learning or memory in isolation. The processes of learning and memory are interdependent and inseparably linked.

2

Classical Conditioning: Learning about Stimuli as Signals

In Chapter 1 we characterized learning as a process by which organisms associate events that are related in some way. We said that by discovering these relationships and by forming these associations, organisms appear to acquire new meanings for the events involved. As a result, organisms begin to respond to these events in entirely new ways. The type of learning we will discuss in this chapter is called *Classical* or *Pavlovian conditioning*. And, as we will see, Classical conditioning fits this characterization of learning almost precisely.

In Classical conditioning organisms come to recognize *predictive relationships* that exist between stimuli in the environment. This means that they discover that certain stimuli can serve as *signals* for the occurrence of other, biologically significant events. In this context the term "biologically significant event" is applied to a certain type of stimulus. This is the kind of stimulus, discussed in Chapter 1, that is capable of naturally producing reflexive or involuntary reactions. In other words, stimuli that naturally elicit muscle reflexes, glandular secretions, and general emotional reactions all qualify as biologically significant events because they automatically produce adaptive responses. Thus, in Classical conditioning, organisms learn to predict when these response-eliciting stimuli will occur by using other, less significant stimuli as signals for their occurrence.

The full importance of this kind of learning becomes evident when we consider how Classical conditioning alters an organism's behavior. Through conditioning, an organism comes to respond differently to the signaling stimulus. In most cases this stimulus, which originally produces little or no responding, begins to produce a reflexive or involuntary reaction similar to the one produced naturally by the response-eliciting stimulus. In effect, an organism begins to react to these two stimuli in similar ways because of the association that has been formed between them.

Now that we have described Classical conditioning in an abstract sense, let's consider a specific example of how the conditioning process works. It is well known that very young children often exhibit natural fear reactions when they see unfamiliar faces. This reaction normally involves crying, turning away from the stranger, and reaching out for the nearest familiar adult. This set of responses occurs as a natural and automatic reaction to the sight of a strange face.

Imagine for a moment that a child going through this stage of development is at home, playing inside near the front door. The doorbell rings, but except maybe for a tilt of the head in the direction of the sound, the child shows no particular reaction. When the parent answers the door, however, an unfamiliar person appears in the doorway and the child immediately begins crying. A few days later the same sequence of events occurs. The doorbell rings, a stranger appears at the door, and the child proceeds to cry and reach out for the parent. After a few such experiences, the parents begin to notice a distinct change in the child's behavior. Now, whenever the doorbell rings, the child begins to react by crying and seeking out one or both parents. The sound of the doorbell, which originally produced little or no response, now elicits the same response that was once reserved for strange faces.

In this example, one stimulus, the unfamiliar face, naturally produces a fear response. The doorbell, on the other hand, originally produced no significant response of any kind. By virtue of experiences with these stimuli, however, the child learns that the doorbell is a reliable signal for the appearance of strangers. Whenever the bell rings, strangers appear. Once the doorbell has become a reliable signal for the fear-eliciting stimulus, the bell becomes capable of producing fear on its own.

Similar examples of Classical conditioning may be found, of course, in adults as well as children. Certainly you salivate naturally when food is in your mouth, but you may also salivate in response to hearing or reading about the foods you enjoy. Although fear may be a natural reaction to physical pain, fear may also occur when you speak to an audience, when you take an exam, or even when you contemplate riding a crowded elevator. Even sexual arousal, which can be elicited naturally by certain kinds of physical contact, can occur in response to a photograph, a particular aroma, or even a spoken phrase. In all these cases we make reflexive or emotional responses to stimuli that do not naturally produce them. In each case we respond to such stimuli because we have learned that they are signals for other stimuli that naturally produce such responses. These responses, and numerous others we make every day, arise through the process of Classical conditioning.

The Concept of Contingency

We have stressed the idea that Classical conditioning depends to some degree on one stimulus becoming a signal for another. In effect, stimuli that become reliable signals for important events become capable of producing new responses. In the present section we will discuss briefly how a stimulus becomes a reliable signal. As we will see, not only does the *degree* of conditioning depend on how effective a signal is, but also the *type* of conditioning that occurs depends on the type of signal a stimulus becomes.

For any stimulus to become a signal for another event, that stimulus and that event must have a *contingent relationship.* Very simply this means that the occurrence or nonoccurrence of the significant event must be contingent, or dependent on, the prior occurrence of the stimulus. That is, the occurrence of the stimulus and the occurrence of the significant event must be *correlated* in some fashion.

When a signaling stimulus is consistently followed by the occurrence of some event, we say that a *positive contingency* exists between them. This means that the two stimuli tend to occur together and that neither tends to occur when the other is absent. One example of a positive contingency in a real life setting is the relationship between turning on your television set and the appearance of a picture on the screen. Unless, of course, your set is broken, these events always occur together. As you can easily see, with a positive contingency in effect you can use one of the events (turning your set on) as a reliable predictor or signal for the occurrence of the other (the appearance of the picture).

In a Classical conditioning situation, when a positive contingency exists between some signaling stimulus and a response-eliciting stimulus, the type of learning that occurs is called *Classical excitatory conditioning,* where "excitatory" refers to the signal's acquired capability of exciting or producing a response like the one that is naturally produced by the signaled event. The example of Classical conditioning discussed earlier, involving the doorbell and the child, is really an example of Classical excitatory conditioning. In this example a positive contingency existed between the doorbell and the appearance of strangers. As a result, the doorbell began to produce the same fear response in the child that originally had been produced by the strangers.

A second type of contingent relationship is a *negative contingency.* This refers to the situation in which one stimulus is regularly accompanied by the *absence* of another stimulus that might otherwise be expected to be present. For example, we all know that dogs tend to exhibit aggression when strangers enter their territories. However, if you are approaching a house and encounter a dog that is wagging its tail, you can be fairly certain that you will not be bitten. Tail wagging seldom precedes aggressive behavior. It more often precedes play or affectionate responses. Thus, you can observe a strange dog's movements as you approach it, interpreting tail wagging as signal that aggressiveness is likely to be absent.

The existence of such a contingency in Classical conditioning can be seen when the signaling stimulus is regularly accompanied by the *absence* of some response-eliciting stimulus we have come to expect. Such negative contingencies result in what is termed *Classical inhibitory conditioning.* When Classical inhibitory conditioning occurs, the signaling stimulus begins to produce a new response just as in excitatory conditioning. However, unlike what is found in excitatory conditioning, the response produced by the signal bears little similarity to the response produced naturally by the signaled stimulus. In fact, the response the signal begins to produce is normally one that *opposes* or *inhibits* the response that is elicited by the signaled event.

To illustrate this kind of conditioning let's return to our doorbell example, in which a positive contingency existed between the doorbell and the entrance of strangers. As a result, the doorbell began to produce a fear response. Let's assume now that when familiar persons come to the door they ring the bell and also call out "Is anybody home?" In this case, the verbal sound would come to signal the *absence* of strangers, and the child would learn to respond to the verbal sound by actively suppressing fear. In other words, the verbal sound would come to produce a response such as relaxation, and this new response exemplifies the inhibitory type of conditioning.

In the pages that follow, we will look at both the excitatory and inhibitory forms of Classical conditioning in more detail. In each case we will begin by considering the experimental situations used to study that particular form of conditioning. Then we will outline the factors or variables that affect the degree to which these types of conditioning occur. We begin by discussing how Classical excitatory conditioning was discovered and how it was first studied.

Methods for Studying Classical Excitatory Conditioning

Pavlov's Original Experiments

The discovery of Classical conditioning was made by the Russian physiologist Ivan Pavlov, in the course of an investigation into the physiology of the digestive system. Indeed, Pavlov received the Nobel Prize in 1904 for his contributions to our understanding of how the digestive system functions.

One aspect of Pavlov's work concerned the role of the salivary glands in digestion. To study salivation Pavlov placed dogs in a harnesslike apparatus such as is pictured in Figure 2.1. He then inserted glass fistulas or tubes into the dogs' salivary gland ducts. Thus, when the dogs salivated for any reason, the saliva would run through the fistulas instead of into their mouths. This allowed Pavlov to collect and measure the amount of saliva that was produced under certain conditions.

In one of these experiments, Pavlov was attempting to measure salivation in response to meat powder placed in an animal's mouth. After a few sessions, however, precise measurements became impossible because the dogs began to salivate as soon as the experimenters entered the room with the meat powder in hand. By the time the meat powder had been placed in their mouths, the dogs had already produced significant amounts of saliva.

Pavlov hypothesized that this premature salivation was occurring in response to stimuli that preceded the presentation of the meat powder. To test this idea, he began to present discrete stimuli before each presentation of food. He used stimuli such as clicking sounds or tones, which he knew would not naturally produce the salivation response. After a few pairings of the sound and the meat powder, the dogs began to salivate to the sound itself. These tests constituted the first experimental demonstration of what we now call Classical or Pavlovian conditioning (Pavlov, 1927).

Aside from providing an initial analysis of the conditioning process, Pavlov gave us a terminology we still use today to describe the elements of the conditioning situation. He chose the term *unconditioned stimulus* (*US*) to denote the stimulus that naturally or automatically elicits some reflexive reaction. In Pavlov's experiments, the meat powder served as the US because the presentation of the meat naturally produced salivation. Such stimuli are called "unconditioned" because they produce the reflexive response without the aid of any conditioning or learning experience.

The reflexive response that is naturally elicited by the US was called the *unconditioned response* (*UR*). In Pavlov's situation the UR, of course, was the salivation, as produced initially by the exposure to the meat powder. As with the US, the response is termed "unconditioned" because it will occur when the US is presented without any prior conditioning or learning.

The stimulus Pavlov presented before the meat powder (for example, the clicking sound) was labeled the *conditioned stimulus* (*CS*). The term indicates that a stimulus so labeled becomes capable of producing the reflexive reac-

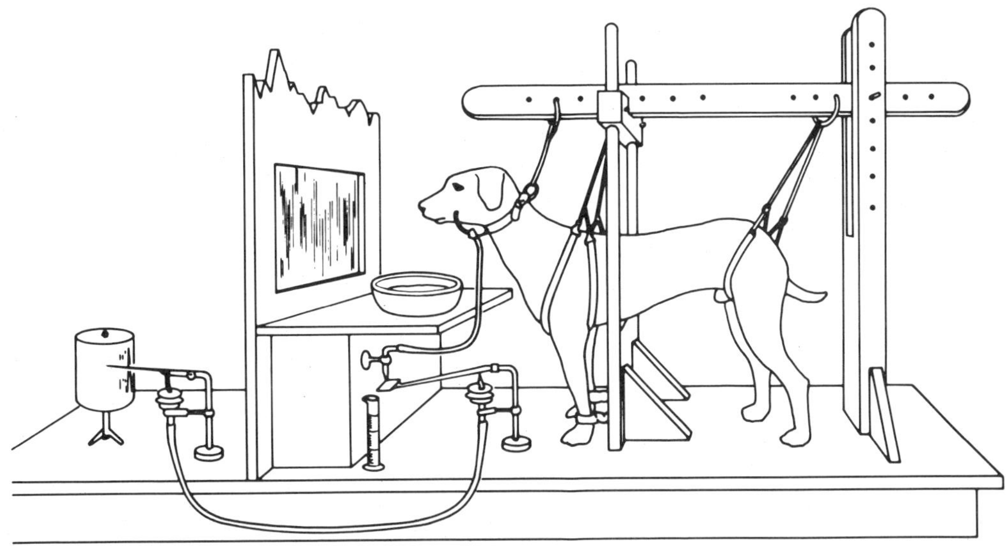

FIGURE 2.1 Pavlov's salivary conditioning apparatus. Notice that the saliva from the salivary gland is collected by a tube that runs to a recording device. (From Yerkes and Morgulis, 1909.)

tion only after conditioning or learning has occurred. For this reason the CSs chosen for most Classical conditioning experiments are often described as being relatively neutral. This means that before being paired with the US, this stimulus produces no reflexive reaction of the kind that is naturally elicited by the US. You might also note that the CS is equivalent to what we have been calling "the signal" in our discussions of the conditioning process thus far.

The final element of the conditioning situation is the new response that comes to be produced by the signal or CS. This response Pavlov called the *conditioned response* (*CR*), since it is a response that can be produced by the CS only after some conditioning has occurred. In Pavlov's experiment, the salivation produced by the clicking sound represented the conditioned response. As we have noted before, the conditioned and unconditioned responses may be identical or at least similar in many ways. Even when this is the case, however, the response is labeled an unconditioned response when it is produced naturally by the US and a conditioned response when it comes to be produced by the CS after conditioning.

These terms, coined by Pavlov, will be used not only throughout our discussion,but also are used throughout the research literature on Classical conditioning. To facilitate your familiarity with these terms, Figure 2.2 (page 18) represents the stages of the conditioning process as they occurred in Pavlov's experiment and as they might have occurred in the doorbell example discussed earlier. In each case, the elements of the conditioning situation are identified with their more technical labels.

Other Classical Conditioning Paradigms

Since Pavlov's original studies, several experimental situations have been developed to study the nature and the laws of the conditioning process. These situations, called *paradigms*, have evolved because they represent efficient procedures for studying conditioning in a given species. The following is a brief description of some of the paradigms researchers have used.

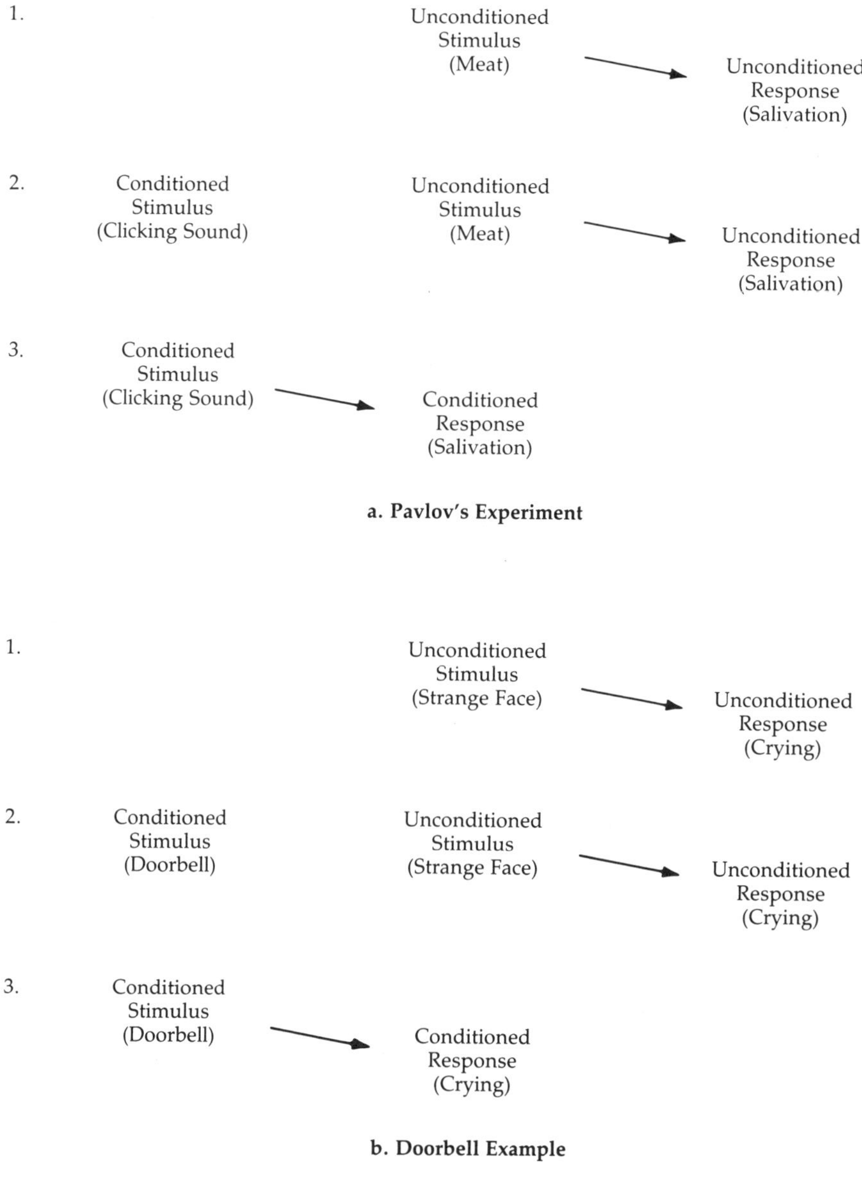

FIGURE 2.2 Elements of the conditioning situation as seen (a) in Pavlov's experiment and (b) in the doorbell example discussed earlier.

Human conditioning paradigms Among the more common responses studied in human conditioning experiments are the eye blink reflex, the galvanic skin response, and the reflexive withdrawal of the finger in response to pain. In *human eyelid conditioning,* a subject is usually seated in a dimly lit, sound-attenuated chamber and is fitted with a padded headband. The headband contains a nozzle pointed toward the corner of the subject's eye and a potentiometer. A flexible wire from the potentiometer is attached to the subject's eyelid so that any movement in the lid causes the electrical resistance in the potentiometer to change. Thus, changes in electrical resistance can be used as a measure of eyelid movement. Typically, subjects are presented a light or tone as the CS. The US is normally an airpuff directed toward the outside corner of the eye via the nozzle in the headband. The airpuff produces an immediate blinking response (the UR). After several pairings of the light or tone and the airpuff, the subjects begin to blink whenever the light or tone is presented.

One point concerning the conditioned eye blink response is worth noting, since it is also true of most other conditioned responses we will discuss. The eye blink that occurs to the CS in this situation does not appear to be a voluntary reaction made to prevent the airpuff from reaching the eye. As it happens, the form of the blinking response, as well as the rapidity of the response, differ when a blink is voluntary and when it occurs in response to a CS (Spence & Ross, 1959). Thus, conditioned responses to a CS are more like reflexive than voluntary reactions.

A second paradigm involving human subjects is conditioning of the *galvanic skin response* (*GSR*). It is well known that the electrical resistance of the skin decreases markedly when a subject senses some form of aversive stimulation or undergoes emotional stress.Thus, some researchers have used this naturally occurring reaction to study the conditioning process (see Grings, Lockhart, & Dameron, 1962). Usually, electrodes are placed on the palms of the hands to measure changes in electrical resistance. Since these changes depend on changes in perspiration, the electrodes may be placed anywhere that the sweat glands are located. Typically, a visual or auditory CS is presented just prior to an aversive stimulus such as a shock or a loud buzzer. On the initial trial a decrease in skin resistance is seen only after the aversive stimulation. As the trials progress, however, the change in resistance tends to occur with greater and greater frequency as a response to the visual or auditory CS.

One other paradigm used to study human conditioning involves the reflexive withdrawal of the finger when a painful stimulus is applied. One might imagine that this technique has been more popular among experimenters than among subjects. In any event, the technique is similar in many ways to the eyelid conditioning procedure. A wire from a potentiometer is attached to the finger along with an electrode for delivering a mild shock. An auditory or visual CS is normally followed by a shock, which causes the finger to curl or withdraw. The movement of the finger is measured by changes in resistance within the potentiometer. After several CS–shock pairings, withdrawal begins to occur in the presence of the CS alone.

These, of course, are not the only responses that have been conditioned in human subjects. Pupillary constriction, changes in heart rate and blood pressure, and leg flexion are but a few of the other responses that have been studied (Beecroft, 1966). In addition to these various response systems, several types of CSs have been used in human conditioning studies. For example, some experimenters have investigated how conditioning progresses when words, visual forms, or numbers are used as CSs (see, for example, Grant, 1973). Still, since the mid-1960s there has been a general decline in the number of conditioning studies employing human subjects. Most studies in the past 10 to 15 years have looked at the conditioning of response systems in nonhuman species.

Conditioning paradigms used with animals

Most of the contemporary studies of Classical conditioning have been done with animal subjects in paradigms specifically suited to the species involved. Three of the most commonly used procedures are the nictitating membrane paradigm utilizing rabbits, the conditioned emotional response procedure using rats, and the autoshaping paradigm involving pigeons. It should be noted that these procedures have not been chosen because they involve responses that are particularly relevant to human behavior. They have been selected because they are efficient procedures for studying the laws of conditioning—laws that should be applicable to human conditioning situations.

The first of these procedures, the conditioning of the *nictitating membrane* in the rabbit, is a direct analog of the human eyelid conditioning paradigm. Besides having an outer eyelid similar to that of humans, rabbits and some other rodents have an inner eyelid called a nictitating membrane. This membrane closes or blinks naturally in response to air movements or other forms of stimulation around the eye. Using procedures similar to those used for eyelid conditioning, Gormezano (1966) has demonstrated that this membrane will close in response to a CS that regularly precedes the presentation of an airpuff. This procedure has proved to be invaluable in recent years in the study of brain mechanisms involved in conditioning (see, for example, Thompson, Hicks, & Shvyrok, 1980).

The second procedure, known as the *conditioned emotional response* (*CER*) paradigm, involves conditioning rats to fear a previously neutral stimulus (see Estes & Skinner, 1941). The conditioning procedure itself is very simple. Rats are usually presented with an auditory or visual stimulus as the CS, which is followed by the presentation of an aversive stimulus such as a mild shock or a loud noise. The shock or noise, which serves as the US, naturally produces a number of internal responses such as increased heart rate, elevated blood pressure, and the release of certain hormones. In addition, rats react to such aversive stimuli by freezing or halting whatever responses they were making when the aversive stimulus appeared. It is this freezing reaction that is used to determine whether the rats have associated the neutral CS with the aversive US. After the CS–US pairings, the question of interest is whether the CS becomes capable of producing a freezing reaction on its own.

Determining whether a rat freezes when a CS is presented sounds simple enough. In reality, however, it can be difficult because an animal's natural level of activity may be low even before any conditioning has occurred. If this is the case, it can be particularly difficult to assess when an animal is freezing and when it is simply not doing much. For this reason, most researchers train rats to perform some active response before giving them the CS US pairings. The rats may be trained, for example, to press a lever in order to receive food, or they may be taught to lick a drinking spout for water. After such training, rats tend to make these responses with a high probability and at a reasonably high rate. The researcher allows the animal to begin making the active response and then presents the CS that had been paired with the aversive US. If conditioning has in fact occurred, the presentation of the CS will cause the rats to freeze. This freezing in turn disrupts the bar pressing or licking the animals were engaged in before the CS occurrence.

Table 2.1 summarizes the stages of the CER paradigm. Note that in stage 1 rats are trained to perform some active response, so that during testing a high level of responding will be assured. In stage 2 the rats receive conditioning trials involving pairings of a neutral CS with an aversive US. Stage 3 involves returning the animals to the situation in which they learned the active response. After responding has begun, the CS from conditioning is presented and any change in the active responding is measured. Decreases in the rate of responding due to CS presentation are interpreted as evidence that the CS has become capable of producing a freezing reaction.

One additional point concerning the CER paradigm should be made explicit. The actual measure of conditioning used in this paradigm is usually a ratio. This measure, termed a *suppression ratio,* compares the responding that occurs in the interval before the CS presentation to the responding that occurs while the CS is present. Specifically, it involves dividing the number of responses made during the CS by the total number of responses the rat makes both before and during the CS.

To clarify the use of this measure, let's assume that an experimenter allows a rat to begin responding and then presents a CS lasting 30 seconds. To measure suppression or freezing related to the CS, the experimenter records the number of responses the rat makes in the 30 seconds before CS occurrence, as well as the number of responses made during the CS. The experimenter would then set up the following ratio:

$$\frac{\text{responses during the CS}}{\text{responses before CS + responses during CS}}$$

As you can see, if a rat freezes almost totally during the CS presentation, the numerator of this ratio will be very small, and the ratio itself will be small. An animal that never responds during the CS, for example, would have a suppression ratio of 0. This would, of course, indicate successful conditioning, since the CS would be producing a high level of freezing. An animal that responds the same number of times during the CS as it does in the period before the CS would have a suppression ratio of 0.5. Thus, a higher ratio would reflect little conditioning, since the CS would be producing little in the way of freezing behavior.

Our final paradigm is the *autoshaping paradigm* in pigeons. Pigeons, like many other birds, make a natural pecking response when food is presented. In this case food can be considered to be a US that naturally elicits the response of pecking. It is now also known that pigeons tend to peck other objects when these objects regularly precede the presentation of food (Brown & Jenkins, 1968). For example, if a pigeon is presented with a lighted disk on several occasions and on each occasion the disk is followed by a food presentation, the pigeon will begin to peck the disk just as it had previously pecked at the food. In this case the disk represents a CS, since it is not a stimulus that naturally elicits pecking. Pecking at the disk is a CR, since it is a response that occurs only because of the disk–food pairings. This autoshaping paradigm has been used increasingly in recent years to study the variables that affect Classically conditioned responding (see, for example, Hearst & Jenkins, 1974).

Measures of the CR In describing these basic paradigms, we have detailed the measurement of the conditioned response only in the case of the CER procedure. This was done because the CER paradigm involves an indirect measure of conditioned responding. In most other paradigms the assessment of whether a CS produces a reliable CR is more straightforward. Still, there are a few points concerning CR measurement that we should note.

First, researchers usually measure condi-

TABLE 2.1 Stages of Training in the Conditioned Emotional Response (CER) Paradigm

Stage	*Procedure*	*Example*
1	Train the animal to perform a voluntary response at a high rate.	Train the animal to press a bar for a food or water reward.
2	Expose the animal to a series of fear conditioning trials.	Give the animal a series of tone (CS)–shock (US) pairings.
3	Allow the animal to resume the previously learned voluntary response. Then present the CS used in fear conditioning.	Allow the animal to resume bar pressing. While it is pressing, present the tone used in fear conditioning.
4	Compare the rates of voluntary responding with and without the CS.	Compare the rate of pressing before the tone presentation to the rate of pressing during the tone.

tioned responding using either of two procedures. One procedure is simply to assess the presence of a CR on each conditioning trial. Each time a CS–US pairing is presented, the experimenter measures the responding that occurs between the time of CS onset and the beginning of the US. This procedure gives us a trial-by-trial look at how the CR develops. However, this procedure becomes difficult to employ when a brief CS duration is used or when the CS and the US occur close together in time. In such cases it becomes almost impossible to measure responses to the CS before the US begins to produce its own reaction.

As a result of this problem, some researchers use what are called *test trials* to assess the presence of a CR. A test trial is an occasional presentation of the CS by itself. Such trials are usually presented at various times during the course of conditioning in place of regular CS–US pairings. This technique has the advantage of allowing a clear measure of responding to the CS without the measure being interrupted by responses to the US. On the other hand, the test trial technique has at least two disadvantages. It does not allow us to look at the trial-by-trial development of a CR, since measurements do not occur on each trial. More important, as we will discover later, presentations of the CS by itself can decrease the amount of conditioned responding to the CS. Thus, in an attempt to measure conditioning as it progresses, this technique may actually decrease the amount of responding one would otherwise see.

Aside from using different procedures for measuring a CR, the actual CR characteristics that are measured may differ from one paradigm to another. For example, in salivary conditioning the strength of a CR is usually assessed by looking at the *amplitude* or amount of salivation that is produced by the CS. In the case of eyelid conditioning, only responses of a given amplitude are counted as conditioned responses. Thus, in eyelid conditioning, the *frequency* of CRs of certain amplitude is used as a measure of conditioning. There is no one response characteristic that is necessarily better as a response indicator than another. The choice of the characteristic to be measured usually depends on the particular type of response being conditioned.

Variables That Affect Excitatory Conditioning

In our description of conditioning paradigms, we spoke as if pairings of a CS and a US inevitably produce conditioned responding. At best, this is an oversimplification. A wide variety of factors influence the degree to which excitatory conditioning occurs in any given situation. The present section deals with three general categories of variables that appear to be particularly important. The first category involves variables having to do with the physical relationship between a CS and a US. The second concerns factors such as the specific characteristics of the CS and the US. And finally, the third group of factors concerns the presence of stimuli other than the CS and the US at the time of conditioning.

The Physical Relationship between CS and US

In this context, the term "physical relationship" refers to the way occurrences of the CS and the US are arranged in time. In this section we will look at how the temporal order of CS and US occurrence and the temporal distance between these stimuli affect conditioning. We will also be concerned with the effects of the CS–US correlation and with the effects of the number of CS–US pairings. In each of these cases, certain circumstances favor the development of the CS as a signal for the US, while others do not. As we will see, the same circumstances that enable a CS to become a reliable signal also tend to provide an optimal climate for conditioning.

The temporal order of the CS and US In the natural environment, potential CSs and USs can occur at any time and in any number of arrangements. For example, a potential US may occur quite some time after a potential CS has appeared. In some cases, a potential CS may not occur until after a US has already disappeared. Sometimes such stimuli may even occur at precisely the same time. What degree of conditioning should be expected when these different arrangements occur? To answer this question, researchers have analyzed a variety of CS–US configurations. The four most commonly studied arrangements are depicted in Figure 2.3.

The first two arrangements are the delayed and trace conditioning configurations. Both arrangements are examples of what is termed *forward conditioning,* since the beginning (onset) of the CS precedes the onset of the US in both cases. The difference between the forward delayed and forward trace situations has to do with when the end (offset) of the CS occurs relative to the beginning of the US. In *delayed conditioning,* the CS begins before the US, and it does not end until sometime after US onset. In other words, the durations of the CS and the US overlap to some degree. In the *trace conditioning* situation the CS begins *and* ends before US onset. Thus, time elapses between the end of one stimulus and the onset of the other. This procedure is called trace conditioning because at the time the US occurs, only an internal "trace" or memory of the CS remains.

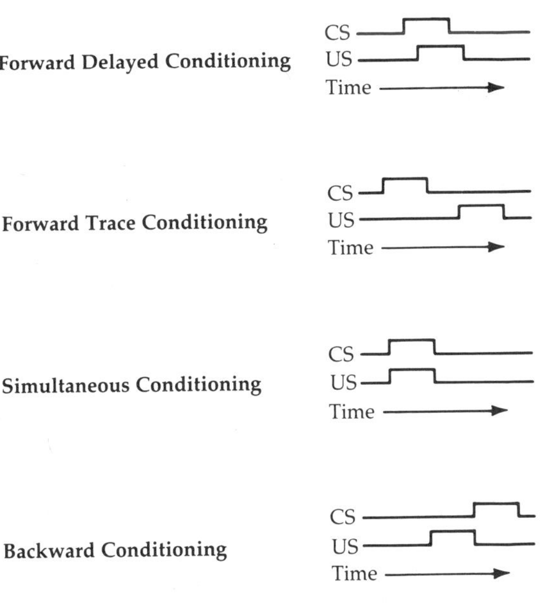

FIGURE 2.3 Common CS–US arrangements used in Classical conditioning experiments.

It is clear that a CS can come to produce a conditioned response when either of these forward conditioning arrangements occurs (see Ellison, 1964). However, most studies have shown that the conditioning produced by the delayed procedure is far superior to that which occurs when a trace conditioning arrangement is used. For example, Schneiderman (1966) compared these two procedures in an attempt to condition the rabbit's nictitating membrane. He found that the delayed procedure produced much faster conditioning of the response than did the trace arrangement. This superiority was particularly evident when the trace procedure involved longer intervals between CS offset and US onset. Similar results have been reported by Kamin (1965), who studied the effect of these arrangements in a CER paradigm.

A third type of CS–US arrangement is termed *simultaneous conditioning,* because the CS and US begin and end at the same time. In comparing the delayed and trace conditioning procedures, we saw that some degree of overlap between the CS and US appeared to aid conditioning. From this, one might assume that simultaneous conditioning would be very effective, since it involves total CS–US congruity. This, however, is not the case. Although the simultaneous procedure has been studied only sparingly, most experiments have shown it to be almost totally ineffective as a conditioning procedure (Bitterman, 1964; Smith, Coleman, & Gormezano, 1969). Although simultaneous conditioning has occasionally been shown to produce small amounts of conditioned responding (see, for example, Burkhardt & Ayres, 1978), this arrangement is clearly not as effective as the forward conditioning configurations.

The final arrangement outlined in Figure 2.3 is called *backward conditioning*. This procedure is in effect whenever the onset of the US precedes the onset of the CS. In general, backward conditioning is inferior to the forward conditioning arrangements in the production of conditioned responding (see, for example, Mackintosh, 1974). However, a variety of factors influence the amount and type of responding obtained with this procedure.

Some researchers have found that backward conditioning produces no evidence of excitatory conditioned responding at all (Terrace, 1973). Others have found that the procedure can result in Classical inhibitory conditioning, especially when a large number of backward pairings are used (Hall, 1984; Moscovitch & LoLordo, 1968; Siegal & Domjan, 1971). Still other studies have reported that backward conditioning can produce excitatory CRs if special conditions exist (Heth & Rescorla, 1973; Mahoney & Ayres, 1976; Spetch, Wilkie, & Pinel, 1981; Wagner & Terry, 1975). Basically, this procedure appears to result in excitatory CRs in two types of circumstances. First, excitatory conditioning is most likely to be found when only a few conditioning trials are used. Second, excitatory CRs may result when the occurrence of the US on each trial is particularly surprising or unpredictable. Why these special conditions seem to enhance the effectiveness of the backward conditioning arrangement will be discussed later in some detail.

In summary, it appears that excitatory conditioning occurs most readily when forward conditioning arrangements are in effect. This finding makes sense given our initial characterization of the conditioning process. We stated earlier that excitatory conditioning seems to depend on a CS becoming a reliable signal for the occurrence of a US. In both the delayed and trace conditioning arrangements, the CS precedes the US and, thus, can serve as such a signal. This is not the case in either the simultaneous or the backward configuration and, as a result, excitatory conditioning with these procedures is relatively poor. Still, the fact that these procedures do lead to excitatory CRs on some occasions is important. It suggests that conditioning may depend on more than simply the degree to which a CS comes to serve as a signal for US occurrence.

The CS–US interval Even in forward conditioning arrangements, the effectiveness of conditioning depends to a large degree on the *CS–US interval*—that is, the time between the onset of the CS and the beginning of the US. The importance of the CS–US interval can be seen in Figure 2.4, which represents the results of an experiment by Smith, Coleman, and Gormezano (1969) in which the rabbit's nictitating membrane response was studied. In this ex-

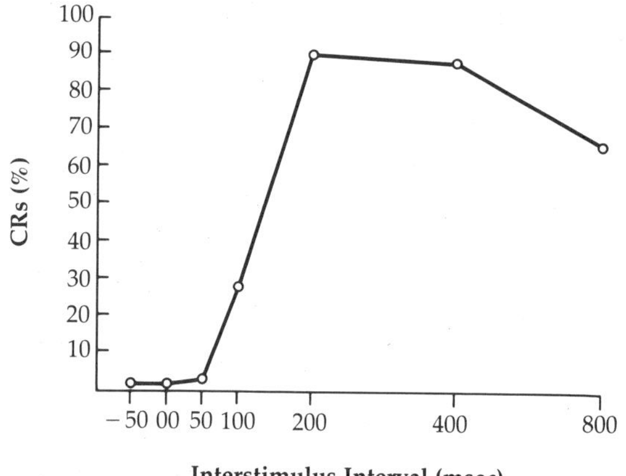

FIGURE 2.4 The percentage of trials on which a CR occurs as a function of the length of the CS–US interval. Note that conditioning is poor when either backward (−50 msec) or simultaneous (0 msec) pairings occur. Maximal conditioning results when the CS–US interval is approximately 200 msec. (After Smith, et al., 1969.)

periment, the rabbits were exposed to a 50-millisecond (msec) tone CS and a 50-msec shock US. The rabbits differed in terms of the number of milliseconds that separated the CS and US onsets. As you can see, when backward (-50 msec) and simultaneous (0 msec) arrangements were used, the percentage of conditioned responses produced was negligible. Animals that received forward conditioning configurations in which the CS–US interval was very short (50 msec) also showed little evidence of conditioning. Maximal conditioning was obtained when animals were exposed to a CS–US interval of approximately 200 msec. Longer CS–US intervals tended to be less effective in producing CRs.

Although the specific time intervals that result in maximal conditioning do vary from one paradigm to another, studies done with virtually all paradigms have shown that the same pattern of effects occurs. Extremely short CS–US intervals seldom result in conditioning. Maximal conditioning usually occurs when the CS–US interval is between 200 msec and 2 seconds. As the CS–US interval is gradually increased beyond this optimal interval, less and less conditioned responding usually results.

Again, just as we noted when we discussed the order of stimulus occurrence, the CS–US intervals that produce the best conditioning are the same intervals that seem to favor the CS becoming a reliable signal. For the CS to develop this capacity, it must precede the US by some finite period of time. However, with extremely long CS–US intervals, it becomes difficult for an organism to recognize the CS as a signal for some discrete, future event. When CS–US intervals are long, the CS tends to signal a period of US absence rather than signaling the impending onset of the US.

There is one clear exception to the rule that long CS–US intervals fail to promote conditioning. This exception occurs in a situation that is usually termed the *taste aversion* or *poisoning paradigm* (see, for example, Garcia, Ervin, & Koelling, 1966). In this paradigm, an animal is allowed to drink a liquid or consume food that has a distinctive odor or flavor. The animal is subsequently injected with a chemical that produces nausea, such as lithium chloride. When tested later, the animals usually show a clear avoidance of the odor or taste they experienced before they became ill. In this paradigm the odor or taste functions as the CS, while the US is the chemical that produces nausea. The avoidance of the odor or taste represents the conditioned response.

One of the unusual features of this paradigm is that several hours may elapse between the time the taste or odor is experienced and the time the chemical begins to produce nausea. In effect, this means that the CS–US interval in this situation often lasts for several hours. Despite this lengthy interval, conditioning obviously occurs, and the strength of the conditioning is often remarkable. Anyone who has ever eaten spoiled food and has later become ill can attest to how aversive the taste of a particular food can become. It is not at all clear how this particular form of conditioning can occur when such long CS–US intervals are involved. As we will see, however, the taste aversion paradigm presents an entire range of problems for theorists in the field of Classical conditioning.

The correlation of CS and US occurrence We have noted that a CS becomes an effective signal for a US whenever a strong positive correlation exists between the two stimuli. In other words, the CS becomes a reliable signal when it regularly precedes the occurrence of the US. From this, you might predict that the degree of conditioning would also depend on the degree to which the CS and the US are positively correlated. This prediction is clearly supported by data from a variety of conditioning paradigms.

To illustrate the importance of the CS–US correlation, let's consider an extreme example. Assume that you are studying conditioning in two groups of organisms. Both groups receive the same number of exposures to the CS and the US. However, one group receives a +1.0 correlation between the CS and the US. In other words, in this group the US is *always* preceded by a presentation of the CS. The second group receives a 0.0 correlation between the two stimuli—that is, the presentations of CS and US occur totally at random. This means that for the second group sometimes two CSs might occur in sequence. At other times two USs might occur together. And, at still other times, a CS might precede a US presentation by chance. How would you expect these two groups to compare in terms of conditioned responding to the CS?

Several researchers have made this kind of comparison and the results are clear (see, for example, Gamzu & Williams, 1971; Rescorla, 1966, 1968, 1969a; Weisman & Litner, 1969). A strong positive correlation between a CS and a US usually produces substantial conditioning. However, a zero correlation produces virtually no evidence of conditioning even when some CS–US pairings do occur by chance. At first glance, these findings appear to be convincing evidence that a positive CS–US correlation is necessary for conditioning. There is, however, another way to interpret this finding. The group that receives the positive correlation is exposed to a greater number of CS–US pairings than the zero correlation group receives. Thus, the superior performance of the positive correlation group may be due simply to its having received more pairings, rather than the greater CS–US correlation in this group.

To choose between these alternative interpretations, it is necessary to conduct an experiment in which two groups receive the same number of CS–US pairings but are exposed to different CS–US correlations. Several experiments of this type have been carried out by Rescorla (1968, 1969). In one of these studies (Rescorla, 1968: experiment 2), rats were trained in a CER paradigm using a tone as the CS and a mild shock as the US. Four of the groups in this experiment received the same number of tone–shock pairings. However, these groups differed in terms of the probability that shock would also occur when the tone was absent. Since the CS–US correlation depends on how consistently the US is preceded by the CS, groups that received large numbers of US-alone presentations actually experienced low CS–US correlations.

The results of this experiment are plotted in Figure 2.5. Recall that better conditioning is reflected by lower suppression ratios in the CER paradigm. As you can see, the group that received no shocks in the absence of the CS exhibited substantial conditioning. However, as the probability of shock-alone presentations increased, the amount of conditioning decreased. This result illustrates that conditioning depends to a large degree on the CS–US correlation, or on how reliably the CS signals a US occurrence. As the positive correlation between a CS and a US increases, so does the

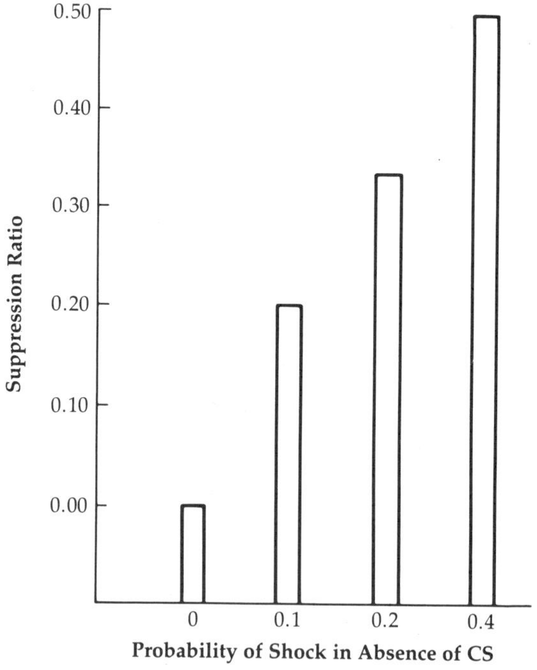

FIGURE 2.5 Amount of conditioning as a function of the probability that the US will occur alone. (From Rescorla, 1968, Exp. 2.)

amount of conditioned responding. Importantly, CS–US correlations influence conditioning even when the number of CS–US pairings is taken into account.

The number of CS–US pairings If we assume that all other factors that affect conditioning are optimal, the amount of conditioned responding depends directly on the number of CS–US pairings. In general, the more CS–US pairings an organism experiences, the greater the probability that a CR will occur. There is, however, a limit to this effect. After a substantial number of CS–US pairings have occurred, this increase in conditioned responding will level off or reach *asymptote.* Asymptote is simply the maximal amount of responding that can be obtained with a particular set of conditioning circumstances.

In some cases asymptote is determined by the measure of responding used. For example, if the measure of responding is the percentage of times the CS produces a CR, this measure must obviously level off at 100 percent. In other cases, however, asymptote will depend either on the physical limitations of an organism or on the physical characteristics of the CS and US. Figure 2.6 illustrates the relationship between conditioned responding and the number of CS–US pairings in three of the paradigms we have discussed thus far. These graphical representations are usually called *learning* or *acquisition curves,* since they reflect the degree to which a CR is learned or acquired as a function of CS–US experiences.

Characteristics of the CS and the US

We have seen that the physical arrangement of a CS and US can determine the degree to which conditioning occurs. It is also the case that conditioned responding depends on the particular characteristics of the CS and US that are used. In this section we will look at the effects of certain CS and US characteristics on the conditioning process. Specifically, we will be concerned with three factors: the intensity or salience of these stimuli, the organism's prior experience with these stimuli, and, the relationship between the CS and US characteristics.

CS and US intensity When we talk about the intensity of a stimulus, we are referring to where that stimulus falls on some physical scale or dimension. For example, visual stimuli vary in brightness just as auditory stimuli differ in terms of loudness. Tactile stimuli vary in

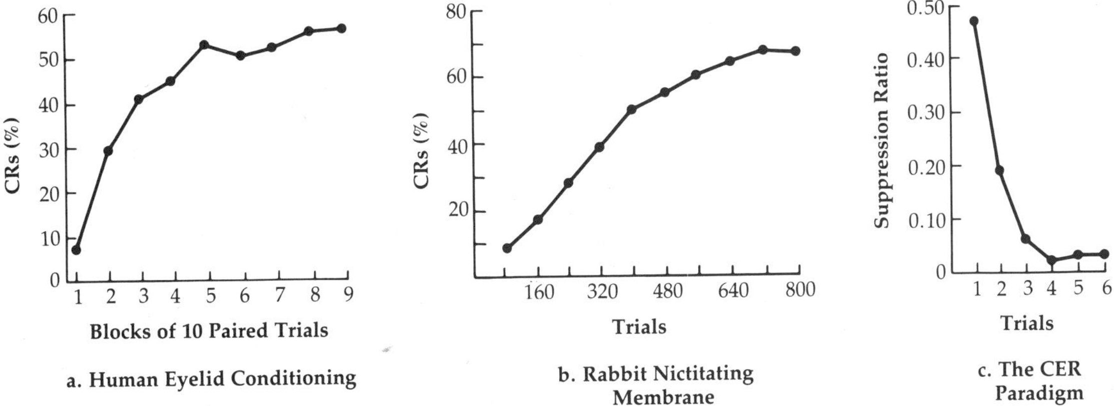

FIGURE 2.6 Amount of conditioning as a function of the number of CS–US pairings. (After (a) Trapold and Spence, 1960; (b) Gormezano, 1965; and (c) Lovibond, Preston, and Mackintosh, 1984.)

terms of the pressures they can exert on the skin, whereas foods may differ in terms of amount or sweetness. In all these cases we are really referring to the potential a stimulus has for activating an organism's sense receptors.

The effects of CS and US intensity on conditioning are reasonably straightforward. Conditioning normally improves as the intensity of either the CS or the US increases. Although most research has been clear on this point, there has been some disagreement about *why* the intensity of these stimuli affects the conditioning process.

In the case of the CS, it now appears evident that the *absolute* intensity of the stimulus is relatively unimportant. In other words, the use of a very loud tone as a CS does not necessarily ensure better conditioning than would be obtained if a moderately loud tone were used. What appears to be important is the intensity of the CS relative to the background stimuli that are present when the CS occurs. Better conditioning usually results when the CS is clearly discriminable from the stimulus background (see, for example, Logan, 1954).

This difference between absolute intensity and discriminability can be seen in a study conducted by Kamin (1965) using a CER paradigm. In this study the CS was not the presentation of a discrete stimulus. Rather, the CS was a decrease in the level of background noise that normally existed in the experimental chamber. All rats were exposed to white noise in the chamber at the level of 80 decibels. Then different groups were given varying decreases in this background noise level as their CS. The noise decrease was always followed by shock. Kamin found that the groups that experienced the largest noise decreases as a CS showed the greatest evidence of conditioning. This occurred even though the groups with large noise decreases were actually being exposed to less intense noise levels at the time of shock delivery. In effect, this finding shows that conditioning does not depend to any great extent on the intensity of the stimulus that precedes the US. What is important is that the CS be clearly different from the remaining stimuli present in the environment.

As we have noted, US intensity also appears to affect the conditioning process. In this case, however, the mechanism by which US intensity has its effect is less clear. One early idea was that low-intensity USs are less effective, because they are less capable of eliciting a reflexive reaction. However, several studies have shown that the degree to which a US elicits a UR has little relationship to whether the US effectively promotes conditioning (Bruner, 1969; Soltysik, 1971). Most likely, US intensity has its effect by directly influencing the learning process itself. However, what this influence might be is not presently understood.

Prior experience with CS or US It is not unusual in a laboratory experiment for both CS and US to be novel. How many times, for example, are rats exposed to a particular tone or shock before they take part in a conditioning experiment? In our day-to-day lives, however, the potential conditioning situations we encounter often involve CSs or USs with which we are already familiar. How does our prior experience with a CS or a US affect the degree to which these stimuli will promote conditioning?

It is well known that pre-exposures to a CS by itself often retard later conditioning involving that CS. In other words, if a CS such as a tone is repeatedly presented to an organism without any US, later attempts to pair the tone with some US usually result in poor conditioning. This phenomenon is called *latent inhibition* (Lubow & Moore, 1959). Similarly, prior experience with a US also appears to interfere with the conditioning process. Several studies have demonstrated that when an organism is exposed to a series of US-alone presentations, later conditioning involving that US tends to be slowed (see, for example, Randich & LoLordo, 1979). This phenomenon is termed the *US pre-exposure effect.*

Why do pre-exposures to CSs and USs retard later conditioning involving these stimuli? The most likely reason in the case of the CS is that prior exposures cause an organism to learn that the CS signals nothing of consequence. In other words, when the CS occurs regularly without a US, the organism learns that the CS is irrelevant. This "learned irrelevance" then interferes with later attempts to learn that the CS signals something of significance (Baker & Mackintosh, 1977).

The effects of US pre-exposure have been explained in at least two ways. First, some researchers have suggested that during US-alone presentations, an organism learns that the US is unpredictable. In effect, an organism learns that there is no reliable signal for the US occurrence. This learning is then presumed to interfere with later attempts to learn that some CS does signal the US (Baker & Mercier, 1982; Baker, Mercier, Gabel, & Baker, 1981).

The second explanation of this effect is based on the notion that US pre-exposures never really occur alone. Such pre-exposures occur in the presence of background or contextual stimuli such as room lighting, background noise levels, and odors specific to the situation. According to this view, these background stimuli function in much the same way as regular, discrete CSs. These background stimuli become signals that the US will occur and, thus, become capable of producing conditioned responses. Later, when a discrete CS is paired with the US, the organism has no need to learn about the CS as a signal, since it already has background stimuli that signal the US occurrence (see, for example, Tomie, 1976).

This view of the US pre-exposure effect is based on another conditioning phenomenon called *blocking*. We will discuss this phenomenon in greater detail later. For present purposes, blocking simply refers to the tendency of organisms that already have a reliable signal for a US not to learn about additional, redundant signals. This "blocking interpretation" of the US pre-exposure effect has been widely supported in recent years (see, for example, Hinson, 1982; Randich, 1981; Randich & Ross, 1985; Tomie, 1976). Even so, research continues into the question of how US pre-exposure affects subsequent conditioning.

The CS–US relationship For a number of years researchers viewed Classical conditioning as a relatively automatic, invariant process. It was assumed that CSs were essentially interchangeable. That is, given a particular US, any stimulus that was capable of becoming a signal would begin to produce a conditioned response. It was assumed, for example, that if the US were an airpuff to the eye, tones, lights, tastes, odors, and tactile stimuli would all be equally effective as CSs. Furthermore, it was assumed that the conditioned response produced by all these stimuli would be essentially the same.

We now know that the rules of conditioning are not so simple. First of all, it is clear that the conditioned response produced by a CS depends on more than the characteristics of the US. The nature of a CR depends instead on the *combined* characteristics of the CS and US. This is illustrated in a series of experiments conducted by Holland (1977) in which rats were presented with food pellets as the US. This experimenter found that if each presentation of the food were preceded by a tone CS, the rats would come to respond to the tone with an increase in motor activity. In effect, the CR in this case consisted of increased movement, especially in the vicinity of the food delivery location. However, if a light were used to signal the food occurrence, an entirely different CR developed. Instead of increased activity in response to the light, the rats actually decreased their motor movements. The typical response to the light involved orienting toward the food receptacle, rearing on the hind legs, and remaining relatively still until the food delivery. These and similar findings (see, for example, Rescorla, 1980) indicate that it is the combined characteristics of the CS and the US that determine the nature of the conditioned response.

Not only does the interaction of CS and US

characteristics determine the *type* of response that is learned, it also may determine whether *any* CR is produced. In recent years, there has been much discussion of what is termed *CS–US relevance.* This term refers to whether a CS and a US belong to the same category or class of stimuli. For example, some stimuli such as tastes, hunger pangs, and feelings of nausea have been termed *interoceptive stimuli* because they are all related in some way to internal hunger or digestive processes. Other stimuli such as lights, tones, and shocks have been labeled *exteroceptive stimuli* because they arise from an organism's external environment and have an impact on peripheral sense receptors. With these distinctions in mind, many researchers have asked whether CSs and USs from different categories are as likely to become associated as CSs and USs from the same category.

One problem with asking such a question is that it is often difficult to categorize stimuli in any meaningful, consistent fashion. For example, many birds use visual stimuli rather than taste cues to seek out appropriate foods. Does this make a visual stimulus in the bird an interoceptive stimulus, or is it still exteroceptive because it arises outside the bird itself? No one has been able to provide a clear classification system into which stimuli can be placed. Still, research into the role of stimulus categories has focused attention on an important principle. Some combinations of CSs and USs appear to promote effective conditioning while others do not.

The classic example of this principle is contained in a study conducted by Garcia and Koelling (1966). These researchers trained rats to drink a solution from a tube. As the animals drank, they were exposed to two types of stimuli. First, the solution had a distinctive flavor. Second, as the animals drank, a light and a clicking sound were presented. Thus, both taste and audiovisual stimuli occurred as CSs. Shortly after drinking, half the rats were exposed to a shock US while the other half received an injection of lithium chloride. As explained earlier, lithium chloride can serve as a US on a delayed basis because it naturally produces nausea some time after its injection.

To measure conditioned responding to the CSs in this study, Garcia and Koelling gave the rats from these two groups access to the drinking tubes once again after conditioning. Half the shocked rats and half the poisoned rats were allowed to drink a solution having the original taste. The other half of each group was allowed to drink a tasteless solution but was confronted with the audiovisual stimulus while they were drinking. The question of interest was the degree to which the rats would show a fear of, or an aversion to, the taste and the audiovisual CSs.

From the partial results of this study shown in Figure 2.7, it is clear that rats that had been shocked drank very little when drinking was accompanied by the audiovisual stimulus. They drank a great deal, however, when the distinctive taste was the only CS present during testing. Rats that had been poisoned exhibited exactly the opposite behavior. They tended to avoid drinking when it involved contacting the distinctive taste, but they readily drank a tasteless solution that was accompanied by lights and clickers. These results indicate that certain combinations of CSs and USs (for example, a visual stimulus paired with shock or a taste paired with poison) result in effective conditioning. However, other CS–US combinations (for example, a taste paired with shock) produce little evidence of conditioned responding.

The finding that conditioned responding depends on particular CS–US combinations has now been well established (see Domjan, 1983). However, the question of why only certain combinations of stimuli result in conditioning remains unanswered. According to some theorists, organisms come "genetically prepared" to make certain kinds of associations and not others (see, for example, Bolles, 1970; Seligman, 1970). Such an interpretation

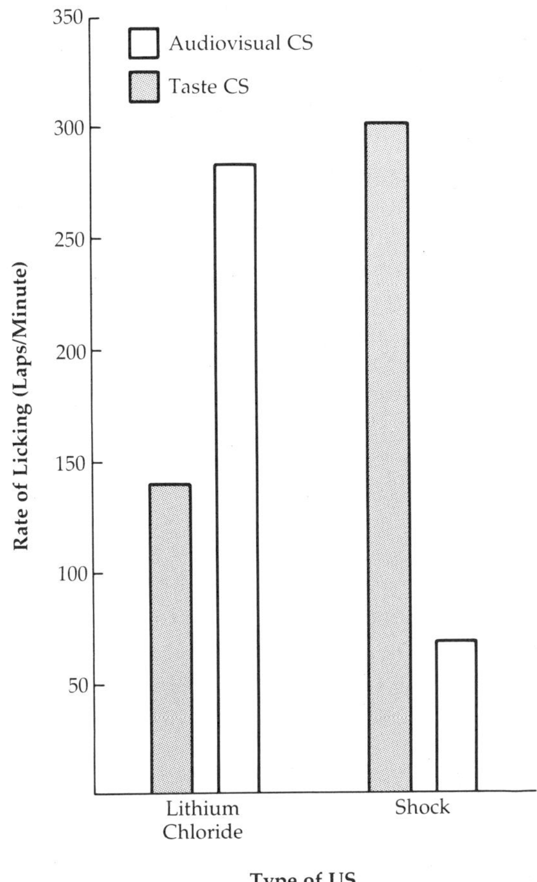

FIGURE 2.7 Avoidance of either taste or audiovisual CSs by animals receiving either lithium chloride or shock as a US. (From Garcia and Koelling, 1966.)

is appealing, given what we know about evolutionary processes. Most genetic predispositions seem to have evolved because they contribute in some way to an organism's survival. Certainly, the potential for survival would be enhanced if organisms were genetically predisposed to make certain associations rather than others. Obviously an organism that associates sounds with illness is not as likely to avoid toxic foods as is an organism that associates tastes with illness.

Still, using the notion of genetic preparedness to explain the differential associability of stimuli is problematic. The major problem is that no one has been able to determine in advance of conditioning which stimuli should be associable and which should not be, based solely on what we know about an organism's nervous system or its evolutionary background. Thus, the preparedness hypothesis gives us no way to predict when conditioning should be successful and when it should not be. The tendency has been to try conditioning with certain stimuli and when it is successful, to assume that an organism was prepared to associate those particular stimuli. This does not mean, of course, that the notion of genetic preparedness is incorrect. As we have said, it is an appealing idea. For it to be a useful explanation, however, we need to be able to determine in advance of conditioning which stimuli are likely to be associable and which are not, based on what we know about an organism's genetic makeup.

One other explanation advanced for these findings is that all combinations of CSs and USs may promote conditioning, but the rules for conditioning may differ depending on which combination occurs. One example of this rationale can be seen in a study by Krane and Wagner (1975). These researchers reasoned that stimuli such as tastes may leave an internal trace that lasts for a long time after the ingestion of the experimental food or liquid. Thus, when an animal experiences a taste that is followed by a shock, the internal trace of the taste may remain within the animal long after any trace of the shock has disappeared. This means that the taste will function not only as a signal for the occurrence of shock, but it will remain to signal the absence of shock as well. As we will see, a CS that signals both the presence and absence of a US promotes little observable conditioning.

Based on this notion, Krane and Wagner exposed rats to a distinctive flavor and afterward shocked different groups of rats at various intervals. They found that groups given shocks several seconds after the taste did form an aversion to the taste. However, rats shocked immediately after the taste formed no aversion. This, of course, is exactly the opposite of what has been found using CSs such as tones or lights. Such studies are interesting because they suggest that certain CS–US combinations may promote conditioning, but only when the accepted rules of conditioning are changed in some way.

In summary, it is clear that not all CSs are interchangeable in the conditioning process. Certain CSs may come to produce one response when paired with a US, while other CSs paired with the same US may produce an entirely different CR. It is also evident that using a given set of conditioning parameters, some CS–US combinations result in evidence of conditioning while others may not. A complete understanding of conditioning requires an understanding of why these phenomena occur. An abundance of current research is aimed at investigating these issues.

The Presence of Other Stimuli during Conditioning

To this point we have discussed conditioning situations in which a single CS is paired with a single US. In the natural environment, however, CSs rarely occur by themselves. In fact, even in laboratory settings it is virtually impossible to present a CS in isolation from other stimuli. When we talk about a particular CS, we are usually referring to one component of the stimulus complex or compound that is present to signal the US.

Consider the following example of conditioning. You arrive home one evening and find that your puppy has gnawed into the living room couch. In an effort to modify the puppy's behavior (and probably to vent your own anger), you roll up a newspaper, hold the puppy's nose against the gnawed upholstery, and proceed to spank the puppy with the paper. The next evening you come home, sit on the damaged couch, and begin to read the newspaper. As you read, you notice that the puppy is not in its accustomed place next to your feet but is instead cowering in a corner of the room.

Clearly, the spanking episode has resulted in a conditioned fear reaction. The dog exhibits fear to some stimulus that has not before elicited such a response. But, what stimulus in particular is producing the fear CR? Is it the sight of the menacing newspaper? Is it you? If it is you, then what specific aspect of you does the dog fear? It could be your facial expression, your odor, your physical build, or your shoes. All these stimuli were present when the dog was spanked, and any one or any combination of these stimuli could have become a signal for the punishment.

In the present section we will find that the degree to which conditioning occurs to one stimulus often depends on what other stimuli are present at the time of conditioning. In other words, conditioning to one component of a stimulus compound is usually affected by the nature of the other stimuli in that same compound. We will concentrate on three conditioning phenomena. In the first, called *overshadowing*, one part of a compound is more salient or noticeable than another part. In the second phenomenon, called *blocking*, one component of a compound has already undergone some conditioning to the US. Third, we will consider situations in which conditioning to one stimulus component depends on how well other stimuli in the compound are correlated with the US.

Overshadowing Some stimuli in a compound are more salient or noticeable to an organism simply because they are more intense than other stimuli. For example, some stimuli may simply be brighter, louder, or more odorous than others. In other cases, however, the relative salience of stimuli may depend on the organism that experiences them. In other words, certain organisms, by virtue of their sensory apparatus, appear to be predisposed to notice stimuli of certain kinds, rather than others. Dogs and rats, for example, appear to rely on odors more than visual stimuli in their natural environments. The exact opposite is true of humans and pigeons. How does the differential salience of stimuli in a CS compound affect the degree to which the elements in that compound come to produce conditioned responding?

Several experimenters have studied how the salience of one stimulus affects conditioning to other stimuli in a compound (see, for example, Kamin, 1969; Kasprow, Cacheiro, Balaz, & Miller, 1982; Mackintosh, 1971; Pavlov, 1927). In one of these experiments, Kamin(1969) trained rats in a CER paradigm using either single or compound stimuli to signal shock. Three groups of rats were given pairings of a single CS with shock. For one group the CS was a light, for another it was a loud noise (80 decibels), and for the final group it was a less intense noise (50 decibels). All three groups developed fear responses to their respective CSs, indicating that all three stimuli were effective CSs when presented alone.

The groups of primary interest were the two groups given compound CSs paired with shock. One group received the light in compound with the loud noise. Half of this group was later tested with the light alone and the other half with the loud noise alone. Kamin found that the animals exhibited a strong fear response to the light but only a mild fear response to the loud noise. This indicated that the light had somehow lessened conditioning to the noise when the two stimuli had occurred in compound as a signal for shock. In the other group, the compound CS consisted of the light and the less intense noise. Here the effect of the light was even stronger. Animals tested with the light alone again showed strong conditioning to the light. However, those rats tested with the low intensity noise showed almost no evidence of conditioning to this stimulus.

Since the 50-decibel noise used in this study was shown to be an effective CS when it alone was paired with shock, the failure for it to condition when presented in compound must have been due to the presence of the light at the time of conditioning. Pavlov (1927) originally labeled this phenomenon *overshadowing*, to indicate that more salient stimuli in a CS compound can diminish the effectiveness of less salient stimuli. As a result, less salient stimuli often fail to acquire the capacity for producing a CR when they occur in compound with more salient stimuli.

Although overshadowing is a phenomenon that occurs readily in a variety of conditioning situations, at least one conditioning paradigm appears to be an exception. As you might guess from our previous discussions, this exception is found in the taste aversion or poisoning paradigm. In this situation it has been found that odors as well as tastes may become associated with nausea. However, in many cases odors are less effective than tastes as CSs in this type of conditioning situation. Surprisingly, one technique that has been used to enhance conditioned aversions to odors consists of placing the odors in compound with a novel, salient taste. For some reason, rats that experience taste–odor compounds before becoming nauseated do develop strong aversions to the odors (see, for example, Kucharski & Spear, 1984; Palmerino, Rusiniak, & Garcia, 1980; Rusiniak, Hankins, Garcia, & Brett, 1979). This phenomenon has been labeled *potentiation,* to indicate that a salient element of a compound can sometimes enhance conditioning to less salient elements. Why overshadowing occurs in some situations and potentiation occurs in others is not well understood (see Durlach & Rescorla, 1980). However, it is clear that conditioning to one element of a compound often depends on how salient other elements happen to be.

Blocking We have seen that when one stimulus in a compound is more salient than another, the more salient stimulus may prevent the other from developing a conditioned response. The same is true when one element of a compound has undergone conditioning before being placed in that compound. The previously conditioned stimulus prevents the novel stimulus from becoming an effective CS. This form of overshadowing is given the specific label of *blocking*.

The initial demonstration of blocking came from a series of studies by Kamin (1968, 1969) in which, again, rats were trained in a CER paradigm. The treatments for the most critical groups in these experiments are outlined in Figure 2.8. The first two groups were exposed to pairings of a compound CS (noise–light) with shock. However, group 2 was given several pairings of the noise and the shock before the compound trials began. After the compound CS–shock pairings, both groups were tested to assess fear responding to the light. Only group 1 showed substantial fear in the presence of the light. In group 2 the prior conditioning to the noise enabled the noise to overshadow the light when the two stimuli were placed in compound.

The last two groups were treated comparably to the first two groups in that both groups received a series of compound CS–shock pairings. In this case, however, group 4 received prior conditioning to the light. Furthermore, after compound conditioning, both these groups were tested to assess their fear of the noise. In this instance, group 3 showed evidence of fear to the noise while group 4 did not.

These findings indicate that if one stimulus is already a reliable signal for the US by virtue of prior conditioning, this stimulus will block conditioning to other stimuli with which it is compounded. We might conceptualize this effect by saying that during compound con-

	Stage 1	**Stage 2**	**Stage 3**
Group 1	(No Pre-Exposure)	Noise + Light } Shock	**Test:** Light
Group 2	Noise–Shock	Noise + Light } Shock	**Test:** Light
Group 3	(No Pre-Exposure)	Noise + Light } Shock	**Test:** Noise
Group 4	Light–Shock	Noise + Light } Shock	**Test:** Noise

FIGURE 2.8 The main conditions in Kamin's blocking experiment. (From Kamin, 1968, 1969.)

ditioning, if one stimulus already reliably signals the US, an organism will simply view other stimuli as redundant. It may be that organisms have no need to learn about new signals if a reliable signal for the US is already present.

One bit of evidence that supports this interpretation is that blocking does not occur if the intensity of the US increases between the time of single stimulus and compound training. In other words, if a light is paired with a low-intensity US and then a tone–light compound is paired with a higher intensity US, conditioning to the tone is seldom blocked (Kamin, 1969). Kamin has suggested that prior pairings of the light and the low-intensity shock did not establish the light as a signal for the higher intensity shock presented during compound training. Thus, during compound training, since neither CS had previously become a reliable signal, both CSs developed CRs.

Correlation of the compound elements with the US As we have seen, blocking may occur when one stimulus appears in compound with another stimulus that already signals the US. Blocking, however, is only one example of how conditioning to one stimulus may depend on the *signal value* of other stimuli present at the same time. The term "signal value" refers to the degree to which one stimulus allows us to predict the occurrence of another. There is one principle that normally will enable us to predict how much one element in a compound will become conditioned. In most cases, *the degree of conditioning to one element of a compound is inversely related to the degree to which other elements in that compound already signal US occurrence.* In other words, on a given conditioning trial, an element is likely to gain in its capacity to produce a CR as long as other elements in the compound are poor signals for the US. On the other hand, an element is likely to gain little capacity for producing a CR when other elements in the compound are good signals for US occurrence.

This principle is illustrated rather well by the results of a set of experiments by Wagner, Logan, Haberlandt, and Price (1968). One study in this series involved nictitating membrane conditioning in the rabbit, while another utilized the CER paradigm with rats. The procedures for these experiments were, however, the same. For this reason we will discuss these procedures in general terms.

Each experiment involved two primary conditions, as outlined in Table 2.2. In the *correlated condition,* animals were exposed to two different compound CSs. On half their trials the animals received a compound consisting of a particular tone (T_1) and a light. We will designate this compound as T_1L. For this group T_1L was always followed by the US. On the other half of their trials, the correlated group received a CS compound consisting of the same light with a different tone. We will designate this compound as T_2L. The compound T_2L was never followed by the US.

In the other condition, the *uncorrelated condition,* animals were exposed to the same two CS compounds. On half their trials T_1L occurred and on the other half T_2L was presented. The only difference between the correlated and uncorrelated conditions was in terms of the degree to which each compound was correlated

TABLE 2.2 The Main Conditions Used in the Conditioning Experiment of Wagner, Logan, Haberlandt, and Price: T_1 = Tone 1, T_2 = Tone 2, and L = Light

	Correlated condition
50% of trials	T_1L: US
50% of trials	T_2L: no US
	Uncorrelated condition
25% of trials	T_1L: US
25% of trials	T_1L: no US
25% of trials	T_2L: US
25% of trials	T_2L: no US

with US occurrence. Whereas the correlated animals always received a US following T_1L, the uncorrelated animals received a US following only half of the T_1L presentations. And, whereas the correlated animals never received a US after T_2L, the uncorrelated animals again received a US on half of the T_2L trials.

In effect, then, both conditions involved US presentations on half of the conditioning trials. This means that in both conditions the light was followed by the US 50 percent of the time. However, in the correlated condition T_1 always signaled the occurrence of the US, while T_2 always signaled US absence. In the uncorrelated condition neither T_1 nor T_2 served as a reliable signal for the likely occurrence of the US. Both T_1 and T_2 sometimes preceded US occurrence and sometimes preceded the omission of the US. The question of interest was the degree to which the light would develop a CR in these two conditions.

The results of these experiments were clear. The light acquired the capacity to produce a CR in the uncorrelated condition but not in the correlated condition. This difference occurred even though the light had preceded the US 50 percent of the time in both conditions. The difference in the conditions was in terms of whether the different tones could be used as reliable signals for US occurrence. In the correlated condition the different tones served as effective signals, making the light redundant. Thus, in this condition there was little conditioning to the light. Light did acquire the capacity to elicit a CR, however, in the uncorrelated condition, where the tones did not function as reliable signals.

Results such as these have now been found in a variety of experimental situations (see, for example, Rescorla & Wagner, 1972). From such findings it is clear that the amount of conditioning to a given stimulus cannot be predicted solely on the basis of the correlation between that stimulus and the US. It also is necessary to know how well the other elements of a compound are correlated with US occurrence.

Conditioning without an Explicit US

Now that we have completed our discussion of factors that influence excitatory conditioning, we are ready to discover that conditioning can take place in some cases even when no explicit US appears to be present. Our discussion will concentrate on two phenomena: *higher order conditioning* and *sensory preconditioning*. The occurrence of these phenomena is important because it demonstrates how pervasive or widely occurring the conditioning process can be in the natural environment.

Higher order conditioning To serve as an effective US, a given stimulus must reliably produce some reflexive reaction. Normally, the only stimuli that meet this requirement are those that *naturally* elicit reflexive responses. However, once a stimulus has served as a CS in a conditioning situation, that stimulus also becomes capable of producing reflexlike reactions. The only difference is that the CS produces its reaction because of its prior conditioning history, whereas the US produces a response because of its natural characteristics.

This similarity between a US and a previously conditioned CS is important, because once a CS begins to produce a CR, the CS can serve in place of a US in a subsequent conditioning situation. For example, if a light has been paired regularly with shock, the light begins to produce a fear response on its own. At this point, a second CS that reliably signals the occurrence of the light will begin to produce a fear response also.

When conditioning results from the pairing of a novel CS with a previously conditioned CS, we call the process *higher order conditioning* (see Figure 2.9a for a description of the stages involved in this form of conditioning). The occurrence of higher order conditioning is well documented (see, for example, Rescorla, 1980), and the fact that it happens has important implications for human behavior.

We know that a child who has been bitten by a dog may begin to show fear reactions whenever the dog comes into view. This reaction occurs because the sight of the dog was present when the painful bite occurred. However, once the sight of the dog has become capable of producing a fear response, other stimuli associated with the sight of the dog may also begin to arouse fear. The child may begin to fear venturing into the backyard if that is where the dog is normally kept. Likewise, barking sounds may begin to elicit fear if the child associates barking with the dog's presence. In effect, one CS that has been paired with an effective US may then help to condition a variety of additional stimuli.

One difference between regular excitatory conditioning and higher order conditioning involves the strength or permanance of the conditioned response. We noted that when a CS and a US have a positive contingent relationship, the strength of the CR tends to increase, the greater the number of CS–US pairings. This is not the case, however, in higher order conditioning. If a novel CS (CS_2) is paired with a previously conditioned stimulus (CS_1), CS_2 will begin to produce a substantial response after a few trials. As more and more CS_2–CS_1 pairings occur, however, conditioned responding to CS_2 begins to decrease. Most probably this is due to the absence of any genuine US. When CS_1 occurs several times in the absence of the original US, it begins to lose its acquired capacity to produce a CR. As it loses this capacity, it also loses the capacity to serve in place of the US in other conditioning situations. Thus, while higher order conditioning does occur, the response produced in such situations appears to be more fragile than that produced in regular conditioning situations.

Sensory preconditioning Conditioning also appears to occur without benefit of a real US in the *sensory preconditioning* paradigm. Since this situation is often confused with higher order conditioning, the procedures for these two forms of conditioning are compared in Figure 2.9.

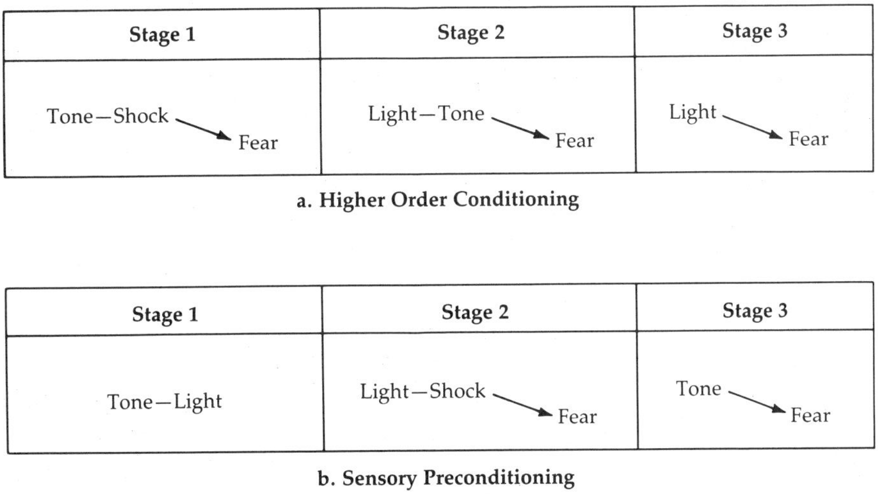

Stage 1	Stage 2	Stage 3
Tone—Shock → Fear	Light—Tone → Fear	Light → Fear

a. Higher Order Conditioning

Stage 1	Stage 2	Stage 3
Tone—Light	Light—Shock → Fear	Tone → Fear

b. Sensory Preconditioning

FIGURE 2.9 Stages in (a) the higher order conditioning procedure, and (b) the sensory preconditioning paradigm.

As indicated in Figure 2.9b, sensory preconditioning first involves the pairing of two CSs. In other words, two stimuli that do not naturally elicit a reflexive reaction are paired in the same manner as a CS and a US would normally be. For example, a light might be used to signal the occurrence of a tone.

In stage 2 of this procedure, the signaled stimulus from stage 1 (the tone) is used to signal the occurrence of a regular US such as a shock. After several conditioning trials, the tone begins to produce a conditioned fear response. This result is not surprising since the tone has become a reliable signal for the shock. What is surprising, however, is that once the tone and shock have been paired, the light from stage 1 also becomes capable of producing a fear response. This happens despite the fact that the light and shock have never been paired (see, for example, Brogden, 1939; Wynne & Brogden, 1962).

The usual interpretation of this result is that during stage 1 the two CSs that are paired become associated. In effect, an organism learns to react to these two stimuli as if they were equivalent. Later, when one of the stimuli is paired with a US and becomes capable of producing a CR, the organism reacts to the other CS as if it, too, had been paired with the US.

This phenomenon raises the possibility that excitatory conditioning may not really depend on a CS acting as a signal for a response-eliciting stimulus. It suggests that an association may be formed between any two stimuli that are paired such that one serves as a signal for the other. It may simply be that unless a true US is involved in conditioning, no measurable response is produced by the signaling stimulus. In general, the occurrence of sensory preconditioning emphasizes that learning may occur without any overt or measurable change in an organism's behavior. This becomes even clearer in other learning situations we will describe subsequently.

One additional point concerning this phenomenon should be made clear. Sensory preconditioning effects, like the effects of higher order conditioning, are relatively weak. Several studies have shown, for example, that sensory preconditioning is strongest when the number of CS_2–CS_1 pairings is small. Large numbers of CS_2–CS_1 pairings often result in little conditioned responding to CS_2 (see, for example, Hoffeld, Kendall, Thompson, & Brogden, 1960). Thus, regardless of what sensory preconditioning may tell us about what is necessary for conditioning to occur, it is clear that conditioning is strongest when a CS signals the occurrence of a biologically significant US.

Classical Inhibitory Conditioning

As we have noted previously, inhibitory conditioning results whenever a CS reliably signals the absence of a US an organism has come to expect. And a CS can become such a signal only when the CS and the US have a negative contingent relationship. The result of such conditioning is that an organism begins to respond to the CS by actively suppressing or withholding the response that the US normally elicits. For example, we know that food naturally produces salivation. A stimulus that reliably signals the absence of food usually begins to produce an active suppression of the salivary response.

From an adaptive viewpoint, it is easy to see why the occurrence of inhibitory conditioning is important. In many instances it is just as critical to learn when some significant event will be absent as it is to learn when such an event is likely to occur. Yet, until very recently, little research on inhibitory conditioning was done. As a matter of fact, many early theories of Classical conditioning dealt only with excitatory effects (see, for example, Bush & Mosteller, 1951). It was assumed in these theories that a CS that reliably signaled a US would become capable of producing a CR. However,

CSs that signaled the absence of a US were treated the same as CSs that signaled nothing. In effect, it was assumed that unless a CS signaled US occurrence, no conditioning of any type would result.

In recent years, interest in inhibitory conditioning has increased markedly (see, for example, Miller & Spear, 1985). Much of this interest has arisen because a number of contemporary theories have begun to treat excitatory and inhibitory conditioning as equally important processes (see, for example, Rescorla & Wagner, 1972). Still, our own discussion of inhibitory conditioning must be somewhat limited, given the relative scarcity of experimental evidence concerning this process. We begin this discussion by looking at the problems inherent in measuring inhibitory conditioned responding. Then we outline the procedures necessary for producing conditioning of this type.

Problems in Measuring the Inhibitory CR

The assessment of excitatory conditioned responding is relatively simple. Following CS–US pairings, all one need do is measure changes in the overt responses that are made to the CS. The measurement of inhibitory conditioned responding has not proved to be this easy. The problem that arises has to do with the nature of the inhibitory response that is learned. In most cases, the response is one of withholding some overt reaction. Thus, when an inhibitory CS is presented to an organism, the organism normally exhibits no discernible reaction. This makes it difficult to know when the CS has become a signal for US absence and when it has simply failed to become a reliable signal for anything.

To illustrate this difficulty, let's turn to a specific example. Assume that a particular stimulus has become a signal for the availability of food. Most organisms will begin to react to that stimulus with salivation and approach responses. Now assume that a second stimulus has become a signal indicating that food will not be presented. When this stimulus occurs, most organisms will withhold salivation and will not approach the stimulus. This failure to approach and salivate is similar to the reaction we would get if we presented a novel stimulus that had never come to signal anything concerning food. How, then, is it possible to distinguish between an inhibitory CS and a stimulus that has no relation whatsoever with the US?

To make such a distinction, researchers have begun to use two tests to determine when a stimulus has become an inhibitory CS. These instruments are usually termed the *retardation test* and the *summation test* for conditioned inhibition. As we will see, to determine conclusively that a stimulus has become an inhibitory CS, the stimulus must meet the requirements of both these tests.

The retardation test Once a single response to a given stimulus has been learned, it is usually difficult to train the organism to make an opposing or conflicting response to that same stimulus. For example, it may be relatively easy for a student to learn to speak out in class as long as such behavior is consistently rewarded. However, it is much more difficult to learn to speak out in class if one has previously learned *not* to raise questions in the classroom setting. Whenever two responses conflict or are incompatible, it is always difficult to learn to perform both responses in the same stimulus situation.

The retardation test for conditioned inhibition takes advantage of this difficulty of performing conflicting responses in the same situation. It is presumed that during inhibitory conditioning a CS comes to produce withholding or suppression of some reflexive reaction. This results because the CS has become a signal for the absence of a US that normally produces that reaction. If the same CS is now paired with that US (so that it now becomes a signal for US occurrence), normal excitatory conditioning should be slowed or retarded. It should take the CS longer to begin to produce the reflexive reaction, if previously the CS had come to produce withholding of that same response.

Thus, one way to determine whether a CS has become a reliable signal for US absence is to assess how long it takes the CS to become a reliable signal for US occurrence. Inhibitory conditioning is said to have occurred if that conditioning experience interferes with subsequent excitatory conditioning of the CS. This test for conditioned inhibition has been used in a variety of experiments (see, for example, Hammond, 1968; Siegel & Domjan, 1971). It is clear from such studies that prior training in which a CS signals US absence does retard later excitatory conditioning involving that same CS and US. As we will see, however, the difficulty in relying on this test alone is that several manipulations can retard excitatory conditioning. And, only a few of these manipulations appear to produce inhibitory conditioning.

The summation test The summation test for conditioned inhibition is also based on the idea that excitatory and inhibitory CRs are incompatible. In this case the test involves presenting a supposed inhibitory CS at the same time an excitatory CS is being presented. The rationale here is that if a CS has become a true response inhibitor, its presentation should decrease conditioned responding to the excitatory CS. In effect, the organism is presented with one stimulus that says "respond" while another stimulus that says "don't respond" is present. This technique was first developed by Pavlov (1927); however, numerous examples of this procedure have appeared in more recent experiments (see, for example, Hinson & Siegel, 1980; Rescorla & Holland, 1977). It is now common to accept a CS as a conditioned inhibitor if it is shown to be capable of reducing the excitatory CR produced by another CS.

Conditions That Promote Inhibitory Conditioning

By using the retardation and summation tests, it is possible to determine the degree to which inhibitory conditioning occurs in various experimental settings. As we will see, two factors appear to be necessary for the production of inhibitory CRs. First, there must be some reason for an organism to expect or predict that a specific US might occur in a given situation. Second, some stimulus must become a reliable signal for the absence of that US in that situation. Experimental settings in which both these requirements are met normally promote inhibitory conditioned responding.

CS discriminations One way to produce inhibitory conditioning is to expose an organism to two different CSs in the same stimulus situation. If CS+ is always followed by a US and CS− is never followed by a US, CS− will begin to evoke an inhibitory CR. Evidence that the CS− becomes a conditioned inhibitor comes from studies using both retardation (Hammond, 1968) and summation tests (Grossen & Bolles, 1968; Hammond, 1967). Apparently, in this kind of paradigm, organisms come to expect the US because it has occurred in the experimental context previously. The CS− becomes an inhibitor because it signals that the US will not occur in that context for some period of time.

In a related procedure that produces somewhat stronger inhibitory effects, first used by Pavlov (1927), organisms are exposed to two types of trials. On one trial type a single CS (CS_1) is paired with a US. On the other trial type, a compound CS consisting of CS_1 and a novel CS (CS_2) is presented. This compound CS is never followed by a US. As you might expect, CS_1 comes to elicit an excitatory conditioned response. However, CS_2 becomes a strong conditioned inhibitor as assessed by both retardation (Hoffman & Fitzgerald, 1982) and summation tests (Rescorla & Holland, 1977).

This procedure produces strong inhibitory effects because it is ideally suited for the development of conditioned inhibition. CS_1 becomes a reliable signal for US occurrence because it reliably precedes US presentation. Thus, when the CS_1CS_2 compound occurs, there is an expectation of US occurrence because the compound contains CS_1. The only part of the compound that uniquely signals US absence is CS_2. As a result, CS_2 takes on inhibitory characteristics.

Long CS–US intervals We have seen that in both trace and delayed conditioning procedures, long CS–US intervals produce only weak excitatory conditioning effects. There is even some evidence that long CS–US intervals can result in inhibitory conditioning to the CS. One example of such an effect comes from a pair of experiments conducted by Hinson and Siegel (1980). Both these experiments looked at the effects of trace conditioning on the rabbit's conditioned eye blink response. In describing these results, we will concentrate on two of the treatment conditions used in these studies.

In experiment 1, one group of animals received a number of trace conditioning trials, while a second group received no conditioning experience. The trace conditioning trials involved a brief presentation of a light or tone CS, followed 10 seconds later by a mild shock to the cheekbone. The mild shock served as the US because it naturally produced eyelid closure. Animals that received the trace conditioning experience showed no evidence of excitatory conditioning during this training.

In the second phase of the study, both the trace-conditioned group and the group given no training were exposed to 8 days of delayed conditioning trials. The CS and the US were the same as those the trace-conditioned animals had previously experienced. In this case, however, the beginning of the US overlapped the end of the CS. From Figure 2.10, which shows the results of this training, you can see that the animals that received no prior training

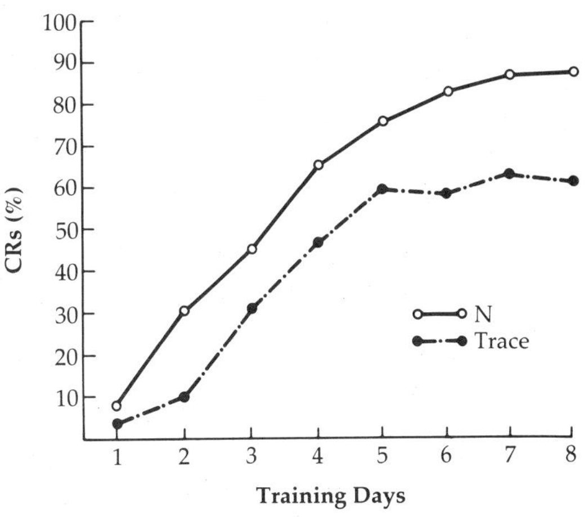

FIGURE 2.10 Conditioning with either a novel (N) or a previously trace-conditioned (Trace) CS. (From Hinson and Siegel, 1980, Exp. 1.)

rapidly acquired a conditioned response to the CS. However, the animals given prior trace conditioning showed retarded acquisition of the CR. This finding indicates that a long trace interval can result in a CS becoming inhibitory and can retard later excitatory conditioning involving that CS.

The second experiment confirmed this conclusion by using a summation test of conditioned inhibition. As in the first study, one group of rabbits received trace conditioning with CS_1 and the shock US. The other group received no conditioning experience. In stage 2 of the experiment, both groups received delayed conditioning trials involving a new CS (CS_2) and a shock US. During this training both groups showed substantial excitatory conditioning to CS_2. Finally, both groups received 6 days of tests in which CS_1 and CS_2 were presented in compound. The conditioned responding to the compound CS for both groups is shown in Figure 2.11 (page 42). Clearly, the group given prior trace conditioning with CS_1 made fewer responses to the compound than did the animals that had no experience with CS_1. Since both groups had shown substantial conditioning to CS_2, this re-

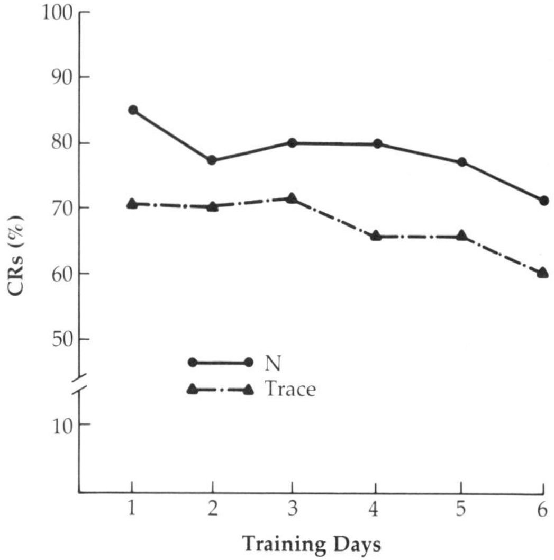

FIGURE 2.11 Summation testing in which an excitatory CS is placed in compound with either a novel (N) or a previously trace-conditioned (Trace) CS. (From Hinson and Siegel, 1980, Exp. 2.)

sult indicates that trace conditioning had promoted inhibitory conditioning to CS_1. In other words, prior trace conditioning made CS_1 capable of interfering with the excitatory CR produced by CS_2.

Although the evidence is not as strong, some studies have suggested that inhibitory conditioning may even occur in delayed conditioning paradigms when extremely long CS–US intervals are used (see, for example, Rescorla, 1967a). This means that a CS may even acquire inhibitory properties when the CS and US overlap, as long as the CS onset precedes the US onset by a substantial period of time.

How is it that inhibitory conditioning can result from trace and delayed conditioning procedures when in these paradigms the CS precedes the US? In such paradigms it would appear that the CS is a signal for US occurrence, not its nonoccurrence. The key factor here appears to be the length of the CS–US interval. When CS onset precedes US onset by several seconds or even minutes, the CS actually signals a period of time during which the US will not occur. Apparently, when this is the case, the CS becomes capable of producing an inhibitory response rather than an excitatory CR.

Other CS–US arrangements One way to present CSs and USs to an organism is to make sure that the two stimuli never occur together in a paired manner. This *explicitly unpaired* procedure normally involves presenting the stimuli such that both CS–US and US–CS intervals are very long. Thus, neither stimulus becomes a reliable signal for the occurrence of the other. As you might imagine, explicitly unpaired presentations often promote inhibitory conditioning to the CS (see, for example, Baker, 1977).

Results are not so clear, however, when backward conditioning trials are used. As we have said previously, some studies using backward conditioning trials have found evidence of inhibitory CRs using a retardation test (see, for example, Hall, 1984; Moscovitch & LoLordo, 1968; Siegel & Domjan, 1971). Others, however, have found that such trials produce excitatory CRs (for example, Mahoney & Ayres, 1976). There is little or no evidence that backward pairings produce inhibition coming from studies using summation tests. In sum, the particular type of conditioning found when backward pairings are used appears to depend on a whole variety of factors such as the number of conditioning trials and the specific characteristics of the US. A complete understanding of backward conditioning effects awaits additional research (see, for example, Gordon, McGinnis, & Weaver, 1985; Hall, 1984).

One final CS–US arrangement we have discussed is the random presentation of CSs and USs. In this procedure CSs and USs occur randomly so that there is a zero correlation between CS and US occurrence. In other words, the CS should not become a signal for US occurrence, nor should it come to signal US absence (Rescorla, 1967b). Nevertheless, some studies have shown that prior random presentations of a CS and a US can retard later excitatory conditioning involving these stimuli (see, for example, Baker & Mackintosh, 1977). It is notable, however, that studies using summation tests have failed to support such findings (see, for example, Hinson & Siegel, 1980; Siegel & Domjan, 1971). Currently, it seems doubtful that random CS and US presentations produce inhibitory conditioned responding.

Latent inhibition procedures In talking about an organism's experience with a CS, we noted that pre-exposures to a CS alone can retard later excitatory conditioning involving that CS. This latent inhibition phenomenon raises the question of whether CS-alone presentations result in inhibitory conditioned responding to the CS. The answer to this question is almost certainly "no." Several studies have shown that a CS that has been presented alone is not capable of interfering with excitatory CRs produced by another CS. In other words, a pre-exposed CS does not pass the summation test for conditioned inhibition (see, for example, Reiss & Wagner, 1972).

That CS pre-exposure does not produce inhibitory conditioning should not be surprising. In a latent inhibition paradigm, at the time the CS is being pre-exposed no USs have ever occurred. Thus, the organism forms no expectation of US occurrence. Without such an expectation, the CS cannot become a signal for US absence and, thus, should not become an inhibitory CS.

Why, then, does CS pre-exposure retard excitatory conditioning involving the pre-exposed CS? One suggestion is that during the pre-exposure an organism learns that the CS is irrelevant or that it signals nothing of significance. In effect, an organism may come to ignore the CS, and this inattention may be what makes subsequent conditioning so difficult. In this regard it is worth noting that CS preexposure retards both excitatory *and* inhibitory conditioning involving the pre-exposed CS (Baker & Mackintosh, 1977).

Extinction

Quite obviously, conditioning is an adaptive process that favors an organism's adjustment and survival. When new relationships among stimuli become apparent, an organism is capable of altering its behavior accordingly. As we have seen, once a CS has begun reliably to signal something of biological significance, that CS begins to elicit a new response.

Even so, relationships among stimuli seldom remain static throughout an organism's lifetime. A CS that has signaled a US for some period of time may cease being a reliable signal for US occurrence. When this happens, it may no longer be adaptive to respond to the CS in the same manner. That is, the conditioned response learned when the CS was a signal may no longer be appropriate when the CS has lost its signal value. How do organisms adjust to these changing stimulus relationships?

One mechanism that allows organisms to adapt to such changes is called *extinction.* In this context the term does *not* refer to an organism's death or to the vanishing of a species. It does, however, refer to the demise of a conditioned response once a CS has ceased to be a reliable signal. Technically, extinction is defined as the gradual decrease in the performance of a conditioned response that results from CS-alone occurrences. This means that once a CS has come to produce a CR, the performance of that response will diminish to the extent that the CS occurs alone. One way to conceptualize extinction is to think of it as a decrease in the CR as an organism learns that the CS is no longer a reliable signal.

To clarify how extinction works, let's consider once again our example of the child and the doorbell, which had become a signal for the appearance of strangers. How might a parent go about extinguishing this fear response conditioned to the sound of the bell? Actually, the procedure would be simple. All the parent would need to do is ring the doorbell regularly, making sure that no strangers ever appeared immediately after the sound. Gradually, as the child heard the bell more and more often without strangers appearing, the fear response would diminish. Finally, after several experiences with the bell alone, the child would no longer show evidence of fear to the bell sound. At this point we would say that the fear response had been extinguished.

Although the occurrence of extinction is well documented, for years researchers have argued about the precise mechanisms that control this phenomenon. Why do responses diminish when CS-alone presentations occur? Is the conditioned response forgotten? Does the learned association that led to the response become broken? Might it be that extinction simply results from the suppression of the learned response? Our current understanding of what extinction involves is incomplete. We can, however, answer some of these questions at least tentatively.

First, it is clear that extinction does not result from forgetting. As we will see later, forgetting is a decrease in the performance of a learned response that occurs with the passage of time. Forgetting does not depend on CS-alone presentations, which are necessary for extinction. Thus, although extinction and forgetting both involve a reduction in CR performance, the variables that control these phenomena appear to be different.

Second, it seems clear that extinction does not involve a loss of the association formed during conditioning. At least two facts suggest that the learned association remains intact even after extinction of a response has occurred. First, once a CR has been extinguished, the original CS can usually be reconditioned faster than a novel CS can be conditioned (Konorski & Szwejkowska, 1950). This suggests that even after extinction, some association involving the original CS remains intact.

Another fact that leads to the same conclusion is that after extinction, *spontaneous recovery* of the response often occurs. That is, if time is allowed to pass after extinction, the conditioned response to the CS returns to some degree. In most cases, the degree of responding that occurs is less than that which the CS produced before extinction. In other words, recovery of the response is not complete. Furthermore, spontaneous recovery usually can be eliminated by extinguishing the CR several times. Still, the occurrence of spontaneous recovery does suggest that extinction does not abolish the learned association responsible for the CR. If it did, we would not expect an extinguished CR to return in the absence of additional conditioning trials.

A final point concerning extinction is worth noting. CS-alone presentations after conditioning do not cause the CS to become a conditioned inhibitor. Even after several extinction sessions, a CS will not pass either a summation or a retardation test for conditioned inhibition (see Rescorla & Wagner, 1972).

Summary Statements

We have seen in this chapter that a stimulus that signals either the occurrence or the nonoccurrence of a biologically significant event becomes capable of producing a new response. When a positive contingent relationship exists between a CS and a US, the result is called Classical excitatory conditioning. When a negative contingent relationship holds for these stimuli, inhibitory conditioning develops.

In the case of excitatory conditioning, we found that the development of a CR depends on a variety of factors. Among these factors are the physical arrangement of the CS and US, the specific characteristics of these stimuli, and the presence of stimuli other than the CS and US during conditioning. We also found that in some instances excitatory conditioning seems to occur even when no explicit US is present.

With respect to inhibitory conditioning, we noted two factors that appear to be critical for a CS to become an inhibitory stimulus. First, there must be an expectation of US occurrence, and second, the CS must signal the absence of the US. Most situations in which these conditions are met produce CSs that pass both retardation and summation tests for conditioned inhibition.

We completed our discussion by noting that conditioned responses extinguish or decrease when a previously conditioned stimulus is presented alone. We noted that spontaneous recovery of extinguished responses does occur, however, when time passes after extinction.

3

Classical Conditioning: Theoretical Issues

In Chapter 2 we discussed the empirical facts of the conditioning process, outlining the various factors that influence the development of a CR. In the present chapter, we turn our attention to the interpretations of these facts. That is, we will look at different explanations for why these factors have their effects. We will be interested primarily in two questions. First, how have different theoretical explanations of conditioning guided research into the variables that affect the process? Second, how has this research led to the modification of our theoretical explanations? Before we focus on a few of the most critical theoretical issues in Classical conditioning, however, some comments on the role of theory in the study of conditioning are in order.

When we ask an *empirical question* we are asking how one observable event affects another. Such questions can be answered simply by performing a laboratory experiment involving the events. *Theoretical questions,* on the other hand, ask how nonobservable factors might be used to explain empirical relationships. In other words, theories are proposals about what may be occurring inside an organism that would explain why one event affects another.

For example, if we ask *how* the number of CS–US pairings influences the development of a CR, we are asking an empirical question. To answer such a question, we can conduct an experiment in which the number of CS–US pairings is varied, then measure the degree of CR development in each case. On the other hand, if we ask *why* CS–US pairings affect the growth of a CR, we are asking a theoretical question. We are asking about how CS–US pairings affect an organism in such a way that the organism will make a CR when a CS is presented. Since we can't observe what goes on inside the organism, the answer to such a question involves speculation. Based on all the evidence we have at our disposal, we speculate or theorize about how the organism may change as the number of CS–US pairings increases.

When we make tentative suppositions about how some process inside an organism operates, we are actually theorizing about the nature or the characteristics of the organism itself. We are saying that variable *X* has a certain effect because organisms function in a particular way. Thus, while a theory may be based on a specific empirical finding, it does more than simply attempt to explain that finding. It provides a broad characterization of some process that suggests to us how an entire range of variables should function. We can then assess the accuracy of a theory by testing experimentally these suggestions or implications about how a set of variables should work.

To clarify this point let's consider a concrete example. We know that a CR usually becomes more probable as the number of CS–US pairings increases. This is an empirical, observable finding. Based on this finding alone, we could theorize about how the learning process works within an organism. One simple speculation might be that organisms begin to make CRs once they have been exposed enough times to a CS and a US. In other words, as exposures to a CS and a US increase, an organism changes in some manner, so that it is more likely to exhibit a CR. This speculation or theory is one way to account for the observation that increased numbers of CS–US pairings result in more CRs. However, such a theory goes beyond simply attempting to explain the effects of CS–US pairings on conditioning. It suggests that a variety of other factors should also affect conditioning.

For example, if we take the position that CS–US pairings produce conditioning because they provide exposures to the CS and US, we could make at least two other predictions. We could predict that the number of CS–US pairings could be reduced without affecting CR development, as long as the duration of the CS and US were increased. We might also predict that a CR would be produced if we simply exposed an organism to several CSs and then later exposed the organism to a number of USs. By testing these implications of our theory, we would discover that it is an *inaccurate* explanation. The theory provides an explanation of one finding, but it fails to account for the effects of other variables.

As we begin our discussion of theoretical issues in Classical conditioning, keep one point clearly in mind. All these theories are tentative versions of how the conditioning process might work. They are rather like working copies or rough drafts of a manuscript. When you write a manuscript you often begin by putting down on paper the information you have at that time. As you do more research and as you study the components of your draft, you revise your original version of the paper, or even discard it. You do this because the work you have done since your first draft has enabled you to provide a clearer picture of your topic.

Theory formulation and testing works the same way. Theorists assess all the evidence available at a given time and formulate explanations to account for that evidence. As researchers test the implications of these explanations, they discover more about the variables that affect a process. These new discoveries then allow the theorists to modify their explanations so that they provide a clearer picture of the world as it really is. Thus, the mere fact that elements of a theory have been disproved does not mean that the theory has failed to contribute to our understanding of some process. The true worth of a theory is gauged by whether it provides us with implications or predictions that when tested, give us a better understanding of how some process works.

The Necessary and Sufficient Conditions for CR Development

Any theory that attempts to provide a general explanation of the conditioning process must begin by stating when conditioning will occur and when it will not. Such a theory must specify the minimum conditions that are necessary for a CR to develop. In this section we discuss two theory types that have attempted to specify these conditions. The first, which we will call *contiguity theory*, concentrates on the temporal arrangements of a CS and a US. The second type, which can be labeled *contingency theory*, concerns itself with how adequately a CS serves as a signal or predictor for US occurrence. We begin by looking at the basic elements of the contiguity position.

Contiguity Theory: Basic Assumptions

The contiguity view of conditioning was first proposed by Pavlov in an effort to explain the results of his early studies. However, this position has since been restated in several other theories (see, for example, Bush & Mosteller, 1951; Hull, 1943) and until the early 1970s served as the prevailing view of conditioning.

According to this theoretical position, two conditions are essential for the development of a CR. First, conditioning depends on the occurrence of an effective CS and US. An effective CS was defined as any stimulus that could be sensed by an organism, while an effective US was viewed as a stimulus that reliably produced a reflexive reaction. Second, the CS and US must occur in a temporally contiguous manner. This means that for conditioning to be effective, the two stimuli must be presented close together in time. Specifically, Pavlov proposed that conditioning occurs to the extent that neural activity provoked by a CS overlaps neural activity associated with the UR. For such an overlap to occur, it was assumed that the CS had to precede the US in time. Thus, the contiguity principle suggests that optimal conditioning should occur whenever the CS and the US are temporally contiguous and the CS occurs just before the US.

Based on our discussion in Chapter 2, it should be clear that when these two assumptions are met, conditioning usually results. It should also be evident from the data we reviewed that when either of these assumptions is not met, conditioning becomes less likely. We know, for example, that conditioning normally results when forward CS–US arrangements (such as delayed and trace conditioning procedures) are used. Simultaneous and backward arrangements of the CS and US are relatively ineffective in promoting CR development. Likewise, we found that conditioning tends to be most effective with short CS–US intervals. In other words, temporally contiguous CS–US occurrences produce better conditioning (in most cases) than do noncontiguous occurrences. These basic facts about conditioning are obviously consistent with the contiguity theory.

Remember, however, that according to contiguity theory, these assumptions constitute the necessary and sufficient conditions for CR occurrence. This means that when these assumptions are met, conditioning should *always* occur. It also means that if either of these conditions is not in evidence, conditioning should be relatively ineffective. Thus, to truly test this theory we need to ask two questions. First, does conditioning ever fail to occur when these assumptions are met? Second, to what extent does conditioning result when these conditions are not in effect? In the next section we explore the answers to these questions.

Contiguity Theory: The Evidence

Since we know that contiguity theory is consistent with some of the most basic findings from conditioning studies, we will concentrate now on findings that appear to be inconsistent with this view. We begin by looking at situations in which conditioning fails to occur, although the assumptions of the theory have been met. This discussion includes situations in which conditioning differs in two groups even though these assumptions are met equally in both. We end this section by describing some findings indicating that conditioning can occur when these assumptions are not valid.

Conditioning deficits not predicted by contiguity theory Given that a CS and a US are properly arranged, contiguity theory proposes that conditioning should depend on whether the two stimuli are effective. Conditioning should result as long as the CS is sensed and the US reliably produces a reflexive reaction. This prediction appears not to hold true in all cases. Several studies have shown that even when clearly effective stimuli are used, conditioning may not occur.

One example of such conditioning failures comes from a study of salivary conditioning in the dog conducted by Colavita (1965). Colavita used a tone as the CS, but instead of using food as the US, he used a mildly acidic solution. He found that whenever the acidic solution was injected into a dog's mouth, salivation reliably occurred. Thus, the acidic solution fit the definition of an effective US. Still, even though both CS and US were effective, the CS failed to produce a salivary CR. Only when the solution was injected into both the mouth and the stomach of a dog did salivary conditioning occur.

This finding is not unusual. Several stimuli that reliably elicit a UR fail to serve as effective USs in a conditioning situation (see, for example, Bruner, 1965; Gerall & Obrist, 1962). This occurs even when the CS being employed is effective when paired with USs of other types. Thus, not all pairings of effective CSs and USs result in conditioning as one would predict based on contiguity theory.

Even when a given CS and US are known to promote conditioning, researchers have found that the amount of conditioning cannot be determined solely on the basis of CS–US arrangement and temporal contiguity. As we have seen, when two groups of organisms receive the same number of CS–US pairings, but one also receives several US-alone presentations, conditioning in the two groups will differ (Rescorla, 1968). The group with the US-alone presentations will condition less strongly than the group without these experiences. This finding is clearly inconsistent with contiguity theory, since according to this position, US-alone presentations should have no effect on conditioning. And, since both groups have the same number of CS–US pairings, they should show equivalent CR development.

Another finding that is inconsistent with the contiguity view is the occurrence of the blocking phenomenon (Kamin, 1968, 1969). As you may recall, blocking is the failure of one element of a compound CS to become conditioned when the other element of the compound already has been conditioned. Specifically, Kamin demonstrated that when a CS compound such as a light and a tone is paired with shock, both elements of the compound normally begin to produce a conditioned fear response. However, if one of the elements has been paired with shock before the compound was established, conditioning to the novel element is blocked. This shows that the amount of conditioning to a given CS cannot be predicted solely by looking at the number of times the CS has occurred in a temporally contiguous manner with the US. Conditioning may also depend on the learning history associated with other stimuli that are present at the time of conditioning. The same conclusion can be drawn from other experiments we have discussed (see, for example, Wagner, Logan, Haberlandt, & Price, 1968).

These findings indicate that even when the assumptions of contiguity theory are met, conditioning may not occur. Furthermore, even when two groups of organisms have equal numbers of CS-US pairings, conditioning may differ. We can conclude, then, that the conditions suggested by contiguity theory are not *sufficient* to predict when conditioning will occur. Obviously, other assumptions are needed. However, we can still ask if these conditions are *necessary* for CR development. In other words, must at *least* these conditions be met for conditioning to be effective?

Conditioning in the absence of contiguity assumptions In Chapter 2 we reviewed several studies suggesting that CRs can develop even when the assumptions of contiguity theory are violated. The most notable example comes from the work of Garcia and colleagues on the taste aversion or poisoning phenomenon (Garcia & Koelling, 1966). These researchers have shown that when particular CSs and USs are employed, conditioning results even when several hours separate the stimuli. Specifically, when a taste CS is followed by the administration of an illness-producing toxin, organisms later avoid the taste as if it were an illness producer itself. Since the toxin or US does not become effective until long after the taste has been experienced, it appears that in some situations conditioning can develop without temporal contiguity between the CS and US.

Another example of conditioning that occurs when these assumptions are not met comes from some studies of backward conditioning. Certainly, the more typical finding is that backward arrangements of a CS and US produce no evidence of conditioning (see, for example, Mackintosh, 1974). However, it is equally clear that certain backward conditioning situations do promote excitatory CRs. Ayres and his associates, for example, have found evidence of excitatory conditioning when only a few backward trials are presented (see Mahoney & Ayres, 1976). Likewise, other researchers have shown that backward CS–US presentations can result in excitatory CRs when each occurrence of the US is surprising to an organism (Heth & Rescorla, 1973; Wagner & Terry, 1975). Later in this chapter, we will discuss why the surprisingness of the US may produce such an effect. In any event, it is clear that contiguity theory cannot account for these findings. According to the contiguity approach, only forward CS–US pairings should ever result in the acquisition of a conditioned response.

Finally, one of the major difficulties with the contiguity approach is that none of its assumptions deals with the occurrence of inhibitory conditioning. We have seen that when a CS reliably signals the absence of an expected US, the CS begins to produce an inhibitory CR. For a CS to become such a signal, CS and US must occur in an unpaired manner. According to contiguity theory, such unpaired CS–US presentations should produce no evidence of conditioning. The theory is partially correct in that such presentations produce no excitatory conditioned responding. However, there is obviously a big difference between a prediction of no conditioning and the observation that conditioning of an inhibitory nature does take place. This is a clear example of conditioning that occurs despite failure to meet the assumptions of contiguity theory.

Contingency Theory: Basic Assumptions

In the late 1960s, the above-mentioned problems with the assumptions of contiguity theory led to the development of what we can call the contingency view of Classical conditioning. Various aspects of the contingency approach were proposed by Kamin (1968, 1969), Rescorla (1969), and Wagner (1969). However, by far the most influential statement of this view came in a paper by Rescorla and Wagner (1972). The particular contingency theory outlined in this paper has come to be called the *Rescorla–Wagner model of conditioning*. Although other versions of contingency theory have been proposed (see, for example, Pearce & Hall, 1980), we will use the Rescorla–Wagner model as a prototype for discussing the contingency approach.

Basically, the Rescorla–Wagner model proposes four related assumptions:

1. Classical conditioning occurs only to the extent that the occurrence or nonoccurrence of a US is surprising to an organism. In other words, if the occurrence or nonoccurrence of a US takes an organism by surprise, the potential for conditioning is present. If the occurrence or nonoccurrence of a US is already fully predictable or expected, no conditioning will occur.
2. A given CS acquires the capacity for producing a CR to the extent that it can be used as a reliable signal for the occurrence or nonoccurrence of a US. If a CS can be used as a reliable signal for the occurrence of a US, the CS can acquire the capacity for producing an excitatory CR. If a CS can be used as a reliable signal for the nonoccurrence of a US, it can become capable of producing an inhibitory CR.
3. A given CS loses the capacity for producing a CR when it loses its ability to function as a signal for US occurrence or nonoccurrence. If a CS already is capable of producing an excitatory CR, it loses this capacity to the extent that it loses its ability to signal US occurrence. Likewise, if a CS is capable of producing an inhibitory CR, it will lose this capacity to the extent that it becomes incapable of signaling US nonoccurrence.
4. The degree to which a CS acquires the capacity to produce a CR depends not only on how well it signals US occurrence or nonoccurrence, but also on how well other stimuli in the environment already serve as signals. Actually, this assumption follows logically from the first assumption. If other stimuli in the environment already signal US occurrence or nonoccurrence, these events will not be surprising. Therefore, conditioning to a novel CS will not occur.

At first glance, these assumptions may seem to be unnecessarily complicated. They are, however, relatively simple in their application. Let's look at the four assumptions in less formalized terms.

According to this model, conditioning is really a mechanism by which organisms come to anticipate important events such as USs. In effect, the model assumes that it is adaptive in some manner for an organism to be able to anticipate or predict when a US is likely to occur. Thus, when an organism is exposed to an unexpected or surprising US or when it is surprised by the nonoccurrence of an expected US, the conditioning process is initiated. To paraphrase Kamin (1968, 1969), when a surprising US occurs, the organism "scans back" through its memory of recent events to discover if there are any stimuli that might have served as a signal for the US. To the extent that such signaling stimuli are discovered, those stimuli become capable of producing a conditioned response. Thus, the first and fourth assumptions of this model are based on the existence of a need for learning only when a US is surprising. There is no need to learn about new signals if a US can be predicted by stimuli already present in the environment.

Assuming that the US occurrence or nonoccurrence is surprising, what determines the degree to which a particular CS becomes conditioned? Basically, the conditioning of a given CS depends on how well that CS signals the surprising event. As we learned earlier, a CS becomes a reliable signal to the extent that it is correlated with US occurrence. In other words, when a CS and a US have a contingent relationship, the CS can be viewed as a reliable signal. If, then, an organism is surprised by the occurrence of a US and discovers that a CS had been present before the US, the organism notices the positive contingent relationship. When such a relationship is discovered, the CS acquires some capacity to produce an excitatory conditioned response. If an organism is surprised by the absence of a US, it also searches for a stimulus that might have been present to signal the nonoccurrence. When such a negative contingent relationship is noted, the CS acquires some capacity for producing an inhibitory CR. So, conditioning to any CS depends first on an event being surprising and second on the CS being correlated with that surprising event.

To some extent, this approach appears to be a radical departure from the contiguity view of conditioning. However, the Rescorla–Wagner model does retain some of the basic ideas from this approach. It is still assumed, for example, that conditioning will not occur in the absence of an effective CS–US pair. It is further assumed that the temporal contiguity of events is a critical factor. Unless a CS and a US occur close together in time, an organism will be unable to recognize the CS as a signal for US occurrence. Thus, in some senses the Rescorla–Wagner model represents an expansion or modification of the contiguity position.

The Formal Expression of the Rescorla-Wagner Model

One advantage of the Rescorla–Wagner model is that its assumptions have been incorporated into a formal, mathematical expression. By substituting numbers for the symbols in this mathematical equation, it is possible to predict with great clarity the degree to which conditioning should occur in a given situation. It is, of course, not necessary to use the mathematical model to make general predictions. However, understanding the basic rules in the mathematical formulation should enhance your understanding of the model itself. For this reason, we discuss briefly how this formulation works.

The purpose of the mathematical model is to enable us to predict the change in conditioning to a particular CS on any given conditioning trial. Thus, the first symbol in the formula is ΔV_a, which stands for the change in conditioning to stimulus A (or CS_a) on a given trial. This change in conditioning to a given CS can be either positive or negative. That is, the capacity a CS has for producing a CR may either increase or decrease on a given trial depending on the circumstances.

What are these circumstances that determine the change in conditioning to a particular CS? Three factors are built into the formula. First, conditioning to CS_a depends on the salience of that CS. Second, conditioning varies depending on the intensity of the US. Third, and most important, conditioning will vary as a function of how surprising a US is on a particular trial. In the formula itself, CS salience is represented by the symbol α (alpha), while US intensity is represented by the symbol β (beta). The degree to which the US is surprising on a given trial is represented by the expression $\lambda - V_{ax}$. The symbol λ (lambda) in this case stands for the total amount of conditioning a given US can promote—that is, the total amount that a US can be predicted or signaled. The symbol V_{ax} stands for the degree of conditioning that has already occurred to all stimuli in the situation. Again, this may also be viewed as the total amount the US is already signaled by all stimuli present at the time of conditioning. If λ represents the degree to which a US *can* be predicted and V_{ax} represents the degree to which the US is *already* predicted, then obviously $\lambda - V_{ax}$ represents the degree to which the US is surprising. In effect, surprise is the difference between how much an event can be predicted and how much it is already being predicted or signaled. These symbols and their definitions are summarized as follows:

Δ = change
V = associative strength of a stimulus or the degree to which a stimulus signals the US
V_a = associative strength of CS_a or degree to which CS_a signals the US
V_x = associative strength of all other stimuli in the conditioning situation, or degree to which these stimuli signal the US
V_{ax} = $V_a + V_x$, or degree to which all stimuli in the conditioning situation signal the US
α = salience of the CS
β = intensity of the US
λ = amount of conditioning the US can support or total amount that the US can be signaled
$\lambda - V_{ax}$ = degree to which the US is surprising in a conditioning situation

The associative strength of CS_a changes on any given conditioning trial according to:

$$\Delta V_a = \alpha\beta(\lambda - V_a x)$$

This formula, as proposed by Rescorla and Wagner, is simple to use. It states that the change in conditioning to a CS on a given trial (ΔV_a) is equal to the CS salience (α) multiplied by the US intensity (β), multiplied by the degree to which the US is surprising ($\lambda - V_{ax}$). As we noted, surprise is quantified as the amount a US can be signaled (λ) minus the amount it is already signaled by stimuli present in the conditioning situation (V_{ax}).

To use this formula for making predictions, it is necessary to keep two rules in mind. First, it is assumed that the value of $\alpha\beta$ will always be a number between 0 and 1; $\alpha\beta$ will not be 0 unless no CS occurs on a given trial. Second, λ has a value of 0 whenever a US is absent on a conditioning trial. In all other cases λ has a positive value greater than 0.

To illustrate, let's consider a few examples. Let's assume that a CS is paired with a US for the first time, and that no other stimuli present are reliable predictors for US occurrence. How will the ability of the CS to produce a CR change as a result of this first pairing? Since we are not specifying the real nature of the CS and US, we will choose arbitrary numbers to insert in the formula. For purposes of illustration, we select 0.5 as the value for $\alpha\beta$ and 100 as the value of λ. Since no stimuli in the conditioning situation already signal the US, $V_{ax} = 0$. According to the formula, then,

$$\Delta V_a = 0.5\ (100 - 0)$$
$$\Delta V_a = 0.5\ (100)$$
$$\Delta V_a = 50$$

This means that the capacity of the CS to produce a CR will increase by 50 units.

This number is, of course, relatively meaningless until we compare it to what happens in other situations. Thus, let's assume that several CS–US pairings have occurred, so that the CS (in combination with other stimuli in the environment) has become a completely reliable predictor for US occurrence. What would happen if one additional trial were given? In this case, the value of $\alpha\beta$ would still be 0.5 and the value of λ would remain at 100. However, because of all the prior conditioning, V_{ax} would now have a value of 100. This means that the CS and other stimuli present already fully predict the US. The occurrence of the US is no longer surprising. According to the formula, the result of this additional conditioning trial would be as follows:

$$\Delta V_a = 0.5\ (100 - 100)$$
$$\Delta V_a = 0.5\ (0)$$
$$\Delta V_a = 0$$

In effect, the additional CS–US pairing would lead to no change in the capacity of the CS, since the US was already fully predicted by the stimuli available. This contrasts sharply with the large increase in conditioning (+50 units) that occurred on the initial conditioning trial.

As you can see, by using this formula it is possible to say how much a CS will become conditioned on any given trial, based on how much conditioning has occurred in the past. In addition, however, the formula enables us to predict what will happen to a CS when it occurs alone, without a US. Recall that when a US is omitted, the value of λ becomes 0. Let's assume that a CS has been paired with a US several times so that the value of the CS is 80 units. This means, of course, that the value of V_{ax} will also be 80 units. What happens if we now present the CS alone? The values in the formula would be as follows:

$$\Delta V_a = 0.5\ (0 - 80)$$
$$\Delta V_a = 0.5\ (-80)$$
$$\Delta V_a = -40$$

In other terms, the capacity of the CS to produce a CR would decrease. Before the trial began, the CS had a value of 80, but its value decreased by 40 due to the CS-alone presentation. This, of course, is what happens to the value of a CS when it is extinguished.

One final example is worth noting. According to this model, a CS produces an excitatory CR to the extent that the CS has a positive value. When the value of the CS is negative, however, the CS becomes capable of producing an *inhibitory* CR. Under what circumstances does the model predict that a CS will become inhibitory? As we know from our previous discussions, a CS becomes an inhibitory stimulus when it reliably signals the absence of an otherwise expected US. This means, first of all, that there must be some stimuli present that signal US occurrence. Otherwise, there would be no expectation of the US. Second, some CS must then occur as a signal that the US will be absent. This means that the CS must occur alone. If we translate these conditions into numbers in our formula, we find that λ is 0, since no US occurs. We also find that V_{ax} has a positive value, because some stimuli in the environment already signal US occurrence (for present purposes we'll assume that $V_{ax} = 50$). What would happen then if a novel CS (with a value of 0) were presented without the US?

$$\Delta V_a = 0.5\ (0 - 50)$$
$$\Delta V_a = 0.5\ (-50)$$
$$\Delta V_a = -25$$

As you can see, on such a trial the CS value decreases by some amount. Since before the trial the CS had a value of 0, this decrease means that the CS takes on a negative value or becomes inhibitory.

These examples help you to form some idea of how the formal model works to make predictions. As long as you understand the basic assumptions of the contingency approach, it will be possible to assess how well such a model accounts for Classical conditioning phenomena. We now begin that assessment by determining how experimental evidence squares with the predictions of contingency theory.

Contingency Theory: The Evidence

Most of the basic conditioning phenomena we have discussed are handled rather easily by the contingency approach. For example, we have seen that conditioning is most effective when salient CSs and intense USs are employed. In the Rescorla–Wagner model, increased CS salience results in a higher value for α , whereas increased US intensity leads to increased β values. According to this model, when either α or β values are higher, conditioning will occur to a greater degree on any given trial.

Likewise, this model predicts that long CS–US intervals should produce less effective conditioning than shorter intervals, because longer intervals tend to obscure the contingent relationship between a CS and a US. As we have seen, in most cases, this prediction is upheld by the experimental data.

Finally, we have seen that forward conditioning arrangements produce better CR developments than either simultaneous or backward configurations. This finding is clearly consistent with the contingency view, which states that a CS must be a reliable signal for US occurrence in order for conditioning to occur. The CS can be a reliable signal only if it precedes the US in time.

Thus, the contingency approach is able to account for the same basic findings that the contiguity theory was developed to explain. The major appeal of contingency theory, however, is its ability to account for a variety of phenomena that cannot be explained using a contiguity approach. Let's briefly consider three such phenomena.

The degree of positive CS–US correlation As we learned earlier, the development of a CR depends not only on the number of CS–US pairings, but also on the degree to which CS and US occurrences are correlated. Recall that Rescorla (1968) manipulated this correlation in a CER paradigm by varying the number of US-alone presentations each group of rats received in addition to their conditioning trials. In essence, each group had the same number of CS–US pairings, but the groups that received more US-alone presentations had lower correlations between CS and US occurrence. Rescorla found that conditioning was a direct function of how well the CS was correlated with US occurrence. The higher the correlation, the better the conditioning. The critical importance of CS–US correlation has been found in a number of experiments (see, for example, Gamzu & Williams, 1971; Rescorla, 1966, 1969; Weisman & Litner, 1969).

This finding is precisely what one would predict based on the contingency position. According to this view, conditioning should occur only to the extent that a CS becomes a *reliable* predictor for US occurrence. When a CS and a US are highly correlated, the CS becomes a reliable predictor. When the correlation is low, the CS fails to signal US occurrence on at least some occasions. Thus, the contingency approach clearly predicts that CR development should depend on the degree of positive correlation between a CS and a US.

Effects of stimuli other than the CS Earlier we reviewed a number of studies showing that conditioning to a given CS often depends on other stimuli present at the time of conditioning. One example of this finding comes from Kamin's studies (1968, 1969) of the blocking phenomenon, which showed that conditioning to one element of a compound CS depends on whether the other element has already been paired with the US in question. If one element of a compound has been associated with the US, subsequent conditioning to the other element is blocked or impeded.

Again, findings such as this can be accounted for by the basic assumptions of a contingency approach. One of these assumptions is that conditioning to a given CS will occur only if the US occurrence is surprising. A novel CS paired with a US will not develop the capacity to produce a CR if, at the time of the pairing, the US is already predicted by other stimuli in the environment. The blocking paradigm is, of course, a clear example of just such a situation. As a result of prior pairings with the US, one CS becomes a reliable signal for US occurrence. When that CS is later compounded with a novel CS in a conditioning situation, the occurrence of the US is not surprising because it is being signaled by the previously conditioned CS. Since the US is not surprising, no conditioning will occur to the novel CS, even though it is paired with the US on a regular basis.

It is notable that the same logic allows the contingency view to account for a variety of other conditioning phenomena. For example, this "lack of surprise" explanation has been used to explain the occurrence of the US preexposure effect. Recall that if an organism is exposed to a US several times before that US is used in a conditioning situation, conditioning to the CS is usually ineffective (Randich &

LoLordo, 1979). According to the contingency explanation, this occurs because during US pre-exposures the stimuli in the pre-exposure room (contextual stimuli) come to signal the occurrence of the US. In other words, an organism comes to expect that in a particular environment, the US will occur. Later, if a novel CS is paired with the US in the same environment, the occurrence of the US is not surprising. For this reason, the novel CS will not become capable of producing a CR (see, for example, Tomie, 1976). This explanation is supported by studies indicating that US pre-exposure will have little effect on subsequent conditioning as long as pre-exposure and conditioning occur in different environments (see, for example, Hinson, 1982).

The occurrence of inhibitory conditioning One of the major difficulties associated with the contiguity approach was its failure to account for inhibitory conditioning. According to the contiguity position, whenever a CS signals the absence of a US, no conditioning should result. However, as we have seen, this does not appear to be the case. A CS that signals the absence of an expected US does not become capable of producing an *excitatory* CR. It does, however, gain the capacity to produce an *inhibitory* CR.

The development of inhibitory responding under these conditions is clearly predicted by the contingency position. According to this kind of theory, conditioning depends on CS–US correlations. Positive CS–US correlations result in excitatory CRs, while negative CS–US correlations promote inhibitory conditioning. Only zero correlations between a CS and a US are assumed to result in conditioning failures. Thus, one of the major advantages of the contingency view is that it predicts the occurrence of inhibitory conditioning in certain situations.

This recognition of inhibitory conditioning by contingency theory has had a major impact on Classical conditioning research. Not only has it stimulated interest in the conditions that promote inhibitory CRs, but also it has changed the kinds of treatment conditions used in most Classical conditioning experiments.

Let's assume that we are doing a simple experiment to determine how CRs develop as a function of the number of forward CS–US pairings. We need one group of organisms (the experimental group) that is simply given a number of CS–US pairings, and we measure the CR that occurs on each trial. We then compare the CR development in this group to the responding that occurs in a baseline or control group. The control group will receive all the same treatments as the experimental group (for example, equivalent handling, equivalent stimulus exposures), except that the control organisms will not receive actual forward CS–US pairings. If CR development were greater in the experimental group than in the control group, we could attribute the increased conditioned responding to the forward CS–US pairings, not just to stimulus exposures.

The question of interest in this kind of experiment is: How can control organisms be given the same stimulus exposures as the experimental organisms without allowing conditioning to occur? Early experiments, done in the framework of contiguity theory, simply gave control organisms either backward pairings or explicitly unpaired CS and US presentations. According to the contiguity view, this should provide the control organisms with the same number of CS and US exposures given the experimental organisms, but it should not result in conditioning.

However, Rescorla (1967b), working from a contingency position, questioned the appropriateness of such controls in conditioning experiments. He pointed out that organisms receiving backward pairings or explicitly unpaired CS and US exposures are likely to undergo inhibitory conditioning. In other words, these organisms will become less likely to respond to the CS than organisms that have never undergone any stimulus exposures. Thus, when the responding of the experimental group is compared to the responding of the control group, the difference will actually be larger than it would have been if experimental organisms had been compared to nonconditioned subjects.

For this reason, Rescorla proposed what has been termed the *truly random control procedure* for conditioning studies. This procedure involves giving control organisms the same number of CS and US exposures that occur in the experimental group; however, the control group receives these exposures in a completely random sequence. The rationale for the procedure is that random CS and US occurrences should produce a zero correlation between the stimuli, and this should result in neither excitatory nor inhibitory CRs. In effect, this procedure should provide a truly neutral baseline against which to compare the responding of an experimental group. Although some arguments have been advanced against this view (see, for example, Kremer, 1971; Seligman, 1969), the truly random control procedure is now commonly used in contemporary studies of conditioning.

Problems associated with the contingency approach Contingency theory has contributed a great deal to the study and explanation of the conditioning process. Still, such theories have not been without problems. For example, the Rescorla–Wagner model, as originally stated, fails to account for certain details of the blocking phenomenon. For this reason, some of the assumptions of the model have been modified in more contemporary versions of contingency theory (Pearce & Hall, 1980).

More important, the Rescorla–Wagner formulation fails to deal with some of the apparent anomalies that occur in certain conditioning situations. It does not, for example, account for the excitatory conditioning that sometimes occurs when backward conditioning trials are used. It also fails to explain the unusual findings that have been reported in experiments featuring the taste aversion paradigm. For example, the Rescorla–Wagner model is silent when it comes to explaining how conditioning can occur in the taste aversion paradigm when such long CS–US intervals are used. It also offers no explanation of why aversions are formed only to stimuli such as tastes and odors, not to stimuli such as lights and tones. Such difficulties have led to the development of a new kind of contingency theory. Although it is unnecessary for us to consider these recent models in detail, it is useful to look briefly at the directions they have taken.

Wagner's priming theory In the past few years, several modifications in contingency theory have been proposed by Wagner (1976, 1978, 1981). Although these various proposals have differed to some degree, a few important themes have emerged. The basic notion common to all these hypotheses is that once a stimulus has ceased to exist in the environment, it may continue to be processed in an organism's short-term or primary memory. In other words, even though a stimulus itself may no longer be present in the outside world, a representation or copy may persist in an organism's short-term memory for some finite period of time. We will discuss the concept of short-term memory in some detail in a later chapter. For present purposes, we can characterize short-term memory as the part of an organism's memory that is active at any particular moment. Items in short-term memory are the items an organism is currently aware of, thinking about, or rehearsing.

The critical assumption in Wagner's position is that conditioning does not occur between stimuli out in the environment. Conditioning involves associations that are formed between stimuli that are represented in short-term memory. According to Wagner, excitatory conditioning occurs whenever a CS and a US are represented and rehearsed *jointly* in short-term memory. In effect, the development of an excitatory CR depends on the degree to which the CS and US are rehearsed in memory at the same time. Alternatively, excitatory associations are broken down and inhibitory associations may be formed to the extent that a CS and US are rehearsed separately. Thus, extinction of an excitatory CR or the formulation of an inhibitory CR can occur when CS and US are represented in memory at different times.

By focusing on an organism's memory for stimuli rather than on just the occurrence of the stimuli themselves, Wagner introduces an important principle. According to this view, it is not possible to predict when a certain type of conditioning will occur solely on the basis of how stimuli are temporally arranged in the environment. To make such predictions, it is necessary to understand the factors that influence the rehearsal or processing of a stimulus in short-term memory. Only then will we be able to predict when two stimuli are and are not likely to be rehearsed jointly in memory. To illustrate the importance of this principle, let's look briefly at a few of the factors that might determine the degree to which a stimulus is rehearsed in memory.

First, Wagner has proposed that whether any stimulus is rehearsed will depend on how surprising the stimulus is. If a stimulus such as a US is surprising to an organism, that stimulus will "engage" or initiate the rehearsal process. This means that a surprising stimulus will be rehearsed in short-term memory for a substantial period of time. However, a stimulus that is expected or is nonsurprising will be represented in short-term memory only briefly. Nonsurprising stimuli are thus rehearsed for a shorter time than surprising ones, and this means that nonsurprising stimuli have less chance to be rehearsed jointly with other events. Several studies conducted by Wagner and his colleagues seem to support this notion that surprising stimuli are rehearsed longer than nonsurprising stimuli (see, for example, Terry & Wagner, 1975; Wagner, Rudy, & Whitlow, 1973).

But if this is the case, how does such knowledge improve our ability to explain conditioning phenomena? One example of the application of this view is found in the area of backward conditioning research. As we have seen, backward conditioning trials sometimes result in excitatory CRs when only a few trials are presented (Mahoney & Ayres, 1976). However, when several backward pairings occur, the typical finding is either no evidence of excitatory conditioning or, in some cases, the development of an inhibitory CR (see, for example, Moscovitch & LoLordo, 1968; Siegel & Domjan, 1971). Wagner attempts to explain these divergent findings by suggesting that in backward conditioning situations, the probability of joint CS–US rehearsal changes as more conditioning trials occur.

Specifically, Wagner hypothesizes that on the first few backward conditioning trials, the occurrence of the US is surprising to an organism and is thus rehearsed for a long period of time. Therefore, even though the CS occurs after the US, the rehearsal of the US is still going on when the CS is presented. In other words, joint rehearsal of the two stimuli will indeed occur, and some evidence of excitatory conditioning should be found. As more and more backward pairings occur, however, the US will become less and less surprising in that situation. The organism comes to expect the US because the US has occurred previously in the presence of the situational or contextual stimuli. As the US becomes less surprising, it is rehearsed for shorter and shorter periods of time. This means that after several backward pairings there is an increased likelihood that US rehearsal will be ended by the time CS rehearsal begins. Because the stimuli are rehearsed separately in memory, any excitatory associations formed on the initial trials will begin to break down. If enough trials of this type occur, inhibitory CRs may even begin to develop.

To test this interpretation, Wagner and Terry (1975) conducted a backward conditioning experiment in which they attempted to maintain the surprisingness of the US over several conditioning trials. Their rationale was that if the US remains surprising throughout backward conditioning, the US will continue to be rehearsed long enough to overlap with CS rehearsal. This should result in better excitatory conditioning than that which is usually found when backward pairings occur.

In brief, this experiment consisted of two phases. In phase I, rabbits were exposed to two different auditory stimuli we will call CS_1 and CS_2. CS_1 was always followed by a mild shock under the eye, while CS_2 was never followed by a shock. As a result, CS_1 began to produce a conditioned eye blink response, whereas CS_2 did not. The purpose of the first phase was to establish CS_1 as a signal for shock occurrence and to assure that CS_2 became a signal for the absence of shock.

Once these CSs had been established as signals for shock occurrence or nonoccurrence, the experimenters began phase II, a series of backward conditioning trials. However, each trial in phase II was preceded by a signal saying that the US would or would not occur. On half the trials the signal for shock occurrence preceded the pairing of shock and a novel CS (CS_3). Thus, the sequence of events on these trials was: (1) the presentation of the signal for shock, (2) the presentation of the shock, and (3) the presentation of the novel CS_3. It was assumed that on these trials the occurrence of the shock would be expected because it was being signaled. Thus, CS_3 should show little in the way of excitatory conditioning.

On the other half of the trials the shock was always paired with another novel CS (CS_4). Just before each of the shock–CS_4 trials, the experimenters presented the signal for shock absence. Thus, the stimulus sequence on these trials was: (1) the presentation of the signal for shock absence, (2) the presentation of the shock, (3) the presentation of the novel CS_4. The experimenters assumed that on these trials the occurrence of the shock would be surprising. Thus, they predicted that CS_4 would develop a substantial ability to produce an eyeblink response.

As indicated in Figure 3.1, which summarizes the results of this study, the prediction made by Wagner and Terry is confirmed. Both CS_3 and CS_4 occurred *after* the shock US. However, CS_4 developed a strong capacity to produce an excitatory CR, while CS_3 did not. The main difference between the CSs was that CS_4 was always preceded by a surprising shock, whereas CS_3 always followed an expected shock. This result is consistent with Wagner's notion that backward conditioning trials can produce excitatory CRs if the US is rehearsed long enough to overlap with CS rehearsal.

It is notable that this view of conditioning has also been applied to other phenomena that have been difficult to explain by means of contiguity and contingency theories. For example, in the taste aversion situation, Wagner has tentatively attributed the puzzling results to the rehearsals of different kinds of CS for dif-

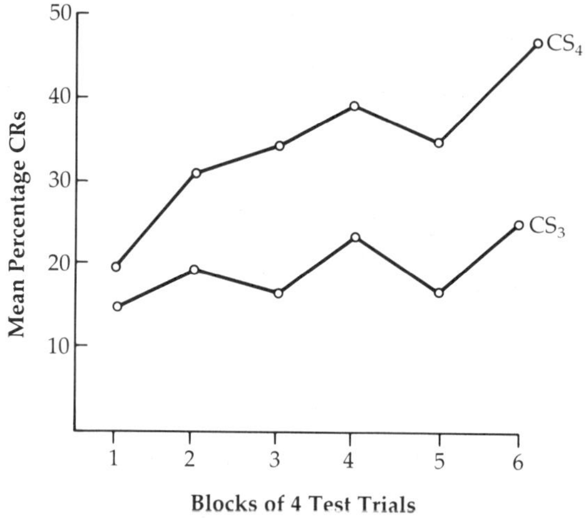

FIGURE 3.1 Conditioned responding to two CSs used in backward conditioning arrangements. CS_4 is preceded by a surprising US and CS_3 is preceded by an expected US. (From Wagner and Terry, 1975.)

ferent periods of time (see, for example, Whitlow, 1976). Specifically, he has proposed that externally based stimuli such as lights and tones may be rehearsed in short-term memory only briefly. However, other stimuli such as odors or tastes may remain in short-term memory for much more extended periods. If we accept this suggestion that different CSs may be rehearsed differentially, it becomes possible to explain some of the more perplexing phenomena found in taste aversion research.

For instance, the hypothesis of different rehearsal times would help to explain why flavors can become associated with events that occur long after exposure to the flavor. According to Wagner, the memory of a flavor lasts long enough to be rehearsed jointly with, for example, illness-producing toxins. This joint rehearsal then results in the development of an excitatory CR to the flavor. The same reasoning has been used to explain why stimuli such as flavors do not appear to become associated with shock and why stimuli such as tones do not appear to become associated with illness (Garcia & Koelling, 1966).

Wagner explains this apparent lack of associability between certain stimuli by pointing out that we do not know exactly how these stimuli are rehearsed. He believes that tones do not become associated with illness-provoking toxins because tones are rehearsed only briefly and the toxins do not produce any effects until long after they have been administered. This means that the tone and the toxic effects are never jointly rehearsed in short-term memory. Similarly, when experimenters have attempted to induce associations between flavors and shock, they have normally presented the shock shortly after the flavor. This means that the two stimuli undergo joint rehearsal. However, if the flavor continues to be rehearsed for long periods after shock presentation, there is significant rehearsal of the CS in the absence of US rehearsal. This separate rehearsal is thought to result in the breakdown of any of the excitatory CRs that form during joint rehearsal. The rehearsal of the flavor CS, which continues to occur after rehearsal of the shock US, makes this situation similar to a backward conditioning arrangement.

In a study conducted by Krane and Wagner (1975) that attempted to test the foregoing view, rats were trained to drink a solution from a drinking tube. For half of the animals the solution had a distinct flavor (saccharine), and for the remaining rats the solution was accompanied by a tone–light compound. In each of these groups a shock followed exposure to the solution by 5, 30, or 210 seconds. Krane and Wagner wanted to determine the degree to which animals exposed to each of these conditions would later suppress or avoid drinking the solution. In other words, to what degree would shock become associated with the flavor and the tone–light compound? Figure 3.2 shows the results of this experiment.

Clearly, shock was capable of producing suppression to both the flavor and the audiovisual characteristics of the solution.

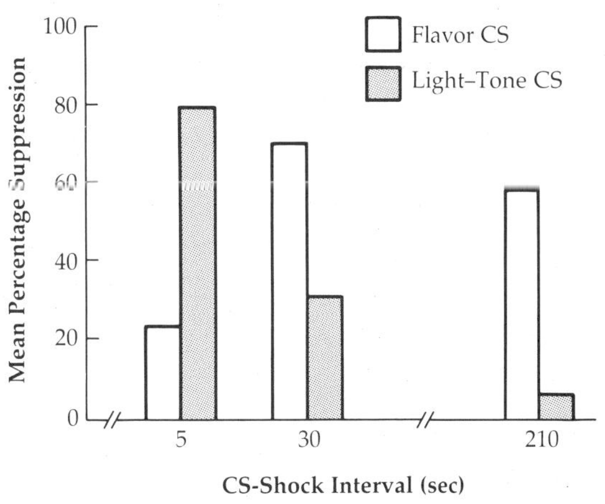

FIGURE 3.2 Conditioned aversions formed to either a flavor CS or a light–tone compound CS when shock is used as the US. The degree of conditioned aversion is shown as a function of the CS–shock interval used during training. (Adapted from Krane and Wagner, 1975.)

However, maximal suppression to these two kinds of CSs occurred under different conditions. Suppression in the presence of the light–tone compound occurred only when the CS–shock interval was short (5 seconds). Maximal suppression to the flavor, however, developed only when longer CS–shock intervals were used (30 and 210 seconds). This result is consistent with Wagner's hypothesis that some stimuli such as flavors may be rehearsed for long periods of time. In effect, these stimuli can become associated with USs only when the CS–US intervals are relatively long. Otherwise, rehearsal of the CS will occur well after the US rehearsal has been completed, by which time excitatory associations will have broken down.

In many instances, it is too early to assess the validity of Wagner's theoretical formulations. His most recent proposals have not been tested systematically enough to warrant final conclusions. It is evident, however, that these models have had a major impact on the study of Classical conditioning. Most important, this view has suggested that to understand even relatively simple learning situations, it may be necessary to base our explanations on complex memory processes. By raising this suggestion, these models have provided a link between Classical conditioning research and work on memory processes in humans and other species. In later chapters we will look at this work on memory processes in greater detail.

What Is Associated in Classical Conditioning?

Thus far, we have devoted much of our discussion to the question of the conditions necessary for CR development. Now we address a second theoretical issue that has been debated throughout the history of Classical conditioning research. It is widely assumed that a CS acquires the capacity to produce a CR because during conditioning, the CS becomes associated with some other element of the learning situation. Historically, however, there has been disagreement over what the association entails. Specifically, theorists have disagreed about what the CS becomes linked to in a conditioning situation. As we will see, there have been two primary points of view as to which elements become associated in Classical conditioning. We begin by describing these points of view, and then we will assess the evidence that is related to each.

Stimulus–Response or Stimulus–Stimulus Associations?

One way to conceptualize conditioning is to assume that the CS becomes linked directly to the reflexive response produced by the US (see, for example, Hull, 1943). According to this position, a CS and a US must normally occur close together in time, because these conditions assure that CS and UR will occur contiguously. It is this contiguous pairing of CS and UR that leads to the CS–UR association. Once this association has been formed, presentations of the CS automatically lead to the same reflexive reaction that originally was produced by the US alone. Thus, in this view, the CS simply becomes a second stimulus (in addition to the US), which is linked to and is capable of producing the reflexive response.

A somewhat different interpretation is that during conditioning the CS becomes associated with the US. This means that once conditioning has occurred, the presentation of a CS stimulates or arouses an organism's representation or memory of the US. This arousal of the US representation then provokes the appropriate conditioned response. Thus, instead of the CS actually coming to produce a response directly, the CS simply triggers a memory of the US and the response occurs as a reaction to this memory (see, for example, King, 1979; Wagner, 1981).

These two positions actually represent two different conceptual traditions in the study of learning. The notion that learning involves stimulus–response associations is derived from the behaviorist tradition, which emphasizes the importance of overt, observable events in the explanation of behavior. It also emphasizes the cause–effect relationships among observable events. Thus, when in conditioning a CS begins to produce some new response, the most parsimonious explanation is that the observable stimulus is causing the observable response to occur. Furthermore, the CS achieves its capacity to cause the response by virtue of its association or link with that response.

On the other hand, the suggestion that conditioning results from stimulus–stimulus associations reflects a more cognitive view of the learning process. The cognitive approach is concerned more with how individuals organize stimulus inputs to gain information about the environment. Responses are then produced in accordance with this information about how stimuli are related. The emphasis here is clearly on associations between stimulus representations in an organism's brain or memory system. Just because an organism responds in the presence of one stimulus does not necessarily mean that the stimulus and response are directly linked. It may mean that the organism is responding on the basis of what it has learned about stimulus relationships.

Evidence concerning the Elements in an Association

It is difficult to resolve the question of which elements become linked in Classical conditioning. Speculations about the nature of associations within an organism are easier to state than to test. Still, as we will find, much of the available evidence does appear to favor the view that conditioned responding depends on stimulus–stimulus associations.

Effects of blocking the UR The stimulus–response view of conditioning clearly assumes that for a CR to develop, both a CS and a UR must occur at the time of learning. Thus, one way to approach this issue is to determine whether conditioning can occur in the absence of a UR. One of the earliest studies of this type was conducted by Light and Gantt (1936), who were studying conditioned leg flexion in the dog. The US in this case was a shock to the dog's paw and the normal UR involved lifting the leg. In one of their groups, Light and Gantt exerted pressure on the motor nerves involved in the leg-lifting response, such that the dogs temporarily lost motor function in the legs they were being conditioned to lift. Thus, when the CS was followed by shock, no leg withdrawal (the UR) could occur. Later, however, when the dogs recovered the use of their legs, presentation of the CS led to a pronounced leg withdrawal CR. Apparently, conditioning had occurred even though no UR was present during conditioning.

Similar results have been reported when URs have been blocked with certain drugs (see Finch, 1938; Solomon & Turner, 1962) and when apparatus arrangements have prevented URs during conditioning (see Hearst, 1978; Moore, 1973). In all these cases, a CR clearly develops even when overt URs are absent at the time of conditioning. At first glance, this evidence appears to argue strongly against a stimulus–response version of conditioning. However, researchers holding this position have argued otherwise, suggesting that the blocking of a peripheral, overt UR does not necessarily block all the internal responses an organism makes that are related to that UR. For example, a dog that is prevented from moving its leg is not necessarily unable to make internal responses that normally produce leg–lifting. Thus, conditioning may occur in these situations because of an association between the CS and some internal response that is produced by the US (see Rescorla & Solomon, 1967, for one version of this argument).

Sensory preconditioning Aside from situations in which the UR is blocked, there appear to be instances of conditioning in which no overt UR can be observed. One example comes from the sensory preconditioning paradigm. Recall that in this paradigm two neutral stimuli such as a tone and a light are first paired. Then one of the stimuli (for example, the tone) is paired with a US. In this case, not only does the tone begin to produce a CR, but also the light, which has never been paired with the US, becomes capable of producing a conditioned response (see, for example, Wynne & Brogden, 1962).

The usual interpretation of this phenomenon is that the two neutral stimuli become associated during stage 1 of training. Later, when one stimulus acquires the capacity to produce a CR, the other stimulus that is linked to it acquires the same capacity. If this interpretation is correct, the occurrence of sensory preconditioning would constitute strong evidence that stimuli can become associated without a reflexive response occurring. Still, this interpretation is not without detractors. Some theorists have argued that when the two neutral stimuli are paired, an organism is bound to make at least some reaction to the stimuli. For example, if a light occurs followed by a tone, the organism may orient its ears toward the tone. Thus, the light may become associated with the orienting response rather than to the tone itself (see, for example, Kimble, 1961).

In effect, this argument is similar to the one advanced by stimulus–response theorists to explain how conditioning occurs when the UR is blocked. In other words, it is suggested that stimulus–response associations are actually occurring in these situations, but the responses in question are difficult to observe.

The occurrence of different CRs depending on the nature of the CS A third phenomenon that brings the stimulus–response position into question has to do with variations in conditioned responding as a function of CS characteristics. It is well known that the specific nature of a CR does not depend on the US alone. When different CSs are paired with the same US, the CRs may differ dramatically. One example of this phenomenon can be seen in the activity conditioning paradigm. In this situation rats are presented with food as the US. The normal reaction to the food is increased motor activity as the animal approaches the food. Holland (1977) has demonstrated that if a tone is used to signal the delivery of food, the tone becomes capable of producing increased activity as a CR. However, if a light is used to signal food availability, the CR that develops to the light is one of *decreased* activity. Specifically, when the light is presented animals tend to rear on their hind legs and then remain still.

This finding, which occurs with some regularity in other paradigms (see, for example, Rescorla, 1980) presents problems for a stimulus–response interpretation of conditioning. According to this view, the CR should closely approximate the UR, since conditioning involves the association between a CS and that UR. To explain this finding using a stimulus–response view, we would need to make two assumptions. First, we would assume that the US produces multiple URs. This assumption is almost certainly the case. Second, however, we would assume that because of their varying natures, some CSs are more likely to become associated with one UR, while others tend to become associated with other URs. The second assumption may be correct. However, if this is the case, the stimulus–response position must delineate the conditions under which these different associations will occur.

Postconditioning changes in the US According to the stimulus–response view of conditioning, the US is important for one reason. It produces the response with which the CS becomes associated. The stimulus–stimulus view, however, suggests that the US is part of the association itself. One set of experiments that tends to differentiate these views involves changing the nature of the US after conditioning. For example, let's assume that a tone has been paired regularly with a medium-intensity shock so that the tone begins to produce moderate fear responses. After conditioning has occurred, the shock alone is presented to the organism, but the intensity of the stimulus is either substantially stronger or weaker than it was during conditioning. Will this change in the intensity of the shock alter the fear response that is later produced by the tone?

The two views of conditioning we have discussed would appear to make different predictions in answer to this question. The stimulus–response view would say that during conditioning the tone becomes associated with the moderate fear response produced by the medium-intensity shock. Since later presentations of the altered shock occur without the CS present, the CS should not become associated with any new UR. Thus, responding to the tone should be unchanged. According to the stimulus–stimulus position, however, it is the internal representations of the CS and the US that become associated. In other words, an organism's memories of the two events become linked. Responses to the CS depend on an organism's memory for what the US was like. If we assume that presenting different intensity USs to an organism alters its memory of the US, then such presentations would be expected to alter responding to the CS.

Although all the evidence pertaining to this question does not fall on the same side, the great majority of results tend to favor the stimulus–stimulus prediction. In other words, postconditioning alterations in a US often result in changes in responding to a CS. One example of this effect can be seen in a study by Rescorla (1974: experiment 2). In this experiment rats were given pairings of a tone and a 0.5 milliampere shock. After the pairings, the rats were divided into four groups. Animals in three of these groups received eight shock-alone presentations. For one group the shocks were of the same intensity as those used during conditioning (0.5 mA). In the other two groups, shocks of either 1.0 or 3.0 mA were presented. The final group received no shocks after conditioning. Rescorla then determined the degree to which the tone from the conditioning phase would lead to suppression of a bar pressing response.

Figure 3.3 summarizes the results of this experiment. Keep in mind that better conditioned responding to the CS is reflected by low suppression ratios in the CER paradigm. At least two findings evident in this graph are worth noting. First, the rats that received shock-alone presentations of the same intensity they received during conditioning (0.5 mA) responded less than rats that received no additional shocks. Rescorla interprets this finding as an example of habituation to that shock intensity. In other words, when animals are exposed to the same stimulus several times, they tend to become less and less responsive to it.

The second finding of interest in Figure 3.3 is directly related to our discussion. Rats that were exposed to shocks of greater intensity than they had experienced during condition-

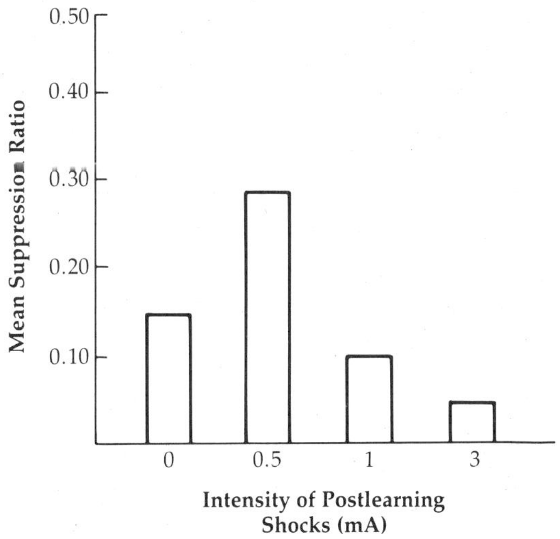

FIGURE 3.3 Conditioned responding to a CS after varying intensity of exposures to US-alone presentations. (From Rescorla, 1974.)

ing showed enhanced CRs to the tone CS. According to Rescorla, this enhanced responding is probably the result of a change in the rats' memory of the shock. After the high-intensity shock presentations, the animals' memory of shock changes from that of a low-intensity shock to a recollection of a high-intensity shock. Since the CS is associated with that memory (according to the stimulus–stimulus view), responding to the CS increases. This finding, then, clearly favors the idea that the CS and US representations become associated during a conditioning experience.

Conclusions from the evidence The questions of whether CS–US or CS–UR associations are formed during conditioning cannot be answered with great confidence. The evidence we have reviewed clearly favors the stimulus–stimulus position over the stimulus–response interpretation. It is notable, however, that the stimulus–response interpretation can be stretched to account for most of the individual bits of evidence we have discussed.

This fact illustrates an important point. Seldom are complex theoretical issues resolved by a single experiment or by a single set of experiments. In many cases, researchers must make an educated judgment about the relative merits of two theoretical positions by considering all the evidence that is available. This is why researchers often conduct experiments of several different kinds, which converge on the same theoretical question. In the present case all we can really say is that a stimulus–stimulus conception of conditioning accounts for the majority of evidence more easily than does a stimulus–response view.

The Role of Context in Conditioning

Thus far, we have considered two very broad and historically significant theoretical issues in Classical conditioning. Basically, we have dealt with the necessary conditions for this type of learning and with the elements involved in a Classically conditioned association. Now we look at an issue that has a more limited scope but has provided a significant amount of research in recent years: namely, the role of contextual stimuli in the conditioning process.

Contextual stimuli are the background stimuli that are present throughout a conditioning experience. When CS–US pairings are presented in a given room, for example, the background noise, odors, and lighting conditions in that room qualify as contextual stimuli. The same is true of stimuli that arise from an organism's internal state at the time of conditioning. In effect, any stimulus that remains relatively constant during conditioning and does not vary along with the CS or US presentation can be considered to be a contextual stimulus.

Although this description seems to suggest that contextual stimuli are incidental to the conditioning process, it is clear that this is not the case. Conditioned responses that are learned in one context tend to be relatively context specific. If a CR is acquired in one stimulus context, that CR occurs most readily when the CS reoccurs in that same context. The tendency for an organism to make a conditioned response is often diminished when a CS occurs in a context that is substantially different from that used for conditioning.

The importance of contextual stimuli in controlling learned behaviors can be appreciated by looking at any number of everyday situations. For example, many people have come to fear the sight of a hypodermic needle because of their experiences with injections. These conditioned fear responses occur most readily, however, when individuals are confronted with a hypodermic needle in a physician's office or a hospital. They tend not to exhibit fear when they see a hypodermic needle for sale in a drug store or when they see a needle in a veterinarian's office. Clearly, the fear response to the needle is greatest when the object appears in the same context in which the original injections took place.

This kind of contextual control is evident from the results of numerous conditioning experiments. Some of the best examples of contextual influence come from studies that are often called "switching experiments" (see, for example, Asratyan, 1965). In one such experiment, Rescorla and his colleagues used an autoshaping paradigm with pigeons (Rescorla, Durlach, & Grau, 1985). On some occasions the pigeons were trained in one experimental chamber (context 1) and at other times the training occurred in another chamber (context 2). In context 1 the pigeons received exposures to two different CSs (CS_A and CS_B). CS_A was always followed by food and CS_B was never followed by food. In context 2 the reverse was true. Food never followed CS_A but always followed CS_B. The results of this training are shown in Figure 3.4. As you can see, the pigeons responded to CS_A when in context 1 and

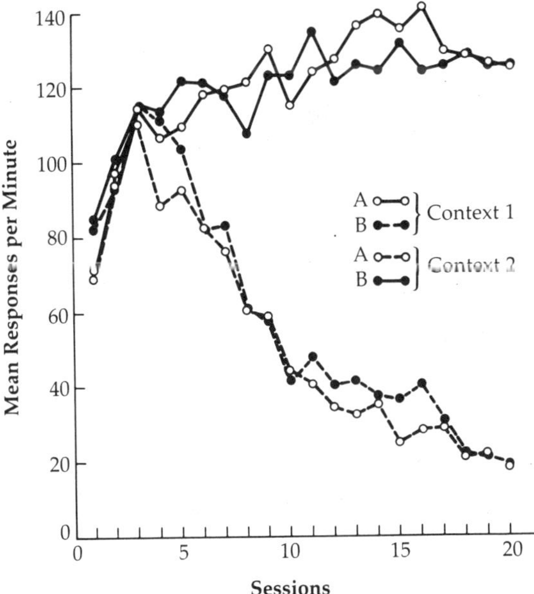

FIGURE 3.4 Differential responding to two CSs that were trained differently in contexts 1 and 2. (From Rescorla, Durlach, & Grau, 1985.)

to CS_B in context 2. Although both contexts contained all the same stimuli, the pigeons obviously learned to use the contexts as cues for responding to the respective CSs.

The strength of the control that contextual stimuli exert over conditioned responding indicates that at the time of conditioning, organisms learn something about the context they are in. What is not clear, however, is what organisms actually learn about contextual stimuli. In the present section we will discuss two points of view concerning the role of the conditioning context. The first view is that contextual stimuli function in the same manner as CSs. That is, contextual stimuli are capable of becoming associated with the US in the conditioning situation. The second view suggests that contextual stimuli act as cues to remind an organism of the relationship between the CS and US that was in effect during conditioning.

Contextual Stimuli as CSs

Many contemporary theories of conditioning view contextual stimuli in the same way as they view the CS in a conditioning situation (see, for example, Frey & Sears, 1978; Rescorla & Wagner, 1972; Wagner, 1978). According to these theories, contextual stimuli, along with the CS, actually constitute a compound CS that comes to signal US occurrence. Because contextual stimuli are part of the CS compound, these stimuli can become associated with the US and can become capable of producing a conditioned response on their own. In most cases, it is assumed that contextual stimuli are not as effective as the CS in producing a CR. The reason is that the CS reliably signals US occurrence, whereas the context is present even when the US is unlikely to occur. Still, in many cases contextual stimuli retain some capacity for producing conditioned responding because they are at least partially reliable in signaling US occurrence.

By viewing contextual stimuli in this manner, these theories have been able to explain why conditioned responding is better in the conditioning context than it is in a novel context. After conditioning, if the CS reoccurs in the conditioning context, there are several stimuli present that are capable of producing a CR (the CS plus all the original contextual stimuli). Thus, the likelihood of a CR occurring in this situation is very great. If, however, the CS occurs in a novel context, only the CS is present to produce a CR. The contextual stimuli that had become capable of producing a CR are no longer present. Thus, in a novel environment, conditioned responding to the CS will be less likely. In effect, the more stimuli in a situation that are capable of producing a CR, the more likely the CR is to occur.

Evidence for Contextual Stimuli as CSs

There is substantial evidence to support the notion that contextual stimuli can become capable of producing a CR during conditioning. One example of such evidence comes from a study by Balaz, Capra, Hartl, and Miller (1981). Although this CER experiment involved several groups of rats, we will concentrate on two groups. As outlined in Table 3.1, both groups of rats were given *tone–shock* pairings in one distinct chamber (context X). Both groups also received a comparable number of *click–shock* pairings in a distinctly different chamber (context Y). Later, both groups were tested to determine the degree to which the clicker would suppress a drinking response. One group was tested in a completely novel chamber (context Z). The other group was tested in context X where they had previously received tone–shock pairings. So, neither group was tested in the chamber in which the clicker had been paired with shock.

TABLE 3.1 Training Procedures Used by Balaz, Capra, Hartl, and Miller (1981), to Assess Conditioned Responding to Contextual Stimuli

	Stage 1 (Tone–shock pairings)	*Stage 2 (Click–shock pairings)*	*Stage 3 (Test for suppression to the click CS)*
Group 1	Context X	Context Y	Context Z
Group 2	Context X	Context Y	Context X

The results of the experiment were clear. The group tested in context X suppressed drinking to a greater extent than the group tested in novel context Z. This occurred even though the groups had had an equivalent number of clicker–shock pairings and even though neither group was tested in the context in which these pairings had occurred. The groups differed in that one was tested in a context that had been used for tone–shock pairings while the other was tested in a novel context. The difference, apparently, resulted because context X became capable of producing fear during the tone–shock pairings. Thus, when the clicker and context X were combined on the test, conditioned responding was greater than when the clicker and context Z were combined. This result supports the idea that during conditioning, contextual stimuli can come to produce a conditioned response.

Another, more direct approach to the same issue can be seen in a study by Bouton and King (1983). These researchers gave rats CS–shock pairings in a distinctive chamber (context A). Later, they placed the same rats in context A but allowed the animals to have access to a novel chamber (context B). They found that these rats now showed a distinct preference for context B over context A, where they had been conditioned. No such preference was found in animals that had not been conditioned in context A. This finding indicates that after receiving CS–shock pairings in context A, the rats were fearful not only of the CS, but also of the contextual stimuli present at the time of conditioning.

These and similar experiments leave little doubt that contextual stimuli can begin to elicit a CR if they are present at the time of conditioning. According to some theorists, this alone is enough to explain why CRs are more probable in the conditioning context than in totally novel contexts. The CR-producing capacity of the conditioning context simply combines with that of the CS to enhance conditioned responding. Some theorists have disagreed, however, that this is the entire explanation for contextual control.

Contextual Stimuli as Cues for the CS–US Relationship

Few theorists question that contextual stimuli can come to elicit CRs. Recently, however, a number of theorists have suggested that this may not be the main mechanism by which context controls learned responding. According to these theorists, during conditioning contextual stimuli may become more than signals for US occurrence. They may become cues or signals for a particular CS–US relationship. In effect, contextual stimuli may become capable of signaling to an organism when a CS is likely to be followed by a US and when it is not. Thus, these stimuli served as cues to remind an organism when it should respond to a CS and when it should not (see, for example, Estes, 1973; Medin, 1975; Nadel & Willner, 1980; Spear, 1973; also see Rescorla, Durlach, & Grau, 1985, for a similar view).

Evidence That Context May Serve as a Cue for a Specific CS–US Relationship

If context can act as a cue for a specific CS–US relationship, then over and above any CRs produced by contextual stimuli, these stimuli should aid responding by signaling when a CS–US relationship is in effect. For this reason, much of the evidence in support of this position comes from studies showing that contextual stimuli affect responding even when they do not produce observable CRs. Several studies of this type have been conducted by Miller and his associates (see, for example, Miller & Schachtman, 1985). The rationale for these experiments was to use procedures that would minimize or eliminate the contextual production of CRs during conditioning. The question of interest was whether under these circumstances the conditioning context would continue to affect conditioned responding to the CS.

In one of these experiments, for example, rats were given CS–shock pairings in a distinctive context (Balaz, Capra, Kasprow, & Miller, 1982). However, before conditioning, some rats were given extensive exposures to the conditioning context alone. We know from our previous discussions that prior exposures to a CS alone usually result in retarded conditioning to that CS (latent inhibition). The purpose of the contextual exposures in this study was to retard the subsequent development of CRs to the conditioning context. These experimenters found that animals given these prior exposures developed little or no conditioned responding to the context. Still, when responding to the CS was measured, responding was best when the CS occurred in the conditioning context. Responding to the CS was diminished when the CS was presented in a novel context. This suggests that the conditioning context aids responding to the CS even when the context itself produces no observable conditioned responding.

In a similar vein, Balaz, Capra, Hartl, and Miller (1981) gave rats CS–shock pairings in one context and then attempted to extinguish any CRs that might have developed to the contextual stimuli. They did this by exposing animals to the contextual stimuli alone *after* the conditioning session. As in the previous experiment, they found that extinction virtually abolished CRs to the conditioning context. Still, responding to the CS was better when the CS was presented in the conditioning context than when it occurred in a novel situation. Again, this finding suggests that contextual stimuli need not produce CRs themselves to facilitate responding to the CS. It is notable that several recent experiments in other laboratories appear to agree with this conclusion concerning contextual effects on responding (see, for example, Bouton & Swartzentruber, 1986).

Conclusions about Contextual Stimuli

At the present time there is some disagreement with respect to the precise role of contextual stimuli in the conditioning process (see Balsam & Tomie, 1985). On the one hand, it appears clear that at the time of conditioning, contextual stimuli often acquire the capacity to produce CRs on their own. It seems equally evident, however, that contextual stimuli can affect responding to a CS even when these stimuli produce little in the way of conditioned responding. This latter conclusion is consistent with the notion that contextual stimuli may function to signal when a certain CS–US relationship is in effect.

In this regard, it is interesting that several recent experiments have demonstrated that noncontextual stimuli can sometimes act as signals for particular CS–US relationships (see, for example, Holland, 1983, 1985; Rescorla, Durlach, & Grau, 1985). These discrete stimuli appear to acquire no capacity to produce CRs themselves, yet they clearly influence responding to the CS from conditioning. Such stimuli have been termed "occasion setters" because they identify points at which a particular CS is likely to be followed by a US. This line of research on discrete stimulus signals may help to clarify the mechanism by which contextual stimuli influence conditioned responding.

Summary Statements

In this chapter we have considered three theoretical issues in the study of Classical conditioning. The first issue concerned the necessary and sufficient conditions for development of a CR. We found that although CS–US contiguity is an important factor, the degree of conditioning seems to depend more strongly on the contingent relationship between the CS and US. Our second concern was to determine the elements in the conditioning situation that become associated. We saw that the preponderance of evidence favors the view that CS–US associations, not CS–UR associations, underlie the conditioning process. Finally, we considered the role of contextual stimuli in the conditioning process. The evidence on this issue was found to be somewhat mixed. It appears that contextual stimuli act like CSs in that they become capable of producing CRs. Still, contextual stimuli appear to affect responding to a CS even when the context produces no observable CRs. Thus, the precise mechanism for contextual effects remains unclear.

4

Instrumental/Operant Conditioning: Learning about the Consequences of Responding

We have noted that Classical conditioning involves learning about the relationships between stimuli. Specifically, it entails learning that one stimulus can serve as a signal for another. We found that as a result of such learning, a behavior that is naturally elicited or produced by one stimulus comes to be produced by a completely different stimulus.

The present chapter deals with a different learning situation, which is usually termed either *Instrumental* or *Operant conditioning*. In this type of situation, organisms learn about the relationships between their responses and the consequences of those responses. Specifically, organisms learn that their voluntary or *emitted* behaviors produce changes in the environment. By coming to understand which behaviors lead to which changes, organisms learn to adjust or modify their responses to produce a more favorable outcome.

In asserting that Instrumental or Operant conditioning involves changes in emitted or voluntary behaviors, we must be careful to distinguish between responses of these kinds and the reflexive behaviors discussed earlier. Emitted responses are behaviors that an organism engages in voluntarily. They are *not* behaviors that can be produced automatically by any given stimulus. When you choose to speak to a friend or to write a letter, you act of your own accord. When you attend class or drive a car or watch a movie, you emit these behaviors voluntarily. In Instrumental or Operant conditioning situations, you learn to modify responses analogous to these, depending on the outcomes they produce.

Examples of this type of learning are numerous. Any time you learn a new motor skill, such as typing, Instrumental conditioning is involved. You begin by moving your fingers in a certain way and by observing the outcome that appears on paper. You learn that you can adjust your patterns of responding in particular ways so that the product of the response is a word instead of a meaningless string of letters. Thus, by learning how different responses are related to different outcomes or consequences, you modify your responses to achieve the desired result. The same procedure is used by children when they learn appropriate social behaviors and by students when they learn to study more effectively. By emitting responses and then recognizing what consequences these responses produce, it becomes possible to alter and refine our behaviors so that they more effectively produce changes that we desire.

In the present chapter we will discuss this type of learning in some detail. We begin by looking at the kinds of consequences that commonly follow responses and the kinds of contingencies that can exist between our behaviors and these outcomes. Then we will discuss the experimental paradigms that have been developed to study Instrumental or Operant conditioning. Finally, we will catalog the range of variables that influence this learning process.

Consequences of Responding

We have noted that organisms learn to alter their responses depending on the outcomes these responses produce. One type of outcome that affects responding is called a *reinforcement* or a *reinforcing event. A reinforcement is any event that increases the probability that a prior response will reoccur.* In other words, if an organism makes a response and a reinforcing event follows, the organism tends to repeat that response in the future.

Two types of response outcome tend to have reinforcing effects on behavior. First, when organisms respond and receive some reward or some desirable stimulus, they usually repeat the response. Whenever a response is reinforced by *giving* or *presenting* some rewarding stimulus to an organism, we say that *positive reinforcement* is in effect. The term "positive reinforcement" is used to indicate that a positive contingency or correlation exists between an organism's response and the appearance of a rewarding stimulus.

We find examples of positive reinforcement or reward throughout our daily experiences. Children clean their rooms and receive praise from their parents. The praise is a reward that increases room cleaning responses in the future. A student studies for an exam and receives a high grade from the instructor. The high grade serves as a reward that increases subsequent studying. When your dog comes to you when you call, that response can be rewarded by giving the dog a piece of meat. In all instances of positive reinforcement, an organism repeats some response because it *receives* some stimulus as a consequence of that response.

Aside from the occurrence of a reward, there is a second kind of response outcome that can serve to reinforce responding. This type of outcome is labeled *negative reinforcement*—that is, the removal or disappearance of some aversive stimulus following a response. Here "aversive stimulus" refers to any stimulus that an organism dislikes or would attempt to avoid. Thus, in negative reinforcement situations an organism responds, and this response leads to the removal of some aversive stimulus. As a result of this removal, the organism tends to make the same response again. This type of response outcome is called negative reinforcement because there is a negative correlation or contingency between responding and the occurrence of a stimulus. The response occurs and the aversive stimulus disappears.

Examples of negative reinforcement are almost as common as examples of reward. If you are bored, you tend to find that state aversive. For this reason you may begin to jog or go to movies regularly because these activities reduce your boredom. Likewise, most of us find tension or anxiety to be an extremely aversive state. Many of our behaviors, such as smoking, listening to music, drinking, and even visiting a therapist, originate because we learn that these responses reduce or eliminate anxiety. Clearly, removal of an aversive stimulus works in the same way as the presentation of a reward. Both reinforce the behaviors that precede them.

To this point we have discussed only response outcomes that reinforce or increase the tendency to repeat a response. There are, however, certain consequences of responding that have the opposite effect. These response outcomes are labeled *punishments.* Technically, a punishment is any consequence of responding that leads to a *decrease* in the probability that the response will reoccur. Obviously, punishment involves the occurrence of some state of affairs that an organism would rather avoid. Thus, when an organism perceives that a certain response leads to punishment, the organism is likely to refrain from repeating that response.

Just as with reinforcers, we can talk about two types of punishment—positive and negative. *Positive punishment* is what most of us think of when we use the term in our daily conversations. It occurs when an organism responds and then *receives* some form of aversive stimulation that causes the response to decrease. For example, when a child misbehaves and is spanked, the spanking causes the misbehavior to decrease, because the child views the misbehavior as having led to an undesirable consequence.

In *negative punishment,* the undesirable consequence results from the *removal* of something the organism finds pleasurable. By following a response with removal of some desirable stimulus, the response can be decreased. Parents often punish adolescents by "grounding" them or removing certain privileges. If a certain behavior is followed by the removal of privileges or the cessation of an allowance, the behavior that led to the removal tends to decrease. Thus, both positive and negative punishers tend to decrease those behaviors that precede them. The difference is that positive punishment involves the administration of an aversive stimulus, while negative punishment entails the removal of a desirable stimulus.

These, then, are the types of consequences that can affect emitted responses. By learning which responses lead to which consequences, organisms are capable of modifying their behavior accordingly. Still, the particular response adjustments organisms make depend on a variety of factors. Before commenting on these factors, however, it will be useful to examine some of the experimental paradigms that have been used to study Instrumental or Operant conditioning effects. We begin by distinguishing between "Instrumental" and "Operant," two terms we have used synonymously thus far.

Paradigms for Studying Instrumental/Operant Conditioning

The Instrumental–Operant Distinction

In both Instrumental and Operant conditioning situations, organisms learn the relationship between emitted behaviors and their consequences. However, these situations differ in subtle ways, and as a result researchers often study these two types of conditioning differently. The fundamental difference between instrumental and operant situations involves the degree to which an organism is *free* to make a response at any given point in time.

In an *Instrumental conditioning* situation, there are environmental constraints on the organism's opportunities to respond. In these situations organisms can emit a behavior only at a particular time. For example, let's assume that we are having difficulty getting a child to eat breakfast before going to school. We are convinced that the child needs a nourishing meal to start the day, so we decide to begin rewarding good eating habits at breakfast time. We can do this by praising the child when she eats well, by telling her how strong she is getting, or we can even do something crass like giving her money (money rewards are always considered crass except by the child).

In any event, we are rewarding a voluntary response that can only occur at a certain time. We will not reward the child for eating a large breakfast in the afternoon or late at night. The response of eating well will be noted and rewarded only if it occurs early in the day before school. Thus, since the opportunities to make a response are limited in some way, in this example we are dealing with an Instrumental conditioning situation.

In *Operant conditioning* situations, an organism is free to emit a given response as many times as it wishes while in that situation. In other words, given that an organism is in the appropriate situation, no constraints are placed on when or how often a response can be emitted. For example, instructors often subtly reward their students for being attentive during a lecture. They do this by joking, varying their tone of voice, moving, and making eye contact when students appear to be paying attention. During the lecture, the students are free to attend to the speaker as often as they want. They are not constrained to make attentive responses only at a particular time. Thus, the opportunity for responding and receiving a reward is virtually unlimited during the lecture period.

A similar example can be seen in the field of obedience training. The standard procedure for training a dog to walk on a leash is to walk with the leashed dog and to reward the animal when it remains at your side or heel. This can be done by praising the dog or by giving it food when it performs correctly. During a given session of walking, the dog is free to make the correct response as often as it wishes. It has numerous opportunities to respond and to be rewarded. Thus, this type of learning qualifies as an example of Operant conditioning.

Because both instrumental and operant situations occur in the real world, researchers have devised different paradigms for studying them. In Instrumental conditioning paradigms, organisms are given discrete, limited opportunities to respond. As a result, researchers study the *probability, speed,* or *accuracy* of an organism's responses when the opportunities for responding are present. In Operant conditioning paradigms, organisms are placed in a situation and are given unlimited opportunities to emit a response. The primary measure of learning in these paradigms is an organism's *rate* of responding. The experimenter measures how often an organism responds correctly in a given period of time. Obviously, it would make no sense to measure the rate of responding in an instrumental paradigm, since in this kind of situation the experimenter controls when an organism can respond and when it cannot.

Now that we have differentiated between learning situations of two types, we can look specifically at the paradigms that have been developed to study Instrumental and Operant conditioning. We begin with paradigms used to study the conditioning of instrumental behaviors.

Instrumental Conditioning Paradigms

The straight runway for rats One of the simplest paradigms for studying instrumental learning in the rat is the straight runway procedure. The experimenter places a rat in a small chamber called a start compartment. When the door to the start compartment is opened, the rat has the opportunity to enter a straight runway that is often several feet long. At the end of the runway is a goal compartment, in which the experimenter usually places a reward such as food. When the rat reaches the goal compartment and consumes the reward, it is removed from the apparatus to await subsequent trials or opportunities.

Typically, when rats begin runway training they remain in the start compartment for a time after the door is opened. They also spend a great deal of time exploring the runway itself. However, as more trials occur, the rats begin to traverse the runway at a faster and faster pace. This increase in speed apparently results from learning that running or moving is correlated with receiving a reward. Thus, learning is measured by assessing changes in a rat's speed as more and more learning trials are given. In most cases the rat's speed in leaving the start compartment (start speed), its speed in traversing the runway (running speed), and its speed in the terminal portion of the runway (goal speed) are all recorded.

Maze learning tasks In a maze learning task an organism must choose one response rather than another in order to receive some desirable outcome. One of the simplest maze tasks utilizes an apparatus called a *T maze* (Figure 4.1a). Typically a rat or other small animal is placed in a start compartment that opens onto a straight runway. This runway terminates in a dead-end choice point, such that instead of continuing forward, the rat must choose to turn right or left. Each of the short runways, or right and left "arms," ends in a goal compartment. In most cases a reward is present in the

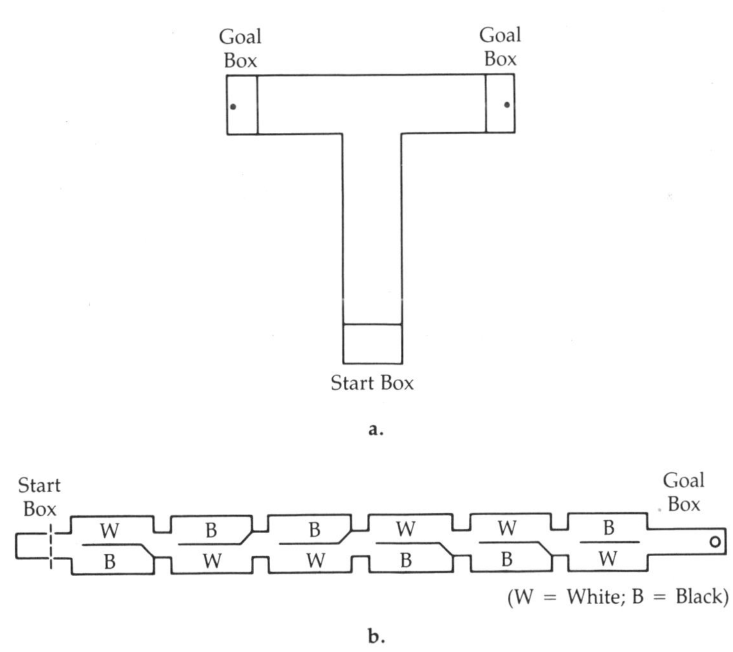

FIGURE 4.1 Diagram of (a) the T maze, and (b) a complex maze. (From Brennan and Gordon, 1977.)

goal compartment of one arm but not in the other. The rat must learn which arm to enter to receive a reward. The usual measures of learning are the time to reach the appropriate goal compartment and the number of errors made in reaching that goal. Normally, as the number of learning trials increases, both the time and the number of errors decrease substantially.

The use of the T maze allows researchers to assess the factors that influence the choice of one emitted behavior over another. This is critical because in many real-life settings the behaviors we emit are based on such choices. In other cases, however, our emitted behaviors are actually complex chains of responses that involve several choices. For example, if you park your car and walk several blocks to an office building, you may encounter numerous choice points along the way. At each point you can proceed in more than one direction—some will bring you closer to your destination, others will take you further from it. The first time you make the trip you may make a number of wrong turns. But, as you take the same path more often, you decrease your error rate and reach your destination more quickly.

To study how these chains of behaviors are learned, researchers employ more complex maze apparatuses. One such maze, pictured in Figure 4.1b, has several choice points between the start and goal compartments. A correct choice at any one of these points leads to the next choice point, while an incorrect choice usually leads to a dead end. A correct turn at the final choice point leads to the goal compartment, where some reward is normally present. As with the T maze, learning is usually assessed by measuring the time taken to reach the goal and by the number of errors made along the way.

Escape and Avoidance Paradigms

Both the straight runway and the maze learning tasks are usually employed to study the effects of reward or positive reinforcement on Instrumental conditioning. Researchers study the effects of negative reinforcement in *escape* or *avoidance learning* paradigms.

In an escape learning paradigm the experimenter exposes an organism to some form of aversive stimulation such as a loud noise, a bright light, or a mild shock. The organism must then learn to perform a specific response to secure the removal of the aversive stimulus. One simple apparatus often used to study escape learning (Figure 4.2) has two chambers, separated by a door. In a typical study the experimenter places a rat in one chamber and exposes it to shock. When the shock is initiated, the door to the other chamber opens, and to terminate the shock, the rat must move into the other chamber. The usual measure of learning in this paradigm is the speed with which the animal moves into the "safe" chamber after the door opens.

Whereas in escape learning the organism must learn a response to terminate an aversive stimulus that is already present, in avoidance learning paradigms the organism learns to perform a response that prevents the aversive stimulus from ever being presented. By responding correctly, that is, the organism can avoid the aversive stimulus altogether. Many avoidance learning paradigms involve the use of a stimulus that signals the impending pre-

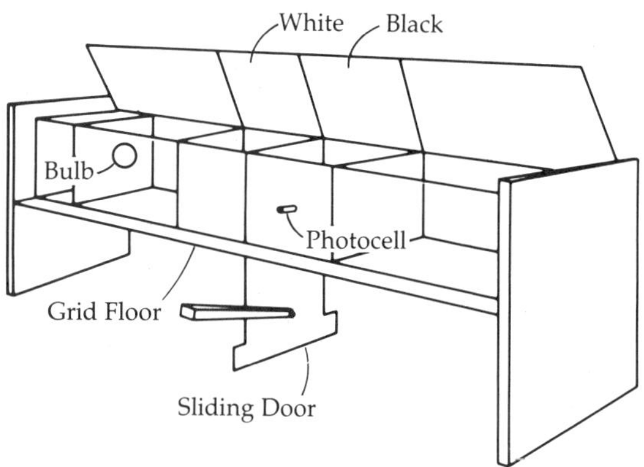

FIGURE 4.2 Diagram of a two-chamber apparatus used for escape and avoidance learning studies. (From Spear, 1971.)

sentation of the aversive stimulus. For example, an experimenter may place a rat in a chamber and present a tone that signals the impending administration of shock. In most cases the signal will precede the shock by several seconds. The animal must learn to perform some response in the presence of the signal in order to avoid the shock. If the desired response does not occur, the shock is administered as scheduled.

To exemplify the usual sequence of events in an avoidance paradigm, let's consider how a rat might be trained to avoid in the two-chamber apparatus described earlier. An experimenter places the rat in one compartment of the two-chamber apparatus, whereupon a tone sounds and the door to the other chamber opens. Five seconds after the tone begins, a shock occurs and remains on until the rat moves into the other chamber. If the rat happens to move to the other chamber before the shock is scheduled to begin, it does not receive the aversive stimulus.

As you might imagine, most animals fail to avoid the shock on the first few learning trials. The shock comes on and the animal simply emits various responses until it finds one that enables it to escape from the shock. However, after several trials, most animals begin to respond in the presence of the signal alone, thereby avoiding the shock altogether. The usual measure of learning in this paradigm is the time it takes for an animal to respond once the signal has begun. Times that are *shorter* than the signal–shock interval reflect the performance of a true avoidance response.

What we have just described is a prototypical avoidance procedure known as a *one-way avoidance paradigm*. We apply this label to situations in which an organism must physically move in the same direction each time it attempts to avoid the aversive stimulus. In other words, an organism must always move from an aversive chamber located in one place to a safe chamber located somewhere else.

Another avoidance procedure that is frequently used is termed a *two-way avoidance paradigm*. This paradigm, too, makes use of a two-chamber apparatus. As before, a signal comes on in chamber 1, where the experimental animal is located. If the animal does not move into chamber 2 during the warning signal, it receives a shock in chamber 1 until it does respond. Now, instead of moving the animal back to chamber 1 to begin the second trial, we leave the organism in chamber 2. On the second trial the signal comes on in chamber 2 and the animal must respond by moving back to chamber 1. The third trial commences in chamber 1 and requires a movement into chamber 2. Thus, there is no single permanently aversive chamber, nor is there a single chamber that is always safe. On some trials a given chamber is safe, while on others that same chamber is aversive. Thus, in this type of paradigm the organism cannot simply learn that some places are good and others are bad and respond accordingly. It must learn to move to another location whenever the signal comes on in the place it presently occupies.

Finally, it is possible to study avoidance learning in situations that do not require an organism to physically leave its environment in order to avoid an aversive stimulus. For example, the experimenter may confront an animal with an aversive stimulus that cannot be avoided until the animal has pressed a bar or pokes its nose into a hole in the wall (see, for example, Spear, Gordon, & Martin, 1973). In some such paradigms no explicit signal precedes the aversive stimulus. Instead, organisms receive aversive stimulation on some set schedule unless they make an appropriate response. In these *unsignaled avoidance* situations, animals must use the passage of time as the signal for determining when the aversive stimulus is likely to occur (see Sidman, 1962).

We should make explicit one important point regarding all these avoidance paradigms. Although each paradigm requires that an organism learn an instrumental avoidance response, there is also the potential for Classical fear conditioning in virtually all avoidance situations. In these paradigms the warning stimulus and other contextual stimuli regularly signal the occurrence of a fear-eliciting event. Thus, these stimuli can, themselves, become capable of producing conditioned fear reactions. We will discuss in a later chapter how important this fear conditioning may be in helping an organism learn an avoidance response. It is clear, however, that in most avoidance paradigms such conditioning does occur.

The study of avoidance learning has taken on special significance in recent years as many researchers have discovered parallels between how animals learn avoidance responses and how humans acquire neurotic behaviors such as phobic reactions (see, for example, Peterson & Levis, 1985). As a matter of fact, many contemporary therapies used to treat phobic responses are based directly on research into how avoidance responses are eliminated in the laboratory. As we will see, there has been some controversy concerning what is involved in the learning and extinction of avoidance responses.

Operant Conditioning Paradigms

In each of the instrumental learning paradigms discussed above, an organism receives single, discrete opportunities to emit some response. Once one of these opportunities has passed, the organism cannot respond again until another trial commences. In contrast, Operant conditioning paradigms involve placing organisms in a particular setting and then giving them unlimited or free opportunities to respond while in that setting. One of the most common of the Operant conditioning paradigms involves the bar press response in rats.

The bar press response Rats normally learn the bar press response in an apparatus called an *operant chamber* or a *Skinner box* (Figure 4.3), named because it was conceived originally by the Experimental psychologist B. F. Skinner. Skinner has used this apparatus extensively to investigate the variables that control operant responding (see, for example, Ferster & Skinner, 1957).

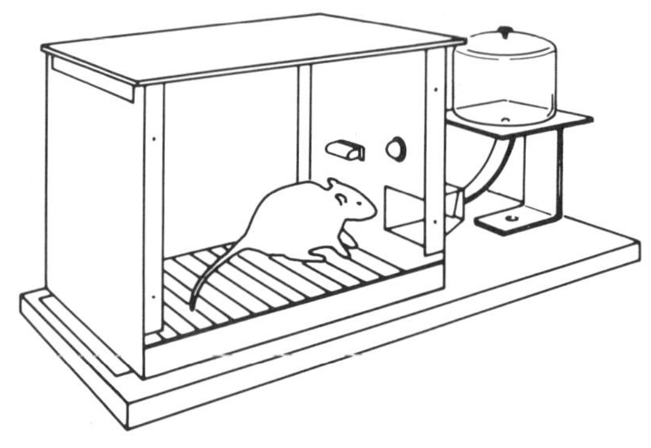

FIGURE 4.3 Diagram of a typical Skinner box.

In most Skinner boxes, one wall of the chamber contains a bar or a lever that can be depressed by the rat. Depression of the bar usually results in the delivery of a food or water reward through a hole in the wall next to the bar. Once the experimenter has placed the rat in the box, the animal is free to press the bar and receive a reward as often it wants. It is not unusual for a well-trained rat to position itself with one paw on the bar and its head near the opening in the wall. In this way it can respond repeatedly and consume the rewards as soon as they appear. The principal measure of responding in this paradigm is the rate at which the bar is depressed. The rate is derived by dividing the number of bar depressions by some unit of time. As we will see, the rate of bar pressing depends greatly on how rewards are scheduled by the experimenter.

The key peck response in pigeons As we mentioned earlier in connection with the autoshaping paradigm, pigeons have a natural tendency to peck round disks. It is possible to modify this tendency by following each pecking response with some consequence, such as a reward. The apparatus used to assess key pecking is similar to the Skinner box. There is an opening in one of the chamber walls through which rewards can be delivered. However, instead of a bar or lever, a round disk called a *key* is mounted on the chamber wall. When the pigeon pecks the key, the response is usually followed by a food reward. As with the bar press, the *rate* of key pecking is the usual measure of operant responding in this situation.

Measuring Instrumental and Operant Responses in Humans

As with Classical conditioning, much of the research on instrumental and operant learning has been conducted with animals. The typical procedure has been to investigate the laws of instrumental and operant behavior using animal subjects and then to apply these laws to human subjects in natural settings. This enterprise has had numerous successes, including the development of therapeutic techniques in the clinical setting, the use of biofeedback procedures for treating medical disorders, and the formulation of teaching principles that have been applied in classroom settings.

In addition, some paradigms have been developed to study Instrumental and Operant conditioning directly in humans. Many of these techniques have been used to study motor skill learning. For example, humans are often asked to perform some task involving hand–eye coordination, after which feedback is provided to allow them to assess the accuracy of their responses. One example of such a paradigm is the *pursuit rotor task.* The pursuit rotor is a flat, round disk not unlike a phonograph record. On the surface of the disk is a metal circle about the size of a small coin. The task of the subject is to keep a metal pen in contact with the metal circle as the disk revolves on a turntable. Feedback often consists of a buzzing sound that occurs only when the pen and the metal circle are in contact. Most studies of motor skill learning show that the subjects respond more accurately with practice, especially when feedback is received (see, for example, Dore & Hilgard, 1937).

Aside from studies of motor skills, human subjects have been used in studies of operant responding for different schedules of reward. Typically, subjects are seated in front of a keyboard and allowed to press one of two keys. It may take only a few presses of one key to receive a reward, while several presses of the other key may be required. Subjects soon adjust their key pressing behavior to maximize their rewards much as pigeons or rats do when they are confronted with such choices (see, for example, Bradshaw, Szabadi, & Bevan, 1976; Dougher, Crossen, & Garland, 1986).

The Shaping Procedure

In discussing Instrumental and Operant conditioning paradigms, we have made the learning of emitted behaviors sound very simple. Organisms respond, they receive some consequence, and they modify their subsequent responses. The only problem with this description is that it assumes that an organism will always make the appropriate response, which then can be either reinforced or punished. Seldom can we actually make this assumption.

When a rat is first placed in a Skinner box it normally explores, pokes its nose into the food delivery opening, and grooms itself. The likelihood that it will spontaneously press the bar is very low. Likewise, when you are toilet training a child, if you simply wait for a correct toileting response to occur in order to reward it, you will be in for a long wait. The problem with many emitted behaviors that we wish to increase or decrease is that they often do not occur spontaneously so that they can be reinforced or punished.

For this reason the training of instrumental and operant responses usually requires a procedure called *shaping*. By shaping we mean that we have to gradually coax or bias an organism toward making the appropriate response. This is normally done by rewarding any response that makes it more probable that the correct response will be performed. By a series of rewards and nonrewards, we guide the organism to closer and closer approximations of the response we deem appropriate.

To exemplify the shaping procedure, let's look at how we might shape the rat's bar press response. In the beginning, we reward the rat each time it moves to the side of the chamber that houses the bar. After several rewards, the rat usually remains on the bar side of the chamber. We then stop rewarding this behavior. Next we require that the rat do something else that brings it closer to the bar press response. We may, for example, require the rat to stand next to the bar to receive a reward. Once the rat has acquired this response, we cease rewarding it and require that the animal be in physical contact with the bar itself. Finally, we reward the rat only when it depresses the bar.

By using shaping procedures, we can train an organism to perform even very complex, low-probability behaviors. When you see a dog begging for food on its hind legs or a whale jumping through a hoop held high above the water, you can be sure that extensive shaping has preceded the response. The key to shaping any behavior is understanding what the components of that behavior are. Then it is possible to build in, through reward, each component that brings the organism closer to the desired response.

The Development of Superstitious Behavior

Even when two organisms undergo the same shaping procedures, there is no guarantee that they will end up performing the desired response in the same way. One rat may consistently press the bar with its left paw, while another may approach the bar, turn in a circle, and press the bar with both paws. Both make the response that produces the reward (depression of the bar), but they differ substantially in the other behaviors that accompany the bar press response. Why do these differences develop?

As we have said, *any* behaviors that precede a reward tend to be repeated. Thus, whatever behaviors happen to accompany the appropriate response when it is first rewarded tend to be present whenever that appropriate response reoccurs. It is almost as if the organism is not sure which of its behaviors actually produced the reward. Therefore, instead of taking a chance on not being rewarded, the organism repeats *all* the behaviors that might have been responsible. These irrelevant behaviors that are repeated even though they do not produce the reward are called *superstitious behaviors* (Skinner, 1948). The term is used because such behaviors appear to develop in much the same way as the superstitions we form in our daily lives.

For example, we have all heard stories of athletic coaches who continue to wear a particular hat or pair of socks as long as their teams are winning. They superstitiously attribute the winning streak to the "lucky" garment and believe that to change the hat or the socks might result in a loss. Such superstitions usually develop because the coach happened to be wearing a certain article of clothing when the team won a particular game. Of course the coach also had recruited good players, devised successful plays, and organized practices, and it is these behaviors that probably produced the favorable record. However, the coach tends to repeat *all* the behaviors that preceded the rewarding experience.

Once learned, such superstitious behaviors can be difficult to eliminate. Often, extensive reshaping is necessary to get an organism to perform the appropriate response without the irrelevant behaviors. This is accomplished by ceasing to reward the appropriate response whenever it is accompanied by the superstitious behavior. We reward the appropriate response only when it occurs alone. By doing this we give the organism the opportunity to discriminate between behaviors that produce some reward and those that do not.

Variables That Affect Instrumental Responding

To this point we have examined the basic conditions under which Instrumental and Operant conditioning occur. Also, we have described the paradigms used to study these forms of conditioning. Now we will look at the factors that influence responding in Instrumental conditioning paradigms, moving from the variables that affect responding in positive reinforcement situations to certain negative reinforcement and punishment paradigms.

Positive Reinforcement Situations

In Instrumental conditioning situations that involve positive reinforcement, responding is influenced most strongly by the characteristics of the reward. Of particular importance are the amount of reward, the quality of the reward, and the time that elapses between a response and the presentation of reward. In this section we consider the effects of these variables, as well as some others that influence responding in instrumental, positive reinforcement situations.

Amount and quality of reward In most cases, instrumental responding occurs faster and becomes more accurate as we increase the amount of reward given after each response. This principle has been illustrated by any number of studies that have varied the magnitude of reward in instrumental learning paradigms.

In one such experiment, Crespi (1942) trained five groups of rats to run down a straight runway for a food reward. The groups differed in terms of the number of small food pellets they received in the goal compartment on each trial. The groups received either 1, 4, 16, 64, or 256 pellets for each correct response. Crespi found that after 20 trials, the running speeds of the groups corresponded directly to the number of pellets received. The fastest running occurred in the group receiving the largest reward, and the speeds of the other groups decreased in direct proportion to the size of each group's reward. In addition, Crespi found that the animals that received the largest rewards improved their performance more quickly than did the other animals.

Although such findings have been replicated numerous times, there is one complicating factor in the results of reward magnitude studies. Some experimenters have disagreed as to the definition of "reward magnitude." Is it the absolute size of the reward, the amount of time it takes to consume the reward, or is it the number of objects the organism receives? Several studies have shown that if an experimenter gives two groups the same amount of food for each response, but for one group the food is simply broken into more pieces, the group receiving the most pieces will respond faster (see, for example, Campbell, Batsche, & Batsche, 1972). While such findings do not detract from the basic principle that larger rewards lead to better performance, they do suggest that organisms may not always perceive the amount of reward as the experimenter intended.

Size or amount of reward notwithstanding, organisms also perform better when the "quality" of reward is higher. We can define quality by assessing how vigorously an organism consumes a reward when it is presented. High-quality rewards are consumed quickly by organisms, whereas low-quality rewards are consumed less quickly. For example, it is well known that when rats are allowed to drink solutions that vary in sweetness, they drink faster, the sweeter the solution is. Likewise, when rats are rewarded for an instrumental response by being presented with sweet solutions, groups that receive the sweetest solutions perform best (see, for example, Flaherty & Caprio, 1976).

Delay of reward Just as reward magnitude and quality affect instrumental responding, so does the delay of any reward that follows a correct response. The longer a reward is delayed after a response has been performed, the poorer the performance of the instrumental response. This conclusion is illustrated clearly by the results of a runway experiment conducted by E. J. Capaldi (1978). Two groups of rats received the same amount and quality of food reward on each trial. However, one group received the reward immediately upon entering the goal box while the other group experienced a 10-second delay. The results of this study are shown in Figure 4.4, which plots the start speed in the runway a function of learning trials and delay conditions. At the end of training, the speed of the immediate-reward group is substantially higher than is the speed of the delayed-reward group.

There are probably a number of reasons for why delay of reward adversely affects instrumental responding. One reason is that

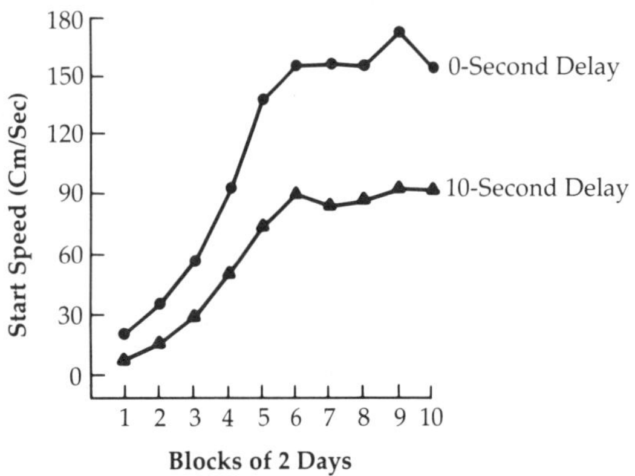

FIGURE 4.4 Acquisition of a running response as a function of the length of time reward is delayed on each trial. (From E. J. Capaldi, 1978.)

long delays almost certainly make it more difficult for an organism to recognize that the reward is a consequence of the instrumental response. When long delays occur, an organism has the opportunity to engage in a number of responses between the instrumental response and the reward. This means that responses that do not actually produce the reward may be superstitiously repeated in the future instead of the appropriate response. It is notable that some studies have shown very efficient instrumental learning even with very long reward delays, as long as the procedures used aid animals in remembering the instrumental response over the delay period (see, for example, Lieberman, McIntosh, & Thomas, 1979).

Contrast effects In general, the effects of quantity, quality, and delay of reward on instrumental responding appear to be rather simple. However, these effects can vary depending on an organism's past experiences with different reward characteristics. For example, a given magnitude of reward may influence instrumental responding differently, depending on the reward magnitude an organism has come to expect. This phenomenon was first demonstrated by Crespi (1942) in his experiments involving the runway performance of rats.

In Crespi's experiment one group of rats was trained to traverse a runway for a large amount of reward, while a second group received a small reward for the running response. After several trials the rats receiving the large reward were running consistently faster than the small-reward group. Crespi then switched half of the large-reward animals to the small reward being given the other rats (large–small group). He also switched half the small-reward rats to the large reward magnitude—the small–large group. The results of this switch in reward magnitude were surprising.

The animals that were switched from the large to the small reward slowed their running speeds to such a degree that they ran *more slowly* than the rats that had received the small reward all along. This phenomenon has been labeled the *"depression"* or *negative contrast effect.* Likewise, animals that were shifted from the small to the large reward began to run *faster* than the animals that had been receiving the large reward since trial 1. This phenomenon is called an *elation* or *positive contrast effect.* Figure 4.5 illustrates the kind of reward shift effects found by Crespi.

The kind of paradigm employed by Crespi has been termed a *successive contrast paradigm,* to denote that one reward magnitude succeeds or follows another. Contrast effects have also been found, however, in *simultaneous contrast paradigms.* In these types of paradigms, one group consistently receives one reward magnitude. The other group receives the same reward magnitude as the first group on some trials but either a larger or a smaller reward on other trials. For example, one group may receive 5 food pellets on all its trials. A second group may receive 5 food pellets on half its trials and 10 food pellets on the remainder. If you compare the running speeds of the two groups on the 5-pellet trials only, you will usually find that the group that receives 10 pellets on some trials runs more slowly than the group that receives 5 pellets on all trials (see, for example, Bower, 1961).

The occurrence of contrast effects is not limited to different experiences with reward magnitude. Contrast effects have been obtained with shifts in reward quality (Elliot, 1928), as well as when reward quality is varied in simultaneous contrast paradigms (see, for example, Flaherty, Riley, & Spear, 1973). Likewise, there is some evidence that contrast effects may occur when organisms experience more than one delay of reward condition (see, for example, Beery, 1968; McHose & Tauber, 1972).

There is presently some confusion about the precise mechanisms underlying these contrast effects (see, for example, Black, 1968; Flaherty, 1982), largely because not all changes in reward characteristics produce contrast effects equally in all paradigms (Mackintosh, 1974). Still, these findings make it clear that instrumental responding depends on more

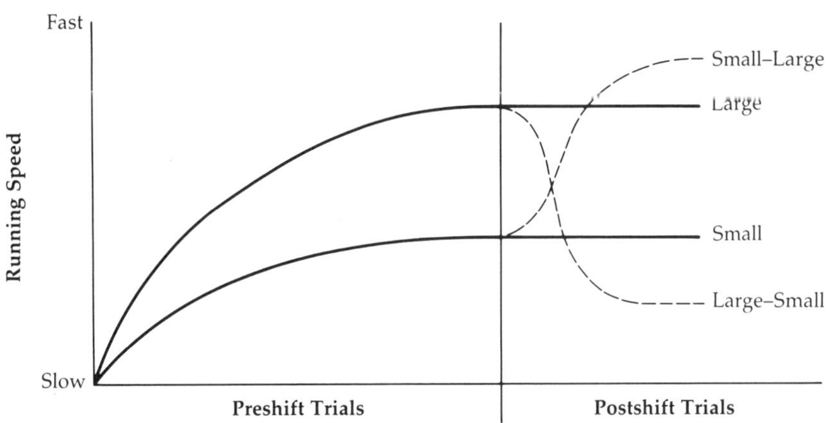

FIGURE 4.5 Contrast effects of the type found by Crespi (1942). Rats shifted from a large to a small reward (Large–Small) ran more slowly than rats given a small reward (Small) throughout training. Rats shifted from a small to a large reward (Small–Large) ran faster than rats receiving a large reward (Large) throughout.

than the reward characteristics an organism experiences on a given trial. Responding is also influenced by the reward characteristics an organism has come to expect in its past.

The schedule of reward In real-life settings we seldom receive rewards each time we emit an appropriate response. For example, it may be our plan to reward a child each time the child picks up her toys. However, once this plan has been initiated, the child is likely to begin to pick up her toys even when we are not around to give praise. What is the effect of such reward inconsistency on the performance of an instrumental response?

To answer this question, several researchers have compared the performance of organisms given *continuous reinforcement* (reward after each correct response) to that of organisms given *partial reinforcement* (reward after only a percentage of the correct responses). One might expect that in such comparisons continuously reinforced organisms would outperform organisms given partial reinforcement. Somewhat surprisingly, this has not always been the case.

Some studies have found that as long as a substantial percentage of responses is rewarded, partially reinforced responses develop almost as fast as continuously reinforced responses (see, for example, Brown & Wagner, 1964; Mikulka & Pavlik, 1966). In still other experiments, results indicate that partial reinforcement actually produces better responding than reinforcement after each response (Goodrich, 1959; Wagner, 1961). This rather mixed pattern of findings does not allow us to draw any firm conclusions. However, it is clear that instrumental learning is not dependent on continuous reward. Instrumental responding develops quite efficiently even when reward occurs after only some of the correct responses.

Deprivation conditions One final variable that influences instrumental responding for rewards is the degree to which an organism has been deprived of the rewarding substance before learning. Several studies have shown that, up to a point, the hungrier a rat is when it responds for a food reward, the more vigorously it responds in order to receive food (see, for example, Cotton, 1953; Stabler, 1962; Weiss, 1960). Likewise, the longer rats have been deprived of water, the faster or more vigorously they respond to receive a water reward (see, for example, Kintsch, 1962).

The effects of deprivation on instrumental behavior have been interpreted in several ways. One notion, proposed by Hull (1943), is that deprivation increases an organism's motivation to perform any responses in its repertoire. As the organism learns the instrumental response, this simply becomes one of the behaviors that is energized by the organism's motivational state. Support for this idea comes from a number of studies showing that deprivation increases activity in general, not simply instrumental responses (see, for example, Collier, 1969).

Although this view of deprivation effects has enjoyed some support, there appear to be problems associated with such an interpretation. According to this view, after an organism has learned a particular instrumental response, the deprivation conditions present at a given time determine the degree to which the response is energized. There is evidence, however, that organisms may actually learn responses differently, depending on deprivation conditions (E. D. Capaldi, 1971). Such studies show that organisms that learn under one deprivation condition continue to perform at a particular level even when the deprivation conditions are changed. If deprivation acted only to energize the instrumental response, one would expect the performance of the response to change each time the deprivation conditions were altered. This does not appear to be the case.

Regardless of the final interpretation of deprivation effects, it is clear that this variable can have a strong influence on instrumental performance. This suggests that when we attempt to instrumentally condition a behavior in the real world, we should choose rewards that have not been constantly available to an organism in its recent past. Praise is unlikely to be an effective reward for an organism that has been praised for everything it has done.

Negative Reinforcement Situations: Escape Learning

Amount of reinforcement Just as the amount of reward affects performance in positive reinforcement situations, so does the amount of reinforcement influence escape learning performance. In escape learning, the amount of reinforcement corresponds to the degree to which the aversive stimulation is reduced after a successful response.

In one study conducted by Trapold and Fowler (1960), rats escaped shock by running from an alleyway into a safe compartment where no shock was present. Different groups of rats were exposed to different shock intensities in the alleyway. The results of this study showed that the speed of the escape response was directly related to the shock intensity in the alleyway. Rats that received the highest shock intensity ran the fastest, whereas lesser shock intensities led to slower speeds.

This finding can be interpreted in two ways. One is that animals exposed to high shock intensities received the highest reduction of shock when they entered the safe compartment. According to this interpretation, escape speed depends on the amount of negative reinforcement. Another view is simply that escape speed depends on the intensity of the aversive stimulation regardless of how much the stimulation is reduced upon completion of the escape response. Which of these interpretations is correct?

The answer appears to be provided in another experiment by Campbell and Kraeling (1953), who exposed all rats to the same shock intensity in the runway and reduced this shock by varying degrees in the "safe compartment." That is, all animals received shock reduction after responding, but most animals still received some shock in the safe compartment. Campbell and Kraeling found that rats would learn the escape response under these conditions. Furthermore, the speed of the escape response was a direct function of the degree to which shock was reduced. It appears, therefore, that escape learning depends more on the amount of negative reinforcement than on the intensity of the aversive stimulus per se.

Delay of reinforcement If all organisms receive the same amount of negative reinforcement for an escape response, performance then depends strongly on the delay of reinforcement. Here, "delay of reinforcement" refers to the time between the escape response and the reduction of the aversive stimulation. The effect of this variable is clearly illustrated by the results of a study conducted by Fowler and Trapold (1962).

These experimenters exposed rats to shock in an alleyway and required the animals to run to a safe compartment to escape the shock. Once in the safe compartment, however, the groups differed in terms of the time it took for the shock to go off. The delay in shock offset varied between 0 and 16 seconds. The results, shown in Figure 4.6 (page 86), indicate that as the delay of shock offset increased, escape speeds correspondingly decreased. Thus, the effects of delay of negative reinforcement are similar to those of delay of reward in positive reinforcement situations.

Negative Reinforcement Situations: Avoidance Learning

In our original description of avoidance learning, we said that in most such situations a stimulus signals the impending presentation

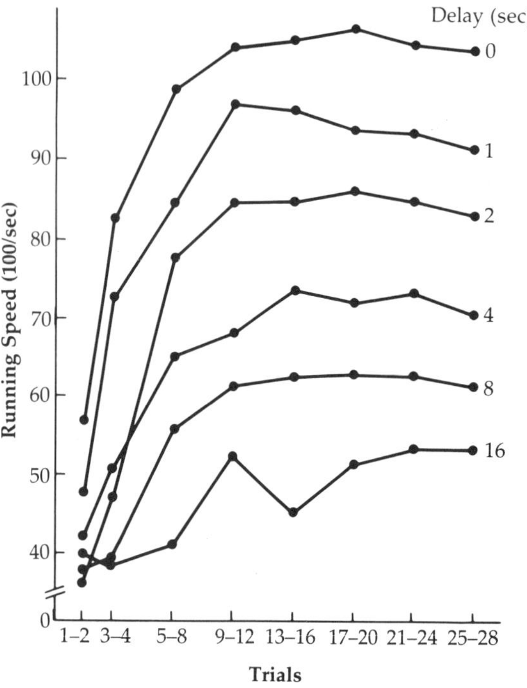

FIGURE 4.6 Acquisition of an escape response as a function of the delay of shock termination on each trial. (From Fowler and Trapold, 1962.)

of the aversive event. To avoid the aversive event, the organism must respond in the presence of the signal. In effect, avoidance learning usually involves two stimuli—the signal and the aversive stimulus—that are critical for correct responding. As you might expect, then, the characteristics of both these stimuli are important determinants of avoidance learning.

The intensity of the aversive stimulus The rate at which avoidance responses are learned does appear to vary with the intensity of the aversive stimulus that is used. However, the manner in which intensity affects the rate of learning depends on the type of avoidance paradigm being considered. For example, earlier we discussed the one-way avoidance paradigm in which the same start chamber is used for each trial. In this type of situation, the more intense the aversive stimulus, the faster the avoidance response is learned (see, for example, Dieter, 1976).

On the other hand, we also discussed the two-way avoidance procedure, where each of the compartments of a two-chamber apparatus serves as the start compartment on some trials and the safe compartment on others. In this paradigm, as we increase the intensity of the aversive stimulus, we actually retard or slow the rate of learning (see, for example, McAllister, McAllister, & Dieter, 1976). The same is true of avoidance situations that require responses such as a bar press to avoid the aversive stimulus. The higher the intensity of the aversive stimulus, the more slowly the avoidance response is acquired (see, for example, D'Amato & Fazzaro, 1966).

Why does the intensity of the aversive event affect avoidance learning so differently in these different paradigms? The answer to this question most likely involves a factor mentioned earlier. That is, in every avoidance paradigm there is the potential for Classical fear conditioning. In the one-way avoidance paradigm, both the signal and the stimuli in the single-start chamber become associated with the aversive event. Thus, all these stimuli become capable of producing fear. As the intensity of the aversive stimulus is increased, this fear conditioning becomes stronger and the organism becomes increasingly fearful whenever it is placed in the start chamber in the presence of the signal. The choice for the organism is to remain in a very aversive chamber or to move to another chamber where the stimuli have never been associated with an aversive event. The organism readily chooses to move to the safe compartment, and this tendency is even greater when the signal and the start chamber stimuli have been associated with an aversive event of high intensity.

In the two-way avoidance paradigm the picture is more complex. Organisms receive the aversive stimulus in one chamber of the apparatus on one trial and in the other chamber on the next trial. This means that stimuli in both chambers of the apparatus become capable of eliciting fear. Thus, on any given trial the organism must choose between remaining in one chamber that is fear provoking or moving to another chamber in which aversive stimuli also have been experienced. As you might imagine, two-way avoidance tasks are difficult for an organism to learn under any circumstances. There is always a tendency for the avoidance of one chamber to be interfered with by the organism's desire to avoid the other chamber as well. This interfering tendency is heightened when the aversive stimulus is more intense, because with a more intense stimulus, the chamber the organism must run into is simply more fear provoking.

The same type of explanation can be applied to situations in which the organism must press a bar or poke its nose into a hole to avoid aversive stimuli. In these paradigms the organism never physically leaves the chamber in which the aversive event occurs. Thus, the stimuli in that chamber come to produce fear. To the degree that an organism freezes in that environment because of its fear, no avoidance response will occur. The likelihood that a freezing response will occur increases as the intensity of the aversive stimulus increases. Thus, in both this and the two-way avoidance situation, the intensity of the aversive stimulus has a paradoxical effect. As the stimulus becomes more intense, organisms are more highly motivated to avoid it. However, high-intensity aversive stimuli tend also to impair performance by producing responses or tendencies such as freezing, which interfere with avoidance behavior.

The signal–aversive stimulus interval Avoidance responding is clearly related to the temporal relationship between the signal and the aversive stimulus. In our discussion of Classical conditioning we spoke of trace conditioning procedures in which the signaling CS terminates before the onset of the US. In avoidance learning, if the signal terminates before the aversive stimulus begins, the development of avoidance responding is considerably retarded (see Kamin, 1954; Warner, 1932). Avoidance learning appears to occur most efficiently when the signal and the aversive stimulus overlap, as in a delayed conditioning procedure.

When the signal and the aversive stimulus do overlap, the rate of learning depends on the duration of the signal before the onset of the aversive event. In general, signals of longer duration tend to facilitate the learning of the avoidance response (see, for example, Low & Low, 1962). The reason for this effect seems reasonably simple. Very short signal–aversive stimulus intervals do not allow an organism ample time to respond before the aversive stimulus occurs. Longer intervals afford the opportunity for a true avoidance response.

The termination of the signal Even when the organism's response results in avoidance of the aversive stimulus, the rate of learning depends on whether the response also leads to the termination of the signal. For example, Kamin (1957a) conducted a two-way avoidance experiment using rats as subjects. In this study all rats were able to avoid shock by moving to the safe chamber during the signal–shock interval. For one group of animals the signal terminated as soon as the avoidance response occurred (0 second delay). In the remaining three groups the signal ended either 2.5, 5, or 10 seconds after the avoidance response. It is clear from the results of this study in Figure 4.7 (page 88), that avoidance responding suffers rather dramatically when the response does not result in immediate termination of the signal. This suggests that for organisms in avoidance situations, elimination of the aversive stimulus is not the only important response

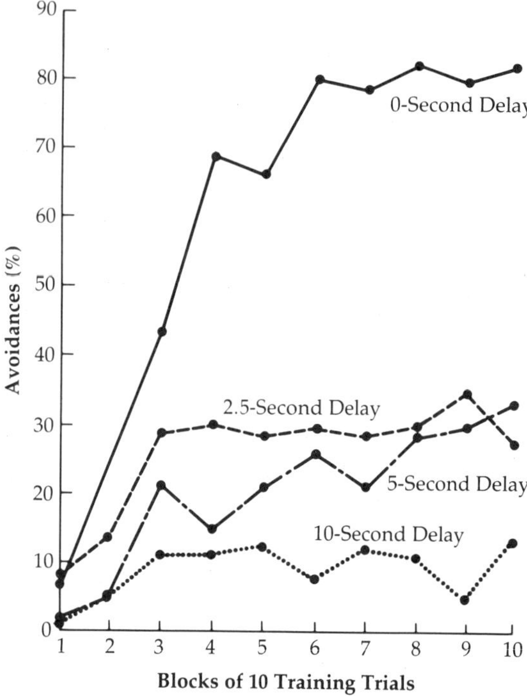

FIGURE 4.7 Acquisition of a signaled avoidance response as a function of how long termination of the signal is delayed following each response. (From Kamin, 1957.)

consequence. It also is important that the response terminate the stimuli that signal the aversive stimulus.

Punishment Situations

It is important to understand the variables that control instrumental responding when either positive or negative reinforcement is used. The reason is that we constantly utilize positive and negative reinforcement procedures to modify the behaviors of ourselves and others. Still, no form of behavior control is chosen more often than the punishment procedure. When an organism behaves in a manner we deem inappropriate, our first inclination is often to follow that response with some form of aversive stimulation. Whether we inflict physical pain, use hurtful language, or attempt to deprive an organism of something it desires, we often seek to eliminate behaviors through punishment techniques.

Although punishment procedures are used with great frequency, we often find that they fail to reduce the behaviors we wish to eliminate. For example, a teacher may find that scolding a child for being disruptive in class may actually result in an increase in the disruptive behavior. Likewise, a dog's habit of defecating in the house is seldom modified by spanking the animal whenever the owner discovers the deed. Does this mean that punishment is less effective than reinforcement in altering behaviors? The answer is no. In most cases, our attempts at punishment fail because we do not fully understand how punishment works. It fails when we fail to apply it correctly.

In the present section we will detail the variables that are most critical in making punishment effective. In discussing these variables we will point out some of the more common misapplications of the punishment procedure. We begin by looking at the effects of the intensity and duration of the punishing stimulus.

The intensity and duration of punishment

As the intensity of the punishing stimulus increases, punishment becomes more effective in suppressing a target response. Although this finding has been reported in several experiments, it is illustrated most clearly in a study by Church, Raymond, and Beauchamp (1967). These experimenters first trained rats to press a bar for a food reward. Once this response had been well established, they punished a certain percentage of the bar depressions with shocks of low, medium, or high intensity. They found that bar pressing was only slightly affected by the low-intensity shock. However, rats that received the higher intensity shocks showed substantial suppression of bar pressing, and the amount of suppression was directly related to the shock intensity.

In the same experiment, Church and his colleagues also demonstrated the importance of punishment duration on response suppression. For each of the shock intensities used, different groups of rats were exposed to shocks of lasting 0, 0.25, 0.3, 0.5, 1, or 3 minutes. The suppressing effects of each shock intensity increased significantly as the duration of the shock was increased. Thus, punishing stimuli become more effective in suppressing target responses as either the intensity or duration of the stimulus increases.

These findings concerning the intensity and duration of punishment are hardly surprising. However, it is clear that in applying punishment procedures we often fail to take these effects into account. Mild punishers such as minor scoldings or looks of dissatisfaction are often used by adults in an attempt to punish aggressive or disruptive behaviors in children. As we noted earlier, such "punishers" sometimes increase rather than decrease the target behaviors. One reason is that these adult reactions are not intense enough to effectively reduce the undesirable responses. Furthermore, they involve attending to the child, which may be interpreted as a reward. Obviously, most of us avoid using punishers that are too severe or debilitating. Still, we should be aware that the use of very low-intensity punishers may sometimes increase rather than reduce a target response.

Delay and noncontingent delivery of punishment Several studies have shown that punishment is most effective in reducing a target behavior if it occurs immediately after the behavior (see, for example, Baron, 1965; Camp, Raymond, & Church, 1967; Kamin, 1959). The results of one such experiment conducted by Randall and Riccio (1969) are shown in Figure 4.8. In this study albino rats were allowed access to a dark compartment. Since these rats normally seek out dark environments, movement into the dark chamber was a highly probable response. Once each rat had entered the dark compartment, it was shocked either immediately or 5, 10, 30, or 60 seconds later. Then the animals were returned to the original environment, and the experimenters measured the latency to "cross through" (that is, to move back into the dark compartment) on a subsequent trial. As you can see, rats that received the immediate shock suppressed moving into the dark chamber. This tendency not to move was less, however, when the original shock had been delayed. Animals that had experienced the longest delay in punishment reentered the dark chamber readily.

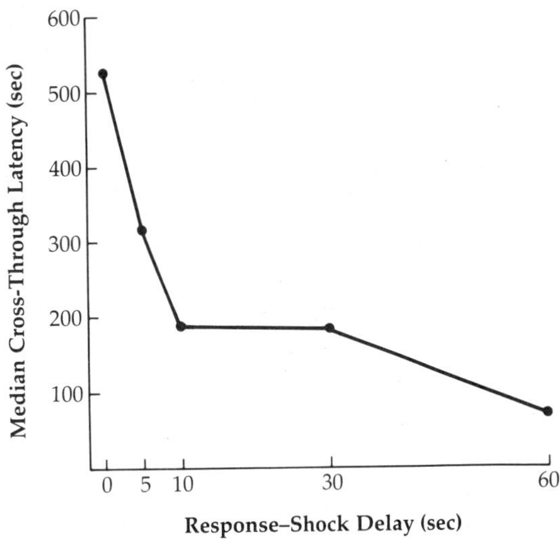

FIGURE 4.8 The latency to perform a previously punished response as a function of how long after responding the punishment occurred. (From Randall and Riccio, 1969.)

Delayed punishments are less effective than those given immediately because, for one thing, substantial delays reduce the contingent relationship between the target response and the punishment. Since with long delays organisms can make numerous responses between the time of the target response and the punisher, it becomes unclear which response is being punished. The clearest contingency exists between the punishment and the last response the organism remembers having made before the punishing stimulus. Contingencies between the punisher and other responses are less clear, the further these responses are removed in time from the punisher.

This raises the question of what happens to responses that are not clearly viewed as being responsible for the punishing stimulus. In other words, when punishing stimuli occur, what happens to the behaviors that have no clear contingent relationship to the punishment? In some cases behaviors that are uncorrelated with punishment do not seem to be affected. For example, in one study by Boe and Church (1967) rats were trained to bar press. Then separate groups either were shocked for bar pressing or were given noncontingent shocks every 30 seconds regardless of what responses they were making. Rats given the shocks contingent on bar pressing showed a long-lasting reduction in responding even after the punishments ceased. On the other hand, rats given noncontingent shocks resumed the normal rate of bar pressing once the shocks had stopped.

In other cases, organisms seem to increase nonpunished responses when some other response in their repertoire is clearly associated with punishment. Dunham (1971), for example, gave gerbils an opportunity to either drink, eat, or shred paper. All these behaviors are highly probable for gerbils. The experimenter shocked some gerbils when they approached food, others when they approached water, and still others when they began shredding paper. In each case he found that the punished behavior decreased in probability. However, if animals were shocked for eating, they tended to increase drinking and paper shredding. In other words, nonpunished behaviors increased to take the place of the punished response.

Finally, organisms that receive unavoidable intense aversive stimuli that are not clearly contingent on any response often exhibit what has been termed *learned helplessness.* In effect, organisms exposed to such stimulation often appear to give up making responses of any type. This occurs even when the investigator changes the conditions of the experiment such that some of their responses would enable them to avoid or escape from the aversive stimulus. This phenomenon was first demonstrated by Overmeir and Seligman (1967), using dogs as subjects.

In this experiment the dogs were administered unavoidable and inescapable shocks that were not contingent on any particular response. Then the dogs were placed in an avoidance apparatus in which shock could be avoided by crossing from one compartment into another. Overmeir and Seligman found that these animals showed significant deficits in learning to avoid. The typical response was to simply sit in the shock compartment and submit to the aversive stimulation. This behavior has often been likened to depressed behavior in humans who feel that they are being punished regardless of what they do and regardless of their attempts to avoid unpleasantness (see, for example, Seligman, 1975). In any event, the occurrence of learned helplessness has prompted numerous studies into the effects of uncontrollable aversive stimulation on the behavior of humans and other organisms (see, for example, Maier & Jackson, 1979; Maier & Seligman, 1976).

The practical implications of the findings discussed above should be clear. First of all, punishments will be most effective in reducing a specific target behavior when the punishing stimulus is clearly contingent on the performance of the target response. Punishments that occur in a noncontingent manner can be ineffective, or they can decrease activity in general.

Second, punishers are most effective when they follow a target response immediately.

When children misbehave excessively, while being watched by a babysitter, the sitter often tells them they will be punished when the parents get home. In such cases, punishment does not occur until well after the inappropriate behavior has ceased. Such punishments are rarely effective in eliminating an undesirable response. The behavior that is actually punished is the children's anticipation of the parents' arrival, which is the response they are making just before the administration of the punishing event. In such situations, punishers may reduce certain behaviors, but they seldom reduce the behaviors we actually wish to eliminate.

Responses produced by the punishing stimulus A punishing stimulus is more than simply a consequence of some prior emitted behavior. Punishers usually elicit or automatically produce behaviors themselves. For example, speaking harshly to a friend may automatically produce a negative emotional response. Spanking a child may produce fear and crying. Physically punishing a dog may produce natural aggressive reactions in the animal. As it happens, the particular responses produced by a punisher often help to determine whether the punisher will reduce a prior emitted behavior.

In most cases a punisher will be most effective when the responses produced by the punisher are incompatible with the response we wish to eliminate. In other words, if we wish to reduce a specific target response, we should select a punisher that produces responses that interfere with that target response. If our punisher produces the same behavior we are trying to eliminate, it is likely to be ineffective.

This general principle is illustrated by an experiment conducted by Fowler and Miller (1963). These experimenters trained rats to run down a straight runway to a goal compartment to receive a food reward. Once this response had been established, the experimenters began to punish it by shocking the rats in the goal compartment. One group received a shock on their front paws when they stopped running. The shock caused these animals to jump backward away from the food location—a response that was incompatible with moving toward the goal compartment. The second group received a shock to the hind paws as they entered the goal compartment. This shock caused the animals to jump forward toward the food location. Obviously, this response was similar to the running response the animals were making at the time the shock was delivered. Fowler and Miller found that the running response was reduced much more in the rats that received shock on the front paws. In effect, the punisher was more effective when it produced a response that was incompatible with the target behavior.

Such findings suggest that specific punishments should be selected on the basis of the particular behaviors we wish to eliminate. Slapping a child's hand when the child reaches out toward a hot stove may be effective because the punishment produces hand withdrawal and fear. These responses are incompatible with reaching out and exploring. However, if a child who is already fearful is crying or clinging to a parent, slapping the hand may be an ineffective punisher for these behaviors. In these cases the punisher produces fear and crying, which are the same responses we are trying to reduce.

Variables That Affect Operant Responding

As we have noted, there are strong similarities between instrumental and operant behaviors. For this reason one might expect that the same variables that influence instrumental responding would affect operant responses in a like manner. In most instances this is the case. For example, amount and delay of reward affect operant responding in much the same way as these variables affect instrumental responding. On the other hand, the one variable that appears most strongly to influence operant responding is one that we mentioned only briefly in connection with Instrumental conditioning paradigms. This variable is the schedule of reinforcement. We detail next the effects of reinforcement schedules on the performance of operant behaviors.

Schedules of Reinforcement

When we discussed schedules of reinforcement in Instrumental conditioning situations, we differentiated between "continuous" and "partial" reinforcement. The term *continuous reinforcement* was applied to situations in which each correct response was reinforced. *Partial reinforcement* was used to describe instances in which only a percentage of the correct responses was reinforced. The emphasis in the Insrumental conditioning paradigm was on how these different schedules affected the development of correct instrumental responding.

In Operant conditioning paradigms, researchers have been interested primarily in how different schedules of partial reinforcement influence the performance of a response that has *already* developed. In other words, once a rat has learned to press a bar, how will the *rate* of bar pressing be affected by the schedule of partial reinforcement?

This emphasis on well-learned responses alone and on partial reinforcement schedules only may sound somewhat arbitrary until one considers the practical significance of such work. Most of our important operant behaviors (for example, working, studying, and talking) are behaviors we already know how to perform. The variable to be explored is how reinforcement affects the rate at which we perform these well-learned responses. And, since most real-world behaviors are reinforced only on certain occasions, it becomes particularly important to look at the effects of partial reinforcement schedules on operant performance. As we will see, the rate at which rats, pigeons, and even humans perform operant behaviors depends considerably on the schedule of reinforcement that is in effect at a given time.

Although several types of partial reinforcement schedules have been studied, we will focus on two major types—ratio and interval schedules. These types of schedules differ in terms of the rules used to determine which responses should *not* be reinforced. We begin by looking at the effects of ratio schedules on the performance of operant responses.

Ratio schedules In a *ratio schedule* of reinforcement, the experimenter requires that an organism make a certain *number of responses* to receive each reward. This guarantees that instead of being reinforced for every response, an organism will be reinforced for only a proportion of its responses. Two types of ratio schedules have been studied in detail. The first, termed the *fixed ratio (FR)* schedule, is so named because the organism is required to make the same number of responses for each reward it obtains. For example, a rat may be required to press a bar 10 times to receive its first reward. Then it must press the bar 10 more times to obtain its second reward. Thus, each reward is contingent on the same number of bar press responses.

We find examples of fixed ratio reward schedules throughout society. A political campaign worker may be paid a certain sum for each 100 posters mailed out to prospective voters. In this case, 100 responses are required for each reward. Likewise, some reading programs for children give out a gold star or a certificate for each 10 books that a child has read. In this example, 10 responses are required for each reward. The critical feature of the fixed ratio schedule is that an organism must make the same number of responses to acquire each reward.

To demonstrate how reinforcement schedules affect responding, most researchers rely upon a *cumulative record,* which is simply a graph showing the number of responses that have been made by an organism as a function of the time that has elapsed. The line on this graph moves vertically whenever a response is made and horizontally whenever a pause in responding occurs. Thus, in a cumulative record, continuous responding would be represented by an almost vertical line, whereas no responding would be reflected by a horizontal line. Figure 4.9 depicts a cumulative record of the kind normally found when organisms are placed on a fixed ratio schedule. The small diagonal slashes on the response line show when reinforcements were obtained. As you can see, fixed ratio schedules produce a fairly high, constant rate of responding (see, for example, Ferster & Skinner, 1957). Typically, however, organisms on FR schedules do pause in their responding, usually just after a reward is obtained. The duration of these *postreinforcement pauses* is dependent on the number of responses required for reward. The pauses tend to be short when only a few responses are necessary, but they can be relatively long when many responses are required for each

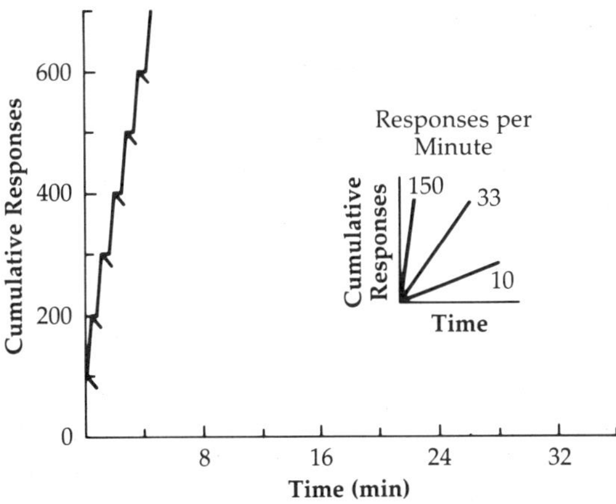

FIGURE 4.9 Typical cumulative record of operant responding on a fixed ratio schedule of reinforcement.

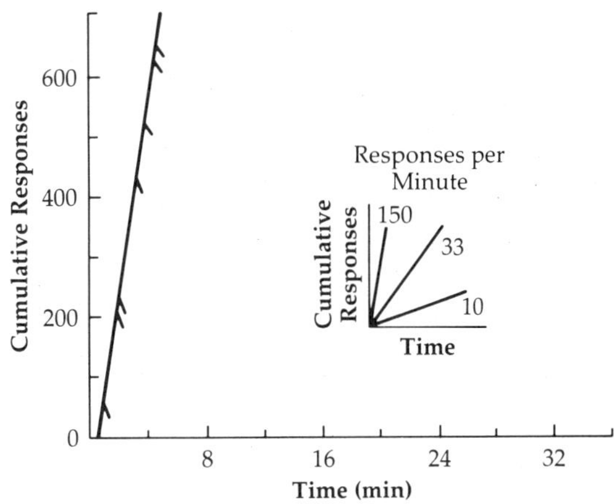

FIGURE 4.10 Typical cumulative record of operant responding on a variable ratio schedule of reinforcement.

reward. The same pattern of responding tends to occur whenever an organism, regardless of species, is placed on a fixed ratio schedule.

The second major type of ratio schedule is called the *variable ratio (VR) schedule* because the number of responses required for each reward changes from one reward to the next. For example, a pigeon may have to peck a key 10 times to receive its first reward, 30 times to obtain its second reward, and 15 times to receive the next. When an organism is on this type of schedule, there is no way to learn or predict how many responses will be necessary to obtain a given reward. Some rewards may be obtained with only a few responses, while others may require numerous responses.

Figure 4.10 is an example of a cumulative record that might be found using a variable ratio schedule. As you can see, such schedules produce an extremely high rate of responding. The rate of responding on a VR schedule is usually at least as high, and often higher, than that found with FR schedules. As with FR schedules, organisms on VR schedules do tend to pause occasionally. However, these pauses do not appear to occur in any set relation to the time of reinforcement. Furthermore, the VR schedule produces fewer and shorter pauses than are often found with FR schedules (see, for example, Ferster & Skinner, 1957). Again, it is notable that virtually all species show this typical pattern of VR responding. Humans, for example, respond this way when they are playing slot machines. Most slot machines are programmed to give payoffs on a variable ratio schedule. Some payoffs require hundreds of lever pulls, whereas others may occur after only a few such responses. When confronted with such a payoff schedule, humans tend to pull slot machine levers at a high rate, pausing only very occasionally. Obviously, casino owners are aware of the strong control reinforcement schedules exert over operant responses.

Interval schedules As we have noted, partial reinforcement is assured in ratio schedules by reinforcing only a certain fraction of the responses made. Interval schedules accomplish the same end by establishing a time period after each reward during which no responses are rewarded. In the typical interval schedule, once a reward has been obtained, a "time-out period" of preset duration goes into effect. During this time-out period no response is reinforced. However, the first response that occurs after the time-out period has elapsed results in a reward. Then a new time-out period begins. It is important to note that in an interval schedule, reinforcement is not programmed to occur as soon as the time-out period ends. Just as in ratio schedules, interval schedules require a correct response before reinforcement is given. However, in the interval schedule it is the first response following the time-out period that leads to reinforcement.

The first type of interval schedule we will describe is a *fixed interval (FI)* schedule, in which the length of the time-out period that follows each reward is the same. For example, after its first reward a rat may receive a 30-second time-out period during which no bar press responses are reinforced. When the 30 seconds has elapsed, the rat's first bar press is rewarded. Then another 30-second time-out period begins. When this type of schedule is used, it becomes at least theoretically possible for an organism to estimate how long it must wait after one reward before making another rewarded response. The optimal strategy would, of course, involve receiving one reward and then waiting to respond again until just after the time-out period has elapsed. In most cases this appears to be the strategy most organisms attempt.

Figure 4.11 represents the kind of cumulative record normally obtained when an FI schedule is used. This record shows that organisms tend to respond very little soon after receiving a reward. However, responding gradually increases as the end of the time-out period approaches. Finally, responding reaches a high point at the end of the time-out period. This well-known pattern of responding is referred to as the "FI scallop," since the cumulative record obtained with the FI schedule resembles a series of arcs or scallops. These

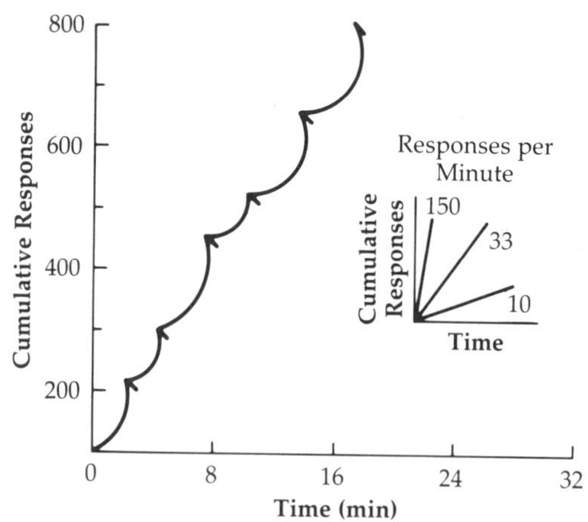

FIGURE 4.11 Typical cumulative record of operant responding on a fixed interval schedule of reinforcement.

scallops suggest that organisms attempt to wait until the end of a time-out period before making responses.

Fixed interval schedules occur widely in our everyday life. For example, most people receive their mail at approximately the same time daily. Thus, after one visit to the mailbox results in finding mail (the reward), there is a 24-hour time-out period during which visits to the mailbox will not be rewarded. However, the first time you visit the mailbox after the time-out period, your response will again be reinforced. To see how this schedule affects human behavior, you need only watch someone who is expecting an important letter. After the mail has been picked up on one day, the person seldom visits the mailbox again for several hours. However, as the time for the next day's mail delivery approaches, the person may begin to check the box more regularly. Constant checks of the box begin to occur at the end of the time-out period. This, of course, is the same FI scallop pattern we see when the rat or pigeon is placed on an FI schedule.

The second type of interval schedule that is commonly studied is the *variable interval (VI) schedule.* In this schedule, the length of the time-out period following each reinforcement varies. For example, a pigeon may experience a 20-second time-out period after its first rewarded response and a 60-second time-out period after its second reward. In this type of schedule it is, of course, impossible for an organism to anticipate when the time-out period will end.

Figure 4.12 shows the kind of cumulative record usually obtained with a VI schedule. Note that the pattern of responding is not scalloped like the FI pattern. Instead there is a moderate, fairly consistent rate of response throughout the course of each time-out period. This is the same response pattern you show when you are trying to reach someone on the telephone but continue to receive a busy signal. You know that if you wait long enough, the other party will get off the phone. However, you do not know how long this reward will be in coming. Faced with this dilemma, most of us continue dialing at regular intervals until we get an answer.

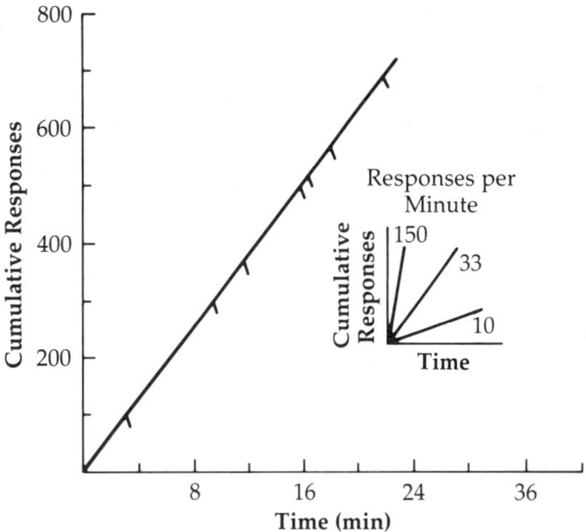

FIGURE 4.12 Typical cumulative record of operant responding on a variable interval schedule of reinforcement.

Concurrent schedules In real-life settings we are seldom confronted with single reinforcement schedules. More typically, we are faced with a choice of reinforcement schedules for the same operant response. For example, if you are engaged in a conversation involving several people, some individuals will attend to your words (that is, they will reinforce your verbal responses) more often than others. In effect, you will be differentially reinforced for your verbal output depending on the person in the group to whom you speak. When we are faced with such choices between different schedules of reinforcement, how do we respond?

To answer this question experimentally, several researchers have studied *concurrent schedules of reinforcement.* In such situations organisms are allowed free access to two separate manipulanda (for example, bars to press or keys to peck). Each bar or key is associated with a different schedule of partial reinforcement. For example, by pressing one bar an animal may be rewarded on a VI schedule with a 1-minute time-out period. Responses on the other bar may be rewarded on a VI schedule having a 5-minute time-out period. The question of how organisms allocate their responses when given such a choice was answered by a series of experiments conducted by Herrnstein (1961).

Herrnstein measured the rate at which pigeons pecked keys that were associated with different reinforcement schedules. Surprisingly, he found that pigeons did not simply choose the key having the most favorable schedule of reward. That is, they did not make the vast majority of their responses to the key that provided the most reinforcement in the shortest period of time. Instead, the rate of responding on each key was directly related to the rate of reinforcement on that key. For example, if responding on key number 1 was reinforced three times as often as responding on key number 2, the pigeons responded on key number 1 three times more than on key number 2.

From these data, Herrnstein proposed what is called the *matching law,* which states that when an organism has free access to two different schedules of reinforcement, it will allocate its responses in proportion to the rate of reinforcement on each schedule. This law has been shown to hold in a wide variety of experimental settings involving human subjects (McDowell, 1981, 1982) as well as other species (see, for example, deVilliers, 1974). In recent years, there has been great interest in understanding the mechanisms by which organisms match responding to reinforcement schedules (Commons, Herrnstein, & Rachlin, 1982) and in discovering how extensively this law may be applied to instances of choice behavior (see, for example, McSweeney, Melville, Buck, & Whipple, 1983). Regardless of the final outcome of such research, however, the occurrence of matching provides one more example of how strongly reinforcement schedules control the rate of operant responding in humans and other organisms.

Extinction

In our discussion of Classical conditioning we found that a well-learned conditioned response can be eliminated or reduced by presenting the CS regularly without the US. This decrease in the performance of the conditioned response was called extinction. In a like manner, well-learned instrumental and operant responses may be extinguished. In this case extinction occurs when an organism performs a response and *no reinforcement* occurs afterward. For example, if a rat has learned to press a bar or run through a maze for a food reward, these responses can be reduced by eliminating the food reward that normally follows responding. In negative reinforcement situations, extinction is produced by failing to eliminate the aversive stimulus after a correct response. Thus, an animal that has learned to jump to a safe compartment to escape shock finds that the shock remains present even after the escape response occurs.

We also noted earlier that when some period of time is allowed to elapse after a CR has been extinguished, the conditioned response tends to reoccur. We termed this phenomenon *spontaneous recovery.* Spontaneous recovery also tends to occur in Instrumental and Operant conditioning paradigms. Once an instrumental response has been reduced by elimination of the reinforcement, the response tends to recover over time. As in Classical conditioning, the spontaneous recovery of instrumental and operant responses can be eliminated by giving a series of extinction treatments.

Although extinction occurs readily in most Instrumental or Operant conditioning paradigms, the rate of extinction can vary dramatically depending on a number of variables. How resistant a response is to extinction can be influenced by the conditions that were present when the response was learned. Similarly, resistance to extinction is affected by the conditions present when extinction itself occurs. Let's look now at a few of these variables that influence extinction of instrumental and operant responding.

Variables That Affect Extinction of Positively Reinforced Responses

Conditions present during learning How quickly a response extinguishes depends in large part on the conditions under which it was learned. Common sense would lead us to predict that any condition that promotes rapid or strong learning should result in slower extinction. We make this prediction because it would seem that the stronger a learned response, the more difficult it should be to eliminate. Although this prediction appears logical, it is *wrong*. As we will see, virtually any condition that slows learning or makes learning more difficult also makes a response more difficult to extinguish. Although this general rule seems counterintuitive, it clearly holds in many cases.

As we have seen, animals learn instrumental responses faster when large magnitudes of reward are used. Small amounts of reward produce slower rates of learning. Still, several experiments have shown that responses learned with small reward amounts are more difficult to extinguish than responses learned for large rewards (see, for example, Armus, 1959; Hulse, 1958; Wagner, 1961). This type of finding is illustrated clearly in a study conducted by Roberts (1969). Roberts trained rats to traverse a runway for rewards ranging from 1 to 25 food pellets. He then proceeded to extinguish the running response. The results of this experiment are shown in Figure 4.13, which plots the extinction performance of each reward magnitude group in terms of both starting and running speeds. As indicated, the group that received 1 pellet for each run during learning extinguished very slowly. Groups that had received greater reward amounts during training extinguished progressively faster.

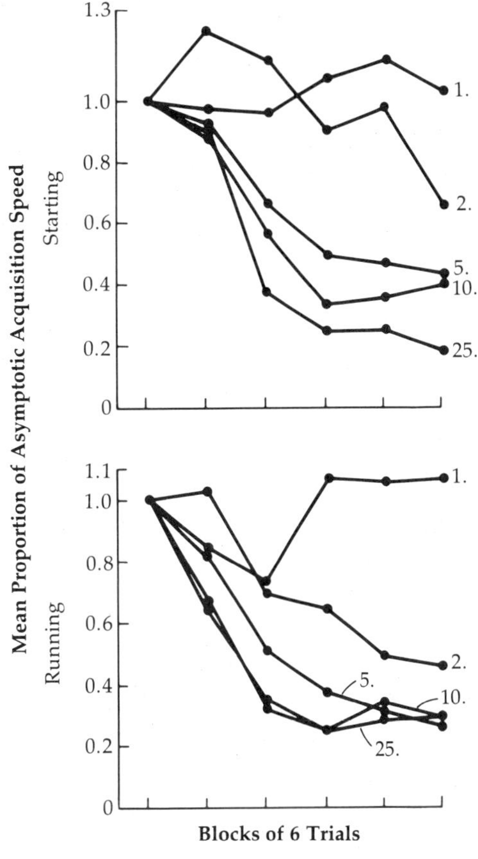

FIGURE 4.13 Rate of extinction for a running response as a function of amount of reward during learning, where 1., 2., 5., 10., and 25. refer to the number of food pellets given during learning for each response. (From Roberts, 1969.)

Another condition that tends to slow learning but makes extinction more difficult is delay of reward. Here the data are conflicting in many cases. For example, some studies have shown that longer reward delays during learning slow extinction of the learned response (see, for example, Capaldi & Bowen, 1964; Fehrer, 1956; Tombaugh, 1966). However, other experimenters have failed to replicate this effect (see, for example, Renner, 1963; Tombaugh, 1970). In one situation, however, delay of reward in learning clearly slows extinction: namely, when animals are exposed to delay of reward on some, but not all, learning trials. The data consistently show that intermittent reward delays during learning make extinction of the learned response more difficult (Knouse & Campbell, 1971; Tombaugh, 1970; Wike, Mellgren, & Wike, 1968).

Although both magnitude and delay of reward can affect extinction, probably the most powerful influence on extinction is the schedule of reward during learning. In almost every case, organisms that are partially reinforced during learning extinguish more slowly than organisms that have received continuous reinforcement. This well-known finding is termed the *partial reinforcement extinction effect* (*PREE*).

The PREE can be seen in the data from an early study by Hulse (1958). Hulse trained rats to run in a straight runway. He rewarded one group with food on 100 percent of its trials and a second group on only 46 percent of its trials. Hulse then extinguished the running response in both groups. The results of the extinction treatment are presented in Figure 4.14. It is clear from these data that the rats given continuous reinforcement extinguished running very quickly. However, rats trained on a partial reinforcement schedule exhibited high resistance to the extinction treatment.

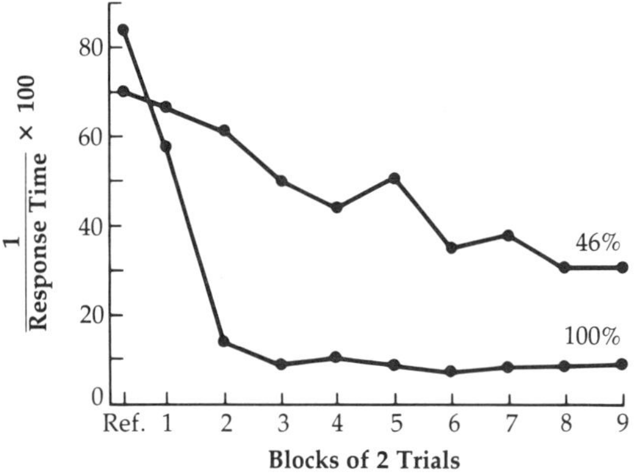

FIGURE 4.14 Rates of extinction for rats given continuous and partial reinforcement during learning. (From Hulse, 1958.)

In recent years it has become clear that the partial reinforcement extinction effect is not a simple phenomenon. For example, it is now known that it depends on the particular arrangement of reinforced and nonreinforced trials during learning (see, for example, Capaldi & Kassover, 1970; Spivey & Hess, 1968). As we will see when we assess different theories of extinction in Chapter 5, the analysis of the PREE has been critical to our understanding of the extinction process.

A final learning variable that appears to affect extinction is the number of learning trials an organism receives before extinction. In the case of this variable, however, the conclusions suggested by the data differ depending on the specific type of response that is studied. Several researchers have found that when rats are trained to traverse a runway, the more learning trials they receive, the more rapidly extinction occurs (see, for example, Ison, 1962; Madison, 1964; North & Stimmel, 1960). On the other hand, in studies of the bar press response, researchers have typically found that increasing the number of trials either slows extinction (Perin, 1942; S. B. Williams, 1938) or has no effect on the extinction process (D'Amato, Schiff, & Jagoda, 1962; Dyal & Holland, 1963; Uhl & Young, 1967).

For some time this conflict in evidence was attributed to the larger reward amounts usually involved for runway paradigms as opposed to bar press paradigms. Presently, however, it appears that the different effects in the two paradigms do not result simply from differences in reward magnitude (see, for example, Likely & Schnitzer, 1968). As yet, there is no clear explanation of why different levels of learning affect extinction differently depending on the type of response that is studied.

Conditions present during extinction The extinction of an instrumental response depends not only on how the response was learned, but also on how the response is extinguished. Probably one of the most important variables during extinction is the *intertrial interval,* the period separating the extinction trials. In general, extinction is faster when extinction trials occur close together in time. Long intertrial intervals normally slow the extinction process significantly (see, for example, Birch, 1965; Hill & Spear, 1962; Krane & Ison, 1971).

Although this rule holds in most cases, there is an important exception. If the intertrial interval used during extinction varies widely from the intertrial interval used during learning, extinction tends to be faster. This occurs even when long intertrial intervals are used during extinction. One example of this effect comes from a study by Teichner (1952). This experimenter trained rats to perform an instrumental response using a 45-second intertrial interval. During extinction, the animals had an intertrial interval of 60, 45, or 30 seconds. Both the 30- and 60-second intertrial interval groups extinguished faster than animals exposed to a 45-second intertrial interval. As we will see in our later discussion of extinction, most significant changes between learning and extinction conditions tend to hasten the extinction process.

Variables That Affect Extinction of Negatively Reinforced Responses

Technically, extinction of a negatively reinforced response should involve allowing an organism to make the response and then not removing the aversive stimulus the organism is attempting to escape or avoid. In effect, once the organism has made the learned response, it should continue to receive aversive stimulation. Although this procedure is clearly analogous to elimination of reward in positive reinforcement situations, few experimenters have utilized this approach to study extinction of negatively reinforced responses. The reason is obvious. If an organism responds and the response is accompanied by continued aversive stimulation, the response is actually being punished. Thus, it is impossible to determine whether the response is decreasing because it is being extinguished or because it is being punished.

For this reason, researchers have used other approaches to study the extinction of negatively reinforced responses. In one such procedure the contingent relationship has been removed between an organism's response and the elimination of the aversive stimulus (see, for example, Reynierse & Rizley, 1970). In this type of procedure the termination of the aversive stimulus no longer regularly accompanies the learned response. Sometimes the termination of aversiveness occurs before the response, sometimes it occurs during the response, and sometimes it occurs after the response. Such procedures usually result in a rapid decrease in the performance of the learned behavior.

At least two other extinction procedures have been used in avoidance learning paradigms. Both are based on the idea that avoidance responding depends on an organism's Classically conditioned fear of the warning signal. In other words, organisms avoid because they have associated the warning stimulus (the CS) with an aversive event (the US). It is the fear of the warning stimulus that causes the organism to respond before the aversive stimulus occurs. According to this view, it should be possible to eliminate the avoidance response by extinguishing the learned fear to the signal. In other words, exposing an organism to the signal alone should extinguish fear to the signal and should thus reduce the avoidance response.

One extinction procedure based on this view was developed by Solomon, Kamin, and Wynne (1953). These researchers trained dogs to avoid shock by presenting a warning stimulus before each shock presentation. When the response was well established, they attempted to extinguish the avoidance behavior by continuing to present the warning stimulus without any shock. They found that even though the shock was being omitted, the dogs continued to show the avoidance behavior in the presence of the signal. In effect, the procedure had virtually no effect on the avoidance response.

This result is not surprising if we consider the nature of the avoidance response. Once an avoidance response has been well learned, organisms always respond in the presence of the signal. This means that the organisms seldom, if ever, experience the aversive event itself even during learning. If we try to extinguish the response simply by omitting the aversive event, the organisms will never realize that the aversive event is being omitted. Unless an organism discovers that the warning stimulus no longer signals an aversive event, there is really no reason to expect extinction to occur.

To deal with this problem, several researchers have used *response prevention* procedures to extinguish avoidance responses (see Baum, 1970). In effect, these procedures force organisms to confront the fact that the warning stimulus no longer signals an aversive event. This is accomplished by exposing an organism to the warning stimulus and preventing the avoidance response. By preventing the response, the experimenter forces the organism to remain in the presence of the signal long enough to experience the omission of the aversive stimulus. Such procedures provide organisms with an opportunity to learn that the warning stimulus and the shock are no longer correlated.

When shock omission trials are given after these response prevention procedures, extinction of the avoidance response often occurs rather rapidly (Mineka & Gino, 1979). In general, extinction is more rapid, the greater the number of response prevention trials preceding extinction (see, for example, Baum & Myran, 1971; Bersh & Keltz, 1971). Also, extinction is more rapid when longer duration response prevention trials are used (Schiff, Smith, & Prochaska, 1972). These conditions appear to be particularly important for response prevention to promote extinction of avoidance behavior. There is some evidence that if too few trials or trials of very short duration are used, subsequent avoidance responding may be enhanced rather than extinguished (see, for example, Gordon, Smith, & Katz, 1979).

The development of these response prevention techniques has had a substantial impact on the treatment of certain maladaptive behaviors in humans. Earlier we noted that certain neurotic reactions such as phobias are often viewed as being similar to avoidance responses learned in the laboratory. The phobic person is presumed to have developed a fear to a particular stimulus or situation and because of that fear to have learned some maladaptive behavior to avoid what he or she fears.

To treat these phobic reactions, several therapists have begun to use techniques similar to those used by researchers to extinguish avoidance responses. Two such therapeutic techniques, *flooding* and *implosive therapy*, are based directly on response prevention procedures. In flooding, the phobic person is forced to contact physically the feared object without any avenue of escape. For example, someone with a neurotic fear of germs may be forced to place his or her hands into a container filled with dirt. In implosive therapy, the phobic person is forced to imagine the feared object in vivid detail and is given no way to avoid these images. Both techniques assume that confrontation with the feared object will result in discovery that the object is not really associated with anything aversive. When the phobic places his or her hands in dirt and nothing bad results, fear of the dirt extinguishes. Once fear has been extinguished, the often bizarre responses that had been used to avoid contact with dirt also diminish. Both techniques have been successful in eliminating or decreasing phobic reactions that had been resistant to other forms of therapy.

Summary Statements

We have seen that organisms modify their emitted behaviors based on what the consequences of those behaviors happen to be. Generally, emitted behaviors are increased when they are followed by either positive or negative reinforcement, and they decrease to the extent that they are followed by punishment.

We discovered that the effectiveness of reinforcement depends on a number of variables. In positive reinforcement situations, the magnitude, quality, delay, and schedule of reward were all noted as influencing the performance of instrumental and operant behaviors. In negative reinforcement situations, amount and delay of reinforcement, as well as characteristics of any warning stimuli, were shown to affect emitted responses. In punishment paradigms, we found that the effectiveness of punishment depended on factors such as the intensity and delay of the punishing stimulus, as well as the response that is produced by the punisher.

Finally, we noted that instrumental and operant responses can be reduced by extinction procedures. Specifically, we found that extinction occurs when emitted responses are no longer followed by either positive or negative reinforcement.

5

Instrumental/Operant Conditioning: Theoretical Issues

In the preceding chapter we looked at a number of variables that influence Instrumental and Operant conditioning. In the vast majority of cases, these variables had to do with some characteristic of the reinforcing event. Clearly, the success of this form of conditioning depends heavily on the nature and characteristics of reinforcement.

The present chapter deals with some of the major theoretical issues that have arisen in the study of Instrumental and Operant conditioning. And, as you might expect, most of the issues raised again concern reinforcement. First, we will examine the theories that have attempted to identify the characteristics that an event must have in order to be reinforcing. In essence, these theories have attempted to delineate the characteristics that are common to all effective reinforcing events.

Second, we will discuss the function the reinforcing event serves in the conditioning process, focusing on the question of whether reinforcement is necessary for an organism to learn or whether reinforcement simply provides a reason for organisms to perform what they have learned.

Third, we will examine the major theories that deal with the extinction of instrumental and operant responses. Basically, these theories attempt to explain why the elimination of reinforcement results in the decrease of a previously learned behavior.

Finally, we will consider the nature of the reinforcing event in the avoidance learning situation. This issue has arisen because once an avoidance response has been learned, organisms no longer experience the primary aversive stimulus (for example, shock). Thus, it is impossible to maintain that well-learned avoidance responses are reinforced by the termination of the aversive stimulus. We will address the question of how the avoidance response is reinforced in the absence of a primary aversive event.

All these issues have been of great historical significance in the study of Instrumental and Operant conditioning, and controversies continue to surface in the contemporary research literature. For us, these issues serve to focus our attention on important aspects of the research in this area. And, by doing so, they help to increase our understanding of the learning process.

The Nature of Reinforcement

Primary and Secondary Reinforcers

Earlier we defined a reinforcer as any event that causes preceding behaviors to reoccur. We have not been very explicit, however, about the kinds of events that function as reinforcers. We should begin by noting that there are two general classes of reinforcing events. The first consists of all those events that can serve as reinforcers simply by virtue of their natural characteristics. These events, called *primary reinforcers,* include food, water, sexual stimulation, and the reduction of pain. Such events increase the occurrence of emitted responses regardless of an organism's experiences, and they work the same way in virtually all species. In other words, primary reinforcers are like unconditioned stimuli. Both are capable of producing behavior changes naturally without the benefit of any prior learning.

In the preceding chapter we saw how variations in primary reinforcement can influence instrumental and operant behaviors. Still, many of our everyday emitted behaviors appear to be reinforced by a different kind of event. For example, we perform certain work duties because these responses are rewarded with money. Likewise, children may learn table manners because their parents give verbal approval for appropriate behavior. In the same way, a dog may learn to retrieve a ball just because the response is followed by a word of praise. In all these cases emitted responses are repeated and learned, but the reinforcers used do not qualify as primary reinforcers. None of these events that follows responding has an inherent or natural capacity that causes emitted behaviors to reoccur.

Consider money as an example. There is nothing about a piece of green and white paper engraved with the image of a former president that is inherently rewarding. To convince yourself that money is not a natural reinforcer, try to imagine reinforcing a rat's bar press response by dropping a dollar bill into its food cup. Similarly, consider how effective money would be as a reinforcer for an infant's smile. Money, praise, and verbal approval are not naturally reinforcing events. They serve as reinforcers only when they have been associated or linked in some way to primary reinforcers in the past. In other words, these events called *secondary reinforcers* acquire the capacity to reinforce responses only through their prior associations with primary reinforcing events.

To see how a stimulus becomes a secondary reinforcer, let's consider some examples from the laboratory. In one well-known experiment, Saltzman (1949) trained rats to run down a straight runway for a food reward. The goal box in which the food was delivered was white for some animals and black for others. After this training, Saltzman placed the rats in a maze that contained two goal boxes. One goal box was identical to the one used in the runway, while the other was a neutral color. Although no primary reward such as food was ever delivered, the rats learned to navigate through the maze to reach the goal box that was like the one previously used in the runway. That is, during the maze learning phase of this experiment, the goal box stimuli alone served to reinforce the choice response. These stimuli acquired their reinforcing capacity because of their prior association with a food reward.

A similar result was obtained in an early experiment by Bugelski (1938). This experimenter trained rats to press a bar for a food reward that was always accompanied by a clicking sound. Later he attempted to extinguish the bar press response by eliminating the food. During these extinction trials, some animals continued to receive the clicking sound after every response while others did not. Bugelski found that the presentation of the clicking sound continued to reinforce responding even though food was no longer available. Apparently the clicking sound had acquired the capacity to reinforce responding through its prior association with food.

These examples indicate that when a stimulus regularly accompanies or signals a primary reinforcer, that stimulus acquires reinforcing properties of its own. The most common assumption is that secondary reinforcers acquire these properties through Classical conditioning. According to this view, almost every Instrumental or Operant conditioning situation contains all the necessary elements for Classical conditioning to occur. The primary reinforcer can serve as a US because in most cases it is capable of naturally eliciting certain responses. Stimuli that regularly accompany or signal the primary reinforcer are like CSs. These stimuli become capable of producing responses similar to those elicited naturally by the primary reward. Thus, in Bugelski's experiment the clicking sound acquired the same properties as the food reward because this sound regularly signaled the presentation of food. In recent years numerous studies have supported this idea that secondary reinforcement develops through the process of Classical conditioning.

We have just seen that some events are natural reinforcers while other events must acquire this capacity through prior association. In addition, we have given some examples of stimuli that fall into the primary reinforcer category. However, we have not determined what these primary reinforcing events have in common. Now we examine some of the hypotheses concerning the nature of primary reinforcers that have been suggested over the years.

Theories of Primary Reinforcement

Hull's drive-reduction hypothesis One of the earliest and most influential views of primary reinforcement was stated by Clark Hull in his now classic book, *Principles of Behavior* (1943). Hull conceived of learning as an adaptive process that allows organisms to cope with the biological need states that threaten survival. According to this view, biological needs develop whenever an organism's body becomes depleted in terms of any life-supporting substance (for example, fluids or nutrients). Need states also arise when an organism encounters physical stimuli that are capable of producing tissue damage (for example, painful stimuli). Hull felt that these biological needs give rise to psychological states of tension called *drives*. For example, the biological need for nutrients leads to the psychological state we call hunger. Likewise, the need for fluids results in the drive state we know as thirst.

Hull viewed these drives as motivational states that are capable of energizing, increasing, or driving behavior in general. Thus, organisms that are hungry, thirsty, or in pain become more active because of these drives, and their enhanced activity increases the likelihood that they will encounter stimuli or situations that will fill their biological needs. An active organism is simply more likely than a quiescent one to contact food, water, or safety. When an organism encounters a stimulus that fills some biological need, the associated drive state is reduced and the organism's motivation to respond decreases.

For present purposes, the most important point in Hull's analysis is that organisms do not respond in a random manner each time a drive state arises. Instead, organisms learn to repeat the behaviors that lead to need-fulfilling or drive-reducing stimuli. When an organism responds and its response leads a drive-reducing stimulus, the organism will tend to repeat that response whenever the same drive state arises. Thus, according to Hull, stimuli that fulfill biological needs and, therefore, reduce drives, are capable of reinforcing emitted behaviors. In this sense, Hull defined a primary reinforcer as a drive-reducing stimulus.

By equating primary reinforcement with drive reduction, Hull gave us one of the first testable hypotheses concerning the nature of reinforcement. Furthermore, this hypothesis appears to be a powerful one, since it seems to describe so many of the primary reinforcers we commonly encounter. Obviously, food reinforces responding if a rat is hungry just as water will reinforce the behavior of a thirsty organism. Both food and water qualify as need-fulfilling stimuli, and both are capable of reducing certain drive states. Clearly, a number of reinforcing events fall into the category of drive-reducing stimuli. The question one must ask is whether *all* reinforcers reduce drives.

One of the first complications with the drive-reduction hypothesis was noted by Miller and Kessen (1952), who trained hungry rats to go to one goal box of a T maze. They rewarded one group for this response by allowing them to drink milk in the goal box. Two other groups were fitted with fistulas or tubes that allowed the experimenters to pump fluids directly into the animals' stomachs. One group received milk in their stomachs for visiting the correct goal box, while the other received a saline-and-water solution. Miller and Kessen found that the task was learned best by the rats that actually drank milk in the goal box. Rats that received milk through the fistulas learned faster than those receiving saline, but not as fast as those that had been allowed to consume the milk.

This finding is important because the two groups that received milk should have been equivalent in terms of need fulfillment and, thus, drive reduction. In other words, according to the drive-reduction hypothesis, reinforcement in these two groups should have been the same. On the contrary, Miller and Kessen found that the milk was a more effective reinforcer when the rats were allowed to taste it than when it was simply pumped into the stomach. This result suggests that there may be more to reinforcement than the reduction of needs and drives.

Other problems associated with the drive-reduction idea have been pointed out in a series of studies conducted by Sheffield and his colleagues. In one such set of studies, Sheffield and Roby (1950) demonstrated that rats would learn to repeat emitted responses for a saccharine reinforcer. This finding does not fit well with the drive-reduction hypothesis, since saccharine is a nonnutritive substance that fills no biological need. This means that a substance that is incapable of reducing a hunger drive is still capable of reinforcing the responses of a hungry animal. To explain this finding within a drive-reduction framework, it is necessary to argue that saccharine is a secondary, not a primary, reinforcer. For example, one might argue that sweet-tasting substances are rewarding because the taste has been present when the animals have ingested substances (sugars) that *are* drive reducers. Such a mechanism is possible, but it appears unlikely to operate in this case. Sheffield and Roby showed that saccharine continued to reinforce instrumental responding even when numerous learning trials were used. They argued convincingly that ample experiences were given to allow the rats to learn that the taste of saccharine was not associated with hunger reduction. Still, saccharine remained an effective reinforcer (see, also, Sheffield, Roby, & Campbell, 1954).

A second experiment also argues against the drive-reduction view of reinforcement. Sheffield, Wulff, and Backer (1951) trained male rats to traverse a runway and enter a goal box. To reinforce this response they allowed the males to mount female rats in the goal box and to begin copulation. They did not, however, allow the males to ejaculate. Rather, the copulating males were removed from the females before ejaculation could occur. These experimenters found that the males rapidly learned the instrumental response that led to this so-called reward. Clearly, the opportunity to begin copulation was reinforcing, even though the opportunity for orgasm was blocked.

Sheffield and his colleagues argued (and most reasonable persons would agree) that the reinforcer in this case was not drive or tension reducing. On the contrary, this form of reinforcement appears to involve an *increase* in the drive or tension state. One might, of course, argue that the rats in this study continued to respond because they anticipated that copulation would ultimately lead to drive reduction. It is notable, however, that none of the male rats in this study had ever copulated before the experiment. Thus, there was no prior experience upon which such an anticipation could have been based. It appears clear that the behavior of these animals was being reinforced by the pleasant sensations of copulation, which could only have served to increase their sexual tension states.

A final group of studies that presents problems for the drive-reduction hypothesis concerns the tendency of organisms to seek out variety or additional sources of stimulation. We all know that individuals ride roller-coasters, jump out of airplanes, and drive at high speeds simply because of the excitement these activities generate. It is clear that such activities are reinforcing because we tend to repeat the behaviors that lead to these forms of stimulation. This phenomenon has been demonstrated numerous times in laboratory experiments. For example, some studies have shown that rats would learn to press a bar if the only reward for doing so was the onset of a light (see, Kish, 1966). Similarly, Moon and Lodahl (1956) found that monkeys would learn a bar press response in order to have a room light turned off. The same kinds of findings have been reported when the onsets and offsets of auditory stimuli have been used (see, for example, Kish & Antonitis, 1956).

Probably one of the best-known studies of this type was conducted by Butler (1954), who trained monkeys to push open the door to their cage enclosures. The reward for this response was the opportunity to view another cage in the laboratory. In some cases the other cage was empty, while in other cases it contained either a food arrangement, a moving toy train, or another monkey. Each of these stimulus arrangements elicited the door-opening response. However, response frequency was highest when another monkey or the toy train was used.

These studies and numerous others suggest that increases in stimulation can reinforce instrumental responses (see Eisenberger, 1972, for a review of these studies). Such findings are inconsistent with the drive-reduction hypothesis for two reasons. First, we know of no identifiable biological need for increases in stimulation, except in young, developing organisms (see Wiesel & Hubel, 1965). In general, a lack of stimulation has little negative impact on an organism's functioning unless the stimulus deprivation is severe (see Bexton, Heron, & Scott, 1954). This makes it difficult to argue that the opportunity to increase visual or auditory stimulation satisfies any primary biological need. Second, like the sexual reinforcement findings of Sheffield, these studies indicate that increases in an organism's overall level of tension may be just as reinforcing as reductions in such tension. This conclusion is clearly at variance with the drive-reduction hypothesis.

To account for these anomalous findings, some drive-reduction proponents have hypothesized the existence of additional drive states such as the "drive to explore" (see, for example, Fowler, 1965). Obviously, if such a drive existed, we could say that exploring or seeking out stimulation was reinforcing because it reduced the exploratory drive. Most researchers, however, have been unconvinced by these explanations. The most common conclusion is that Hull identified a condition that is *sufficient* for reinforcement, but not one that is *necessary*. In other words, all events that reduce drives will act as reinforcers, but an event need not reduce a drive in order to function as a reinforcing event.

Optimal stimulation hypotheses From our discussion thus far, it would appear that events of at least two kinds qualify as reinforcers. First, organisms that possess high drive or tension states tend to repeat the responses that lead to the reduction of those drives. In other cases, organisms appear to respond for the sake of increasing their levels of stimulation. Given this diversity of reinforcing events, we might question whether it is possible to find a common mechanism for all primary reinforcers. One proposal featuring the existence of such a common mechanism has been termed the *optimal stimulation hypothesis.*

In actuality, several variations of the optimal stimulation position have been proposed (see, for example, Berlyne, 1963; Fiske & Maddi, 1961; Hebb, 1955; Leuba, 1955). Most of these individual hypotheses do, however, share a common theme: namely, that organisms function optimally under an intermediate level of environmental stimulation. According to these hypotheses, an organism's internal state of arousal is linked to the amount of stimulation received. Furthermore, organisms are motivated to achieve a certain amount of arousal that can occur only under intermediate levels of stimulation. These hypotheses suggest that either increases or decreases in stimulation can serve as reinforcers, as long as these changes help the organism to maintain an intermediate amount of stimulation and, thus, an optimal level of arousal.

For example, if an organism is hungry, the hunger produces a high level of internal stimulation. Food serves as a reinforcer in this case because it satisfies the hunger and reduces the amount of internal stimulation to an intermediate level. On the other hand, organisms that are bored experience low levels of internal stimulation. Thus, for these organisms stimulus changes and opportunities for exploration are reinforcing because such events increase stimulation to an intermediate level. Obviously, such hypotheses appear, on the surface at least, to be capable of explaining almost any reinforcing effect. If an increase in stimulation is reinforcing, we need only assume that the organism's original level of stimulation was too low. If a response is reinforced by a decrease in stimulation, we simply assume that the level of stimulation was too high. In effect, such hypotheses appear to provide a ready explanation for the apparent reinforcing effects of any event.

Despite its seeming advantages, the optimal stimulation notion has never had a major impact on the thinking of most learning researchers. This lack of interest most probably results from two factors. First, although it is suggested that reinforcement depends on changes in an organism's state of arousal, these hypotheses have never explained clearly how an organism's arousal level should be measured. As a matter of fact, there has been some disagreement among proponents of this view concerning what the term "arousal" really means. Obviously, this confusion over the concept and the measurement of arousal presents a real problem. If we are unable to measure an organism's arousal level before a learning trial, how can we predict whether an increase or a decrease in stimulation is likely to be reinforcing? In effect, these hypotheses fail to provide us with a means of predicting when a certain event will be reinforcing and when it will not. Instead they offer a way of accounting for effects that have already been observed.

The second problem associated with these hypotheses is that they appear to make incorrect predictions in certain situations. For example, these hypotheses state that hunger produces a high level of internal stimulation. Thus, this view must predict that a hungry organism always should seek to reduce its level of stimulation in order to attain an optimal level of arousal. Furthermore, a hungry organism should be able to be reinforced only by events that reduce stimulation. Neither of these predictions is upheld by the data. Several studies have shown, for instance, that hungry animals explore novel stimuli to a greater extent than satiated animals (see, for example, Fowler, Blond, & Dember, 1959; Glickman & Jensen, 1961). That is, animals that supposedly are already overstimulated seek out additional forms of stimulus input. Also, it has been shown that the opportunity to explore is a more effective reinforcer for hungry rats than for those that are satiated (Richards & Leslie, 1962). Clearly, such a result is inconsistent with the optimal stimulation view. It indicates that the opportunity to explore can serve as a reinforcer even when organisms are already highly stimulated.

Defining reinforcement in terms of responses
Both the drive-reduction and optimal stimulation hypotheses represented attempts to define reinforcement in terms of stimulus characteristics. By focusing on the nature of the stimulus an organism experiences in the wake of some response, both attempt to specify the characteristics that enable a stimulus to serve as a reinforcer. As we have seen, such attempts have had only partial success. For this reason, some theorists have proposed that we should focus on the nature of the consummatory response an organism makes following an instrumental response, rather than the stimulus the organism consumes. For example, instead of regarding food as a reinforcing stimulus, we should look at eating as a reinforcing event, such that organisms are seen as learning responses because these responses afford an opportunity to eat, not because they lead to a stimulus such as food.

In one of the first hypotheses that dealt with responses as reinforcers (see Sheffield, Roby, & Campbell, 1954; Sheffield, 1966), Sheffield proposed that reinforcement depends on the vigor or persistence of a consummatory response. According to Sheffield, when an instrumental behavior is followed by a vigorous or persistent consummatory behavior, reinforcement of the instrumental behavior is strong. The less vigorous or persistent the consummatory response, the less well it can serve as a reinforcer.

In one sense, this hypothesis is not very different from the theories of reinforcement that concentrated on the characteristics of a "rewarding stimulus." Sheffield himself notes that the vigor of a consummatory response depends on the characteristics of the stimulus being consumed. For example, very palatable foods elicit stronger eating responses than do less tasty foods. Still, this hypothesis emphasizes the dependence of reinforcement on the response elicited by some goal stimulus, *not* on what the goal stimulus does for the organism's state of motivation or arousal. If the stimulus plays any role in reinforcement, it influences the consummatory response, which itself serves as the reinforcer.

Obviously, such a view has the advantage of making it unnecessary to look for some common effect that all rewarding stimuli have on an organism's internal state. According to this view, it makes no difference that saccharine fails to reduce hunger, whereas sugars do reduce hunger. It also makes little difference that novel stimuli and sexual stimulation appear to enhance rather than decrease states of tension. What is important is that each of these stimuli elicits a consummatory reaction—each, in other words, is capable of producing a reinforcing event.

To bolster this view, Sheffield published results from studies in which stimuli of several types were presented to rats after an instrumental running response. Some of the stimuli were nutritive substances; others were not. Some of the substances were novel, and others were familiar. Sheffield and his colleagues found that none of these characteristics influenced the degree to which the running response was reinforced. Rather, these researchers found a direct relationship between the speed of the running response and the vigor with which the animals consumed the presented stimulus (Sheffield, Roby, & Campbell, 1954).

Clearly, Sheffield's consummatory response hypothesis seems to have substantial power in identifying reinforcing events. There are, however, two problems with this notion. First, several researchers have failed to find a direct correspondence between the vigor of consummatory responding and the degree of instrumental behavior preceding that responding (Collier, Knarr, & Marx, 1961; Goodrich, 1960; Snyder & Hulse, 1961). This failure suggests that the vigor of consummatory responding may not be related directly to the amount of reinforcement in an Instrumental conditioning situation. Even more problematic are some data we discussed earlier. Recall that Miller and Kessen (1952) found that allowing animals to drink milk was more reinforcing than simply pumping milk into the rats' stomachs. *However*, loading milk directly into the stomach *did* serve as a reinforcer even if it was less effective. Such a finding is difficult to explain if it is accepted that reinforcement depends on consummatory responding, since the stomach-loading technique circumvents the opportunity to make such a response (see also Hull, Livingston, Rouse, & Barker, 1951). Thus, even the proposition that reinforcement depends on consummatory behavior has difficulty accounting for all the data on reinforcing events.

A final point of view that has received increasing attention in recent years is the reinforcement theory proposed by Premack (1965, 1971). Premack's view is similar to Sheffield's in that reinforcement is defined in terms of response, not stimulus, characteristics. A major difference, however, is that Premack proposes that any kind of emitted response (not just a consummatory response) can serve to reinforce an instrumental or operant behavior. Basically, Premack suggests that any response that is preferred by an organism can serve to reinforce the performance of any less preferred response. For example, if a child prefers eating to doing her homework, the opportunity to eat can be used to reinforce studying behavior. By the same token, if the child prefers studying to washing the dishes, the opportunity to study will reinforce dishwashing. This hypothesis is unique in that it views reinforcement as a relative matter. There are no responses that are simply labeled "reinforcers" or "nonreinforcers." Whether a given response can act as a reinforcer depends on an organism's momentary preference for that response relative to others.

To test this kind of hypothesis, one must be able to determine an organism's preference for different behaviors. Premack suggests that the most reliable measure of preference is simply the percentage of some time period an organism spends engaged in different behaviors. For example, we might place a rat in a cage that contains a bar and a running wheel. Then, for the next hour we could measure the amount of time spent running and the amount of time spent bar pressing. If the rat spends a significantly greater proportion of its time engaging in activity A than in performing activity B, we can presume that activity A is preferred to B.

Over time, Premack and others have conducted numerous experiments that demonstrate the utility of this theory of reinforcement. In one such experiment, Premack (1959) allowed first graders free access to a pinball machine and a candy dispenser. For each child he recorded the time spent operating each machine, to determine each child's preferences. Several days after the preference test, the children were returned to the experimental setting. Premack found that he could increase the children's performance of their less preferred behavior by following this behavior with the opportunity to engage in the more preferred response. For example, if a child preferred the operation of the candy machine, he was able to increase pinball playing by following this behavior with an opportunity to operate the candy machine. Importantly, he also demonstrated that opportunities to perform the less preferred response would not function to reinforce the preferred behavior.

Similar findings have been reported in studies involving manipulatory behaviors in monkeys (Premack, 1963), consummatory behaviors in rats (Bauermeister & Schaeffer, 1974), and social behaviors in nursery school children (Homme, DeBaca, Devine, Steinhorst, & Rickert, 1963) and schizophrenic patients (Dougher, 1983). In all these cases, the opportunity to engage in a preferred behavior has been used to reinforce less probable or less preferred responses.

One additional point concerning this reinforcement theory should be made. Premack recognized that preferences for different behaviors do not remain static. First of all, he suggested that depriving an organism of the opportunity to make a response tends to increase an organism's preference for that response. This increase in preference is particularly evident if an organism is unable to respond at the level at which it normally would choose to respond. The effects of *response deprivation* on the reinforcing capacity of a preferred behavior have been emphasized by other theorists in recent years (see Allison, 1983; Timberlake, 1980; Timberlake & Allison, 1974).

Second, Premack has indicated that once the performance of a response has been allowed to occur, an organism's preference for that response can decrease as a result of *satiation*. Thus, it is possible that response A can reinforce response B for a period of time, but at some point response A may become less preferred simply because it has been performed so often. When this occurs, not only will response A cease being a reinforcer, but it will become possible for response B to reinforce response A. In effect, Premack emphasizes that response preferences can shift over time as a function of how much a response has been performed. Thus, to use this theory effectively, it is necessary to assess the preference for a given response at the time the response is to be used as a reinforcer. Only by looking at these *momentary response probabilities* can we make accurate predictions concerning the reinforcing properties of a given response.

The kind of theory developed by Premack and extended by others (see Allison, 1983; Staddon, 1979; Timberlake, 1984) has had great practical utility and has been applied successfully to a wide variety of situations. Still, such theories cannot satisfactorily account for some of the same kinds of data that were difficult to reconcile with Sheffield's view. For example, in a study such as Miller and Kessen's (1952), how does reinforcement occur when the organism makes no overt response after an instrumental behavior, but instead simply receives a milk injection into the stomach?

Other problems have arisen from studies showing that under some conditions low-probability responses can reinforce responses having a higher probability of occurrence (see, for example, Eisenberger, Karpman, & Trattner, 1967). Still, this theory represents a clear break from attempts to define reinforcement in terms of stimulus characteristics, and it has encouraged the performance of numerous experimental tests in recent years.

Conclusions about Primary Reinforcement Theories

All the theoretical views described in this section attempt to characterize the nature of primary reinforcing events. And, as we have seen, no single theory provides a truly adequate account of reinforcement. It is clear that events of numerous kinds can serve to reinforce emitted behaviors. It is also clear that it is difficult to find any characteristics that are common to all these reinforcing events. In recent years there has been a move toward looking at the types of responses that follow emitted behaviors rather than concentrating on the kinds of stimuli that occur. These "response oriented" approaches appear promising; however, it is only recently that such theoretical views have been explored seriously. For the present, at least, an adequate characterization of reinforcing events awaits the development of new theories and additional theoretical tests.

The Role of Reinforcement in Instrumental and Operant Conditioning

We have just discussed the nature of reinforcement, seeking to identify the kinds of events that will function as reinforcers in learning situations. Now we turn to a different question: What role does the reinforcer play in an Instrumental or Operant conditioning paradigm? We will examine three possible answers. The first is the proposal that reinforcers "stamp in" or strengthen the association between an organism's stimulus situation and a particular response. The second possibility is that reinforcers help to motivate an organism to perform emitted responses. And third, there is the view that reinforcers acquire associations with emitted behaviors, so that organisms come to expect certain consequences for their responses. We will examine each of these possibilities.

Reinforcement as a Necessary Condition for Stimulus–Response Associations

In one of the earliest views, Instrumental conditioning was thought to involve the formation of associations between environmental stimuli and emitted responses. For example, when a rat learned to press a bar in a Skinner box, it was said to be learning to associate stimuli such as the sight of the bar with a pressing response. The basic idea was that correct responding will gradually increase as the stimuli in a learning situation become more strongly linked to the appropriate behavior.

This view, first proposed by Thorndike (1913) and later expanded upon by Hull (1943), contained an interesting idea concerning the role of reinforcement. According to this view, reinforcers are events that *strengthen* the associations between prior stimuli and responses. In other words, stimulus–response associations are formed *only* when an emitted response occurs in a particular stimulus situation and *only* when the response is followed by reinforcement. Thus, according to this view, reinforcement is a necessary condition for the formation of a stimulus–response association.

As support for this notion, Hull cited numerous experiments that indicated a strong relationship between reinforcement and the performance of instrumental behaviors. For example, we have already seen that organisms tend to increase instrumental responding as more and more reinforced trials occur. We have also seen that the performance of such behaviors decreases when reinforcement is eliminated. It is also clear that the degree to which instrumental responding occurs depends on such factors as the amount, the delay, and the quality of the reinforcer. In all these cases, Hull proposed that variations in reinforcement produce changes in performance, because different experiences with reinforcement result in different levels of learning.

Although this position remained influential for a number of years, several findings suggest that reinforcement does *not* influence specific stimulus–response associations. For instance, some experimenters have conducted studies that are usually labeled *latent learning* experiments (see, for example, Blodgett, 1929; MacCorquodale & Meehl, 1951; Seward, 1949; Tolman & Honzik, 1930). Tolman and Honzik (1930) trained three groups of rats to run through a 14-unit maze. One group (the rewarded control group) received a food reward in the goal box of the maze on each of their daily trials. A second group (the unrewarded control group) never received a reward in the goal box. The third group (the nonreward/reward group) received no reward on the first 10 daily trials but did receive a reward on each subsequent trial. The results of these treatments can be seen in Figure 5.1.

As this figure indicates, the rewarded control group steadily improved its performance (decreased its errors) as it received more and more reinforced trials. The unrewarded control group showed only a slight decrease in errors over the course of its trials. The nonreward/ reward group performed like the unrewarded animals for the first 11 trials. However, on the trial after reward was introduced, these rats improved their performance to the level of the rats that had been rewarded from the start. In effect, the nonreward/reward rats performed just as well after 1 reward as the other group performed after 12 rewards.

Such a finding is totally unexpected if we assume that learning (and, thus, performance) depends on the number of reinforced trials an organism receives. Tolman and Honzik suggested that the rats in the nonreward/reward condition had learned how to navigate through the maze during their nonrewarded trials. However, they did not perform what they had learned until a reinforcer was provided. These latent learning studies indicate that reinforcement may not be necessary for

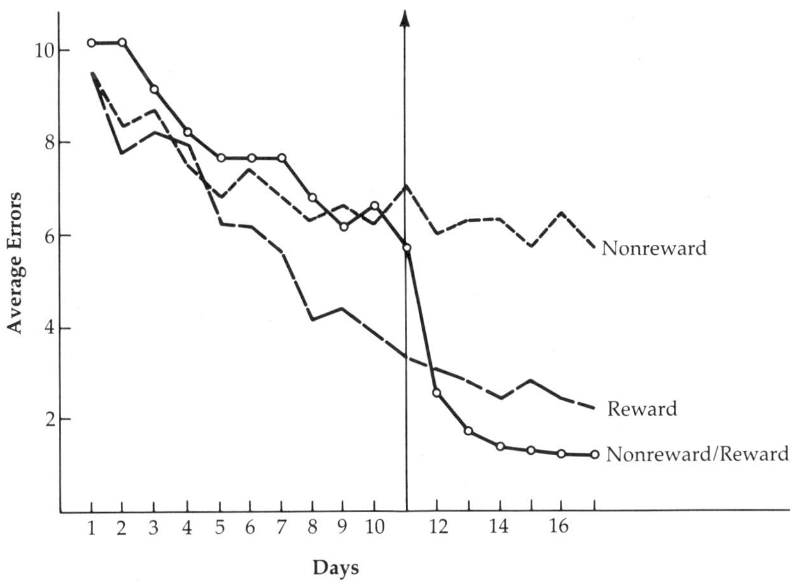

FIGURE 5.1 Maze learning in groups given reward on all trials, no reward on any trials, and no reward on first 10 trials but reward on trials 11–17. (From Tolman and Honzik, 1930.)

learning an instrumental response, although it seems to be necessary to elicit the performance of a learned response.

Making the same point are the contrast effect experiments described in Chapter 4. Recall that in this kind of experiment organisms learn some response that is followed by a given amount or quality of reinforcement. Then the quality or amount of the reinforcer is changed, whereupon organisms usually exhibit a swift change in performance. Figure 5.2 illustrates a typical set of results from a contrast effect experiment in which rats were trained to lick a drinking spout to obtain a sucrose solution (Gordon, Flaherty, & Riley, 1973). For one group the solution was very sweet (32 percent sucrose) and for the other group the solution was much less sweet (4 percent sucrose). As is typical, the licking response rate was much higher in the rats receiving the 32 percent solution.

On day 11 of this experiment, the rats that had been receiving the sweeter solution were shifted down to a 4 percent concentration. These rats exhibited an immediate decrease in licking such that their rate of responding was *lower* than that of the rats that had received the 4 percent solution all along. This phenomenon is, of course, what we have previously called a *negative contrast effect*.

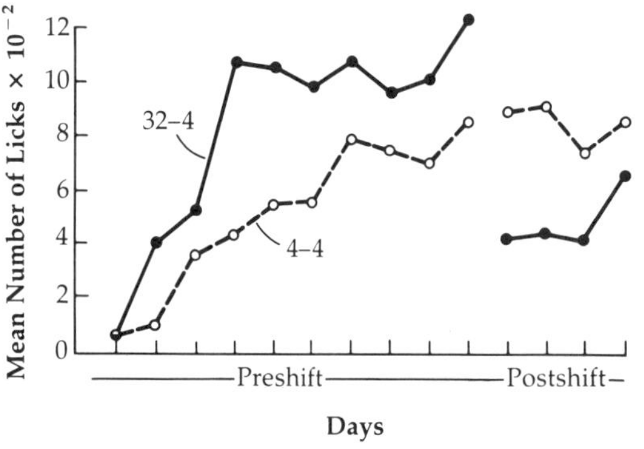

FIGURE 5.2 Lick rates for rats consistently given 4 percent sucrose and for rats shifted from 32 percent to 4 percent sucrose. (From Gordon, Flaherty, and Riley, 1973.)

At least two points concerning such contrast effects bear on our present discussion. First, when the amount or quality of reward is shifted, animals *immediately* shift to a new level of performance. If the amount or quality of reinforcement had affected the level of learning, one would expect such changes in performance to be gradual, not immediate. We would expect a gradual change because learned changes in performance normally occur gradually. The fact that shifts in reward result in an immediate change suggests that the characteristics of reinforcement influence the momentary performance of a response, not the level of learning per se. This rationale becomes even clearer when we see animals shifted from a low- to a high-quality reward. In such cases, animals immediately begin responding as well as animals that have received the high-quality reward all along. If the high-quality reward were simply strengthening the stimulus–response association, we would expect responding to have increased gradually as the association became stronger. Instead, performance increases immediately.

A second point concerning contrast effects is worth noting. Recall that according to the Thorndike–Hull hypothesis, a reinforcer should always strengthen the association between a prior stimulus and response. Thus, the occurrence of a reinforcer should always strengthen an organism's tendency to perform an instrumental response in the appropriate stimulus situation. The contrast effect experiments demonstrate that this assumption is not always valid. If an organism makes a response and it is followed by a 4 percent sucrose solution, subsequent responding will depend on whether the organism has been rewarded for the same response before. The 4 percent solution usually will strengthen the tendency to respond the first time a given response is rewarded. However, an organism that has been receiving a 32 percent solution for making the response and now is given a 4 percent solution will tend to *decrease* its response instead of increasing it. The observation that a reward can sometimes decrease responding is very damaging to the Thorndike–Hull notion of how reinforcers function.

The existence of positive and negative contrast effects suggests that an animal's performance depends on more than its current level of reinforcement. Performance also depends on an organism's previous experiences with reinforcement. Obviously, contrast effects depend on some kind of comparison between a prior reward level and the level of reinforcement currently in effect. To make such a comparison, an organism would have to learn something about the characteristics of reinforcement during its Instrumental conditioning trials. In other words, based on the contrast effect data, it appears that when organisms learn an instrumental response, they also learn to expect a given type of reward. This suggests that the reinforcer itself may be a critical element in an instrumental association. This, of course, is different from the Thorndike–Hull position, which views the reinforcer as a strengthener of associations, but not a part of any association per se.

Reinforcement as a Motivator for Responding

The studies reviewed in the preceding section emphasize the distinction between learning and performance. For example, the latent learning studies indicate that organisms do not always perform in accord with what they have learned. Contrast effect experiments suggest the same conclusion. In both cases, the data indicate that the characteristics of reinforcement may influence the performance of a response rather than the degree to which a response is learned.

Based on such findings, Spence (1956; see also Hull, 1952) proposed a change in the prevailing view of reinforcement. Spence retained the notion that Instrumental conditioning involves associations between stimuli and emitted behaviors. However, he suggested that such associations result simply from the temporal contiguity of these events. In effect, stimuli and responses that occur close together in time automatically become associated even in the absence of a reinforcing event. According to this view, the function of the reinforcer is to help motivate an organism to respond, so that responses can occur contiguously with situational stimuli. Reinforcement *aids* learning, but it is not *necessary* for learning.

Specifically, Spence proposed that the characteristics of a reinforcer provide *incentive motivation,* a motivational state that is aroused by the characteristics of external stimuli. For example, we eat certain foods partially because we are hungry. Hunger is a motivational state produced by periodic changes in our biological condition. We are also motivated to eat by the odor, the taste, and the sight of certain foods. When it is the characteristics of some food that lead us to seek out that food, we are experiencing incentive motivation. Thus, Spence viewed a reinforcer as a stimulus that arouses incentive motivation and helps to promote emitted behaviors that lead to that reinforcer.

The proposed mechanism by which reinforcers motivate responses was elucidated in some detail by Spence. Basically, he viewed a reinforcer as functioning like a US in a Classical conditioning situation. When an organism encounters a reinforcer, that stimulus naturally elicits a given reaction Spence called a *goal response* (R_g). The goal response is analogous to an unconditioned response made to a US. For example, if the reward is food, the goal response may involve approach behaviors, salivation, or chewing movements. Since these goal responses occur in the presence of goal box stimuli (S_g), these goal stimuli, like CSs, become capable of eliciting goal responses on their own. Thus, stimuli in the goal box become capable of producing responses that are

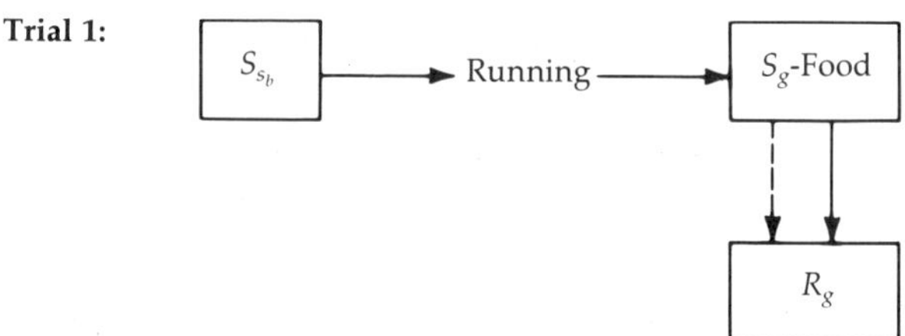

Animal leaves start box stimuli (S_{s_b}) and runs to goal box, where it encounters goal box stimuli (S_g) and food. The food naturally produces goal responses (R_g) such as salivation. Goal stimuli come to produce goal responses through Classical conditioning.

a.

Trial 2:
S_{s_b}
Running
S_g-Food
r_g-s_g
R_g

Since the start box stimuli (S_{s_b}) are similar to the goal box stimuli, S_{s_b} produces a fractional or partial goal response (r_g). This fractional goal response leaves stimulus aftereffects (s_g), which can become attached to running. Thus, the occurrence of r_g in the start box provides an additional set of stimuli that can aid in the production of running.

b.

FIGURE 5.3 Spence's conceptualization of how reward influences performance in Instrumental conditioning: (a) trial 1 and (b) trial 2.

normally elicited only by the reward itself. Figure 5.3a illustrates how this Classical conditioning of the goal response was presumed to occur.

According to Spence, once this conditioning has occurred, the conditioned goal response can help to elicit the responses that normally lead to the goal. To see how this happens, let's assume that we are training a rat to run down a runway for a food reward. On trial 1 the rat explores the runway and finally encounters food in the goal box. The food elicits a goal response (R_g) and the stimuli in the goal box (S_g) become capable of producing the same response via Classical conditioning. On trial 2 the rat is placed in the start box of the runway (see Figure 5.3b). The stimuli in the start box (S_{sb}) are similar to those in the goal box (S_g). Thus, the start box stimuli elicit a partial goal response (r_g) because of *stimulus generalization*—the tendency of an organism to respond in the same way in the presence of similar stimuli. Spence called the partial goal response produced by start box stimuli a *fractional anticipatory goal response*. Keep in mind that the fractional anticipatory goal response (r_g) occurs only because the start box stimuli are usually similar to the goal box stimuli and the goal box stimuli have come to elicit a goal response through prior conditioning.

Spence hypothesized that these partial goal responses are important because they result in stimulus aftereffects (s_g). For example, when an animal begins to salivate in the start box, it can feel its mouth becoming wet. Such stimulus aftereffects are important because they can become associated with the running or movement responses the organism is making in the runway. And, once the stimulus aftereffects have become associated with the emitted response, they can help to elicit that response on subsequent occasions. In effect, the start box stimuli set off a chain of responses and stimuli that can aid in promoting the instrumental behavior. Start box stimuli (S_{sb}) elicit fractional goal responses (r_g), which produce stimulus aftereffects (s_g) that can become associated with instrumental responding.

Many researchers, as well as many beginning students, have viewed this analysis as needlessly complex. The hypothesis, however, is logically consistent and is totally in keeping with a stimulus–response interpretation of learning. According to such an interpretation, complex emitted behaviors always consist of chains of stimulus–response associations in which each stimulus elicits a response and each response has stimulus consequences that can become attached to other responses. Spence's hypothesis clearly reflects this explanatory tradition.

Until the mid-1960s, the Spence view of reinforcement enjoyed wide popularity among learning researchers. This conceptually elegant theory appeared to account for a substantial number of reinforcement effects and had the clear advantage of viewing reinforcement as an influence on learned performance, not as a necessary condition for learning. Thus the theory was able to accommodate data such as those found in the latent learning and contrast effect experiments.

In the case of latent learning, this theory simply states that organisms learn stimulus–response associations in the absence of reinforcement. However, it is only when reinforcement is introduced and fractional anticipatory goal responses begin that the instrumental response will be elicited strongly enough to occur with regularity. In contrast effect experiments, reinforcement shifts are presumed to affect the strength of Classical conditioning in the goal box. Thus, according to this view, reinforcer shifts affect the strength of the fractional anticipatory goal response and lead to changes in how strongly an instrumental response is elicited. Reinforcer shifts do not directly affect the association between stimuli and the instrumental response; they affect the degree to which the incentive for responding is present.

Aside from providing an explanation for latent learning and contrast effects, this theory also suggested a mechanism that would account for a variety of other reinforcement phenomena. For example, we know that small rewards, low-quality rewards, and long reward delays all produce poor instrumental responding. This theory suggests that all these circumstances lead to poor Classical conditioning of goal responses. Thus, under all these conditions, fractional anticipatory goal responses are less likely to occur. This means that under these conditions there will be fewer stimuli available to elicit or promote performance of the instrumental behavior. Thus, small rewards do not reduce associations between stimuli and emitted responses, they produce less in the way of incentive motivation for responding.

Despite the power and early appeal of the Spence position, this view of reinforcement is no longer favored by most researchers (see, for example, Adams & Dickinson, 1981; Bolles, 1975; Mackintosh, 1983). The reason for this loss of favor is clear. The main premise in the Spence theory is that Classically conditioned goal responses help to motivate or promote instrumental behaviors. If we accept this basic assumption, Spence's theory is able to account for a number of reinforcement effects. However, there is little or no experimental support for this most basic premise. Researchers simply have been unable to find evidence that conditioned goal responses affect the performance of instrumental behaviors.

For example, several researchers have tested this assumption by conducting two-stage experiments. In stage 1, animals receive pairings of a specific CS with a food US, to condition goal responses such as salivation to the CS. Upon completion of this conditioning, the animals enter stage 2 of the experiment, in which they are trained to perform some instrumental or operant response for a food reward. During training, some of the animals receive the CS from stage 1 while they are performing the instrumental response. According to Spence, the presentation of the CS should produce goal responses, which should act to enhance the instrumental behavior. Yet most such studies have found either that the CS has no effect on responding or that the CS actually retards performance of the instrumental behavior (Azrin & Hake, 1969; Hake & Powell, 1970; Miczek & Grossman, 1971).

Another approach to testing this premise of Spence's theory has been to measure conditioned goal responding and instrumental responding concurrently in the same experiment. If the Spence notion is correct, we should find that conditioned goal responses develop before instrumental responses, since the goal responses presumably help to produce the instrumental behaviors. We would also expect to see a strong correlation between these two kinds of responses. That is, instrumental responding should increase as the occurrence of goal responding increases. These predicted relationships between instrumental and goal responses have seldom been found.

In one study that typifies this approach, D. R. Williams (1965) trained dogs to press a lever to obtain a food reward on a fixed ratio schedule. As you may recall, organisms placed on a fixed ratio schedule usually make no responses for a short period of time after each reward. However, once they have resumed responding, they normally respond at a reasonably constant rate until the next reward occurs. In this particular study, Williams measured both the rate of lever pressing and the amount of salivation that occurred throughout training. He was interested in how long it would take the dogs to resume pressing after each reward. He also wanted to know when salivation would occur relative to the pressing response.

According to the Spence theory we would expect the dogs to begin salivating before resuming the lever press response on each trial. Yet Figure 5.4 shows that this is not what Williams found. This figure illustrates lever press and salivary responding by one of the dogs in this experiment. We see that on average, the dog resumed the lever press response within 4 seconds after each reward. However, no significant salivation tended to occur until about 10 seconds after each reward. In other words, the goal response of salivation, which according to Spence should be helping to promote the operant response, did not begin to occur until well after the operant response was occurring maximally (see Deaux & Patten, 1964, for a similar result in a runway experiment).

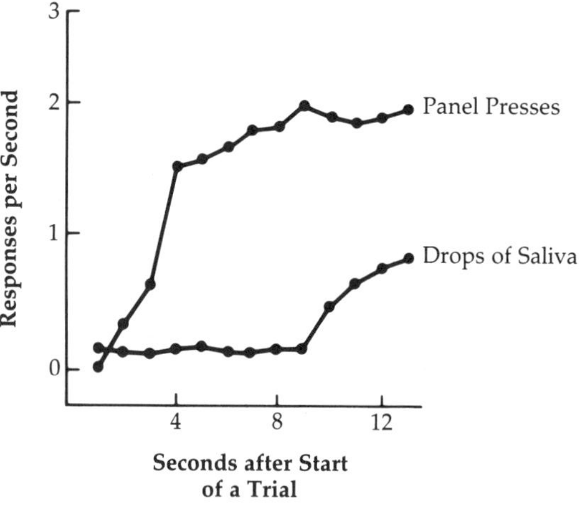

FIGURE 5.4 Number of panel presses and drops of saliva as a function of time since the start of a fixed ratio trial. (From D. R. Williams, 1965.)

It is notable that the Spence prediction also appears to fail in studies that have attempted simply to correlate instrumental and goal responding. Several studies that have measured responses of both kinds in the same situation have found that the degree of instrumental responding is often unrelated to the degree of goal responding (see, for example, Kintsch & Witte, 1962; Miller & Debold, 1965). Such findings have done little to bolster the Spence version of reinforcement effects.

Reinforcement as an Element in the Instrumental Association

Both the reinforcement theories we have discussed so far take the position that stimulus–response associations are formed during Instrumental conditioning. Reinforcement is viewed as an event that either strengthens these associations or helps to translate them into performance. Most contemporary theories of reinforcement take a different view of instrumental associations and of the role of reinforcement. Probably the most common notion is that Instrumental conditioning involves an association between an organism's response and the consequences of that response (see Mackintosh, 1974). In this view an organism learns to expect that certain kinds of behaviors will have certain outcomes. Performance then depends on which outcomes an organism prefers. According to this approach, reinforcement no longer plays a secondary role, but instead (as a response outcome) is part of the association that is formed.

The idea that the reinforcer may be one of the elements in an instrumental association is entirely consistent with the evidence we have discussed. For example, the results of contrast effect experiments strongly suggest that during Instrumental conditioning organisms learn about the characteristics of the reinforcer. If this is true, it seems reasonable to conclude that an instrumental association includes some representation of the reinforcer itself. Likewise, the latent learning experiments suggest that an organism's performance will change as soon as an organism is given an opportunity to associate its response with a certain outcome. Again, this phenomenon is consistent with the view that during Instrumental conditioning organisms change their responses because they come to associate their responses with reinforcing events.

This characterization of Instrumental conditioning has much in common with modern theories of Classical conditioning. In Classical conditioning, the most common contemporary view states that a CS and a US become associated to the extent that the CS serves as a reliable signal for the US. The same kind of idea is now being applied in an attempt to characterize Instrumental conditioning. Responses that reliably signal reinforcing events become associated with those reinforcers. There are several lines of evidence that tend to support this view.

First, it is clear that Instrumental conditioning depends on response–reinforcer contingencies, just as CS–US contingencies are critical for Classical conditioning. When a response regularly signals some reinforcer, the instrumental response tends to increase. The response decreases when it regularly signals the absence of reinforcement. When the response occurs and the reinforcer is delayed, conditioning is slowed. One reason for this effect may be that the delay makes a positive response–reinforcer contingency more difficult to detect.

Second, we saw that in Classical conditioning a given CS–US association is formed only if no other reliable signal for the US is already present. That is, an existing CS–US association can block or overshadow the formation of a new association. The same kind of finding has been reported in Instrumental conditioning paradigms. Several researchers have found that instrumental responding for a given reinforcer is retarded or blocked if a reliable signal for that same reinforcer is already present in the conditioning situation (see St.Claire-Smith, 1979).

For example, Pearce and Hall (1978) trained

rats to press a bar for a food reward on a variable interval schedule. As you may recall, on a VI schedule the correlation between responding and reinforcement is relatively low, since several responses usually occur before a single reinforcement is delivered. During this training, the researchers presented a tone each time the rats made a reinforced response. Therefore, the tone was perfectly correlated with reinforcement and could be used as a completely reliable signal for the reinforcing event. Pearce and Hall found that the presence of the tone slowed the acquisition of the bar press response. This finding is consistent with the notion that organisms fail to learn about one signal for a reinforcer (the response) when a more valid signal (the tone) is already present. Thus, such findings indicate that instrumental responding may increase only to the extent that the response can be used as a reliable signal for reinforcement.

A third type of evidence that favors the view of reinforcement as an element in the instrumental association comes from studies that attempt to change the value of a reinforcer outside the conditioning situation. Recall that in Classical conditioning, conditioned responding can be influenced by changing the intensity or value of the US outside the conditioning situation (see Rescorla, 1974). If an organism experiences CS–US pairings and then is exposed to presentations of a higher or lower intensity US by itself, conditioned responding to the CS changes accordingly. This evidence is often used to support the notion that Classical conditioning involves an association between CS and US representations. The same approach has been used to show that Instrumental conditioning involves a response–reinforcer association.

One series of experiments using this rationale has been conducted by Adams and his colleagues (see Adams, 1980, 1982; Adams & Dickinson, 1981). Basically, Adams trained rats to bar press for sucrose pellets and later paired sucrose consumption with a lithium chloride injection. As we have seen, lithium chloride usually results in nausea, and organisms normally form aversions to tastes experienced prior to injections with this substance. Thus, the point of the treatment was to make the taste of sucrose aversive or less palatable. After the treatment, the rats were returned to the operant chamber and were given the opportunity to press the bar. This phase of the experiments actually involved extinction, since no sucrose pellets were ever delivered. Adams found that rats that had associated sucrose with illness pressed much less than did the control animals. This finding suggests that the rats' memory of the sucrose value had been altered by the lithium chloride and, thus, responding for the expected sucrose was decreased. One would expect such a decrease only if, during the bar press training, the rats had learned that their responses would lead to an outcome of sucrose pellets.

In summary, all these lines of evidence suggest that reinforcers play more than a supporting role in Instrumental conditioning. Such data are consistent with the notion that in Instrumental conditioning the reinforcer is actually part of the association that is formed. In effect, Instrumental conditioning seems to involve the formation of an expectancy that a particular response will lead to a particular outcome.

Theories of Extinction

Thus far, we have discussed the characteristics of a reinforcer and the role reinforcement plays in Instrumental conditioning paradigms. In turning now to the mechanisms that underlie the extinction of a learned response, we will examine the question of why the elimination of reinforcement causes learned responding to decrease or disappear. Numerous theories of extinction have been proposed, but no single theory adequately explains the empirical facts of extinction. For this reason we will focus on only two of the theories that have been suggested. These theories represent different approaches to explaining extinction, and each theory contains ideas that have contributed to our understanding of the extinction process.

Amsel's Frustration Theory: A Competing Response Hypothesis

It is well known that during the extinction of a learned response, organisms often begin to perform new alternative responses. For example, when a bar press response undergoes extinction, rats often exhibit an increase in such behaviors as grooming, exploration, and rearing. Based on this occurrence of alternative behaviors, several theorists have suggested that during extinction organisms develop responses that compete or interfere with the behavior being extinguished. According to these theories, the instrumental response diminishes because other incompatible responses develop and become more probable.

Without doubt, the most influential competing response theory that has been proposed is Amsel's *frustration theory* of extinction (Amsel, 1958, 1967, 1972). Amsel's ideas were initially influenced by the observation that during extinction, animals display a number of reactions that appear to be emotionally charged. To the casual observer, such animals appear to be "frustrated" or "angry" when reinforcement is eliminated. Thus, Amsel proposed that the elimination of an expected reward results in a motivational state of frustration that produces a number of new responses. These responses are usually incompatible with the ongoing instrumental behavior. As extinction progresses, organisms become increasingly frustrated, and the incompatible responses begin to block the performance of the instrumental response. Thus, extinction is viewed as resulting from competition between the previously learned response and incompatible behaviors produced by frustration.

In partial support of this view, several researchers have reported that the elimination of an expected reward does appear to produce a motivational state that is capable of enhancing an organism's behaviors (see, for example, Amsel & Roussel, 1952; Amsel & Ward, 1965; Hug, 1970; Peckham & Amsel, 1967; Wagner, 1959). Furthermore, by extrapolating certain ideas in this theory, Amsel has been able to account for a variety of extinction phenomena. For example, we saw earlier that extinction is usually fastest when the magnitude of reward during learning is large. According to Amsel, the larger the reward during learning, the greater is the frustration state produced when the reward is eliminated. This means that when large rewards cease, frustration-produced incompatible responses in extinction are stronger and more numerous. For this reason, the instrumental response is more quickly replaced or extinguished.

Although this theory does an adequate job of explaining a number of extinction phenomena, the notoriety of the theory is based largely on its ability to account for the partial reinforcement extinction effect (PREE). As you may recall, the PREE refers to the fact that organisms given partial reinforcement during learning extinguish more slowly than those given continuous reinforcement. Amsel explains this effect by suggesting that partially reinforced organisms learn to respond in the presence of frustration during learning. In other words, on nonreinforced trials these organisms experience frustration and exhibit frustration-produced responses. However, the organisms continue to perform the instrumental response because they are rewarded on some occasions. This means that the frustration-produced responses occur contiguously with the instrumental response, and the stimulus aftereffects of frustration become associated with the instrumental behavior. In effect, frustration becomes attached to the ongoing instrumental response and actually helps to motivate or promote the response.

When extinction begins, both partially and

continually reinforced organisms experience frustration. In the case of the continually reinforced animal, frustration-produced responses begin to interfere with the instrumental behavior and extinction occurs rapidly. However, in partially reinforced organisms, the frustration of extinction actually helps to maintain responding, since initially it was associated with the instrumental behavior. Thus, during extinction, partially reinforced organisms continue to perform the instrumental behavior for a substantial period of time.

As we have noted, Amsel's frustration theory successfully accounts for a variety of extinction effects, and it is compatible with our observations of animal behavior during extinction. Still, this theory cannot stand as a complete explanation of the extinction phenomenon. The first problem is that one would expect frustration to decrease during extinction as an organism's expectation of reward decreases. And indeed, there is substantial evidence to suggest that the frustration resulting from reward elimination begins to diminish as more experiences with nonreward occur (see, for example, McHose, 1963). This means that the continued decrease in an instrumental response over extinction trials must result from some other mechanism.

The second problem is that the theory fails to account for some of the finer aspects of the PREE. For example, Amsel emphasizes that frustration should begin to occur only after a clear expectation of reward has been formed. To support this idea, Hug (1970) has shown that the elimination of reward has no motivating effects unless an organism has had approximately 8 to 12 prior experiences with reinforcement. Still, a significant PREE has been obtained in studies using only 5 or 6 learning trials. This means that after only 2 or 3 reinforcement experiences intermingled with 2 or 3 nonreward experiences, animals exhibit slower extinction (see, for example, McCain, 1969; Ziff & Capaldi, 1971). This suggests that a PREE can occur in the absence of frustration.

Similarly, it is now clear that the occurrence of a PREE depends not only on partial reinforcement but also on the specific sequencing of the reinforced and nonreinforced trials. Amsel would say that the only critical sequence effect should be that some reinforced trials precede the nonreinforced trials during learning. Otherwise, no expectation of reward would precede nonreward and no frustration would occur. Aside from this prediction, Amsel's theory is silent concerning other trial sequence effects. As we will now see, there is another extinction theory that is particularly adept at accounting for such trial sequence effects.

Capaldi's Sequential Theory: A Generalization Decrement Hypothesis

Although several theories of extinction have relied on the notion of competing responses, others have been based on the idea that extinction is primarily the result of a *stimulus generalization decrement.* We will discuss the topic of stimulus generalization in greater detail in Chapter 7. However, for present purposes, stimulus generalization simply refers to the fact that when organisms learn a response in one stimulus situation, they tend to perform that response best when they are confronted with the same or a similar stimulus situation. When learning occurs in the presence of one stimulus set and testing occurs in the presence of a different stimulus set, performance of the learned response tends to decrease. This decrease in learned responding that results from stimulus change is called a stimulus generalization decrement.

Extinction theories based on this effect suggest that during learning the reinforcer becomes a critical part of the stimulus situation. In this sense the reinforcer is analogous to contextual stimuli that are present when an organism learns a response. In extinction, the elimination of the reinforcer changes the stimulus situation dramatically. Thus, organisms cease responding for the same reason they would fail to respond if they were placed in a novel apparatus. They stop responding because the stimulus situation is different from the one in which they learned.

Probably the most compelling extinction theory of this type is the *sequential theory* proposed by E. J. Capaldi (1967, 1971). First of all, Capaldi proposes that a reinforcer always strengthens the association between an instrumental behavior and any stimuli that are present when the behavior occurs. Thus, if an organism runs through a runway and receives food in a goal box, the food strengthens the association between the runway stimuli and the running response. Just as important, however, once an organism has encountered a reinforcer, it will form a memory of the reward (M_R), which can remain within the organism for a substantial period of time. Thus, reinforcers serve to strengthen stimulus–response associations *and* to set up memory traces that can carry over to subsequent learning trials.

To better understand how these two functions of the reinforcer affect instrumental learning, let's consider Figure 5.5, which describes a typical sequence of learning trials. On trial 1 a rat is placed in a runway and wanders to the goal box, where it finds food. The food strengthens the association between the apparatus stimuli (S_A) and the running response.

Trial 1:

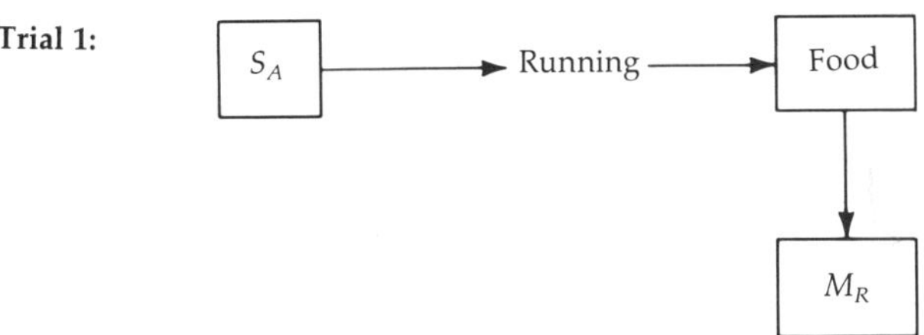

Animal runs in the presence of apparatus stimuli (S_A) and encounters food in the goal box. The food reward strengthens the association between S_A and running. The food also leaves behind a memory trace of reward (M_R) that can carry over to the next trial if the intertrial interval is not too long.

a.

Trial 2:

$S_A + M_R$ → Running → Food

M_R

The animal is confronted once again with apparatus stimuli (S_A) as well as its own memory of reward (M_R) from the previous trial. This means that the total stimulus complex on trial 2 is (S_A + M_R). The animal runs in the presence of this stimulus complex and again encounters food. The food strengthens the association between the stimulus complex (S_A + M_R) and the running response.

b.

FIGURE 5.5 E. J. Capaldi's view (1967, 1971) of how the memory of reward becomes associated with the instrumental response: (a) trial 1 and (b) trial 2.

The food also triggers a memory of reinforcement (M_R). On trial 2 the animal is placed back in the runway, where it notices the apparatus stimuli (S_A) as well as its own memory of reward (M_R) from trial 1. Thus on trial 2 the entire stimulus complex consists of $S_A + M_R$. In effect, the memory of reinforcement from trial 1 becomes part of the stimulus situation on trial 2. When the rat runs to the goal box and encounters food, the food strengthens the association between running and the $S_A + M_R$ complex. Thus, the organism's memory of reinforcement becomes one of the stimuli associated with responding. As more and more reinforced trials occur, the M_R builds up as a result of reinforcement exposures and becomes a larger and larger part of the stimulus complex that controls the instrumental response.

In extending this view to extinction, Capaldi proposes that nonreinforcement triggers a memory trace of its own (M_{NR}) that is distinctly different from the M_R. Thus, on an organism's first extinction trial, M_{NR} is formed, and this memory carries over to the next extinction trial to become part of the stimulus complex. This means that on trial 2 of extinction, an organism notices S_A, which has been associated with running, and the M_{NR}, which has not. Since the stimulus complex $S_A + M_{NR}$ is different from the $S_A + M_R$ complex that was present during learning, performance decreases as a result of a stimulus generalization decrement. As more extinction trials occur, M_{NR} builds up and becomes a larger part of the stimulus complex on each extinction trial. Thus, as extinction trials progress, the stimulus complex becomes increasingly different from the one present during training and the running response decreases accordingly.

Using this theoretical framework, Capaldi has been able to account for an impressive array of extinction data. For example, Capaldi's theory, like Amsel's, is able to explain why organisms often extinguish faster after training with large rewards than they do after training with small rewards. Capaldi simply asserts that the M_R for a small reward is more similar to M_{NR} than is the M_R for a large reward. Thus, during extinction, the occurrence of M_{NR} constitutes a major change in the stimulus situation for organisms that have previously experienced large rewards. As a result, the stimulus generalization decrement is large and performance drops dramatically. Because the M_R for a small reward is more similar to M_{NR}, animals that have been trained using small rewards experience a less significant stimulus generalization decrement during extinction. Thus, performance decreases more slowly in these organisms.

As with Amsel's theory, Capaldi's view has created interest primarily because of its capacity for explaining the PREE. As a matter of fact, Capaldi's position does an excellent job of accounting for the particulars of this phenomenon. Basically, Capaldi suggests that partial reinforcement affords an organism the opportunity to associate the MNR with the instrumental response during training. For this to occur, however, it is not enough for an organism to experience some rewarded and some nonrewarded trials. These trials must occur in a particular sequence such that at least some nonrewarded trials (*N* trials) are followed by a rewarded trial (*R* trial). Capaldi calls such a trial sequence an *N–R transition* to denote that a nonrewarded trial is followed by a rewarded trial.

The importance of *N–R* transitions for associating M_{NR} with responding should be apparent. When a nonrewarded trial occurs, an M_{NR} is formed and is carried over to the next trial. If on this next trial the organism responds and is reinforced, the reinforcement will strengthen the association between the M_{NR} and the response. When extinction begins and the M_{NR} occurs as a result of nonreward, the M_{NR} has previously been associated with responding and the response will continue to occur during extinction. Thus, according to Capaldi, the PREE does not result simply from experience with a partial reward schedule. It results from the *N–R* transitions that often occur within such schedules.

This prediction that *N–R* transitions are critical for producing a PREE holds up well under experimental tests. For example, in one experiment by Spivey and Hess (1968) rats were trained to run in a straight alleyway for a food reward. Each animal received four trials per day for 3 days. Rats differed in terms of the sequence of rewarded (*R*) and nonrewarded (*N*) trials. One group, which served as a continuously rewarded control, received four reinforced trials each day (*RRRR*). The remaining two groups each received two reinforced and two nonreinforced trials per day. For one group the sequence of trials was *NNRR*, while the other received the sequence *RRNN*. The latter two groups differed in terms of *N–R* transitions. The *NNRR* group received three *N–R* transitions over the 3 days of training (one N–R transition per day). The *RRNN* group received no *N–R* transitions. (It does not count as an *N–R* transition that the last trial on each day is nonreinforced and the first trial the following day is reinforced. Over a 24-hour period it is presumed that the M_{NR} goes away and is not present at the beginning of the next day.) After this training regimen, each group was exposed to extinction trials.

From the results of the extinction procedure (Figure 5.6), you can see that the *RRNN* group extinguished just as quickly as the *RRRR* group. In other words, this group showed no evidence of a PREE even though these animals were partially reinforced during training. The only group that exhibited a PREE was the *NNRR* group, which was exposed to *N–R* transitions during training.

Several studies have confirmed that *N–R* transitions are necessary for the production of a PREE (see Mackintosh, 1974). Such findings are clearly consistent with Capaldi's view of extinction. Additional support for this theory

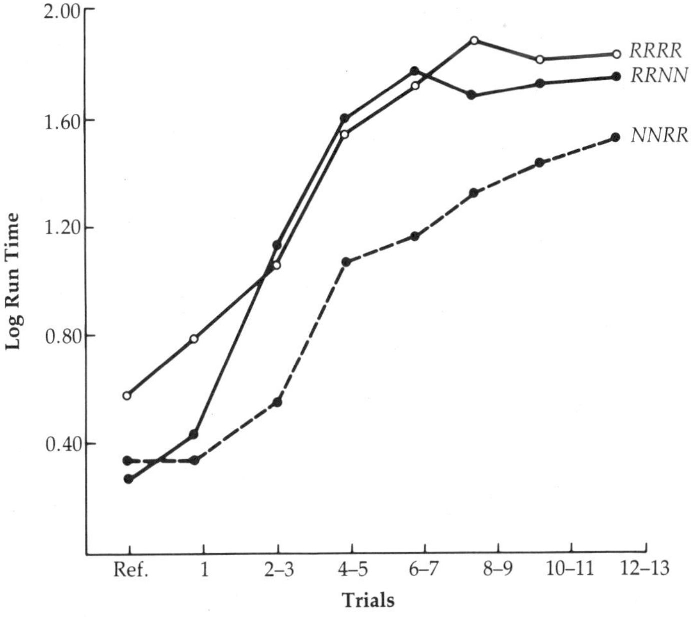

FIGURE 5.6 Extinction performance by rats given different reward–nonreward sequences during learning. (From Spivey and Hess, 1968.)

comes from other experiments that have looked at the effects of a variable called *N-length.* Capaldi defines *N*-length as the number of consecutive nonreinforced trials that precede a reinforced trial in a partial reward schedule. According to Capaldi, as more and more consecutive nonreinforced trials occur during training, the M_{NR} builds up and becomes more similar to the M_{NR} that will occur over repeated extinction trials. If many nonreinforced trials occur before a reinforced trial (that is, if the *N*-length is long), then the M_{NR} associated with responding will be similar to the M_{NR} an organism will experience in extinction. This means that responding will continue during extinction for a longer time. In effect, Capaldi predicts that longer *N*-lengths during training will lead to a more substantial PREE than will shorter *N*-lengths. Again, several studies have confirmed this prediction (see, for example, Capaldi & Stanley, 1965; Gonzalez & Bitterman, 1964).

Despite the obvious success of Capaldi's theory in accounting for extinction phenomena, some theorists have questioned whether this or any other stimulus generalization decrement theory can stand as a complete explanation of extinction (see Mackintosh, 1974). For example, several studies have shown that extinction occurs readily even under circumstances in which generalization decrements should be minimal (Rescorla & Skucy, 1969; Uhl & Garcia, 1969). Other studies have shown that extinction occurs even when only one extinction trial per day is given (see, for example, Hill & Spear, 1962). This finding is difficult for Capaldi's theory to explain, since with this procedure the M_{NR} should not last long enough to be available as part of the stimulus situation on each extinction trial. In sum, stimulus generalization decrements appear to contribute substantially to the extinction of instrumental behaviors, but such decrements may not provide a complete account of extinction phenomena.

Conclusions concerning extinction theories Currently it appears that Capaldi's generalization decrement approach accounts for the widest range of extinction data. However, there are also studies suggesting that frustration plays a role in extinction. Most likely, extinction is a phenomenon that results from a variety of factors such as generalization decrements, competing emotional responses, and even learning that responding no longer leads to a rewarding consequence. Future theories of extinction may need to include all these mechanisms to provide a complete account of why the elimination of reinforcement abolishes instrumental responding.

Reinforcement in Avoidance Learning

Historically, one of the most widely debated issues in the Instrumental conditioning literature has been the question of what constitutes reinforcement in an avoidance learning paradigm. To better understand this issue, it is helpful to consider an example of a typical avoidance learning procedure. Let's assume that a rat is placed in the start compartment of a two-chamber avoidance apparatus. In this apparatus a hurdle separates the start compartment from the other chamber. After several seconds a tone comes on to signal the impending delivery of a shock. To avoid the shock successfully, the rat must jump over the hurdle into the safe compartment before the shock occurs—that is, during the presentation of the tone signal.

Typically, a rat in this situation fails to respond correctly on the first few trials. That is, the rat remains in the start compartment until the shock occurs. When the shock is delivered, the rat often jumps and runs until it finally leaps over the hurdle and the shock goes off. On the next few trials the rat again waits for the shock to occur, but now it begins to jump the hurdle as soon as the shock is initiated. In effect, the animal has learned a response that allows it to *escape* from the shock. Finally, after several successful escape responses the rat makes its first true avoidance response. In other words, it jumps the hurdle during the tone presentation before the shock is administered. These avoidance responses then continue to occur on subsequent trials, usually with very few errors.

In an effort to explain how avoidance responding is learned, theorists have had little trouble accounting for an organism's initial escape responses. These responses are clearly motivated by the presence of shock, and the termination of the shock after each escape response obviously serves to reinforce the escape behavior. What has been more difficult to explain, however, is the occurrence of avoidance responses in the first place, and their continuation, trial after trial. The crux of the problem is this. We have said that to avoid an aversive stimulus successfully, an organism must respond *before* the stimulus (shock) is presented. This requirement raises two questions in the present case. First, since shock is not yet present, what element in the situation motivates the organism to make an avoidance response? Second, since the response occurs in the absence of shock, shock termination cannot serve as the reinforcer for the avoidance behavior. What, then, does reinforce avoidance responses, ensuring that they continue to occur?

Numerous theories of avoidance learning have been proposed to answer this question (see, for example, Bolles, 1970; Denny, 1971; Herrnstein, 1969; Hilgard & Marquis, 1940; Hull, 1929). Clearly, it is beyond the scope of this discussion to explain the details of each of these accounts and to review the data pertinent to all these theories. Thus, in an effort to provide at least an introduction to this issue, we will concentrate on two very different theoretical approaches. The first, which is usually termed the *two-factor theory of avoidance* (see N. E. Miller, 1948; Mowrer, 1947; Schoenfeld, 1950), is discussed for two reasons. First, for years this was the most widely accepted theory of avoidance learning, and as such it provided a framework for much of the research done on this type of learning. Second, the two-factor theory represents a clear example of a behavioral approach to understanding avoidance phenomena. Our second theory, the *cognitive theory of avoidance learning* proposed by Seligman and Johnston (1973), represents a radically different approach. This theory, however, demonstrates some of the advantages that cognitive theorizing can bring to an analysis of basic learning phenomena.

The Two-Factor Theory

The major proponent of the two-factor theory was Mowrer (1947), although other theorists have contributed important variations of the same idea (see, for example, Schoenfeld, 1950). The "two-factor" label is applied to this approach because the basic idea is that avoidance learning really involves both Classical and Instrumental conditioning.

According to Mowrer, the development of an avoidance response first involves learning a Classically conditioned association in which the signal in the avoidance situation functions as a CS and the aversive stimulus acts as a US. Since the signal regularly precedes the aversive stimulus in time, the signal becomes capable of eliciting a fear CR. This Classical conditioning has two results. First, it ensures that an organism will become fearful in the presence of the signal even *before* the primary aversive stimulus occurs on each trial. This fear provides a motivational state that increases the probability that an organism will make some response during the signal presentation. Second, this conditioning establishes the signal as an aversive stimulus in its own right. It becomes aversive because of its association with the primary aversive event.

Once this Classical conditioning has occurred, the second factor in avoidance learning is triggered. The organism now learns an instrumental escape response—that is, a response that allows it to get away from the signal that has become aversive. Thus, organisms respond during the signal, not to avoid the primary aversive stimulus which is still to come, but rather to escape from the aversive signal that is already present. According to this view, the instrumental response is reinforced by the termination of the signal and by the reduction of the fear the signal produces.

The appeal of this approach is that it identifies a plausible reinforcer for the avoidance response even though such responses ensure that the primary aversive stimulus itself will never occur. The two-factor theory also gained prominence because many predictions derived from the theory were upheld by the empirical data. For example, the theory predicts that avoidance responding will be learned only to the extent that the warning signal terminates when a response is made. To test this prediction Kamin (1957a) trained four groups of rats in a two-chamber avoidance apparatus. One group was given typical avoidance learning trials in which moving from one compartment to the other during the signal led both to avoidance of shock *and* to the termination of the warning signal. A second group was trained so that responding led to avoidance of the shock but not to the termination of the signal. Responses in the third group terminated the signal, but shock was delivered nevertheless. In the last group both the signal and the shock occurred regardless of the response. Thus, this group received only Classical conditioning trials with no instrumental contingencies in effect.

From the results of this experiment (Figure 5.7), it is obvious that a significant amount of avoidance responding occurred in the first group only. It is particularly notable that responding was poor in the group that was able to avoid shock but could not terminate the signal. This is precisely the kind of result predicted by the two-factor theory.

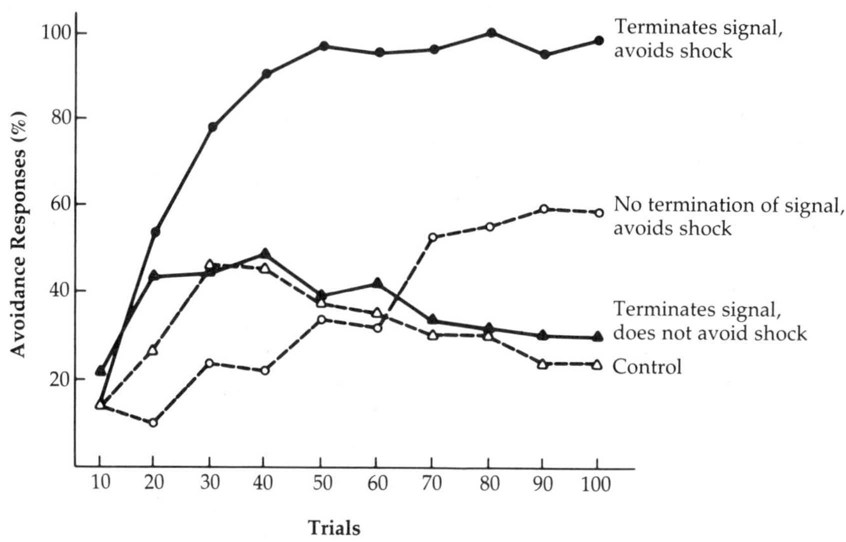

FIGURE 5.7 Avoidance responding by rats whose responses result in different outcomes. (From Kamin, 1957a.)

A similar prediction that can be derived from this theory is that avoidance responding should develop as long as the response is followed by a stimulus that reduces the fear associated with the signal. In other words, one way to reduce the fear is to terminate the signal that produces the fear. The same effect should occur, however, if a conditioned inhibitor of fear (that is, a "safety signal") were to follow the avoidance response. This prediction has been confirmed in a number of studies (see, for example, D'Amato, Fazzaro, & Etkin, 1968; Weisman & Litner, 1969). Basically, these studies show that it is not necessary for the warning signal to terminate when the avoidance response occurs as long as the response is followed by an additional stimulus that has previously been associated with the absence of shock.

Finally, in our discussion of Classical conditioning we noted that the development of a CR is better with a delayed conditioning procedure than with a trace procedure. If, as two-factor theory claims, avoidance responding depends on Classical conditioning of the signal, we would expect avoidance learning to depend on the signal–aversive stimulus arrangement. This is clearly the case. When the signal terminates before the aversive stimulus is presented (a trace conditioning arrangement), avoidance learning is significantly retarded (Kamin, 1954).

Although the two-factor theory has much to recommend it, it also has encountered a number of problems that have diminished its appeal. Many of these problems have been outlined in some detail by Herrnstein (1969). According to Herrnstein, three major difficulties with the two-factor approach are evident: (1) the "elusiveness of the CS," (2) the "elusiveness of the fear CR," and (3) the persistence of avoidance responding even during extinction. Let's look at these problems and the difficulties accompanying each one.

First, Herrnstein uses the term "elusiveness of the CS" to indicate that many avoidance responses are learned in the apparent absence of any warning signal. For example, Herrnstein and Hineline (1966) conducted an experiment in which rats were exposed to two different schedules of shock: a "high-density" schedule in which shocks were presented with high regularity, one after another, and a "low-density" schedule in which shocks were widely spaced in time. All rats were originally placed on the high-density schedule. Whenever a rat pressed a lever, however, the animal was switched to the low-density schedule, where it remained until another shock occurred. If an animal failed to respond, it was switched back to the high-density schedule; if it did respond, it remained on the low-density schedule. Thus, by making an appropriate response, the rats could avoid the high-density stimuli and receive shocks only very occasionally. Importantly, no signals ever occurred to tell the organism when one schedule had been substituted for another.

As you might imagine, the animals required numerous trials to learn to avoid the high-density shock schedule, since shock *did occur* to some degree even when they responded correctly. Still, the animals did learn, and they did so without any explicit warning signals (see also Sidman, 1953, for an example of avoidance learning without a warning stimulus). When we recall that the two-factor theory relies on the assertion that organisms associate some warning stimulus with shock in order to learn avoidance, we see that for this theory to explain such findings, some stimulus that may have served as a warning signal must be identified in the situation.

To reconcile these results with the two-factor approach, some theorists have proposed that the stimulus feedback (proprioceptive stimuli) from "not responding" can serve as a warning signal. In other words, when an organism fails to respond, a certain set of sensations occurs in its muscles and joints. These sensations regularly precede the occurrence of the aversive event, and this experience can begin to elicit fear just as an explicit warning stimulus might do. In effect, this explanation proposes that warning stimuli *are* present in all avoidance situations, but in some cases the stimuli are inside the organism, hence invisible. Although such an explanation could be accurate, it relies on a notion that is difficult to test. Because we cannot confirm than an organism's internal stimuli serve as reliable warning signals, it becomes impossible to determine whether warning signals are necessary for avoidance learning.

The second problem the two-factor approach faces is based on what Herrnstein calls "the elusiveness of the fear CR." Clearly, the two-factor theory is based on the notion that organisms learn to avoid aversive stimuli because they become fearful before the onset of the primary aversive event. One difficulty with this proposition is evident to virtually any researcher who has conducted an avoidance experiment. In most such studies, organisms exhibit all the external signs of fear in the early trials of learning. Rats, for example, will defecate, squeal, and show freezing behavior when the warning stimulus occurs. Yet once the avoidance response has been acquired, these external signs of fear disappear. As a matter of fact, most organisms that have learned an avoidance response will appear to become very nonchalant about performing the response. They avoid, but they show few signs of being fearful.

Obviously, we cannot test a theory by relying on our casual observations. However, experimental evidence suggests that these observations are correct. For example, Black (1959) measured certain autonomic responses normally associated with fear while his dogs were learning avoidance. He found that fear reactions, evident in early avoidance trials, tended to disappear when the avoidance response had been learned. Similarly, Kamin, Brimer, and Black (1963) found little evidence of fear related to a warning stimulus once avoidance responding had begun. These researchers trained rats in a typical avoidance paradigm and used the warning stimulus in a CER paradigm to see whether the stimulus would suppress operant responding. They found that the warning stimulus did lead to suppression (an indication of fear) if animals were tested after only a few avoidance learning trials. However, if the experimenters waited until the avoidance response was well learned, the warning signal led to almost no suppression in the CER paradigm.

Findings like these suggest that avoidance responding can occur in the absence of any indication of fear. Such findings are of course difficult to explain by means of a two-factor theory, according to which the avoidance response occurs only because the organism is fearful before the primary aversive stimulus. Some researchers have suggested that although the external signs of fear vanish, the emotion may be continuing *inside* an organism during avoidance learning (see, for example, Rescorla & Solomon, 1967). Again, such an explanation may be valid, in which case the two-factor theory could continue to be viable. However, such a theory becomes less plausible when it requires us to accept a major premise that is impossible to test.

The final problem for the two-factor theory arises from the following logical inconsistency. According to this view, the warning stimulus acquires the capacity to produce fear through Classical conditioning and it is this fear that maintains the avoidance response. However, when the avoidance response is occurring regularly, the organism regularly encounters the warning stimulus and does *not* encounter the primary aversive event. In effect, the warning stimulus occurs alone. We have already seen that when a CS that has become conditioned is presented alone, the CR is extinguished. Thus, once the avoidance response has begun to occur, the fear response initiated by the signal should begin to diminish, as extinction proceeds. As we have just seen, fear does appear to extinguish during avoidance learning. But if we attribute this phenomenon to extinction, how can the two-factor theory explain the persistence of the avoidance behavior in the absence of the aversive event? If there is no aversive event and if the fear related to the warning signal extinguishes, what motivates the organism to respond, and what reinforces that response? Basically, the persistence of avoidance behavior when the aversive event has ceased to occur presents a major difficulty for the two-factor approach (see Solomon & Wynne, 1954, for an attempt to reconcile this problem within the two-factor theory framework).

There are numerous variations of the two-factor approach, and some are more capable of handling avoidance phenomena than others. There are also other behavioral theories that fare reasonably well in attempting to account for these phenomena. Next, however, we will look at a different kind of theory, which represents a much different approach to understanding avoidance behavior, namely, the cognitive theory proposed by Seligman and Johnston (1973).

A Cognitive Theory of Avoidance Learning

Behavioral theories of learning always emphasize associations between environmental stimuli and responses. Thus, according to such theories, stimuli always come to trigger or elicit appropriate behaviors. In this sense behavioral theories are somewhat mechanistic because once stimulus–response associations have been formed, an organism's behaviors are determined by the particular stimuli that are present.

Cognitive theories, on the other hand, emphasize learning about the relationships among stimulus events. According to such theories, organisms form expectancies about which events go together and which do not. An organism may learn, for example, that one event may lead to outcome A, while another event may result in outcome B. An organism's behavior then becomes a matter of choice. It chooses one behavior over another not because it is forced to do so, but because it prefers the outcome produced by one response to the outcome produced by another.

Seligman and Johnston (1973) have proposed just such a cognitive theory to explain avoidance behavior. According to this view, avoidance learning involves the formation of two related expectancies. The first expectancy is that responding leads to the outcome of no shock (or more generally, no aversive event). This expectancy is denoted as $rE\bar{s}$, where r = responding, E = expectancy, $\bar{s}$ = no shock. The second expectancy, $\bar{r}Es$, is that no response leads to an outcome of shock. Each of these expectancies is strengthened whenever it is confirmed. In other words, the expectancy $\bar{r}Es$ is strengthened whenever a failure to respond does, in fact, result in shock. Each of the expectancies is weakened whenever it is disconfirmed. Thus, the expectancy $\bar{r}Es$ is weakened whenever a failure to respond does *not* lead to shock. In avoidance learning, when these two expectancies are strong, an organism will be equipped with the information needed to produce either outcome as desired.

Although the formation of these expectancies provides information about which behaviors lead to which outcomes, the expectancies themselves do not necessarily lead to one behavior as opposed to another. The behavior an organism chooses to engage in depends on its innate preferences for the possible outcomes. Seligman and Johnston make the reasonable assumption that most organisms prefer no shock ($\bar{s}$) over shock (s). This preference is denoted as $\bar{s}Ps$, where P = preference. Thus, this view states that avoidance behavior can be explained by understanding which variables influence an organism's expectancies and outcome preferences in the avoidance situation. Let's try to use this view to account for the acquisition of avoidance responding and related avoidance phenomena.

At the outset of learning, an organism has the built-in preference $\bar{s}Ps$. Before the first trial, however, neither of the important outcome expectancies has been formed. On trial 1, an organism experiences a signal, it makes no response, and shock occurs. This sequence of events strengthens the expectancy $\bar{r}Es$. This sequence of events *also* leads to an association between the signal and shock, so that through Classical conditioning the signal begins to elicit a fear reaction. On the next few trials, the same sequence of events occurs. This leads to further strengthening of the $\bar{r}Es$ expectancy and to further fear conditioning with respect to the signal.

After several trials, the fear related to the signal becomes strong enough to motivate the organism to make a response before the shock occurs. This response results in the absence of shock, and this sequence of events strengthens the expectancy $rE\bar{s}$. As more trials occur, fear of the signal continues to motivate responding and $rE\bar{s}$ grows stronger because it continues to be confirmed. At this point the organism is now equipped with two strong expectancies—$\bar{r}Es$ and $rE\bar{s}$—as well as the preference $\bar{s}Ps$. Based on the expectancies and the preference for a given outcome, the organism continues to respond before shock onset. This responding does two things. First, it continues to strengthen the $rE\bar{s}$ expectancy. Second, it leads to the extinction of fear related to the signal because the signal is no longer followed by shock. The avoidance behavior continues in the absence of fear because of the innate outcome preference and because of the expectancies that have been formed.

One important point concerning this analysis should be reiterated. According to this view, Classical fear conditioning to the warning signal does play a role in avoidance learning. However, this role is a limited one. Fear of the signal causes an organism to respond early in training so that the $rE\bar{s}$ expectancy can be confirmed. Once this has happened, however, fear no longer plays a role in promoting the avoidance response. Fear extinguishes, and the response is then motivated simply by the organism's outcome preference.

Such an analysis has much to recommend it. First, this approach is consistent with the observation that organisms appear fearful early in avoidance learning but not after several trials. This view acknowledges that fear is present early in avoidance training, but it states that fear should extinguish after several successful avoidance responses. Second, this hypothesis provides a mechanism for responding once the fear related to the signal has extinguished. After extinction has occurred, an organism still has its preferences and expectancies with which to generate a response.

Aside from providing an adequate explanation for the acquisition of avoidance responses, Seligman and Johnston's theory makes clear predictions about the conditions necessary for eliminating avoidance behaviors. According to these theorists, learned avoidance responses should decrease only when the original expectancies are weakened through disconfirmation. In other words, avoidance responding should be eliminated if organisms learn that responding now leads to shock or that not responding now leads to no shock. Whenever the original expectancies are disconfirmed, an organism's bases for responding should disappear.

These predictions hold up very well. For example, one of the best procedures for eliminating a learned avoidance response is the *response blocking* or *response prevention* technique (Baum, 1970). In this procedure an organism is exposed to a familiar stimulus situation in which it normally makes an avoidance response. However, the experimenter arranges the apparatus so that it is impossible for the organism to make the usual response. While this response prevention is in effect, no shock is ever presented. By disallowing the response for some period of time, the experimenter facilitates the extinction of avoidance behavior, which tends to occur fairly rapidly. According to Seligman and Johnston, the reason for this extinction is simple. The experimenter has arranged the environment to disconfirm the expectancy $\bar{r}Es$. The organism does not respond (because it is prevented from doing so), yet no shock occurs. By disconfirming the original $\bar{r}Es$ expectancy, the experimenter has weakened one of the bases for the organism's avoidance behavior. Likewise, there is some evidence that avoidance responding will decrease if an organism receives a shock after making an avoidance response (see, for example, Brush, 1957; Seligman & Campbell, 1965). Again, Seligman and Johnston would predict this result, alleging that this procedure is serving to disconfirm the $rE\bar{s}$ expectancy.

Although this theory is consistent with a number of avoidance phenomena, it does have difficulty accounting for some of the more anomalous avoidance findings (see Seligman & Johnston, 1973). Still, its explanatory power should be obvious. We can account for a wide variety of learning effects simply by assuming that organisms form expectancies based on event relationships and that organisms prefer certain outcomes over others. It is because of this breadth and flexibility that contemporary learning theories have increasingly favored a more cognitive orientation.

Summary Statements

We have examined four theoretical issues concerning Instrumental/Operant conditioning. We found, first of all, that there is no really adequate theory to characterize the nature of reinforcement. However, recent theories that emphasize the kinds of response that occur after the instrumental response appear promising.

Second, we noted the various attempts to explain how reinforcement functions in Instrumental conditioning. We saw that there are problems associated with the view that a reinforcer strengthens stimulus–response associations. We also found that the notion that a reinforcer provides incentive motivation does not cover all situations. Here, the best explanations appeared to be those in which the reinforcer is viewed as an element in the instrumental association itself.

Third, we looked at two different types of instrumental extinction theories. One was based on a competing response notion, while the other emphasized stimulus generalization decrements. We found that Capaldi's generalization decrement theory accounts for a wide range of extinction data. Still, we noted the possibilities that extinction may be caused by multiple factors and that a combination of theoretical ideas may be necessary to provide a satisfactory explanation.

Finally, we examined the traditional two-factor theory of avoidance learning and encountered important difficulties in explaining the basic data. We also described a more cognitive explanation of avoidance behavior, which handles most avoidance phenomena reasonably well. This theory, proposed by Seligman and Johnston, was used to exemplify the direction that some theorists have taken in recent years.

6

Verbal Learning and Transfer

One of the most distinctive features of human behavior is its heavy reliance on language or verbal symbols. We use language not only to communicate with each other, but also as a medium for our own thought processes. For this reason, when most of us consider the way human beings learn, we quite naturally think of how humans process and use verbal information. More specifically, we think of how humans learn and remember relationships between words and how they derive meanings from these relationships.

As you might imagine, a complete analysis of how we process verbal information is a very complex endeavor. It involves questions about how we learn concepts, how we derive meaning from text material, and how we represent verbal symbols in memory. We will discuss these and several related issues in subsequent chapters. In the present chapter, we confine our discussion to the question, apparently simpler, of how we learn verbal lists. How, that is, do humans link together individual verbal items to form complex verbal sequences?

Researchers have been interested in how verbal lists are learned for at least two reasons. We mention first the practical consideration that humans are constantly called on to learn verbal lists in their day-to-day lives. When children first learn the alphabet or learn to count they are, in essence, learning verbal lists. The same is true of adults learning recipes or learning which television programs occur on a given night. Even the acquisition of something as simple as your social security number involves learning a sequence of verbal units. Thus, one reason for studying how lists are learned is the pervasiveness of this kind of learning in our daily lives.

A second reason for the interest of researchers in list learning is that such paradigms enable us to look directly at how individual words become associated. We can, for example, have subjects learn lists of items that vary along a number of dimensions. Subjects can be given lists of meaningful or nonmeaningful words. They can be given lists in which the words are either related or unrelated. It is even possible to present lists in which the words are widely separated in space or time. Thus, in list learning paradigms it is possible to monitor the influence of a variety of factors on the formation of verbal associations.

Manipulations of these types are often difficult to do within the context of a sentence or a text passage. How, for example, could one construct a sentence in which all the words were unrelated? The very fact that all the words occur in the same sentence means that the words will at least have some syntactic relationship. It is also more difficult to manipulate the meaningfulness of words in a sentence or paragraph. Even strings of letters that are meaningless in isolation can take on plain meanings in the context of a sentence. For example, "Xral" means nothing when it occurs alone, but it can be translated into a familiar word in the sentence "The Xral barked when the postman came to the door." In effect, it becomes very complicated to study the effects of certain variables within a sentence learning paradigm. This is why many researchers have turned to list learning as a way of studying verbal associations.

In our discussion of this topic, we will focus on three sets of factors that appear to influence the learning of verbal lists. The first set consists of *procedural variables,* which have to do with the way verbal items are presented to an individual for learning. Second, we will examine the effects on list learning of the *characteristics of the verbal items* themselves. Finally, we will outline the *learning strategies* subjects use when they attempt to learn a list. As we discuss these factors, one point will become clear. The effects of different variables often depend on the particular type of verbal list that is being learned. Thus, we begin our discussion by looking at the types of list learning paradigms most commonly used by researchers.

Methods for Studying Verbal Learning

The Paradigms

Basically, all Verbal learning paradigms were developed to capture at least the flavor of everyday human learning situations. For example, we know that we are sometimes called on to learn lists of verbal items in a particular order. At other times we must learn all the items in a list, but the order is unimportant. On still other occasions we are required to learn that certain items are related while others are not. As we will see, each of these common learning situations forms the basis for an important Verbal learning paradigm. We begin by looking at the *serial learning* paradigm, which was developed by the German psychologist Hermann Ebbinghaus in 1885.

Serial learning When children learn the alphabet, they must first learn that a set of verbal symbols (in this case, 26 letters) exists and then that these symbols occur in a given order. The same applies when children learn to count or when high school students learn the order in which the U.S. presidents served. In each of these cases and in numerous others, we learn not only that certain verbal items are related, but also that these items occur in a given order. How we accomplish such a task is studied in the Verbal learning paradigm called serial learning.

In serial learning, a list of items is presented one at a time. The mode of presentation can be auditory or visual, such as on a computer monitor. When the first list presentation or trial is completed, the subject is re-exposed to the same list of items in precisely the same order. These trials continue until the subject is able to recite the entire list in the given order. Errors are recorded whenever a subject fails to place an item in its appropriate serial position or misses an item altogether.

In most cases subjects are tested using one of two techniques. In the *study–test technique,* the subject is exposed to the entire list and is then given an opportunity to try to reproduce it. If an error occurs, the subject is given a second exposure to the entire list, along with another opportunity to list the items. The cycle is repeated until the list has been mastered. In the second technique, called the *anticipation method,* the subject is first presented with the entire list of words just as in the *study–test* procedure. Then, at the beginning of the second trial, the subject is asked to produce the first item in the list. Whether or not the subject is successful, the first item is then presented and the subject is asked to produce (or anticipate) the second item. This second item is then presented and the subject is asked for the third. The procedure continues until the subject can correctly anticipate all the items on the list.

In both procedures subjects are usually given a *trials-to-criterion score,* which reflects the number of attempts the subject needed to learn the list perfectly. As we will see, a subject's ability to learn a serial list depends on a number of factors, such as the characteristics of the verbal items and the way the items are presented.

Free recall learning Often we must learn a set or group of verbal items, but the order in which the items are produced is not critical. For example, when you attempt to learn a grocery list, your only goal is to remember all the items. The order in which they are learned is relatively unimportant. The same is true when you learn the names of the states or the names of all the people in your class. To study how a set of items is learned without regard to order, researchers have developed a paradigm called *free recall learning.*

In the free recall situation, a subject is presented with a list of verbal items and is asked to recall them in any order. Since order is not critical, the study–test procedure, not the anticipation method, is used. Assuming that more than one trial is needed, the second trial usually involves presenting the same items, but not in the same order used in trial 1. Each learning trial usually involves a different presentation order.

Even though there is no requirement to learn the sequence of items in free recall learning, researchers have found that subjects often impose some order on the items as they learn them. For example, study the following list of items:

apple, train, shirt, pants, orange, shoes, automobile, peach, bus

Typically, when subjects are asked to recall such a list, the order of recall goes something like this:

train, automobile, bus, shirt, pants, shoes, apple, orange, peach

In other words, subjects often learn lists by grouping together items that are similar in some way, just as modes of transportation, articles of clothing, and types of fruit have been grouped in the example above. Thus, even when the experimenter imposes no order on a free recall list, subjects often provide an ordering of their own. As a matter of fact, one purpose of the free recall paradigm has been to examine the strategies subjects use for ordering items in a set.

Paired associates learning When you learn a foreign language, you must acquire a new vocabulary. But how do you go about learning the meanings for an unfamiliar set of words? For the most part, you learn new vocabulary words by associating each foreign term with its English language equivalent. For example, you learn the meaning of the French word "très" by associating it with the English word "very." We follow the same procedure when we learn the meanings for unfamiliar words in our own language. We associate the unfamiliar word with a synonymous term we already know. This procedure is one example of what Verbal learning researchers call *paired associates learning*.

In a paired associates learning paradigm, the subject is presented with a list of word (or verbal item) pairs. For example, the following list of word pairs would constitute a paired associates list:

book–desk
chalk–radio
car–dog
lamp–flower

Each trial in this paradigm consists of a single presentation of *all* the pairs in the list. Usually, however, the order of the pairs changes from trial to trial. For example, the initial pair "book–desk" might appear third in a subject's list on trial 2.

The first word in each pair is normally called the *stimulus term* for that pair, and the second word is called the *response term*. Thus, in our example list the words "book," "chalk," "car," and "lamp" are stimulus terms, while "desk," "radio," "dog," and "flower" make up the response terms. The subject's task in this paradigm is to associate each stimulus term with the appropriate response term. Thus, the subject must learn that a given stimulus term goes with one response term and not with others in the list.

As in serial learning, a subject may be tested using either the study–test or the anticipation procedure. When the study–test method is used, the subject usually is allowed to see the list of item pairs and then is presented with a list of the stimulus terms alone. The subject attempts to recall the response term for each of the stimulus items. If errors occur, the subject is shown the entire list again and is given a second opportunity to produce the response items. When the anticipation method is used, trial 1 involves presenting a stimulus item followed by a short delay period. After the delay, the appropriate response term is presented. Then the next stimulus term occurs, and so on. On trial 2, the same procedure is used, except that during the delay after each stimulus term, the subject attempts to produce the appropriate response term before it is presented. Trials continue until the subject is able to anticipate correctly the appropriate response item for each stimulus term. As in serial learning tasks, subjects are usually given a "trials-to-criterion" score that reflects the number of trials required to learn the entire list.

We will discover later that the paired associates paradigm has been used extensively to study how verbal associations are formed. We will also see that such learning depends on much more than simply the characteristics of the verbal items and the method of item presentation. Paired associates learning clearly involves the use of cognitive strategies on the part of the subject as a way of linking verbal items.

The Verbal Items

When Ebbinghaus began to study verbal associations, his primary interest was in the effect of procedural variables on rate of learning. For example, he was concerned with how factors such as the spacing and number of learning trials influenced acquisition of a serial list. Ebbinghaus recognized very early the difficulty of studying the effects of these procedural variables using real words as the items to be learned. He realized that his own familiarity with the words he used had a powerful effect on the rate of learning and that this effect often overshadowed the influence of the procedural variables he wanted to study.

For this reason, Ebbinghaus decided to use lists of syllables instead of real words in his learning experiments. He developed a set of three-letter syllables called *trigrams,* which consisted of either a consonant–vowel–consonant sequence (a CVC trigram) or three consonants in a row (a CCC trigram). He believed that all these syllables would be relatively meaningless to a human subject, and thus, learning would not be as contaminated by a subject's prior verbal experiences. In general, these trigrams were called *nonsense syllables.*

The use of nonsense syllables in Verbal learning experiments has been extensive, especially when such research has focused on procedural variables. It should be noted, however, that even trigrams have differential meanings among subjects. Glaze (1928), for example, presented 2000 nonsense syllables and asked subjects to indicate whether the syllables were meaningful to them. He found wide variations in the meaningfulness of different trigrams. As you might imagine, even though neither "BAL" nor "ZEQ" constitutes a real word, the syllable BAL is very meaningful to most subjects, whereas ZEQ has little meaning. Thus, most of the syllables commonly used in Verbal learning studies have been carefully scaled with respect to their meaningfulness (see, for example, Archer, 1960). By scaling these syllables, it is possible to make certain that one list of syllables is no more meaningful than another, so that procedural variables may be studied without the distorting effect of word meanings.

Although nonsense syllables have been used by a number of researchers, many studies have been conducted with real words. Obviously, the frequent focus of such research has been on the effect of the characteristics of the words themselves on the learning process. As in the case of nonsense syllables, the words used in these experiments usually are compared or scaled on a variety of stimulus dimensions (see, for example, J. L. Bradshaw, 1984; A. S. Brown, 1976). Such scales are invaluable in studying the effects of different word characteristics on a subject's ability to learn.

Tests for Learning

Thus far, we have concentrated on how the Verbal learning paradigms have been used to study the acquisition of verbal associations. Many Verbal learning experiments, however, have been concerned with the *transfer* and *retention* of such associations. "Transfer" refers to the degree to which learning one set of verbal items influences the learning of a subsequent set. The measures used to study transfer effects are essentially the same as those used to study acquisition. Subjects simply learn one set of items and are then given a different set to learn. Transfer is assessed by measuring the trials necessary to learn the second set.

The study of the retention of verbal associations usually focuses on how well a learned association can be retained over time once it has been acquired. In such a study a subject learns some set of items such as a free recall list. Then, after a period of time called a *retention interval* has passed, the subject is given a *retention test* to assess how well he or she remembers the items in the list. Several different retention test measures have been employed.

In a *recall test,* for example, subjects are asked to recall, without any explicit cues, the list originally learned. A second measure used is termed a *recognition test.* Here subjects are given the original items embedded in a larger set of items. From the larger set, the subject must recognize which items were in the originally acquired set. Finally, some retention tests follow a *relearning* format, in which a subject has the opportunity to learn the set of items again, after the retention interval. The relearning trials are the same as those used for original learning. The actual measure of retention used with this procedure is called a *savings measure*. That is, the experimenter compares the number of trials a subject needed to relearn the items to the number of trials needed to learn the items originally. If the subject relearns the items faster than he originally learned them, we say that a savings has occurred. The amount saved is usually expressed as a percentage and is computed by the formula:

$$\frac{\text{original learning trials–trials to relearn}}{\text{trials for original learning}} \times 100$$

Using this formula, it is assumed that the higher the percentage of savings, the more the subject has remembered. This is the measure Ebbinghaus used to measure retention in his initial learning experiments.

In this chapter we deal exclusively with the acquisition and transfer of verbal materials without talking specifically about retention performance. Still, these retention tests will be important in our discussion, since several researchers have used such tests to assess how much a subject has learned after a given number of trials.

Variables That Influence Verbal Learning

Procedural Variables

Procedural variables are factors having to do with how verbal materials are presented to a subject for learning. Such variables as the number of presentations, the spacing of the presentations, and the organization of the items on each presentation fall into this category. We begin our discussion of Verbal learning factors by looking at the effects of these procedural variables.

The effects of list repetition Just as in Classical and Instrumental conditioning, the learning of verbal items increases as more and more learning trials occur. Ebbinghaus (1885) was the first to demonstrate this phenomenon in his study of serial learning. In his experiment, Ebbinghaus learned a serial list of nonsense syllables. He attempted to relearn the same list once each day, and he measured the percent savings in relearning the list on each occasion. From the results of this study (Figure 6.1), we see that the percentage saved in relearning the list increased as more and more learning trials were completed. This relationship between the number of learning trials and learned performance holds in all Verbal learning paradigms regardless of the learning measure used.

This effect of list repetition should come as no surprise. We all know that the more opportunities we have to learn a set of materials, the better we usually perform. What is surprising is that there is still no widely accepted explanation for how repetition improves learned performance. The theoretical explanations for this finding have continued to change as our views of list learning have evolved.

For example, early researchers viewed list learning as involving the formation of a series of simple stimulus–response associations (see, for example, Hull, 1935; Lepley, 1934; Postman, 1962a; Rock, 1957). It was assumed that paired associates learning simply required that a subject form associations between the corresponding stimulus and response terms in a list. Serial learning was thought to involve associations between each pair of adjacent items in a list. Based on this view, at least two explanations were advanced for how repetition might affect list learning performance.

According to one interpretation, the first trial of a list learning procedure leads to the formation of several weak associations. As

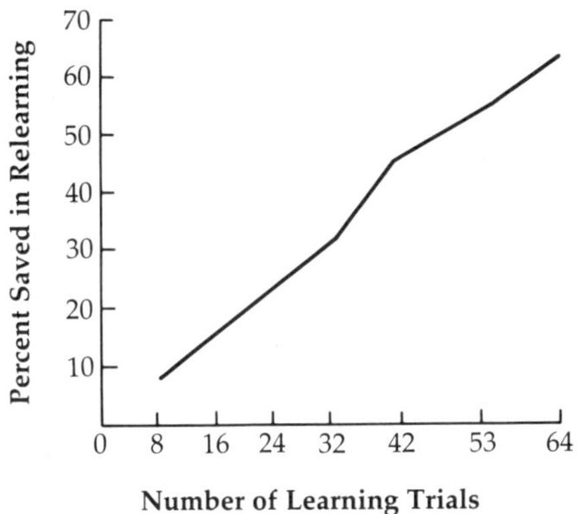

FIGURE 6.1 The percent saved in relearning a serial list as a function of the number of learning trials. (From Ebbinghaus, 1885.)

more trials occur, these multiple associations become gradually stronger, resulting in an increased probability that a subject will make the correct response to each stimulus item in a list (see, for example, Hull, 1943; Postman, 1962a; Underwood & Keppel, 1962). This explanation is usually called the *incremental hypothesis,* since it states that the various associations in a list grow stronger by small amounts from trial to trial.

The second explanation, usually called the *all-or-none hypothesis* (see, for example, Estes, 1960; Rock, 1957), states that on a given trial, subjects either form an association completely or do not form one at all. Thus on trial 1 of a list learning procedure, one or two of the associations in a list might be fully formed, but the other associations would gain no strength at all. As trials progressed, more and more of the associations would be formed and a subject would get progressively more responses correct. Thus, this view holds that list repetitions improve performance simply by giving a subject more opportunities to form the required associations in a list.

These two hypotheses generated a heated controversy among researchers in the 1960s, and several inventive techniques were devised to test the implications of the two positions (see Estes, 1960; Postman, 1962a; Rock, 1957). However, no clear resolution to this debate evolved. Instead, the view of list learning on which these hypotheses were based began to change. One idea that was instrumental in this change was the *encoding variability hypothesis* proposed by Martin (1972). At the crux of this hypothesis is the notion that there is no such thing as a simple stimulus–response association in a list learning paradigm, because verbal stimuli may be viewed differently by a subject from one trial to the next.

To illustrate this point, consider a typical word pair such as "boy–toy," which might occur in a paired associates list. Martin proposed that the stimulus term "boy" cannot be viewed as a single stimulus item but is instead a compound stimulus composed of a variety of features. The word "boy" has a particular sound, it has a dictionary definition, it consists of letters that have visual features, and it may have a variety of connotations for a given subject. Thus, in associating "boy" with "toy," a subject may actually form a number of different associations. On one trial a subject might associate the sounds of the two words, while on subsequent trials the meanings or visual features of the words may be associated in various combinations. This means that a subject may *encode* or represent the "boy–toy" pair in memory in a variety of different ways.

The encoding variability hypothesis has important implications for how we view the learning of a verbal list. It suggests that identifying the specific associations a subject is forming on a given trial of a list learning procedure may be difficult. It also suggests that to understand list learning we must understand how subjects rehearse and encode verbal items in memory. In other words, we must understand the various ways in which a verbal item can become represented in a subject's memory store.

As our conception of list learning has changed, interpretations of list repetition effects have shifted accordingly. For example, contemporary explanations often suggest that repetition affords a subject the opportunity to encode a verbal item in a variety of ways (see, for example, Anderson & Bower, 1974; Hintzman, 1976; Howell, 1973; Whitlow & Skaar, 1979). In such views, each trial results in an independent memory trace for a verbal item, and each trace is encoded in a slightly different manner. It is assumed in these theories that recall of a learned item will be better the more variously encoded the item is. In effect, when items are encoded in multiple ways, there are more ways to access or retrieve them from memory at the time of testing.

Several studies have tended to support this interpretation of repetition effects (see, for example, Hintzman, 1976; Hintzman & Block, 1971; Whitlow & Estes, 1979). However, this interpretation is still being examined in current research programs. What is clear is that repetition does not influence performance in any simple fashion. Thus, a complete understanding of this effect probably awaits further theorizing and experimentation.

The spacing or distribution of trials A second factor that appears to influence the rate of verbal learning is the spacing or *distribution of learning trials.* Ebbinghaus, again, was the first to report this effect. He found that a serial list was learned more rapidly when he distributed his learning trials over time than when he massed his trials together. Thus 10 learning trials spaced over 10 days were more effective then 10 learning trials all occurring on the same day. This superiority of *distributed practice* over *massed practice* has not been found in all experimental situations (see, Spear, 1970); however, it does occur in a wide variety of circumstances (see, for example, Underwood, 1961; Waugh, 1970).

It is also notable that distributed practice effects appear to occur when items are repeated within one list presentation. To illustrate this point, imagine that you are given a single presentation of a word list in which the word "house" occurs twice. You are more likely to remember this repeated word if the two presentations are widely spaced in the list than if they occur close together (see, for example, Shaughnessy, 1976). This variation of the distributed practice phenomenon has been called the *lag effect* (Melton, 1970).

There have been several attempts to explain why distributed practice is generally better than massed practice (see Hintzman, 1976). One view, suggested by Rundus (1971), is that when learning trials are spaced, subjects have more time to rehearse the items than they have when trials are massed. As we will see in a later chapter, most researchers assume that rehearsal plays a critical role in committing verbal materials to memory. This explanation simply states that distributed item presentations allow more time for effective rehearsal before items are presented again.

Although the foregoing explanation seems reasonable, several studies suggest that distributed practice may improve performance even when subjects do not rehearse the items they are given (see, for example, Rowe & Rose, 1974). For the most part these studies have used *incidental learning paradigms,* in which subjects are given lists of words and are told simply to rate the words on certain dimensions. They are not told that they will later be asked to recall the words. Thus, there is little reason to expect subjects to try to rehearse the words in order to commit them to memory. Still, when surprise recall tests are given after lists have been presented under these conditions, subjects perform better if the word presentations have been spaced rather than massed.

Other explanations for the distributed practice effect have been based, at least loosely, on Martin's encoding variability hypothesis. Recall that, according to this hypothesis, the more different ways an item is encoded or represented in memory, the easier it will be to recall that item later. Thus, several researchers have speculated that distributed practice may facilitate recall by producing greater encoding variability.

According to one version of this explanation, the contextual stimuli in our environment change as time passes. Thus, when practice is distributed we tend to encounter the same item in several contexts. As a result, we form different representations or encodings for a single item (the item is encoded with a different context on each trial), and the item is relatively easy to recall. When massed practice occurs, encodings are less variable, because each item presentation tends to occur in the same context (see, for example, D'Agostino & DeRemer, 1973).

Other variations of this hypothesis have suggested that when learning trials are spaced in time, subjects tend to attribute slightly different meanings to a word from one trial to the next (see, for example, Hintzman, 1974). That is, when practice is distributed, a single word will tend to occur in a variety of contexts, each of which helps to encourage a slightly different meaning for the word. In effect, encoding variability occurs because on each trial the meaning of an item is encoded differently.

To this point these encoding variability explanations have been supported in some experiments, but not in others (see, for example, Elmes & Bjork, 1975; Hintzman, Block, & Summers, 1973; Hintzman, Summers, & Block, 1975; Hintzman, Summers, Eki, & Moore, 1975). Most probably the effects of distributed practice are at least partially the result of greater encoding variability. However, it is equally likely that other factors we do not yet understand contribute to this effect (see, for example, Elmes, Dye, & Herdian, 1983; Rose, 1980). Current research on this problem should help to clarify the nature of the distributed practice phenomenon.

The order of item presentation If you have ever attempted to teach the alphabet to a child, you have no doubt seen a particular learning pattern emerge. Most children quickly learn to recite the letters "A, B, C, D." It also takes very little time for most children to learn that the series "W, X, Y, Z" comes at the end. However, children often require numerous recitations before the letters in the middle of the alphabet are committed to memory.

This pattern of learning illustrates an important phenomenon also found in adults. Whenever a set of items is presented in a given order, we almost always learn the first and last items in the list before learning the items in the middle. This learning pattern is called *the serial position effect*. Although such an effect is most often found in serial learning paradigms, it also occurs in free recall learning situations when only a single list presentation is given.

One example of the serial position effect can be seen in the results of a study conducted by Murdock (1962). Murdock gave one group of subjects a single presentation of a list of 20 common words. He then asked the subjects to recall the list in any order they desired. Figure 6.2 shows the probability of recalling a given

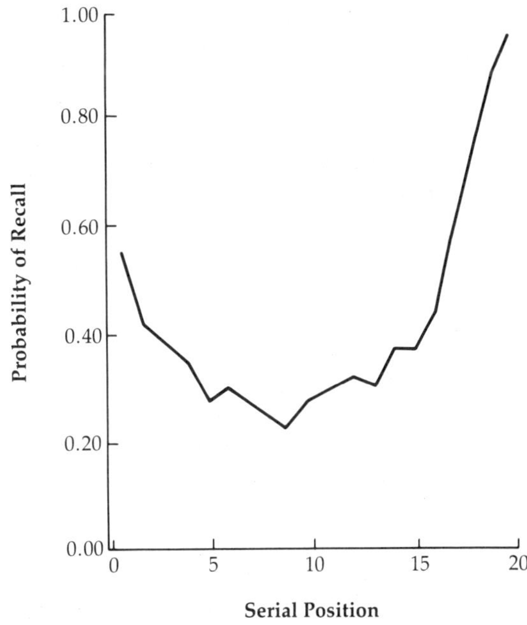

FIGURE 6.2 The probability of recalling an item depending on the serial position of that item in a list. (After Murdock, 1962.)

item depending on the serial position of the item in the presented list. As you can see, the subjects recalled the latter items in the list best. They also showed reasonably good recall for the initial items. However, recall of the intermediate items was generally poor. This phenomenon is extremely robust, and it occurs under a wide variety of circumstances.

One of the earliest attempts to account for this effect was based on a view of serial learning first proposed by Ebbinghaus (1885), who assumed that subjects form two kinds of associations when learning a serial list. First, subjects associate each item in the list with the next adjacent item. Thus, if the list "house–car–man–apple" is presented, subjects will associate "house" with "car," "car" with "man," and so forth. In effect, this view states that each item in a serial list serves as the stimulus for the next item in the list and the response for the preceding item.

In addition to these adjacent associations, Ebbinghaus proposed that subjects form weaker associations between nonadjacent items. He called these additional item links *remote associations*. From our list of items above, an association between "house" and "apple" is an example of a remote association. Ebbinghaus claimed that to learn a serial list in the correct order, a subject must strengthen adjacent associations and weaken remote associations. Only then will each item serve to trigger the memory of the next item in a list, rather than some other item.

In an effort to explain the serial position effect within this theoretical framework, Hull (1935) and Lepley (1934) suggested that remote associations might be responsible for the phenomenon. Specifically, they hypothesized that an adjacent association is always weakened when it falls between two items that are remotely associated (see Hull et al., 1940, for a complete description of how remote and adjacent associations interact). For example, in the list "house–car–man–apple," the association between "car" and "man" is weakened because these items fall between the remotely associated items "house" and "apple." In effect, remote associations that span or surround an adjacent association always interfere with the formation of that adjacent association.

To understand how this idea accounts for the serial position effect, it is useful to refer to Figure 6.3, which illustrates all the remote associations that can be formed in a seven-item serial list. Numerous remote associations span the middle items in the list, while relatively few remote associations overlap the first and last items. According to Hull and Lepley, it is for this reason that the middle associations in a serial list are normally weaker than associations elsewhere in the list.

Although this explanation of the serial position effect predominated for several years, few contemporary researchers still adhere to this view. One reason for the lessened popularity of this explanation is that the Ebbinghaus view of serial learning has been challenged on several grounds. For example, some studies have indicated that subjects may not learn serial lists by associating adjacent items (see, for example, Jensen & Rohwer, 1965; Young, 1962; Young & Casey, 1964). Still other studies have questioned whether remote associations are even formed during serial list learning (see Slamecka, 1964). In effect, few researchers still accept the notion that serial learning involves the formation of simple item associations.

Today, it is commonly assumed that serial learning involves the formation of an integrated memory set (see Feigenbaum & Simon, 1962; Jensen & Rohwer, 1965; Lashley, 1951). That is, a subject simply rehearses the items in a serial list in the presented order. The result of this rehearsal is a single memory, consisting of items ordered in a particular way. In effect, it is now assumed that to understand serial learning, we must first understand how items are processed in memory.

This view of serial learning has led to a number of new explanations for the serial position effect. For example, Feigenbaum and Sim-

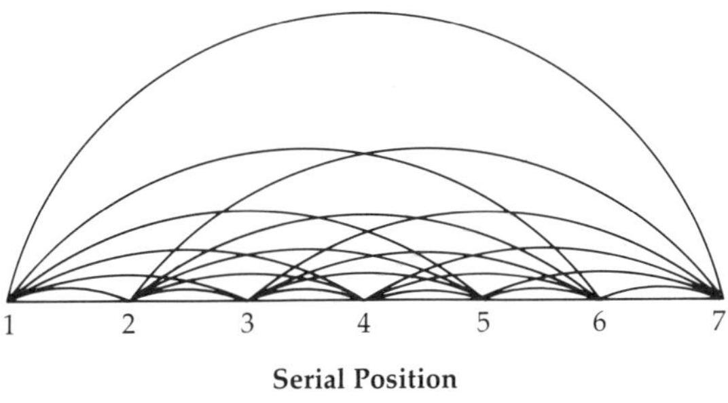

FIGURE 6.3 A schematic illustration of the adjacent and remote associations that are possible in a seven-item serial list. (From Hull, 1935.)

on (1962) have proposed that humans can rehearse only a limited number of items at any given time. Thus when given long list of words to learn, a subject must select a subset of the words for rehearsal on the initial learning trials. Only when these items have been stored in memory will the subject be able to select additional items for rehearsal. According to this view, subjects tend to select initially the first and last items in a serial list, since these items are the most distinctive. Once the first and last items have been stored, items located near these items in the list are rehearsed. The last items to be rehearsed are the middle items in a serial list. Thus, the serial position effect occurs because of the order in which items are selected for rehearsal. This idea is often called the *anchor point hypothesis* because of the assumption that the first and last items serve as anchors or points of reference for the other items in the memory.

Although several experiments tend to support this interpretation of the serial position effect (see, for example, Coppage & Harcum, 1967; Glanzer & Dolinsky, 1965), some researchers have suggested that rehearsal order may be only partially responsible for this phenomenon. For example, it has been proposed that the serial position effect may really consist of two separate phenomena that occur for different reasons. The first phenomenon, called the *primacy effect*, is the subject's tendency to show superior recall for the initial items in a list. The second phenomenon, the superior recall of the last items in a list, is called the *recency effect*.

In recent years it has become popular to offer different explanations for these two effects. To explain the primacy effect, most researchers assume that the initial items in a list receive more rehearsal time simply because they were presented first. This increased rehearsal time means that the initial items will be the most strongly encoded items in permanent memory. Explanations for the recency effect usually center on the idea that the last items in a list are often still being rehearsed at the time of testing. In other words, subjects show superior recall for the last items because these items are still undergoing conscious rehearsal when recall is required. According to this interpretation, the middle items in a serial list should always be more difficult to recall, because these items were not rehearsed as much as the first items and are not being consciously rehearsed at the time of testing.

This interpretation of the serial position effect makes a number of testable predictions. One such prediction is that the recency effect should go away if a recall test is delayed after presentation of a list. Delaying the recall test should decrease the probability that a subject will still be rehearsing the end items at the time of testing. Several studies have confirmed this prediction (see, for example, Craik, 1970; Glanzer & Cunitz, 1966). When subjects who have been given a serial list are tested after a long delay, they still show superior recall for the initial items in the list, but the recency effect tends to disappear. This and numerous other findings lend strong support to the idea that the serial position effect may really consist of two effects that occur for different reasons. In any event, it is now clear that a complete explanation for the serial position phenomenon requires an understanding of how we process items in order to store them in memory.

Characteristics of the Verbal Items

It is obvious from personal experience that certain kinds of verbal materials are easier to learn than others. Still, in most cases, we simply accept this circumstance without considering what it is that makes some items "learnable" and others difficult to learn. Researchers have identified at least two item characteristics that have a powerful influence on ease of learning. The first is the meaningfulness of the items and the second is the degree to which items in a given set are similar to each other. Let's begin by examining the role of item meaningfulness.

Meaningfulness Among Verbal learning researchers, the term "meaningfulness" has had several definitions. Some term an item meaningful when a subject can think of several word associates for that item. For example, the word "mother" would be thought of as meaningful because it immediately reminds us of "father," "family," "brother," "sister," "love," and so on. The word "gyroscope" would be less meaningful because it is associated with far fewer words in our vocabulary. As we mentioned earlier, both words and nonsense syllables have often been scaled in terms of meaningfulness by assessing the number of word associates subjects have for a given item (Archer, 1960; Glaze, 1928; Noble, 1952).

When meaningfulness is defined in this manner, it is clear that the rate of learning is directly related to the meaningfulness of the verbal items. For example, Cieutat, Stockwell, and Noble (1958) presented a different paired associates list to each of four groups of subjects. One group was given a list in which both the stimulus and response terms were highly meaningful according to Noble's (1952) scale of word associates (H/H). A second group received a list having low meaningful stimulus and response terms (L/L). The list presented to the third group had highly meaningful stimulus terms and low meaningful response terms (H/L). The final group's list consisted of low meaningful stimulus terms and high meaningful response terms (L/H). The rates of learning for each of these lists are shown in Figure 6.4. Clearly, learning was fastest in the group having highly meaningful stimulus *and* response items. When both the stimulus and response terms were low in meaningfulness, learning was slow. Intermediate rates of learning occurred when the lists were mixed in terms of meaningfulness. The same effect of meaningfulness is commonly found in the other Verbal learning paradigms (see Underwood, 1966).

Meaningfulness also can be defined in terms of word familiarity. According to this view, words that occur with greater *frequency* in our written or verbal communications become more familiar or more meaningful to us. And, just as researchers have rated words in terms of their association value, others have scaled common words with respect to their frequency in the written language (see, for example, Thorndike & Lorge, 1944). When meaningfulness is defined in terms of frequency of use, the effect of meaningfulness on rate of learning is again clear. Words that are frequently used are learned faster than words

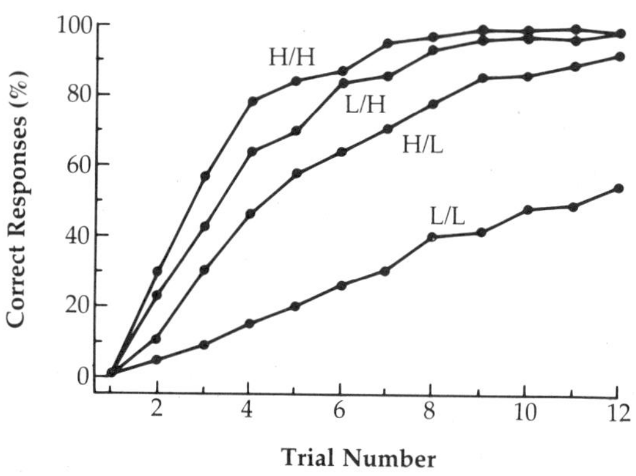

FIGURE 6.4 The rate of paired associates learning as a function of the meaningfulness of the stimulus and response terms: H = high meaningfulness and L = low meaningfulness. (From Cieutat, Stockwell, and Noble, 1958.)

that occur less frequently (see, for example, Deese, 1959; Hall, 1954; Postman, 1962b).

Still another way to define meaningfulness is in terms of the *imagery value* of a word —that is, the degree to which a word elicits a clear mental picture in a subject. If you hear the word "automobile," for example, you can easily form a vivid image of the object represented by that word. The term "freedom," however, does not evoke such a well-defined image. According to this definition, "automobile" is more meaningful than "freedom" because the first term evokes a sharper image than the second. Several studies have shown that words that are high in imagery values are easier to learn that those with low imagery values (see, for example, Paivio, Smythe, & Yuille, 1968).

In addition to these definitions, researchers have identified other variables that probably contribute to item meaningfulness. For example, some have suggested that pronounceability affects the meaningfulness of an item (Underwood & Schulz, 1960). Others have proposed that items are more meaningful when they contain letter strings that occur with great frequency. For example, the trigram RQN is less meaningful than REN, simply because we are used to seeing the letter E rather than the letter Q following an R (Underwood & Schulz, 1960). As with other measures of meaningfulness, these measures also are related directly to the rate of learning verbal items. The more pronounceable a word is or the more familiar a word's letter strings are, the faster the word is learned.

Researchers have never actually agreed on a single "best" measure of meaningfulness. It is obvious that all the measures used are highly related. For example, words with common letter strings are likely to be easier to pronounce. When words are easy to pronounce, they are likely to be used more frequently in written and verbal communication. And, the more often we use a word, the more likely it is that we will have word associates and images attached to it. Thus, all these measures probably reflect some aspect of a word's meaningfulness. Furthermore, all these measures are strongly related to the rate of Verbal learning.

Item similarity A second variable that has robust effects on Verbal learning is the degree of similarity among items in a list or set. As we have seen, item meaningfulness facilitates acquisition in all Verbal learning paradigms. The effects of item similarity are not nearly as consistent. First of all, these effects depend on the way in which items in a list are similar. Second, the similarity of items affects acquisition differently depending on which paradigm is studied. As a matter of fact, these differential effects of similarity have contributed greatly to our understanding of how the Verbal learning paradigms differ. We will begin by looking at the different kinds of similarity that can exist between items. Then we will examine the effects of these different kinds of similarity in the various Verbal learning paradigms.

For the most part, researchers have concentrated on three types of item similarity. The first type, called *formal similarity,* refers to the degree to which items share the same letters. For example, the words "run," "gun," and "sun" have a high degree of formal similarity because all three words contain the letters "un." The words "run," "lip," and "set," which contain no common letters, have low formal similarity. In most cases, words that are high in formal similarity look and sound the same.

A second way in which items may be similar is in terms of their meanings. *Meaningful similarity* refers to the degree to which items are synonymous. The words "gun," "pistol," and "revolver" have high meaningful similarity, since all three may refer to the same object. You should note that these three words have very little formal similarity, because they contain almost none of the same letter strings.

Finally, some words are similar because they refer to objects that belong to the same conceptual category. This type of similarity, called *conceptual similarity,* can be seen in the words "gun," "knife," and "spear." These three words share few common letters and refer to very different objects. They are similar, however, in that they designate weapons. In the same sense, the words "bus," "train," and "car" are conceptually similar, since each refers to a mode of transportation.

Now, assume that you are attempting to learn a set or a list of words that are either formally, meaningfully, or conceptually similar. How will these different kinds of similarities affect your ability to learn? As we have mentioned, the effects of similarity are rather complex, and they depend a great deal on the requirements of the learning task. Probably, the simplest effects of similarity can be seen in a free recall learning situation.

In free recall learning, if the items to be learned are high in either meaningful or conceptual similarity, the rate of acquisition will be faster (see, for example, Ekstrand & Underwood, 1963; Underwood, Runquist, & Schulz, 1959). The reason for this facilitation of learning should be obvious, given our previous discussions. In free recall learning, subjects usually group similar items together, to be able to recall them more easily. Let's assume, for example, that all the words in a set belong to the same conceptual category. Thus, if subjects simply remember the conceptual category name (for example, weapons), they will have a cue that helps to remind them of all the individual words in the set. If all the items belonged to different categories, no one cue would be available to help the subjects recall the individual items. Thus, it is not surprising that high meaningful or conceptual similarity facilitates learning a free recall list.

The effects of formal similarity on free recall learning are less clear. In some cases this type of similarity seems to have little effect on such learning (Horowitz, 1961), while in other cases it even appears to retard acquisition (Underwood, Ekstrand, & Keppel, 1964). To understand this effect, consider that thousands of words can share at least one common letter. How many words, for example, contain the letter "e"? Just because words have one or two common letters does not necessarily make this information useful to a subject who is trying to remember the particular words in a given list. In some cases, attempting to use this information to recall the individual items may actually retard learning by preventing the subject from using a more effective strategy.

In paired associates learning, the effects of item similarity are particularly complex. This is partly because we can vary the similarity of either the stimulus terms or the response terms in a paired associates list. In addition, however, paired associates learning is usually presumed to involve *at least* two separate learning stages that can be differentially influenced by variations in similarity. Thus, before examining the effects of similarity in this paradigm, it will be useful to look briefly at how the learning of a paired associates list is usually conceptualized.

According to many researchers, the paired associates task involves at least two distinct learning stages. First, subjects attempt to learn the response terms in the list, much as they would learn a free recall set. By doing this, each subject forms a pool of possible responses to the stimulus terms. Second, after the response terms have been learned as a set, subjects begin to associate individual responses from that set with the appropriate stimulus terms. This involves differentiating the stimulus terms from each other (so that they represent distinct stimulus items) and then joining the appropriate response to each distinct stimulus (see Polson, Restle, & Polson, 1965; Underwood, Runquist, & Schulz, 1959).

Given this conceptualization of the paired associates task, we can now more readily understand some of the similarity effects in this paradigm. First, if the stimulus terms in a paired associates list are similar, the rate of learning is retarded. Retardation occurs regardless of whether the stimulus terms are similar formally (Joinson & Runquist, 1968), meaningfully (Beecroft, 1956), or conceptually (Underwood, Ekstrand, & Keppel, 1965). The reason for this debilitating effect of similarity appears obvious. The more similar the stimulus terms are, the more difficult it is for a subject to discriminate between the items. For example, a subject who associates the stimulus term "run" with the response term "lamp" will tend to make the same response (that is, "lamp") to any similar stimulus (for example, "fun"). As we mentioned in Chapter 5, this tendency is called stimulus generalization. Thus, paired associates learning is easier, the more distinctly different the stimulus terms are.

Variations in the similarity of the response terms in a paired associates list usually have little or no effect on the overall rate of learning (see, for example, Underwood, Ekstrand, & Keppel, 1965). However, this does not mean that the similarity among response terms has no effect at all. Underwood, Runquist, and Schulz (1959) conducted an experiment in which two groups received different paired associates lists. For one group the stimulus terms were all nonsense syllables, while the response terms were synonymous (for example, "cheerful," "carefree," and "pleasant"). The list presented to the second group contained the same stimulus terms used for group 1. However, this group's response terms consisted of a set of unrelated words (for example, "spicy," "modern," and "rounded").

Each of these groups was to learn the appropriate paired associates list. However, after every few trials, each subject was also given a free recall test for the response terms alone. The researchers found that the group exposed to the related response terms learned the set of responses much faster than the group exposed to the unrelated terms. This confirms our previous conclusion that similarity can enhance free recall learning. However, the paired associates list was learned somewhat faster by the group that had the unrelated response terms. This suggests that high similarity can enhance one stage of paired associates learning—namely, the response learning stage. However, this advantage is clearly offset by some negative influence of similarity on the stimulus–response association stage of learning. Since response item similarity affects the two stages of paired associates learning differently, the overall effect of similarity is usually negligible.

Finally, the effects of item similarity on serial learning are generally disruptive. Underwood and Goad (1951) had subjects learn serial lists consisting of either similar or dissimilar adjectives. They found that learning was significantly faster for the dissimilar adjectives than for the similar words. The same results have been obtained in studies varying the formal similarity among items in a serial list (see, for example, Underwood, 1952).

One factor that may contribute to this effect is a subject's tendency to group similar items together. In serial learning, subjects must learn items in the order provided by the experimenter. However, if the serial list contains items that are similar, subjects may group the items on the basis of their similarities. This grouping strategy may lead subjects to learn the items in an order that is different from the one required. In effect, the grouping strategy that is fostered by item similarity may interfere with learning items in an experimenter-supplied order.

In summary, the effects of item similarity on Verbal learning are often robust, but these effects differ substantially depending on the particular learning paradigm that is used. These paradigm-specific effects suggest at least two conclusions. First, high similarity among items seems to enhance learning whenever the learning paradigm allows for a subjective grouping of the items. Thus, both free recall learning and the response learning stage of paired associates learning seem to benefit from similarity among items. On the other hand, high item similarity usually retards learning when a subject must associate an item with a particular stimulus term or a specific position in a serial order. For this reason, item similarity tends to have negative effects on both serial learning and the associative phase of the paired associates task.

Subject Strategies

We have noted previously that humans take an active role in learning verbal materials. Thus, subjects often modify items or restructure item sets in some manner as they attempt to learn the set more efficiently. Now we are ready to describe some of the strategies subjects use and to assess the effectiveness of these strategies in different learning situations.

Coding: The transformation of verbal items

We have already seen that one factor that influences learning is the meaningfulness of verbal items. Highly meaningful words are learned more easily than words with low meaningfulness. Thus, one strategy subjects use in learning a group of items is to transform low meaningful items into similar words having more meaning. For example, one way to learn a list of nonsense syllables such as "yob," "nus," and "piz" is to rearrange the letters in each syllable to form a common word (in this case, "boy," "sun," and "zip"). Similarly, a real word such as "psalm" that is low in meaningfulness can be transformed into the word "palms," which is a more meaningful word. This strategy is called *coding* because it involves learning a code for a given item rather than learning the item as it is presented. In some Verbal learning experiments it has been estimated that more than half of all subjects employ such a strategy, even when they have received no instructions to do so (see, for example, Underwood & Keppel, 1963).

The advantage of a coding strategy is obvious. Less obvious, however, are the disadvantages. Whenever we code an item in order to learn it, we must be able to decode the transformed item in order to remember the item that was actually presented. For example, transforming the syllable "yob" into "boy" is an easy way of learning the three letters in the syllable. However, we must be able to remember that "boy" actually stands for "yob" and not for the syllable "oyb" if this strategy is to be effective. In some cases decoding problems can offset the advantages of transforming an item into a meaningful term.

Both the advantages and the disadvantages of the coding strategy have been seen in laboratory experiments. In one study, for example, Underwood and Keppel (1963) required their subjects to learn a list of 10 nonsense syllables in a free recall situation. Each of the 10 syllables contained three letters that could be rearranged to form a common word. The experimenters instructed half the subjects to use the letter rearrangement as a coding strategy and gave no instructions to the remaining subjects. On the free recall test, half the subjects in each of these conditions were given a standard test in which they were asked to recall the syllables as they were presented originally. This test required decoding of any coded items. The remaining subjects in each condition were allowed to recall the letters in the items in any order they desired. Obviously, this test required no decoding of the transformed items.

The results of the study were clear. Subjects who were instructed to code showed better recall of the items when they were able to recall the letters in any order. However, if the test required decoding of the transformed items, subjects using the coding strategy actually performed more poorly. These results indicate that coding can facilitate the learning of an item's letters. However, coding does not necessarily facilitate recall of the items actually presented. In some cases, difficulties in decoding a transformed item may even make the coding strategy detrimental. This conclusion raises an important question. Since recall almost always requires the decoding of a transformed item, is a coding strategy ever useful?

This question has been addressed in an excellent series of experiments by Underwood and Erlebacher (1965). These experimenters assumed that the successful use of a coding strategy involves two steps. First, subjects must be able to transform an item into a more meaningful term. Second, they must be able to remember a rule for decoding that item. For example, a subject learning the syllable "nus" must first transform the item into a word such as "sun." Then, however, the subject must decode "sun" by using a rule. In this case, the rule would be simply to reverse the letters in the code to retrieve the original item. Underwood and Erlebacher hypothesized that coding strategies should facilitate learning and recall in situations featuring simple decoding rules. However, this strategy should be less successful as the difficulty of the decoding rules is increased.

To test this hypothesis, they gave subjects lists of syllables that could be transformed into common words. Some subjects were given a list of items that could be coded and decoded using a single rule. For example, all the items "yob," "nus," and "piz" can be coded simply by reversing the letters in the syllable and decoded by reversing the letters in the code. Other subjects received lists of items that would involve multiple decoding rules. For example, "yob," "uns," and" "pzi" also can be transformed into common words. However, a different letter rearrangement rule is required to decode each of the common words. Underwood and Erlebacher found that coding clearly facilitated learning when a single rule could be used to decode every transformed item in the list. However, coding produced no advantages when subjects had to use multiple rules for decoding their coded items. The conclusions from these studies are clear. Coding is a popular strategy for learning verbal items. However, coding facilitates learning only when the decoding of a transformed item is easy. When decoding becomes difficult, the coding strategy may even interfere with a subject's ability to learn.

Clustering: The transformation of item order
In our discussion of free recall learning we noted that subjects seldom recall a list of items in the presented order. Instead, subjects tend to group similar items together regardless of where in the presented list these items originally appeared. When a subject reorganizes the order of a free recall list such that similar items are learned together, we call the process *clustering*.

The discovery of the clustering strategy is most often attributed to Bousfield (1953). In one experiment Bousfield presented subjects with a 60-word free recall list. Each word in the list could be placed in one of four different conceptual categories (for example, a type of food or a type of furniture). However, the 60 words were presented in random order without regard to category membership. Bousfield found that virtually all subjects recalled the words in four distinct groupings that corresponded to the four conceptual categories. In other words, all items belonging to category 1 were recalled together, then all items in category 2, and so forth. This grouping together of conceptually similar words is a clear example of the clustering strategy (also see Jenkins & Russell, 1952, for an example of clustering based on word associations).

Aside from the clustering that occurs when items belong to obvious categories, subjects also attempt to cluster words even when a list contains no apparent item similarities. This type of clustering has been termed *subjective organization* (Tulving, 1972). The term subjective organization refers to the fact that a subject given a list of unrelated words often does two things. First, the subject recalls the items in an order different from the one that occurred during item presentation. Second, the subject recalls the items in a consistent order on each trial. Thus from one trial to the next, a given subject groups the same items together even though these items may have little relationship in the eyes of the experimenter. The occurrence of subjective organization illustrates an important point. A subject's tendency to cluster a free recall list is so strong that this strategy is used even when words are very dissimilar and are difficult to group by any obvious means.

As we saw in our discussion of coding, the mere fact that a subject uses a strategy does not make that strategy effective. Thus, we are led to ask whether clustering actually facilitates the learning and retention of a free recall list. While this question seems straightforward, it is difficult to answer with any confidence. Clustering, after all, is an internal strategy or process that cannot be observed. It is, therefore, impossible to manipulate clustering directly in an experiment. We can only manipulate variables that we presume will affect clustering and then measure the effects of these variables on learning. Most studies that have taken this approach point to the same conclusion. Factors that presumably enhance clustering also facilitate free recall learning. In other words, clustering appears to be positively correlated with effective learning and recall.

One example of this correlation can be seen in an experiment by Underwood (1964) in which one group of subjects was given a single presentation of a free recall list consisting of 16 words. Each of the words could be placed into one of four conceptual categories. Thus, the words in this list could be clustered easily. A second group of subjects received a list of 16 unrelated words. Underwood found that the clustering strategy was used extensively by the subjects who received the categorized list. He also found that subjects recalled significantly more words from this list (14.6) than from the unrelated list (11.3). In effect, subjects recalled more words when the list was easy to cluster than when unrelated words were presented.

Similar findings have come from studies in which subjective organization has been measured. For example, Tulving (1962) devised a measure of subjective organization that depended on whether a subject recalled unrelated items in a consistent order from trial to trial. He found that recall performance increased, the more a person used subjective organization. Likewise, subjects who are encouraged to cluster an unrelated group of items recall better than subjects who are not instructed to cluster (Mayhew, 1967). Finally, recall performance often decreases when subjects are instructed to remember each item in a list individually and not to group items together (Allen, 1968). Thus, almost any procedure that encourages the clustering strategy also improves recall performance.

One final piece of evidence that illustrates the correlation between clustering and recall comes from a study by Thompson, Hamlin, and Roenker (1972). These experimenters presented three 48-item lists to their subjects. Each list could be clustered by splitting the items into four 12-item categories. On the basis of recall order, the subjects were divided into those who used clustering (high clusterers) and those who did not (low clusterers). It was found that the high clusterers recalled significantly more items than the subjects who clustered less often.

In an effort to understand how clustering might affect recall, several researchers have attempted to analyze the clustering process in more detail. Probably the best analysis of clustering has been proposed by Bower (1972a). Bower suggests that clustering involves three distinct steps. First, a subject must recognize that the words in a list can be placed into different categories. If no obvious categories exist, a subject must devise some subjective categories into which the words can be placed. Second, once the categories have been delineated, a subject must associate each word in the list with the appropriate category name. Finally, at the time of testing, a subject must recall each category name. Recalling each category name should act as a cue for all the words associated with that category name. Thus, according to this view, clustering facilitates recall by giving a subject a cue (the category name) that helps a subject remember specific items in a list.

Several studies tend to support this characterization of clustering. For example, if the first step in clustering involves recognizing possible categories of items, any manipulation that facilitates this recognition should enhance both clustering and recall. We have already seen that lists having obvious categories are clustered to a greater extent than those in which categories are less obvious. Also, we have seen that subjects show better recall for lists that have easily recognizable categories (Underwood, 1964). There are also studies in which categories have been made more recognizable by presenting all the words in a given category together, rather than presenting items in a random order. This manipulation increases both clustering and recall performance (Cofer, Bruce, & Reicher, 1966).

Second, if Bower's view is correct, clustering and recall should be enhanced by any manipulation that makes it easier for a subject to associate items with a category name. Several studies indicate that this is the case. For example, Cofer, Bruce, and Reicher (1966) constructed two free recall lists that could be categorized by subjects. One list contained words that were frequent examples of each category (for example, "dog" and "cat" are frequent examples of the animal category), while the other list consisted of words that were less frequent examples of each category ("camel" and "zebra" are less frequent examples of the animal category). They reasoned that high frequency example words should be easier to associate with a category name than the low frequency example words. They found that both clustering and recall were better using the high frequency list.

Finally, according to Bower's hypothesis, the effects of clustering on recall should be more pronounced when the category names in a list are easier to recall during testing. This prediction also has been supported. In one study, for example, Tulving and Pearlstone (1966) presented subjects with free recall lists consisting of either 12, 24, or 48 items. For each list length they also varied the number of categories into which the items could be placed (one, two, or four categories). For example, some subjects who received the 12-item list could cluster the items into a single category, while others would have to cluster the list into two or four categories. Most important in the present context were the manipulations used at the time of testing. Some subjects were actually given the category names as cues (cued recall group), while the remaining subjects (noncued recall group) received no such suggestions. Figure 6.5 shows the results of these manipulations. Clearly, subjects given the category names as cues performed much better on the recall test.

In summary, the data we have reviewed are consistent with the notion that clustering can facilitate the learning and retention of a free recall list. Furthermore, these data suggest that clustering may influence recall in a particular manner. Apparently, clustering works by pro-

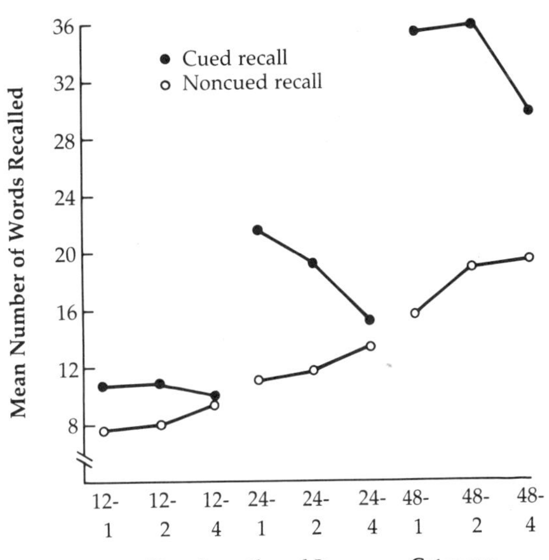

FIGURE 6.5 The number of words recalled from a free recall list when subjects are either cued or not cued with category names. (From Tulving and Pearlstone, 1966.)

viding a subject with category name cues that help the person recall the individual words in a list.

The use of mental imagery Each year when I discuss learning strategies with the students in my own course, I give them two paired associates lists to learn. Both lists contain 12 pairs of commonly used nouns. I present the first list of pairs once at the rate of about one pair every 3 seconds. I then present the stimulus terms and ask the students to write down the response terms. On the average, students correctly recall between five and seven responses. Almost no one remembers all the items.

Next, I present the second list of pairs in the same manner. However, before presenting the list I instruct the students to use a particular strategy. They are told that when they hear a word pair such as "hammer–lamp," they should try to form a mental image or picture of these two items together. For example, they might try to imagine a hammer smashing into a lamp. When students use this technique, they are often surprised at its effectiveness. The vast majority of students recall all the correct responses. The few who do not usually miss only one or two. Obviously, this demonstration is not a controlled experiment. It does, however, illustrate an important point. The use of mental pictures or images is one of the most powerful strategies a subject can employ to learn verbal items.

To study the effectiveness of imagery in Verbal learning paradigms, researchers have available two approaches. The first is to manipulate the imagery value of items in a list to see whether learning and recall of the items are affected. We have alluded to these studies before in our discussion of item meaningfulness. In one such set of experiments conducted by Paivio and his colleagues (Paivio, Smythe, & Yuille, 1968), subjects were presented with paired associates lists consisting of noun pairs of four different types. In one type both the stimulus and response items were rated high in imagery value (high/high type). That is, previous subjects had rated these items as easy to imagine. A second type of pair consisted of stimulus and response terms that were low in imagery value or were difficult to imagine (low/low). The two remaining types had either high imagery value stimulus terms (high/low) or high imagery value response terms (low/high). Figure 6.6 shows the results of this study.

Clearly, when it is easy to form images of both the stimulus and response terms (high/high type), recall of the pairs is excellent. Intermediate recall performance occurs when one of the terms has high imagery value and the other does not. When both terms are difficult to imagine, recall is very poor. These findings obviously suggest that a subject's ability to use imagery can facilitate the learning of verbal items. Such findings are made even more impressive, however, when we consider one other aspect of this experiment, namely, that the words used were all equated in terms of association value. That is, all these words were equally meaningful based on the number of word associates they produced, such that the imagery value of each word affected learning over and above any effects of meaningfulness.

A second approach to studying the effects of imagery has been to vary the instructions given to subjects. This is essentially the type of manipulation used in the classroom demonstration described above. Again, the results of such studies have been consistent. Subjects who are instructed to learn a paired associates list by forming images of the stimulus and response terms perform much better than subjects who are given no instructions (see, for example, Bower, 1972b). Likewise, instructions to use imagery have even been found to facilitate serial learning. In one such study, Delin (1969) instructed some subjects to link adjacent items in a serial list together using images, while other subjects were not so instructed. Subjects who received the imagery

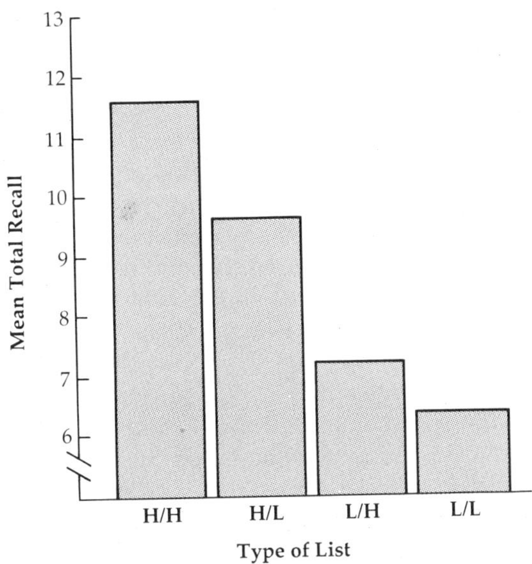

FIGURE 6.6 The recall of paired associates as a function of the imagery value of the stimulus and response terms: H = high imagery value and L = low imagery value. (From Paivio, Smythe, and Yuille, 1968.)

instructions learned the list faster and recalled it better than the noninstructed group.

A specific type of imagery instruction appears to be particularly effective when subjects are learning a serial or a free recall list. These instructions are to use an imagery technique called the *Method of Loci,* which involves forming a mental image of a familiar set of spatial locations. For example, if you know the route between your house and the house of a friend, you can easily picture yourself driving between the two houses. You know that as you drive you pass certain cross-streets in a particular sequence. For example, the first major cross-street after your house may be Elm Street. The next cross-street may be Central Avenue, followed by Princeton Drive. In other words, simply by making the familiar trip in your imagination, you automatically remember a well-ordered sequence of spatial locations.

Now, assume you have the following serial list of items to learn: "dog," "lamp," "book," "flower," "sofa," "horse," "table," and "chalk." To learn the list you must not only learn each word, but you also must remember the order of presentation. One simple procedure for learning the list is to imagine each item at one of the spatial locations in your imaginary trip. For example, you might begin by forming an image of a dog (the first word in your list) standing on the corner of Elm Street (the first cross-street in your imaginary trip). You would then form an image linking the second word in your list to the second cross-street in your trip. Once comparable images have been formed for each item, remembering the items in order is simple. All you must do is imagine yourself driving to your friend's house. Each cross-street you pass reminds you of the corresponding word in the list. In effect, you maintain the order of a new list by linking it to an imaginary list of spatial locations that already has a familiar order.

This imagery strategy may sound complex. However, with minimal practice subjects usually become proficient at its use. Groninger (1971), for example, instructed college students to imagine a sequence of 25 spatial locations on their campus. He then gave the subjects a list of 25 words to learn using the Method of Loci. Students who used this technique showed significantly better recall of the 25 words than subjects who were given no imagery instructions. Similar facilitation using the Method of Loci has been reported in other experiments (see, for example, Ross & Lawrence, 1968).

A second imagery technique that is highly related to the Method of Loci is the *pegword technique.* To use this technique, a subject must begin by knowing a list of items in some order. For example, if you have a favorite major league baseball team, you probably know the names of the starting players and the order in which they usually bat. Alternatively, you may remember the grammar school teachers you had in each of the first six grades. If you know such a list, you can use it to learn a novel list in much the same way as you would use the Method of Loci, simply by forming an image that links the first item in your familiar list with the first item in the novel list. You would then form images for each subsequent pair of items from the two lists. To remember the novel list, you would merely recite the familiar list, and each item on it would serve as a cue for a novel list item. Several studies have documented the effectiveness of the pegword technique (see, for example, G. A. Miller, Galanter, & Pribram, 1960; Paivio, 1969).

It is obvious that under many conditions, manipulations that encourage the use of imagery facilitate Verbal learning. Still, the effectiveness of the image-forming strategy depends on a variety of factors. First of all, of course, some words provoke less vivid images than others. Although it is easy to form an image of a door, it is quite difficult to form an image that represents "justice." Paivio (1971) has suggested that our ability to form an image of a word depends on that word's concreteness. Concrete nouns represent real, visible objects in the environment. On the other hand, words such as "justice", "integrity," and "freedom" are abstract because instead of naming real objects they name states of being or nonphysical characteristics. According to Paivio, image-forming strategies are most effective when concrete terms are used simply because these provoke more vivid images.

A second factor that influences imagery effectiveness is the type of image a subject uses or is instructed to use. This point was illustrated when Wollen, Weber, and Lowry (1972) sought to test the often-cited assumption that bizarre or unusual images are more effective than common images in learning verbal items. The experimenters gave subjects a list of paired associates items to learn. All the items were names for concrete objects. Instead of instructing the subjects to form images of each item pair together, they supplied pictures of each item pair and instructed the subjects to form an image of each picture. For example, if the words to be associated were "cigar" and "piano," the subjects were shown a picture that contained a cigar and piano in some arrangement.

In this experiment, however, the pictures of item pairs differed along two dimensions. First, some pictures contained bizarre or strange illustrations of the objects, while others contained ordinary, common drawings. Second, some pictures showed the two items together so that the items appeared to be interacting in some way. Other pictures showed the items separately. By using such combinations, the investigators had four experimental conditions based on the four types of pictures: bizarre–interacting, bizarre–noninteracting, common–interacting, and common–noninteracting. Figure 6.7 contains examples of these four picture types for the words "cigar" and "piano."

The results of this manipulation were somewhat surprising. Subjects who were encouraged to use interacting images learned the list of words better than those given the non–interacting pictures. However, the use of bizarre images did nothing to improve performance. Apparently, the effectiveness of image formation depends on how close together two objects are within the image. Once an interacting image has been formed, it seems to matter very little whether the image is commonplace or unusual. The same finding has been reported when young children, rather than young adults, are used as subjects (Reese, 1965).

Thus, it is clear that under certain conditions, encouraging subjects to form mental images can facilitate Verbal learning and recall. What is less clear, however, is *how* imagery instructions influence learning. One explanation, proposed by Paivio (1971), is termed the *dual-coding hypothesis.* According to this view, when humans learn about verbal items they often code or represent these items in memory in terms of the items' meanings. However, when subjects are asked to form images, they

Noninteracting, Nonbizarre

Piano Cigar

Noninteracting, Bizarre

Piano Cigar

Interacting, Nonbizarre

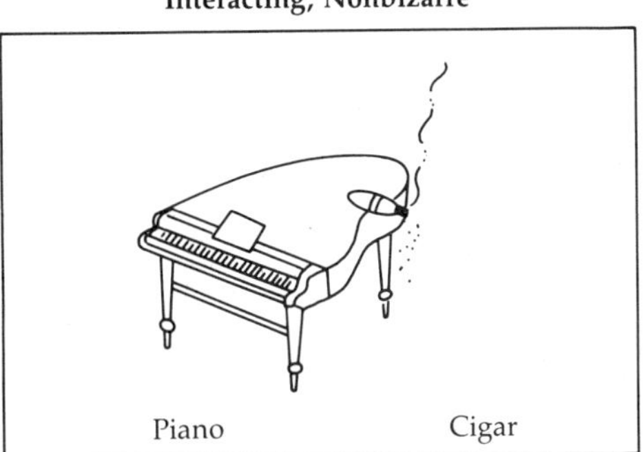

Interacting, Bizarre

FIGURE 6.7 Examples of pictures used by Wollen, Weber, and Lowry (1972) to induce subjects to form images of different kinds.

also represent the items in terms of a visual or pictorial code. In effect, Paivio suggests that imagery facilitates learning and recall because it results in an additional code that a subject can use when trying to remember an item.

An alternative view held by several theorists (Anderson, 1978; Anderson & Bower, 1973; Intraub, 1979; Pylyshyn, 1973) is that all items are represented in terms of a single code in memory. According to this view, imagery instructions do not lead to pictorial codes, but instead cause a subject to form a more elaborate meaning code for a word. In other words, imagery instructions simply force the subject to "think about" or process a word more fully than he or she would have done otherwise. Better recall is presumed to result from the formation of a more elaborate code.

Distinguishing between these views has proved to be difficult. Each hypothesis has garnered substantial experimental support. One experiment, however, is particularly interesting as it relates to this controversy. Jonides, Kahn, and Rozin (1975) used imagery instructions in a typical Verbal learning experiment. Like other experimenters, these researchers found that imagery instructions facilitated learning and recall. This experiment was unusual, however, in that all the subjects had been blind since birth. Thus, it is hard to imagine how they could have formed visual or pictorial images when instructed to do so. Nevertheless, the instructions did result in better recall. These findings suggest that imagery instructions can affect learning and recall even when they do not result in the formation of a visual image. Such a result obviously is consistent with the idea that imagery instructions facilitate performance by promoting more elaborate meaning codes. Still, it is possible that imagery instructions may have different influences on sighted subjects.

Natural language mediation The final Verbal learning strategy we should note is the use of *natural language mediation.* This strategy involves linking items together on the basis of common language associations we have for these items. For example, to learn to associate the words "dog" and "purr," we can place the word "cat" between the words to be linked. Because "cat" is strongly associated with "dog" and with "purr," the word "dog" will help us remember "cat," and "cat" can help us remember "purr." As another case of natural language mediation, we can link two words by interposing a third word to form a phrase or sentence. To remember that "hammer" and "television" go together, for example, we might remember the phrase "hammer hits television."

The effectiveness of natural language mediation has been shown numerous times. In one experiment, Montague, Adams, and Kiess (1966) required subjects to learn a paired associates list and to report any natural language mediators used. At the time of testing, they asked the subjects to recall not only the word pairs, but also the mediators they had used to learn the pairs. Subjects who used mediators for learning and recalled their mediators during testing remembered more than 70 percent of the correct responses. Subjects who failed to use mediators or could not recall the mediators remembered fewer than 6 percent of the correct responses. Obviously, the use of natural language mediation can be a potent Verbal learning strategy.

Conclusions We have seen that a number of variables can affect the learning and recall of verbal items. However, it is the particular strategy a subject uses that seems to have the greatest influence. This is a critical point, since it indicates the importance of active cognitive processing in Verbal learning. In recent years, the interest in such processing has grown considerably, and now it is the major focus in the study of how verbal materials are learned and remembered. We will see this emphasis very clearly in subsequent chapters when we discuss the concept of memory in greater detail.

Transfer Effects in Verbal Learning

To this point we have seen that our ability to learn verbal materials depends on a variety of factors, including the way verbal items are presented, the characteristics of the items themselves, and the types of learning strategies we use. Although each of these factors plays an important role in Verbal learning, the extent to which such variables influence learning often depends on a person's prior learning experiences. Indeed, our experiences often determine which strategies we will select in learning a new set of items. Likewise, the way we interpret or perceive some new set of items depends heavily on items we have seen and heard before. In effect, learning seldom occurs in a vacuum. Aspects of our prior experience always carry over or *transfer* to present learning situations and influence our ability to learn in the new settings. This influence of prior learning on a new learning experience is called a *transfer effect.*

Transfer effects can be seen in a wide variety of real-life situations. For example, let us assume that you are learning to play bridge. Let us also assume that you have never played any other card game before. Therefore you would have to learn what constitutes a suit, which suits have the highest values, what a "trick" is, what people mean by the term "trump," and so on. You would also need to learn a scoring system, a variety of playing strategies, and some methods of bidding. Even learning the rudiments of bridge represents a monumental task for a first-time card player.

On the other hand, let's assume that an accomplished card player is to be introduced to bridge. Since most card games involve suits, tricks, trumps, and bidding, a person who knows about these matters will have an advantage in learning the basics of bridge. The experienced card player may be a bridge novice, but from other games he has learned there is much that can be applied to the new learning experience. Since, in this case, prior learning affects the rate of learning a new set of materials, we say that a transfer effect is operating.

As you might imagine, some transfer effects are helpful while others are not. We have already seen that learning the rules to one card game can facilitate learning about a second game. When prior learning facilitates learning a new set of items, we say that *positive transfer* has occurred. On the other hand, there are numerous situations in which prior learning makes subsequent learning more difficult than usual. Consider, for example, what occurs when an accomplished baseball player first attempts to learn the game of golf. Swinging a baseball bat and swinging a golf club are very different actions. For this reason, the baseball player's swing may at first be incompatible with the swing necessary to hit a good golf shot. As a result, a baseball player may take longer to learn the correct golf swing than a person with no prior baseball experience. Since, in this example, prior learning makes subsequent learning more difficult, we would say that a *negative transfer effect* had occurred.

Finally, we say that *zero transfer* has occurred when the rate of learning some new set of items is unaffected by a prior learning experience. Zero transfer often results when two learning experiences are highly unrelated. We might expect, for instance, that learning to ride a horse would provide zero transfer to the task of learning to type, since these two tasks have almost no elements in common. We should note, however, that zero transfer can also occur when prior learning produces a combination of positive and negative transfer effects, such that one effect tends to cancel out the other.

Obviously, an understanding of transfer effects is critical for predicting how rapidly a given set of materials will be learned in a laboratory setting. Understanding these effects is also important when looking at learning in real-life situations, since the potential for transfer is so great in our everyday experiences. Now we will look at two categories of transfer effects. The first, called *nonspecific transfer,* includes transfer effects that tend to occur even when two sets of verbal items are relatively unrelated. Then we will look at *specific transfer effects,* which result when two sets of materials are related in some specific fashion.

Nonspecific Transfer

Even when we learn two sets of items that are very different, the mere fact that we have had prior practice in learning can result in a transfer effect. For example, college sophomores often find that they learn course materials more efficiently and obtain better grades than they did as freshmen. This tends to be the case even when the freshman and sophomore courses have little content in common. The reason for this improvement is that sophomores have usually spent a year learning some general skills and study strategies that facilitate later attempts to learn. Such an improvement resulting from general learning factors is one example of a *nonspecific transfer effect.*

In Verbal learning situations, at least two types of nonspecific transfer have been identified. The first of these is termed a *warmup effect.* It is assumed that when learning a group of verbal items, a subject must first get into a particular "set" or "frame of mind" for learning. This set includes a particular posture, a degree of attentiveness, and even a rhythm for studying the items. This set is reached only by practice, and when it has been attained, the subject is ready to learn. Thus, prior learning can influence later learning by, for example, allowing a subject time to "warm up" or acquire the proper set before learning a second group of items. Several studies have shown that allowing subjects to warm up by learning one set of items can have *brief* facilitating effects on learning a second set. For example, Thune (1950) had subjects learn a paired associates list consisting of 10 noun pairs. All subjects had previous experience learning a list of 10 adjective pairs. All subjects were given the same number of trials to learn the adjective pairs, but Thune varied the number of adjective learning trials that directly preceded learning the noun list. Thus some subjects received all the adjective learning trials just before learning the noun list, while other subjects received only a few of their adjective learning trials just before noun learning, having received most of their adjective trials on the previous day. The results of this study are summarized in Figure 6.8, which shows the rate of learning the noun list as a function of the number of adjective learning trials given just beforehand.

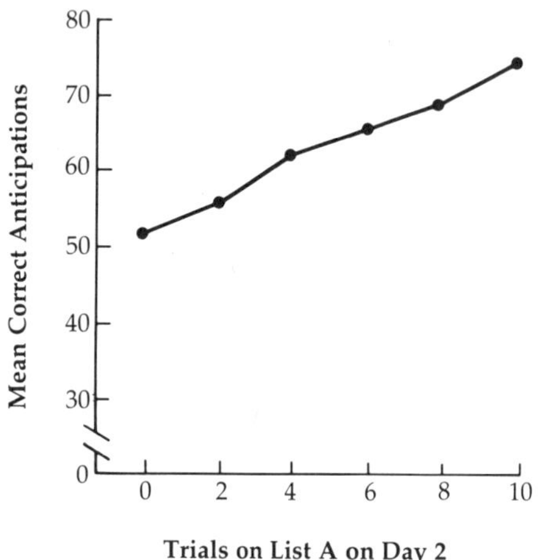

FIGURE 6.8 List learning performance as a function of the number of immediately preceding trials spent learning another list. (From Thune, 1950.)

Two points are evident from Figure 6.8. First, learning the list of adjective pairs produced positive transfer in learning the list of noun pairs. Second, this facilitative effect depended on the amount of first-list practice that shortly preceded learning list 2. This means that learning an unrelated first list can produce a warmup effect that will facilitate learning a second list. However, such effects do not last long. If warm up occurs 24 hours before learning, little positive transfer results.

A second type of nonspecific transfer that occurs in Verbal learning paradigms results from *learning-to-learn*—that is, the tendency of subjects to acquire specific strategies in learning one set of items that can later be used in learning a second set. For example, if a subject learns two serial lists in sequence, the learning of the initial list may make learning the second list easier, even if the items in the two lists are completely unrelated. Furthermore, at least some part of this positive transfer may result because in learning list 1, the subject may acquire serial learning strategies that can be used in learning list 2. Unlike warmup effects, which are relatively short-lived, learning-to-learn effects are relatively long-lasting. In other words, if a subject acquires certain strategies through learning one list of words, these strategies usually can be applied to learning other lists hours or even days later (see, for example, Ward, 1937). It is this learning-to-learn effect that often makes college sophomores more efficient learners than their freshman counterparts.

Specific Transfer

We have seen that nonspecific transfer can occur whenever a subject is given the opportunity to practice with one group of items before learning a second group. These effects depend very little on the specific characteristics of the items that are learned. Still, we should know from our own experiences that transfer effects can also be based on how two sets of items are related. Your ability to learn concepts in a math course may well be facilitated by other courses you have taken in math. However, prior history courses may aid you very little in attempts to master mathematical concepts. Such effects, which depend on the specific characteristics of two item sets, are called *specific transfer effects.*

The study of specific transfer has a long history among Verbal learning researchers. This research has looked at how a variety of list learning procedures affect subsequent list learning attempts (see, for example, Ellis, 1969; Jensen, 1962; Jensen & Rohwer, 1965). We should note, however, that the most thorough analysis of specific transfer has been carried out using the paired associates learning paradigm. The most common procedure has been to have subjects learn first one paired associates list and then a second paired associates list that differs from the first in certain respects. For example, the two lists may have different response terms or different stimulus terms. By using this procedure, researchers are able to assess the transfer that occurs when two lists of items share certain features and differ in terms of others.

The first list a subject learns is usually called an A–B list, where "A" designates a specific set of stimulus terms and "B" refers to a specific set of response terms. The designation applied to the second list in a transfer paradigm tells how the second list differs from the first. If the second list is called an A–C list, for example, it has the same stimulus terms as the first list (A), but the response terms (C) are different. If the second list a subject learns is designated C–B, it has different stimulus terms (C) from the first, but the response terms (B) are the same. Obviously, a second list designated C–D would have both stimulus *and* response terms different from those in list 1.

Two other second-list designations have also been commonly used. These are the A–B' and A–Br designations. A second list that is designated A–B' has the same stimulus terms as list 1 and it has response terms that are similar. For example, if "car" is one of the response terms in list 1, the corresponding response term in list 2 might be "automobile." In a second list of the A–Br type, both the stimulus and response terms are the same as those in list 1; in list 2, however, the response terms are rearranged so that the stimulus–response pairings are different from those used in list 1. The following example shows a typical A–B list and how various transfer lists might vary from A–B.

A–B List
car–book
dog–pen
pipe–paper

C–D	A–C	C–B
ink–boy	car–home	fan–book
rat–sled	dog–lip	hip–pen
cup–chalk	pipe–cake	lock–paper

A–Br	A–B'
car–pen	car–pamphlet
dog–paper	dog–pencil
pipe–book	pipe–page

To understand the specific effects that occur in these various transfer paradigms, it is best to begin by considering the A–B, C–D sequence. When a subject learns an A–B list followed by a C–D list, all the items in the two lists are different. This means that there should be no specific transfer effects in this paradigm, since none of the specific items learned in list 1 are represented in list 2. Still, this does not mean that this paradigm is devoid of transfer. Subjects who learn A–B followed by C–D usually learn C–D faster than those subjects who learn only the C–D list. This facilitation in learning C–D is due to nonspecific kinds of transfer such as the types we have discussed.

Since the A–B, C–D paradigm results in nonspecific transfer, this sequence is often used to provide a baseline against which the other sequences are compared. For example, we can compare subjects who learn an A–B, A–C sequence to those who learn an A–B, C–D sequence. Both sequences should produce nonspecific transfer. This means that any differences in transfer that occur between these sequences should be due to specific transfer effects. How then do these other sequences compare to the A–B, C–D sequence?

The one sequence that produces a reasonably clear positive transfer effect is the A–B, A–B' paradigm. Recall that in this paradigm list 2 responses differ from the list 1 responses, *but* each list 2 response is similar to the corresponding response in list 1. For example, if the pair "ball–dog" occurred in list 1, the corresponding pair in list 2 might be "ball–canine." To understand why learning an A–B list facilitates learning an A–B' list, consider what a subject must do when learning the A–B' list. First of all, from prior A–B learning the subject already has learned the stimulus terms and has associated each one with a particular response. Since the A–B response is similar to the new A–B' response, the A–B response can help to cue the subject to the correct new response. Clearly, the prior learning of an A–B list should make learning the A–B' list easier.

An entirely different effect occurs when either an A–B, A–C, or an A–B, A–Br sequence is learned. In both these paradigms, prior learning of the A–B list retards second-list learning. This effect can be seen in the results of a study by Postman (1962c) in which several transfer paradigms were compared. Figure 6.9 plots the performance of a subject who had already learned an A–B list in learning either a C–D, an A–C, an A–Br, or a C–B list. The fact that A–C and A–Br learning is retarded relative to C–D learning indicates that the first two paradigms produce specific negative transfer effects.

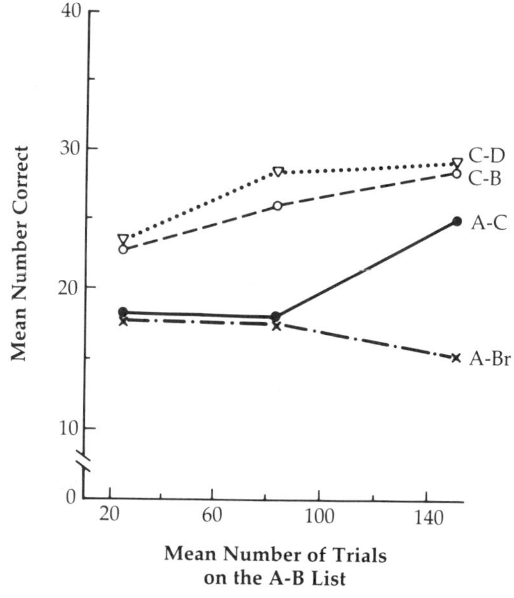

FIGURE 6.9 Correct responses subjects made while learning various types of paired associates lists after varying numbers of A–B list learning trials. (From Postman, 1962c.)

Again, we can see generally why such effects might occur. In both the A–B, A–C and the A–B, A–Br paradigms, subjects must learn to associate a new response to a stimulus that has been associated with another response. In these cases, however, the A–B response should not be similar to the new response that must be learned. Thus, a subject attempting to learn the second list who remembers the old A–B response finds that the old response does not help in remembering the new response. The old response simply serves as a distraction or a source of interference with learning the new appropriate response term. Thus, we would expect negative transfer to occur in these paradigms.

The final paradigm we should mention is the A–B, C–B sequence. Here the stimulus terms in the second list differ from those in the first list. The response terms, however, are the same. The transfer effects found in this paradigm have been mixed (see Figure 6.9). In general, depending on variables such as the meaningfulness of the response terms, such paradigms have produced either slight amounts of positive or negative transfer (see, for example, Jung, 1963; Twedt & Underwood, 1959). Apparently, learning A–B is helpful to learning C–B in that the appropriate responses have already been acquired. On the other hand, A–B learning may also retard C–B learning because subjects must learn to associate the former responses with a new set of stimulus terms. It may be that these multiple effects tend to counteract each other, such that large negative or positive transfer effects seldom occur.

Rules that govern specific transfer effects In this brief introduction to specific transfer effects, we have hinted at a few possible explanations of why some paradigms produce positive transfer while others result in zero or negative transfer. We have not, however, stated any general rules that would allow us to predict when a certain type of transfer is likely to occur. The reason for this omission is the tendency of transfer effects to be somewhat complex. It is simply difficult to devise a set of rules that apply to every transfer situation.

This difficulty is illustrated by some of the early attempts to account for transfer effects. For example, Osgood (1949) proposed that specific transfer could be explained solely on the basis of the similarity of items in two paired associates lists. He suggested the following principles, which he believed should govern all specific transfer effects.

1. In any transfer paradigm, we should find positive transfer when the two lists contain the same response terms. This positive transfer will grow greater, the more similar the stimulus terms are in the two lists.
2. In any transfer paradigm, we should find negative transfer when the two lists contain different response terms and the same stimulus terms. This negative transfer will increase, the more dissimilar the response terms are in the two lists.
3. When both the stimulus and response terms in two lists are different, negative transfer will occur. This negative transfer will increase, the more similar the stimulus terms are in the two lists.

Clearly, these rules hold quite well in a number of transfer situations (see Dallett, 1962). For example, rule 1 predicts that positive transfer should always result in an A–B, C–B paradigm, while rule 2 predicts that an A–B, A–C paradigm should always produce negative transfer. As we have seen, such paradigms do produce these predicted effects in many cases. However, several researchers have demonstrated that the specific transfer effects in these paradigms often depend on certain characteristics such as the meaningfulness of the items in a list.

For instance, some researchers have found that the A–B, A–C sequence produces strong negative transfer when the items in the two lists are highly meaningful. However, this negative transfer is greatly diminished when low meaningful items make up the two lists (see, for example, Richardson & Brown, 1966). Likewise, the A–B, C–B paradigm is most likely to produce positive transfer when the listed items have low to intermediate levels of meaningfulness. When the items are highly meaningful, this paradigm often results in zero transfer (see, Merikle, 1968). The difficulty of predicting specific transfer from a simple set of similarity rules is clear from such results.

More recent explanations of transfer have attempted to take into account the complexities of these effects. For example, the *component analysis approach* begins with the assumption that paired associates learning involves much more than simply learning to associate response terms with appropriate stimuli. According to this view, an individual attempting to learn a paired associates list must go through a series of steps. Each step involves learning about a different aspect or component of the list (see Postman, 1972). For instance, most researchers seem to agree that at least the following steps occur during most paired associates learning tasks:

1. *The formation of forward associations.* This step involves associating response terms with appropriate stimulus terms, so that each stimulus term will help the subject recall a particular response.
2. *The formation of backward associations.* In this step, subjects associate stimulus terms with corresponding response terms, so that each response term will remind the subject of a particular stimulus.
3. *Response learning.* Here subjects learn the list of response terms much as they would learn a free recall list. The purpose of this step is to form a pool of responses from which correct responses for each stimulus term can be chosen.
4. *Response differentiation.* This step involves learning to distinguish one response term from another so that individual responses can be associated with individual stimuli.
5. *Stimulus differentiation.* In this step subjects learn to distinguish one stimulus term from another. Again, the purpose of this step is to enable a subject to associate individual stimuli with individual responses.

This idea that paired associates learning involves several distinct steps has important implications for explaining transfer effects. According to this view, transfer paradigms involve more than simply learning one thing about list 1, which then transfers to the learning of list 2. Instead, it is assumed that subjects learn several things about list 1, and each of these things can provide either positive, negative, or zero transfer to the learning of list 2. In this view, an overall transfer effect is really based on a combination of transfer effects, each stemming from one aspect of list 1 learning. Thus, it is possible to understand transfer only if we look at how each component of list 1 learning affects the learning of a second list.

To exemplify this approach, consider what occurs when a subject learns an A–B list followed by an A–C list. Since the stimulus terms are the same in both lists, the stimulus differentiation that occurs in learning list A–B will help the subject with stimulus differentiation in learning list A–C. Thus, there should be some positive transfer in this paradigm due to a subject's prior familiarity with the "A" terms when A–C learning occurs. On the other hand, the forward associations formed when A–B is learned should make learning the A–C forward associations more difficult. This difficulty is expected because each time a subject tries to learn an A–C association, the previously formed A–B association is likely to be recalled, interfering with learning the new connection. Thus it is predicted that the forward associations formed in learning A–B will produce negative transfer in learning A–C. Finally, we expect that the other components involved in learning A–B will produce zero transfer when A–C is learned. These components—response learning, response differentiation, and the formation of backward associations—all depend on a knowledge of the response terms. Since the response terms in these two lists are different, whatever is learned about the responses in the A–B list will be irrelevant when the A–C responses are learned. In sum, the overall transfer effect in an A–B, A–C paradigm will be based on a combination of positive, negative, and zero transfer effects.

All that we now need to predict overall transfer is a rule for how these individual transfer effects combine. Most component analysis approaches simply assume that overall transfer effects can be predicted by adding together the effects produced by the individual components. There is, however, an important exception to this rule. Most such approaches assume that the formation of a forward association is the most important step in learning a paired associates list. Thus, the transfer provided by this component is weighted more heavily than that provided by the other components.

To illustrate this point, consider again the A–B, A–C paradigm. We have found that in such a paradigm the forward association produces negative transfer, while stimulus differentiation produces positive transfer. If we were simply to combine these effects with the zero transfer provided by the remaining components, the net effect would be zero transfer in this paradigm. However, if we weight the negative transfer produced by the forward association more heavily, the overall transfer effect will be negative. This, of course, is the type of transfer normally obtained in the A–B, A–C paradigm.

Although the component analysis approach is somewhat cumbersome to use, certain variations of it have been very successful at predicting transfer effects in specific learning situations. Such approaches have even been able to account for the influence on transfer effects of variables such as item meaningfulness. This view simply assumes that meaningfulness can affect the ease with which certain learning steps occur. Thus, variables such as item meaningfulness help to determine the amount of transfer a given component provides.

A complete discussion of how this approach applies to each transfer situation is beyond the scope of our discussion (see Postman, 1972, for a description in greater depth). Nevertheless, our brief discussion of the component analysis view has made one point very clear. Even something as seemingly simple as learning a paired associates list probably involves a number of complex processes. And, unless these processes are taken into account, it is virtually impossible to understand completely the nature of specific transfer effects.

Summary Statements

In attempting to understand how individuals learn lists of verbal items, we concentrated on three types of list learning paradigms: serial learning, free recall learning, and paired associates learning. We found that an individual's ability to learn a verbal list depends on factors of three kinds. First, list learning is influenced by the way items are presented during learning. For example, we noted that subjects learn to different degrees depending on variables such as the number of learning trials and the distribution of these trials in time. Second, the characteristics of the verbal items in a list help to determine how easily a list will be learned. We saw, for instance, that learning almost always is easier, the more meaningful the verbal items are. We also noted that variables such as item similarity influence the rate of list learning. Third, we found that the success of list learning depends in large part on the learning strategies a subject uses. In our discussion we mentioned the relative merits of strategies such as coding, clustering, and various imagery techniques. We found that although most strategies facilitate learning, the use of some strategies can be counterproductive in some situations.

The last part of this chapter was devoted to the study of transfer effects in Verbal learning paradigms. We began by distinguishing between specific and nonspecific forms of transfer. Then we described the paradigms most commonly used to study specific transfer effects. We found that it is difficult to explain transfer effects solely on the basis of list similarity. To account for such effects, it appears to be necessary to use some type of component analysis approach.

7

Generalization, Discrimination, and Concept Learning

A few years ago we were dressing our two young sons in snow suits so we could take them sledding. These were the kinds of suits that have long zippers that extend from a child's feet to the chin. While dressing one child, Jason, I was distracted by his brother Scott, and I inadvertently pinched Jason's neck with the zipper. His reaction was immediate. He jerked his head downward and shrieked while I struggled to separate the zipper from his neck.

From what you already know about conditioning, it should come as no surprise that subsequent attempts to put Jason in the snow suit always resulted in a wrestling match. Whenever I began to zip up the snow suit, he would jerk his head forward, cover his neck with both hands, and scream at the top of his voice. Clearly, he had associated this zipper with painful stimulation and he was not about to let his father abuse him any further.

Before long, we noticed that Jason was exhibiting a number of curious behaviors. First, whenever we attempted to zip up his pants he would cover his neck and begin to cry. We also noticed that Scott had learned a new trick: he could make Jason cry simply by zipping his own pants up and down. Obviously, Jason's fear of the snow suit zipper had extended to zippers of any kind, even though only the snow suit zipper had ever actually attacked him.

This set of behaviors illustrates an important principle that we have alluded to in several of the preceding chapters. When, through experience, an organism learns some new response to a particular stimulus, the organism tends to make the same response in the presence of other similar stimuli. This tendency is called *stimulus generalization,* and its occurrence has important implications for the behavior of humans and other organisms.

The tendency to generalize from one stimulus to another means that organisms do not have to experience all possible stimulus situations in order to make appropriate responses in those situations. For example, if you are bitten by one dog you will quickly develop a healthy respect for that particular animal. Because of stimulus generalization, you will show similar respect for other dogs without having to be bitten by each of them.

Quite obviously, stimulus generalization can be a highly adaptive process insofar as many stimuli that are similar do require the same adaptive response. On the other hand, the natural tendency to generalize can sometimes result in inappropriate or maladaptive responses. I once heard a therapist relate a case study of a client who had almost drowned in the ocean. Not only did the client thereafter avoid swimming in the ocean, but she also avoided going near any body of water. She reported for therapy because she could no longer take baths without experiencing an extreme fear reaction. In this case, the tendency to generalize had resulted in a clearly inappropriate set of responses.

Similar inappropriate reactions can be seen in the way we respond to certain ethnic, religious, or racial groups. Through our experiences with one member of such a group we may come to react to that person in a particular way. It is common, however, to generalize the same reactions to other members of the group simply because all the members share certain characteristics. Thus, racial and ethnic stereotypes often develop through stimulus generalization and can lead to inappropriate reactions to individual members of a given group.

The fact that stimulus generalization can result in inappropriate responses draws our attention to another very important learning process called *discrimination learning.* In this process we learn to make a response in the presence of one stimulus and not to make the same response to other similar stimuli. Thus, in one sense, discrimination learning can be viewed as a process that helps us counteract our natural tendency to generalize. Through discrimination learning we can learn that a fear of swimming in the ocean may be adaptive, but that we need not fear sitting in a bathtub. Likewise, discrimination learning allows us to respond differently to different members of various demographic groups, rather than responding the same way to all individuals having similar characteristics.

For humans, as well as other organisms, discrimination learning plays another important role. It is through processes like discrimination learning that we are able to form and use *concepts.* A concept is a group of objects or ideas that fall into a given category because they share certain characteristics or features. For example, the concept of "automobile" includes a number of objects that all have wheels, seats, and engines and move along the ground. To form a concept, an individual must be able to attach labels or feelings to one set of stimuli and not to others. As we will see, this can be a rather complex endeavor. However, the ability to discriminate is almost certainly essential for the process of concept formation.

In the present chapter we discuss the processes of stimulus generalization, discrimination learning, and concept formation in greater detail. We will learn how these processes are studied in the laboratory and we will become aquainted with some of the factors that influence each process. We will also examine some of the theoretical explanations for how these processes work.

Stimulus Generalization

Methods for Studying Generalization in the Laboratory

Generalization has been studied in learning situations of virtually every type. For example, some of the earliest stimulus generalization experiments were carried out by Pavlov (1927) within the Classical conditioning paradigm. Basically, these experiments involved training dogs to salivate to a particular CS and later assessing the amount of conditioned responding to other similar stimuli.

Numerous generalization studies have also been done using Instrumental and Operant conditioning paradigms. In these experiments organisms are usually trained to perform some emitted response in the presence of one stimulus, whereupon they are tested to see whether they will respond in the presence of similar stimuli. One rather common paradigm of this type involves training pigeons to peck a key for reinforcement when a light of a particular color is present. Key peck responses that occur in the absence of this light are not reinforced. Finally, after the training is completed, the pigeons are tested by presenting lights of different colors and assessing the amount of responding to the lights on which the birds were not trained.

Figure 7.1 illustrates some representative findings from a generalization study of this type. The curve that is drawn, which shows the amount of responding to both the original training stimulus (a 600-nm light) and other similar but nontrained stimuli, is called a *stimulus generalization gradient.* Most such gradients have a generally similar form. That is, the greatest amount of responding usually occurs to the previously trained stimulus or to some stimulus that is very similar to the trained stimulus. Progressively less responding usually occurs as the test stimuli grow more dissimilar to the original training stimulus.

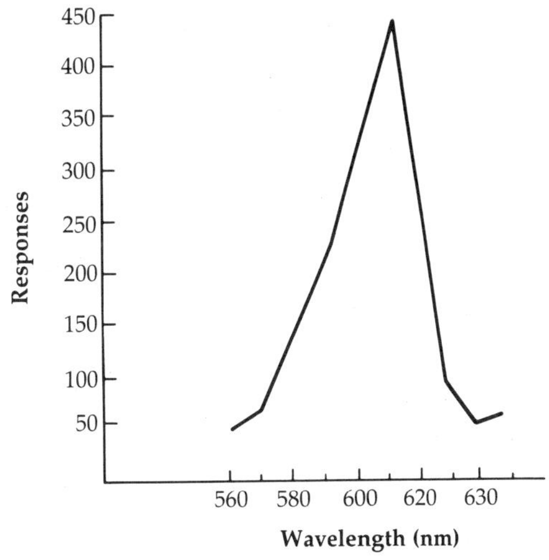

FIGURE 7.1 An example of a stimulus generalization gradient. (From Guttman and Kalish, 1956.)

The amount of generalization an organism exhibits on a particular test is reflected by the *slope* of the generalization gradient. Figure 7.2 (page 170) illustrates two gradients having very different slopes. Gradient A is termed a *steep gradient* because responding decreases substantially even when minor changes in the training stimulus occur. Obviously, a steep gradient indicates very little stimulus generalization. Gradient B, on the other hand, is called a *shallow gradient,* indicating that substantial responding occurs even to stimuli that are highly dissimilar to the training stimulus. The occurrence of a shallow gradient shows that significant stimulus generalization has taken place. Thus, the shape of any generalization gradient reflects the degree of stimulus generalization that an organism exhibits.

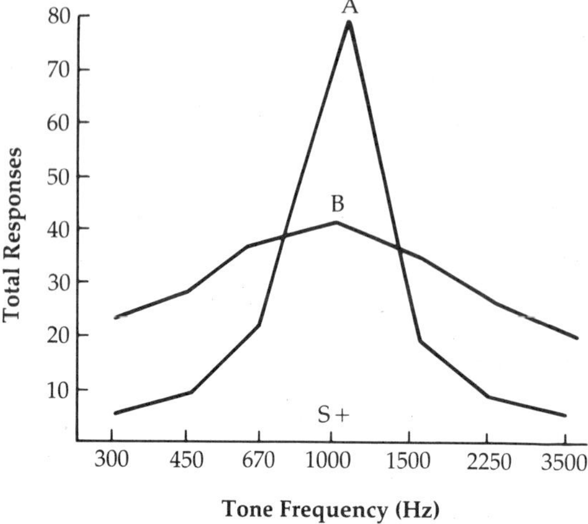

FIGURE 7.2 Examples of steep (A) and shallow (B) generalization gradients after training on a 1000-Hz tone.

Three further points concerning generalization gradients should be noted. First, the abscissa or *X*-axis of a gradient always represents some kind of *stimulus dimension*—that is, a scale along which stimuli can be ordered according to some characteristic. For example, color, size, height, and loudness are all stimulus dimensions, since stimuli can differ in terms of these characteristics and we can order stimuli according to these characteristics. The stimulus dimensions used in many generalization experiments, represent a physical scale (for example, color or size). However, in some cases stimulus dimensions such as stimulus meaning have been employed (see, for example, Staats, Staats, & Heard, 1959). In such studies subjects may be trained to respond to a particular word and then tested with words having either similar or dissimilar meanings.

A second point concerns the ordinate or *Y*-axis of the generalization gradient. We have considered thus far only gradients based on an absolute measure of the number of responses made to each stimulus. A gradient based on total number of responses is called an *absolute generalization gradient*. This type of gradient is, of course, valuable because it tells us precisely how many responses a subject makes to each test stimulus. In some cases, however, a slightly different measure of responding is useful.

We might, for example, wish to know how some variable, such as the amount of reward during training, affects subsequent generalization. To answer this question we might give two groups of organisms different amounts of reward during training and then test both groups on the training stimulus and on a set of nontrained stimuli. What we are likely to find if we measure the absolute number of responses is that the small-reward group makes fewer responses to *all* stimuli, including the training stimulus. In other words, the height of the generalization gradient will be depressed in the small-reward group. This means that the gradient will tend to flatten out or become shallow, not necessarily because of any change in generalization, but because overall responding has been depressed.

To rectify this measurement problem, several researchers have used what are termed relative measures of generalization. In other words, on a generalization test the experimenter notes the total number of responses made and then calculates the percent of this total that was made in the presence of each stimulus. This procedure results in a *relative generalization gradient*. The shapes of such gradients are less affected by changes in absolute responding to all stimuli. Figure 7.3 shows an absolute and a relative gradient based on the same data.

Our final point concerning generalization gradients is that we can measure either *excitatory or inhibitory gradients*. Excitatory gradients are formed when organisms are first trained to *emit or produce* some response in the presence of a given stimulus. Then, during testing, we determine whether this tendency to emit a response generalizes to other stimuli. All the types of gradients we have discussed thus far fall into the category of excitatory gradients.

On the other hand, an organism may also

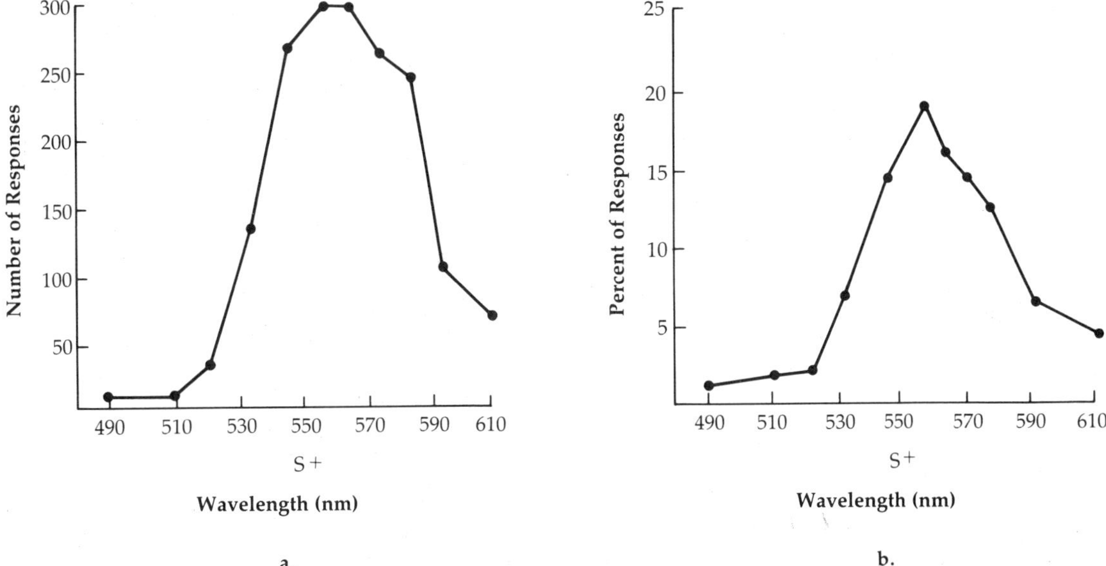

FIGURE 7.3 Examples of an absolute (a) and a relative (b) generalization gradient based on the same data. (From Thomas and Switalski, 1966.)

be trained to inhibit or withhold a response in the presence of a given stimulus. This is the kind of training that occurs in Classical inhibitory conditioning, in punishment paradigms, and even during extinction trials. If an organism is trained to inhibit responding in the presence of one stimulus, this tendency to inhibit responding will generalize to other similar stimuli. The curve in Figure 7.4 (page 172), a graphical representation of an organism's tendency to generalize the inhibition of responding, is termed an inhibitory generalization gradient.

Variables That Affect Stimulus Generalization

Earlier it was noted that whenever we learn some new response, we tend naturally to generalize that response to novel stimulus situations. We also noted that the tendency to generalize can have important consequences for our everyday behaviors. For this reason it is helpful to understand which circumstances tend to promote generalization and which factors tend to inhibit it. To make such a determination, researchers have examined how a variety of variables affect the shape of generalization gradients. Many of these studies have been concerned with a single question: Does the way we learn influence our tendency to generalize? We will attempt to answer this question by looking at some of the learning variables that have been studied in generalization experiments.

Degree of original learning It seems reasonable to assume that our tendency to generalize depends on how well we have learned a particular response. At least some experiments do support this assumption. For example, Hearst and Koresko (1968) trained pigeons to peck a key that had a vertical black line on its surface. Pecking in the presence of this stimulus was reinforced on a variable interval schedule. In this study various groups of pigeons received either 2, 4, 7, or 14 sessions of training. Then all pigeons were tested for generalization by being presented with a key having either a

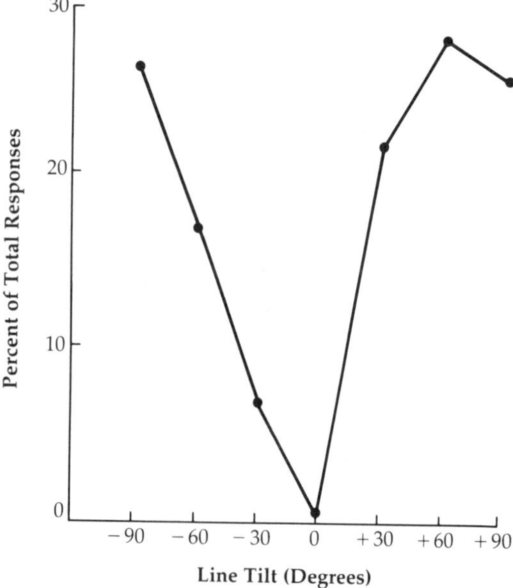

FIGURE 7.4 Example of an inhibitory generalization gradient from a study in which pigeons were trained to peck a blank key and were not reinforced for pecking a key with a vertical line (0° tilt). Then they were tested using different line tilts. (From Zentall, Collins, and Hearst, 1971.)

vertical line or lines that were tilted away from the vertical position. During testing none of the responses were reinforced. The results of this test can be seen in Figure 7.5. Clearly, the more training given with the vertical line stimulus, the more the pigeons responded to this stimulus on the test. Increased training also appeared to reduce generalization, as evidenced by the steepened generalization gradient.

This effect of degree of training on absolute generalization gradients is reasonably common (see, for example, B. L. Brown, 1970). There is, however, some disagreement as to whether increased training on the original stimulus (S+) reduces generalization in a relative sense. The data produced by Hearst and Koresko suggest that increased training does decrease the relative proportion of responses allotted to the nontrained stimuli. However, other studies have reported that in some cases increased training can actually *increase* relative generalization (that is, flatten the relative generalization gradient) (see, for example, Margolius, 1955). Thus, although the effects of degree of training on absolute generalization are clear, how relative gradients are affected remains an open question. Increased training clearly enhances responding to the training stimulus, but it does not necessarily enhance responding to this stimulus relative to others.

Motivational level Another variable that appears to influence the shape of generaliza-

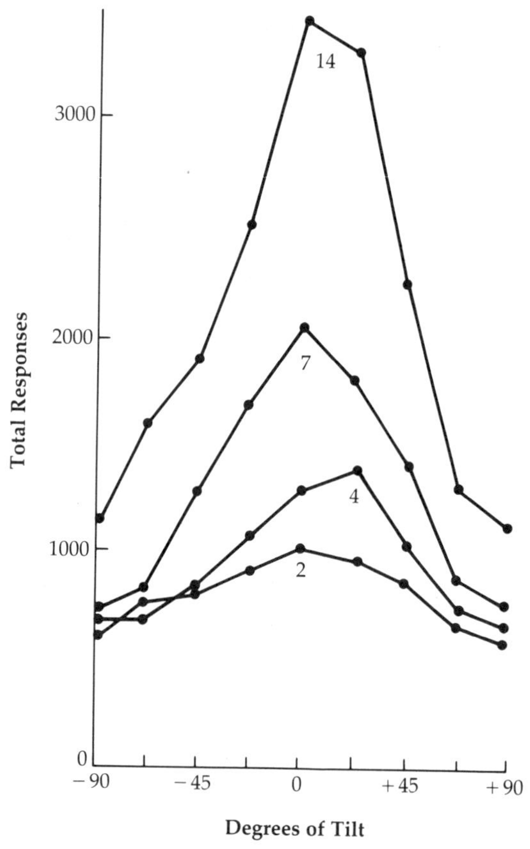

FIGURE 7.5 Generalization among tilted lines after 2, 4, 7, and 14 training sessions with a vertical line as S+. (From Hearst and Koresko, 1968.)

tion gradients is an organism's level of motivation at the time of original learning. However, just as with the degree of learning variable, the effects of motivational level have not always been consistent. For example, Kalish and Haber (1965) trained pigeons to peck a key of a certain color and then tested for generalization using a range of different colored keys. Before training, these experimenters reduced their pigeons to either 90, 80, or 70 percent of normal body weight. The presumption was that motivational levels should be higher, the greater the reduction in normal body weight, since greater reductions involve greater degrees of food deprivation. Using this manipulation, Kalish and Haber found that increased levels of motivation resulted in greater responding to the S+ during the generalization test. They also found that higher levels of motivation tended to produce steeper absolute generalization gradients. Similar findings have been reported by Newman and Grice (1965), who assessed size generalization in rats.

Thus, some studies involving absolute gradients show that generalization is reduced by higher levels of motivation during learning. This finding is reasonably common, but there are some notable exceptions (see, for example, J. S. Brown, 1942; Thomas & King, 1959). The major exceptions to this conclusion come from work in which relative generalization gradients are used. Here, several studies have found that increases in motivation can actually flatten relative gradients or increase the tendency to generalize (see, for example, Jenkins, Pascal, & Walker, 1958; Thomas & King, 1959; see also, Coate, 1964).

These conflicting conclusions, as well as the mixed results found with the degree of learning variable, illustrate an important point. The effects of some variables on generalization are complex, and they depend heavily on how generalization is defined and measured. To this point there is still no general agreement with respect to which measure best reflects the underlying process of stimulus generalization. Fortunately, the effects of most other variables we will discuss tend to be more consistent.

Schedules of reinforcement If we train an organism to respond in the presence of one stimulus (S+) and then test for generalization to other stimuli, the amount of generalization is strongly influenced by the schedule of reward used in training S+. This conclusion is illustrated clearly in a study conducted by Hearst, Koresko, and Popper (1964). These experimenters trained five groups of pigeons to peck a key marked with a vertical line. The groups differed in terms of the reinforcement schedule used to train the pecking response. Although all pigeons were exposed to a variable interval schedule, the average length of the time-out interval was 30 seconds or 1, 2, 3, or 4 minutes in the five groups, respectively. After training, all pigeons were tested using a variety of tilted lines on the response key. Figure 7.6 (page 174) shows the relative generalization gradients for these five groups. As you can see, the different training schedules produced markedly different gradients. Basically, the tendency to generalize was greater when subjects had been trained using longer time-out intervals. Shorter time-out intervals reduced generalization significantly. In general, schedules of reinforcement that are relatively rich or dense (that is, schedules that allow more frequent reinforcement) tend to reduce subsequent generalization to nontrained stimuli (see also, Haber & Kalish, 1963).

Duration of the training–test interval Another variable that has a consistent effect on generalization is the length of time that separates training on S+ and the subsequent test for generalization. Several studies have shown that the tendency to generalize increases as the training–test interval is lengthened (see, for example, Burr & Thomas, 1972; McAllister & McAllister, 1963; Perkins & Weyant, 1958; Thomas et al., 1985). One example of this effect can be seen in a study by Thomas and Lopez

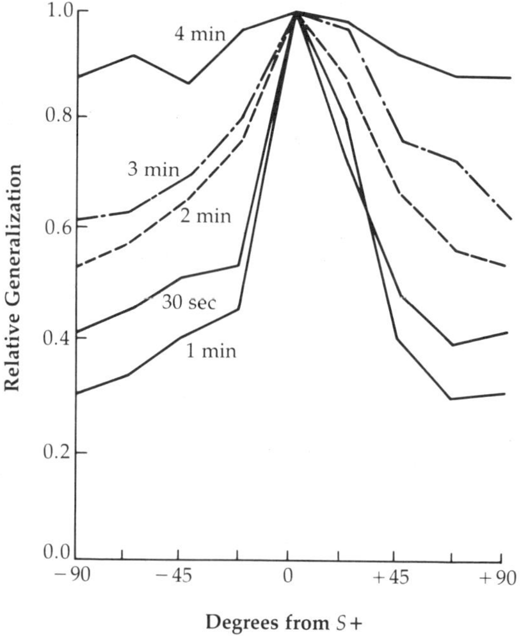

FIGURE 7.6 Generalization on a line tilt dimension after training on a vertical line using different VI schedules of reinforcement. (From Hearst, Koresko, and Popper, 1964.)

(1962), in which pigeons were trained to peck a colored key and were later tested using keys of different colors. Pigeons in this experiment were tested either 1 minute, 1 day, or 1 week after training. Figure 7.7 shows the results of these tests in terms of relative generalization gradients. It is clear that the pigeons tested after 1 minute exhibited very steep generalization gradients. Those tested 1 day and 1 week after training showed somewhat flatter gradients. This effect is often interpreted as an example of forgetting. That is, over time subjects forget the specific characteristics of the S+ and tend to respond more often to relatively similar stimuli.

Prior discrimination training In our introduction to this chapter, we noted that discrimination learning is one process that can counteract the tendency to generalize. Thus, it should come as no surprise that generalization gradients are affected by whether an organism has had discrimination training before being subjected to a generalization test. To this point we have dealt only with learning situations in which organisms are reinforced when they respond in the presence of a given stimulus. In contrast, discrimination training involves presenting two or more stimuli to an organism during the training phase. For example, an organism may be confronted with one stimulus on some trials and another stimulus on the remaining trials. Basically, the organism is reinforced for responding in the presence of one of these stimuli (the S+) and is not reinforced for responding to the other stimulus (the S−).

The effect of such discrimination training on subsequent generalization is usually pronounced. For example, Jenkins and Harrison (1962) trained pigeons to peck in the presence of a 1000-Hz tone by reinforcing these re-

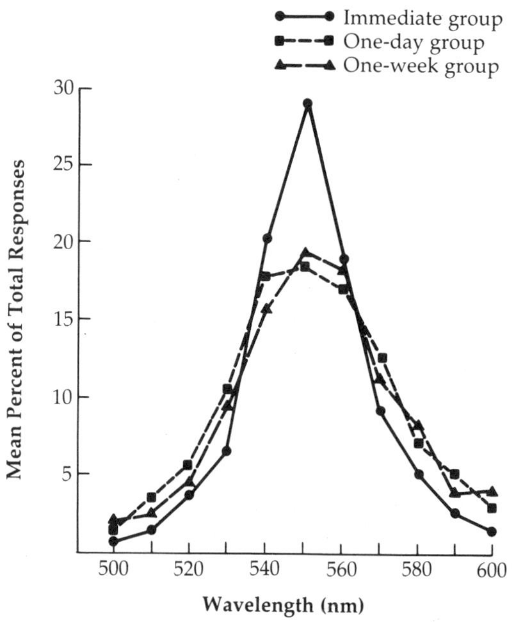

FIGURE 7.7 Generalization as a function of the training–test interval. (From Thomas and Lopez, 1962.)

sponses. They also trained the pigeons not to respond to a 950-Hz tone by giving no rewards for responses to this tone. Subsequently, they tested the pigeons for responses to a range of tone frequencies. They found that this discrimination training led to very steep generalization gradients relative to those produced by pigeons that had been trained to respond to the 1000-Hz tone only. In effect, prior discrimination training between two tones (1000 and 950 Hz) reduced later generalization along the tone frequency dimension. The same effect has been reported in numerous experiments involving a wide variety of stimulus dimensions (see, for example, Friedman & Guttman, 1965; Hanson, 1959; Thomas, 1962).

Aside from reducing generalization, prior discrimination training can result in two other effects, as illustrated in a study with pigeons conducted by Hanson (1959). Although this experiment actually involved several treatment conditions, for present purposes we concentrate on only two of Hanson's groups. One group of pigeons (the no-discrimination group) was simply reinforced for responding to a colored light having a wavelength of 550 nm. A second group (the discrimination group) was reinforced for pecking a 550-nm key (the S+) and was not reinforced for pecking a 560-nm key (the S–). Both groups were then given a generalization test in which no responses were reinforced. The test consisted of presenting a variety of keys having different wavelengths and measuring the response to each. Figure 7.8 shows the results of this generalization test.

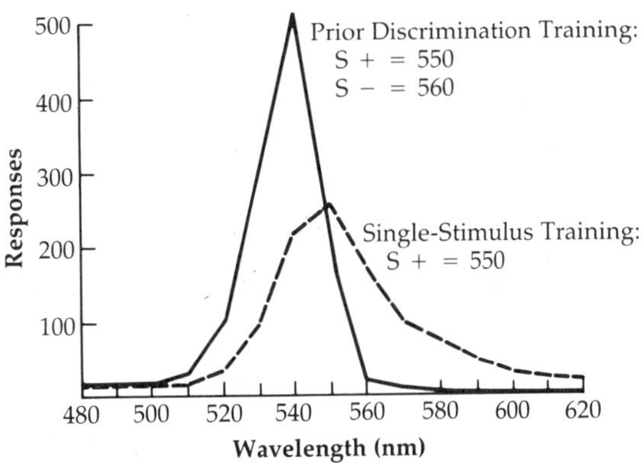

FIGURE 7.8 Different generalization gradients resulting from single-stimulus and discrimination training. (From Hanson, 1959.)

Clearly, as in the study by Jenkins and Harrison (1962) cited above, prior discrimination training resulted in a significantly steeper generalization gradient. In addition, however, two characteristics of Figure 7.8 are notable. First, in the no-discrimination group maximal responding occurs to the previously trained wavelength (550 nm). In the discrimination group, however, maximal responding occurs not to the original S+ (550 nm) but instead to a key having a wavelength of 540 nm. In other words, the peak of the generalization gradient is not at the original S+ but is shifted *away from* the original S– (560 nm). This effect, called the *peak-shift phenomenon,* has been found in a number of studies and is the direct result of prior discrimination training (see, for example, Purtle, 1973). It is important to emphasize that the peak shift always occurs in a direction away from the S– that was used in discrimination training.

One explanation for this effect is that during discrimination training, organisms form an excitatory generalization gradient around the S+ and an inhibitory gradient around the S– (see Spence, 1937). In effect, subjects learn not to respond to the S–, and this tendency generalizes to other similar stimuli. To understand how the interaction of these generalized tendencies results in a peak shift, consider Hanson's findings. In this study the pigeons should have had a strong tendency to peck the 550-nm key because it was the S+. They should also have tended to peck at the 540-nm key because of excitatory stimulus generalization. However, the inhibitory tendency formed to the 560-nm key (the S–) should have generalized more to the 550-nm key than to the 540-nm key simply because of the greater similarity of the 560- and 550-nm wavelengths. This means that the inhibitory tendency that generalizes from the S– will depress responding to the 550-nm key to a relatively great extent. The result is that peak responding occurs at 540 nm, not at 550 nm. Generally, this kind of explanation has gained wide support (see, for example, Klein & Rilling, 1974).

A second notable feature of Hanson's findings is that discrimination appears to enhance peak responding substantially. Hanson's discrimination group had a mean of more than 500 responses to the 540-nm key, whereas the no-discrimination group had between 200 and 300 responses to the 550-nm key. This phenomenon, termed a *behavioral contrast effect*, results from giving organisms a comparison between the reinforcing values of two stimuli. In other words, if two organisms receive the same percentage of reinforcement for responding to a stimulus (S_1) and one organism is also given a lower percentage of reinforcement for responding to another (S_2), the organism that experiences both stimuli often responds most to S_1. This is the case even when responding to S_2 does result in some degree of reinforcement (see, for example, Reynolds, 1961). Thus, aside from reducing generalization and producing a peak shift, discrimination training can elevate peak responding on a generalization test.

To this point we have considered only situations in which discrimination training occurs among stimuli that will later be present on the generalization test. Somewhat surprisingly, discrimination training can apparently affect generalization gradients even when the stimuli an organism must discriminate are not the same as the stimuli on the generalization test. One example of this effect comes from a series of experiments conducted by Thomas, Freeman, Svinicki, Burr, and Lyons (1970). In one of their experiments, one group of pigeons (true discrimination group) learned a discrimination between two different colored keys. They were rewarded for responding in the presence of one color and not rewarded for responding to the other. Superimposed on both the S+ and S– keys was a vertical white line. A second group of pigeons (pseudodiscrimination group) also was presented the different colored keys bearing a vertical line. However, for this group, responding to either key resulted in reinforcement on the same VI schedule. Thus, this group was not required to learn any discrimination between the two colors.

After this training both groups were given generalization tests using keys marked with lines that were either vertical or tilted from the vertical position. Recall that even though all pigeons had seen a vertical line during training, the discrimination task involved a discrimination based on colors. These researchers found that the true discrimination group exhibited a steep generalization gradient, with peak responding occurring for the vertical line. The pseudodiscrimination group produced an extremely flat generalization gradient, with no clear response advantage for the vertical line. This study shows that discrimination training on one stimulus dimension can reduce later generalization along a totally different stimulus dimension. This finding has been replicated in number of experiments (see, for example, Honig, 1970; Mackintosh & Honig, 1970). It suggests that practice in discriminating among stimuli may result in some general set or predisposition that makes organisms more discriminating even in different stimulus situations.

Conclusions The studies we have discussed make it clear that the tendency to generalize is not invariant. In effect, this tendency depends on how a new response is acquired. Generalization effects can be decreased by having organisms learn under a rich schedule of reward or by testing organisms shortly after learning. Such effects can also be diminished by giving organisms discrimination training before they undergo a generalization test. There is some indication that protracted training and high levels of motivation may also lead to less generalization. Thus, while generalization is a natural consequence of all learning experiences, we can use certain training procedures to modify this tendency.

The Basis for Generalization Gradients

Certainly you were not surprised when we began this chapter by saying that organisms respond in the same way to similar stimuli. The phenomenon of generalization is so common that we accept it almost as a basic characteristic of living organisms. We should not, however, let our familiarity with the phenomenon obscure the important question of *why* we generalize. Why do we respond the same way to similar stimuli instead of responding the same way to dissimilar stimuli? Does it have to do with how our sensory systems are constructed, or is it the result of the way we learn? Could generalization depend on our emotional reactions to stimuli, or does it result from some combination of factors?

We examine now a few of the ideas that have been advanced to explain why generalization happens. We will find that it is easier to identify generalization when it occurs than to explain why it occurs. Although a number of hypotheses have been proposed, there is no general agreement regarding the mechanisms underlying generalization.

Traditional explanations for generalization

For several years there were two predominant theories that attempted to explain generalization phenomena. One theory, proposed by Hull (1943), suggested that generalization results because during learning, organisms associate several different stimuli with the correct response. According to this view, although an experimenter may attempt to condition a response to a single stimulus, such an endeavor can never succeed completely. On many occasions the subject's sensory system senses the level of the stimulus the experimenter actually intends. On other occasions, however, the subject senses the stimulus as being slightly different from the one presented. This means that conditioning actually occurs to a "zone" or range of stimuli instead of to a single stimulus. Maximal conditioning occurs to the nominal stimulus, but some conditioning also occurs to variations of this nominal stimulus (that is, to stimuli that are similar to the nominal stimulus). This, according to Hull, is the basis for the stimulus generalization gradient.

Hull's position was directly opposed by Lashley and Wade (1946), who offered a somewhat different explanation. These theorists rejected the idea that several stimuli acquire associative strength during learning. They suggested that subjects generalize because of confusion at the time of a generalization test. In other words, at the time of testing subjects are often unable to distinguish the training stimulus from similar testing stimuli. As a result, responses are made to test stimuli as well as to the original training stimulus.

This view states that such test confusions can be eliminated by giving a subject prior discrimination training with the stimulus dimension involved. That is, if a subject has learned to discriminate between the training and testing stimuli, the tendency to confuse these stimuli during testing will be diminished. Thus, Lashley and Wade hypothesized that generalization will always depend on an individual's prior experiences with the stimulus dimension in question. The more discrimination experience a subject has, the less generalization the subject should show.

Clearly, both the foregoing theories provide reasonable potential explanations for the occurrence of generalization effects. Unfortunately, researchers have found it difficult to distinguish between these views experimentally. In many cases these two theories simply make the same predictions concerning the effects of experimental manipulations. One of the few differences between these theories concerns the role of prior discriminative experience.

According to Hull's position, such experience should play an insignificant role in determining the shape of a generalization gradient. Lashley and Wade, however, viewed prior discriminative experience as a critical variable.

In an attempt to determine whether prior experience affects generalization gradients, several experimenters have varied the rearing conditions of organisms before training with a given stimulus. For example, in some studies animals have been reared in environments that are virtually devoid of color in an attempt to prevent them from learning to discriminate colors. The question of interest is whether such a manipulation does in fact affect later generalization along the color dimension.

The results of such studies have been mixed. Some experimenters have found that prior experience manipulations clearly influence the shape of generalization gradients (see, for example, Ganz & Riesen, 1962; N. Peterson, 1962; Walk & Walters, 1973). However, others have reported that these manipulations have little effect on generalization performance (see Riley & Levin, 1971; Rudolph & Honig, 1972; Tracy, 1970). These conflicting results obviously provide little basis for choosing between Hull's explanation and the interpretation proposed by Lashley and Wade.

Aside from the difficulty in distinguishing between these theories, it is also clear that neither view can provide a complete explanation of generalization phenomena. For example, we have seen that generalization along one stimulus dimension can be influenced by prior discrimination training on a totally different dimension (see Thomas, Freeman, Svinicki, Burr, & Lyons, 1970). Such a result cannot be predicted from either the Hull or the Lashley–Wade position.

These difficulties do not necessarily invalidate the ideas proposed by these early theorists. It is possible that both multiple associations formed during training and stimulus confusions at the time of testing contribute to generalization performance. However, the problems just outlined have led other theorists to search for additional generalization mechanisms. One promising contemporary approach focuses on the role of incidental or contextual stimuli in producing generalization.

The role of "incidental stimuli" in generalization Another approach to explaining generalization is suggested by contemporary learning theories such as the Rescorla–Wagner model (Rescorla & Wagner, 1972). You may recall that these theories view contextual or background stimuli as functioning like the nominal CS in a conditioning experiment. Thus, in any conditioning situation, not only will the CS acquire the capacity to produce a response, but contextual stimuli will also acquire this capacity to a lesser degree.

Based on this view, Mackintosh (1974), among others, has suggested that these incidental or contextual stimuli may be critical for understanding generalization phenomena. According to this view, responding during a generalization test will always be determined by the associative strength of all the stimuli present on that test. Let's assume that an organism has been trained to respond to a vertical line on a green key and is then tested by being shown a number of green keys, each marked with a tilted line. During training, not only the vertical line but also the green key will become associated with responding. On the test, the greatest responding will occur when the vertical line and the green key are present. However, some responding will occur to a slightly tilted line because the green key is still present. Somewhat less responding will occur to a horizontal line because it changes the organism's view of the green background, making the incidental stimuli different. The result is that a generalization gradient is exhibited.

This contextual view further states that prior discrimination learning (even on a dimension different from the test dimension) should steepen the gradient by reducing associations to the background stimuli. In other words, during discrimination training, responses in the presence of the background stimuli are sometimes reinforced and sometimes not reinforced. This means that such stimuli will become poor predictors for reinforcement and will not acquire much associative value relative to the S+ that is always followed by reinforcement. On a subsequent test, S+ will produce substantial responding. However, any change in S+ will decrease responding drastically, since the background stimuli present will have little capacity to produce a response.

In a rather extensive review of generalization experiments, Mackintosh (1974) demonstrates that this approach is consistent with a large proportion of generalization findings. Clearly, such an explanation is promising, and it deserves increased attention by experimenters in the field. Still, the explanation deals primarily with generalization based on physical stimulus dimensions such as color or loudness. It is unclear how an approach of this kind deals with phenomena such as generalization along a word meaning dimension.

Generalizations mediated by internal responses Earlier in this chapter we mentioned that humans generalize not only between physically similar stimuli but also between words that have similar meanings. The classic experiment demonstrating this effect was conducted by Lacey and Smith (1954). These experimenters first had subjects free associate to each word in a list. Through this technique they were able to determine clusters of words with similar meanings. They then chose one word such as "cow" and followed the presentation of the word with a shock. They found that the word "cow" began to elicit a conditioned elevation in heart rate. They also found that words in the same conceptual category (for example, "plow," "corn," and "tractor") would produce a conditioned response even though these words had never been paired with shock. No responding occurred to unrelated words such as "paper." This example of "semantic generalization" is one of many that have been demonstrated using a variety of techniques (see Maltzman, 1977).

In many regards these findings are reminiscent of the generalization that occurs among physically similar stimuli. However, it is difficult to account for such findings with any of the explanations of generalization we have discussed thus far. The problem is that all these theories are based on the physical differences between training and test stimuli. As a result, theoretical explanations of semantic generalization have differed somewhat from theories of the kinds we have described.

Basically, attempts to explain semantic generalization have centered on the idea that a meaningful word always produces certain internal responses within an individual (see J. J. Jenkins, 1963). These internal responses may be conceptualized as either thoughts or emotional reactions triggered by the meaning of a word. So, for example, the presentation of the word "cow" may trigger thoughts about farms or rural settings. This implies that if a given word is paired with a US, not only will the word itself become capable of eliciting a CR, but also any thoughts provoked by that word will become conditioned. Following our example, if the word "cow" is presented and is followed by shock, both the word "cow" and thoughts about farms will become associated with shock.

According to this analysis, the conditioning of these internal thoughts or reactions to a word is responsible for semantic generalization. If by pairing the word "cow" with shock, we associate thoughts about farms with shock, then any other word that produces thoughts about farms should also produce a fear response. For example, the word "tractor" produces a fear response not because it is physically similar to "cow", but because it provokes thoughts about farms, which have already been associated with shock. In effect, subjects will generalize responding between any words that provoke the same thoughts or emotional reactions. These internal responses *mediate* or provide a link between physically dissimilar words.

In general, this kind of theorizing accounts rather well for semantic generalization effects. However, there have been few attempts to use such analyses to explain generalization between physically similar stimuli. In effect, we still have different theories to explain generalization depending on whether stimuli are physically or semantically similar. This may well be appropriate, since generalization between different kinds of stimuli may occur for different reasons. It will be interesting to see whether future research confirms this assumption or leads us in the direction of a unitary generalization theory.

Discrimination Learning

In our discussions of generalization, we have described some of the necessary conditions for discrimination learning. We know, for example, that such learning involves presenting different stimuli to an organism and then differentially reinforcing responses to those different stimuli. In other words, responses in the presence of one stimulus are reinforced, while responses in the presence of other stimuli are not reinforced. As a result of such differential reinforcement, we begin to establish *stimulus control* over behavior. That is, we cause responding to begin to occur in the presence of one stimulus and not in the presence of others. As we have seen, the occurrence of stimulus control is reflected by the steepening of a generalization gradient.

On the surface, at least, the process of discrimination learning appears to be rather simple. All that it seems to entail is the strengthening of one stimulus–response association and the extinction of others. However, discrimination learning in the real world is seldom this simple. The complicating factor is that in our day-to-day lives we never actually encounter stimuli in isolation. What we encounter are *objects* that are comprised of *several stimuli.* Thus, we are never differentially reinforced for responding to isolated stimuli. We receive differential reinforcement for our responses to different objects or stimulus compounds.

To illustrate how this fact of our environment complicates the discrimination process, consider how a child might learn to tell the color red from all other colors. If it were possible to present the child with colors by themselves, we could simply praise the child for making the verbal response "red" in the presence of the color red and withhold praise when the child responds "red" to other colors. But, as we know, such a procedure is not actually possible. All we can do is present colored *objects* to the child and then reinforce correct responding to red objects and not to others.

For example, we might place a red ball and a green block next to each other on a table. Each time the child points to the red ball and says "red," we could offer praise. We could withhold praise whenever the child says "red" while pointing to the green block. After a while, the child will consistently label the ball as red and the block as not being red. Does this mean, however, that the child has learned to discriminate red from the green? In many cases, the answer would be no. Since the child has been reinforced for responding to an object, not a single stimulus, the child may be saying "red" in response to the object's color, its size, its shape, its texture, or even its relative position on the table. After such discrimination training, a parent may be discouraged to find that the child is now calling all round objects red instead of attaching this label to objects that are red, regardless of shape.

The same kind of complication arises even in relatively simple laboratory experiments. We may, for example, attempt to train a rat to choose the white arm of a T maze as opposed to the black arm. We might do this by rewarding the animal each time it enters the white arm and not rewarding entries into the black arm. Even this discrimination problem is complicated by the fact that on any given trial the white arm must be either on the left or the right of the central maze runway. Thus, if the rat turns right, enters the white arm, and is reinforced, it may well be learning to turn right instead of learning to enter the arm that happens to be white instead of black.

These examples raise an important question. How is it ever possible to attach a response to one specific stimulus and not to others when the specific stimulus never occurs alone? (In other words, how is it possible to learn to discriminate one stimulus from another when it is our responses to objects that are differentially reinforced?) For years this question has perplexed researchers interested in discrimination learning. Let us now examine two possible answers, looking as well at some of the discrimination learning data that have made it possible to choose between these explanations.

Spence: A Continuity Theory of Discrimination Learning

In 1936 Spence proposed that discrimination learning can be explained solely on the basis of the way reinforcement and nonreinforcement affect stimulus–response associations. Central to this theory were two simple principles. First, *whenever an organism is reinforced for responding in the presence of a stimulus object, the association between that response and all the stimuli making up that object will be strengthened.* Thus, when a child is reinforced for making the response "red" in the presence of a red ball, several associations are strengthened. The response of "red" becomes associated with the color, the size, the shape, and even the spatial location of the ball. This means that in the future each of these stimuli will have some capacity to produce the response "red."

The second principle concerns the effects of nonreinforcement. *Whenever an organism makes a response in the presence of an object and is not reinforced, the association between that response and all stimuli comprising that object will be weakened.* In effect, all stimuli present when a response is not reinforced become inhibitory. That is, these stimuli tend to produce inhibition or suppression of that response. Thus, if a child makes the response of "red" to a green block and is not reinforced, all features of that object—the color, the shape, the size, and so on—will, in the future, tend to inhibit the response of "red."

By using these simple reinforcement principles, Spence was able to account for the occurrence of specific discriminations even in relatively complex situations. To demonstrate the power of this approach, let's return to our example of the child who is learning to discriminate colors. Assume that on trial 1 the child is presented with two small rubber balls that are identical except that one is red and the other is green. The child selects the red ball, labels it as "red" and is reinforced. This means that the small size, the round shape, and the red color of that ball all become associated with the "red" response. On trial 2 the child labels the green ball as "red" and is not reinforced. This means that the association between the color green and the response "red" will be weakened. It also means that the associations between "red" and the small size and the round shape are also weakened. Thus, after two trials the child has an excitatory association between the color red and the response "red." There is also an inhibitory association between the color green and the response "red." The other stimuli in the situation—the small size and the round shape—have both excitatory and inhibitory associations that tend to cancel each other out.

Thus, as more and more reinforced and nonreinforced responses occur, a clear pattern will emerge. The only strong excitatory association will be between the color red and the "red" response, since the child is consistently reinforced for labeling red objects correctly. The only strong inhibitory association will be between the color green and the "red" response, since the child is consistently nonreinforced for saying "red" in the presence of a green object. All other stimuli that comprise these objects will be reinforced sometimes and not reinforced sometimes, depending on whether they occur in compound with the color red or the color green. Thus, these stimuli will have a net association of zero with the response "red."

Spence's view of discrimination learning is termed a continuity theory since it assumes that discrimination learning is a continuous process. In other words, the formation of a discrimination begins on trial 1 and emerges gradually over several reinforced and nonreinforced trials. The appeal of such a view is that it can account for discrimination learning solely on the basis of reinforcement principles. Such a theory contrasts sharply with a second type of theory, which claims that discrimination phenomena cannot be accounted for simply by understanding how stimulus–response associations become stronger or weaker. Theories of the latter type, termed *non-continuity theories,* focus on the role of attentional mechanisms in the discrimination learning process.

Noncontinuity Theories: The Concept of Attention in Discrimination Learning

Spence assumed that when an organism is confronted with a stimulus object, it notices or perceives a large number of the individual stimuli that make up the object. This assumption is the basis for the idea that a simple reinforcement can affect numerous stimulus–response associations. Other theorists, however, have questioned this assumption. Rather, they believe it is impossible for an organism to learn about all the stimuli that impinge on its sense receptors at any given time. It is felt that because organisms have a limited capacity for processing stimulus information, they have developed filtering mechanisms. Such mechanisms, which allow an organism to select or notice only a small subset of the stimuli actually present in a given instance, ensure that the organism's processing capacities will not be overwhelmed. It is this process of selecting out only a portion of the total stimulus array that we call *attention.*

Several theorists have suggested that attention plays a major role in discrimination learning (see, for example, Krechevsky, 1932; Lashley & Wade, 1946). Basically, these theorists have proposed that discrimination learning involves two distinct but interacting stages. One stage involves learning to attend to the correct stimulus dimension. Thus, when an organism is reinforced for responding to a given object, the organism must learn whether its response applies to the color, the shape, the size, or some other aspect of that object. To do this, the organism initially focuses its attention on one dimension (for example, shape) and through its experience with reinforcement determines whether this dimension is critical for solving the discrimination problem. If attending to this dimension does not increase the probability of reinforcement, the organism shifts its attention to a second dimension (for example, color).

Once the organism has determined that it is attending to the dimension on which reinforcement depends, it begins the second stage of the discrimination process, which proceeds in basically the same manner suggested by Spence. That is, at this point the organism begins to associate the response with *one stimulus* on the correct dimension (for example, red) and to weaken the association between responding and another stimulus on that dimension (for example, green). As in Spence's theory, these associations are strengthened or weakened depending on the occurrence of reinforcement.

This kind of theory has usually been called either a *noncontinuity* or a *hypothesis-testing theory.* The term "noncontinuity" is often applied because such theories view discrimination learning as occurring in two stages, not as a single process that works in a continuous fashion. The term "hypothesis-testing theory" denotes that in learning to attend to the correct dimension, organisms begin by forming a hypothesis about what the correct dimension might be. They then test the hypothesis by determining whether their attention to the dimension specified increases their probability of reinforcement.

One difficulty with the early noncontinuity theories is that they were not explicit concerning what was involved in learning to attend to the correct dimension. They also were not entirely clear about how the two stages of discrimination learning were supposed to interact. Later versions of the noncontinuity position have been far more precise in their formulations (see, for example, Lovejoy, 1968; Sutherland & Mackintosh, 1971; Zeaman & House, 1963, for details on contemporary noncontinuity approaches).

The critical difference between the continuity and noncontinuity views stems from the degree to which individuals learn to focus on a given stimulus dimension during discrimination learning. Aside from learning specific stimulus–response relationships, do individuals learn that certain stimulus dimensions are important while they are solving a discrimination problem? Experiments of several types have been done to examine this question (see Sutherland & Mackintosh, 1971). For the most part, these studies have led to the same conclusion. Just as the noncontinuity view suggests, subjects learning a discrimination problem do appear to learn about stimulus dimensions as well as about stimulus–response relationships. To illustrate this point, let's consider two kinds of studies that have been used to deal with this issue.

Two Tests of the Noncontinuity Position

The acquired distinctiveness of cues One type of finding that is clearly in accord with the noncontinuity approach comes from a series of experiments conducted by Lawrence (1949, 1950, 1952) to evaluate what he called the *acquired distinctiveness of cues.* In the first experiment of this type, Lawrence (1949) trained three groups of rats on a discrimination problem in a T maze. For one group, the arms differed in terms of brightness and the S+ was either a black arm or a white arm. For the second group the critical cue was floor texture. Specifically, the S+ was either a rough floor or a smooth floor. The final group learned to discriminate between arms that were of different widths, such that the S+ was either a narrow arm or a wide arm.

After this training, all three groups were given a very different discrimination problem to learn. The animals were placed in a T maze that had two white arms on some trials and two black arms on other trials. Their task was to learn to turn in one direction (for example, right) when the arms were black and to turn in the other direction when the arms were white. Lawrence reasoned that none of the groups had learned a specific stimulus–response association in problem 1 that should help them learn the discrimination in problem 2. However, the group that had learned the black–white discrimination in problem 1 would have an advantage in learning problem 2 if, in learning problem 1, they had learned to attend to the brightness dimension. This advantage was expected because for the black–white group, the second problem would be like the first in that the use of brightness cues was needed to learn the correct discrimination.

Lawrence's prediction was well supported by his data. The second problem was learned fastest by the group that had previously learned the black–white discrimination. Similar findings have supported Lawrence's conclusions (see, for example, Mackintosh & Holgate, 1967; Mumma & Warren, 1968). These data clearly indicate that when an organism learns a discrimination between, for example, a black stimulus and a white stimulus, it does more than simply attach specific responses to these stimuli. These data suggest that, in addition, an organism learns to attend to the stimulus dimension on which these stimuli are located.

Intradimensional versus extradimensional shifts A second set of data clearly favoring the noncontinuity position comes from studies that compare *intradimensional* and *extradimensional shifts.* Basically, any discrimination shift paradigm involves two stages. A subject is trained first, to discriminate between two stimuli and then to discriminate between two other stimuli not encountered in the first stage. In an *intradimensional shift,* all the stimuli used in both stages are from the same stimulus dimension. One example of an intradimensional shift would be to train an organism to discriminate between the colors red and green and then to shift the organism to a discrimination problem involving the colors yellow and blue. In an *extradimensional shift,* on the other hand, the stimuli used in stage 1 and stage 2 are from different stimulus dimensions. For instance, if we train an organism to discriminate first between red and green and then require it to discriminate squares from circles, we are providing an example of an extradimensional shift.

The question of interest in most studies using shift paradigms has been whether subjects will learn the second stage of an intradimensional shift faster than the second stage of an extradimensional shift. That is, if a subject first learns a red–green discrimination, will that subject later learn a yellow–blue discrimination faster than a circle–square problem? The interest in this question has arisen because the continuity and noncontinuity positions make entirely different predictions concerning stage 2 learning.

Spence's continuity view clearly predicts no difference in the rate at which intradimensional and extradimensional shifts will be learned. Since in both paradigms the stage 1 stimuli are entirely different from the stage 2 stimuli, no associations formed in stage 1 of either paradigm should carry over to aid learning in stage 2. On the other hand, noncontinuity theories predict clear advantages for subjects learning an intradimensional shift. According to this view, in stage 1 a subject learns to attend to a particular stimulus dimension. If the stage 2 problem involves stimuli from the same dimension (as in the intradimensional paradigm), subjects will learn very quickly because they have already learned to attend to the stimulus dimension that is critical for solving the stage 2 problem.

Many experiments have been conducted to test these differing predictions. And, in most cases, the evidence favors the conclusion that intradimensional shifts are learned faster than extradimensional shifts. One experiment by Mackintosh and Little (1969) will serve to illustrate these findings. Mackintosh and Little first trained two groups of pigeons on a discrimination task that involved pecking one of two keys. Group 1 was trained on a red–yellow discrimination, while group 2 received a problem involving horizontal and vertical lines. After these discriminations were learned, half the group 1 pigeons were taught a second color discrimination between blue and green (group color–color), while the other half were trained to discriminate between two obliquely tilted lines (group color–line). The same procedure was followed by the group 2 birds. Half received a blue–green discrimination task (group line–color) while the other half discriminated between the oblique lines (group line–line).

Mackintosh and Little found that the blue–green discrimination was learned faster by the group that had previously discriminated red and yellow (group color–color). The oblique line discrimination was acquired faster by the group that had originally learned a horizontal–vertical discrimination (group line–line). In other words, both stage 2 problems were learned faster when they were part of an intradimensional shift than when they occurred as part of an extradimensional shift. Similar findings have been reported using rats (Shepp & Eimas, 1964), monkeys (Shepp & Schrier, 1969), children (Dickerson, 1966), and college students (N. P. Uhl, 1966) as subjects. Only a few experiments, using very young children, have failed to find a clear advantage for intradimensional shift learning (see, for example, Trabasso, Deutsch, & Gelman, 1966).

Conclusions

One of the obvious advantages of Spence's original discrimination theory was its simplicity. Using only principles of reinforcement, this theory was able to explain how a subject, confronted with two complex objects, might form a discrimination between specific stimuli embedded in those objects. In this way, continuity theory encouraged the notion that even complex learning phenomena might be explicable on the basis of relatively simple associative mechanisms. However, as we have seen, this is apparently not the case. Most experiments suggest that discrimination learning involves more than simply associating a specific stimulus and response. It also seems to involve learning to attend to stimulus dimensions that are important in solving the discrimination problem.

Concept Learning

Unless you live in the southwestern United States or have access to a particularly good zoo, it is unlikely that you have ever seen a roadrunner that was not a cartoon character. Still, if someone were to point out a roadrunner to you, you would immediately recognize it as a bird. To make this judgment you would not need to observe the roadrunner's mating rituals or its food-gathering behaviors. Likewise, you would not need to read about the physiology of the roadrunner, nor would you need to have someone describe its diet. You would make your judgment based on your idea or your *concept* of what a bird is. You would note that the roadrunner has a beak, two scrawny legs, feathers, wings, and eyes on the sides of its head. Since all these features probably fit your concept of what it is to be a bird, the roadrunner would quickly be identified as fitting this concept.

This example illustrates an important point. Much of our knowledge about the world and many of our reactions to novel objects depend on concepts that we have formed from our experiences. We can define a concept as a *distinct category of objects or events that are all generally related on the basis of certain features or characteristics.* In other words, every concept is defined in part by a set of stimulus features. Objects that contain these features are usually viewed as part of that concept, while objects that do not have these features are usually excluded. The "automobile" concept, for example, contains for most people a wide variety of objects. Sports cars, station wagons, and limousines all fit into this concept, even though the objects named differ along a number of dimensions. All are usually included because they share certain features, such as four wheels, seats, and engines, that tend to define our concept of "automobile."

Just from this brief description, it may be obvious why some researchers feel that concept formation is related to the processes of generalization and discrimination. On the one hand, in order to form a useful concept we must be able to distinguish between objects having different features and then respond to these objects accordingly. Certainly, such a process is similar to what we do when we learn a discrimination. At the same time, learning a concept involves learning to respond similarly to related objects even if they differ in some ways. This, of course, is similar to the process of generalization.

Now we will examine some ideas about what concepts consist of and about concept formation. We will find that theories of concept formation range from treatments of concepts as simple discriminations to views of concepts as complex abstractions. We will also find that while concepts play a key role in an organism's interaction with its environment, we have no completely adequate explanation for how concepts are derived. The first position we describe, the notion that concepts are learned via simple stimulus–response associations, is reminiscent of the earliest discrimination learning theories.

Associations as the Basis for Concept Learning

One of the earliest studies of concept formation was conducted by Hull (1920). Hull hypothesized that the formation of a concept begins with the association of certain stimulus features with a particular response. This response was assumed to generalize to a number of objects containing these stimulus features. That is, Hull assumed that a subject would form the concept of "bird" by first associating some critical feature such as wings or feathers with the verbal response "bird." Hull believed that once such an association had been formed, the same response would generalize to other objects containing these features. Thus, the tendency to group objects together into a concept was presumed to result from a stimulus–response association that generalizes to other similar stimuli.

To test this notion, Hull presented his subjects with a series of paired associates lists, each containing 12 stimulus–response pairs. In all these lists, the stimulus terms were Chinese language characters and the response terms were nonsense syllables. Before describing Hull's complete procedure we should note an important attribute of written Chinese. Although different characters are used to represent different words, several characters often share a common element or feature called a "radical." Figure 7.9 illustrates some of the characters Hull used and shows the radicals common to groups of characters.

Radical	List 1	List 2	List 3	List 4	List 5	List 6
氵	[illegible]	[illegible]	[illegible]	[illegible]	[illegible]	[illegible]
歹	[illegible]	[illegible]	[illegible]	[illegible]	[illegible]	[illegible]
力	[illegible]	[illegible]	[illegible]	[illegible]	[illegible]	[illegible]
弓	[illegible]	[illegible]	[illegible]	[illegible]	[illegible]	[illegible]
石	[illegible]	[illegible]	[illegible]	[illegible]	[illegible]	[illegible]
穴	[illegible]	[illegible]	[illegible]	[illegible]	[illegible]	[illegible]

FIGURE 7.9 Some of the Chinese characters used by Hull to study concept learning. (From Hull, 1920.)

In this study, each list Hull presented had the same 12 nonsense syllables as response terms. However, each list had a different group of characters as stimulus terms. So the response term "ZPQ" had one character as a stimulus term in list 1, and a different character as its stimulus term in list 2. One facet of the stimulus terms did remain constant, however, from list to list. If a character with a given radical had been paired with "ZPQ" in list 1, a different character containing that same radical was paired with "ZPQ" in list 2 (see Figure 7.9). Thus, while the stimulus terms themselves changed from list to list, each list contained the same pairings between radicals and nonsense syllables.

Hull found that as more and more lists were presented, subjects learned the correct responses faster. For example, on list 1, subjects could remember very few of the responses after a single list presentation. On later lists, however, subjects were able to remember a substantial number of responses after one presentation. Hull saw this result as indicating that subjects associate the radical (one facet of the stimulus term) with the correct response. Thus, when the same radical is later seen, the subject tends to make the same response, which is then correct. In effect, these results indicate that subjects associate a verbal response with features of an object and then generalize that response to other objects containing the same features. This, of course, is precisely how Hull proposed that concepts are formed.

In the ensuing years, several theorists have suggested variations of Hull's original position. For example, Bourne and Restle (1959) proposed that as individuals learn a concept, they do more than learn to respond similarly to a set of common features. They also learn to *ignore* the features that are irrelevant to a given concept. For example, in learning the concept "automobile," subjects learn to attach this label to many objects that have engines, seats, four wheels, and doors. However, they also learn to ignore the size and shape of an object in determining whether it fits the concept. Although this and other proposals have made Hull's position more appealing (see also, Kendler & Kendler, 1962), the basic idea has remained the same. Concepts are presumed to result from stimulus–response associations that generalize to other similar stimuli.

Hypothesis Testing as the Basis for Concept Learning

The hallmark of the associationistic view was that concept learning is a relatively passive, automatic process. The association between a stimulus feature and a concept label was presumed to occur automatically when the subject's response to a stimulus was reinforced (that is, labeled as correct). The generalization of this concept label to other stimuli was also viewed as being a natural, automatic process. This view contrasts sharply with a second theory of concept learning often called the hypothesis-testing theory.

The notion of hypothesis testing was first proposed by Bruner, Goodnow, and Austin (1956), who suggested that concept learning is closely related to problem solving. The problem involved in such learning is discovering which stimulus features actually define a particular concept. Only by discovering these defining features is an individual able to determine which objects belong to a given concept and which do not. Thus, in learning the concept of "bird," a person must determine that feathers are important features, which define that concept. Unless this determination is made, the individual may end up including airplanes and kites in the same concept as robins and eagles, since all these objects fly.

To solve this problem of defining features, it is proposed that individuals form hypotheses concerning which features are critical and then test these hypotheses. For example, let's assume that a child is learning the concept of "bird." The child may be told that a canary is a bird and a German shepherd is not a bird. Beginning with this information, the child might assume that several features are involved in the bird concept. Birds may be small, they may be yellow, they may sing, or they may have feathers.

To learn which features are critical to the "bird" concept, the child may begin with the hypothesis that all yellow objects are birds. This hypothesis will soon be rejected, however, when the child labels a taxicab and a lemon as birds and is told these labels are incorrect. Having rejected this hypothesis, the child may test a second feature, and then a third, and so on, until she learns that feathers are among the important features defining the concept. At this point, the child can begin to call feathered objects birds and usually will be correct. Of course, the first time the child labels a feather duster a bird and is not reinforced, further hypothesis testing will be necessary to refine the concept.

Although the theoretical approach just described was tested first by Bruner, Goodnow, and Austin (1956), it was Levine (1966, 1975) who most thoroughly developed and tested this point of view. Levine reasoned that it is one thing to assume that subjects form and test hypotheses, but quite another to demonstrate this process in action. Thus, Levine developed the *blank trials procedure* for studying hypothesis testing in concept formation experiments.

To begin, a subject is shown two objects and is told that one of them represents some unknown concept. For example, the subject may be confronted with a small, white letter "T" on the left and a large, black letter "X" on the right. He is then instructed to guess which of the objects belongs to the concept. The experimenter determines ahead of time which stimulus is the correct one in this task. For example, the experimenter may determine that *white letters* represent the concept and black ones do not. Thus, if the subject chooses the white letter "T," he is told he is correct. According to the hypothesis-testing theory, this beginning trial should leave the subject with four hypotheses with respect to what stimulus defines the unknown concept. The subject may assume that white letters, T-shaped letters, small letters, or letters on the left define the concept. And, according to this theory, the subject should begin testing these hypotheses systematically.

Therefore, Levine followed the initial trial with four additional presentations of the stimulus objects. On each of these presentations, the experimenter changed the size, position, and color of every letter. So, for example, on the first of the additional trials the subject might receive a large, black "X" on the left and a small, white "T" on the right. The next trial might consist of a small, white "X" on the left and a large, black "T" on the right. Figure 7.10 illustrates how the initial trial and the four additional presentations might be given. On each of these additional presentations the subject is asked to choose the letter he believes represents the concept. However, the subject is given no feedback about the correctness of his responses. The term "blank trials" refers to this lack of feedback.

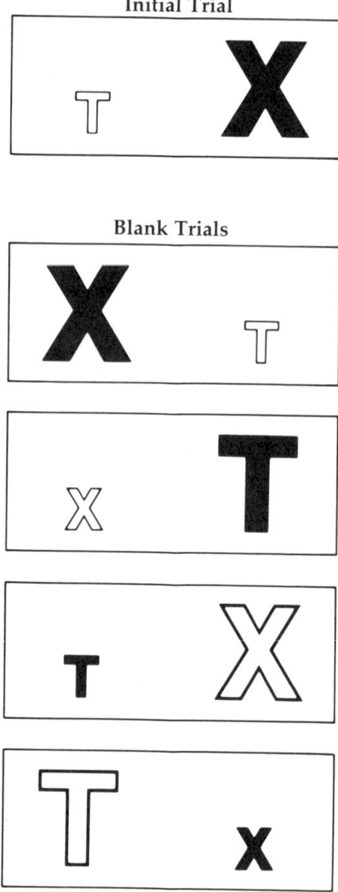

FIGURE 7.10 An example of an initial trial and four blank trials used by Levine in his concept learning studies. (From Levine, 1966.)

Levine assumed that if subjects actually do form and test hypotheses, these hypotheses should be evidenced by how the subject responds on the blank trials. He assumed that since the blank trials involve no feedback, the subject should stay with the same hypothesis on all trials regardless of how the stimuli are changed. For example, let's assume that after the first trial the subject forms the hypothesis that all letters on the left fit the concept. If this is the case, the subject should choose the left letter on the four subsequent blank trials, regardless of whether that letter is a "T" or an "X," black or white, large or small. Thus, by tracking responses on the blank trials, it becomes possible to determine whether a subject has formed a hypothesis after trial 1, and, if so, what that hypothesis is. Furthermore, by presenting a series of feedback trials followed by blank trials, it becomes possible to see how subjects reject incorrect hypotheses and select new ones.

Using this procedure, Levine found evidence in support of the general hypothesis-testing notion. First, he found that after a given feedback trial, virtually all subjects would stay with a single hypothesis over the next four blank trials. They would, for example, choose "T's" or white letters or small letters consistently across these trials. Second, he found that the hypothesis used on a set of blank trials virtually always was consistent with what had been learned on the feedback trial. Thus if a subject learned that a small, white "T" on the left was correct, he always chose either small letters, white letters, "T's," or letters on the left during the blank trials. Finally, Levine found that once a hypothesis used on blank trials had been shown to be incorrect, the subjects would reject it on future trials. Furthermore, they would turn to a new hypothesis that was part of the original pool of hypotheses that might have been correct on trial 1. So, for example, if four hypotheses were possible after trial 1 and the one chosen was found to be incorrect, subjects would shift to one of the remaining three possible hypotheses.

Based on these findings, Levine was able to refine the hypothesis-testing theory. He suggested that after a first experience with two objects, an individual forms a pool of hypotheses concerning the defining features in a concept. These hypotheses are retained in memory so that they can serve in additional object comparisons. On subsequent comparisons the individual retrieves these hypotheses from memory and selects one as a working hypothesis. If this hypothesis is incorrect, it is deleted from the pool represented in memory. Only hypotheses that still may be correct are carried over to the next comparison experience.

Levine's work on the hypothesis-testing theory is important for several reasons. First, it indicates that concept learning involves more than simply the formation of an association that generalizes to similar stimuli. On the contrary, concept learning appears to involve the active formation and testing of hypotheses concerning what stimuli define a concept. Second, this work suggests that memory plays a key role in concept formation. To arrive at a concept, a subject must be able to remember what hypotheses were originally possible and which hypotheses have previously been rejected. Finally, this proposal is stated clearly enough to permit the making of testable predictions. This property is obviously critical if any theory is to generate useful research.

This is not to say that Levine's position has gone unchallenged. For example, some researchers have questioned the idea that successful hypotheses remain in memory, while unsuccessful hypotheses are deleted. Kellogg, Robbins, and Bourne (1978) have shown that if subjects are asked to recall their hypotheses during concept learning, they recall recent successful hypotheses no better than earlier rejected ones.

Another problem with Levine's approach is that when subjects are asked to verbalize the rules they use for categorizing stimuli, concentrating on these rules can sometimes disrupt the categorization process (see, for example, Reber & Allen, 1978). This finding makes it difficult to believe that individuals would use hypotheses or rules in learning a concept, if the recognition of these rules makes the task more difficult.

Thus, some experimental evidence clearly supports the idea that hypothesis testing is part of the process of concept learning. Other data, however, indicate that the use of hypotheses is unlikely and can even be detrimental. This conflicting evidence has led to the development of a new set of concept learning theories. The important idea in these theories is that concept learning can proceed in different ways depending on the constraints of the experimental procedure. In some cases, it involves the formation and testing of hypotheses, and in other cases it depends on how frequently a subject has correctly associated a response with a specific stimulus feature (see, for example, Hasher & Zachs, 1979; Kellogg, 1982). These theories suggest that both Hull's associative idea and Levine's hypothesis-testing notion have merit in explaining how subjects learn concepts in the laboratory.

Natural versus Laboratory Concepts

Both the associationistic and the hypothesis-testing views were developed to explain the results of concept learning experiments conducted in a laboratory. This circumstance raises an important question. Are the concepts learned in a laboratory setting truly representative of the concepts we learn in the natural environment?

According to at least some researchers, the answer to this question may be no (see, for example, Rosch, 1977; Rosch & Mervis, 1975). The concepts subjects usually learn in a laboratory experiment tend to consist of objects that all share specific stimulus features. That is, all the concepts are clearly defined by the presence of some features and the absence of others. To illustrate this point, consider the concepts learned in Levine's blank trials experiments. In these studies concepts were specifically defined by a single feature such as the color of a letter, the size of a letter, or the position a letter occupied. All stimulus objects that shared a given feature were considered to be part of a concept, while those not having this feature were considered not to be part of the concept. The same was true of Hull's experiment, in which concepts were defined in terms of a specific radical in a Chinese character. Laboratory concepts usually are very simple in that they include only objects having specific stimulus features.

In contrast to these simple concepts, the concepts we learn in our day-to-day lives often lack clarity. "Natural concepts" seem to include objects that are related only vaguely. In other words, many natural concepts do not appear to be based on a specific set of stimulus features. Consider, for example, our concept of "games" (see Wittgenstein, 1953). We all know a game when we see or play one. But, is it possible to think of a specific set of features that will distinguish games from other activities? Games are often fun, they may be interesting, they are usually competitive, and most involve achieving some goal. Still, there are numerous activities that are not classified as games that nevertheless contain these features. There are also many activities we label as games that do not contain all the features just mentioned. A game is like many natural concepts. It is simply difficult to define precisely based on a list of distinguishing stimulus features.

This distinction between natural and laboratory concepts is supported by several facts (see, for example, Mervis, 1980; Rosch, 1977; Rosch & Mervis, 1975). First, if natural concepts simply included all objects with a given set of features, it should be easy to determine which objects belong to a concept and which do not. To make such a determination, we would simply match the features of a concept with the features of the object in question. In the real world, however, it is often difficult to determine whether or not an object belongs to a given concept. Take, for example, the object "ant." Clearly, it fits the concept "insect." But does the object "ant" fit the concept "food"? In some cultures ants clearly fit this concept, but in our own it is a questionable fit at best. What about the object "lamp"? Is it an "appliance" or does it fit better in your concept of "furniture"?

Is a "bat" a "bird" or a "mammal"? If all our concepts were neatly defined on the basis of specific features, such judgments would be simple. Yet, subjects often have great difficulty deciding on concept membership.

A related issue has to do with the observation that some objects seem to be better examples of a concept than others. If natural concepts were all neatly defined in terms of stimulus features, then all objects containing those features should be equally good examples of a concept. As a practical matter, however, even though both a lamp and a television set can be considered to be pieces of furniture, neither comes to mind as quickly as "sofa" when someone says "furniture." Likewise, most people feel that a robin is a very good example of the concept "bird" and that although an ostrich is clearly a "bird," it is not a particularly good example of the concept.

This difference between natural concepts and concepts learned in laboratory settings has important implications for theories of concept formation. All the theories we have discussed so far make the assumption that concepts always contain objects that have common stimulus features. These theories do not explain how we might form concepts that contain vaguely related objects. To explain the formation of natural concepts, many researchers have turned to *prototype* or *exemplar theories.*

Prototype or Exemplar Theories of Concept Formation

The *prototype* or *exemplar theories* have been developed to explain how vaguely related objects become part of the same concept. Basically, these theories suggest that through our experiences with objects, we tend to form an abstraction that represents the best example of a concept. This "best example" is usually termed a *prototype.* According to some such theories, these prototypes are based on an averaging of all the features objects in a concept usually have (see, for example, Posner & Keele, 1970). Thus, in forming the prototype for "bird" we might form an average representation for what feathers look like, as well as an average representation for the characteristics of wings. Our mental picture of the prototype, however, may not match any real bird we have ever seen.

Other theories of this kind (see, for example, Rosch, 1977) propose that prototypes are usually the most common instances of a concept that we have encountered. Thus, our prototype of a bird may be a robin, not an ostrich, because we frequently encounter robins as examples of the bird category. We seldom encounter ostriches as examples.

Regardless of how prototypes are formed, these theories suggest that decisions about concept membership are *based on how well an object matches a given prototype, not on whether an object contains a given set of features.* It is presumed that objects in the same concept or category share what is called a *family resemblance* (see Rosch & Mervis, 1975; Wittgenstein, 1953). This means that each object in a concept shares at least some features with other objects in that category. If an object has a close family resemblance to the prototype, it will be considered to be a good example of that concept. An object that has only a slight family resemblance to the prototype is usually considered to be only a marginal member of that concept.

Experimental support for this general prototype view has come from a variety of sources. First of all, there is evidence that subjects do form abstract prototypes on the basis of their experience with a number of related objects. In one set of experiments, Posner and Keele (1968, 1970) constructed four geometric shapes with black dots. These shapes were considered as prototypes. They then created a series of distorted shapes by rearranging some of the dots used to form each of the original prototypes. Figure 7.11 shows one of the prototypes used, as well as some of the distortions created for that prototype.

The subjects in these studies were first given all the distorted figures in a random

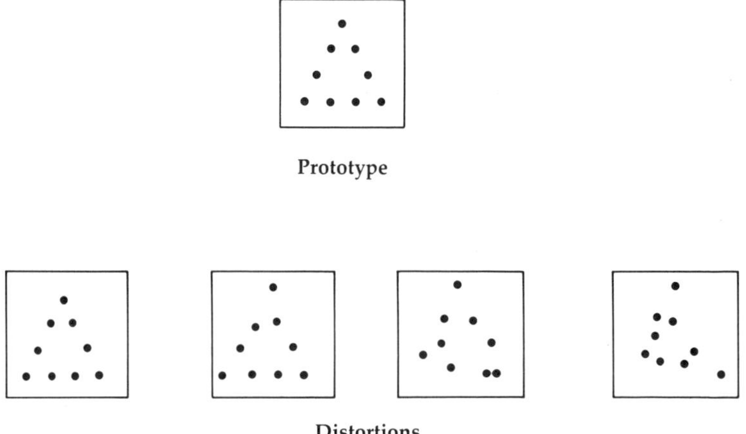

FIGURE 7.11 An example of one prototype and distortions of that prototype used by Posner and Keele to study prototype formation. (From Posner, Goldsmith, and Welton, 1967.)

order and were asked to sort them into four categories. It is important to note that at this point the subjects had not seen the prototypes. Still, in order to be correct they had to learn to sort all the distortions of a given figure (for example, the triangle) into one group, all the distortions of a second figure into another group, and so forth. Once the distorted figures had been sorted correctly, the subjects were given a second set of figures to sort. Some of these figures were the old distortions they had already sorted, while some were new distortions of the same prototypes. Also included in set 2 were the four prototype figures, which the subjects had never seen.

Posner and Keele found that the subjects sorted the prototypes into the correct categories along with their distortions. They were able to sort the prototypes much more easily than the new distortions, even though they had never seen either type of item before. This suggests that in the original sorting task, the subjects had formed some mental representation for each category that approximated the prototype for that category. Otherwise, it is difficult to explain how the previously unseen prototypes could be categorized so easily. Similar findings have been reported by other experimenters using a variety of stimulus configurations (see, for example, Bomba & Siqueland, 1983; Reed, 1972).

Aside from these prototype formation experiments, other studies have confirmed that not all objects belonging to the same concept are equally good examples of that concept. For example, Rosch (1973) conducted a reaction time experiment in which both children and adults were asked to determine whether an object was a member of a given concept. They were asked to make their decisions as quickly as possible. Rosch found that certain objects were consistently identified as members of a concept and that these decisions were made very quickly (that is, reaction times were short). The classification of other objects required a much longer decision time. Rosch's results indicate that although two objects may both contain features normally associated with a concept, one object may be viewed as a better example of that concept than another. This finding is consistent with the idea that subjects judge concept membership on the basis of similarity to a prototype, not on the basis of the specific stimulus features an object contains.

The conflict between prototype and feature-based theories of concept learning has generated substantial research interest in recent years. For example, certain feature-based theories have been developed to incorporate the findings that led to the notion of prototypes (see, for example, Bourne, 1982; Neumann, 1974). As yet, however, there is no clear resolution to this conflict. Feature-based theories are clearly adequate in explaining how simple concepts are formed, but prototype theories seem to be necessary to account for the learning of complex natural concepts. This recent research has given us a much better idea of the complexities of concept formation and has raised a number of interesting questions concerning the structure of concepts. In the next few years this promises to be an active and important research area—an area that is critical for our understanding of how we gain and structure knowledge of the world.

Natural Concepts in Nonhuman Species

Prototype theories were developed around the notion that many of our natural or real-world concepts cannot be defined on the basis of one or two critical stimulus features. Natural concepts, unlike the concepts often learned in a laboratory experiment, are often fuzzy and ill-defined (see, for example, Rosch, 1977). This distinction raises an interesting question. We have already seen in our discussions of discrimination learning that rats and pigeons can form "concepts" based on a few stimulus features. For example, a pigeon can learn to respond to red objects and not to green ones. But are nonhuman organisms capable of acquiring natural concepts, which are less easily discriminated?

Some of the best work on this question has been conducted by Herrnstein and his colleagues, and the answer appears to be yes (see, for example, Herrnstein, 1979; Herrnstein & deVilliers, 1980; Herrnstein, Loveland, & Cable, 1976). For example, in one experiment, Herrnstein and deVilliers (1980) presented a set of 80 slides to a group of four pigeons. Half the slides showed underwater pictures of fish. These slides differed dramatically in terms of the type of fish shown, the position and size of the fish, and the physical context. The remaining 40 slides also showed underwater scenes, but no fish were represented. The pigeons were reinforced on a variable interval schedule for pecking at the fish slides and were given no reinforcement for pecking at the others. Herrnstein and deVilliers found that all four pigeons rapidly acquired this discrimination even though the fish slides shared few common features and the features in the fish and nonfish slides overlapped considerably.

Even more impressive was the behavior of the pigeons when they were presented with an entirely novel set of fish and nonfish slides. Based on their discrimination training, the pigeons showed a clear facility for responding to the new fish slides and not to the new nonfish slides. This result suggests that the pigeons had somehow acquired a "fish" concept and were then able to categorize novel objects into the natural concepts they had formed.

Similar experiments have been reported by a number of researchers (see Herrnstein, 1979, for a review of these studies). Pigeons, for example, are capable of distinguishing trees from other plants, oak leaves from leaves of other trees, and pictures of water from pictures having no water. Monkeys and bluejays have exhibited a similar ability to sort objects into natural categories. Thus, it appears that humans are not the only species capable of forming concepts having "fuzzy" or ill-defined sets of features. The ability to form complex natural concepts is an ability that apparently is shared by a variety of organisms.

Summary Statements

In this chapter we found that once an organism has learned to respond to one stimulus, it tends to make the same response to other similar stimuli. This tendency, called stimulus generalization, is affected by a number of factors such as the degree and type of learning, an organism's level of motivation, and the interval that separates learning from generalization testing. In our review of generalization theories, we found that no theory currently provides an adequate account of generalization phenomena. We did find, however, that contemporary theories emphasizing the role of "incidental" stimuli appear to be consistent with a large number of generalization findings.

Our discussion of discrimination learning revealed that stimuli gain control over responding through the process of differential reinforcement. We described both the continuity and noncontinuity approaches to explaining discrimination learning and reviewed data relevant to these positions. We found that most discrimination phenomena are compatible with current noncontinuity theories, which emphasize the role of attentional processes in discrimination learning.

The last phenomenon we discussed was concept formation. We described several concept learning experiments and looked at different theoretical explanations for how concepts are formed. First, we reviewed Hull's notion that concept formation and discrimination learning are essentially equivalent. Then we noted Levine's ideas concerning the role of hypothesis testing in the formation of a concept. Finally, we explored the difference between laboratory and natural concepts and discussed the prototype analysis of how natural concepts are formed. We concluded by describing how nonhuman species acquire natural concepts.

8

Memory Processes: The Formation of a Representation

Most of us become aware of our memories when we have to work to recall something. For example, if I asked you how many doors you have in your house or apartment, you probably could not answer immediately, because most probably you have never counted them. Still, most of us would be able to answer this question after a period of time. We would probably do this by imagining each room in the house and then counting the number of doors in each room.

The process we go through to answer such a question makes several facts obvious. First, through our experiences we have formed some internal representation of what our homes look like. Second, this is an enduring representation that can last for long periods of time. Third, we are able to select or activate this representation from among the thousands of memories we carry in our brains. And finally, we are able to use this representation to answer questions or to guide our behaviors.

Since we tend to become aware of our memories only when we are asked a specific question, it is easy to underestimate the role that memories play in our everyday behaviors. When we walk across a room, for example, we seldom consider that this is a learned behavior and that each step requires a memory for which motor movement occurred last and which one should follow. Likewise, carrying on a simple conversation involves remembering how to form sounds with our mouths, which sounds represent appropriate words, and which words we have already spoken. It also involves remembering which social cues signal that it is our turn to talk. In effect, we use our memories not only to answer specific questions, but also to perform behaviors so simple that we consider them to be automatic.

Given the pervasive role of memory in our lives, it is not surprising that the study of memory has become very important among psychologists. In the past 15 years alone, thousands of studies have been done to examine various aspects of the memory system. In the chapters that remain, we will discuss some of the most important theories and experiments that have come out of this work. We will look first at the question of how memories are formed. Then we will address the question of how memories are organized or structured. Finally, we will examine various ideas concerning how we remember and why we forget.

We will begin our discussion in this chapter by focusing on the processes involved in memory formation. By way of introducing this topic, it is helpful to take note of one of the more important developments in the study of memory—the use of the computer analogy as a way of conceptualizing the memory system.

Information Processing: The Computer Analogy

As we will see in Chapters 9 through 11, the memory system in humans and other species is extremely complex and often mysterious. To understand these complexities, researchers have found it useful to look at simpler memory systems to get some idea of how our own systems might operate. Since the mid-1960s, many researchers have concentrated on the memory capabilities of computers as a way of conceptualizing memory in living organisms. This approach has not been founded on the idea that computers and living organisms function in the same way. Rather, it has been thought that by understanding how computers handle information, we may gain some clues to how organisms form and use memories.

This conceptual framework, which is usually called the *information processing approach*, takes the position that both computers and living organisms can be viewed as information processing systems. In other words, both computers and living organisms begin by acquiring information from the environment in the form of stimulus inputs. Next, they convert these inputs into a format or code that can be used by their respective systems. The next step is to store this coded information in the memory system in a particular file or location. Later, when the information is needed, the file containing it is retrieved and the information is used.

Through the use of this computer analogy, memory researchers have come to realize that an understanding of memory requires a knowledge of at least two aspects of the system: memory processes and memory structures. First, we must understand the processes we use to handle information. *Memory processes* include the operations we perform on stimulus inputs to convert them into usable memories, as well as the operations we go through to search memories out and retrieve them when they are needed. Most researchers agree that three processes are of critical importance: encoding, storage, and retrieval.

The *encoding process* is characterized as the set of operations we perform on incoming stimuli to convert them into a usable format or code. Just as the computer converts the depression of a letter key on its keyboard into a numerical symbol, organisms must modify incoming stimuli into codes that the brain can understand and use. In addition, encoding involves organizing or tagging stimuli by relating them to other bits of information in memory. Just as computers create files for inputs that belong together, we organize our own inputs into groups of related bits of information. All these operations that result in an organized format are called encoding processes.

The second major memory process is *storage*. Very simply, "storage" refers to the operation of placing information into the memory system and maintaining it there for later use. Anyone who has ever used a computer for word processing will quickly recognize the difference between encoding and storage. When you type a document into the computer, you can give that document a particular file name so that it will be kept separate from documents you have previously entered. This procedure is, of course, analogous to encoding, since the document is being organized or tagged in a certain way. However, until you direct your computer to save or store the new document, it does not become a permanent part of the computer's memory. Until a document is actually stored, it can be written over or lost from the system regardless of how well it has been encoded. Storage, then, involves the registration of information in the memory system.

After a memory has been encoded and stored, it becomes subject to the process of *retrieval*, which involves the operations necessary for locating and calling up specific information from a memory store. Again, computers, like living organisms, are capable of storing thousands and thousands of individual memories. Yet, by giving a computer an individual file or code name, we make it possible for the computer to find the information attached to that name and display it on a screen. The same is apparently true of our own memory systems. When we attempt to learn a person's name, we often relate the name to the person's facial features or to environmental stimuli that are present when the person is introduced. Later, when we see these facial features or stimuli, we are able to use the cues to help us retrieve the name from among all the other memories we have represented in storage. The operations we go through to locate a particular memory in storage are called retrieval processes.

Obviously, the storage, encoding, and retrieval processes are highly interrelated. Retrieval is impossible without storage, since unless storage has occurred there will be no memory in the system to be retrieved. However, retrieval is equally dependent on the encoding process. For example, a memory in storage that is not properly encoded may be impossible to find. Just because we have stored a document in a filing cabinet does not mean we will be able to locate the document when we need it. Our retrieval of the document depends on whether we have filed it correctly; otherwise, when we search the filing cabinet in the logical, or proper place, we will not find the document. Finally, as we will see later, retrieval operations may result in more than simply finding a memory. These operations may also lead to the re-encoding of the memory once it is found.

As we have said, our interest in these memory processes has been stimulated by the use of the computer analogy. However, this analogy has also drawn our attention to *memory structures*, a second aspect of memory that must be considered. We know, for example, that a computer has certain prewired circuits that are designed to hold information at various stages in our work. For example, we have "buffer" circuits to hold temporarily new information we are entering into the computer. While information is held in buffer circuits we can make changes in a document, add one document to another, or change the file or code name attached to a document. In effect, these buffers hold our "rough drafts" of a document long enough for us to make whatever changes we desire to make.

When we are satisfied with the form of a

document that is located in a buffer, we can save the document or store it permanently in the computer's memory. Permanent storage requires shifting the document from the buffer circuits to another set of circuits designed to hold information indefinitely. Once located in the permanent storage circuits, a document can no longer be changed unless it is returned to the buffer circuits, where modifications are performed.

The prewired circuits are often referred to as computer "hardware." These are the structural components of the computer that never change, regardless of the operations we happen to be performing at a given time. The existence of such structural components has led researchers to look for like components in our own memory systems. Thus, several theories of memory have proposed that our own memories reside in different buffers or holding areas at different points in the memory processing sequence. "Short-term memory," "working memory," and "long-term memory" are but a few of the terms suggested to denote different holding areas in which memories might reside.

In the chapters to come, we will closely examine the various memory processes and structures that have been implicated in memory function. Since in this chapter we are concerned with memory formation, we will deal primarily with the processes of encoding and storage, as well as the structures involved in memory formation. To focus this discussion, we will begin by looking at a *stage model* of memory formation—that is, the notion that a memory must pass through a sequence of structures and processes between the time of stimulus input and the time of permanent memory registration.

The Atkinson–Shiffrin Model

Several theorists have proposed memory models that have been based at least loosely on the computer analogy (see, for example, Broadbent, 1958; Waugh & Norman, 1965). However, the information processing model proposed by Atkinson and Shiffrin (1968, 1971) is probably the best-known model of this type. According to Atkinson and Shiffrin, the human memory system is best conceptualized as a series of memory structures through which information must pass. In other words, information from the environment moves through a set sequence of memory structures before the memory of that information can become permanently stored. A basic assumption of this model is that information is processed differently in these various memory structures.

To illustrate how this model works, Atkinson and Shiffrin devised a flowchart that characterizes how information might move through the memory system. This flowchart (Figure 8.1) shows three memory structures, lists the processes that can occur in certain structures, and includes directional arrows showing how information flows from one structure to another. We will use this chart as the basis for our description of the Atkinson–Shiffrin model.

The model begins with a very simple assumption. When an individual first notices a stimulus in the environment, only the raw physical features of that stimulus become represented in memory. These physical features are stored in a memory structure called the *sensory register* or the *sensory memory store.* Atkinson and Shiffrin suggest that stimulus features remain represented in sensory memory only briefly (0.5–1.0 sec). They further propose that there are different sensory registers for stimulus features of different types. Thus, the visual features of a stimulus are presumably represented in a visual register, the auditory characteristics are thought to reside in an auditory register, and so on, down to the characteristics experienced through the sense of touch, which would belong in the haptic register.

Basically, the sensory registers are thought to provide us with a brief stimulus aftereffect

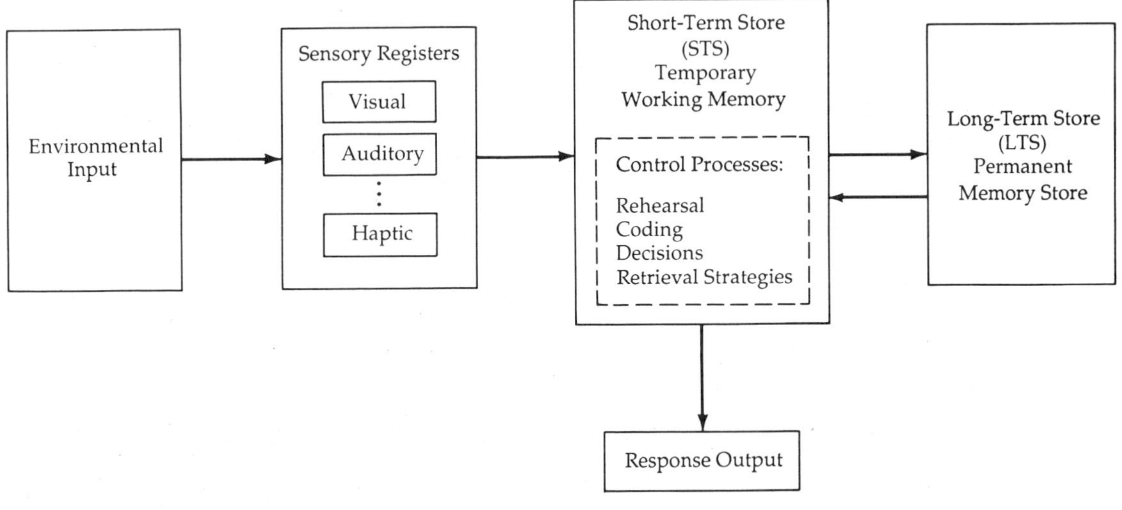

FIGURE 8.1 The Atkinson–Shiffrin information processing model. (From Atkinson and Shiffrin, 1971.)

for each stimulus an organism encounters. For example, it is presumed that once an auditory stimulus has disappeared, its sound will remain briefly in the auditory register much like a short-lived echo. Likewise, visual stimuli are presumed to leave behind a brief image in the visual register. Although these registers are thought to hold sensory information only briefly, Atkinson and Shiffrin propose that the sensory memory store has an extremely large capacity, permitting the holding of many bits of sensory information at any given time.

The importance of the sensory registers can best be understood by realizing that we constantly encounter new and varied sources of stimulation. For this reason we cannot process simultaneously all the incoming stimuli we sense at any given time. Basically, we cope with this limitation by attending to only a small proportion of the stimuli our sensory systems detect. According to Atkinson and Shiffrin, this selection process occurs while stimuli are represented in sensory memory. They propose that our attentional mechanisms scan through the stimuli represented in the sensory registers and select certain stimuli for further processing in the memory system. Stimuli that are not selected are lost from the sensory memory store and never become represented permanently in memory. In other words, sensory information that is not attended to cannot be maintained in the sensory registers and simply decays or deteriorates in fractions of a second. Sensory information that *is* selected by our attentional mechanisms is transferred to the short-term memory store for further processing.

According to this model, the first time we become consciously aware of a stimulus input is when that input enters the short-term memory store. This store holds all the information we are currently thinking about or are conscious of at any given time. For this reason, Atkinson and Shiffrin suggest that the short-term store must have a very limited capacity. They assume that because we can be conscious of only a limited number of items at one time, the short-term store must be able to hold only a few bits of information at once.

Aside from being a structure of limited capacity, the short-term store is viewed as being a temporary facility. That is, unless information is actively processed upon entering this store, it can remain there for only a matter of seconds. If information in the short-term store is not processed, it is presumed to decay or fade, never to become represented permanently in the memory system. Unlike information in the sensory store, however, information in the short-term store can be maintained there indefinitely if it is processed or rehearsed.

The true importance of the short-term store is that this is where we consciously or purposely rehearse and encode information for permanent storage. This model suggests that the short-term store contains a separate system called a *buffer.* As suggested earlier, information in the short-term store can be selectively placed into this buffer, where it can be rehearsed and encoded. The buffer is presumed to have a very limited capacity, such that only a few items can be actively rehearsed at once. New information placed into the buffer automatically displaces information already there. This displaced information then goes back into the short-term store, where it decays over time. Information that remains in the buffer and is actively processed becomes transferred into the *long-term memory store,* where it is permanently represented. Thus, much of the active memory processing that we do is presumed to occur in short-term memory. For this reason, several researchers have called short-term memory the *working memory store.*

Although as we have seen, Atkinson and Shiffrin assume that information processed in the short-term buffer is transferred to long-term memory, they also suggest that under some circumstances it may be possible for information to reach long-term storage without such processing. They seem to presume, for example, that some information may be transferred to long-term storage simply by remaining in short-term memory for some period of time (see Atkinson & Shiffrin, 1968). This point, which is not made entirely explicit, suggests that we may store some information that we have not consciously processed. Thus, we may sometimes be surprised by the contents of our permanent memories.

The long-term memory store is characterized in this model as having an unlimited capacity. In other words, long-term memory is capable of holding as many memories as we can acquire in a lifetime. This model also assumes that once represented in long-term storage, memories can be maintained there almost indefinitely without any need for active processing. This model does presume that memories can be lost from the long-term store through processes such as decay or interference resulting from the storage of new memories. Still, this store is thought to be a relatively permanent storage place, which serves as a vast repository for our formed memories.

To this point we have discussed how the Atkinson–Shiffrin model views the formation of a permanent memory. However, two additional points about this model should be mentioned. First, the flowchart (Figure 8.1) shows that information can move not only from the short- to the long-term store but also from long- to short-term memory. This bidirectional flow of information is meant to represent the retrieval of memories from the long-term store. In other words, it is presumed that when a long-term memory is retrieved, at least a copy of that memory re-enters short-term storage, where we become conscious of it. This process has one very important implication for the formation of a memory. Once information has been retrieved into the short-term store, it can be rehearsed along with new information that has entered short-term storage via the sensory registers. Thus, this model presumes that some memories may be the product of the combination of new information with old information from long-term storage.

A second point worth noting is that the Atkinson–Shiffrin model views the decision-making process as occurring in short-term memory. That is, we decide how to respond based on information that is in that store at a given time. As we have seen, some of our decisions may be based on new information coming from the sensory registers, while others may be determined by information retrieved from long-term memory. Once again, these points emphasize the important role of short-term memory processes in the formation and use of our memories.

Evidence Supporting the Atkinson–Shiffrin Model

Although the Atkinson–Shiffrin model is based to some degree on how computers process information, it would be misleading to imply that the computer analogy was the only source of this model. In constructing this approach, Atkinson and Shiffrin relied heavily on several lines of experimental evidence. This evidence suggested that the characteristics of a memory appear to change, the longer a memory remains in the system. Based on such evidence, these theorists concluded that a memory must move through different structures and processes as a function of the time since stimulus input. Now we review some of the evidence Atkinson and Shiffrin used in formulating their hypothesis, as well as other pertinent studies.

Evidence for the Existence of Sensory Memory

Atkinson and Shiffrin based their notions of sensory memory on the pioneering work of Sperling (1960), who studied memory for visual stimuli. Since brief visual memories are often referred to as *icons,* Sperling's work is usually described as dealing with *iconic storage.* Basically, Sperling was interested in two questions. First, when an individual sees a visual display, how much of that display is stored in the sensory registers? Second, how long does this visual information last in storage?

To address these questions, Sperling conducted a series of experiments in which subjects were briefly presented with an array of 12 letters such as the following:

A R Q N
Z L P F
M B E V

In his first experiment, Sperling presented the array for 0.05 second. The subjects had been instructed to write down as many of the letters as they could as soon as the array disappeared. Sperling found that his subjects consistently recalled an average of 4 to 5 letters from the array.

Sperling realized that this finding could be interpreted in one of two ways. First, the results could indicate that when a visual display is presented, subjects store only 4 to 5 of the items in memory. Another possibility, however, is that subjects store a much larger number of items, but the memory for these items decays rapidly. By the time a subject has written down 4 or 5 of the items, the remaining items may have decayed from memory. To distinguish between these two interpretations, Sperling devised what is called the *partial-report procedure.* Once again, a 12-letter array was presented. When the array had disappeared, however, the subjects were presented with one of three tones. Each tone stood for one row of 4 letters in the array. If tone 1 was presented, the subjects were to report the top row in the array. Tone 2 indicated that the second row should be reported, and tone 3 signaled that a report of the bottom row would be required. Thus, subjects did not know which row would be tested until after the array had disappeared.

Sperling reasoned that if subjects were storing only 4 or 5 items from the entire array, then on the average they should be able to report only 1 or 2 items from a given row. If, instead, subjects were storing all the items in the array but simply were having difficulty reporting more than 4 or 5 before memory decay set in, a different result would be expected. Under these circumstances, one would predict that a subject should be able to report almost all the items in a given row, since each row contained only 4 letters.

In his second experiment, Sperling used this partial-report procedure. He also varied the time between the disappearance of the array and the onset of the tone. On various trials the tone occurred either 0, 0.15, 0.30, or 1 second after the offset of the letters. The purpose of this manipulation was to determine how quickly visual memories are lost from the sensory register.

This experiment resulted in two important findings. First, when subjects were given the tone immediately after the offset of the letters, they were able to recall 3 to 4 of the letters from whatever row had been signaled. Since this level of recall occurred regardless of which row had been signaled, the result suggests that for a brief period of time virtually all the letters in the array had been represented in the sensory store. The second significant finding was that recall of the letters decreased as the onset of the tone was delayed. For example, when a full second elapsed between the array offset and the tone onset, subjects were able to recall only 1 or 2 letters from the signaled row instead of 3 to 4. This result indicates that while several letters are originally stored in sensory memory, the memory for these stimuli decays very rapidly. Subjects who have to wait even 1 second before reporting the letters show very poor levels of recall. Sperling concluded from this study that iconic memory has a reasonably large capacity for the storage of items, but items can remain in iconic storage for only a brief time.

A final experiment conducted by Sperling was directed at still another characteristic of sensory memory—specifically, the type of information that is stored in the sensory registers. On the one hand, it is possible that the sensory store contains only the physical features of the stimuli we sense (for example, the size, color, or shape of an object). Alternatively, sensory memory might include information about the meanings of sensory events, as well. It is possible, for example, that when we see a set of items, these items may be automatically classified in sensory memory according to what the visual symbols mean. We might, for instance, organize our sensory information into groupings such as vowels and consonants, letters and digits, or uppercase and lowercase letters. In effect, the question of interest is whether we analyze or process the information in sensory memory or whether these memories are little more than pictures or traces of environmental stimuli.

To answer this question, Sperling presented his subjects with a smaller array such as the following:

R 4 6 C
3 B 9 S

As you can see, half the symbols in each row were letters and the other half were digits. On some trials the subjects were asked to report all the symbols in the array. On other trials they were asked to report only the symbols in a given row. This, of course, is analogous to the partial-report procedure. Finally, on some trials the subjects were asked to report either all the digits or all the letters in the array. This is like a partial-report procedure, except that subjects must analyze the difference between letters and digits instead of simply responding on the basis of location within the array.

Sperling found that when subjects were asked to report the symbols in a given row, they consistently recalled 3 to 4 symbols correctly. When asked to report all the digits or letters, however, most subjects gave only 1 or 2 correct responses. This result indicates that subjects are able to use sensory memory to identify items having specific physical features, such as items appearing in a particular spatial location. However, they are unable to use sensory memory to identify items according to a meaningful category such as letters or digits. This finding is consistent with the idea that sensory memory is like a brief picture of stimulus input. It is not a place in which items are organized in terms of meaning or conceptual class.

Since Sperling's original experiments, several researchers have replicated and extended his basic findings. For example, Averbach and Coriell (1961) presented letter arrays to subjects and asked for the recall of a single letter after the array had disappeared. One procedure they used was to present the array on a visual field for 50 msec. When the array had disappeared, they presented a black bar over the position one of the letters had occupied in the array. The subject was required to identify the letter marked by the position of the bar. The investigators found that subjects were able to recall the letter with a high degree of accuracy as long as the bar was presented immediately after the offset of the letter array. However, if more than 0.25 second elapsed between the offset of the array and the presentation of the bar, recall performance dropped to a very low level. This finding replicates Sperling's data and attests to the brief duration of iconic storage.

A related procedure used by Averbach and Coriell points out another important characteristic of sensory memory. This procedure was identical to the one discussed above except for the kind of marker used to denote the target letter. Instead of placing a bar next to a letter's position, the experimenters placed a circle around the position a letter had occupied in the array. They found that if the circle was presented immediately after the array, subjects were able to recall the letter very easily. However, as soon as any delay occurred between the array offset and the onset of the circle, performance dropped to extremely low levels. In other words, the circle marker resulted in much poorer letter recall than did the bar.

In discussing this finding, Averbach and Coriell suggested that since the circle surrounded the entire position in which the letter had been, the circle was perceived as a new stimulus occupying the same position. They proposed that if one stimulus is stored in sensory memory and another stimulus occurs in the same physical location shortly thereafter, the second stimulus will erase the first from the sensory register. In other words, the second stimulus was thought to *mask* the first by being stored on top of it. This phenomenon has now been reported in numerous experiments and is called *backward masking* (see, for example, Breitmeyer & Ganz, 1976). The importance of backward masking is that it indicates that sensory memories may be lost not only by decay, but also by being displaced when new stimuli are sensed.

One final procedure we should note comes from a study conducted by Haber and Standing (1969). These experimenters estimated the duration of iconic storage using a procedure very different from the ones we have discussed thus far. Very simply, they presented their subjects with a series of circles projected on a screen. Each circle was presented for only 10 msec, and the interval separating the appearances of consecutive circles was varied. The subjects were asked to note whether each circle in the series was still visible when the next circle appeared. They found that when only a quarter-second (0.25 second) separated the offset of one circle and the onset of another, subjects invariably reported that the first circle was still visible when the second was presented. This finding is clearly in accord with Sperling's notion that visual stimuli remain very briefly in the sensory store even after the stimuli themselves have disappeared.

Although much of the evidence pertaining to the sensory store has dealt with visual stimuli, there is also evidence for the existence of an auditory sensory register. This auditory register has been termed an *echoic store,* since it appears to hold an echo of any sound we sense from the environment (see Neisser, 1967). Although the results of several studies argue for the existence of such a store, there has been little agreement with respect to how long auditory information is held there.

For example, Darwin, Turvey, and Crowder (1972) performed an experiment with auditory stimuli that was much like Sperling's studies using visual stimuli. These researchers presented strings of spoken symbols (letters or digits) to subjects through earphones, using the protocol illustrated in Figure 8.2. One string of 3 symbols was presented through the left earphone, while a second string of 3 symbols was spoken through the right. A third string of 3 symbols was presented simultaneously through both earphones so that the subjects perceived this string as being spoken in front of them. The three different strings were presented simultaneously, such that all the first symbols in each string occurred together, then the second symbols in each string, and finally the third. All symbols were presented in a span of 1 second.

On some occasions subjects were asked to recall as many of the 9 symbols as possible immediately after the presentation was over. As in Sperling's experiments, subjects averaged about 4.2 correct symbols on this kind of test. On other occasions, however, a partial-report procedure was used. Subjects were given a visual signal indicating that they should report only the symbols presented to the left ear or to the right ear, or in front of them. The visual signal occurred either 0, 1, 2, or 4 seconds after the symbols had been heard. When a 0-second interval was used, subjects were able to report approximately 2 of the 3 symbols from a given string. This suggests that the subjects had more than 4.2 symbols in the auditory register immediately after the symbol presentation. Recall dropped steadily, however, as the symbol–signal interval was increased. The experimenters estimated that symbols remain in the auditory register for up to 2 seconds. When 4 seconds elapsed between the symbols and the signal, subjects performed no better than they did when they were asked to recall all the symbols.

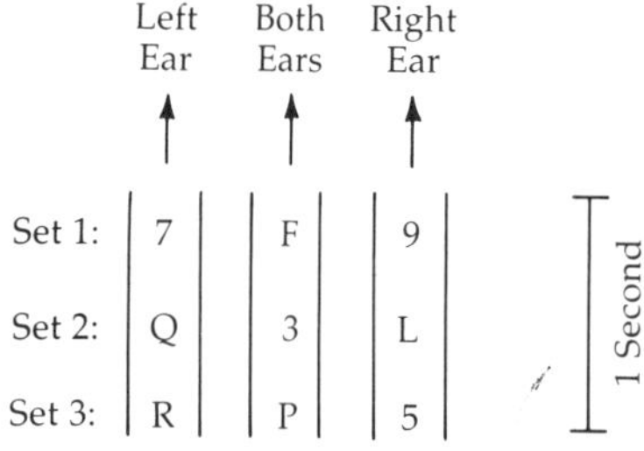

FIGURE 8.2 Procedure used by Darwin, Turvey, and Crowder (1972) to study auditory sensory memory. In each set, which consisted of three symbols presented simultaneously, one symbol went to a subject's left ear, another to both ears, and the last to the right ear. Then the next set was presented. Total time for all set presentations was 1 second.

Although Darwin, Turvey, and Crowder estimated that information remains in auditory sensory memory for approximately 2 seconds, other researchers have arrived at different estimates using different procedures. Efron (1970a and 1970b) used a procedure similar to that used by Haber and Standing (1969). He administered auditory stimuli followed by a light presentation and asked the subjects when the offset of the auditory stimulus coincided with the onset of the light. Using such a procedure, Efron estimated that auditory stimuli remain in sensory memory for only 130 msec.

In recent years, the duration of auditory memory has been studied most extensively by Crowder and his associates using still another procedure (see, for example, Crowder, 1971, 1976; Crowder & Morton, 1969; Morton, Crowder, & Prussin, 1971). This technique is based on certain characteristics of the serial position effect, which are best illustrated by the results of a study by Conrad and Hull (1968). Conrad and Hull presented subjects with a list of 7 digits visually. Some subjects were asked to simply look at the digits, while others were required to repeat each digit aloud as it was presented. Shortly after the last digit disappeared (400 msec), the subjects were asked to recall the digits in order.

As the results shown in Figure 8.3 suggest, a typical serial position effect occurred only when subjects repeated the digits aloud. Subjects who received only the visual presentation did not show the usual excellent recall of the most recently occurring item (digit number 7). Conrad and Hull attributed their finding to differences in the duration of auditory and visual memories in the sensory memory store. They suggested that visual information concerning the last few digits decays rapidly, preventing subjects from remembering these digits any better than digits in the middle of the list. However, the digits stored in the auditory register (such as occurs when digits are spoken aloud), remain there much longer, making it relatively easy for subjects to remember the last item in the list.

Given this finding, Crowder began to use the serial position paradigm as a way of studying the duration of memories in the auditory register. In these experiments, Crowder presented a list of 8 digits to subjects auditorially. At the end of the list the word "zero" or "naught" (the British term for zero) was presented as a signal that the subjects should recall the digits in order. Subjects had previously been told that "zero" or "naught" was simply a signal and should not be recalled as one of the digits. Crowder found that the use of the word "zero" as a signal disrupted a subject's ability to recall the last digit in the serial list. In other words, subjects performed as if the list had been presented visually instead of having been spoken. They did not show the usual excellent recall for the last digit (Crowder & Morton, 1969).

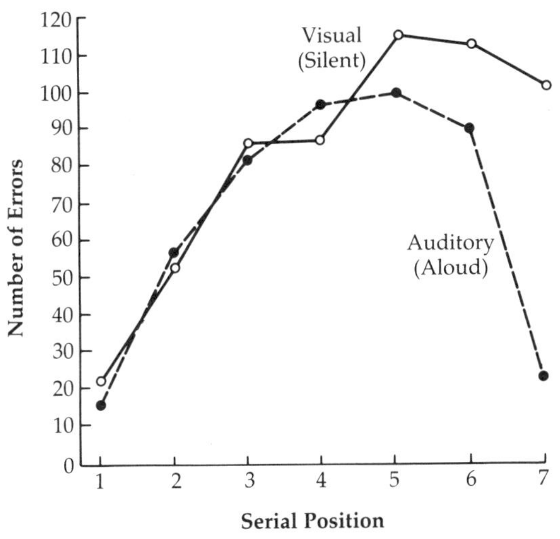

FIGURE 8.3 Retention of a 7-digit serial list when the digits are seen, as opposed to being spoken aloud. (From Conrad and Hull, 1968.)

This phenomenon has been labeled the *suffix effect* by Crowder. That is, if an auditory suffix is attached to the end of a list that is spoken, the suffix blocks out the auditory memory of the final listed item. In effect, Crowder and Morton suggest that the suffix replaces the last digit or pushes it out of the auditory register.

Using this procedure, Crowder and his associates have attempted to assess how long memories remain in the auditory sensory store. For example, in one experiment (Crowder, 1971) subjects were given a digit list followed either by no word or by the suffix word "zero." Some subjects received the suffix 0.5 second after the end of the list, while others received the word 2 seconds after the list was complete. Figure 8.4 (page 206) shows the results of this manipulation. Basically, subjects receiving no suffix word (control group) exhibited excellent recall of the last digit. Slightly poorer recall of the last digit was found when the suffix word occurred 2 seconds after the list. When only 0.5 second elapsed between the list and the suffix, subjects showed very poor recall of the final digit.

This finding suggests that when subjects hear a digit list, the final digit remains in auditory memory for only a few seconds. For this reason, if a suffix occurs almost immediately after the final digit, the memory of this digit will be displaced and forgotten. Apparently if at least 2 seconds elapses between the final

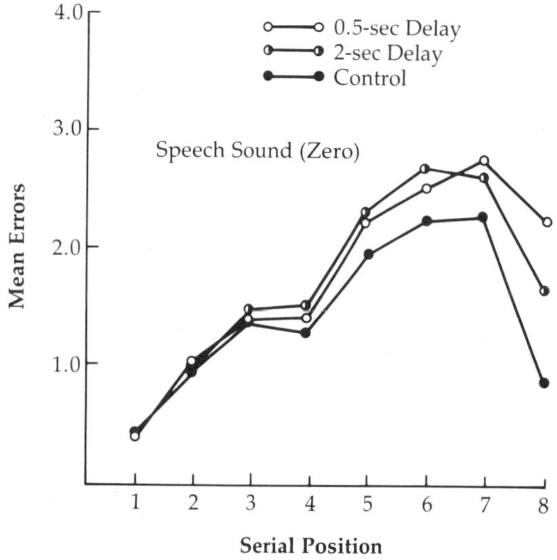

FIGURE 8.4 Retention of a serial digit list when the word "zero" is heard at various delays after the list presentation. (From Crowder, 1971.)

digit and the suffix, the final digit has time to transfer into short-term storage and the suffix has little or no effect on its subsequent recall. Various experimenters using this procedure have estimated that memories remain in the auditory register for 2 to 6 seconds.

In summary, there is substantial evidence for the existence of both a visual and an auditory sensory store. The visual store, which appears to have a reasonably large capacity, is believed to maintain items for a very brief period. While the auditory store also appears to hold items only briefly, estimates of the duration and capacity of this store vary widely. Both the visual and auditory stores seem to be structures that hold only the physical characteristics of stimuli. Thus, most of the available evidence suggests that the Atkinson–Shiffrin view of sensory memory is substantially correct.

Evidence for Selection by Attentional Mechanisms

Atkinson and Shiffrin also proposed that we attend selectively to items in sensory memory and that items move from sensory to short-term storage for processing through this focusing of attention. We look now at some of the evidence pertaining to this proposed role for attentional mechanisms.

Attention as a filtering mechanism Many of the early experiments concerning attention supported the view that we select only a limited number of items from sensory memory for processing. In other words, these studies suggested that attention works like a selective filter, permitting us to focus on only some information in the sensory registers. Information we focus on enters our conscious awareness (that is, short-term memory), while information not attended to is lost.

Most of these early experiments used the so-called *shadowing procedure,* in which two messages, usually prose passages, are presented to a subject simultaneously. One message is usually presented to one ear via a set of earphones, while the other message goes to the other ear. The subject is instructed to attend to the message entering one ear and not to attend to the other. To ensure attention to only one message, the subject is instructed to "shadow" or speak aloud the words in the attended message while it is being presented.

Using this procedure, several experimenters found that the unattended message had little effect on a subject's ability to shadow the attended message. Furthermore, subjects asked to recall information from the unattended message usually were unable to do so. Moray (1959), for example, had subjects shadow a prose passage presented to one ear while he presented a list of common words to the other ear. The list of words was presented a total of 35 times during the course of the experiment. Later, subjects were given a recognition test to see if they remembered any of the words in the unattended list. He found that recognition of the unattended words was no better than one would expect by chance. He concluded that subjects simply have no memory for nonattended information.

In a similar kind of experiment, Treisman and Geffen (1967) had subjects shadow one message, but instructed them to tap on a table whenever they heard one of a set of target words presented in either the attended or the nonattended ear. Subjects correctly responded to more than 85 percent of the target words that occurred in the attended message. However, they correctly identified only 8 percent of the target words in the nonattended ear.

Finally, Cherry (1953) also found evidence suggesting that subjects block out the content of an unattended message. He began by simultaneously presenting two messages spoken in English. During the course of the presentation, however, the nonshadowed message was switched to the German language. When later queried about the unattended message, subjects reported being unaware that the message had changed from one language to another. The same was true when the nonattended message was changed to a string of nonsensical words that only approximated the English language. This result suggests that subjects are often totally unaware of the meanings of words in a nonattended message.

Another finding consistently reported in these earlier studies was that subjects *do* seem to be aware of the gross physical characteristics of unattended stimuli. For example, Cherry (1953) found that subjects were able to recognize when a nonattended message was switched from a male to a female voice. Likewise, they were able to recognize when an unattended prose passage was replaced by the presentation of a pure tone. Others found that shadowing appeared to be more difficult when both messages were spoken by the same voice than when the messages were spoken by different voices (see Treisman, 1964). In other words, the meanings of unattended messages are usually not recognized, but the physical characteristics of these messages usually are noticed.

These findings are, of course, consistent with the Atkinson–Shiffrin hypothesis. Subjects should be able to recognize physical differences even in unattended incoming stimuli, because these differences are evident while the stimuli are located in sensory memory. To derive meaning from an input, however, that input must be attended to and transferred to short-term memory. Since nonattended information presumably is never transferred into short-term memory, we should not be aware of the meanings of such stimuli.

Based on these early findings, Broadbent (1958) proposed the *selective filter theory* of attention. He hypothesized that attention works like a tuning or channel selection mechanism in a radio. A radio, like sensory memory, is capable of taking in signals from a number of channels or stations. However, when we tune the radio to a given channel, we are selecting one input to be heard or processed and at the same time we are blocking out all other inputs. Broadbent proposed that attention works in much the same way. We scan through the inputs in sensory memory and select one channel or stream of input, which then goes into short-term memory for processing. Other inputs are effectively blocked, and we are never consciously aware of their meaning. This notion is, of course, the same idea Atkinson and Shiffrin incorporated into their model.

Problems associated with the selective filter hypothesis As we have seen, the main support for the selective filter idea is the frequent unawareness of subjects of the content of a nonattended message. If you carefully consider your own experiences, however, you may have cause to doubt that the attentional system always works in this manner. Picture yourself at a large party, where people are standing around in small groups talking. In such a situation you usually find yourself attending to the conversation in your own group, and your only awareness of the other conversations going on is an auditory perception of a garbled buzzing sound in the background. What happens, however, if someone in a group nearby mentions your name (or the name of your spouse)? Almost instantly you recognize that your name has been spoken, and you are very likely to switch your attention to what the people in the other group are saying.

This fact that we sometimes notice important nonattended inputs is appropriately labeled the "cocktail-party phenomenon." This phenomenon is so common that we often take it for granted. Yet, it has important implications for understanding how attention works. It shows that under certain circumstances we are indeed aware of the *meaning* of certain unattended messages. You do not switch your attention because your name has been spoken in a loud voice or because it was spoken by a specific person. You do not switch your attention because of the location of the speaker. You switch your attention because your name has special meaning for you and you recognize this meaning even when the sound of your name occurs in a nonattended conversation.

One of the earliest experimental demonstrations of this effect was provided by Moray (1959), who asked subjects to shadow a prose passage presented to one ear and then embedded the subjects' names in the nonattended message. Invariably, subjects were able to recognize that their names had been spoken in the nonattended ear. This suggests, just as in our example, that individuals can become aware of the meaningful content of nonattended inputs.

A similar conclusion can be drawn from a study that focused on attention to visual stimuli. In this study (Neisser, 1969), subjects were shown two lines of printed words—one in black letters and the other in red. The subjects were instructed to read the black words aloud and to ignore the red words. The subjects did attend to the black words, as demonstrated in later recall tests. They were able to recall the content of the messages written in black, but showed almost no evidence of recall for the red messages. Still, Neisser found one exception to this pattern of results. When a subject's name appeared in the red-lettered message, most subjects were able to remember that their names had been presented.

The studies by Moray and Neisser provide evidence that is damaging to the selective filter hypothesis because both sets of results indicate that at least some nonattended information does enter awareness. This conclusion is strengthened by several other experiments in which nonattended information was shown sometimes to influence a subject's behavior.

For instance, in one study Treisman (1960) had subjects shadow one of two messages, but in the middle of the presentation switched the shadowed message to the nonattended ear. For example, if a subject were shadowing a message beginning "He went to the grocery store," the rest of this sentence ("to buy milk and eggs") would be presented to the nonattended ear, while in the attended ear a phrase such as "He rode the red pony" would follow the phrase about going to the grocery store. Treisman reasoned that if subjects are aware of the input to an attended ear only, they should repeat the phrase "He went to the grocery store, he rode the red pony." However, Treisman's subjects tended to switch to the nonattended ear to complete the more meaningful sentence: "He went to the grocery store to buy milk and eggs." In effect, these subjects combined the phrases from the attended and nonattended ears. This suggests that the subjects were aware of the content in the nonattended ear, even while they were shadowing a message presented to the other ear.

In still another study conducted by McKay (1973), subjects were asked to shadow sentences that had ambiguous meanings. For example, subjects were presented with sentences such as "They threw stones toward the bank yesterday." While subjects shadowed these ambiguous sentences, McKay presented words in the nonattended ear that could have been used to clarify the meanings of the sentences. For example, while shadowing the sentence above, the word "river" or the word "money" might have been presented to the nonattended ear.

After this task, McKay gave the subjects a number of sentences and asked them to identify which ones they had heard before. Some of the test sentences were actual duplicates of sentences the subjects had previously shadowed. Others, however, were only similar to shadowed sentences. McKay found that subjects often falsely identified similar sentences as ones they had heard before. Furthermore, the similar sentences falsely recognized almost always depended on the words the subjects had received in their nonattended ears. For example, if the subjects had received "river" while shadowing "They threw stones at the bank yesterday," they were likely to say that they had previously heard "They threw stones toward the side of the river yesterday." On the other hand, if subjects had received "money" while shadowing "They threw stones at the bank yesterday," they were more likely to say that they had previously heard "They threw stones at the savings and loan association yesterday." This finding indicates that the subjects had used the nonattended words to interpret the meanings of the sentences they were shadowing. Thus, these findings add to the evidence that subjects are sometimes aware of the content of a nonattended message.

Obviously, such findings present problems for the selective filter hypothesis proposed by Broadbent and used by Atkinson and Shiffrin. As a result of such findings, several modifications of the Broadbent hypothesis have been proposed in recent years. Treisman (1969), for example, suggests that nonattended information is not totally blocked but is simply attenuated or weakened. This view states that when we attend to information in sensory memory, that information is transferred to short-term memory for conscious processing. Other information in the sensory registers may also enter short-term memory, but this information arrives there in a weak or attenuated form.

Treisman suggests that attenuated information is usually difficult to recognize and process, just as a weak signal from a radio is difficult to decipher or hear. Sometimes, however, attenuated information is recognized and processed. Such will be the case when the attenuated information is already a salient part of permanent memory (such as one's own name), or when cues to the content of the attenuated information are available from the context (such as when nonattended information follows directly from information we are attending to). Treisman's model helps to explain how we are able to recognize nonattended messages of certain types, while we apparently remain oblivious to others.

Some other models of attention have dropped the notion of a filtering mechanism altogether. According to these models (Deutsch & Deutsch, 1963; Norman, 1968, 1973), all information in sensory memory is processed at a relatively unconscious level until it reaches long-term or permanent memory. When sensory information reaches permanent memory, it activates the part of permanent memory that is relevant to that information. For example, if the word "camel" is spoken, the representation of "camel" is activated in permanent storage. The degree of permanent memory activation depends on two factors. One is the salience or importance of a given representation in permanent memory. For example, a very salient or important representation located in permanent storage is the memory of one's own name. Thus, if you hear your name spoken, the degree of memory activation will be greater than if you had heard a word such as "camel" spoken.

A second factor that determines the degree of memory activation is the momentary importance or *pertinence* of a given memory representation. This means that if an individual has just been discussing camels, the representation of the word "camel" will be highly pertinent. Thus, if the individual hears the word "camel" again, the word will activate the camel representation to a high degree. Alternatively, if one hears the word "camel" and he has just been discussing physics, the camel representation will be less pertinent and the activation of this representation will be weaker.

This view suggests that we selectively attend to stimuli that produce strong activations in permanent memory. It is these strongly activated representations that are returned to short-term memory for conscious processing. Thus, we are more likely to become aware of an input when that input is capable of activating a permanent memory representation. Figure 8.5 illustrates how these models view the attentional process. As you can see, the major difference between the memory activation models and the earlier attentional models is the location of the attentional mechanism in the information processing sequence. Earlier models viewed attention as a bottleneck that kept most inputs from being processed in memory. Models such as the one proposed by Norman (1968, 1973) allow for substantial processing of virtually all stimulus inputs. However, only inputs that produce a strong activation in permanent memory are selected for complete processing in the short-term memory store.

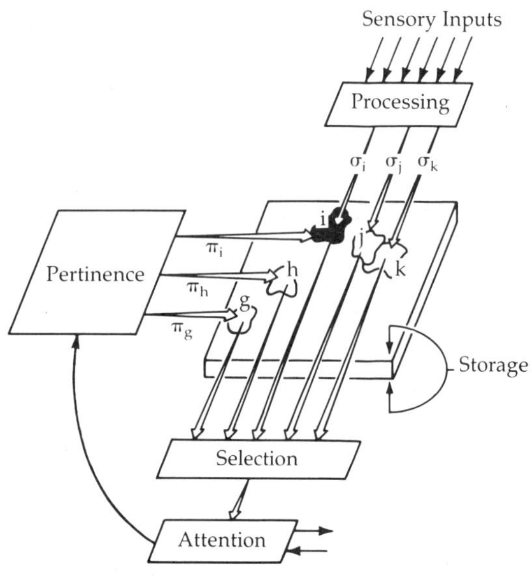

FIGURE 8.5 The model of attention proposed by Norman (1973). Note that sensory inputs (σ) activate stored representations (*i–k*) in memory. The degree of activation depends on the strength and current pertinence (π) of each representation. Only those inputs causing strong activations are selected for attention. (From Norman, 1973.)

Today, the prevailing view of attentional mechanisms is captured in what are called *capacity models of attention* (see, for example, Kahneman, 1973). The key feature of these models is that attention is no longer seen as a mechanism for stimulus selection, per se. According to this view, we are capable of processing several stimulus inputs simultaneously. That is, virtually all inputs stored in sensory memory can be processed to some degree. We do, however, have a limited pool of processing resources, hence a limited capacity for processing information. Thus, in some circumstances we may choose to process several inputs to a small degree, while at other times we may decide to process selected inputs to a greater degree. The more processing effort we devote to one input, the less effort or capacity we have available for processing other inputs. This position emphasizes that the degree to which we become aware of a given input depends on the degree to which that input is processed. Thus, attention is not seen as an all-or-none bottleneck. Instead, it is presumed that attention can be allocated to different inputs in varying amounts.

This kind of model is clearly consistent with the finding that nonshadowed inputs can sometimes be remembered. According to this view, the mere fact that we devote processing capacity to a shadowed input does not preclude us from allocating any of this capacity to a nonshadowed message, as well. When we shadow one input, this simply means that we are devoting more processing capacity to that input than to others.

Such a model also predicts that our awareness of a nonshadowed message should depend on the degree of processing devoted to a shadowed message. In other words, as it becomes more difficult to shadow a given input, the shadowing task will require more and more of our processing capacity. And, as more capacity is devoted to the shadowed input, less capacity should be available for a nonshadowed message. As a result, when a shadowing task is very difficult, we should show little awareness of nonshadowed inputs. Several studies have supported this prediction (see, for example, Zelniker, 1971).

In summary, our notions concerning attentional mechanisms have changed substantially since Broadbent's original selective filter model was proposed. Thus, Atkinson and Shiffrin's view of how information is selected from sensory memory is no longer the prevailing interpretation. It is now obvious that attention to a selected input does not preclude the processing of other inputs that occur at the same time.

Evidence for a Separate Short-Term Memory Store

The hallmark of the Atkinson–Shiffrin model is the idea that a distinction can be drawn between short- and long-term memory. Regardless of how information is selected from sensory memory, this model proposes that the information must be stored and processed in short-term memory before a permanent record of that information can be registered. According to this model, the short-term memory store differs from the long-term store in a number of important respects. First, while the capacity of long-term memory is apparently very large, short-term memory is believed to have a very limited storage capacity. Second, it is suggested that the short-term store can hold memories only for a limited period unless rehearsal is used to maintain information in that store. Obviously, the long-term memory store is capable of holding memories for years. Finally, Atkinson and Shiffrin hypothesized that short-term memory is the locus for the important controlled processing of information, whereas long-term memory involves no such processing.

Although these are the primary distinctions proposed by Atkinson and Shiffrin, others have suggested that short- and long-term memories may differ in additional ways. For example, some researchers have suggested that short- and long-term memories may be represented in terms of different memory codes. Others have hypothesized that these two memory stores may be susceptible to different sources of forgetting. We examine next the evidence that bears on these proposed distinctions, beginning with the possibility that these memory stores have different storage capacities.

The capacity of short-term memory How many bits of information can we hold in conscious awareness at any given point in time? Since Atkinson and Shiffrin equated short-term memory with conscious awareness, this is the question we must answer in assessing the capacity of short-term memory. The most common answer comes from a paper by G. A. Miller (1956) entitled "The magic number seven, plus or minus two: Some limits on our capacity for processing information." As the title suggests, Miller proposed that on average it is possible to hold 7 separate bits of information in short-term storage at one time. Miller based his estimate on numerous experiments in which subjects heard long lists of words, digits, or numbers and then tried to recall as many items as possible (see, for example, Hayes, 1952; Pollack, 1953). These studies showed that invariably subjects were able to report 5 to 9 items accurately. Such results suggested that this was the maximum number of items a subject could hold in short-term memory at once. Several later studies have tended to confirm this earlier estimate (see, for example, Cavanagh, 1972).

The only real ambiguity in this literature concerns the definition of "bits of information." Miller proposed that it is possible for an individual to maintain approximately seven "chunks" of information in short-term storage. His term "chunk" refers to a single indivisible idea. Thus, a chunk may be a single letter when we are focusing on recall of individual distinct letters, or it may be a grouping of letters that form a single word or idea, depending on the focus of the task at hand. A word, for example, is actually a grouping of letters that represents one chunk of information. Therefore, it is possible to maintain about 7 words in short-term memory even though these words may contain 30 or more individual letters.

This notion of "chunks of information" is important because it points to a strategy we often use to retain more information in short-term storage. When called on to remember a long string of letters or digits, we often chunk related items together and then remember the chunks rather than attempting to recall each item individually. In many ways, chunking is similar to the technique of clustering that we have discussed previously. To show how this strategy works, consider the following string of 12 letters: A, P, E, X, S, H, U, T, F, R, O, G. If these letters were presented one at a time in a different order, it would be difficult to remember accurately more than 7 of them. However, when the letters are presented in the order shown above, it is easy to chunk them into three words: APEX, SHUT, and FROG. These words represent three chunks of information, and they easily fit the capacity of short-term memory. By using this chunking strategy, we can remember all 12 letters without difficulty.

Regardless of the precise estimate of short-term memory capacity and regardless of how we define a "bit of information," one point is clear. The capacity of conscious awareness is strictly limited. This restriction is one of the major reasons for distinguishing between short-term memory and the long-term store, which can hold an unlimited number of representations at any given time.

The temporal limits of short-term memory Atkinson and Shiffrin proposed that short- and long-term memory differ not only in terms of capacity but also in terms of storage duration. They suggested that while memories may remain in long-term storage for several years, memories that are not rehearsed can remain in short-term storage for only a matter of seconds. They presumed that memories are lost from short-term storage via two mechanisms. First, they hypothesized that in the absence of rehearsal, memories simply fade or decay from the short-term store. Second, since the short-term store has a limited capacity, they assumed that memories in that store can be displaced or pushed out by incoming information. Because of the combined effects of these two mechanisms, short-term memories were presumed to be short-lived.

Support for the notion that short-term memory is a brief-duration store comes from a classic study by Peterson and Peterson (1959; see also, J. A. Brown, 1958). In this study, subjects were given a single trigram such as "RZL" and were asked, after a retention interval, to recall it. The retention intervals used in this experiment varied between 0 and 18 sec. The Petersons had wanted to determine how long a subject could retain the trigram in short-term memory if the trigram were not rehearsed. Thus, to prevent rehearsal, subjects were given a 3-digit number immediately after the trigram and were told to repeat this number and begin counting backward by 3's. The counting was done aloud and subjects were required to say a 3-digit number about every half-second. If you try this procedure yourself, you will notice that counting backward by 3's requires a great deal of concentration. It is virtually impossible to rehearse an item such as a trigram and at the same time count backward accurately. Thus, by means of such a procedure it becomes possible to determine the fate of the unrehearsed trigram.

The results of this study (Figure 8.6) indicate that retention of the trigram decreases

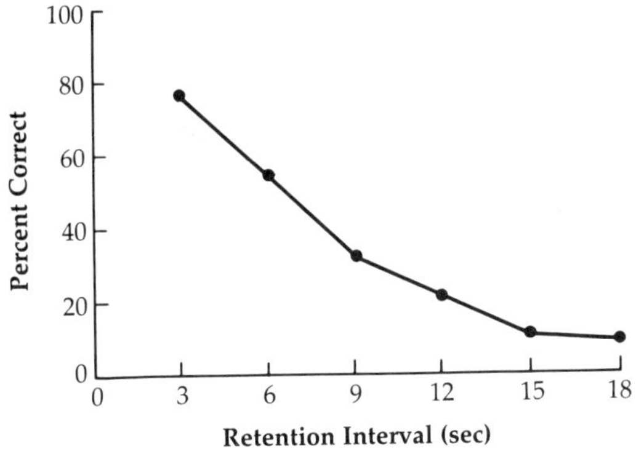

FIGURE 8.6 Retention of trigrams over short retention intervals when a distractor task is used to block rehearsal. (From Peterson and Peterson, 1959.)

rapidly as the retention interval is lengthened. Retention is excellent using a 0-second interval, but after 18 seconds recall of the trigram occurs on only about 10 percent of the trials. Peterson and Peterson interpreted these results as an indication that short-term memories rapidly decay unless they are rehearsed. They estimated that within 15 to 18 seconds, nonrehearsed memories become lost from short-term storage.

These findings show unambiguously that short-term memories can be lost in a matter of seconds. However, this experiment does not necessarily show that short-term memories decay without rehearsal. An alternative interpretation of these results is that short-term memories may be lost simply by being displaced from short-term storage by incoming information. In other words, subjects may have had difficulty remembering the trigram because counting backward placed into short-term memory a series of digits that displaced the trigram from the short-term store. According to this interpretation, forgetting of the trigram is greater after longer retention intervals because longer intervals permit more incoming stimuli and a greater probability for displacement of the trigram.

As we will see in a later chapter, there is substantial evidence to support this latter interpretation of the Petersons' result (see, for example, Reitman, 1971, 1974). Thus, we can only conclude that the duration of short-term storage is normally very brief. This may result partially from the decay of memories in that store when rehearsal does not occur. However, it may also be a function of the limited capacity of short-term memory, which necessitates, in the normal course of events, the constant displacement of older memories from storage.

Evidence for control processes in short-term memory Another idea advanced by Atkinson and Shiffrin is that the fate of information in short-term storage depends on how that information is processed. In effect, they viewed the short-term store as the location for conscious manipulation of memories. They assumed that the way an individual chooses to process short-term memories determines how these memories are encoded and whether they are stored permanently. They called these conscious manipulations *control processes.*

In our discussion of rehearsal, we saw some evidence for the existence of control processes. We know, for example, that individuals can choose whether to rehearse the information of which they are consciously aware. And, as we have seen, a failure to rehearse can lead to rapid forgetting, while rehearsal can prolong a memory's availability. There is additional evidence, however, that the fate of a memory depends on more than whether the memory is or is not rehearsed. It also appears to depend on the type of rehearsal that occurs.

Some of the best evidence for the existence of different types of rehearsal comes from experiments called *directed forgetting studies* (see, for example, Bjork, 1972, 1975; Geiselman, 1975), in which subjects are presented with items and told to retain them in memory. After a retention test, the subjects are then told to forget the old items and to retain a new set of items in memory. After several sets of items have been presented and tested, the subjects are given a surprise retention test over the items they have been instructed to forget. Subjects are usually unable to recall these items even though often they have rehearsed the items for a substantial period of time. This suggests that it is possible to rehearse items solely to keep them in awareness without this rehearsal leading to the storage of the items in long-term memory.

One study by Bjork and Jongeward (see Bjork, 1975) illustrates this procedure. The subjects were given a sequence of 6-word sets. Each set was rehearsed for 20 seconds, after which a retention test was given. Some subjects were instructed to forget each set immediately after the retention test. Others were instructed to keep all sets in memory even after testing. When all sets had been presented and tested, a surprise retention test was given for all the word sets.

Bjork and Jongeward found that the two groups of subjects performed equally well on the immediate retention tests. That is, the two groups were equally capable of remembering each set of 6 words after 20 seconds of rehearsal. However, on the surprise retention test the two groups differed dramatically. The group told to retain all the words performed very well on this test, while the group told to forget did just that. The latter subjects showed very poor recall even though they had rehearsed the words for the same period of time as the subjects in the other group.

Since in this experiment total rehearsal times were equal, the results suggest that the two groups must have rehearsed the words in different ways. One group apparently rehearsed the items solely to keep them in conscious awareness for a brief period of time. The other group seemingly managed their rehearsals to ensure that the words were encoded and stored in long-term memory. The first type of rehearsal has been called *maintenance rehearsal*, while the second type has been termed *elaborative rehearsal* (see, for example, Craik & Watkins, 1973).

As we will see later, other researchers have suggested additional rehearsal distinctions (see Craik & Lockhart, 1972). Such distinctions have been based on the apparent capacity of subjects sometimes to process only the physical features of items, while at other times to process items in terms of meaning. These findings, combined with the data from directed forgetting studies, provide strong evidence for the existence of control processes. It is apparent that once we have become aware of a bit of information, we can choose to rehearse that information in different ways. Furthermore, the way we choose to rehearse determines how well information can be recalled and what aspects of that information remain in memory.

Other distinctions between short- and long-term memory We have now discussed the major distinguishing features of short-term memory according to Atkinson and Shiffrin. We should note, however, that other researchers have suggested that the short- and long-term memory stores may differ in still other respects. One notion popular during the early 1960s was that memories in these two stores may be forgotten for different reasons. It was suggested that short-term memories are forgotten because they decay from storage, whereas long-term forgetting results from interference effects (see, for example, Peterson & Peterson, 1959). As we have seen, this turns out to be a questionable distinction, since there is evidence that short-term memories can also be forgotten via displacement or interference.

Another distinction sometimes drawn between short- and long-term memory stores concerns how the memories in these two stores are coded or represented. As we will see in Chapter 9, there is substantial evidence to suggest that long-term memories may be stored in terms of *meaning codes*. Over long periods of time, that is, we may tend to remember the meaning of a stimulus input much more readily than the physical features of that input. On the other hand, some have suggested that the information in short-term storage is usually represented in terms of *acoustic codes.* This proposal states that even visual information is transformed into sounds or acoustic codes once the information has entered short-term storage.

Early evidence for the view that short-term memories are acoustically coded comes from an experiment by Conrad (1964), who presented a group of letters to his subjects visually. In attempting to recall these letters after short retention intervals, the subjects made a number of errors that seemed to result from acoustic confusions. For example, instead of recalling a previously seen "E," subjects often incorrectly stated that they had seen a "G" or a "P" (letters that sound like "E"). Errors seldom involved the incorrect reporting of the letter "F," even though the "E" and "F" share many of the same visual characteristics. Conrad concluded that while the letters were in short-term memory, they had been rehearsed and coded acoustically, not in terms of visual features (see also, Glanzer & Clark, 1963).

More recently, however, the idea that short-term memories are always coded acoustically, while long-term memories are always coded meaningfully, has come under fire. For example, it now seems evident that at least some short-term memories may be coded in terms of visual features (see, for example, Brooks, 1968; Shepard & Metzler, 1971). There is also the suggestion that some long-term memories may be coded in terms of acoustic or visual characteristics (see Craik & Kirsner, 1974; Hintzman, Block, & Inskeep, 1972). Thus, it has become increasingly difficult to distinguish between short- and long-term memories on the basis of memory codes.

A final distinction that has been offered concerns the possibility that different neural mechanisms underlie short- and long-term memory stores. This distinction is based on clinical evidence from individuals having various types of brain injury. For instance, there have been several reports that individuals having hippocampal or temporal lobe damage appear to maintain normal long-term memory function but show evidence of short-term memory impairments (see, for example, Milner, 1966; Shallice & Warrington, 1970).

Of particular interest has been the patient called "HM" (see Milner, 1966), who sustained temporal lobe damage during a neurosurgical procedure. HM showed no loss in IQ as a result of the damage. He also showed excellent recall of events prior to his surgery. Milner reported, however, that after the surgery HM exhibited tremendous difficulty in transferring new information from short- to long-term memory. He would, for example, work on the same jigsaw puzzle day after day with no evidence of any recall for his work done on preceding days. He also could not remember for more than a few minutes where he had put things. These observations indicate that certain brain mechanisms involved in the short-term processing of information for permanent storage may have little to do with memories already in the long-term store.

A summary of the evidence We have noted that the distinction between short- and long-term memory is crucial to the Atkinson–Shiffrin model. To support such a distinction it is necessary to show that the characteristics of the memory system differ depending on how long a memory has been in storage. Although several distinctions between these stores have been suggested, only a few of them appear to be viable. For example, it does appear that we can be aware of only a few memories at any given time. However, it is also obvious that we can hold countless older memories in storage at the same time. This known property supports Atkinson and Shiffrin's idea that the short- and long-term memory stores differ in terms of capacity.

Additionally we found that shortly after information input, individuals can choose to process this information in various ways. Information may be processed solely to maintain it in conscious awareness, or it may be elaboratively processed for permanent storage. This finding is consistent with Atkinson and Shiffrin's notion that control processes operate in short-term, but not in long-term memory. Such results are also consistent with the idea that control processing in short-term storage may be necessary before a memory can become permanently stored.

Finally, we saw that certain types of brain damage appear to affect short- and long-term memories differently. This evidence supports the idea that short- and long-term memories may be represented differently in the brain. Thus we have additional support for a distinction between short- and long-term memory stores.

When we consider all this evidence together, it becomes clear why Atkinson and Shiffrin proposed the kind of model they did. This evidence suggests that we do, in fact, have different memory stores and that information does have to pass through these stores to become permanently registered in memory. Still, as we are about to see, this evidence does not necessarily imply that multiple memory stores exist. It is quite possible to incorporate these findings into an entirely different kind of memory model—a model that assumes the existence of only a single memory store.

The Levels of Processing Approach

We have noted that the Atkinson–Shiffrin model contains two important ideas. One idea is the notion that the memory system contains distinctive memory structures or memory stores. The second idea in this model is that certain control processes exist and are involved in the encoding and permanent storage of a memory.

In recent years, several theorists have argued that an understanding of these control processes is central to our understanding of memory formation. In fact, some of these theorists have suggested that an explanation of memory phenomena requires *only* the understanding of control processes. According to this view, there is little need to hypothesize the existence of different memory structures as long as we understand how control processes operate. These theorists take the position that distinctions between structures such as short- and long-term memory are superfluous and serve only to complicate the picture of how memory formation occurs.

Although this idea is rooted in earlier theoretical papers (see, for example, Melton, 1963), this general approach to memory theory is usually attributed to Craik and Lockhart (1972) and is called *the levels of processing approach*. What Craik and Lockhart actually proposed is more a set of ideas than a formal model or theory. First of all, they questioned the proposition that memories must move through a sequence of structures or stores on the way to permanent registration. Instead, they proposed that there is a single memory store which holds all memories regardless of when those memories entered the system. In many respects this single store was presumed to be similar to the long-term store suggested by Atkinson and Shiffrin. That is, it was presumed to have an unlimited capacity and to be capable of holding memories for extremely long periods.

A second idea proposed by Craik and Lockhart was that we are capable of applying control processes to only a small subset of memories in this single store at any given time. In other words, our capacity for actively processing information is limited. In most cases we choose to process information that has just entered storage, since we must always adjust our behaviors to new incoming stimuli. We can, however, choose to focus our processing on memories that have been in storage for a longer time.

To illustrate this idea, imagine yourself seated in a darkened classroom with a flashlight, facing a blackboard that contains hundreds of words, or perhaps hundreds of symbols. The blackboard is similar to Craik and Lockhart's single memory store in the sense that it has a large capacity and can hold information almost indefinitely. Since the room is dark, you cannot access the information without your flashlight. You can read any of the symbols on the board, however, by using the flashlight to focus light in a particular direction. You can choose to focus on symbols that have been on the board for several hours or on symbols that have just been written. In any event, the width of the flashlight beam is restricted. This means that at any one time only a limited number of symbols can be read. Your beam of light is like your capacity for processing. It can be focused anywhere on the board you choose, but you can illuminate and read only a few symbols at a time. Thus, according to this view, it is our ability to select and process information that is limited, not our memory structures or stores.

The subset of stored memories we choose to process at a given time was called *primary memory* by Craik and Lockhart. They gave the label *secondary memory* to the part of memory that is not chosen for processing. It is important to note that primary and secondary memory were not thought of as analogues for short- and long-term memory. Both primary and secondary memories were presumed to be subsets of the memories stored in a single structure. They themselves were not viewed as being different structures or stores.

The most important idea in this approach concerns the nature of the processes we employ once certain memories have been selected for processing. Craik and Lockhart proposed that we are capable of processing selected memories in a variety of ways. First, they distinguished two types of rehearsal. As we have noted, maintenance rehearsal is a process by which we keep a memory in conscious awareness for a period of time, whereas elaborative rehearsal involves the encoding of a memory so that it can be recalled even after long retention intervals. Craik and Lockhart suggested that we can choose to rehearse a memory in either of these ways and that our choice will often determine how well a memory can be retained over time.

Importantly, Craik and Lockhart also assume *different levels of processing*. For example, if we hear a spoken word, we may choose to process it at a very shallow or surface level, focusing on only the physical features of the word such as how it sounds. We might also decide to process the word at a somewhat deeper level, perhaps taking note of whether the word begins with a consonant or a vowel. This would constitute a deeper level of analysis, since it would require a recognition of the word's first letter and a categorization of that letter as either a vowel or a consonant. Finally, we might choose to process the word in terms of its meaning or its symbolic characteristics. This would call for a comparison of the word to similar words stored in memory, followed by a decision of what the word is comparable to in terms of meaning.

According to Craik and Lockhart, these different levels of processing are not necessarily sequential. That is, given enough processing time we do not necessarily move from the surface to a deeper level of processing. Two individuals may, for example, rehearse the same item for the same period of time. However, one may spend the entire time processing at a surface level, while the other may spend the whole interval processing meaning. In effect, we can choose how a given memory is to be processed. This choice will depend on a variety of factors, such as our individual characteristics, how we plan to use the memory later, and the features of a given input that seem most pertinent at the moment.

The true importance of these different processing levels is that Craik and Lockhart assume that the processing level we choose determines how a stimulus input will be coded or represented in memory. That is, the level at which we process a given stimulus determines which features of that stimulus become stored in the memory system. For example, a word we choose to process at a surface level may end up being represented in memory only in terms of its sound. On the other hand, if a deeper level of processing is used, the same word might become represented in terms of its meaning.

Assuming that this view is correct, we might ask whether it really matters how a stimulus is coded as long as the stimulus does get represented in memory. Craik and Lockhart suggest that the type of representation we form is critical for at least two reasons. First, the type of input representation formed determines which features of an input we will be able to remember later. If a stimulus is represented in terms of its sound alone, then later we will be able to remember its sound but not its visual features or its meaning. Second, Craik and Lockhart propose that certain types of representations are longer lasting than others. Specifically, they hypothesize that meaning codes last longer than physical feature codes. This implies that an input represented in terms of meaning should be remembered longer than an input represented in terms of its sound.

Evidence Supporting the Levels of Processing Approach

Probably the most salient point in the levels of processing approach is that the fate of a memory depends on how a memory is processed, not on how long. In recent years this point has been supported in a number of different experiments. We have already seen that long-term retention appears to depend on whether individuals engage in maintenance or elaborative rehearsal (see, for example, Bjork, 1975). Such a result is clearly consistent with this general view. However, there is equally strong evidence that when subjects process the same input, but process it at different levels, they form memories that are forgotten at different rates.

In one such study, Hyde and Jenkins (1969) presented four groups of subjects with the same list of 24 words. Some subjects were instructed to search through the list and mark all the letter "E's" in the list. A second group was instructed to count the letters in each word. A third group was asked to rate each word in terms of its "pleasantness." The fourth group was told to memorize the words for later recall.

Upon completion of these tasks, all subjects were given a recall test for the words in the list. This was a surprise test for the first three groups, since none of them had been told that they would be tested later. Still, Hyde and Jenkins found that subjects who had rated the words in terms of "pleasantness" recalled just as many words as the subjects told to memorize the list (both groups averaged more than 16 correctly recalled words).

The first two groups, however, exhibited a much poorer level of recall (both groups averaged 9–10 correct words). This result is clearly in accord with the predictions of the levels of processing approach. Since the first two groups were instructed to note only the physical features of the words, this approach predicts that these groups should have processed the words at a shallow or surface level, and poor recall would be expected.

On the other hand, group 3 had to deal with the meanings of the words in order to rate each word on the "pleasantness" scale, a process that should have resulted in a deeper level of processing and a relatively long-lasting memory code. This, of course, is precisely what the data of Hyde and Jenkins indicate.

Additional support for this interpretation comes from a series of experiments done by Craik and Tulving (1975). In one of these studies, subjects were first asked a question about a word, without being told what word the experimenters had in mind. Then they were given a brief visual presentation of a specific word and were asked to answer the preceding question with a "yes" or a "no" as quickly as possible. Some of the questions used concerned only the physical features of the words that followed (for example, "Is the word in capital letters?"). A second set of questions dealt with the sounds of the target words (for example, "Does the word rhyme with "weight"?). A final group of questions concerned whether the target word would fit a blank in a given sentence (for example, "Does the word fit the following sentence? He met a ____ in the street").

The purpose of the questions of different kinds was to bias subjects toward processing the words at different levels. It was assumed that questions concerning features such as capital letters would lead to a shallow level of processing for the word that followed. Questions about whether a word would fit a sentence were intended to prompt a deep level of processing, by requiring subjects to attend to the meanings of words. The questions having to do with word sounds were intended to result in an intermediate processing level, since to answer these questions one would need to at least sound out the entire word.

After all the questions had been answered, Craik and Tulving gave the subjects a surprise recognition test to determine how many words they remembered. Figure 8.7 shows the results of this test for each of the word categories, as well as the subjects' reaction times to answer each type of question. At least two important results are contained in this figure. First, it is clear that subjects take longer to answer the sentence questions than questions concerning letter cases or rhymes. Second, the recognition results are precisely what one would predict from the levels of processing approach. Retention is best for words that had to be processed

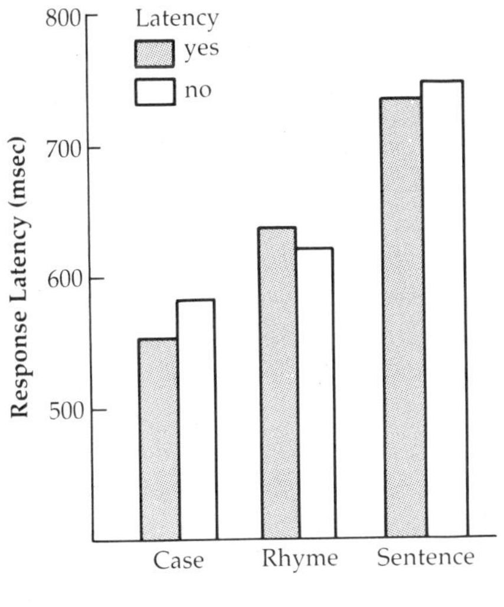

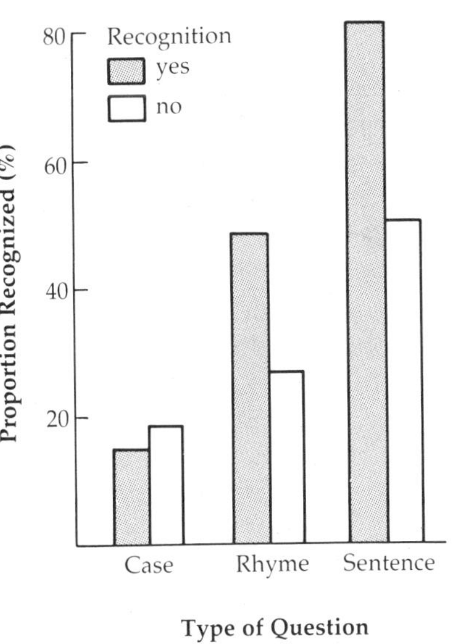

FIGURE 8.7 (a) Mean latency to answer questions about the case of a word, whether a word rhymed with another, or whether a word fit a particular sentence. (b) Proportion of these words that were recognized on a subsequent test. (From Craik and Tulving, 1975.)

for meaning (sentence condition). Retention is somewhat poorer in the rhyming condition and is very poor in the condition requiring a decision on letter case.

There are two possible interpretations for these results. One is that different levels of processing led to different levels of retention. The second possibility is that different *amounts* of processing led to different levels of retention. The latter interpretation is feasible because subjects took more time to answer the rhyme questions than they did to answer the letter case questions, suggesting subjects took longer to process words for the rhyme condition than for the letter case distinction. The longest processing time apparently occurred in the sentence completion condition, since these were the questions eliciting the longest reaction times.

To distinguish between these interpretations, Craik and Tulving next attempted to disentangle depth of processing and total time of processing. The procedure used was similar to the one employed in the first study. That is, subjects received a question followed by a word, whereupon they were to answer the question as quickly as possible. In this study only two types of questions were used. The first type was intended to induce surface processing; however, these questions were also designed to require extensive processing time. These questions concerned the sequence of vowels and consonants in a word ("Does the word match the pattern: vowel–consonant–vowel–consonant?"). The second type of question was similar to the sentence completion questions in the experiment summarized in Figure 8.7. These questions were relatively easy to answer, so that processing time would be minimal, but they required a deep level of semantic processing.

The results of this experiment strongly supported the idea that it is the level rather than the amount of processing time that is critical. Reaction times to the vowel-consonant questions were actually longer than those to the sentence completion questions. Still, words that followed the sentence completion questions were recognized much better on the retention test than the words that followed the vowel–consonant questions. This finding indicates that retention may depend very little on how long a word is processed, but it may depend a great deal on the type of processing that occurs. Similar conclusions have come from a variety of experiments in recent years (see, for example, Bellezza, Cheesman, & Reddy, 1977; Moeser, 1983; Packman & Battig, 1978).

Current Status of the Levels of Processing Approach

As we have discovered, there is much to recommend the levels of processing approach to the study of memory formation. First of all, it is able to account for different degrees of retention, as well as capacity limitations in memory and even differences in memory codes, without having to propose the existence of multiple memory structures. In addition, there is substantial support for the idea that different types of processing result in differential retention of memories. Still, this approach has not gone without criticism, much of which has centered on the definition of the term "level" or "depth" of processing.

In the studies we have reviewed thus far, the rules for defining different processing levels have seemed to be self-evident. For example, it makes intuitive sense to say that an analysis of meaning represents a deeper level of processing than does an analysis of visual features. Still, Craik and Lockhart were somewhat vague in discussing what really constitutes a given level of processing. They did not say, for example, whether there are different levels of processing for meaning. Likewise, they did not explain fully why dealing with the sound of a word should involve a deeper level of processing than dealing with a word's visual characteristics. This lack of explicitness has been viewed by some theorists as a serious flaw in the levels of processing approach (see Baddeley, 1978; T. O. Nelson, 1977; see Lockhart & Craik, 1978, for a different view).

Clearly, the absence of general agreement about what constitutes a level of processing has made it difficult to interpret a number of experimental findings. Packman and Battig (1978), for instance, had subjects rate each word on a list on one of several dimensions. Words were rated in terms of concreteness, meaningfulness, imagery value, familiarity, or pleasantness. Certainly, Craik and Lockhart would have to agree with the notion that each of these rating tasks should promote deep semantic processing. Yet, Packman and Battig found that words rated in terms of pleasantness were recalled much better than words rated along the other dimensions. Does this mean that a pleasantness rating involves a deeper level of processing than a rating in terms of meaningfulness? Without a more explicit definition for processing levels, we have no way of answering this question.

A similar question about the precision with which "level of processing" can be defined arises in connection with the results of Craik and Tulving (1975), discussed earlier. Recall that in these experiments subjects were given questions designed to induce different processing levels for different words, and the only answers possible were "yes" and "no." The results clearly showed that words could be retained differentially depending on the level of processing induced. We should note, however, an additional result of these experiments, which was passed over in our original discussion. As Figure 8.7b indicates, in both the sentence completion and the rhyming conditions, subjects remembered words that required a "yes" response much better than they remembered the words requiring a "no" response.

How might we attempt to explain such a finding? Does it imply that different levels of processing are involved in making "yes" and "no" decisions about the fit of a word in a sentence? Again, the levels of processing approach would seem to suggest that this is true, since the decisions resulting in these two responses produce different levels of retention. However, there seems to be little basis for suggesting that a "yes" decision should require deeper processing than a "no" decision. In effect, Craik and Lockhart have failed to provide a set of rules or conditions for determining when processing levels are deep and when they are shallow. Without such a set of rules, it becomes difficult to use this hypothesis to make predictions concerning retention performance.

Another problem associated with the levels of processing approach is that some findings seem to contradict the idea that deep processing is always necessary for good long-term retention. In contrast to the conclusions drawn by Craik and Tulving (1975), some recent studies have shown that retention sometimes is improved by increases in processing time, regardless of the level at which processing occurs (see, for example, Dark & Loftus, 1976; T. O. Nelson, 1977; Rundus, 1977). Other studies have shown that such physical features of stimuli as the location of a sound or the voice in which a word is spoken can be recognized long after the presentation of the stimuli (see Craik & Kirsner, 1974; Kolers, 1979; D. L. Nelson, 1979; Rothkopf, 1971). These studies seem to refute the notion that only meaning codes remain in memory for long intervals.

As a result of such problems, there have been several recent attempts to modify or make more explicit the levels of processing hypothesis. In most cases the goal of these efforts has been to specify what actually occurs when we process inputs at different levels. Instead of simply showing that different types of processing lead to different degrees of retention, these hypotheses have addressed the question of why processing levels influence retention.

One idea that has gained increasing support is that retention depends primarily on the distinctiveness of a memory code. That is, the more distinctively a memory is coded, the easier it will be to recall that memory later. According to this view, semantic or meaningful processing usually leads to better retention because it increases the distinctiveness of the memory code that is formed. To illustrate this point, consider what we normally do when we read a printed page. While we read, we normally think about the meanings of the words we are reading. That is, we process the printed words at a semantic level. By doing this we create a set of very distinctive memory codes. The meaning found on one page is very seldom the same as the meaning found on another page. Thus, each meaning code is reasonably distinct from the others we form.

Now consider what would happen if we simply noticed the letters in each word we read. We would be processing the words at a shallow level and would be creating memory codes based on the physical features of the letters. Since the same letters occur over and over again, each of these codes would overlap significantly with numerous other codes from the same page. In other words, codes based on physical features are less distinct from one another than are codes based on meaning. As a result, at the time of recall it is much easier to remember the semantically processed words, because they can be differentiated easily from other coded words. It is difficult to recall specific words processed in terms of physical features because so many words are coded in terms of the same features.

In effect, the foregoing view disputes the rather circular idea that meaning codes are remembered better because they last longer in memory. Meaning codes are remembered better because they are usually more distinctive. This view implies that words processed at a surface level should also be recalled better if the physical features of the words are made particularly distinctive. This implication has been supported in a number of experimental situations (see, for example, Kolers & Ostry, 1974; Stein, 1978).

A second idea that has been proposed is that the effects of processing levels may really depend on the amount of effort or processing capacity involved in coding a given memory (see Craik & Simon, 1980; Ellis & Hunt, 1983; Ellis, Thomas, & Rodriguez, 1984). This idea is based on the notion that we have a limited capacity for processing new inputs (see Kahneman, 1973). It is hypothesized that retention will depend on how much of our processing capacity we allocate to the coding of a given memory. The more capacity we use or the more effort we devote to processing a particular input, the better we will retain that input over time. According to this view, semantic processing usually produces better retention, because it involves a greater amount of effort than does processing in terms of physical features.

At least two lines of evidence lend support to this hypothesis. First, some studies have shown that a subject's ability to detect and process one stimulus depends on the level at which he is processing a second input. If, for example, a subject is processing words at a semantic level, it is difficult for that subject to detect other stimulus inputs. However, if a subject is processing words in terms of physical features, detection of a second incoming stimulus is much easier (see, for example, Eysenck & Eysenck, 1979). This suggests that semantic processing may require a greater allocation of processing resources than other types of processing do.

Second, there is growing evidence that retention does depend on the amount of processing effort involved in coding a memory. One example of this line of research comes from studies dealing with a phenomenon called the *generation effect* (see, for example, Graf, 1982; Jacoby, 1978; McFarland, Frey, & Rhodes, 1980; Slamecka & Graf, 1978). In such studies subjects are usually asked a question that requires a one-word answer. Then either they are given a word that answers the question or they must think of the answer themselves. For instance, they may be asked "What is a word that rhymes with *house?*" Some subjects are then given a word, such as *mouse,* while others must decide on a rhyming word on their own. These studies show that subjects remember words much better if they generate the words themselves, rather than being supplied with answers. Such findings suggest that words that require more processing effort are recalled better than words that require little effort.

Thus, one way to interpret the levels of processing data is to say that deeper levels of processing require more effort than do shallow processing levels. This interpretation, however is not necessarily incompatible with the coding distinctiveness idea discussed earlier. It is certainly possible that greater processing effort leads to a more distinctive memory code (see, for example, Jacoby, 1978). Thus, these two views concerning processing levels may actually focus on the same underlying mechanisms.

One final idea to be mentioned in this context is that retention almost never depends solely on how a memory is coded. As we will see in Chapter 10, retention almost always depends on whether a given memory code is appropriate, given the conditions of a retention test. This notion is usually called the *encoding specificity hypothesis* (see Tulving, 1968; Watkins & Tulving, 1975), and it has important implications for understanding the effects of different processing levels. According to this hypothesis, semantic processing may simply produce a memory code that is more useful, given the kinds of retention tests normally employed in experiments. It may well be that with retention tests of certain kinds, surface processing may produce the best performance. It is interesting to note that several studies have found that retention performance depends *jointly* on the level of processing and the type of information requested on a retention test (see, for example, Bransford, Franks, Morris, & Stein, 1979; Stein, 1978).

At present there is no clear resolution to this issue. It is obvious that retention is strongly affected by the type of processing in which a person engages. However, it remains unclear *why* different types of processing have these effects. In any event, the levels of processing approach has had two important impacts on the study of memory formation. First, this approach has diminished the interest of most researchers in the role of memory structures. Because of results obtained in investigations using this approach, many researchers no longer adhere to the idea that memories pass through multiple memory stores. Second, in recent years, this point of view has given rise to countless studies concerning the nature of memory processes. Such studies have clearly increased our understanding of how memory formation occurs.

Models of Memory Formation in Nonhuman Species

Much of the work on memory processing has been done with human subjects. There is, however, a sizable literature dealing with memory processes in other species. Although we will not examine this research in great depth, it is important to note its main features for at least two reasons. First, from a comparative perspective it is useful to determine whether there are differences in the ways organisms of various species process information. Second, it is instructive to note the striking parallels that exist between the theoretical accounts in these two areas of research. As we will see, researchers using animal subjects have made the same transition from structural to process-oriented memory models that we have seen in the area of human memory research.

Consolidation Theory

Traditionally, most of the research concerning memory processes in animals was done within the framework of the *consolidation theory* (see Hebb, 1949; McGaugh, 1966; McGaugh & Dawson, 1971). This theory is similar in many respects to the Atkinson–Shiffrin model. In effect, this theory proposes that there are at least two distinct memory structures or stores, which correspond directly to two different modes of memory representation in the brain. Specifically, this theory assumed that when an animal undergoes a learning experience, a memory trace of that experience is temporarily represented in the brain by changes in the brain's electrical activity (that is, changes in nerve impulses). While represented in this way, the memory was assumed to be *malleable*—that is, modifiable or subject to change. Thus, it was assumed that while a memory is represented in malleable form, it is capable of being altered by a variety of environmental circumstances. This temporary form of memory representation is, of course, analogous to short-term memory storage.

According to this view, if a memory trace remains stored in short-term memory for an uninterrupted period of time, the electrical changes in the brain will begin to trigger more permanent changes in either the structure or the biochemistry of the brain itself. It was felt that these structural or biochemical changes were responsible for permanent memory registration or long-term storage. Thus, as the memory trace remains in short-term storage, it gradually begins to consolidate or transform into a permanent, long-term representation. It was assumed that once a memory trace has fully consolidated, it is no longer susceptible to the modifying effects of environmental events.

Support for this position came from a variety of sources. For example, several researchers reported that they were able to record coherent changes in a rat's electrical brain activity after a learning experience (see John, 1967). Furthermore, these changes appeared to last for only a matter of seconds after learning was completed. This evidence is at least consistent with the idea that short-term memories may be represented in terms of changes in neural activity.

The most convincing evidence for this theory came from hundreds of experiments in which treatments were used to alter an animal's brain activity after learning. Several of these studies employed *electroconvulsive shock* (ECS), a treatment in which electrical current is run through an organism's brain, causing massive disruption of ongoing neural activity. ECS also produces a temporary loss of consciousness, from which organisms usually recover in minutes. Thus, it is possible to administer ECS shortly after a learning experience and then to test an organism for retention of that experience within hours or days.

Figure 8.8 illustrates the general pattern of results found in such studies (see, for example, Gibbs & Mark, 1973). First, we see that if rats receive ECS immediately after a learning experience, later they exhibit almost no retention of what was learned. This effect is called *retrograde amnesia.* Furthermore, less and less amnesia occurs (that is, retention gets better and better), the longer the interval between

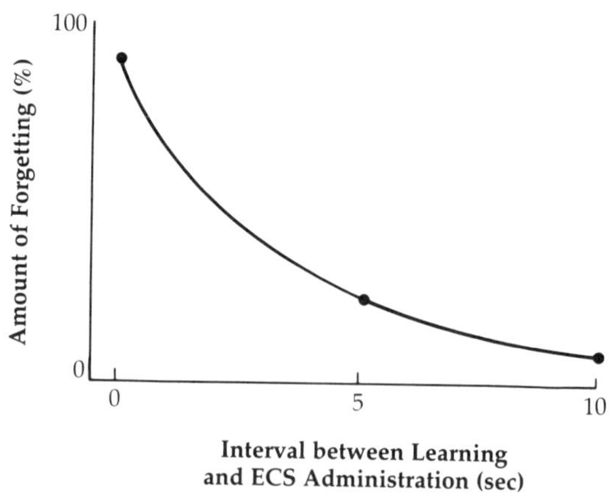

FIGURE 8.8 A typical retrograde amnesia gradient.

learning and ECS administration. In effect, these findings are precisely what one would predict based on the consolidation theory. If brain activity is disrupted by ECS while a memory is still in short-term storage, the memory trace never consolidates or becomes permanently registered, and amnesia results. However, if ECS is delayed for several seconds after learning, the memory trace has time to consolidate and the disruption of brain activity has little or no effect on retention.

It should be noted that a comparable pattern of effects is seen when animals receive drugs that *enhance* the brain's electrical activity. This class of drugs, called central nervous system (CNS) stimulants, includes such agents as strychnine, picrotoxin, and caffeine. Several studies have shown that if rats are injected with CNS stimulants shortly after learning, they later show *enhanced* retention of the learning experience. That is, they perform better on a retention test than animals given a placebo injection. As with ECS, the facilitating effects of these drugs decrease as the interval between learning and drug administration increases (see Calhoun, 1971; McGaugh & Dawson, 1971). These findings suggest that certain drugs are capable of facilitating the permanent storage of a memory. However, this effect can occur only if the drugs are administered while the memory is still represented in short-term storage.

Active and Inactive Memories

For many years the consolidation theory was the prevailing model for the formation of permanent memories by animals. Although this theory still has its adherents today, another view, first proposed by Lewis (1979), has become increasingly influential. Just as we noted the similarities between consolidation theory and the Atkinson–Shiffrin model, we can see clear parallels between the levels of processing approach and the hypothesis advanced by Lewis.

Lewis argues that an animal's memory for an experience is not formed by any progressive movement of the memory from one store to another. Instead, he proposes that there is a single memory store in which all memories are represented. He further proposes that information becomes represented in this single store at the same time it is perceived. Lewis accepts the idea that important memory processes occur shortly after learning. However, he argues that these processes have little to do with memory storage. Instead, they are important for the elaboration or encoding of a memory trace.

Lewis suggests that animals are capable of processing or encoding selected memories found in storage. The part of memory that is selected for processing is called *active memory,* while the subset of memories not being processed is termed *inactive memory.* Obviously, these memory subsets are analogous to the concepts of primary and secondary memory proposed by Craik and Lockhart. Lewis further indicates that memories can undergo processing either at the time of memory formation or when a memory is retrieved from inactive storage.

In recent years, several lines of evidence have tended to support Lewis's processing hypothesis (see, for example, Gordon, 1981; Lewis, 1979; Spear, 1978). At least some of this evidence concerns the actual fate of an animal's memory after the administration of ECS. According to the consolidation theory, ECS disrupts processes that are necessary for permanent memory storage. Thus, the amnesia produced by ECS should be permanent, since ECS is presumed to keep a memory from entering long-term storage. According to Lewis, ECS causes amnesia by disrupting the encoding process that occurs shortly after learning. Thus, the memory is presumed still to be in storage but difficult to retrieve, because it is not properly or completely encoded.

Major support for Lewis's interpretation of ECS effects comes from a number of studies that have used the so-called *reminder paradigm*. In many respects, the reminder paradigm is identical to most procedures for inducing retrograde amnesia. Animals are exposed to either Classical or Instrumental learning trials and are administered ECS immediately afterward. Several hours after ECS, the animals are tested for retention of the learning experience.

What makes the reminder paradigm different is what happens between the time of ECS administration and the retention test. During this interval the animals are briefly exposed to selected stimuli that had been present during the learning trials. For example, if prior learning had involved Classical conditioning, the animals might be exposed to either the CS, the US, or contextual stimuli that had been present during conditioning. This exposure is termed a reminder treatment, since its purpose is to give the animals a cue or prompt with respect to what they had previously learned.

The results of such studies have been reasonably consistent. When tests are administered to animals that were given a reminder treatment after undergoing ECS, the animals perform almost as if no ECS treatment had been given (see, for example, Gordon & Mowrer, 1980; Lewis, Miller, & Misanin, 1968; Miller & Springer, 1972).

To interpret these results within a consolidation theory framework, some researchers have suggested that ECS does block the storage of the original training memory, but the reminder treatments give an animal the opportunity to relearn the correct response (see Gold & King, 1974). That is, reminder treatments may allow an organism to form a new memory to replace the one disrupted by ECS. Although such an interpretation is possible in logic, it seems not to be correct. Several studies show that reminders alleviate amnesia even in cases where no new learning could be produced by the treatments (see Gordon, 1981). Thus, the best explanation for this effect seems to be the interpretation offered by Lewis' processing hypothesis. He suggests that ECS simply disrupts the encoding of a memory, making that memory difficult to retrieve. The reminder serves to activate the training memory, and this activation allows the memory to be re-encoded, hence to be retrievable on a subsequent test.

Additional evidence supporting Lewis's interpretation of retrograde amnesia comes from *familiarization studies*. Recall that Lewis views postlearning processing as having to do with memory encoding or elaboration. That is, when a learning trial is over, Lewis assumes that time is needed to associate key elements of the learning experience (for example, the CS and US) with other aspects of the learning situation (for example, contextual stimuli). He believes that ECS normally causes amnesia by disrupting this encoding process, so that a memory trace becomes difficult to retrieve. According to this view, if an animal has an opportunity to encode most of its memory *before* a learning trial, ECS should have little or no effect on retention. The purpose of the familiarization studies is to test this prediction.

In these studies animals are given extensive exposure to all aspects of the learning situation before a one-trial learning experience. This prior exposure gives the subjects an opportunity to associate most aspects of the learning situation before a learning trial actually occurs. That is, an animal can begin encoding its training memory before the first training trial. After the familiarization experience, animals are given a single learning trial, and ECS is administered immediately upon completion of that trial.

The results of most familiarization studies are clearly in accord with Lewis's prediction. These studies show that familiarization drastically reduces the amnesia normally produced by ECS (see, for example, R. R. Miller, 1970). Apparently postlearning processing is relatively unimportant for later retention if an animal has completed most of its encoding before a learning trial.

Just as Craik and Lockhart's approach has led to an emphasis on encoding processes in humans, Lewis's hypothesis has generated a similar interest among researchers working with animals. Several investigators have even begun to look at the possibility that nonhuman organisms may be able to choose to process or rehearse information in different ways. There are, for example, studies suggesting that pigeons and rats can choose to engage in either maintenance or elaborative rehearsal (see Grant, 1981; Maki, 1981). Such studies, which are basically analogous to the directed forgetting studies using human subjects, indicate that there may be strong similarities between the way humans and other species process and form memories.

Summary Statements

We began by describing the Atkinson–Shiffrin model of memory formation, which emphasizes that a memory must pass through multiple structures or memory stores before permanent registration of the memory can occur. We reviewed evidence in support of this model and also pointed out the difficulties inherent in such a view. We found that one of the foremost problems was the difficulty in distinguishing between short- and long-term storage.

Next we described the levels of processing approach to memory formation proposed by Craik and Lockhart. We saw that this model dispenses with the notion of multiple memory stores and instead emphasizes the role of encoding processes of different kinds. Again, we discussed some of the evidence that is in accord with this position and we examined the problems this approach has encountered. We particularly emphasized the difficulties involved in defining the term "levels of processing." We then discussed various modifications and extensions of this approach that have been proposed in recent years.

Finally, we noted that similar models of memory formation have been suggested to account for memory functioning in nonhuman species. We described the consolidation theory, which emphasizes multiple memory stores, and we outlined a hypothesis propounded by Lewis that bears some resemblance to the levels of processing approach. We ended the chapter by reviewing some of the experimental evidence relevant to these two positions.

9

Memory Codes and Organization

Any complete discussion of memory must include some reference to at least two topics: memory processes and memory content. Memory processes are the activities we must engage in to form and use the internal representations we call memories. In Chapter 8 we began our discussion of these processes by looking at possible mechanisms for the encoding and storage of memories. In Chapter 10 we will examine memory processing further as we discuss how memories are retrieved and used.

Aside from studying memory processes, however, it is also necessary to focus on memory content: what a memory consists of, and how the elements of a memory are organized. In studying memory content, we focus on the characteristics of memories once they have been formed.

Generally, research concerning memory content has emphasized two related issues. First, such research has attempted to determine how memories are coded. When we speak of a memory code, we are referring to the actual format of a memory or to the way in which the memory is represented. For example, some researchers have viewed memories as being constructed out of visual features. Thus, according to this view, a memory for some event is much the same as a picture of that event. Others have suggested that memories consist of acoustic features or of symbols that reflect the meaning of an experience. Still others have proposed that memories may be coded in a variety of ways depending on the constraints of a situation. Research concerning memory codes has sought to understand what aspects of an experience become represented in a memory.

Aside from looking at memory codes, several content-oriented researchers have focused on the question of how the memories contained in storage are organized. Most researchers have assumed that some of our memories are stored as groups of related representations, while others are relatively unrelated. The interest among these researchers has been in determining the organizational scheme we use to relate one memory to another.

In this chapter, we discuss some of the theorizing concerning memory content. We also review experimental studies pertinent to these theoretical positions. We begin by looking at some of the work that has been done to uncover memory codes and to learn how codes may be determined by information already contained in a person's memory store. We will then discuss some of the major ideas about the organization of stored memories.

Memory Codes

In Chapter 8, our discussion of the characteristics of sensory memory included an examination of sensory memory codes. We found that for very brief periods, events we perceive are apparently represented as raw stimulus features. That is, visual stimuli appear to be coded briefly in terms of visual features, while auditory stimuli seem to be represented in terms of sounds. Based on such findings, we characterized sensory memory as being similar to a stimulus aftereffect. That is, after a stimulus has disappeared, we continue to sense that stimulus briefly just as the stimulus was experienced while it was present. Thus, sensory memory codes are most likely direct replicas of the stimulus features we notice when a stimulus occurs in the environment.

In this chapter, we address the question of how memories are coded, once they have been selected from the sensory store for further processing. To answer this question, researchers have concentrated on ways in which memories might be coded at two different points in the information processing sequence. Some of this research has concentrated on the nature of codes while a memory is being actively processed in short-term storage. Other researchers have tried to describe how memories are coded once permanent storage has occurred. Thus, we can begin our discussion by looking at memory codes that are used shortly after items have been selected from sensory storage.

Codes Used in Short-Term Memory

When a representation has been selected from sensory memory, we maintain that representation in storage by rehearsing it. Consider for a moment what we do when we rehearse. Whether we rehearse aloud or subvocally, most of our rehearsal involves the formation of sounds that we speak to ourselves in a repetitive fashion. If, for example, we hear a sentence that we wish to remember, we say those words to ourselves over and over. We go through the same process even if the sentence is presented visually. Instead of trying to visualize the presented sentence, we often read it to ourselves and then speak the material again and again.

Given the acoustic nature of the rehearsal process, many early theorists assumed that all memories are translated into acoustic codes for short-term processing (see, for example,

Atkinson & Shiffrin, 1968). This was presumed to be the case, regardless of how a memory was originally coded in the sensory store. As we saw in our discussion of short-term storage, there is at least some evidence to support this view. For example, recall that Sperling (1960) used a partial-report procedure to study the capacity of sensory memory. In these studies he presented a large array of visual stimuli (letters) and asked subjects to report the stimuli from one location in the array. He found that subjects were able to report small segments of an array quite accurately, indicating that the capacity of sensory memory is reasonably large.

Most pertinent to our present discussion, however, are the errors Sperling's subjects made in attempting to report the letters. When subjects reported a letter incorrectly, it was almost always one that *sounded* like the letter that should have been reported—an "E" for a "V," for example, but seldom an "E" for an "F," which looks like "E" but sounds quite different. Sperling suggested that errors are made in this paradigm when the original letter is no longer in sensory memory to be read. He further suggested that as the visual aspects of a stimulus begin to decay from sensory memory, subjects translate these stimuli into an acoustic code for short-term processing. This, he proposed, was the basis for the acoustic confusion errors his subjects often made.

As we also saw in Chapter 8, similar findings have been reported by R. Conrad (1964), who specifically measured short-term recall of visually presented letters. Subjects were asked to maintain an entire set of letters in memory for a short period of time. Like Sperling, Conrad found that most recall errors involved the incorrect production of letters that sounded like those actually seen. Conrad interpreted this finding as showing that even visual stimuli are transformed to acoustic codes for short-term rehearsal (see also, Conrad & Hull, 1964; Sperling & Speelman, 1970; Wickelgren, 1966). This conclusion is further reinforced by studies that have looked at short-term recall of geometric figures (see, for example, Glanzer & Clark, 1962). These studies have shown that recall of shapes depends more on the names given to the figures than on the shapes of the figures themselves. Again, such findings suggest that humans translate visual stimuli into acoustic codes for short-term processing.

These and other studies provide evidence for the idea that short-term memories are often coded in terms of acoustic features. But does this mean that we use *only* acoustic codes during short-term processing? The answer to this question is quite clearly *no*. The very fact that congenitally deaf people show evidence of short-term memory processing tells us that humans are able to use short-term codes of other kinds. If one has been deaf since birth, it is impossible to use acoustic codes for processing. Yet, congenitally deaf people are clearly able to recall information after either short or long retention intervals. It is interesting to note that R. Conrad (1972) replicated his studies of short-term letter retention using deaf subjects. He found that these subjects made errors based on visual confusions, not on the basis of how letters sound. This suggests that deaf individuals use visual codes during short-term memory processing.

There is also substantial evidence that hearing-intact subjects sometimes use visual codes for short-term memory. Some of this evidence comes from a set of experiments conducted by Posner and his colleagues (Posner, 1969; Posner, Boies, Eichelman, & Taylor, 1969; Posner & Mitchell, 1967). In these studies subjects were shown a letter and then, after a brief interval, another letter. Their task was to state as quickly as possible whether the two letters had the same name. For example, they were to respond "same" to the pair A–A or the pair A-a and "different" to the pair A–B. The data of interest were the subjects' reaction times in making these "same or different" decisions.

Posner found that subjects responded most quickly when the two letters were physically identical (for example, A–A or b–b). Reaction times were somewhat slower on trials requiring a "different" response (for example, A–B), and on trials in which the letters had the same name but were physically different (for example, A–a or b–B). Posner attributed these differences in reaction times to differences in letter coding on the different trial types. He suggested that when letters are physically identical, a subject can use a visual code of the stimuli to determine whether the letters have the same name. However, when letters are not physically identical, subjects must translate the visual code into a name or acoustic code to decide whether they are or are not the same. This translation, according to Posner, requires more time. Thus, a subject responds to A–A faster than to A–a because the first pair can be matched on the basis of visual codes, whereas the second requires some transformation from visual to acoustic codes.

If we accept Posner's interpretation of these findings, one of his results has important implications for our attempt to determine whether visual codes exist in short-term memory. Posner found that the reaction time advantage for the identical letter pairs remained even when the letters in a pair were separated by as much as 2 seconds: that is, subjects still reacted faster to A–A pairs than to A–a pairs. This suggests that subjects were still able to use the visual code for the first letter 2 seconds after that letter had disappeared. Recall that visual stimuli apparently remain in sensory memory for only about 0.5 second. Thus in Posner's experiments subjects apparently were using a visual code beyond the time of sensory storage. Even after a letter became represented in short-term storage, in other words, subjects seemed to be using a visual code. Although such evidence is somewhat indirect, it does suggest that subjects sometimes rely on visual codes for representing short-term memories.

More direct evidence for short-term visual codes comes from a series of studies conducted by Shepard and his colleagues (see Cooper & Shepard, 1973; Shepard, 1978; Shepard & Metzler, 1971). These researchers used a reaction time procedure similar to the one reported by Posner. In one experiment (Cooper & Shepard, 1973), subjects were first given a visual presentation of a letter (for example, "R"). Shortly thereafter, they received a second letter that was either the same as the first ("R") or a mirror image of it ("Я"). Subjects were supposed to declare as quickly as possible whether the second letter was normal or reversed.

What made this task unusual is that the second letter was not always presented in an upright position. Instead, the second letter often was rotated a certain number of degrees from the vertical position. Figure 9.1 shows examples of both normal and mirror-image letters rotated from the vertical. Thus, subjects had to mentally rotate the second letter to the upright position before deciding whether it was normal or reversed. Figure 9.2, which plots the results of this experiment, reveals that reaction times were longer, the further a letter was rotated from the vertical. This suggests that subjects did rotate a "mental image" of the letter and that greater rotations required longer periods of time.

It is difficult to explain these results unless we assume that subjects formed a visual code of the second letter and then worked to rotate that code. Although a letter can be coded acoustically, it is unclear how the sound of a letter might be manipulated to make a correct decision. This point is even clearer in another

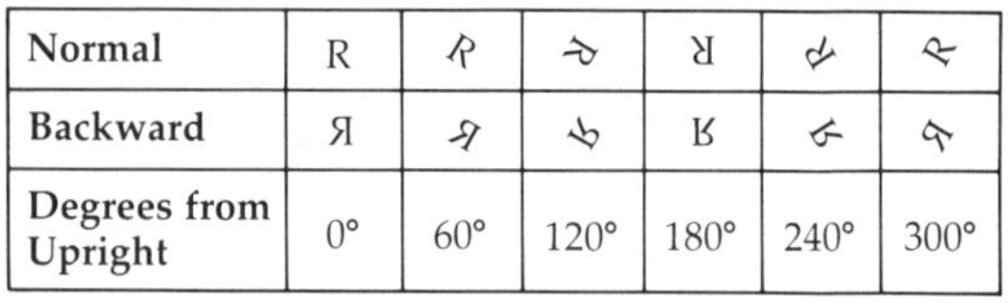

Normal	R	R	R	ᴚ	R	R
Backward	Я	Я	Я	ꓤ	Я	Я
Degrees from Upright	0°	60°	120°	180°	240°	300°

FIGURE 9.1 An example of rotated letter stimuli presented in the experiment by Cooper and Shepard. (From Cooper and Shepard, 1973.)

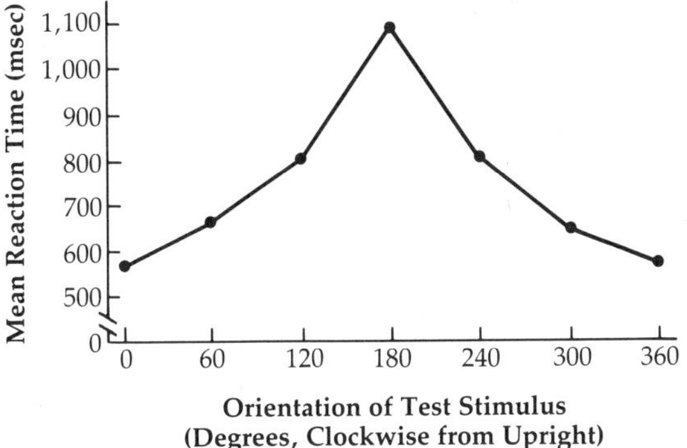

FIGURE 9.2 Reaction times to determine whether a rotated letter is normal or backward depending on the number of degrees the letter is rotated from vertical (0°). (From Cooper and Shepard, 1973.)

experiment done by Shepard and Metzler (1971). Subjects were shown pairs of three-dimensional geometric figures. In some pairs it was possible to rotate one of the figures in space so that it would match the other figure. In other pairs no amount of rotation would result in a match.

Figure 9.3 shows two pairs of figures like those used by Shepard and Metzler. Pair A represents a matching pair, while pair B illustrates a nonmatching pair. In each case subjects were to decide as quickly as possible whether the figures in a pair matched. Again, reaction times increased as a function of the number of rotations necessary to place the figures in the same orientation. In other words, subjects performed as if they were forming a visual image of one figure and then rotating it in space. Here it is even more difficult to explain the results using the notion of acoustic codes. Unlike letters, these were unfamiliar visual stimuli that should have been very difficult to code acoustically. And, even if such acoustic codes could have been formed, it is difficult to imagine how subjects might have used such codes to make their decisions. Such findings are easily interpretable only if we assume that subjects can use visual codes in short-term processing.

These experiments suggest not only that subjects can form visual codes, but also that they can work with these codes as if they were real objects. That is, just as subjects might rotate a real object in space, they also appear capable of rotating the memory code that represents an object. This notion that visual codes and real objects can be manipulated in a like manner is supported by another series of studies done by Kosslyn, Ball, and Reiser (1978). The results of these studies suggest that subjects may scan a visual code in the same way they visually scan a picture.

Subjects in these studies were first shown a map of a fictitious island (Figure 9.4), depicting objects in different locations, which were identified separately by particular names. The studies began by having subjects memorize the map and the location of the objects on the

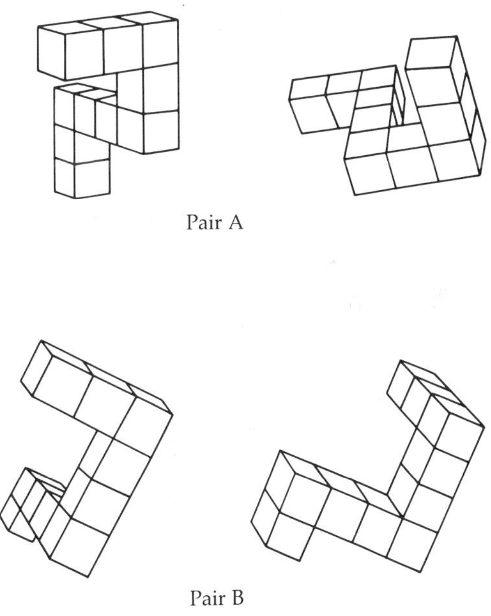

FIGURE 9.3 Examples of the three-dimensional figures used in the experiment by Shepard and Metzler. In pair A one figure can be rotated to match the other. In pair B it is impossible to rotate one figure to match the other. (From Shepard and Metzler, 1971.)

FIGURE 9.4 The map of a fictitious island used in the imagery study of Kosslyn, Ball, and Reiser. (From Kosslyn, Ball, and Reiser, 1978.)

map. When the map had been memorized, the subjects were asked to consciously picture the map in memory, focusing on one particular object. Next they were given the name of another map object and were told to scan from the focused object to the second object as quickly as possible. As soon as they reached the second object, they were to press a button.

The results of this study were clear. Scanning time was directly related to the distance between two objects on the surface of the map. That is, it took subjects longer to scan from one object to a distant one than from one object to another close by. These, of course, are the same results we would obtain if we asked people to scan from one location to another on a real map. Scanning would take longer, the more widely separated the objects. Thus, this experiment is consistent with the notion that subjects use visual codes and that they treat these visual codes like the objects the codes represent.

Finally, we have noted previously that short-term memory is presumed to be a limited capacity system. In other words, we are capable of consciously processing only a certain amount of information at any one time. It is currently believed that if we choose to maintain one set of information in short-term memory via rehearsal, our ability to take in new incoming information is limited to the extent that this set occupies all or part of our short-term memory. Some studies have indicated that there may be capacity limitations specific to memory codes of particular types. Thus, if items are acoustically coded in short-term memory, there may be limits on the processing of new acoustic information. Likewise, the presence of visual codes in short-term memory may interfere with our ability to take in new visual information.

Consider, for example, an experiment conducted by Brooks (1968) in which subjects were given one of two tasks designed to promote either visual or acoustic coding. In the visual coding condition, subjects were shown a block letter such as the one in Figure 9.5, with an asterisk next to one corner. The letter was then removed and the subjects were instructed to maintain an image of the letter in memory. In this condition, the subjects were required to scan their image of the letter clockwise beginning with the corner designated by the asterisk. They were to report whether each

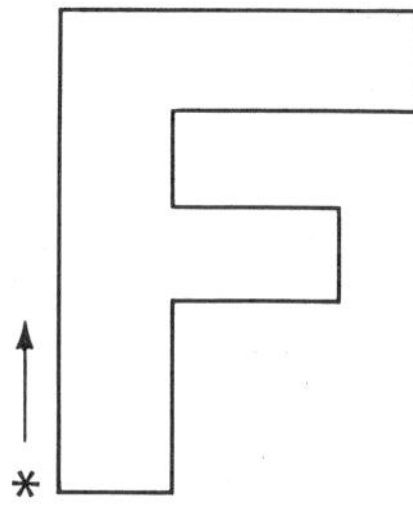

FIGURE 9.5 A block letter of the type used in Brooks's study of visual coding. (From Brooks, 1968.)

corner was at the very top or bottom of the letter (a "yes" response) or not at the top or bottom (a "no" response). For the letter pictured in Figure 9.5, the correct sequence of responses is "yes, yes, yes, no, no, no, no, no, no, yes."

In the acoustic coding condition, subjects were given a sentence such as "The car in the driveway is not in the street." Subjects were asked to remember the sentence, and then, beginning with the first word, to say whether each word was a noun (a "yes" response) or not (a "no" response). For the sentence above, the correct response sequence is "no, yes, no, no, yes, no, no, no, no, yes." Brooks assumed that whereas the letter task would require visual codes for correct responding, the sentence task would involve acoustic coding.

To determine how these codes might interfere with new incoming information, Brooks had subjects make their yes and no responses in one of two ways. In some cases subjects were required to say their responses aloud, which involved the use of acoustic features. In other cases, subjects were to respond by pointing to a "yes" or "no" response printed on a page. This type of response would, of course, involve the use of visual features. Brooks found that a subject's speed in making these different responses depended on the type of code being held in memory. Subjects in the letter task responded much faster when they were allowed to speak their responses rather than pointing to the printed words. On the other hand, subjects in the sentence condition responded faster when they were able to point to the printed responses. These results suggest that it is difficult to process new visual information if we are already maintaining visual codes in short-term memory. Likewise, the processing of acoustic information is more difficult if we are maintaining acoustic codes. Such findings not only support the existence of short-term visual codes, they also suggest that there are capacity limitations for codes of different types. Similar conclusions have been reached by other experimenters using slightly different procedures (see, for example, Baddeley, Grant, Wight, & Thomson, 1975).

To this point we have seen that both acoustic and visual codes seem to exist in short-term memory. Is there evidence that other short-term codes may sometimes be used? Although most of the research concerning codes has focused on acoustic and visual representations, it does appear that we sometimes use codes of other kinds for short-term processing. There are, for example, studies suggesting the existence of kinesthetic or motor codes in short-term memory. In one notable example (Kerr, 1983), congenitally blind subjects performed a task similar to the visual scanning task used by Kosslyn, Ball, and Reiser (1978). Kerr gave subjects a map with a raised outline, which contained raised objects within the outline. The subjects were instructed to feel the map and the objects and to memorize where the objects were located. Next, they were asked to touch one object and mentally scan from that object to another on the map. As in the experiment of Kosslyn, Ball, and Reiser, the greater the distance on the map between the touched and target objects, the longer the subjects took to reach the target object. In other words, scanning time was directly related to how far apart two objects were. In this study subjects could not have used a visual code of the map. Furthermore, it is difficult to imagine how one might do this task using an acoustic code. Apparently, these subjects coded the map locations in terms of some type of movement or motor code and used this code to scan between locations. Other experimenters have also found evidence suggesting that even sighted subjects may use motor codes in tasks requiring specific motor movements (see, for example, Posner, 1967; Posner & Konick, 1966).

Finally, there is also evidence that humans are capable of representing some short-term memories in terms of meaning or semantic codes. Shulman (1972) presented subjects with a series of lists containing 10 words. After each 10-word list, the subjects were asked if a given probe word matched one of the words in the list. On some occasions subjects were told to report a match only if the probe word was identical to a word in the preceding list. On other trials, however, subjects were told to report a match if the probe word was synonymous with a word in the list. The type of match that was required on a given trial was signaled to a subject just before the presentation of each probe word.

Shulman's primary interest in this study was how subjects would respond when the probe word was synonymous with a listed word, but when the subjects were asked for an identity match. He found that under these conditions subjects often reported a match even though the probe word was not identical to any word in the list. These incorrect responses did not occur, however, when the probe word was *not* synonymous with a listed word. Thus, subjects tended to ascribe identity to words that had the same meaning. Shulman concluded that if the subjects had not maintained the meanings of the listed words in short-term memory, this finding would have been unlikely. That is, we would expect such a result only if subjects were capable of coding certain short-term memories in terms of meanings or semantic codes.

We began this discussion with the presumption that most short-term memories are coded acoustically. The evidence we have reviewed in the past few pages does not necessarily invalidate this presumption. Humans rely heavily on language-based information. Since words can be coded acoustically, it seems entirely reasonable to assume that much of our short-term coding is acoustic in nature. Still, there is substantial evidence that humans are capable of using short-term codes of other kinds. Most probably, the codes we employ depend heavily on the constraints of a particular situation. Although acoustic codes may predominate in short-term memory, we appear to be capable of using other codes if the situation warrants or demands.

Codes Used in Long-Term, Permanent Memory

We have seen that the information we hold in short-term memory is usually coded in terms of specific stimulus features or attributes. We may, for example, consciously process a string of letters with respect to how the letters sound or what the string looks like. But how are permanent memories coded? Upon completion of conscious processing, what is done to prepare memories for long-term storage?

In an attempt to answer this question, consider the following familiar situation. You are sitting in a classroom, listening and taking notes. If the lecturer speaks very slowly, you are able to maintain the exact sound of her words in memory long enough to write down verbatim what is being said. This, of course, is consistent with the idea that we can maintain information in short-term memory using acoustic codes. Now imagine that the lecture is over and you are walking to your next class. On the way, you try to remember the information you have just heard. What do you recall? Do you remember the exact sound of the lecturer's words? Do you remember how each sentence was phrased or what the sentences looked like as you wrote them down? Most of us would have great difficulty recalling these specific stimulus features minutes or hours after a lecture. What we would remember is the meaning or the gist of what was said. We would recall the main points or propositions from the lecture. If we recalled specific sentences, these sentences would most likely be our own paraphrases of the lecturer's main points. This suggests to us that many of our long-term memories may not be coded in terms of specific stimulus features such as sounds or visual images. Instead, this example suggests that long-term memories are often coded in terms of meanings or semantic features.

Through the years, several experimenters have found support for this idea that meaning codes predominate in long-term memory. These results can be illustrated by considering an early experiment conducted by Sachs (1967). Sachs's subjects listened to a long prose paragraph concerning the first use of the telescope. Embedded in this paragraph was the following sentence: "He sent a letter about it to Galileo, the great Italian scientist." The point of the experiment was to determine how well subjects would remember specific aspects of this embedded sentence on a later test. To make this determination, Sachs gave her subjects test sentences of different kinds after they had heard the paragraph. Their task was to say whether the test sentence had been the one heard previously. For some subjects the test sentence and the embedded sentence were identical. Other subjects received test sentences that differed from the original sentence in particular ways. For example, some test sentences were changed from the *active* to the *passive voice* ("A letter about it was sent to Galileo, the great Italian scientist.") Other test sentences were different from the target sentence in terms of the *formal structure* ("He sent Galileo, the great Italian scientist, a letter about it.") Still other test sentences differed from the first in terms of meaning or *semantic features* ("Galileo, the great Italian scientist, sent him a letter about it").

Sachs was also interested in whether a subject's memory for the target sentence would change as a function of time or the number of words intervening between the target sentence and the test. Thus, she presented the test sentences either immediately after the target sentence (0 syllables intervening), or she delayed the test until subjects had heard either 80 or 160 syllables beyond the target sentence. From the results (Figure 9.6), we see that when subjects were tested immediately after hearing the target sentence, they performed extremely well regardless of the type of test sentence. In other words, they were able to say that identical test sentences were identical and that different test sentences were different. However, after longer retention intervals this pattern of results changed dramatically. Subjects were still able to correctly state that a semantically changed sentence was different from the target sentence. They tended *not* to recognize that test sentences of other types (formally changed, passive voice) were different from the original sentence. Surprisingly, with longer retention intervals they also tended to say that identical test sentences were not the same as the target sentence.

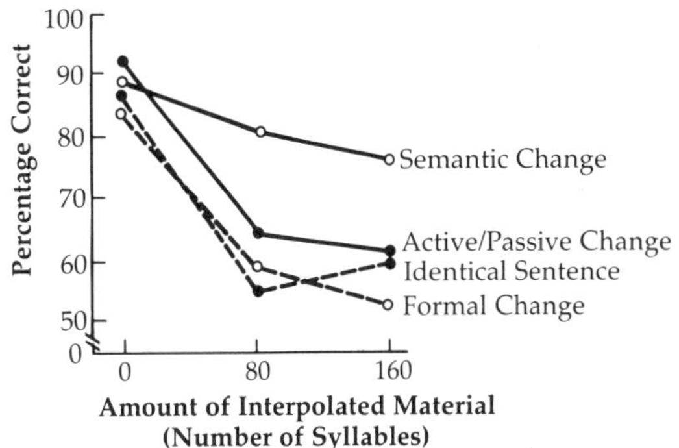

FIGURE 9.6 The percentage of times subjects were able to detect changes in a test sentence as a function of the type of change and the time since the test sentence had been seen. (From Sachs, 1967.)

These findings have some important implications for how memories are coded at different stages of processing. Shortly after a sentence is heard, subjects are able to remember such specific stimulus features as how the words were ordered and what the sentence sounded like. Thus, they are able to state accurately whether test sentences differ from the original in terms of these features. However, after longer intervals only changes in the *meaning* of a test sentence are correctly identified. This suggests that after longer intervals, subjects remember the target sentence meaning but not the specific stimulus features. These findings clearly support the idea that long-term memories are coded in terms of meaning as opposed to features such as sounds or visual images (see also Begg, 1971; James & Abrahamson, 1977).

The nature of meaning codes It is easy to understand what acoustic or visual codes are like. By acoustic coding we simply mean that a stimulus is represented in memory by how the stimulus sounded when we originally heard it. In the same way, a visual code refers to a representation based on how a stimulus originally looked. In both cases there is a direct relationship between the memory code and our original sensation of a stimulus. What is less clear, however, is the intention of theorists when they use the term "meaning code" or when they state that an event is coded in terms of meaning. The meaning of an experience cannot be based solely on the nature of our sensations. The meaning of an event is something we must derive or abstract based on our understanding of the symbolic references in an experience. Thus, meaning is an abstraction, not a direct replica of sensory events. To understand the nature of a meaning code, we must understand how abstractions are represented in memory.

Most contemporary theorists agree that meaning is represented in memory in terms of *propositions*. A proposition can be defined as a small group of words or concepts that express a single idea. For example, consider the sentence "The old man rode the brown horse." This single sentence contains three separate propositions or ideas. We can state these propositions in the following way:

1. The man was old.
2. The man rode the horse.
3. The horse was brown.

Thus, according to this view, when we hear or read a sentence and then code it in long-term memory, we do not form a visual code based on how the sentence looked or an acoustic code based on how the sentence sounded. Instead, we form codes that represent the propositions or basic ideas in that sentence.

This idea that sentences are coded in terms of individual propositions has been supported by a variety of experiments. Kintsch and Glass (1974), for example, presented subjects with sentences having either one or three propositions. Both types of sentences contained the same number of words. Later, the investigators asked subjects for verbatim recall of the sentences. They found that although the sentences were of equal length, verbatim recall was best for sentences having only a single proposition. This is precisely the result we would expect if we accepted the suggestion that subjects code sentences in terms of individual propositions. Recall of the single-proposition sentences should be reasonably easy, since all the information in the sentence is coded as a unit. Recall of multiple-proposition sentences should be more difficult, since recall would require a combination of individual proposition codes. If sentences were coded as whole units, on the other hand, recall should not depend on the number of propositions in sentences of equal length.

Similarly, if subjects are shown a sentence containing multiple propositions, recall of one proposition depends on the particular cues a subject is given at the time of testing. If a subject is given a cue word that is part of the proposition that is to be recalled, recall performance is usually excellent. Recall results are poorer, however, if the cue word comes from one of the other propositions contained in the sentence (Anderson & Bower, 1973). Again, this finding suggests that individual propositions are coded as separate units and that whole sentences are not coded as units.

Finally, Kintsch and Keenan (1973) had subjects study paragraphs of text so that they would be able to recall the meanings of the paragraphs. Although the paragraphs had the same number of words, they contained different numbers of propositions. Kintsch and Keenan found that the more propositions a paragraph contained, the longer the subjects needed to study it to learn the meaning. Thus, this type of study suggests that the basic unit of meaning is the proposition. It also suggests that to code the meaning of a paragraph, we must form representations of each proposition the paragraph contains.

These and numerous other experiments support the idea that meaning codes are actually representations of individual propositions. However, there is currently some dispute concerning the arrangement of the concepts in a propositional code. One point of view has been proposed by Anderson and Bower (1973; see also, Chomsky, 1965). According to this view, each proposition coded in memory consists of two equal parts—a subject and a predicate. The subject of the proposition is really the subject of the simple sentence used to express the proposition. So, for example, in the proposition "The man rode the horse," the subject is represented by "man." The predicate of a proposition contains the verb, any direct or indirect objects, and any modifying words (such as adverbs) in the propositional sentence. Thus, in the proposition "The man rode the horse," the predicate would include "rode" and "horse." Figure 9.7a illustrates the structure of this proposition according to this point of view—that is, the subject and predicate are considered to be equal elements in the propositional code. Note, however, that the predicate may have a substructure of its own, while the subject is usually a single element.

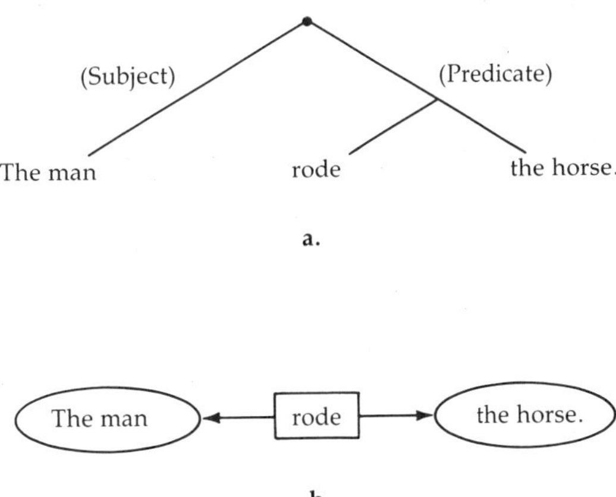

FIGURE 9.7 Views of how two propositional codes, both representing the sentence "The man rode the horse," might be structured: (a) structure in which the subject and predicate of the proposition are equal elements; (b) in which the verb is the central element in the proposition.

Figure 9.7b shows another possible structure for the same proposition. In the view represented here, which is espoused by theorists such as Kintsch (1974) and Norman and Rumelhart (1975), the central element in each proposition is the verb. In this conception the subject, objects, and modifiers in a proposition are all equal elements and are all attached to a central verb representation. This view suggests that each proposition is unique not in terms of its subjects, objects, or modifiers, but in terms of the verb that defines the proposition.

At present these ideas concerning the internal structure of a proposition remain somewhat speculative. Although some experimenters have attempted to check the validity of these hypotheses, there is little evidence now that clearly supports one view over another (see, for example, Wickelgren, 1979). For present purposes the precise structure of a propositional code is relatively unimportant. What is important is that meaning appears to be coded in memory via some shorthand notation, not in terms of complete sentences or chunks of written text.

How meaning is derived from propositional codes We have said that if you read a sentence or a paragraph, you most probably store a series of individual propositions in long-term memory. We emphasize, however, that none of these individual propositions captures the meaning of an entire block of text. To represent the meaning of an entire sentence or paragraph in memory, individual propositional codes must be combined in some fashion. One rather elegant theory of how propositional codes are combined in memory has been proposed by Kintsch and his colleagues

(Kintsch, 1976; Kintsch & van Dijk, 1978; van Dijk & Kintsch, 1983).

Basically, Kintsch proposes that all the propositions in a block of text are organized into a coherent hierarchy called a *text base.* At the top of this hierarchy we place the main idea or proposition in a block of text. This main idea usually consists of the verb that is central to the proposition, as well as the subjects of that verb. Just below the main proposition in the hierarchy are other words that help to clarify the main idea. For example, consider the simple sentence, "The woman drove the car at high speeds." The main proposition, which is represented by "woman drove," would occupy the highest level in the text base for this sentence. Just below this main proposition would be phrases such as "the car" and "at high speeds." These phrases are secondary to the main idea, but they help to clarify the meaning of the higher level proposition.

Lower stages in the hierarchy would be occupied by other propositions from the same block of text. Each of these lower level propositions would again consist of an important verb and its subject. It is presumed that lower level propositions represent ideas that are more secondary to the meaning of the text as a whole. Thus, at each level of the hierarchy we would encounter a proposition followed by defining or clarifying phrases. However, as we move from the top to the bottom of the hierarchy, the propositions would become less central to the overall meaning of a text block.

To illustrate how a text base might be derived from a particular block of text, consider the following complex sentence: "The waves crash heavily onto the beach and wash away the sand on the surface, causing erosion along the shore." The main proposition in this sentence is "waves crash." Other propositions are "waves wash away sand" and "waves cause erosion." The remaining words simply help to clarify the meanings of the three propositions. Thus, the text base for this sentence might be represented by the following hierarchy:

1. Waves crash (proposition based on main verb)
   a. heavily (how)
   b. onto the beach (where)
2. Waves wash away sand (proposition based on secondary verb)
   a. on the surface (where)
3. Waves cause erosion (proposition based on secondary verb)
   a. along the shore (where)

Although this is not the actual format Kintsch proposes to describe a text base, it does contain most of the important features. First, each proposition in the sentence occupies a position in the hierarchy. Second, each proposition is followed by phrases that clarify the meaning of the preceding proposition. Third, the higher a proposition is in the hierarchy, the more central the meaning of that proposition is to the meaning of the sentence.

According to this view, the complete meaning of a text block can be recalled by retrieving the text base from memory. We first retrieve the main proposition in the hierarchy and then progressively read down through the text base to pick up additional meaning. It is interesting to note that such a model makes reasonably accurate predictions concerning memory for meaning. For example, Kintsch and van Dijk (1978) prepared a 1300-word research report and constructed a text base for it. They had subjects read the report and asked them to write a brief summary, either immediately or 1 month or 3 months later. Kintsch and van Dijk found that when subjects were tested immediately, they included a number of lower level propositions in their reports. Subjects tested after longer intervals, however, tended to record major propositions from the top of the text base hierarchy, but very few included propositions or descriptors from the lower part of the hierarchy. These findings suggest that we do not treat all propositions in a text block equally. Instead, the data are consistent with the notion that certain propositions are treated as being central to the meaning of a block and others are treated as being peripheral. This is precisely what one would expect if propositions are arranged in a hierarchical fashion.

The role of inference in constructing a text base One of the ideas that is central to Kintsch's theory is that a text base is a logical, coherent structure. To remember the meaning of a text passage, we must not only store individual propositions, we must interrelate these propositions into a meaningful whole. As you might imagine, the construction of a text base is relatively easy as long as the ideas in a text passage are clearly related, or as long as there is enough overlap to justify treating them as such. For example, consider the following sentences: "John rode the horse" and "The horse was brown." Each sentence contains a single proposition. Furthermore, both contain the word "horse." Because these sentences appear one after the other in the same passage, it is easy to discern that the propositions in these sentences are related. That is, the appearance of the word "horse" in both propositions makes it easy to combine these ideas or to realize that they belong together in a text base.

However, Kintsch proposes that the construction of a text base is more difficult or time-consuming when the ideas in a text passage do not appear to be related or do not share common words or concepts. Again, consider two sentences: "John went riding" and "The horse was brown." Kintsch believes that these sentences are more difficult to combine in a text base because they contain no common words or concepts. To relate these propositions in memory, we are forced to create a proposition that bridges the gap between the sentences. We are forced, that is, to draw an *inference* concerning how these two propositions are related. We might, for example, insert the proposition "he rode a horse" between the propositions "John went riding" and "The horse was brown." In effect we create a proposition that has some overlap with each of the propositions we wish to relate. Our created or inferred proposition tells us that John was riding a horse, not a motorcycle or a bus. Once this intermediate proposition has been created, it makes sense to us for the sentence "The horse was brown" to follow the sentence "John went riding."

The idea that a text base can contain created or inferred propositions is very important. It suggests that when we code the meaning of a passage, we do more than abstract propositions from the text as presented. We also create our own propositional codes that are not contained verbatim in the text but are derived from inferences about the text material. Thus, our memory for meaning is really a construction or a fabrication that includes direct meanings based on presented material and other meanings we attribute to the material. Such a view suggests that it is possible for two individuals to read the same text passage and code its meaning very differently. It also suggests that different memory codes are more likely when a text passage is poorly organized or when the ideas in a passage are not clearly related.

Several studies support the idea that inferences are used to link individual propositions together in memory. For example, Kintsch (1976) presented one group of subjects with a story containing clearly linked sentences such as "A carelessly discarded burning cigarette started a fire. The fire destroyed many acres of virgin forest." Another group was given a story containing sentences that were not clearly linked but which could be linked by using an inference. An example would be: "A burning cigarette was carelessly discarded. The fire destroyed many acres of virgin forest." Thus, the story given to the first group clearly stated that the cigarette caused the fire. The second group could reach this conclusion only by drawing an inference based on the sentences presented. Either immediately or 15 minutes after reading the respective stories, the subjects were given a true–false test concerning the meaning of the sentences. For example, they were asked whether the sentence "A discarded cigarette started a fire" was true or false.

For subjects in group 1 it did not matter whether the test was given immediately or several minutes after reading the story. In both cases they were able to confirm the truth of the statement very quickly. The timing of the test did, however, influence the performance of the second group of subjects. Group 2 subjects tested immediately required a long time to confirm that the statement was true. On the other hand, group 2 subjects tested after 15 minutes confirmed the truth of the statement very quickly. These findings are consistent with the idea that for a short time, subjects remember the precise features of sentences. Thus, group 2 subjects had difficulty on the immediate test because the test sentence did not repeat exactly what the story sentences had said. However, after 15 minutes these subjects had apparently formed an inference that linked the two story sentences together. On the basis of this inference, they were able to confirm the truth of the test sentence quickly.

Other data suggesting that inferences are stored in memory come from a well-known experiment conducted by Bransford and Franks (1971). These experimenters exposed subjects to a long list of sentences and encouraged them simply to read and understand each individual sentence. Contained in each list were several sentences containing one proposition, others containing two propositions, and still others having three propositions. Here, for example, are four of the single-proposition sentences used in this study.

> The ants were in the kitchen.
> The jelly was sweet.
> The jelly was on the table.
> The ants ate the jelly.

The two- and three-proposition sentences were made up of combinations of the single propositions. For example, one of the two-proposition sentences used was "The ants in the kitchen ate the jelly." An example of a three-proposition sentence would be "The ants in the kitchen ate the sweet jelly." Thus, while reading the sentence list, subjects were exposed to four related propositions, but they never saw all four in a single sentence.

After the list had been read, the subjects were given a surprise recognition test in which they were asked which of a series of one-, two-, and three- proposition sentences they recalled having seen before. In addition to these test sentences, the subjects received some four-proposition sentences, constructed from four propositions the subjects had seen previously. One such sentence was "The ants in the kitchen ate the sweet jelly that was on the table." Recall, however, that *no* four-proposition sentences had occurred in the original list.

What Bransford and Franks discovered is somewhat surprising. The test sentences that were most often judged as being old (that is, seen before) were the four-proposition sentences the subjects had never seen, but which had been constructed from previously seen propositions. Subjects were much less likely to recognize single- and double-proposition sentences that they actually *had* seen before. These results provide striking evidence that when subjects read or hear propositions they judge to be related, they infer that the propositions belong together and they appear to store these propositions as a group. This would explain why subjects report having seen a complex sentence, when in fact they had seen only isolated sets of propositions making up that complex sentence. Such findings are important because they suggest that long-term memory consists of more than isolated propositional codes. Apparently, long-term memory also includes inferred propositions and propositions that are grouped on the basis of inference. Several studies have reported similar results, and, thus, also lend support to this conclusion (see, for example, Bransford, Barclay, & Franks, 1972; Singer & Rosenberg, 1973).

Inferences based on schemas The data we have reviewed thus far suggest that long-term memory contains meaning or propositional codes that are derived or abstracted from text. Furthermore, it appears that these propositional codes are not stored in isolation. We seem to organize these codes into meaningful groupings based on inferences we make concerning how individual codes are related. In some cases we appear to infer propositions that are not actually present in text in order to link other propositions together. In effect, we appear to store not what we have seen or heard, but, instead, our own versions of events based on the inferences we make concerning those events. Given the apparent importance of inference in forming memories for meaning, we might ask how inferences arise. In other words, what is the basis for inferring that some propositions are related while others are not?

One of the first researchers to deal with this question was Bartlett (1932). Bartlett was interested in our apparent tendency to store distorted memories rather than direct replicas of experience. We seem to construct or fabricate our memories, rather than simply storing a copy of an experience as it occurred, and Bartlett's primary focus was on whether these memory constructions tend to follow an orderly pattern. In one of his early studies Bartlett had subjects read the following complex story.

> One night two young men from Egulac went down to the river to hunt seals, and while they were there it became foggy and calm. Then they heard war-cries, and they thought: "Maybe this is a war-party." They escaped to the shore, and hid behind a log. Now canoes came up, and they heard the noise of paddles, and saw one canoe coming up to them. There were five men in the canoe, and they said:
>
> "What do you think? We wish to take you along. We are going up the river to make war on the people."
>
> One of the young men said: "I have no arrows."
>
> "Arrows are in the canoe," they said.
>
> "I will not go along. I might be killed. My relatives do not know where I have gone. But you," he said, turning to the other, "may go with them."
>
> So one of the young men went, but the other returned home.
>
> And the warriors went on up the river to a town on the other side of Kalama. The people came down to the water, and they began to fight, and many were killed. But presently the young man heard one of the warriors say: "Quick, let us go home: that Indian has been hit." Now he thought: "Oh, they are ghosts." He did not feel sick, but they said he had been shot.
>
> So the canoes went back to Egulac, and the young man went ashore to his house, and made a fire. And he told everybody and said: "Behold I accompanied the ghosts, and we went to fight. Many of our fellows were killed, and many of those who attacked us were killed. They said I was hit, and I did not feel sick."
>
> He told it all, and then he became quiet. When the sun rose he fell down. Something black came out of his mouth. His face became contorted. The people jumped up and cried.
>
> He was dead.

Bartlett then had subjects try to recall the story 20 hours later. One subject recalled the story as follows.

> Two men from Edulac went fishing. While thus occupied by the river they heard a noise in the distance.
>
> "It sounds like a cry," said one, and presently there appeared some men in canoes who invited them to join the party on their adventure. One of the young men refused to go, on the ground of family ties, but the other offered to go.
>
> "But there are no arrows," he said.
>
> "The arrows are in the boat," was the reply.
>
> He thereupon took his place, while his friend returned home. The party paddled up the river to Kaloma, and began to land on the banks of the river. The enemy came rushing

> upon them, and some sharp fighting ensued. Presently someone was injured, and the cry was raised that the enemy were ghosts.
>
> The party returned down the stream, and the young man arrived home feeling none the worse for his experience. The next morning at dawn he endeavored to recount his adventures. While he was talking something black issued from his mouth. Suddenly he uttered a cry and fell down. His friends gathered round him.
>
> But he was dead.

If you compare these two stories, one of the first things you will notice is that the recalled story is substantially shorter than the original. Some of this abridgement is undoubtedly due to forgetting certain details. However, Bartlett pointed out that the stories differ clearly in other ways. First of all, recalled stories tend to have some of the same themes or meanings as the originals, but the recalled stories tend to have much less detail. This is consistent, of course, with Sachs's finding that long-term recall of meaning is much better than long-term recall of the exact features of text, as discussed earlier.

Second, recalled stories tend to contain some details that did not actually appear in the original story. For example, the recalled story quoted above says that the wounded warrior *"uttered a cry"* just before dying. It also states that the warrior's *"friends"* gathered around him when he fell. Neither of these details appears in the original story. Bartlett suggests that these embellishments were added because they are consistent with the theme of the story. In effect, he proposes that once a coherent theme has been abstracted from a story, we manufacture details that tend to fit this theme or meaning.

Based on these comparisons between recalled and original stories, Bartlett reached certain conclusions concerning how memories become distorted. He pointed out that we never actually read or hear a text passage in a vacuum. Rather, whenever we encounter a text passage we are equipped with a preexisting system of knowledge, concepts, and beliefs called a *schema.* Bartlett proposed that when people read a text passage, they attempt to fit or assimilate the passage into a preexisting schema. In effect, they interpret new passages on the basis of what they already know or expect. When the meaning of a passage is foreign to or different from an existing schema, the process becomes like trying to fit a square peg into a round hole. The meaning of the story is often tailored to fit the reader's schema more closely. Story details that are consistent with the schema tend to be retained, whereas details that do not fit are lost. At the time of recall, individuals report a story that is really a compromise between the original story and the schema into which the story was assimilated. Furthermore, at the time of recall individuals tend to add details that are consistent with this compromise theme or meaning. In other words, they add details that help to make the recollected story more coherent.

Bartlett's view suggests that we infer meanings on the basis of our preexisting knowledge systems or schemas. It is notable that this idea has been supported by a number of experimenters. First of all, some researchers have replicated Bartlett's original studies using stories of different kinds. Basically, these studies have shown that when stories match a subject's preexisting expectations, recalled stories tend to have fewer distortions than Bartlett found (see, for example, Paul, 1959). That is, stories that fit easily into existing schema require less tailoring than stories that do not.

Bartlett's notion is also supported by studies showing that a subject's recall of a passage can be altered by activating certain schemas before the passage is read. In these studies subjects are given some indication of what the passage they are to read might be about. The purpose of the prior indication is to identify a particular schema into which the subject can fit the text block. Probably the best known studies of this type have been those conducted by Bransford and Johnson (1972).

In their first experiment, Bransford and

Johnson had subjects listen to the following prose passage and instructed them to remember as much of it as possible.

> If the balloons popped, the sound wouldn't be able to carry since everything would be too far away from the correct floor. A closed window would also prevent the sound from carrying, since most buildings tend to be well insulated. Since the whole operation depends on the steady flow of electricity, a break in the middle of the wire would also cause problems. Of course, the fellow could shout, but the human voice is not loud enough to carry that far. An additional problem is that the string could break on the instrument. Then there would be no accompaniment to the message. It is clear that the best situation would involve less distance. Then there would be fewer potential problems. With face to face contact, the least number of things could go wrong. (Bransford & Johnson, 1972, p. 719)

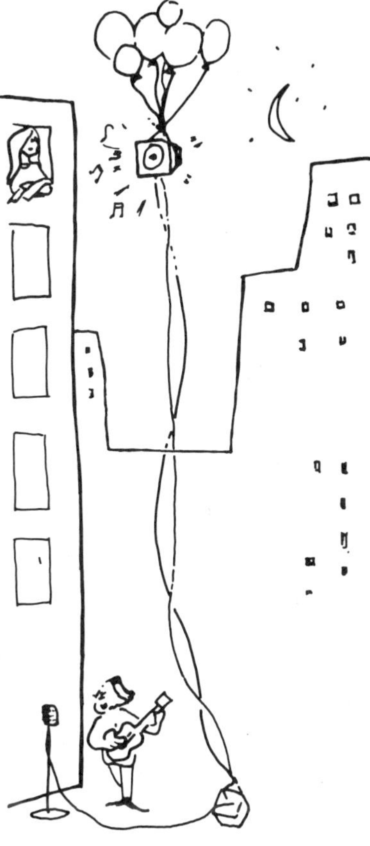

FIGURE 9.8 Bransford and Johnson gave some subjects this sketch as an aid in learning the complicated passage about the balloon, sound, electricity, and so on, displayed in the text. (From Bransford and Johnson, 1972.)

Some subjects in this study were given the passage by itself. However, another group was shown the picture reproduced as Figure 9.8 before hearing the passage. Bransford and Johnson found that the second group recalled significantly more of the passage than the group that received no picture. They interpreted this finding in terms of schema activation. They suggested that the picture activated a schema that made the passage more interpretable or easier to understand. In other words, the picture-induced schema gave the subjects a basis for inferring the meaning of the passage itself.

The foregoing interpretation is consistent with Bransford and Johnson's data, but another interpretation is possible. It may be that both groups forgot the passage to the same degree, but the picture allowed one group of subjects to make more accurate guesses concerning passage contents. According to this interpretation, rather than activating a schema that helped to interpret the passage, the picture may simply have given the subjects a basis for educated guessing. To test this interpretation, Bransford and Johnson conducted a second experiment using three groups of subjects, all of whom heard the following passage:

> The procedure is actually quite simple. First you arrange things into different groups depending on their makeup. Of course, one pile may be sufficient depending on how much there is to do. If you have to go somewhere else due to lack of facilities that is the next step, otherwise you are pretty well set. It is important not to overdo any particular endeavor. That is, it is better to do too few things at once than too many. In the short run this may not seem important, but complications from doing

> too many can easily arise. A mistake can be expensive as well. The manipulation of the appropriate mechanisms should be self-explanatory, and we need not dwell on it here. At first the whole procedure will seem complicated. Soon, however, it will become just another facet of life. It is difficult to foresee any end to the necessity for this task in the immediate future, but then one never can tell. (Bransford & Johnson, 1972, p. 722)

Before hearing this passage, one group was told that the passage would be about *washing clothes.* The second group was not given the topic of the passage before hearing it, but was told what it concerned before being tested for recall. The third group never received the topic of the passage. Bransford and Johnson reasoned that if the topic activated a schema and thus allowed for better interpretation of the passage, only the subjects in the first group should show facilitated recall. However, if the topic only provided a basis for guessing on the test, both groups 1 and 2, which received the clue before testing, should show good recall.

On the test, Bransford and Johnson assessed both recall of specific items in the passage and subjects' comprehension of the passage meaning. They found that both recall and comprehension were much better in the first group than in the other two groups. That is, the group that received the topic before hearing the passage performed much better than the groups that received the topic afterward and not at all, respectively. This finding is consistent with the idea that the topic activates a schema within which a passage can be interpreted. More generally, it supports the hypothesis that our inferences concerning meaning are based at least partially on those preexisting knowledge systems called schemas (see also, Royer, Hambleton, & Cadorette, 1978).

Other codes in long-term memory We have seen that there is substantial evidence for the existence of propositional codes in long-term memory. Is there comparable evidence suggesting that long-term codes of other types are used? As it happens, this is a difficult question to answer at present. First, there has been surprisingly little research into whether other types of codes exist. We know that we are capable of recognizing certain sounds or odors long after these stimuli were originally sensed. Yet few studies have directly dealt with long-term acoustic or olfactory codes. Aside from propositional codes, most research in the area has dealt with the possible existence of long-term visual codes. However, as we will see, evidence that supports visual coding is open to other interpretations.

The evidence for long-term visual coding comes primarily from two sources. First, several studies show that memory for pictures appears to be superior to memory for words. For example, Standing, Conezio, and Haber (1970) presented 2560 complex pictures to their subjects at the rate of one picture every 10 seconds. Later, they administered a recognition test and found that subjects were able to identify correctly almost 95 percent of the pictures seen previously. Similar results have been reported by Nickerson (1965). This extremely high level of recognition is superior to what is found in most studies that assess recognition for words. Based on such differences, some researchers have argued that words and pictures must be coded in different ways. The usual suggestion is that words are coded in terms of meaning, whereas pictures are coded according to visual features.

A second line of support for visual codes comes from the work of Paivio, which we discussed earlier. Recall that Paivio had subjects use mental images to associate items in a Verbal learning paradigm. He also had subjects associate words having either high or low imagery value. Basically, Paivio found that learning and recall were easier when subjects used or could use images than when imagery was either difficult or not suggested. Based on these findings, Paivio (1969) proposed the *dual-coding hypothesis,* according to which it is possible to code words in terms of either meaning or visual images. Furthermore, he suggested that recall is best when both codes are used.

Few theorists deny that humans are capable of generating images that have a "picturelike" quality. However, several researchers have questioned whether this ability to image means that we actually use visual codes in memory. Anderson and Bower (1973), for example, suggest that imagery may well enhance recall not by producing a visual code, but instead by promoting a more elaborate meaning or propositional code. Similar arguments have been expressed by other theorists (see, for example, Intraub, 1979; Pylyshyn, 1973). According to this view, picture memory is superior to word memory because pictures provide an especially effective tool for forming an elaborate meaning code.

Several types of experiments have indeed raised doubts about whether visual codes actually exist. As we have mentioned, Paivio's finding that imagery instructions facilitate recall does not necessarily imply that imagery produces its effect through the establishment of a visual code. This point is emphasized by at least one study showing that imagery instructions tend to aid recall even in congenitally blind subjects (Jonides, Kahn, & Rozin, 1975). Since it is unlikely that the congenitally blind use visual codes, this finding suggests that imagery instructions can influence recall even when these instructions do not result in visual coding. Thus, the mere fact that imagery instructions lead to better recall cannot be taken as strong evidence that visual codes exist.

Questions about the existence of visual codes have also arisen from studies dealing with picture memory. We have noted that the memory for pictures is usually excellent and that this fact is often used as support for the idea that pictures are coded visually. Still, in most studies of picture memory the pictures used are meaningful, hence could be coded in terms of meaning codes. The notion that even pictures may be coded in terms of meaning is supported by a study conducted by Goldstein and Chance (1971), who showed subjects an entire set of very distinctive snowflake patterns. They reasoned that the patterns should lead to distinctive visual codes if such codes are actually formed. However, the patterns should be very difficult to code in terms of meaning. Goldstein and Chance found that their subjects showed very poor recognition of the snowflake patterns. This result suggests that if it is difficult to attach meaning to a picture, memory for that picture is reasonably poor. This should not be the case, of course, if pictures were coded visually in long-term memory.

These results do *not* disprove the existence of visual coding. They do indicate, however, that most of the evidence for visual coding can be reinterpreted to show that only meaning codes may exist. In effect, we are left with an unresolved question. Although the existence of meaning codes is well accepted, the possibility that we also use codes of other types can be neither verified nor dismissed with certainty at this time.

The Organization of Long-Term Memory

To this point we have been concerned with memory codes or the format by which experiences are represented in memory storage. Now we turn to a different aspect of memory representation. Once coded, how are memories organized or arranged in relation to each other? The question of memory organization necessarily focuses on long-term memory. Quite obviously, the capacity of short-term memory is so small that questions of organization have seldom arisen. It is in long-term or permanent memory, however, that we store memories based on a lifetime of experiences. It seems unlikely that we could ever retrieve and use these memories unless they were arranged in some logical or meaningful fashion. In recent years a great deal of research has been directed toward understanding this organizational scheme. Before looking at this research, however, we should point out an important distinction between different types of information that may reside in long-term storage. This is the distinction between *episodic* and *semantic memories*.

Tulving's Episodic–Semantic Distinction

We know that some of our memories concern specific experiences or episodes in our past. Such memories are linked to specific locations and specific times. For example, try to recall what you ate for dinner last night or what you did last weekend. In both cases, your memories for these events contain information about where you were and when you were there. The same would be true if you tried to recall what was said in your most recent lecture or what you read in the preceding chapter of this book. These would all be examples of memories for experiences that occurred in specific times and places.

Aside from memories for individual experiences, you also have memories that allow you to answer more general questions. For example, suppose you were asked to describe an elephant. This is an easy task for almost anyone. We all have some memory for how an elephant looks. However, consider what your memory for an elephant is like. In most cases when we think of elephants we do not try to remember specific experiences we have had with elephants. What we retrieve is a general representation of an elephant that is really a composite of our experiences. This composite may consist of what elephants have looked like at the zoo, in books, and on television. It may also consist of things people have told us about elephants or things we have read. In effect, our memory in this case is not tied to specific locations or times. Rather, it is a compilation of individual bits of information acquired across time and space.

Another example of this type of memory can be seen when we attempt to teach another person to drive. Obviously, this activity requires us to call on our own memory for how a car is driven. Consider, however, what kind of memory you would use in this situation. Would you attempt to recall a specific instance of yourself driving a car and then relate this experience step by step to the other person? Almost certainly you would not. Instead, you would use a generalized memory for how cars are driven. Although this memory might be a composite of your experiences, the memory itself would have little to do with any specific driving experience you have had in your past.

These differences in memory type form the basis for what Tulving (1972) has called the episodic–semantic memory distinction (see also, Tulving, 1983). Tulving proposed that long-term memory is best conceptualized as consisting of two related memory systems. The first system, called *episodic memory*, contains memories of specific experiences from our past. As we have noted, such memories are always linked to specific times and locations. Tulving termed the second system *semantic memory* and described it as being a general knowledge base. In other words, semantic memory consists of composite or generalized memories that are not associated with specific experiences. It is through semantic memory that we are able to answer general questions about the world without referring directly to personal experiences.

Although Tulving views these memory systems as distinct, he also describes them as being related and as having clear influences on each other. For example, he proposes that when we have an experience, this experience will lead to a change in episodic memory but will not necessarily alter the part of semantic memory related to that experience. Thus if you see an elephant in a circus, you will form a memory for that experience in episodic memory. However, this experience does not necessarily impact on the "elephant representation" in your semantic memory. At the same time, however, Tulving presumes that semantic memories are by-products of specific experiences. Thus, while a single experience may alter semantic memory very little, such memories are based on the compilation of individual experiences we have had.

It is also clear from Tulving's analysis that semantic memory can influence our memory for episodes. If, for example, you see an elephant, this experience activates your elephant representation in semantic memory. In effect, you become consciously aware of your general knowledge of elephants. Such knowledge can alter your perceptions of a specific episode or the aspects of an episode you eventually store in episodic memory. Thus, your inferences about a particular experience can be influenced by information stored in the semantic memory system.

Currently there is some controversy over how seriously we should take this episodic–semantic distinction (see, for example, Baddeley, 1976; Hintzman, 1986; Wickelgren, 1977). It is possible, for example, to explain the operation of long-term memory without suggesting the existence of two separate memory systems. It may well be that we store only memories of specific episodes. Then, when we are asked a general knowledge question, we may simply retrieve a number of episodic memories at once and give an answer based on the common aspects of these individual memories. For present purposes, however, it is unimportant whether the episodic–semantic distinction is real or a theoretical figment. The important point is that in recent years, most research on long-term memory representation has incorporated this dichotomy. Thus, in considering how long-term memories are organized, it is useful to look first at episodic memories and then at how semantic memories might be arranged.

The Organization of Episodic Memory

Since the earliest studies of Ebbinghaus (1885) on serial list learning, the vast majority of memory experiments have dealt with the processing and recollection of episodic memories. Given this overwhelming emphasis on the memory for episodes, it is somewhat surprising to learn that relatively little research has been aimed at uncovering the organization of episodic memory. One reason for this lack of interest may simply be that our conceptualization of episodic memories makes their organization seem to be self-evident. Given the nature of episodic memories, that is, there would seem to be only a limited number of ways these memories might be arranged in relation to each other.

It is generally assumed that the memory for a particular experience must contain a whole set of features or attributes. Such memories must contain information concerning time (when the experience occurred), physical context (where the experience occurred), and the sensory or symbolic features of the experience itself (what occurred). Therefore the popular conception of an episodic memory has long consisted of a bundle or grouping of features or attributes, each representing an aspect of an original experience (see, for example, Bower, 1972a; Estes, 1959; Tulving, 1983; Underwood, 1969; Wickens, 1970). The usual presumption is that any number or variety of attributes can be represented in long-term memory. Each individual memory is viewed as being a small, distinct subset of all the possible attributes in long-term memory.

This view that episodic memories are bundles of attributes has led to some general agreement concerning how individual memories might be related. The most common idea is that separate memories are related to each other to the degree that these memories share common attributes. That is, if two memories share many of the same attributes, it is assumed that they overlap substantially in long-term memory. Two memories having completely different attributes are assumed to be more widely separated in memory (see, for example, Underwood, 1969).

To illustrate this idea, consider what your memories would be like for the following three experiences: an evening trip to the movies to see a comedy film, an evening trip to the movies to see a murder mystery, a day trip to the park for a picnic. Figure 9.9 displays the attributes each memory would contain. As you can see, the first two memories are closely related because they share many of the same features (for example, time of day, travel from home, place visited, type of activity). The only features that make these memories distinct are the specific days involved and the specific films seen. On the other hand, the third memory is not as close to the others in the organizational scheme. This is because the third memory shares only a few attributes with the other two. It is more distinct or separate because its features overlap very little with those of the other memories.

We have already seen an example of this view in our earlier discussion of propositional codes and text bases. Recall that Kintsch, among others, suggests that propositional codes (representing individual memories for meaning) are organized into text bases.

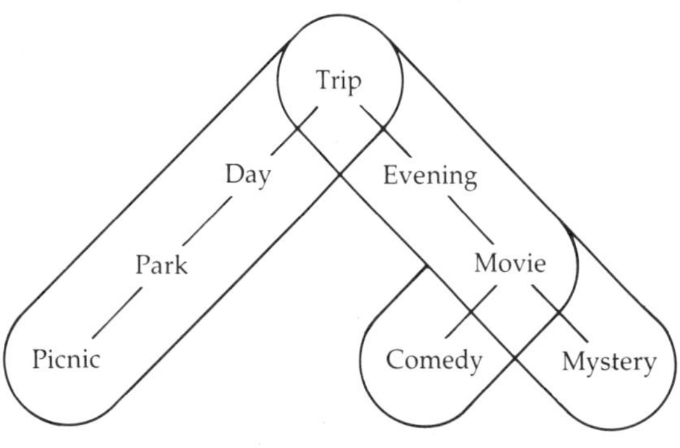

FIGURE 9.9 Schematic representation of memories having overlapping and nonoverlapping attributes.

Kintsch assumes that propositional codes that share important concepts are closely linked in a text base. However, codes that do not share common elements are more widely separated in this organizational scheme.

Thus, while few researchers have dealt explicitly with how episodic memories are organized, we can point to the following common assumption: that episodic memories are organized in terms of the specific attributes they contain. Memories that share attributes are presumed to be more closely related than memories that overlap very little in terms of their features.

The Organization of Semantic Memory

While interest in the organization of episodic memory has been rather subdued, a great deal of research activity has centered on how semantic memories are organized. This interest centers on the idea that we must use semantic memory in order to answer all general knowledge questions. Thus, most models of semantic memory organization have sought to understand how such memories might be related so that we are able to answer questions efficiently . The first model we will consider is one proposed by Collins and Quillian (1969).

The teachable language comprehender (TLC) Collins and Quillian (1969; see also, Collins & Quillian, 1972; Quillian, 1967) began with the goal of devising a computer program that would enable a computer to answer general knowledge questions as efficiently as possible. What they created was a program called the *teachable language comprehender (TLC)*. Although the TLC was constructed for a computer, it contained, by necessity, an organized network of words and concepts. Thus, this program was of interest to semantic memory researchers because it suggested how words and concepts might be related in human semantic memory.

According to this model, the basic elements of semantic memory are *units* that represent specific objects or concepts. For example, the part of semantic memory concerned with living organisms might contain units such as "animal," "bird," "fish," "canary," "ostrich," "shark," and "salmon." Note that some of these units represent broader or more inclusive categories than others. Obviously, "bird" is a broader category than "canary." The most important feature of this model is the arrangement of these units in a logical, hierarchical fashion based on unit breadth (see Figure 9.10). Thus at the top of the hierarchy we find the broadest category (the superordinate category), at the next level we find the next broadest categories that can be included in the superordinate category, and at level 3 we find the next broadest categories that fit into the level 2 categories.

Two other notable features of the TLC model can be seen in Figure 9.10. First, stored along with each unit or concept in the hierarchy is a set of *properties* that help to characterize that unit. For example, along with "animal" we have properties such as "has skin," "can move around," "eats," and "breathes." These properties are stored with the word "animal" because they are properties that most animals share. Note that these properties are not repeated as we move to lower level concepts. We do not, for example, need to store the property "eats" with the concept of "bird," because this property has already been stored with the "animal" concept, of which birds are an example. Thus, properties are stored at the highest point in the hierarchy at which they are true (that is, valid descriptors). This arrangement lessens the redundancy of the system and makes it more efficient.

Although properties stored at one level of the hierarchy are true of *most* of the lower level concepts in the same hierarchy, if a lower level concept does not have a property noted for a higher unit, then one of the properties stored with the lower level concept must be a state-

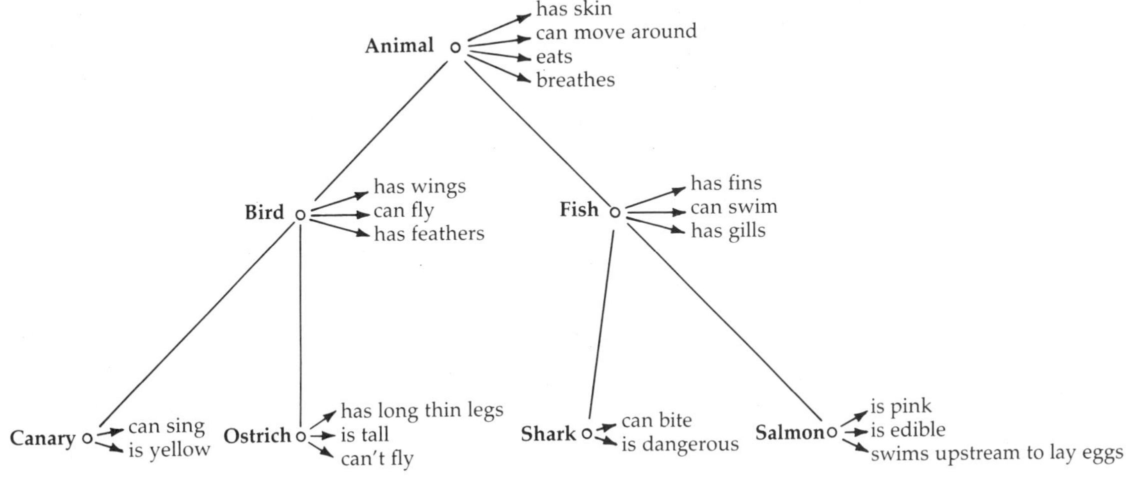

FIGURE 9.10 The organization of semantic memory according to the teachable language comprehender model. (From Collins and Quillian, 1969.)

ment of the exception. For example, consider the concept of "bird" in Figure 9.10. One of the properties stored with "bird" is "can fly." Note, however, that "ostrich," which is subordinate to "bird," does not share this common bird characteristic. Thus, one of the properties stored with "ostrich" is "can't fly."

A second important feature of this organizational scheme is that the components of the hierarchy (the units and properties) are connected by a set of *pointers,* which are used to denote components of the hierarchy that are directly connected. As you can see, each unit is directly connected to its own unique set of properties. Also, each unit is directly connected to the superordinate unit just above it in the hierarchy. Thus, "canary" and "ostrich" are linked directly to "bird," and "bird" and "fish" are directly connected to "animal." Units at the same level (for example, "canary" and "ostrich") are not linked directly to each other. These pointers or connections indicate that units and properties are linked in a specific network-like arrangement.

The importance of this particular arrangement of units and properties can be seen when we consider how we would answer a general knowledge question if semantic memory were organized in this fashion. The TLC model assumes that a specific question will serve to activate one of the units in the hierarchy. For example, the question "Does a canary breathe?" will activate the unit "canary." It is then assumed that one would answer the question by following the pointers in the hierarchy to determine whether breathing is a property of canaries. First, one would search through the properties of the "canary" unit. Since the property "breathes" is not stored with "canary," one would move to the next highest unit in the hierarchy ("bird") and search through its properties. Failing to find the property "breathes" at that level, one would move to the top of the hierarchy to search the properties associated with the "animal" unit. Since the property "breathes" is associated with "animal," since "canary" is a subordinate of the "animal" unit, and since no exception was encountered anywhere in the hierarchy, we can conclude that canaries do, in fact, breathe.

An important assumption of the TLC model is that the time required to answer a question should correspond to the distance one must travel through the hierarchy to find an answer. Thus it should take little time to respond to "Is a canary yellow?" because the property "is yellow" is stored close to the unit "canary." As we have seen, however, to determine whether a canary breathes, it is necessary to search through several levels in the hierarchy or to move a great distance through the hierarchical arrangement. For this reason, the model predicts that this question should take a much longer time to answer.

To test this general assumption, Collins and Quillian (1969) presented subjects with a number of statements, asked them to determine as quickly as possible whether the statements were true or false, and instructed them to register their responses by pressing a "true" or a "false" button located just in front of them. Primarily, Collins and Quillian wanted to know how long it would take the subjects to verify the truth of the true statements. Some of the statements required matching a concept or unit with a certain property (for example, "A canary can fly"). Others required determining whether one concept was part of a superordinate concept (for example, "A canary is an animal"). The statements varied in terms of the number of levels in the hierarchy a subject would have to search in order to verify the truth of the sentence. The results of this study (Figure 9.11) are entirely consistent with the Collins and Quillian hypothesis. Subjects were quickly able to verify that a canary is a canary. It took longer, however, to verify that a canary is a bird (concepts located at adjacent levels), and even longer to verify that a canary is an

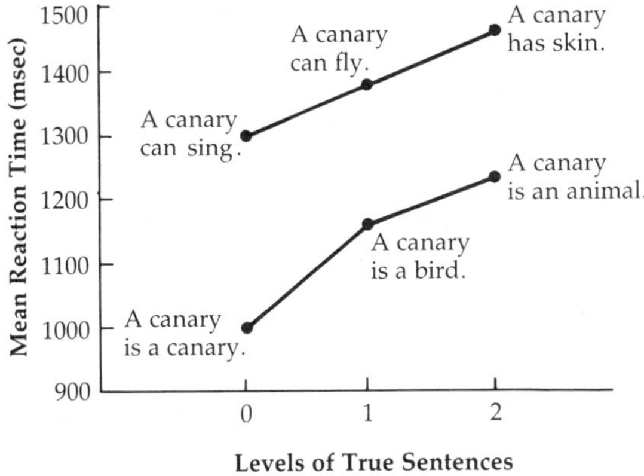

FIGURE 9.11 Reaction times to determine the validity of statements as a function of the hypothetical distances between concepts and properties in the TLC hierarchy. (From Collins and Quillian, 1969.)

animal (concepts separated by one level). Likewise, verification times varied depending on whether a property was stored with a given concept or with a concept located higher in the hierarchy. For example, subjects quickly verified that canaries can sing (singing being a property stored with canary). However, they took much longer to verify that a canary has skin (skin being a property stored with the concept "animal"). These data are consistent with the ideas that in answering a question, subjects search through a semantic hierarchy, and that more time is required to search longer distances.

The Collins and Quillian model is important because it suggests that a *logical* knowledge structure can be used efficiently to answer questions requiring knowledge of the world. And, as we have seen, such a model appears to be consistent with certain data concerning how long it takes to answer questions. Still, problems became evident soon after this model was proposed.

The first problem associated with the TLC model had to do with the assumption that conceptual units are arranged hierarchically, with subordinate units always falling below superordinate units. For example, the Collins and Quillian model states that the concept of "mammal" is subordinate to the concept of "animal," since mammals are members of the animal kingdom. According to this organizational scheme, subjects should be able to verify that a dog is a mammal much faster than they should verify that a dog is an animal. Because dogs are examples of mammals and mammals are examples of animals, verifying that a dog is an animal should require searching through two levels in the hierarchy, whereas verifying that a dog is a mammal should require searching through only one level. Several studies have shown that this prediction is incorrect (see, for example, Rips, Shoben, & Smith, 1973). It usually takes subjects longer to confirm that a dog is a mammal than it does to verify that a dog is an animal. Thus, the way concepts are logically arranged does not always account for how long it takes subjects to answer questions about those concepts.

A second problem with the Collins and Quillian model concerns the idea that a given property is stored only at one level of the hierarchy. Recall that according to this model, the property "breathes" is stored with the "animal" concept but is *not* stored redundantly with concepts subordinate to "animal." In a direct test of this notion, Carol Conrad (1972) had subjects verify statements that contained the same property but differed in terms of the concept level. For example, subjects might be given sentences such as "An animal can breathe," "A bird can breathe," and "An ostrich can breathe." The Collins and Quillian model clearly predicts that of these statements, "An animal can breathe" should be verified fastest because "can breathe" is stored as a property of "animal" only. Contrary to this prediction, Conrad found no differences in the verification times for such sentences. Results of this type question the assumption that properties are stored only with broad, superordinate concepts. Instead, this finding suggests that properties may be stored redundantly with a number of concepts.

Finally, the Collins and Quillian model assumes that all examples of a single superordinate concept are equally representative of that concept. Thus, in this model, "canary," "ostrich," and "robin" would be viewed as equally good examples of the superordinate concept of "bird." In effect, this model predicts that subjects should be able to verify that an ostrich is a bird just as fast as they are able to confirm that a robin is a bird. Such a prediction is clearly not supported by the data. In a variety of tasks it has become clear that subjects view some category members as being better or more central examples of a category than others (see, for example, Roth & Shoben, 1983). Thus, it is easier to confirm that a robin is a bird than it is to verify that an ostrich falls into the same category.

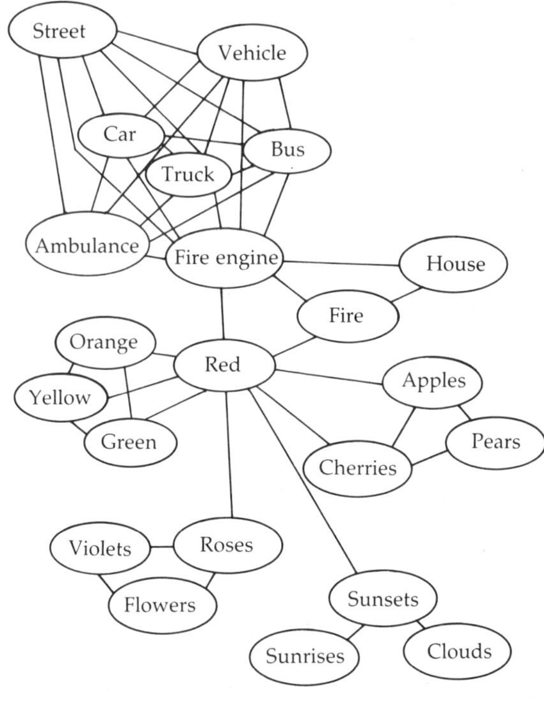

FIGURE 9.12 The organization of semantic memory according to the spreading activation model. (From Collins and Loftus, 1975.)

The spreading activation model In an effort to circumvent some of the problems encountered by Collins and Quillian, several theorists have proposed semantic memory models that do not rely on logical, hierarchical structures. One such idea is the *spreading activation model* formulated by Collins and Loftus (1975). In one sense, this model is an extension of the teachable language comprehender, since it retains the idea that concepts and characteristics are linked together in a network. However, this model differs from the Collins and Quillian model in several important respects. These differences are made evident by Figure 9.12, which shows an example of how concepts and characteristics are organized in the Collins–Loftus model.

One of the first differences we can note is that in the model of Collins and Loftus, concepts and properties are treated equally. The main elements in the Collins–Quillian model were concepts such as "fire engine," and properties such as "red" were simply appendages to these concept units. In the present model, concepts and properties are listed as equally important elements in the semantic memory structure.

Second, properties such as "red" are linked to a whole variety of concepts such as "cherries," "roses," "fire engine," and "sunrises." Properties such as "red" are also linked directly to other properties such as "orange," "yellow," and "green." Thus, in this model the major elements are not linked on the basis of logical semantic relationships. Instead, they are linked to any items with which they are normally associated in our common experience.

Finally, recall that in the Collins–Quillian model, all links between concept units were of equal length, suggesting that all subordinate concepts are equally good examples of a superordinate concept. In the present model, the links among various concepts and properties vary in length. Some concepts such as "car" are closely linked to the superordinate concept of "vehicle." Other concepts, which also have "vehicle" as a superordinate (for example, "fire engine"), are viewed as being linked to "vehicle" but not as closely linked as "car." According to this model, the length of a concept or property link represents how closely two concepts or properties are associated. Thus, while both cars and fire engines fall into the more general category of vehicles, a car is viewed as being a more typical example of this category than a fire engine.

The operation of the spreading activation model centers on a simple assumption. When a concept or property occurs in a question, the unit representing that concept or property in semantic memory is activated. This activation then begins to spread to nearby units in the organizational scheme via the pointers or links. The degree to which related units become activated depends on how closely linked these units are to the originally activated unit. Thus, if "red" is activated, there is greater activation of "cherries" than of "sunsets," since "cherries" is more closely linked to "red" than is "sunsets." This means that when we hear the word "red," we are more likely to think of cherries than of sunsets.

Collins and Loftus assume that our ability to answer questions or to verify the truth of statements depends on whether the activation of two units spreads to some point of intersection in the network. For example, suppose you are asked "Is a car a vehicle?" Both "car" and "vehicle" are activated in this case, and this activation spreads along the link between these units. Thus, the lines of activation spreading from these units quickly meet, allowing a decision to be made. The same procedure allows us to verify that a "fire engine" is a "vehicle." However, this decision takes longer, because the link between "fire engine" and "vehicle" is longer than the link between "vehicle" and "car."

Using this scheme, we can also answer questions concerning concepts that are not directly linked. For example, the question "Is a fire engine a sunset?" will activate both the "fire engine" and "sunset" units, and the lines of activation from these units will finally intersect at the unit "red." This intersection tells us that fire engines and sunsets are related. To determine whether they are the same, we compare the overlap in units linked to these concepts. In this case we would find that the only unit common to "fire engine" and "sunset" is "red"; hence the units are not the same.

This kind of model has several advantages. In particular, it indicates why decisions take longer when we are asked questions concerning an atypical example of a superordinate concept. This model also is able to explain a phenomenon called *priming,* which has been found in so-called *lexical decision* tasks. In such a task subjects are usually presented with two strings of letters. The first string in the pair is called a "prime," while the second is called the "target." The subjects must determine whether the target letter string forms a real word.

In several studies it has been shown that a subject's reaction time in identifying a target as a word depends on the nature of the prime word (see, for example, Meyer & Schvanevelt, 1971). If the prime is semantically related to the target (for example, doctor–nurse), the target is confirmed faster than if the prime is unrelated (for example, butter–nurse). According to Collins and Loftus, this is because the prime activates a given unit in semantic memory. This activation then spreads to adjacent or closely related units, leading to their activations. Thus, when a prime and a target are semantically related, the prime causes the target unit to be activated before the target is ever presented. This enables a subject to respond quickly to the target. When a prime and target are unrelated, however, the prime causes no activation of the target unit, and thus activation of the target does not occur until the target is presented.

Although the spreading activation model represents an advance over the teachable language comprehender, it does lose much of the simplicity inherent in the Collins and Quillian approach. For example, there is no a priori way for determining how semantic memory might be organized in a given individual. The concepts and properties that are closely linked depend on an individual's experiences, not on some logical scheme. This model also suffers from a great degree of complexity with respect to both how concepts may be organized and how decisions are actually made when two concepts are activated. Still, this complexity is not necessarily a detriment, and it may be essential in explaining how semantic memory operates.

A feature comparison model A somewhat different appoach to conceptualizing semantic memory has been proposed by E. E. Smith, Shoben, and Rips (1974; see also, Rips, Shoben, & Smith, 1973). These theorists suggest that concepts in semantic memory are actually represented by groups of properties or features. For each concept there are a few *defining features,* which are so named because they are critical to the definition of that concept. For example, some of the defining features for the concept "canary" might be characteristics such as "is alive," "has feathers," and "is yellow." Each concept also contains certain *characteristic features,* which often are associated with that concept but are not necessary for its definition. Such characteristic features for the concept "canary" might include "it flies," "it is small," and "it sings." According to this view, the more general a concept is, the fewer defining features it will have. For example, the concept of "bird" has defining features such as "is alive" and "has feathers." Specific species of birds have the same defining features, and, in addition, contain other defining features that differentiate them from other birds (for example, "canary" has the additional defining feature "is yellow").

The feature comparison model proposes that statement verifications occur through a two-stage process of matching features. If, for example, you are asked if a canary is a bird, you begin by matching the total features that make up the two concepts. If there is substantial feature overlap, such as exists between canary and bird, you can give a positive response on that basis. If two objects share certain features but not others, it is necessary to go through a second stage of analysis, comparing *only* the defining features of the two concepts. If all the defining features of one concept are contained in the other concept, you are able to verify that one object is an example of the other. If the defining features do not overlap, such a statement must be rejected. In this model, verification times depend on whether it is necessary to go through the second stage of comparison before making a decision.

To better understand the decision-making steps in the feature comparison model, consider two questions: "Is a canary a bird?" and "Is a chicken a bird?" In most cases the answer to both questions will eventually be "yes." However, most people will be able to answer the first question faster than the second, because "canary" and "bird" share many of the same features, allowing a decision to be made without having to match defining features. Although "chicken" and "bird" also share many features, chickens do not fly, they do not sing, and they can be rather large. Thus, there is some discrepancy between the features contained in these concepts. For this reason, we must match the defining features of the concepts to determine that chickens actually are birds. This matching of defining features requires more time, and, thus, slows the answer to the question of whether a chicken is a bird.

This kind of model is able to account for most of the same data handled by the Collins and Loftus approach. In addition, this model has the advantage of being relatively simple, since it deals with specific feature sets, not complex networks. Even so, this approach is not without its own problems. First, it is often difficult to decide which qualities of a concept are defining features and which are only characteristic features. Is the use of language a defining feature of a human adult? If so, what about people who are mute? Do they no longer qualify as members of this concept? Similar questions can be raised about any number of concepts. It is simply difficult to arrive at a clear consensus regarding the defining characteristics of any concept.

A second problem associated with the feature comparison model is its inability to account for a particular kind of finding that comes from studies asking subjects to *disconfirm* certain statements. For example, Glass and Holyoak (1975) gave subjects statements such as "Some chairs are tables" and "Some rocks are tables." They then assessed how long it would take to disconfirm these statements. They found that "Some chairs are tables" was disconfirmed much faster than "Some rocks are tables."

This finding by Glass and Holyoak is exactly the opposite of what one would predict from the feature comparison model, which suggests that when two objects share few characteristics (such as "rocks" and "tables"), subjects should be able to determine quickly that one is not an example of the other. However, when two concepts share a number of characteristics (such as "chairs" and "table"), decision times should be increased because subjects should have to check the defining features of these concepts. This prediction is clearly not in accord with the data.

Current status of semantic memory models In recent years there has been a proliferation of experiments designed to study semantic memory organization. Many of these studies have been aimed at discovering whether concepts may be organized differently depending on a person's expertise in a given knowledge area (see, for example, Engle & Bukstel, 1978; Gammack & Young, 1985; Schvaneveldt et al., 1985). Although most of these studies make the assumption that verification or reaction times can be used to determine how closely related certain concepts are, there is no general agreement about how semantic memory is organized or how it operates. Both the more recent models we have discussed have adherents among contemporary researchers. In addition, models of other kinds have generated great interest. These are the models originally designed to describe how meanings are represented in memory via propositional codes (see, for example, Anderson, 1983; Anderson & Bower, 1973; Kintsch, 1974; Norman & Rumelhart, 1975). Although such models are more explicitly concerned with episodic memory for sentences, some researchers have relied on these approaches for clues to how semantic memory might be structured. Thus the study of semantic memory, although relatively new, is currently one of the most active areas of memory research.

Memory Representations in Nonhuman Species

As we have seen, there has been considerable research on the question of how memories are represented in humans. To this point, however, the question of memory representation has received little attention among researchers working with other species. One reason for this scarcity of data is that interest in animal memory is a relatively recent phenomenon. Another reason, however, is that questions concerning memory representation are often very complex. In many cases it is simply difficult to devise experiments that suggest to us how animals might code and organize information.

Questions about how animals code their experiences have been raised primarily in studies of short-term retention. Most such experiments have employed the *delayed matching-to-*

sample paradigm, in which some animal (usually a monkey or pigeon) is shown a stimulus (the sample stimulus) for a brief period of time. Then the sample stimulus disappears, and there is a retention interval lasting a few seconds. When this interval has elapsed, the animal is presented with a group of stimuli, one of which is the same as the sample stimulus. To gain reinforcement, the animal must choose the original sample from among the alternatives.

The delayed matching-to-sample paradigm is used to assess an animal's short-term memory for a particular stimulus. It is assumed that to respond correctly in the test, the animal must remember something about the sample stimulus that occurred prior to the retention interval. Since both pigeons and monkeys are very adept at this task, the usual interpretation is that both species are capable of representing sample stimuli in memory for short periods of time. This interpretation has led to the question of how animals might code sample stimuli in short-term memory.

Given the nature of the delayed matching-to-sample task, researchers have suggested at least two ways that animals might code the sample information in order to perform the task successfully. One idea shared by many researchers is that animals form memory codes that are exact copies of the stimuli they perceive. Thus, if a visual stimulus is shown to an animal, it is assumed that the animal forms a memory representation having the same visual features as the stimulus itself. According to this view, to solve a delayed matching-to-sample problem, an animal simply forms an exact copy of the sample stimulus in memory and maintains this copy for the duration of the retention interval. On the retention test this "memory copy" is compared to the test stimuli and the test stimulus that best matches the copy is selected as correct (see, for example, Roberts & Grant, 1976).

A second view suggests that when a sample stimulus is presented an animal forms a "rule code" in memory that tells the animal which response to make during testing. That is, instead of representing the sample itself in memory, an animal stores some instruction or rule that can be used to determine responding later. For example, let's assume that a pigeon receives a red disk as its sample stimulus. According to this view, the pigeon does not form a representation of a red disk. Instead, the pigeon stores in memory a rule that says "peck the red disk on the test." At the time of testing the pigeon refers to this rule in order to make a correct response.

Clearly, both these views of coding provide adequate explanations for how an animal might perform appropriately in a delayed matching-to-sample paradigm. To distinguish these views it is necessary to examine how animals perform in other types of short-term memory tasks. One such task is called a *symbolic matching-to-sample* paradigm. In this procedure an animal must learn that a given sample stimulus is to be matched with a comparison stimulus that differs from the sample. That is, an animal might learn to peck a green test stimulus if the sample stimulus had been red or a yellow test stimulus if the sample had been blue. The critical feature of this paradigm is that the sample stimulus never occurs on the matching test. Instead, the test stimuli include only a stimulus that is related to but not identical to the sample.

It is well known that animals are capable of learning symbolic matching problems (see, for example, Maki, Moe, & Bierley, 1977); this fact tends to support the idea that animals may form rule or instructional codes in memory. It is easy to see how a rule code might enable an animal to choose the correct test stimulus in a symbolic matching task. When a red sample occurs the animal would simply form a rule saying "peck the green stimulus on the test." However, it would appear more difficult for an animal to perform this task if the animal were coding the sample in terms of its physical features. Having a copy of a red sample in memory may not be very useful if none of the test stimuli is identical to the red copy.

The notion that animals code stimuli in terms of physical features is also questioned in a study conducted by D'Amato and Worsham (1974). These experimenters presented monkeys with two visual stimuli, successively. On some occasions the two stimuli were identical, while on other trials the stimuli differed. After a retention interval, the monkeys were required to press a key if the stimuli had been the same but to push a lever if the stimuli had been different. The monkeys were able to perform these responses with a high degree of accuracy. Again, if monkeys form rule codes when sample stimuli occur, it is easy to explain these results. When the samples are identical the monkey would simply form a rule code that says "press the key on the test." When the samples are different the rule "push the lever on the test" would be formed. How a monkey might solve this problem by forming copies of the samples in memory is less clear.

This idea that animals code certain stimuli in terms of meanings or rules has received increasing support in recent years (see, for example, Grant, 1981; Honig, 1978; Roitblat, 1980). Although such studies do not preclude the possibility of coding in terms of physical features, they do suggest that there are alternative means by which animals may code stimuli in certain situations. This issue is presently receiving a great deal of attention among experimenters.

Questions concerning how animals organize their memories have been raised in very few experiments. This is not to say that certain theorists have not spoken about this issue. For example, many experiments are based on a particular assumption about memory organization in animals that was proposed by Spear (1973, 1976, 1978). Spear's ideas about memory organization bear strong similarity to the memory attribute idea proposed by Underwood (1969) to explain the organization of long-term memory in humans. That is, an animal's experience is thought to be represented in memory as a collection of attributes or features that stand for visual, auditory, and other sensory aspects of the experience as well as temporal and spatial aspects. Spear suggests that certain attributes (such as those representing a CS or a reinforcer) are central to a memory, whereas other attributes (such as those representing context) are more peripheral. Just as in Underwood's approach, Spear suggests that memories are similar to the degree that their attributes overlap. As we will see in Chapter 10, this view has been used extensively to explain a variety of retention phenomena in animals.

Aside from this general organizational idea, some theorists have proposed more explicit hypotheses about animals' organization of memories for learning experiences of specific types. There are, for example, hypotheses concerning how CS and US codes are connected in Classical conditioning situations (see, for example, Wagner, 1981), as well as models for how different elements of Instrumental conditioning might be organized in memory (see Gallistel, 1980). To this point, however, these models have served primarily as conceptual frameworks for memory research. There have been few attempts to characterize explicitly memory organization in nonhuman species.

Summary Statements

We began our examination of the question of how experiences are represented in memory by focusing on the coding of memories. We saw substantial evidence that many of our short-term or active memories seem to be coded acoustically. We also reviewed evidence suggesting that some short-term codes may be visual. In our discussion of long-term memory codes, we emphasized the idea that most long-term memories appear to be represented in terms of propositional or meaning codes. Moreover, some long-term memories appear to be constructions based on inferences drawn from these propositional codes. Finally, we discussed the idea that long-term memories might be coded redundantly in terms of both meanings and visual images.

The second half of this chapter dealt with possible modes of organization of memory codes. We initiated this topic by distinguishing between episodic and semantic memory, two aspects of long-term memory. We first reviewed some of the ideas concerning how episodic memories might be organized. The majority of our discussion, however, centered on how concepts and characteristics are related in semantic memory. We saw that it is possible to conceive of semantic memory as a logical hierarchy of concepts, a complex network of concepts and characteristics, or groups of features that characterize concepts. We then reviewed some of the data pertinent to these views.

Finally, we discussed the representation of memories in nonhuman species, looking briefly at how animals might code information in a delayed matching-to-sample task and noting some of the current ideas about memory organization in nonhuman species.

10

Memory Processes: Retrieval

Imagine for a moment that you have just purchased a new automobile. The engine is powerful and fuel efficient. The exterior sparkles, and the design is aerodynamically perfect. The steering and suspension systems enable the car to turn on a dime without even a wobble. In short, your new car is ideal for your needs. There is, however, one small problem. The doors are welded shut and the windows won't budge from the closed position. In other words, you can't get in. This automobile is capable of doing everything you would want it to do, but its potential cannot be realized because you are able to gain access to its controls.

In a very real sense, this automobile is what our memory systems would be like without a retrieval process. The processes of storage and encoding enable us to represent experiences in memory. The mere fact that we are capable of forming such representations gives us unlimited potential for profiting from our past experiences. However, unless we are able to access or retrieve these representations from the memory system, the representations themselves are useless. Retrieval is like a key to our memory stores. It allows us to access and use representations at the appropriate time. Quite obviously, the retrieval process is critical if we are to use our memories in an adaptive way.

In our discussions of how memories are formed and represented, we have alluded several times to the process of retrieval. We have seen, for example, that several researchers have used a subject's retrieval speed as a way of determining how memories are organized. In this chapter we examine the retrieval process in more detail, discussing various ideas concerning the nature of retrieval and identifying the factors that appear to influence the procedure by which we access stored memories. We will also discuss how retrieval is involved in the re-encoding of a memory. We begin with the access of short-term or recently acquired memories.

Retrieval of Short-Term Memories

When we use the term "retrieval," we are referring to the process of locating a memory in storage and then activating that memory so that we become aware of it. Thus, the end result of retrieval is to bring a representation into conscious awareness. In earlier chapters we have used terms such as "short-term memory" to describe representations currently being consciously processed. This characterization seems to imply that a retrieval mechanism is unnecessary for the use of short-term memories. If such memories are already in awareness, it ought to be possible to use these representations automatically, without first searching them out.

Since, however, we are capable of holding multiple bits of information in short-term storage at any given time, the isolation and use of a particular bit of information requires us to engage in some type of search process even when we want to access information being held in short-term memory. Several researchers have been interested in the nature of this short-term memory search. By far the most influential work on this subject has been carried out by Sternberg (1966, 1967, 1969).

Sternberg's Memory Search Experiments

The question addressed in Sternberg's experiments is deceptively simple. How do we go about locating or identifying items represented in short-term memory? For example, assume that you are requested to rehearse the letter string "a, r, v, c, l." After a brief interval you are asked if the letter "c" is part of that string. You would, of course, respond "yes" with very little apparent effort. The process of matching the letter "c" with one of the letters in short-term memory appears to occur almost instantaneously. According to some theorists, such a recognition task requires little in the way of retrieval processing (see, for example, Kintsch, 1970). However, Sternberg disagrees with such a conclusion, and the results of his studies tend to support his point of view.

In his earliest experiments, Sternberg presented subjects with a small string of items such as digits or letters. The subjects were instructed to keep these items in memory for later recall. Before being asked to recall the entire set, however, the subjects were given a target item and were told to respond "yes" if the target was part of the original item string and "no" otherwise. They were instructed to respond as quickly as possible by pulling a "yes" or a "no" lever. The purpose of telling subjects that they would be asked to recall the string later was to ensure that they would keep the entire set in short-term storage.

Sternberg was not interested in whether subjects could correctly respond to the target item. He was certain that they would make the correct response in almost every case. Rather, he was interested in reaction times. He wanted to assess how quickly subjects could determine whether a target was present in storage, and his interest in reaction times was based on a particular set of assumptions about what such a task should involve.

Sternberg assumed that to make a correct response, a subject would have to follow three steps. First, encode the target item or enter it into short-term storage. Next, compare the target representation to the representations of the items in the string to determine whether the target matched any of the other items. And finally, respond, based on whether a match had occurred. Sternberg assumed that the time to encode a target item would be the same from trial to trial, since in each case only one target was being presented. He also assumed that the time to respond once a decision had been reached should be relatively invariant from one trial to the next. Thus, within this paradigm, variables that affect reaction times should do so because they affect the process of comparing the target to the item string. That is, differences in reaction times should almost always reflect differences in the time it takes to search through memory to see whether there is a match.

In his initial experiments using this paradigm, Sternberg varied the number of items in the strings. For example, on some trials subjects were asked to keep only a single item in memory, while on other trials they were given 3 or 4 items to process. Regardless of the number of items in the string, however, each trial involved presenting only a single target to be matched. Sternberg's findings are represented in Figure 10.1, where subjects' reaction times to make a "yes" response when the target did match an item in the item string are plotted as a function of the number of items in the string or the number of items being held in memory.

Two points concerning this graph should be emphasized. First, it is obvious that reaction times increase as the number of items in memory is increased. Second, each addition of an item in memory leads to the *same* amount of increase in reaction time. Specifically, Sternberg found that every item added to memory required an additional 38 msec of reaction time to make a response.

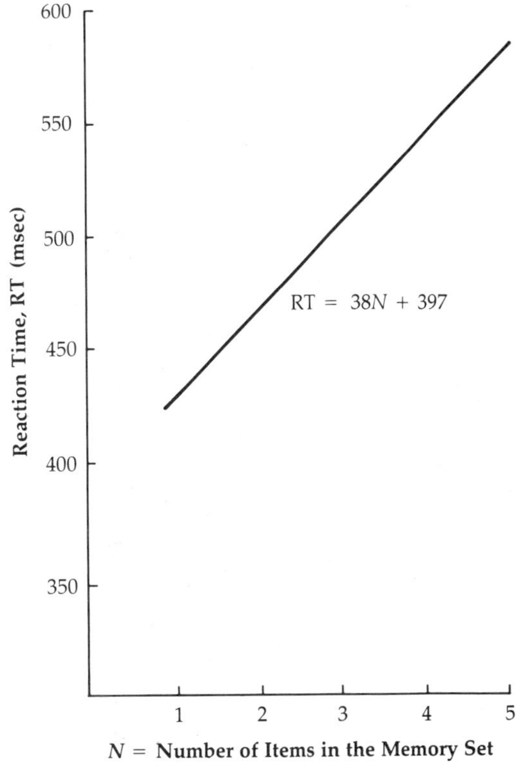

FIGURE 10.1 Reaction time required to decide whether a target stimulus matches a stimulus in memory as a function of the number of items in memory. (From Sternberg, 1966.)

Based on these findings, Sternberg made certain conclusions about how we search through memory to find a particular item. He concluded that searches through short-term memory are not instantaneous. In other words, just because all items are in short-term storage does not mean that we can scan all items simultaneously. If all items in short-term memory could be scanned simultaneously, then reaction times (which reflect search times) should not increase as the items in memory increase. Search times should be the same regardless of how many items are in short-term memory at a given instant.

Instead, Sternberg's data appear to support the idea that short-term memory searches are serial. The term *serial search* refers to the idea that we scan through the items in short-term memory one at a time, looking for an item that matches the target. Scanning each item takes a specific amount of time (38 msec according to Sternberg); thus search time should increase by a fixed amount each time an additional item is represented in memory.

If we accept the idea that short-term memory searches involve scanning items serially, such searches might be carried out in two ways. First, it is possible that we search an item set completely before making a decision about a match. Even if the target matches the first item we scan, we may continue to scan all the items represented before making a decision. This type of procedure has been called a *serial exhaustive search.* The other alternative, which seems more intuitively pleasing, is that we scan items serially until we reach a matching item. As soon as a match is discovered, we terminate the search and make a response. This alternative possibility is referred to as a *serial, self-terminating search.*

To distinguish between these possible search strategies, Sternberg compared subjects' reaction times when a target *did* match an item in memory to their reaction times when the target *did not* match. That is, he compared the times required to make a "yes" response to those necessary for a "no" response. His reasoning was that reaction times to make a "no" response should increase as the number of items in memory increases, regardless of whether the search is exhaustive or self-terminating. In either case, the subject must scan the entire set of items before realizing that the target does not match. On the other hand, reaction times to make a "yes" response should differ depending on whether a search is exhaustive or self-terminating. If searches are exhaustive, subjects should scan all items just as they would do before making a "no" decision. Thus, if searches are exhaustive, reaction times to make "yes" and "no" responses should be the same in each case. On the other hand, if searches are self-terminating, "yes" responses will occur very quickly when the target happens to match one of the first items scanned. Thus, if searches are self-terminating it should take less time on the average to make "yes" responses than to make "no" responses, which always require scanning every item.

To test these predictions, Sternberg presented subjects with strings containing between 1 and 6 digits. He then presented a target digit that either did or did not match one of the digits in the preceding string. Figure 10.2 represents subjects' reaction times to make both "yes" and "no" responses. Clearly, the time required to make both kinds of responses increased as the number of items in the string was increased. This again supports the idea that short-term memory searches are serial. More importantly, there was no difference in reaction times to make "yes" and "no" responses. This finding suggests that our serial searches are indeed exhaustive, that we do spend time scanning each item in memory before we make a "yes" or "no" response. We appear to continue scanning even after we have matched the target to an item in memory.

This conclusion, as we have noted before, seems to be counterintuitive. Why would we continue to scan all items in memory before making a decision if, early in the search, we have formed a match? It seems much more reasonable to assume that we would stop searching as soon as a match occurred. Continuing to scan items would seem to be a waste of time and effort. This conflict between what the data suggest and what seems to be a more reasonable idea has led to a number of experiments designed to test the serial exhaustive search hypothesis.

It is notable that Sternberg's data have now

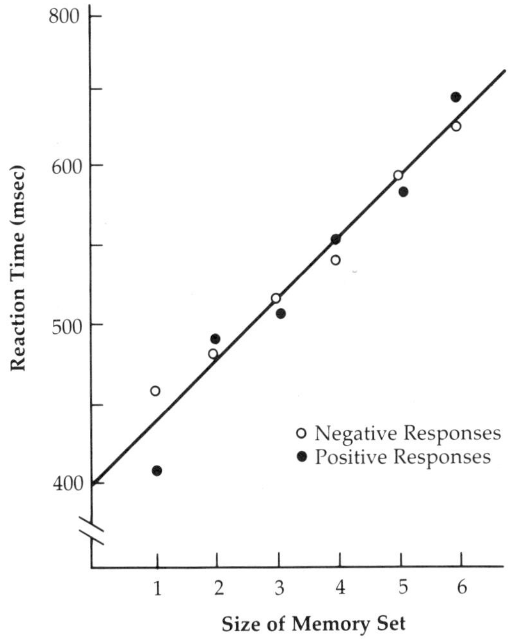

FIGURE 10.2 Reaction times to decide whether a target item is represented in memory. Positive and negative responses are shown as a function of the number of items in memory. (From Sternberg, 1966.)

been replicated in a wide variety of experimental situations. For example, similar data are obtained regardless of whether items are seen or heard (see Wingfield, 1973). Likewise, the exhaustive search conclusion is supported even when the item strings are so long that subjects would need to chunk the items to keep them in memory (see, for example, Naus, 1974). Sternberg himself has demonstrated that a similar pattern of results occurs even when subjects with cognitive impairments are tested (see Sternberg, 1975). Thus, the data supporting the exhaustive search idea are clearly robust.

Still, there have been numerous critics of this interpretation (see, for example, Murdock, 1971; Theios, Smith, Haviland, Traupmann, & Moy, 1973). Also, it is now clear that the exhaustive search model does not apply in every case. For example, in one set of experiments Sternberg (1967) had subjects recall an item from short-term memory rather than asking them to match a target to one of the items. This procedure involved presenting a set of items such as "5, 3, 8, 2" and designating one item in that set as a target. The subjects' task was to recall the item that preceded the target in the original list. Thus, if "8" were given as the target, subjects were to respond with the number "3." Under these conditions, reaction times to recall the correct digit were faster when the target appeared early in the digit string. For example, in the string "5, 3, 8, 2," subjects responded more quickly if the target were "3" than if it were "2." Such a finding suggests that when a search involves specifying the location of an item in a string, searches are self-terminating and not exhaustive. Similar results have been reported when subjects were asked to match multiple probes to item strings in memory (see Wingfield & Bolt, 1970).

To account for these anomalous findings, Sternberg (1967, 1975) has suggested that while short-term memory searches are serial, we are capable of choosing between either exhaustive or self-terminating strategies. In a simple task involving recognition of whether a target is or is not in memory, it is advantageous to use an exhaustive search. Sternberg's rationale is that such a task requires both a search for a match and a decision about that search. He assumes that it requires time and effort to switch from the comparison or matching process to the process of decision making. That is, the easier and faster strategy is to compare a target to all items in a set and then make a decision, as opposed to comparing one pair of items, making a decision, comparing the next pair, and so on. Indeed, the so-called expert computer programs, which make comparisons and offer decisions, are often designed to make exhaustive searches before rendering a response (see Sternberg, 1975). This design is used in such cases because for computers, exhaustive searches are faster than comparisons and decisions on individual items.

On the other hand, exhaustive searches tell us nothing about the position of items in a letter string. We simply scan all items and then decide whether a target matches one of them. Thus, in a task calling for the location of a particular item's position, a self-terminating strategy is appropriate. We scan the items serially until we match the target, then we scan to the item preceding that target in the list and make a response.

Agreement with this interpretation is not universal. There remain a number of different hypotheses about the mechanism(s) of searches through short-term memory. There is little doubt, however, about the contributions of Sternberg's experiments. His procedures, borrowed in part from earlier work by Donders (see Donders, 1868, translation 1969), illustrate how it is possible to use simple reaction time measures to explore complex cognitive processes. His results also provide an important contribution. They show that retrieval from short-term memory may involve a rather complex set of processes and that such retrieval is not necessarily instantaneous.

Retrieval of Long-Term Memories

We all know that in 1980 the incumbent president, Jimmy Carter, ran against Republican candidate Ronald Reagan. In that election, however, an independent third party candidate also received substantial support. Do you remember the candidate's name? If not, does it help to know that the candidate was a Congressman from Illinois? Does it help to know that the candidate had neatly cropped gray hair and wore dark-rimmed glasses? If you can't recall the name, does it help to know that his first name is John and his second name begins with "A"? For those who are still having difficulty, we could ask a simpler question. Do you recognize the name John Anderson?

If you answered "yes" to the last question, or if you recalled the name based on the earlier hints, we can assume that the name "John Anderson" was stored in your long-term memory. Some of you, however, may have recalled the name as soon as you perceived the hint "major third-party candidate in 1980." This information would be called a *retrieval cue* because for many, this information is strongly associated with the name John Anderson. For others, additional retrieval cues were necessary to trigger recall. Since third-party candidates often run in presidential elections, you may have needed to know that this candidate was a man from Illinois, or you may have needed to be reminded of some of his physical features. The ultimate retrieval cue was the presentation of the candidate's name. If you had the name represented in memory at all, hearing or reading that name should have activated some recollection of the candidate.

The process of retrieval from long-term memory is fascinating to almost everyone. The popularity of crossword puzzles and trivia games attests to the satisfaction we get from using subtle cues to retrieve data from long-term memory. By the same token, there are few things more frustrating than not being able to retrieve a fact when we want to. For example, one of the most-watched films in recent years was *E.T.* What was the name of the boy in the movie who befriended the alien? Some of you will recall that name, but others, although they feel that they know it, won't be able to come up with the answer. If you can't recall the name, you may already be experiencing exasperation. This feeling will probably increase as soon as you realize that this paragraph does not contain the answer.

Now we will examine how the process of retrieval works. We begin by looking at different theories of long-term memory retrieval. These theories deal with how we use retrieval cues to locate and activate representations in long-term storage. Then we will focus on retrieval cues themselves, addressing the question of why certain retrieval cues are more effective than others. Finally, we will ask how retrieval can lead to the re-encoding or reconstruction of the memory that is retrieved. Before going on, however, one piece of data should be supplied. The boy's name was Elliot. (If you have spent the past few moments trying to retrieve that name, you probably need to reread this paragraph. The work involved in retrieval can often interfere with the encoding of new material.)

Theories of Retrieval

Most theories of retrieval agree that we use retrieval cues to locate and activate memory representations, whereupon we decide how to respond. There is some disagreement, however, over how this process actually unfolds. Such disagreements have often centered on the issue of whether recall and recognition involve retrieval processes of different kinds. Thus, before examining these ideas, it is useful to look at the recall–recognition distinction.

Recognition versus recall If I were to give you a long list of words to learn, I could later test your memory for that list in two ways. First, I might simply ask you to write down all the words on the list provided. On such an assessment, termed a *recall test,* the subject is given certain retrieval cues that are related to the words on the list. For example, you were told to remember words on a *particular* list (the one I gave you). However, it was left to you to reproduce the exact words that you learned.

The second procedure I might use to test your memory involves a *recognition* test. That is, at the time of testing you are presented with a long list of words that includes items from the list learned previously, as well as new items not contained in the original list. The new items are usually called *distractor items.* Your task is to choose from the test list words that appeared on the list you had been asked to learn. In other words, you see the items you have learned again, and you must simply recognize them among other words on a larger list.

Clearly, both recall and recognition tests represent valid measures of how much you remember. In both cases, in order to perform well, you must have items represented in memory and you must be able to retrieve those representations at the time of testing. Yet, as you might imagine, scores on recognition tests are usually much higher than scores based on recall. As a matter of fact, our ability to recognize items we have encountered before often borders on the amazing.

In one experiment, for example, Shepard (1967) gave subjects more than 500 words printed on cards. Then he tested their recognition of these words by means of word pairs. Each pair contained one word the subjects had seen before and one distractor word. They were to choose the word in each pair that had been presented earlier. Subjects recognized previously presented words about 90 percent of the time, even though they had seen each word only once. Shepard found that if he used pictures instead of words, recognition scores reached almost 100 percent, even though he increased the number of original items to 600 or more. Finally, Shepard found that recognition scores did decrease over long retention intervals. However, most subjects were still accurate more than 90 percent of the time when the test came a full week after viewing the original items.

Not all experiments using recognition tests have shown such outstanding performance. As a matter of fact, there are a few situations we will discuss later in which recall performance is actually better than recognition (see, for example, Watkins, 1974). Still, it is generally accepted that under most circumstances it is easier to recognize an item that has been stored in memory than to recall the same item. Thus any successful retrieval theory must explain why recall and recognition performance often differ.

A single-process model of retrieval One early point of view that developed among memory researchers was that recall and recognition involve the same single process. This is the process of activating a representation in memory. It is assumed that performance on a retention test depends on the degree to which an item in memory becomes activated. The greater the degree of memory activation, the greater the probability that an item will be remembered. According to this view, the degree of memory activation depends on two factors. First, activation depends on the strength of the memory representation. The stronger the memory representation, the easier it is to activate that representation to a high degree. Second, activation levels depend on the effectiveness of retrieval cues. Cues that are particularly effective may result in high levels of activation, while less effective cues may elicit lower levels.

This single-process model makes the reasonable assumption that the retrieval cues on a recognition test are more effective than those on a recall test. After all, on a recall test we usually present cues that are merely related to the target item, whereas on a recognition test we present the target item itself. Based on this assumption, this model makes several predictions. First, if an item is weakly represented in memory, there is little likelihood that it will be recalled, because a weak representation combined with less effective retrieval cues will lead to very low levels of activation. On the other hand, the same item may in many cases be recognized, since even though the representation is weak, the cues contained in the recognition test can lead to a high level of activation. Thus, this model is able to explain why recognition performance is often better than recall performance.

At the same time, the single-process model predicts that when items are strongly represented in memory, recall and recognition performance should be almost equivalent. This makes sense because we can predict that the strong representation will lead to high levels of activation even when less effective retrieval cues are presented. In effect, when item representations are strong, we would expect both recall and recognition performance to be good.

Although the assumptions of this kind of retrieval model are simple, such a view is capable of accounting for a number of recall–recognition differences. However, at least two implications of the single-process model appear to be incorrect. First, the model implies that recognition performance should *always* be better than, or equivalent to, recall performance. There are no circumstances, according to this model, under which recall should exceed recognition. As we will see later, there is now reason to question this implication. Some studies have shown that under certain conditions, subjects are unable to recognize certain items but do appear to be capable of recalling them (see, for example, Tulving and Thomson, 1973; Watkins, 1974).

A second implication of the single-process model is that performance on recall and on recognition should be similarly affected by the same variables. This implication is based on the idea that both recall and recognition procedures result in the same process—the direct activation of a memory representation. The procedures differ only in the degree of activation they produce. Thus, any variable that leads to the increased strength of a representation should improve performance on both recall and recognition. In a like manner, variables that reduce the strength of a representation should decrease both types of performance. Again this implication appears not to be correct. For example, we know that recall is better for words that are frequently used in our language than for less frequently used words. Word frequency has the opposite effect, however, on recognition performance. When asked to recognize words from a previously presented list, subjects tend to perform better with low frequency words than they do with high frequency words (see Kintsch, 1970). Such different effects would be unlikely if recall and recognition tests induced retrieval in the same way.

The generation–recognition hypothesis Because of the foregoing problems associated with a single-process model, another type of retrieval theory has become popular. This view, proposed by Kintsch (1970), is often called the *generation–recognition hypothesis.* According to this view, the recognition of an item proceeds much as suggested by the single-process model. On a recognition test, that is, the presentation of an item can directly activate the representation of that item in memory. If such an activation occurs, an individual decides that the item has been presented before. If there is no activation (or only a weak one), the individual may decide that the item has not been presented in the past. Thus, recognition consists of a decision-making process based on how strongly a representation in memory is activated by some test item. This decision making is simply labeled the *recognition process* in Kintsch's theory.

While Kintsch's hypothesis views recognition as involving only the single decision-making process, it suggests that recall usually requires an additional step before a decision can be made. The additional step is necessary because the retrieval cues presented on a recall test are incapable of directly activating the target memory. Instead, these cues activate their own representations in memory, whereupon the activation spreads to other related representations. Assuming that a given retrieval cue is strongly related to the target stimulus, this spread of activation eventually results in the activation of the target memory, and retrieval of that memory can occur. This spread of activation from the retrieval cue representation to the target memory is called the *generation* or *search process.*

When the generation process has been completed, Kintsch assumes that recognition or decision making begins, working the same way in recall as it does on a recognition test. That is, a subject decides whether an item has been presented before based on the degree to which the target memory is activated. Thus, recall and recognition are presumed to be similar in that both kinds of tests involve a decision-making step. However, recall involves a prior search process that is not necessary when a recognition test is used.

The major advantage of Kintsch's model over the single-process view is the ability to explain why some variables might affect recall and recognition differently. Basically, the generation–recognition hypothesis predicts that any variable that affects the strength of an item representation in memory should affect recall and recognition performance in the same manner. This is reasonable because increasing the strength of an item's representation should lead to greater activation of the target memory and easier decision making. Thus, manipulations such as increasing the degree of learning for an item should improve both recall and item recognition. This prediction is clearly in accord with the existing data.

On the other hand, variables that affect the organization or the relationship between representations in memory would be expected to influence recall, but not recognition. This prediction is based on the idea that the organization of items in memory determines the success of the search process but should have little to do with decision making once the search has been completed. This prediction is supported by data from a number of experiments.

In one study focusing on organizational variables, Kintsch (1968) presented subjects with categorized lists of words. That is, for a given list, all the words belonged to the same conceptual category. Some of the lists contained words that were highly associated with the category name. For example, a list selected from the "fruits" category might have contained "apple" and "orange." Other lists contained words having only weak associations with the category name (for example, "tomato" in the "fruits" list). Kintsch found that recognition of these words was equally good regardless of whether the target words were from a high or low association list. However, recall was much better for words from the high association lists. Kintsch's interpretation of this finding was that words in a high association list are more closely related to the category name and to each other. As a result, the search process involved in recall testing is facilitated for words in these lists.

The generation–recognition hypothesis is also capable of explaining why a variable such as word frequency might affect recall and recognition differently. It is reasonable to assume that frequently used words are more strongly associated with other words than are less frequently used words. These strong associations should facilitate the process of searching through a network of related items. On the other hand, word frequency might be expected to have a detrimental influence on decision making after an item representation has been activated. To illustrate how word frequency might influence decision making, imagine that you are being tested on a list of commonly used words that you have just learned. The test is a recognition test containing both the learned items and, as distractors, words that are frequently used. If a test item leads to the activation of an item representation, it may be difficult to decide whether activation is occurring because the word was on the list or simply because the word is commonly used and is strongly represented in memory. Thus, there is a strong likelihood of incorrectly citing distractor words, since these words should be as strongly represented in memory as the listed words.

Based on this line of reasoning, we might predict that high word frequency will facilitate a search process but might interfere with decision making. On a recall test, the net effect of these influences might be to enhance recall through the facilitation of the search. Recognition performance, however, might well be expected to be poorer, since effectiveness in this task depends solely on decision making.

Clearly, the generation–recognition hypothesis enjoys greater success than the single-process theory. Still, the generation–recognition approach does not overcome all the problems inherent in the single-process view. Implicit in both approaches, for example, is the assumption that recognition performance should always be better than or equal to performance based on recall. We have noted before that this prediction is not always confirmed. There do appear to be occasions of recall performance exceeding recognition. We now turn our attention to this phenomenon and its implications for the generation–recognition hypothesis.

Instances of recall exceeding recognition In 1973, Tulving and Thomson conducted an experiment designed to look at both recognition and recall for a given set of common words. The experiment itself consisted of the following stages.

Stage 1: Pairs of words were presented. Subjects were told to memorize capitalized words and to use lowercase words as cues.

Example: pretty–BLUE

Stage 2: Subjects were told to free associate to given words, using words from stage 1 if desired. Then subjects were asked to list their associations and to circle any they had seen in stage 1.

Example:

Word	Free associations
lake	water
	ocean
	(blue)
	deep

Stage 3: Subjects were given cue words from Stage 1 and were asked to recall the appropriate capitalized words.

Example: pretty–________

Stage 1 was straightforward. Subjects were requested to learn the capitalized word in each pair on a list, and were told that the lowercase word could be used as a cue. Thus, in the pair "pretty–BLUE," subjects were required to remember "BLUE," but were encouraged to use "pretty" as a cue.

Stage 2 did not begin until the word pairs had been studied thoroughly. Then subjects were given a series of target words that had not appeared in stage 1. However, some of the words presented in stage 2 were weakly related to some of the capitalized stage 1 words. The subjects were asked to write down any words that came to mind when each target word was presented. They were specifically told that their free associations could include any of the words they had learned in stage 1. Thus, when "lake" was presented in stage 2, many subjects' free associations included "blue," which had been learned in stage 1. Upon completing the free associations, the subjects were asked to recognize and circle any items that had appeared on the stage 1 list, as shown in the example for stage 2, above.

After this de facto recognition test for the free-associated words, the subjects were presented with the lowercase cue words from stage 1. The task in stage 3 was to recall each of the capitalized words that had been learned in stage 1. Tulving and Thomson found that during the free association stage, several of the capitalized words were given as responses to the target words. However, subjects were able to recognize only about 25 percent of the capitalized words they gave as responses. Surprisingly, when the subjects were given the recall test for these words, on the average they recalled more than 60 percent of the capitalized words. Thus, using these procedures, subjects showed that they were able to *recall* many words that they had not *recognized*. Apparently, retrieval of the capitalized words was easier with the lowercase words as cues than it was when a capitalized word itself was presented.

This finding that some recalled words are not recognizable is, of course, very counterintuitive. We usually assume that if a word can be recalled, it can certainly be recognized. However, these results suggest that such an assumption is not always warranted. Because these results were so contrary to prevailing assumptions about retrieval, the Tulving–Thomson experiment was criticized on a variety of grounds. For example, Martin (1975) argued that the experiment required subjects to encode the capitalized words differently in stages 1 and 2. In stage 1 the words are encoded in terms of the cue word given. In stage 2 the words take on a different meaning because they are responses to a different stimulus. Martin suggests that the words are difficult to recognize because their meanings are essentially different in the original learning stage and in the free association stage.

Although Martin's criticisms are valid, Tulving and Watkins (1977) demonstrated that the Tulving–Thomson kind of result does not depend on a target word having different meanings at different stages of the experiment. In a refined study, the experimenters selected cue words that would give the capitalized words a particular meaning. The words used in the free association phase were designed to evoke the same meaning for the capitalized words. Still, Tulving and Watkins found that recall performance was superior to recognition in this paradigm.

Others have argued that the Tulving–Thomson finding may have resulted simply from the complexity of the procedures used. There is no denying that the Tulving–Thomson procedure can be confusing. However, similar results have been obtained in a variety of experiments using relatively simple sets of procedures (see, for example, Watkins & Tulving, 1975; Wiseman & Tulving, 1976). Apparently, this is a robust phenomenon that can be observed under a variety of conditions.

Although experiments of these kinds continue to be criticized on methodological grounds (see Santa & Lamwers, 1976), the results have raised serious questions about the generation–recognition view of retrieval. This hypothesis, which states clearly that recognition should always be equal or superior to recall performance, is based on the belief that recognition is simply the final step in the recall process. Recall and recognition are said to differ only in that recall involves an additional search process that is unnecessary in recognition. Thus, according to this view, if a word is recallable, a subject must have been able to recognize the word. It should never be the case that a word is recalled and not recognized.

Contemporary retrieval hypotheses Findings such as those reported by Tulving and Thomson (1973) have led several theorists to reexamine the retrieval process involved in recognition testing. As a result, many current theories of retrieval suggest that recognition may entail more than a simple decision-making process. According to these approaches, recognition may involve a preliminary search stage similar to the one proposed for recall. One example of this view comes from the theoretical framework proposed by Anderson and Bower (1974; see also, Anderson, 1976).

Anderson and Bower hypothesize that when a list of words is presented, a subject does not store the words in isolation but instead encodes each one, along with its context. This context includes the meaning the subject attributes to the word at the time the word is presented. For example, if the word "house" appears on a list, the subject may think of his or her own house, which may be constructed of stucco. Thus, instead of simply storing the word "house," the subject will store the proposition "My house is made of stucco." Figure 10.3a illustrates propositions that might be stored with words such as "house" and "car."

In addition to encoding each word as part of a proposition, Anderson and Bower have suggested that each proposition for a listed word is linked to a superordinate proposition, which specifies the list to which these words belong. Thus, if "house" and "car" appear on the same list, the propositions containing these words are linked to a higher level proposition, which says that these words belong to the list recently learned. Figure 10.3b illustrates this link between the word propositions and the proposition denoting list membership. In effect, the list membership proposition is used to differentiate one list or group of words from another.

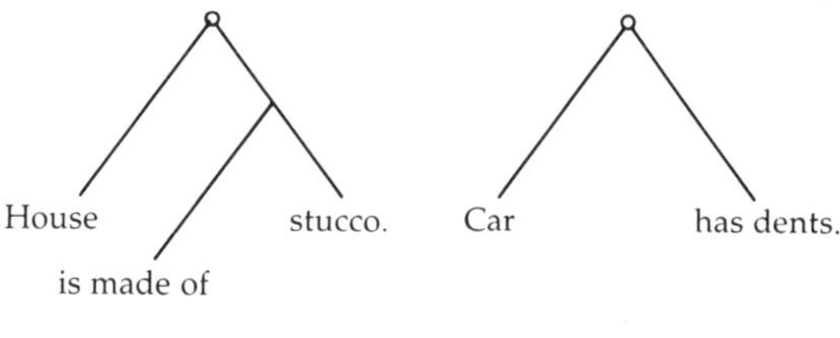

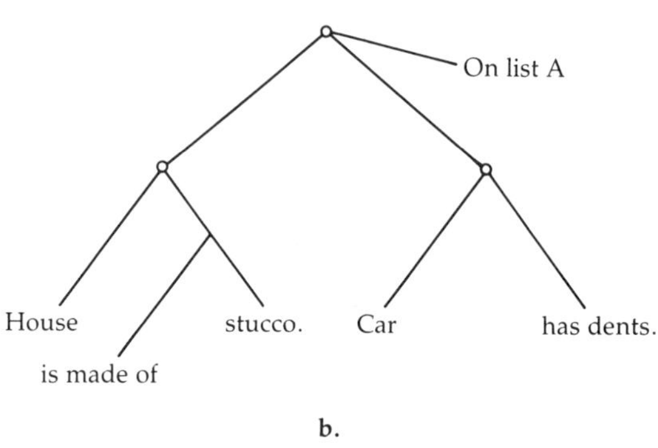

FIGURE 10.3 **a.** Anderson and Bower's conception of propositions we might form for the words "house" and "car." **b.** How these word propositions are linked to a list membership proposition. (Based on Anderson and Bower, 1974.)

According to Anderson and Bower's view, recognition testing involves more than the simple activation of a word in memory. Assume, for example, that the word "house" has appeared on a list and that the subject then sees the word "house" on a recognition test. The subject's task is to determine whether "house" appeared on the list that was recently learned. However, "house" may be stored as part of several propositions in memory. Thus, the presentation of the word on the test may activate several propositions at once. As a result, the subject must search through the connections for these propositions to determine whether any of them are linked to the recently learned list.

For example, the presentation of "house" may activate the proposition "My house is made of stucco." By searching the connections to this proposition, the subject arrives at the proposition stating: "This word belongs to the recently learned list." At this point the subject may conclude that the presented word did appear in the list that was learned. However, the presentation of "house" on a test might have activated instead other propositions in memory, such as "The house is on fire." Since this proposition had been activated, the subject would have to search its connections before arriving at the conclusion that no word on the list was encoded in this manner.

By assuming that recognition involves a search process, Anderson and Bower's theory becomes capable of explaining a number of important phenomena. For example, this theory predicts that the success of a recognition search should depend on at least two factors. One factor is the number of propositions a word belongs to in memory. If a word is stored as part of a single proposition only and that proposition is linked to the recently learned list, recognition should be relatively easy. However, a very common listed word may be part of numerous propositions in memory, most of which will not be linked to the list membership proposition. In this case, recognition of a test word may be very difficult. Such a prediction is supported by the finding that recognition is more difficult when listed words are words that are frequently used in written and oral communication.

Another factor that should influence recognition is the closeness of the links between the listed words and the list membership proposition. Recognition should be facilitated by factors that make it easy to differentiate one list of words from another. To illustrate this prediction, assume that a subject learns a list of common words that are unrelated except insofar as they all appear on the same list. This means that the words may be encoded using very different propositions, which may be linked to a very general proposition, such as "The words were on the list." At the time of recognition testing it may be very difficult to determine whether a test word was on the most recently learned list or on a list of words learned at another time. In effect, it is difficult to differentiate lists in memory because there is little that is distinctive about the particular list of words learned.

On the other hand, assume that a subject learns a list of words that are conceptually related in some way. For example, suppose that all the words represent modes of transportation ("car," "bus," "train," "airplane," and so on). In such a case the propositions used to encode these words would be similar. Furthermore, the list membership proposition would be more specific. Such a proposition might include the phrase "modes of transportation." In this case, one might expect recognition to be easier, since subjects would have at least one means of determining whether a test word belonged to the specific list learned earlier. Such a prediction is supported by some studies, which show that the organization of a list can influence recognition of words from that list (see, for example, Bower, Clark, Lesgold, & Winzenz, 1969).

Finally, the Anderson and Bower approach can help to explain why recall may sometimes be superior to recognition. Basically, this view proposes that under some circumstances a retrieval cue is more closely associated with a list membership proposition than a word itself is. For example, refer to Figure 10.3b, where the proposition "My house is made of stucco" is linked to the proposition "(the word is) on list A." In this particular instance, the word that must be remembered is "house," a common word that may be represented in multiple propositions in memory. Thus, on a recognition test when the word "house" is presented, several propositions may be activated and it may be difficult to determine whether "house" appeared on the learned list or whether it was activated because of its appearance in some other context.

On the other hand, assume a recall test on which the subject is presented with the retrieval cue "stucco." This retrieval cue will also activate the proposition "My house is made of stucco," but it may not activate many other propositions. As a result, the subject may be able to recall easily that "house" was on the list recently learned. Thus, depending on the effectiveness and distinctiveness of a retrieval cue, recall performance can sometimes be superior to recognition performance.

It should be noted that the idea that recognition involves a search process is not confined to the Anderson and Bower approach. Several contemporary theories of retrieval make a similar assumption (see, for example, Atkinson & Juola, 1973; Gillund & Shiffrin, 1984; Mandler, 1972). Interestingly, in one sense theorizing about retrieval seems to have come full circle. Early theories of retrieval stressed the similarities between recognition and recall and viewed these test procedures as simply leading to different degrees of memory activation. Later theories emphasized differences in these tests of retention and specifically proposed that recall involves a process more complex than recognition. More recently, theories have suggested, once again, that recall and recognition involve similar processes. Now, however, it is being suggested that both test procedures lead to complex searches through memory before decisions can be made.

The Tip-of-the-Tongue (TOT) Phenomenon

To this point we have discussed retrieval as if it were an all-or-none process, one by which we either remember some event or fail to remember it. From your own experiences you already know that this is an oversimplification. In our attempts to recall certain events, we are often frustrated by inability to remember the specific thing we wish to recall. In many cases we know that the information is in memory and we can remember aspects of the specific event we wish to retrieve. We cannot, however, activate the particular representation we need. This inability to recall a specific event or item, even though aspects of it are remembered, has been called the *tip-of-the-tongue (TOT)* phenomenon.

To illustrate the TOT phenomenon, consider the following example. A few weeks ago I was working on a crossword puzzle. One clue in the puzzle was an 8-letter word meaning "a symbolic narrative." The first word that came to mind was "parable." It seemed to fit the definition well enough, but it contains only 7 letters. The next possibility I considered was "alliteration." I immediately decided that this word was incorrect for two reasons. First, "alliteration" describes words having the same sound. Thus, although such words might appear in a narrative, "alliteration" did not fit the definition of the correct word. In addition, "alliteration" has the wrong number of letters. The longer I struggled to recall the correct word, the more frustrated I became. I knew that I had the correct answer in memory. However, the more I tried to recall it, the more "alliteration" came to mind. Finally, I gave up and went on to the other word clues. Later, by filling in other words, I found that the word I had skipped ended in "-gory." Then I knew that the correct answer was "allegory," not "alliteration." My earlier attempts at retrieval had allowed me to recall the initial letters in the word "allegory" but not the entire word. Partial retrieval of this type is often a characteristic of the TOT phenomenon.

Studies of the TOT phenomenon in the laboratory have raised interesting questions about how the retrieval process operates. In a now classic set of experiments, R. W. Brown and McNeill (1966), attempted to induce instances of the TOT phenomenon by presenting their subjects with definitions for infrequently used

English words. For example, one definition they presented was "a navigational instrument used in measuring angular distances, especially the altitude of the sun, moon and the stars at sea." Some subjects immediately realized that they did not know the word being defined. Others immediately identified the word defined as "sextant." Importantly, several subjects, upon hearing such a definition, felt that they knew the defined word but were unable to reproduce it. In other words, these subjects felt that the correct words were "on the tips of their tongues."

During the course of these studies, Brown and McNeill induced more than 200 cases of the TOT phenomenon. In these cases they found that subjects were able to identify the first letter of the correct word more often than not. In many cases they were also able to determine the number of syllables in the correct word. Many of the incorrect words offered by the subjects actually sounded like the correct word even though the incorrect responses had totally different meanings. Subsequent studies have reported similar results.

In a recent review of the TOT literature, Reason and Mycielska (1982) have summarized some of the more common findings. First, they conclude that retrieval is not an all-or-none process, but that partial retrieval of certain aspects of a word can occur. Second, they believe that incorrect attempts at retrieval can yield words that either sound like the correct word or have the same meaning. Third, the TOT state often can be resolved by using the incorrect words as cues for retrieving the correct words.

Thus, the results of TOT studies indicate that retrieval is not necessarily a simple search between one representation and another in memory. A cue such as a definition may activate a number of memory representations. Some of these representations may share a common meaning. Other representations may be activated, however, because they are physically similar to the correct word. Once incorrect but related representations have been activated, these representations may be used to launch additional searches through memory. In effect, retrieval may involve various stages of searching in which each stage brings us closer to the correct memory representation. Such findings illustrate that our current understanding of retrieval and memory organization is still incomplete.

The Encoding Specificity Hypothesis

Throughout our discussion of recognition and recall procedures, we have continued to talk about *retrieval cues*. Specifically, the term refers to any stimulus or cue occuring at the time of retention testing that is used by an individual to aid in the accessing of a target representation. When you recall a person's name after seeing her face, the person's facial features seem to serve as retrieval cues for the memory of the name. Likewise, if you cannot remember a list of words, a hint such as "the first word began with the letter A" would constitute a retrieval cue. In some cases retrieval cues are stimuli we notice in the external environment. At other times we seem to provide our own retrieval cues simply by thinking about an event we wish to remember. In any case, retrieval cues play an integral role in the retrieval process.

Now we will look more closely at what makes a retrieval cue effective. In other words, we will try to learn why some retrieval cues lead to immediate recollection, while others are relatively ineffective. Our discussion of retrieval cue effectiveness centers on a deceptively simple hypothesis proposed by Tulving and his colleagues (Flexser & Tulving, 1978; Tulving, 1983; Tulving & Thomson, 1973; see also, Kintsch, 1974). This view is known as the *encoding specificity hypothesis*.

Put simply, Tulving's encoding specificity hypothesis suggests that the success of retrieval depends on the degree to which conditions of retrieval are similar to the conditions of encoding. More specifically, this hypothesis states that whenever a memory is stored, it is encoded in a unique fashion. The way a given memory is encoded depends on the stimuli present at the time of learning as well as on other memories that are activated while learning is occurring. Thus, if one is given a particular word to learn, that word does not occur in memory as an isolated representation. Rather, the representation of the word is connected to representations of environmental features (for example, time, place, odors, and sounds) that are noticed when the word is learned. The representation of the word may also be connected to specific meanings or other words with similar sounds if those meanings or sounds are retrieved at the time of learning. In effect, a memory is always a complex of representations including not only the target event, but also other events that are noticed at the time the memory is formed. The particular set of representations constituting a memory is what makes most memories distinct from one another to at least some degree.

According to Tulving, for retrieval cues to be effective they must be at least similar to the cues represented in a memory. That is, retrieval cues will be effective to the degree that they match the cues noticed by an individual when a memory was first encoded. Thus, if an individual notices the characteristics of a room while learning a list of words, the words will be at least partly encoded in terms of the room characteristics. Retrieval should then be facilitated by testing the individual in the room in which learning occurred. This environment would be expected to enhance retrieval because the retrieval cues would match a portion of the stimuli represented in the memory for those words.

This idea that retrieval should depend on test cues being similar to encoding cues does not seem revolutionary. However, this is a principle that is extremely important and, yet, is often overlooked when retrieval problems occur. To illustrate the power of this hypothesis, we should consider the wide range of circumstances to which it applies.

Evidence favoring the encoding specificity hypothesis Not surprisingly, the earliest work on the encoding specificity hypothesis was conducted by Tulving and his associates. In Chapter 6 we described a pertinent study by Tulving and Pearlstone (1966). Recall that the experimenters presented their subjects with a list of words that could be grouped into several conceptual categories (for example, types of vegetables or modes of transportation). The list they presented had all the words grouped by category, and each grouping was preceded by the appropriate category name. The purpose of this format was to bias the subjects toward encoding the list in terms of specific categories.

Following this procedure, the subjects were asked to recall the words on the list. Half the subjects were given the category names as retrieval cues, while the remaining subjects were given no category names as cues. The subjects who received the category names remembered significantly more words than the subjects who did not receive the cues. Tulving and Pearlstone interpreted these findings in terms of encoding specificity. They suggested that the category names facilitated recall because these names had been presented at the time the list was encoded.

Similar results have been obtained by Tulving and Osler (1968) and by Thomson and Tulving (1970), in experiments involving free recall lists, which subjects were to learn. During learning some subjects were given a meaningful word associate for each list item. For example, the word associate for the listed word "giant" might have been "tall." Other subjects learned the list without word associates. On a later test all subjects were required to recall the listed words. Half the subjects who learned using word associates were tested with the word associates as retrieval cues and half were tested without word associates. Likewise, half the subjects who learned without word associates were given word associates as retrieval cues and half were not.

The results of Tulving's experiments were clear. The best recall performance occurred among subjects who were given the word associates both at the time of learning and at the time of testing. The next best performance was by subjects who received no word associates at the time of learning or testing. The poorest performance was seen in subjects who received the word associates *only* during testing. Such results are consistent with the idea that retrieval depends on the similarity of learning and testing conditions. Retrieval cues are effective to the degree that these cues are similar to those present at the time of encoding.

A more recent study of recognition conducted by Morris (1978) is of particular interest because the results show that for the encoding specificity rule to hold, retrieval cues need not be exact replicas of cues present at the time of learning. In this experiment, Morris presented target words embedded in particular sentences. Some subjects received the words in what were termed "congruous" sentences. These were sentences that described typical or normal situations. For example, for the target word "pickle," Morris used the congruous sentence "The *pickle* was served with the slaw." Other subjects received the target words embedded in "incongruous" sentences, or sentences that described a bizarre or atypical situation—for example, "The *pickle* jammed the saxophone." On the test, subjects received both old and new target words again embedded in either congruous or incongruous sentences. Their task was to recognize the words they had seen before. However, on the test all the sentences were new. For example, a pair of congruous and incongruous test sentences might be "The *pickle* was on top of the sandwich" and "The *pickle* was cut by the chain saw."

The results of Morris's experiment (Figure 10.4) show the probability of correct recognition as a function of encoding and testing conditions. Subjects who learned using congruous sentences clearly performed best when the words were embedded in congruous sentences on the test. However, when incongruous sentences were used during learning, performance was best when testing also involved incongruous sentences. These results occurred even though the actual sentences used in learning and testing were different. Apparently, all that is necessary for successful retrieval is relative similarity of encoding and retrieval conditions.

To this point we have shown that the encoding specificity principle holds very well in studies that use specific verbal cues at the times of learning and testing. Several studies,

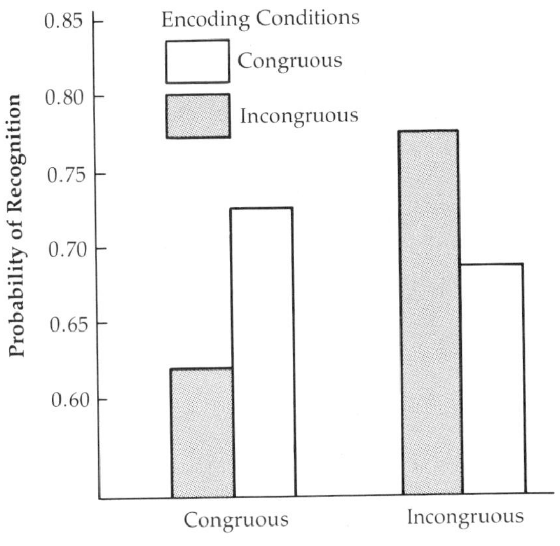

FIGURE 10.4 Recognition performance as a function of the similarity between encoding and retrieval conditions. (Adapted from Morris, 1978.)

however, show that this principle extends to situations featuring the manipulation of more general contextual stimuli. In one rather unusual experiment, for example, Godden and Baddeley (1975) had subjects learn a list of words for later recall. Some subjects learned the words while submerged under water, while others learned on dry land. Retention testing was then conducted either under water or on land. The results of this study are rather dramatic. Recall performance was very good in subjects who were tested under the same conditions present during learning. Performance was relatively poor, however, when subjects learned and recalled under different conditions.

Findings consistent with the encoding specificity principle have also been reported when subjects were asked to learn and remember items in different postural positions. Greenspoon and Ranyard (1957) had subjects learn a list of words either in a distinctive room sitting down or in a different room standing up. Then they tested their subjects under the same or different conditions. Recall was facilitated when room and postural position were the same during learning and testing (see also, Rand & Wapner, 1967; Smith, Glenberg, & Bjork, 1978). The same kind of result has been found when experimenters manipulate the color words are printed in or the backgrounds words are printed on between learning and testing (see, for example, von Wright, 1959).

A final phenomenon that tends to support the encoding specificity view is called *state-dependent learning*. That is, subjects learn items while in one internal bodily state and are tested for retention in either the same or a different state. To illustrate this kind of experiment, consider a study done by Eich, Weingartner, Stillman, and Gillin (1975). These experimenters had subjects learn a list of categorized words after smoking a cigarette containing either marijuana or a placebo. Before testing, subjects smoked another cigarette, which again contained either marijuana or a placebo. They found that subjects tested under the placebo state recalled best if they had learned in that placebo state. However, subjects tested after using marijuana performed better if they had learned after using marijuana. Similar results have been reported when alcohol is used to produce a distinctive internal state (see Petersen, 1974).

Other studies have shown that more naturally occurring internal states can also produce the state-dependent effect. Weingartner, Miller, and Murphy (1977), for example, did an experiment in which bipolar patients served as subjects. A bipolar patient is one whose mood states swing rather violently between depression and mania or elation. The experimenters had their patients learn words in one mood state and asked them to attempt recall in either the same or a different state. They found that recall was superior when the learning and testing mood states were the same. There is some evidence that similar results can be produced in normal subjects whose mood states are varied by experimental manipulations (see Bower, 1981).

We have dealt at length with studies that are consistent with the encoding specificity hypothesis for two reasons. First, it is important to realize the wide range of conditions to which this principle applies. Second, it is difficult to overemphasize the importance of this principle for understanding and predicting retrieval. Clearly, the effectiveness of a retrieval cue cannot be determined simply by looking at the nature of the cue itself. To predict the effectiveness of such a cue, we must know whether the cue is similar to cues present at the time of encoding. The greater the similarity of encoding and retrieval conditions, the more effective the retrieval attempt will be.

Memory Construction at the Time of Retrieval

Virtually all theories of memory processing make the assumption that encoding takes place while memories are in short-term storage or while they are being actively processed (see, for example, Atkinson & Shiffrin, 1968; Craik & Lockhart, 1972). In addition, most such models assume that when a memory is retrieved from permanent storage, that memory or some copy of it re-enters awareness or the short-term memory store. When we combine these assumptions, we are faced with a particular implication. Once a memory has been retrieved, that memory may be susceptible to being re-encoded in short-term storage. In other words, one might predict that a memory that has been retrieved is capable of being altered or modified in some way. This hypothesis raises an interesting possibility. It may be that retrieval is more than simply a process by which we activate and use stored memories. Retrieval may also be a process by which we are able to update or re-encode memories that have long been in storage.

In recent years, several studies have supported the idea that memories may be re-encoded at the time of retrieval. The best known studies of this type have been conducted by Loftus and her colleagues (see, for example, Greene, Flynn, & Loftus, 1982; Loftus, 1979; Loftus, Miller & Burns, 1978; see also, Weinberg, Wadsworth, & Baron, 1983). Basically, Loftus began her studies to look at a very practical question. Is eyewitness testimony of the type given in a courtroom really reliable? To test the reliability of such testimony, she first showed a videotape of an automobile accident. Then she asked her subjects questions about the event they had witnessed. During the series of questions, half the subjects were asked "How fast was the white sports car going while traveling along the country road?" The other subjects received a slightly different question. They were asked "How fast was the white sports car going when it passed the barn while traveling down the country road?" These questions differ only in that one mentions a barn and the other does not. The difference is important, however, because the videotape did not show a barn. Thus, half the subjects were presented with subtle information about the presence of a barn that did not exist in the original stimulus and could not have been in their memory of the tape.

After one week, Loftus asked her subjects another series of questions about the same tape. One of these questions was "Did you see a barn?" Nearly 20 percent of the subjects who had been given the barn question earlier answered "yes." Fewer than 5 percent of the other subjects responded that they had seen a barn. These data indicate that eyewitness accounts can be biased by questions witnesses are asked. More important for present purposes is the implication that information can be added to a memory at the time that memory is retrieved. In the present case subjects were asked questions to get them to retrieve their memories of the tape. One group was given additional information at the time of retrieval. Thus some of these subjects may have incorporated the new information into the memory of the tape, even though this information was not present at the time the memory was originally formed. Such a finding suggests that we sometimes update or alter our memories at the time of retrieval based on any new relevant information that is at our disposal.

In a second, more complex study in this series, Loftus attempted to induce subjects to alter information they had originally stored. To accomplish this she presented two groups of subjects with a sequence of slides showing a red sports car progressively moving toward a collision with another car. Both groups received the same slides in the same sequence, except for one slide, which showed the sports car at an intersection. One group saw a slide that contained a stop sign, while the other group's slide showed a yield sign (Figure 10.5).

Immediately after seeing the slides, the two groups were asked questions about what they had seen. Half the subjects who had seen a stop sign were asked a question in which the

FIGURE 10.5 A pair of photographs used in the experiment by Loftus, Miller, and Burns to test the reliability of an eyewitness account. (From Loftus, Miller, and Burns, 1978.)

term "stop sign" was used (a consistent question). The other half received a question containing the term "yield sign" (an inconsistent question). Similarly, half the subjects who saw a yield sign received a consistent ("yield sign") question, while the other half were asked an inconsistent ("stop sign") question. Several minutes later all subjects were given a recognition test in which pairs of slides were presented. They were to choose the slide seen before. When slides showing the intersection were shown, 75 percent of subjects given a consistent question recognized the correct slide. However, subjects who received an inconsistent question were correct only 40 percent of the time. This result suggests that the inconsistent questions caused many subjects to alter their retrieved memories so that they could no longer correctly recognize what they had originally seen.

In general, we can advance at least two related interpretations for the kind of finding Loftus reports. One explanation is that at the time of retrieval a memory re-enters some active state (possibly short-term storage) and is at that time altered in accord with new incoming information. This altered memory is then restored in its modified form. Another possibility is that retrieval causes a copy of a memory to become active and that this copy is altered. The modified copy may then be stored along with the original memory. Basically, the second interpretation suggests that retrieval is not responsible for altering a memory; rather, it appears that during the retrieval period, another memory can be formed.

These two interpretations for Loftus's results are admittedly very difficult to distinguish experimentally. However, it should be noted that several experimenters have attempted to induce recovery of an original memory once retrieval and alterations have occurred (see Bekerian & Bowers, 1983; Sanders & Simmons, 1983). Generally, such attempts have been unsuccessful. Inability to recover an original memory is not proof that such a memory does not exist. However, such failures are consistent with the idea that retrieval can lead to the alteration of the original memory, not just to the formation of an altered copy. In any event, data such as those reported by Loftus have expanded our understanding of the retrieval process. We now assume that retrieval can induce changes in memories long after the original formation of those memories.

Studies of Retrieval in Nonhuman Species

As we noted in Chapter 9, relatively little research has been done concerning memory codes and structures in animals. In contrast, there has been considerable interest in how animals retrieve memories that have been formed and stored. Now we turn to three issues that have arisen in this area of research: the kinds of retrieval cues animals use to remember food locations in their natural environments, whether the encoding specificity principle governs retrieval in animals, and whether animals alter their memories at the time of retrieval. Throughout our discussion, we will see some striking similarities between human and nonhuman retrieval mechanisms.

Retrieval of Spatial Memories

Most animal species do not have constant or direct access to food sources. For many, food is available only at certain times of the year and only in certain locations. In addition, there is always competition for the limited food resources that are available at a given time. As a result, simple survival in the natural environment requires an organism to use numerous strategies for the location and gathering of food.

Caching or hoarding, a strategy common to many species, involves gathering food while it is plentiful and then storing it in caches or hidden locations so that it will be available when the original food sources are gone. To illustrate this strategy consider the behavior of *Clark's nutcracker,* a small bird that feeds primarily on pine seeds, which are abundant in the late summer and early fall. Tomback (1983), who has studied the food gathering behavior of this species, notes that each bird gathers around 33,000 seeds during the time the food is available. The bird then proceeds to hide the seeds in caches. Tomback estimates that 5 to 6 seeds are left in each cache, which means that each bird stores food in about 6000 different hiding places. About 4 months after the caches are formed, the birds begin to return to the food locations to retrieve the hidden seeds. By carefully monitoring the birds' movements, Tomback has been able to estimate that approximately 75 percent of these retrieval attempts are successful. In other words, when a bird goes out in search of a cache, it finds one of its own caches about 75 percent of the time.

The nutcracker's ability to cache and retrieve its food is truly remarkable. It is not unusual, however, since numerous species exhibit comparable behaviors. Still, when we consider these behaviors several questions arise. First, we might ask why animals bother to spread their food over numerous locations rather than storing it all in one place. The answer to this question appears relatively simple. By forming many caches instead of just one, an organism decreases the chance that an intruder will wipe out its entire food supply. A second question we might ask is how an organism finds its caches months after forming them. One simple possibility is that organisms always store caches in particular categories of locations, such as on tree limbs or in the ground at the bases of trees. Such a strategy would limit the areas to be searched. Another possibility is that organisms might mark each of a variety of cache locations in a particular way. For example, each cache might be marked visually or with an odor of some type.

Although both these possible strategies might make cache retrieval easier, most researchers have dismissed the possibility that such approaches are used. If an organism always stored caches in particular categories of locations or always marked the sites, it should be relatively easy for one organism to find another's food locations. Several studies have shown that when other organisms intrude into a given animal's territory, the intruders are usually unable to find the hidden food in that territory. Thus, it is unlikely that organisms hide their caches in obvious locations or that they mark these locations in any manner that would be recognizable to their conspecifics.

The consensus among most researchers is that many animals are capable of forming elaborate spatial memories (see, for example, Balda & Turek, 1984; Sherry, Krebs, & Cowie, 1981). When these species hide their food, they form memories of the caches' spatial locations and are able to retrieve these memories at the time of recovery. Aside from being a rather impressive memory feat, such abilities have raised questions about the cues an animal might use to remember its cache locations. In other words, what cues are used to retrieve these extensive spatial memories that are formed?

One of the best attempts at answering this question comes from a series of laboratory experiments conducted by Olton and Samuelson (1976), who studied memory for food locations

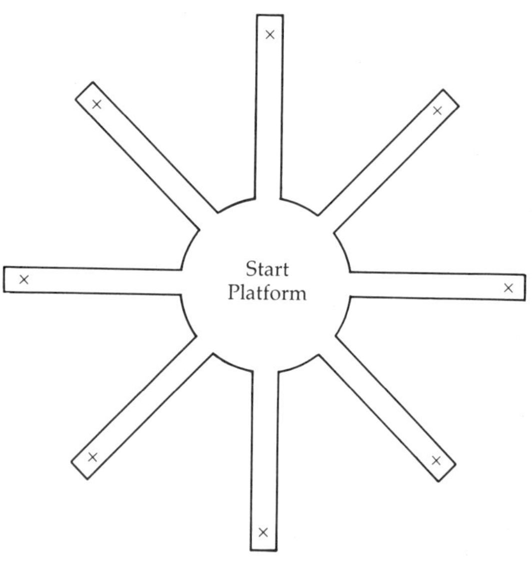

FIGURE 10.6 Eight-arm radial maze of the type used by Olton and Samuelson (1976). Rats begin a trial on the start platform and can choose to enter any one of the eight arms. Food cups at the end of each arm are denoted by crosses.

in the rat. These experimenters used an eight-arm radial maze such as the apparatus pictured in Figure 10.6. The center compartment or start chamber has eight long alleyways or arms radiating away from the center platform; at the end of each arm is a food cup. The experimenters placed food at the end of each arm, released a hungry rat from the center compartment, and monitored the rat's visits to the various arms of the maze.

Olton and Samuelson reasoned that if a rat is capable of remembering specific spatial locations, it should exhibit a particular pattern of behavior in the maze. It should visit one arm in the maze, eat the food, and then go to an arm it had not yet visited, without returning to an already visited arm where there was no more food. That is, it should search only arms it had not searched before. These researchers found that almost every rat used this optimal strategy. In the first experiment they recorded the number of arms each rat visited in its first eight choices. On the average, the animals visited 7.6 different arms in their first eight attempts. Clearly, the rats were able to distinguish the visited arms from those they had not visited before. And clearly, they avoided returning to arms where the food had already been eaten. The experimenters wanted to determine how the rats performed this task.

Olton and Samuelson found that they were able to eliminate certain strategies the rats might have been using to perform in the radial arm maze. For example, it became clear that the rats were not following a single sequence of choices. On one occasion a rat might visit two adjacent arms and then choose an arm on the opposite side of the maze. On the next occasion the same rat tended to visit the arms in a completely different order. It was also determined that the rats were not simply using their own odors or the odors of food to choose the nonvisited arms. In one study rats were allowed to choose a few arms and then were confined in the center platform while the experimenters doused all the arms with a strong masking odor. When the rats were released they still visited the arms they had not visited before. Similarly, in another study rats were confined after making a few choices and one of the previously visited arms was rebaited with food. Nevertheless, upon their release, the rats tended not to revisit the rebaited arm. If the odor of food had been controlling their choices, however, the rebaited arm should have been revisited.

Finally, Olton and Samuelson allowed the rats to choose a few arms, then confined the animals and switched the locations of visited and nonvisited arms. This was accomplished by detaching the arms from the center platform and then reattaching them in a different order. They found that the rats' subsequent choices were based on nonvisited spatial locations, not on the particular arms they had visited before. That is, if a rat had visited the northern-most arm prior to confinement, it did not revisit this location again, even though it now contained an unvisited arm. The experimenters concluded that the rats were performing this task by forming a complex memory of spatial locations they had visited in the past. Furthermore, it appeared that the rats were not using specific cues within the maze to retrieve their memories. This suggests that rats use more distant cues, with a basis beyond the maze, to retrieve their memories of spatial locations.

Olton and Samuelson's conclusion is supported by other studies using the radial arm maze. For example, Suzuki, Augerinos, and Black (1980) surrounded their maze with curtains and hung various objects on the curtains in different locations. They allowed rats to choose a few arms and then confined them in the center compartment. During the confinement they rotated the curtains so that the objects that had been in one location were located elsewhere. They found that this manipulation of "room cues" severely disrupted subsequent correct choices in the maze. This finding indicates that some animals peg retrieval of spatial memories on cues external to the target environment.

Similar findings have been reported by Balda and Turek (1984), who studied the caching behavior of birds. Birds were allowed to cache seeds on a sand floor and were returned 31 days later to the cache locations. Balda and Turek found that the birds were 90 percent accurate in recovering their caches, even though during the 31-day interval the experimenters had disrupted features of the sand floor that might have been used as retrieval cues. Apparently, the birds were using more distant cues to remember where the caches were located.

The foregoing experiments are important for two reasons. First, they suggest that some animals use complex spatial memories to keep track of food locations. Second, they are among the few studies that have attempted to isolate the specific retrieval cues an organism might use when trying to recall these spatial memories. Further work in this area should increase our understanding of how animals use memory processes in their natural environments.

Encoding Specificity in Animals

In this chapter we have seen the importance of encoding specificity for understanding retrieval success in humans. Numerous studies have indicated that the same principle applies to retrieval in other species. Among those doing research with animals, Norman Spear (1973, 1976) has been the strongest advocate for the encoding specificity hypothesis. Spear has stated that at the time of learning, an animal forms a memory that incorporates a wide variety of features or attributes. That is, the memory not only includes representations of the critical elements in the learning situation (such as the CS, the US, or the reinforcer), but also representations of both internal and external contextual stimuli noticed by an animal during the learning experience. Spear hypothesizes that for animals to perform what they have learned, they must first retrieve the memory of the learning experience. He states that the success of an attempt at retrieval depends on whether cues presented during testing match those that were present at the time of learning. The greater the overlap between learning and testing cues, the better the retrieval and the test performance should be.

Spear's hypothesis has been supported by experiments using a wide variety of training and testing cues. For example, it is well known that when animals learn a new response in one context, their later performance depends strongly on whether they are tested in the same or a different context. In one experiment conducted by Gordon, McCracken, Dess-Beech, and Mowrer (1981), rats were trained to perform an avoidance response in an apparatus that required them to run from a white to a black chamber. For some rats the training occurred in one experimental room (context A), while for others it occurred in a room (context B) that differed from the first room in terms of size, odor, lighting, background noise, and other features. Twenty-four hours later all rats were tested for retention of the avoidance response, either in the room in which they had been trained (groups A–A and B–B) or in the alternate room (groups A–B and B–A). Figure 10.7, which shows the results of this experiment, records each group's average latency to avoid after the signaling stimulus was turned on. Shorter latencies reflect better retention of the avoidance response. As you can see, rats trained and tested in the same context or room show excellent retention of the avoidance behavior. Those trained and tested in different contexts exhibit relatively poor performance. These results are clearly in accord with Spear's hypothesis. They are consistent with the idea that successful retrieval occurs when the cues present during testing are similar to those present during learning.

In addition to this kind of experiment, several studies have found that if animals learn competing responses in different contexts, they will invariably perform the appropriate

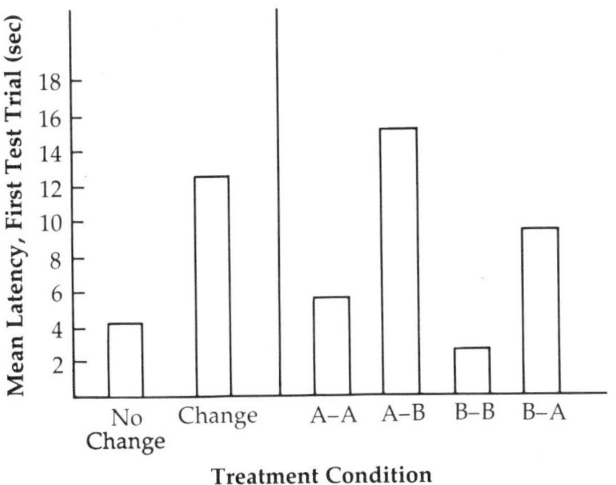

FIGURE 10.7 Mean avoidance latencies of rats trained in one context and tested in either the same (A–A and B–B) or different (A–B and B–A) contexts. (From Gordon, McCracken, Dess-Beech, and Mowrer, 1981.)

response when placed in one of those contexts. Recall that in Chapter 3 we described the *switching paradigm.* In switching experiments, animals discover that in one chamber (context 1) a particular CS (CS_A) is always followed by a US and a second CS (CS_B)is never followed by a US. In a second chamber (context 2) these contingencies are reversed. That is, CS_A always occurs alone, while CS_B is always followed by a US. As training progresses, animals begin to exhibit CRs only to CS_A when in context 1 and only to CS_B when in context 2. Similar results have been reported by Spear (1981) when animals learn competing avoidance responses in different contexts. Such results again are consistent with the encoding specificity principle. Even when animals have learned similar responses, the specific response memory they retrieve appears to depend on contextual stimuli. When tested in a given context, they tend to retrieve the memories that were formed in that specific context.

In our discussion of encoding specificity in humans, we saw that this principle is operative when experimenters manipulate internal bodily states as well as external contextual stimuli. If anything, this effect of internal cues is even stronger in nonhuman species. Overton (1966, 1972) was one of the first experimenters to demonstrate the state-dependent learning effect, working primarily with rats and other animals. He showed quite clearly that animals can learn to discriminate an internal state produced by one drug from an internal state produced by another drug. Using a variety of drug treatments, Overton showed that when animals learn a response in one drug state, retention performance is almost always better when they are tested in the same drug state. Animals in different states at the times of learning and testing often show very poor retention performance.

Similar results have been reported in experiments looking at naturally occurring internal changes. We know, for example, that several of our bodily functions (for example, hormone production and body temperature) change rather dramatically during the course of 24 hours. These cyclical variations in our biological functions are called circadian rhythms. In effect, the occurrence of such rhythms means that our internal states are likely to be very similar at a given hour from day to day. On the other hand, our internal states may be very different if we assess them at different hours of the same day.

Taking advantage of our knowledge of cyclical body changes, some experimenters have looked at what happens when animals are trained and tested at various times of day. In one such experiment, Stroebel (1967) eliminated from the environment all external cues that could be used to determine time of day. He then trained rats in a CER paradigm at one time of day and tested their retention after various intervals. He found that the best retention occurred 24 hours after training, when an animal's internal state should have been most similar to that during learning. Testing after shorter intervals (for example, 6 hours after learning) produced relatively poor performance. Like results have been reported by Holloway and Wansley (1973), using avoidance behavior as an index of retention.

All the studies discussed in this section indicate that the encoding specificity principle applies very well to the retention performance of animals. Apparently, an animal's ability to retrieve a memory depends strongly on the similarity of retrieval cues to the cues present during learning. When retrieval and learning cues are similar, the retrieval process seems to operate more effectively. In recent years, the encoding specificity notion has been used to explain a variety of retention phenomena exhibited by animals (see, for example, Spear, 1978, 1981).

Retrieval and Memory Construction in Animals

We saw earlier in this chapter that for humans, retrieval can serve as an occasion for updating or modifying a stored memory. Specifically, Loftus's studies indicate that if a human retrieves a memory and at the same time is presented with new information, that new information often becomes incorporated into the retrieved memory. In recent years, at least some evidence has suggested that animals also may modify their memories at the time of retrieval.

The first finding of this type was reported by Gordon, McCracken, Dess-Beech, and Mowrer (1981). As we saw in the preceding section, these experimenters began by training rats to perform an avoidance response in a distinctive room (context A). They found that when the rats were later tested for avoidance responding in a different room (context B), the animals performed very poorly. The experimenters interpreted this finding in terms of the encoding specificity hypothesis, suggesting that the rats performed poorly in context B because its stimuli were unlike the contextual stimuli from context A, which were represented in the animals' memory for training. In effect, rats performed poorly in context B because the stimuli in this context were not part of their avoidance memory.

In a subsequent study these experimenters again trained rats to avoid in context A and later tested them in context B. Before testing, however, an attempt was made to remind some of the animals of their avoidance training while in context B (the test context). Thus some of the rats were trained in context A, reminded of this training in context B, and then tested in context B. For the reminder, the experimenters briefly placed the animals in a small white chamber that was similar to the start chamber of the avoidance apparatus. The rats were then removed from the white chamber and were exposed to the stimuli in the context B testing room.

The rationale for this treatment was the same as that followed by Loftus in her experiments with humans. Exposure to the white chamber was used to encourage the animals to retrieve their memory of avoidance training. Retrieval was followed by an exposure to novel contextual stimuli in context B. The question of interest was whether this manipulation would cause the rats to incorporate the context B stimuli into their memory of avoidance training. If so, these rats would be expected later to perform well when tested in context B. That is, they should perform like animals that had been trained in context B originally. We would make this prediction because both the animals trained in context B and those reminded in context B should have context B stimuli represented in their memories for the avoidance experience.

The results of this experiment are shown in Figure 10.8, which shows the latency to avoid on the first test trial for different groups of rats. The first two groups (A–B and B–B) were both tested in context B. However, group A–B was trained in context A while group B–B was trained in context B. As you might expect, group B–B exhibited a much shorter latency to avoid, which indicates that they remembered the avoidance response better. The third group (A–B–B) consisted of the animals that were trained in context A, reminded in context B,

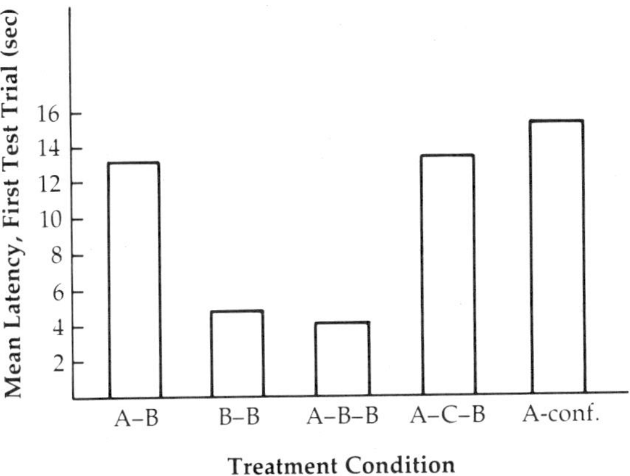

FIGURE 10.8 Mean avoidance latencies for rats in different treatment conditions. Animals trained and tested in the same context (B–B) performed better than animals trained and tested in different contexts (A–B). Note that the poor performance caused by switching contexts was eliminated when rats were reminded of training in the test context before testing (A–B–B). (From Gordon, McCracken, Dess-Beech, and Mowrer, 1981.)

and tested in B. These rats performed the avoidance response just as well as rats that had been trained in context B. Such a result is consistent with the idea that when these animals were reminded, they incorporated the context B stimuli into their avoidance memories.

The last two groups represented in Figure 10.8 were animals that were reminded of avoidance training but not in context B (group A–C–B) and animals that were exposed to context B before testing but were not reminded of avoidance training (group A-conf.). Importantly, neither group performed well on the test. Apparently, to perform well in context B, an animal must learn in that context or retrieve the avoidance memory in that context. Either alternative appears to ensure that context B stimuli will become represented in the memory of training.

In the past few years, a number of experiments have tended to support this conclusion (see, for example, Gordon, 1981, 1983). Animals that are reminded of some learning experience in a novel context usually perform later as if they had learned in that context. Apparently rats, like humans, are capable of incorporating new information into their memories at the time these memories are retrieved.

Summary Statements

In this chapter we dealt at some length with the nature of the retrieval process. We began by looking at how we scan through and retrieve information from short-term storage. We emphasized the experiments by Sternberg, which tended to show that short-term memory scanning involves a serial, exhaustive search.

In discussing retrieval from long-term storage, we reviewed a number of theories concerning the nature of this process. We found that these theories differ primarily in terms of the distinction they draw between processes involved in recall and recognition. We looked at a single-process retrieval theory, the generation–recognition hypothesis, and contemporary theories that propose that both recall and recognition involve searches through long-term memory. We saw that most of the current evidence tends to favor the contemporary theories.

After discussing these theories of retrieval we described the tip-of-the-tongue phenomenon and looked at its implications for understanding retrieval. We then discussed the encoding specificity hypothesis and the possibility that humans re-encode their memories at the time of retrieval. We ended the chapter by reviewing studies of retrieval in animals.

11

Forgetting

In chapters 8 through 10 we have considered how memories are formed, how memories are coded and organized in storage, and how we retrieve memories when we need them. Quite obviously, all these issues are important if we are to understand the way the memory system functions. Still, for most of us, these issues are important only in an academic sense, or only as a result of our natural curiosity about how things work. In our daily lives most of us remain relatively unconcerned about what a memory might look like or about the nature of searches through storage. There is, however, one question about memory function that has great practical significance for each of us. This, of course, is the question of why we forget.

It is safe to say that anyone who has ever learned anything has also forgotten. Forgetting is one of the most pervasive and perplexing problems we encounter on a daily basis. Imagine how different our lives would be if only we could always remember people's names, spouse's birthdays, and even what the perfect golf swing felt like the day we made it. Consider in your own life how many embarrassments, frustrations, arguments, and mediocre test grades you could have avoided if only you hadn't forgotten. Many of us have developed intricate memory devices or even invested money in memory courses to help alleviate such problems. Still, for most of us, forgetting remains an inevitable part of the way we function.

In this chapter we turn our attention to the phenomenon of forgetting, focusing on the various theories that attempt to explain why forgetting occurs. At the same time we will touch on how forgetting is studied in the laboratory and on the conditions that appear to promote the forgetting process. Before we address these issues, however, we need to be more explicit about nomenclature. "Forgetting" and "retention" are so commonly used that it is easy to overlook their more technical meanings. Thus, we begin by defining these terms as they are used by memory researchers.

Forgetting and Retention

How many times have you met someone at a social gathering and later been unable to think of the person's name? Similarly, have you ever been unable to think of the answers to some test questions when you had postponed studying for the exam until the last possible hour? If you have experienced either of these situations, you have probably used the term "forgetting" to explain your difficulty. Although such uses of the term are common, they are technically incorrect. In many such situations what we have actually experienced is a failure to learn or a failure to form a memory at the time an experience occurred. The term "forgetting" should be applied only in circumstances involving a memory that was previously formed, but which we are now unable to remember. We cannot forget what we never really knew or learned. The term "forgetting" always implies that we were able to remember an event at one point in time, but later we were able to remember the event less well.

Another common misuse of the term occurs when individuals form a memory but fail to show evidence of remembering because of some change in their ability or desire. For example, assume that a student who has spent hours preparing for an important exam learns, just before taking the test, of a death in the family. If the student decides to take the exam anyway, he may well perform poorly. Did the poorly performing student "forget" the material? Or did he simply not care or lack motivation to attempt to remember? This example suggests that there may be several reasons for poor individual performance on a memory test. Poor test performance does not necessarily imply that forgetting has occurred.

Having mentioned these common misconceptions, we can now present a more formal definition. *Forgetting is a decrease, over time, in the ability to remember a previously formed memory, which does not result from any sensory, motor, or motivational change.* Granted, this definition is somewhat cumbersome, but it does state clearly when "forgetting" should be used. By adhering to such definitions, researchers have been able to state more accurately when a given variable affects forgetting and when a variable affects retention test performance through some other mechanism.

Another term we will see frequently in this chapter is "retention." In general, when we use this term we are referring to the amount of information an individual remembers on a so-called retention test. Again, however, we need a more explicit definition. Most researchers say that *retention refers to the amount of test performance that is over and above some chance level of performance.* This definition compensates for the fact that an individual may sometimes answer at least a few test questions correctly even when forgetting is complete or even when no memory was originally formed. These correct answers will occur by chance if an individual tends to guess on a test. Thus, retention must always be assessed by looking at the degree to which test performance exceeds these chance levels. Figure 11.1 illustrates this point by

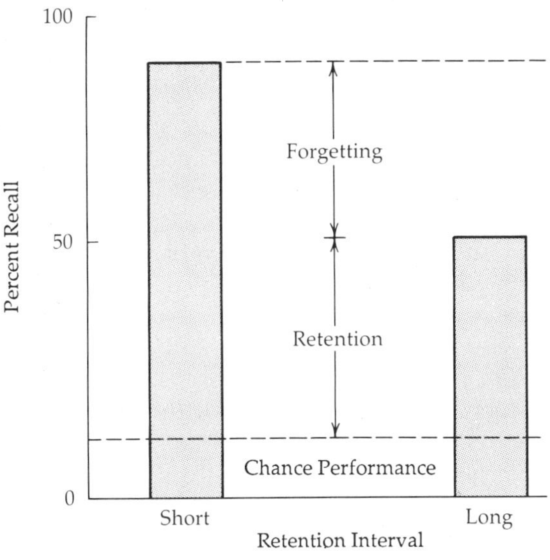

FIGURE 11.1 Schematic representation of what constitutes forgetting and retention in any study of retention test performance.

showing how retention test performance reflects both forgetting and retention.

Aside from clarifying the definitions of these important terms, we need to be aware of the kinds of laboratory situations used to study forgetting. As we will see, researchers have studied forgetting in two general modes. These are called *short-term retention* and *long-term retention paradigms*. These paradigms differ not only in terms of the length of time a subject must remember some event, but also in terms of the kinds of events a subject is usually asked to remember. In most short-term paradigms, subjects receive a single presentation of a stimulus set (for example, one or more digits, letters, or words). Then the subject is usually asked to recognize or recall those stimuli on a test, which normally is begun seconds after the original stimulus presentation. This kind of paradigm is used to determine why we forget when we are attempting to maintain information in short-term storage or in active awareness.

In most long-term retention paradigms, subjects are given several presentations of a stimulus set or several learning trials. In most cases, the stimuli in the set are interrelated to some degree, and the subject must learn to associate or relate the stimuli to each other. For example, a subject may receive several presentations of a paired associates list or a serial list. In such cases the subject is asked to learn either which stimuli go together or what the order of presentation is. Similarly, a subject may be given a story to read. The task is to learn the relationships among the words in the story so that the meaning of the passage becomes clear. After these stimulus associations or relationships have been learned, the subject is usually given a retention test, which may occur hours, days, or even years after the learning experience. The test itself normally requires that the subject answer certain questions that indicate whether the subject remembers the stimulus relationships originally learned. Obviously, this paradigm reflects the kind of forgetting we do after we have attempted to register a memory in long-term or permanent storage. This paradigm looks at the forgetting that occurs once material we have thoroughly studied and rehearsed is no longer being actively processed.

We will find that the factors that influence forgetting in these two paradigms are not always the same. We will also see that separate theories have sometimes been proposed to explain forgetting in these two situations. For this reason, we will discuss the theories of forgetting proposed for these paradigms separately. We begin by looking at theories of short-term forgetting.

Theories of Short-Term Forgetting

We have all had the experience of looking up a telephone number in a directory and trying to remember it just long enough to dial the phone. This is a relatively easy memory task as long as we are able to rehearse the number continuously between seeing it and dialing it. By constantly rehearsing the number, we can usually maintain it in memory for several seconds at a minimum.

We also know, however, that if our rehearsal is disrupted for some reason, we often forget the number completely. For example, if someone asks you a question in the interval between seeing and dialing the number, you usually have to look up the number again before you can make the call. In the present section we will discuss the theories that attempt to explain why forgetting occurs in this very common retention situation.

One theory says that you forget the phone number simply because you have ceased rehearsing it. This view, called the *decay theory,* states that a short-term memory has a limited life span and can be maintained only by constant rehearsal. Another view we will discuss is the *interference theory.* According to this position, you forget when rehearsal is disrupted, not because continuous rehearsal is necessary for maintaining the memory. You forget because the questions or inputs that disrupt your rehearsal interfere with your ability to remember the number. Let's now examine these theories in greater detail and look at the evidence that is pertinent to each view.

The Peterson–Peterson Experiment

To illustrate how decay and interference theories differ, it is useful to consider how these theories interpret a particular retention experiment. For this purpose we will concentrate on a classic experiment conducted by Peterson and Peterson (1959). Although we have described this study in Chapter 8, it may be helpful to restate the basic procedures employed in this experiment.

On each trial of the Peterson–Peterson study, subjects were read a consonant trigram such as "LRG." Immediately after hearing the trigram, they heard a 3-digit number such as "758." They were instructed to repeat this number and then to begin counting backward by 3's, aloud. To assure that the subjects kept counting, they were required to count in time with a clicking sound that occurred at a given rate. Thus, subjects would repeat "758" and then would respond "755," "752," "749," and so forth. This counting task was termed a *distractor task* because it was sufficiently difficult to prevent a subject from rehearsing the trigram presented originally. Peterson and Peterson then had subjects attempt to recall the trigram after retention intervals varying between 3 and 18 seconds.

You may remember the results of this study from our earlier discussion. Peterson and Peterson found that recall of the trigram decreased steadily as the retention interval was lengthened. Specifically, subjects almost always recalled the trigrams when a 3-second retention interval was used. However, when the interval was increased to 18 seconds, correct recall occurred only about 10 percent of the time. The question of interest is why forgetting is so rapid in this paradigm.

The Decay Theory and Its Interpretation

Peterson and Peterson (1959), along with J. A. Brown (1958), proposed a decay theory interpretation for this kind of data. According to this view, a representation that is registered in short-term memory can remain intact for only a short time. As soon as a representation is formed, it begins to deteriorate or decay simply as a function of time. As more time passes, the representation becomes weaker and weaker, hence more difficult to remember. Finally, after several seconds the representation will disappear altogether and it will be forgotten completely.

Although these theorists proposed that memory decay is inevitable, they did state that the onset of decay can be delayed by rehearsal. That is, it is possible to keep a representation strong or intact by repeating a stimulus to oneself over and over again. As soon as rehearsal is halted, however, decay of the representation begins.

The decay theory of forgetting is clearly able to account for the kind of result found by Peterson and Peterson. It simply states that the distractor task used in this study prevents a subject from rehearsing the trigram. Since rehearsal is blocked, the representation of the trigram decays over time. The longer the retention interval used, the more the representation decays and the more complete is the forgetting. Thus, according to this idea, the Peterson and Peterson result is a reasonably pure reflection of the rate of decay when rehearsal is prevented.

The Interference Theory and Its Interpretation

It is more difficult to provide a clear description of interference theory, since several versions have been proposed. Still, these different versions share some common assumptions. The first major assumption is that memory representations do not change in strength simply as a function of time. Once formed, a short-term representation can, at least in theory, remain intact indefinitely. Interference theories also assume that the forgetting of one representation is always due to the presence of other representations we form. In other words, it is the formation of nontarget representations that interferes with our ability to remember a given target representation.

The specific mechanism by which interference causes forgetting varies from one version of this theory to another. Some versions make the assumption that the short-term memory store has a limited capacity (see Atkinson & Shiffrin, 1968). Thus, if we have registered one representation in short-term storage and then another representation is formed, the second representation will tend to bump or displace the first from storage. Other variations of this approach simply say that whenever multiple representations reside in short-term storage at the same time, these representations tend to alter or distort each other. Thus, forgetting would occur because a target representation becomes altered or unrecognizable due to the presence of other representations also in storage. Regardless of the specific mechanism involved, however, all interference theories suggest that forgetting of a target memory always is due to the formation of other nontarget memories.

Finally, the interference theories presume that rehearsal is not necessary for maintaining the strength of a representation. Instead, rehearsal functions to keep us from forming new, interfering representations. The idea is that if you are rehearsing one memory, it is difficult at the same time to attend to new inputs from the environment. Thus, rehearsal prevents forgetting by blocking the registration of new memories in short-term storage.

The interference view of forgetting is also quite capable of explaining the Peterson–Peterson results. According to this kind of theory, subjects tended to forget the trigrams because of the distractor items they received. That is, by giving subjects a number and telling them to begin counting backward, the experimenters were, in essence, instructing subjects to enter number representations into short-term storage. The presence of these number representations served to interfere with the memory of the trigram, which was also being held in short-term storage. Forgetting increased over longer retention intervals because longer intervals involved more counting, and more counting led to a greater number of interfering memories. In effect, this view holds that distractor tasks do more than simply prevent rehearsal. Such tasks can promote the formation of interfering representations, as well.

Evidence Pertinent to the Decay and Interference Theories

Since both decay and interference theories are capable of accounting for simple, short-term forgetting, several researchers have attempted to develop paradigms to distinguish between these points of view. Most of these studies have focused on the question of whether forgetting is caused by the passage of time, per se, or whether it is due to events that occur during the passage of time. One paradigm developed to answer this question is called the *probe-digit procedure.*

The probe-digit paradigm The probe-digit procedure was initially used in a study by Waugh and Norman (1965), who presented subjects with a long list of digits over an interval of several seconds. The final digit in the list was accompanied by a tone. The final signaled digit was called a probe digit because in every case it had occurred earlier in the digit list. For example, subjects might receive the list "7, 3, 9, 4, 6, 9, 7, 2, 1, 8, 5, 0, 4," with the last "4" being signaled by a tone, which served to flag the last digit in the list and to indicate that this number had appeared earlier in the same list. The subject's task was to attempt to remember the digit that had come after the probe in its earlier appearance on the list. Thus, in the list of digits presented above, the correct answer would be "6," since "4" was the probe digit and "6" followed that probe when it first occurred in the list.

Using the probe-digit procedure, it is possible to vary the number of digits that intervene between the probe and its earlier appearance on the list. In the example above, there were 8 digits between the original appearance of "4" and its final appearance as the probe. If, however, we were to vary the original position of "4" in the list, we could evaluate the effect of the number of intervening digits on a subject's ability to remember. This manipulation provides some assessment of how forgetting is influenced by changes in the number of interfering items.

It is also possible using the probe-digit paradigm to vary independently the passage of time between a probe and its prior appearance. To do this, Waugh and Norman sometimes presented the list fast (4 digits per second) and sometimes at a slower rate (1 digit per second). Thus, it is possible to present a list so that the same number of intervening items occurs on each trial, but the time that elapses between a probe and its first appearance differs as a function of speed of presentation.

By manipulating both the position of a probe digit and the rate of presentation, Waugh and Norman made an interesting discovery. Correct recall depended on the number of items that intervened between the probe and its earlier appearance. Recall was unaffected by the time that separated these events. Specifically, subjects' recall performance was poorer, the greater the number of digits that intervened between the probe and its earlier appearance. If on two trials, however, the number of intervening digits was the same, but the rate of digit presentation differed, recall was unaffected by the second variable—that is, the difference in presentation rate. These data suggest that short-term forgetting is controlled by the number of interfering items a subject must keep in short-term storage. The data also indicate that the simple passage of time has little influence on forgetting. Thus, the Waugh and Norman results clearly favor an interference explanation of forgetting over a decay approach.

A modified distractor paradigm In the Peterson and Peterson experiment, subjects were distracted from rehearsing the items to be retained by having to repeat digits aloud. Problems with the interpretation of the Petersons' findings arose because of the nature of the distractor task. It was clear that saying digits led to forgetting of the test material, which consisted of consonant trigrams. However, it was not clear why the distractor produced forgetting. On the one hand, some researchers claimed that the distractor task simply blocked rehearsal and allowed the trigram memory to decay. Others, however, saw the distractor as providing new memories that could have interfered with the trigram memory.

In an effort to circumvent the interpretive problems inherent in the Peterson–Peterson experiment, Judith Reitman attempted to develop a modified distractor paradigm (see Reitman, 1971, 1974). Basically, Reitman's idea was to find a distractor task that would effectively block rehearsal but would not produce interference with the target memory. She reasoned that if such a task could be developed, it would be possible to determine whether memories do, in fact, decay in the absence of rehearsal or whether forgetting occurs only when interfering memories are formed.

In effect, Reitman's earliest experiments were very similar to the one conducted by Peterson and Peterson. She presented her subjects with a set of 3 words and asked for recall after 15 seconds. However, she filled the retention intervals with a distractor activity featuring "white noise" (a mixture of tone frequencies that sounds like static or a rushing of air). Occasionally embedded in this noise was a pure tone signal. Subjects were instructed to monitor the noise during each interval and to press a button whenever the signal occurred. Detection of the tone was so difficult that subjects were able to perceive it only about half the time.

Reitman reasoned that the difficulty of her distractor task would make it almost impossible to rehearse the words and still detect the tones successfully. She also reasoned that this signal detection task should provide little in the way of interference for the word memory. Thus, the use of such a distractor should help to reveal whether short-term forgetting occurs because of decay or whether there must be interfering items. Her results were very clear. Under this paradigm, subjects showed almost no evidence of forgetting even when a retention interval of 15 seconds was used. Using a similar paradigm, Shiffrin (1973) found little forgetting over intervals as long as 40 seconds. These results indicate that the disruption of rehearsal per se does not inevitably lead to forgetting. That is, distractors seem to cause forgetting only if they produce interfering memories. Such results strongly support the interference theory of short-term forgetting and seem to provide overwhelming evidence against the notion that short-term memories decay. In reality, however, the results are not as clear as Reitman had initially hoped.

Reitman herself became concerned about the validity of the foregoing interpretation of her findings. She wondered whether her distractor task had, in fact, blocked rehearsal completely. In a detailed analysis of each subject's data, she found that some subjects had performed rather poorly on the signal detection task, suggesting that they might have been rehearsing the words during the retention interval. She also became concerned that her memory task might have been too easy, so that if subjects had rehearsed even briefly, they would have been able to recall the words.

To compensate for these potential problem areas of the first experiment, Reitman (1974) conducted a study in which the difficulty of the task was increased by using sets of 5 words rather than 3. She also established stringent criteria for determining when subjects might be rehearsing during the distractor task and when they might not. Using these more stringent criteria, she found that only about 20 percent of her subjects actually seemed *not* to rehearse during the distractor task. Thus, she used only the data from the nonrehearsing subjects. The results of this study were not nearly as clear as those from the initial experiment. Reitman found that subjects did show evidence of forgetting, even when the distractor task was noninterfering. That is, at least some forgetting did appear to result from blocking rehearsal per se. On the other hand, Reitman found much less forgetting than Peterson and Peterson had reported earlier. In the 1959 experiment, subjects averaged only 15–20 percent recall after a 15-second retention interval. Reitman found that subjects averaged about 75 percent recall over the same interval.

Based on painstaking analysis, Reitman reached an important conclusion. Some short-term forgetting does appear to result solely from decay when rehearsal is blocked. However, much of the forgetting found by Peterson and Peterson appears to have been due to the interfering effects of their distractor, not to decay of the original memory. Thus, interference appears to be the primary determinant of short-term forgetting, although memory decay also may contribute to this process.

The role of proactive interference in short-term forgetting To this point, we have discussed the possibility that new memories formed during a retention interval may interfere with the retention of another memory formed earlier. This type of interference is called *retroactive interference* (RI), to reflect the capacity of newly formed memories to block the retention of memories previously formed. However, another type of interference appears to play a role in short-term forgetting. This second type of interference is called *proactive interference* (PI).

In *proactive interference*, retention of a memory you are forming now is disrupted by memories you have formed earlier. Assume that I give you a trigram to remember. We have already seen that if you are asked to say digits or letters during the retention interval, these new memories can interfere with your ability to recall the trigram. This is an example of retroactive interference. Assume now that I present you with several trigrams and afterward ask you to remember a target trigram from the end of the list. We would find your ability to remember the target trigram blocked by the trigrams you heard first, and this is an example of proactive interference. Figure 11.2 illustrates the difference between these two types of interference.

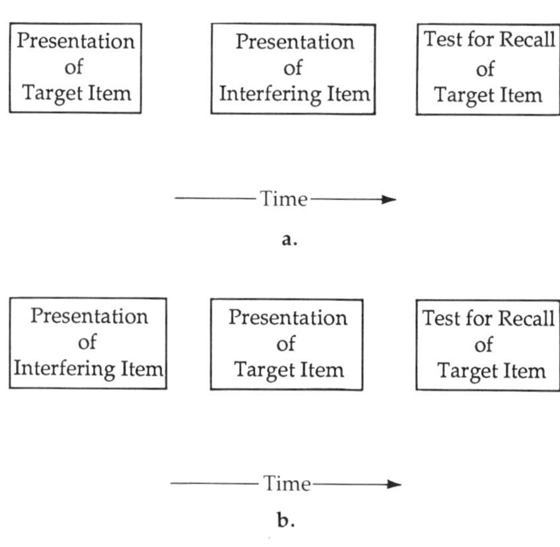

FIGURE 11.2 The arrangement of item presentations than can lead to (a) retroactive interference and (b) proactive interference in a short-term retention paradigm.

We have already seen that much of the forgetting in the Peterson–Peterson study was most likely due to retroactive interference produced by the distractor task selected by these experimenters. Others, however, have offered a rationale for suggesting that at least some of the forgetting may have been caused by proactive interference. Since Peterson and Peterson required their subjects to take part in numerous test trials, all subjects actually received several trigrams, each followed by a retention interval and a test. Thus, it is possible that some of the forgetting that occurred on later trials resulted from the memory of trigrams presented on earlier trials.

To test the foregoing hypothesis, Keppel and Underwood (1962) replicated the Peterson–Peterson experiment and noted the forgetting each subject showed from one trial to the next. Figure 11.3 shows the subjects' forgetting curves on the first three trials. On trial 1, subjects showed very little forgetting even when the retention interval was as long as 18 seconds. On trial 2, however, recall performance was somewhat poorer. Performance decreased even more on the third test trial. This finding supports the idea that the more prior trigrams a subject has heard, the less able

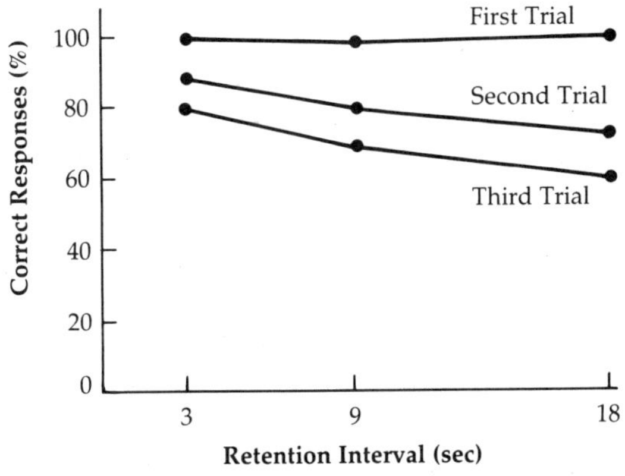

FIGURE 11.3 Short-term retention of a trigram as a joint function of retention interval and number of preceding trials. (From Keppel and Underwood, 1962.)

the subject will be to recall a trigram being heard now. This work, then, indicates that proactive interference can produce short-term forgetting, and it further suggests that such effects were probably at work in the Peterson–Peterson experiment (see also, Loess, 1964).

Since the early experiment by Keppel and Underwood, several studies have confirmed that proactive interference can influence short-term retention. Many of these investigations have focused on the conditions under which such interference effects occur. For example, we know from such experiments that the occurrence of proactive interference depends critically on the interval that separates the presentation of interfering and target items. If a subject is given a target trigram to remember and the presentation occurs very shortly after other trigrams have been seen, interference effects are often very strong. However, if a target trigram occurs more than a few minutes after other trigrams have been presented, the initial trigrams produce very little proactive interference (see, for example, Kincaid & Wickens, 1970). Thus, for proactive interference to block retention, interfering and target items must occur close together in time.

Aside from the temporal interval variable, another factor influencing the degree of proactive interference is the similarity of the interfering and the target items. This was demonstrated convincingly by Wickens (1972), who has conducted "release from PI" experiments. These studies consisted of trials in which subjects were presented with a common word, directed to count backward for 20 seconds, then asked to recall the word. One group of subjects (control group) received four such trials, all involving words belonging to the same conceptual category (for example, names of animals). A second group of subjects (shift group) received the same words as the control group of trials 1–3. However, on trial 4, these subjects received a word from a totally different conceptual category (for example, a type of fruit). Figure 11.4 shows the kinds of results these manipulations produce.

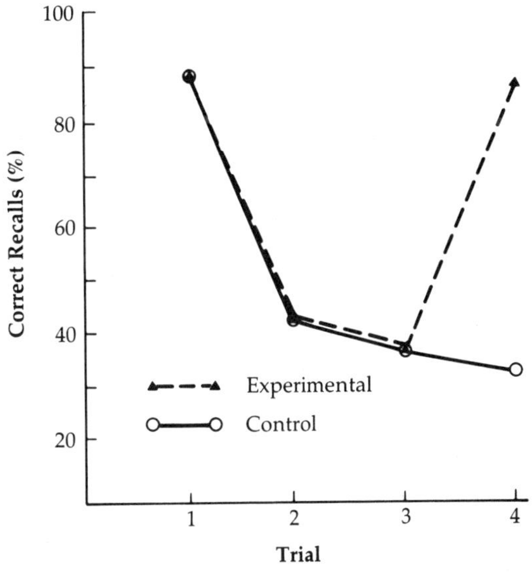

FIGURE 11.4 An example of release from PI. Both control and experimental subjects receive stimuli belonging to the same conceptual category on trials 1 through 3. On trial 4, the experimental subjects are switched to a different category, while the control subjects are not. (From Wickens, 1972.)

First, note the performance of the control subjects in Figure 11.4. These subjects show excellent recall on trial 1, but their performance declines steadily on the subsequent trials. This result is similar to that reported by Keppel and Underwood—performance deteriorates as more and more prior words are accumulated. In effect, proactive interference builds up as more trials occur and this buildup produces progressively more forgetting. We can note the same phenomenon in the first three trials of the shift subjects. However, on trial 4, the shift subjects show a clear *increase* in recall performance. It is as if the effects of proactive interference are lifted or released. Clearly, the detrimental effects of proactive interference are reduced substantially when a subject is shifted to a target word that is dissimilar to the words presented previously. Such results indicate that proactive interference depends on the similarity of the interfering and the target items. When these items are dissimilar, the effects of proactive interference are lessened. It is interesting to note that retroactive interference also appears to depend on the similarity of the target and interfering items (see, for example, Reitman, 1971).

Conclusions Virtually all the studies we have reviewed point to the importance of interference in the production of short-term forgetting. It is clear from these experiments that if a subject is given a target item to remember, the subject's retention can be diminished by either previously presented items (PI) or by items presented during the retention interval (RI). What is less clear is the degree to which memory decay might also contribute to the forgetting process. The studies conducted by Reitman are probably the most informative with respect to the role of decay. These studies suggest that at least some of our short-term forgetting may result from the deterioration of a memory representation over time. Still, even these experiments lead us to conclude that decay contributes only minimally to short-term forgetting. The predominant factor in such forgetting appears to be the presence of interfering memory representations.

Theories of Long-Term Forgetting

We all know that once a memory has been thoroughly rehearsed, encoded, and stored, it may be retrievable years or even decades later. Thus, at least some of our long-term memories are extremely resistant to forgetting. Still, a memory that is well encoded will not necessarily persist. Over long periods of time many of our memories become more and more difficult to retrieve. Other memories may be retrieved very easily minutes after being formed, and totally forgotten in a matter of hours.

Now we will examine some of the theories that attempt to explain how encoded and stored memories are forgotten over time. We will see in this discussion that most theorists have accounted for long-term forgetting by proposing an interference mechanism. For this reason, much of our discussion will focus on how interference theories have evolved over the years. In addition to this analysis of interference theories, however, we will look at the notion that most instances of forgetting, even those resulting from interference, are best viewed as examples of retrieval failure. That is, forgetting may not be due to the actual absence of a memory; rather, it may result from our inability to retrieve a memory that is still present in storage.

The Role of Interference in Long-Term Forgetting

In 1957, Underwood stated: "I know of no one who seriously maintains that interference among tasks is of no consequence in the production of forgetting." In many senses this is a very conservative statement. Historically, most theorists have gone much further than simply believing that interference contributes to forgetting. Many have assumed that virtually all long-term forgetting can be explained on the basis of various interference effects. This belief has been so strong that few researchers have seriously entertained the idea that long-term memories decay or deteriorate over time. It has been generally assumed that once encoded and stored, a memory resides permanently in long-term storage. Such permanence is threatened only by the formation of interfering memories. One reason for this view is the clear evidence that interference of the proactive and retroactive types (PI and RI) produces substantial amounts of forgetting. Although we have described both PI and RI effects in short-term retention paradigms, it is useful to consider how such effects have been assessed in the study of long-term forgetting.

First, in long-term retention studies, subjects are asked to learn a target list of verbal items, often a paired associates list consisting of either word or nonsense syllable pairs. To study the effects of PI or RI, subjects are also given a second (interfering) list of items to learn. In most cases, the interfering list is a paired associates list having the same stimulus terms as the target list. However, the target and interfering lists normally contain different response terms. Thus, if the target list is designated "A–B," the interfering list might be designated "A–C" (see Chapter 6 for a review of paired associates list protocols).

Figure 11.5a shows a typical procedure used for studying PI. Both the experimental and control subjects learn a target list (A–B) at the same time. Then, after comparable retention intervals, the two groups are tested for retention of the "B" responses from the A–B list. The only difference in these two groups is that the experimental subjects learn an interfering A–C list before learning A–B.

Figure 11.5b shows the usual retention performance of experimental and control subjects tested at different intervals after learning the target A–B list. First, note that even the control subjects show evidence of forgetting as the retention interval grows longer. However, subjects in the experimental condition typically exhibit a much faster *rate of forgetting*. Thus the PI effect, which results from the prior learning of A–C, does not show up when very short retention intervals are used. However, this interference effect tends to become more and more evident as the retention interval is lengthened. It is usually assumed that the control subjects forget because of subtle interference from items learned outside the experimental situation. Still, this forgetting can be enhanced significantly if specific prior learning is required by the experimental procedure.

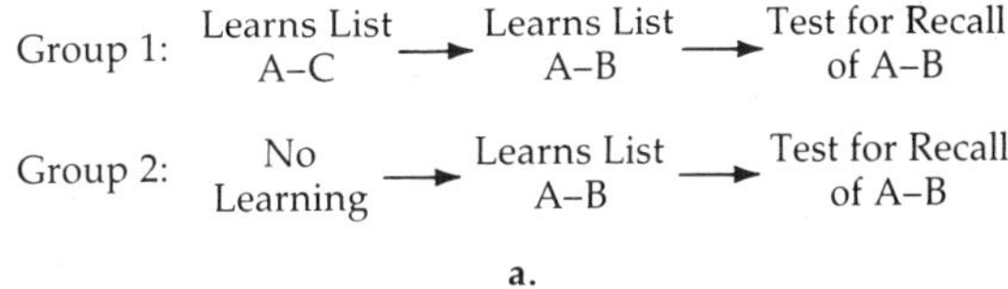

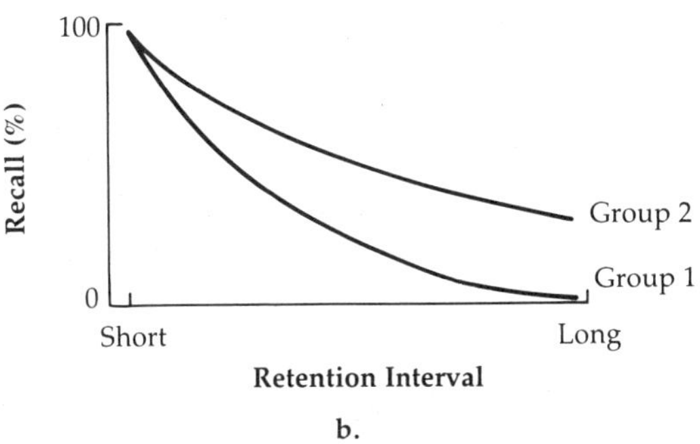

FIGURE 11.5 Example of a proactive interference paradigm (a) and typical forgetting curves found in that paradigm (b).

The usual procedure used to study RI effects is shown in Figure 11.6a. As in the PI paradigm, both experimental and control subjects learn a target A–B list at the same time. Then, after equivalent retention intervals, both groups are tested for retention of the A–B list responses. In this paradigm, however, the experimental subjects learn an interfering A–C

Group 1: Learns List A–B → Learns List A–C → Test for Recall of A–B

Group 2: Learns List A–B → No Learning → Test for Recall of A–B

a.

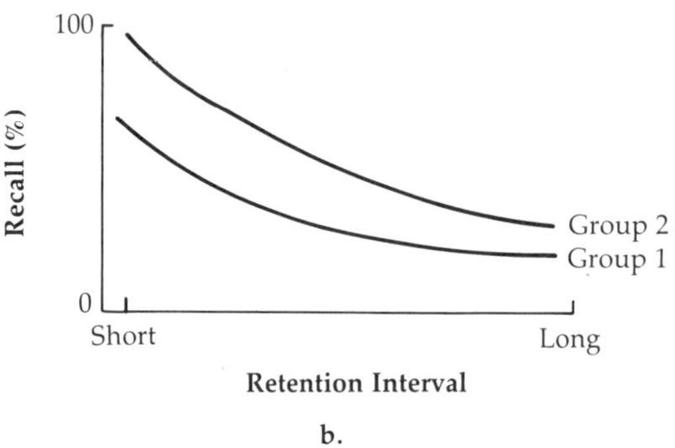

FIGURE 11.6 Example of a retroactive interference paradigm (a) and typical forgetting curves found in that paradigm (b).

list during their retention interval—that is, between the learning of A–B and the test.

Figure 11.6b shows the typical results found when this type of paradigm is used. Once again, the control subjects show evidence of forgetting as the retention interval is lengthened. The experimental subjects tend to exhibit much more forgetting than the controls when the retention interval is relatively short (that is, when they are tested shortly after learning the interfering list). This advantage of the control subjects over the experimental subjects tends to decrease, however, as the retention interval grows longer.

Numerous experiments using these interference paradigms have shown that PI and RI effects can be powerful, even when a target list is learned to a high degree. Thus, most interference theories have attempted to answer two questions. First, what is the mechanism by which an interfering list produces forgetting? Second, why do proactive and retroactive interfering lists produce different patterns of effects? We begin by looking at one of the earliest attempts to deal with these questions.

McGeoch's response competition hypothesis One of the first true interference theories was proposed by McGeoch (1932). McGeoch simply assumed that when learning a paired associates list, a subject forms associations between the stimulus and response terms. The strengths of these associations depend on the number of learning trials a subject has experienced. Now assume that a subject has learned both an A–B and an A–C list and is tested by being presented with the "A" stimulus terms. According to McGeoch, the subject has two responses associated with each stimulus term. Thus, at the time of testing, two responses will be aroused by the presentation of each stimulus term. These responses will then compete with each other for expression. McGeoch assumed that the stronger of the two associations would prevail at the time of testing. Therefore, the learning of an interfering list was thought to produce forgetting because it provided the subject with an incorrect association that might be as strong as or stronger than the target association.

This response competition theory clearly implies that the amount of forgetting produced by an interfering list should depend on the number of learning trials given on the interfering and the target lists. Such a prediction is supported by a number of experiments. For example, Briggs (1957) conducted a retroactive interference study in which he varied the number of learning trials on the target list. He also gave his experimental subjects different numbers of learning trials on the interfering list. Briggs found that in general target list forgetting was greater, the more interfering list trials he gave. He also found that he could reduce RI effects substantially by giving subjects a large number of learning trials on the target list. In essence, RI effects were enhanced when interfering associations were made stronger, but they were decreased by strengthening target list associations.

Although Briggs's data are consistent with a response competition view, this theory makes at least one prediction that appears to be incorrect, and it also is silent concerning some interference phenomena. The problematic prediction concerns test trials on which a subject gives an incorrect response. According to McGeoch, a subject should fail to give a correct target response only when an interfering association is strong enough to compete effectively with the target. This means that failure to give a correct response always should be attributable to an interfering response that is given in its place. Such interfering test responses are usually termed *intrusion errors*.

In one direct test of this intrusion assumption, Melton and Irwin (1940) conducted a retroactive interference study in which they varied the number of learning trials for the interfering list. They found, as Briggs did later, that forgetting increased, the greater the degree of interfering list learning. What is more important in the present case, however, is what Melton and Irwin discovered when they looked carefully at their subjects' errors. They found that very few incorrect responses could be characterized as intrusion errors from the interfering list. The great majority of test errors resulted from response omissions. That is, most errors were recorded when subjects had been unable to give any kind of response. Surprisingly, intrusion errors did not become more evident as more interfering learning trials were given. This means that increases in retroactive interference are not necessarily associated with an increase in intrusion errors, as McGeoch clearly predicts.

In addition to neglecting the anomaly presented by intrusion errors, McGeoch's theory fails to explain why PI effects should increase over time, while RI effects seem to decrease as the retention interval is lengthened. To account for these interference patterns from McGeoch's theory, one would need to assume that target and interfering associations change in strength over time. Yet, McGeoch assumes that the strength of these associations remains constant. Such an assumption appears to invalidate the response competition view.

The two-factor theory of interference The experiment by Melton and Irwin was important because it indicated that the forgetting produced by an interfering list cannot be attributed solely to intrusion errors. This finding led the experimenters to conclude that while response competition may account for some of the forgetting seen in interference paradigms, such competition is only one factor in such forgetting. They suggested that an interfering list also might be responsible for forgetting by causing a subject to *unlearn* the target list. In other words, when a subject first learns list A–B and then learns the interfering list A–C, it may be necessary to unlearn the A–B associations as the A–C associations are formed. Such a mechanism would help to explain why on some occasions subjects are unable to recall any response at the time of testing. Although subjects might realize that they are being tested on the A–B responses, the "B" responses may no longer be accessible in memory in association with the "A" stimuli. This idea that interference effects may result from unlearning as well as response competition has been called the *two-factor theory of interference*.

The notion that the learning of one list leads to the unlearning of another was soon incorporated by other theorists. Underwood (1945), in particular, attempted to elaborate on the unlearning process. He suggested that unlearning was analogous to the extinction process seen in Classical and Instrumental conditioning paradigms. For example, we know that when a CS and US occur together regularly, an association is usually formed. We also know that when a previously conditioned CS occurs regularly without the US, the prior association extinguishes. Underwood viewed the unlearning process as working on the same principles. A subject presented with an A–B list forms associations between the "A" and "B" terms. However, when the subject is later presented with an A–C list, the "A" terms (like CSs) are no longer followed by the appropriate "B" responses. This results in the extinction of the original A–B associations and the learning or acquisition of new A–C associations.

The use of the extinction analogy in interference paradigms represented an important step, because it enabled Underwood to propose that another phenomenon might also occur in interference situations. We have seen that when a CS–US association is extinguished, the association appears to recover spontaneously over time. Thus, Underwood suggested that after the extinction of an A–B association, we might also expect these associations to recover spontaneously. According to this view, if a subject learns A–B and thereafter learns A–C, the A–B associations will extinguish becoming unavailable for immediate recall. However, if time is allowed to pass after A–C learning, the A–B associations will recover and will become capable of competing with the A–C responses on a retention test.

In effect, the two-factor theorists used the unlearning or extinction concept to explain how target associations are weakened in an interference paradigm. In addition to this extinction process, however, they continued to rely on the idea that response competition occurs at the time of testing. Probably the clearest statement of how extinction combines with response competition was provided by Underwood (1945). Underwood suggested that once a target list has been learned, the kinds of errors seen on a retention test will depend on the number of trials a subject is given to learn an interfering list. If a subject learns list A–B and then is given only a few trials to learn A–C, the A–C associations will grow slightly and the A–B associations will begin to extinguish. Thus on a subsequent test, both A–B and A–C associations will be partially available and the subject will not be certain which response is correct. Therefore, some forgetting of the A–B responses will occur because of response competition. In such a case the subject's forgetting should often take the form of intrusion errors from the A–C list.

Now let's try to predict what will happen when a subject learns A–B and is then given numerous A–C learning trials. In this case A–C associations will become very strong and A–B associations will extinguish almost entirely. Thus, on a subsequent retention test, only the A–C responses will be available for recall. At first we might expect a subject to make a number of intrusion errors in such a circumstance. However, Underwood claims that this will not be the case. He states that when several A–C trials are given, a subject has the opportunity to learn to *differentiate* the A–C list from the A–B list. That is, the subject not only forms A–C associations but also begins to recognize that the A–C list is different from the A-B list. For this reason, the subject who is asked for the A–B responses at the time of testing has only A–C responses available and recognizes that these are not the correct responses. Instead of giving obviously incorrect responses, the subject chooses to give no response at all.

It is notable that Underwood's explanation for how response competition works accounts very nicely for the RI effects seen in the study by Melton and Irwin. These investigators found that intrusion errors tend to occur when only a few learning trials are given on the interfering A–C list. However, as more and more A–C trials were given, they found that RI effects increased, while intrusion errors actually decreased. This is precisely what Underwood predicted on the basis of his list differentiation idea.

From this description of the two-factor theory, you can see how both intrusion and omission errors in an interference paradigm can be accounted for. It is important to note, however, that this theory also accounts very nicely for the specific patterns of forgetting seen in both PI and RI situations. Recall that in an RI paradigm, forgetting of a target list is usually very pronounced immediately after the interfering list is learned (see Figure 11.6b). As time passes, the forgetting produced by the interfering list tends to diminish. To explain this pattern of RI effects, the two-factor theory states that just after an interfering list is learned, target associations are very weak due to extinction. Thus, there should be substantial forgetting of the target associations at that time. However, as the retention interval is lengthened, the target associations will begin to spontaneously recover. As a result, these target associations should become increasingly available to at least compete with the interfering associations at the time of testing.

The two-factor explanations of PI and RI effects are very similar. As we have seen, the interfering effects of a previously learned list are very small immediately after the target list is learned (see Figure 11.5b). However, this interference effect tends to increase as time passes after target list learning. According to the two-factor theory, this pattern is also due to extinction and spontaneous recovery. In this case, however, it is the extinction and recovery of the interfering associations that are important. For example, assume that a subject learns the interfering list A–C. Later, when the subject learns the A–B target list, the A–C associations will extinguish. Thus, if a subject is tested for A–B shortly after the A–B list is learned, the A–C associations will not be available to provide interference. On the other hand, if the subject is tested for A–B long after learning this list, enough time will have passed to allow the interfering A–C associations to recover. This means that after a long retention interval, A–C associations will be available to compete with the target associations on the test. This competition results in enhanced forgetting of the A–B list.

The two-factor theory represents an elegant explanation of interference phenomena. It is able to account for the occurrence of both omission and intrusion errors, and it predicts the pattern of RI and PI effects normally found. We have seen in past chapters, however, that just because a theory is *able* to account for a phenomenon does not mean that the theory always provides the correct explanation. It is always possible for a theory to account for some finding via incorrect assumptions. In the section that follows, we review some of the experiments designed to test the specific assumptions made by the two-factor theory.

Direct tests of the two-factor theory assumptions Some of the earliest tests of the assumptions of the two-factor theory were designed to look at the notion that learning one list leads to the extinction of previously formed associations. As we will see, many of these early experiments tended to support this hypothesis.

Briggs (1954) was the first researcher who attempted to chart the strength of one set of associations while another set was being learned. The technique he used has become known as the *modified free recall (MFR) procedure*. First, Briggs had his subjects learn a target paired associates list (A–B). Briggs found that subjects began the experiment with certain preconceived associations to the stimulus terms in his A–B list. Thus when some subjects saw the stimulus term "RAL" on the list, they tended to make a response such as "road" on the first trial ("RAL-road" sounds like "railroad"). As the number of A–B learning trials increased, however, these initial responses decreased and the correct A–B responses took their place, as shown at the left in Figure 11.7.

Next, Briggs had his subjects learn an interfering A–C list. The center panel of Figure 11.7 shows that as the A–C list was learned, subjects gave fewer and fewer responses from the A–B list, demonstrating that they had learned that in this phase of the experiment A–C responses were required.

The final phase of this study involved retention testing, and it was in this phase that the MFR procedure was used. In most interference

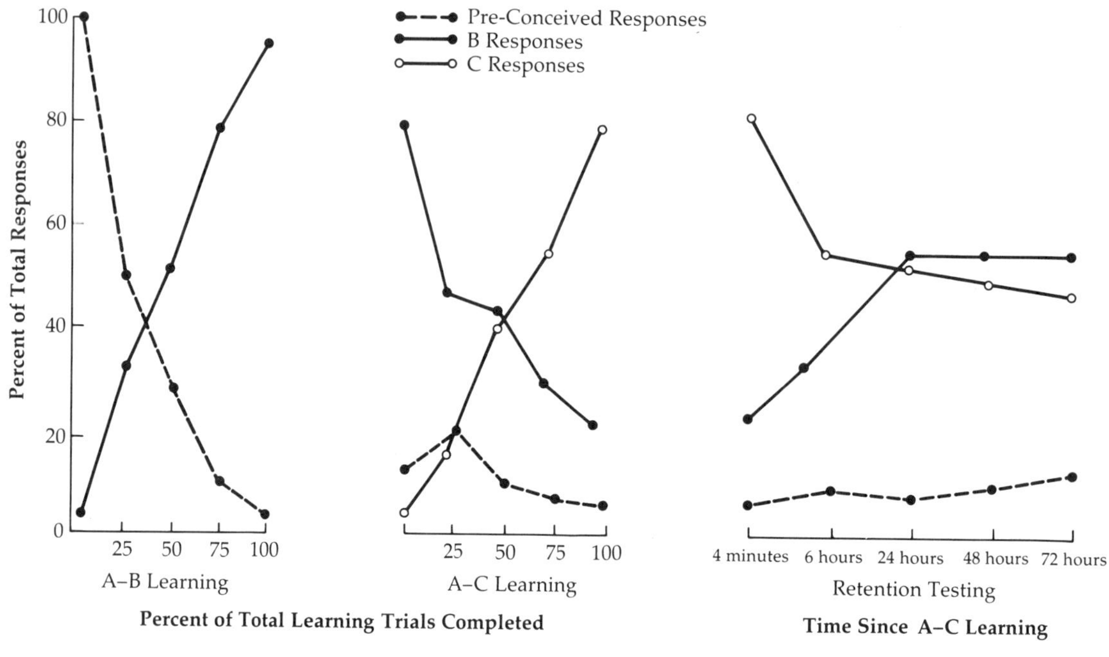

FIGURE 11.7 Results of Briggs's modified free recall procedure. (From Briggs, 1954.)

studies subjects learn two lists and then are told to recall the responses from one particular list. In Briggs's experiment this procedure was altered. He simply presented the stimulus terms, which were, of course, common to both lists. He then asked the subjects to respond with the first word that came to mind. Therefore, subjects produced either A–B or A–C responses without regard to list membership.

Briggs reasoned that if A–B responses had actually extinguished during A–C learning, no A–B responses would be available for recall shortly after A–C learning. Furthermore, if the A–B responses were susceptible to spontaneous recovery, they should become more available after longer retention intervals. His results (Figure 11.7, right) support these predictions. Subjects tested shortly after A–C learning gave numerous A–C responses and very few A–B responses. However, when longer retention intervals were used, the tendency to give A–B responses increased rather dramatically. This is precisely the pattern of results one would expect if the A–B responses had extinguished during A–C learning and spontaneously recovered later.

Even stronger evidence supporting this extinction–recovery notion came from a study conducted by Barnes and Underwood (1959). These researchers noted that Briggs's procedure did not prove that A–B associations had actually extinguished and become unavailable. Since the MFR procedure allowed for only one response to each test stimulus, it is possible that Briggs's subjects still retained both associations at the time of testing, but one association was simply stronger than the other. In other words, Briggs's results may show only a subject's tendency to choose one response over another when both are available.

In an effort to correct for this problem, Barnes and Underwood developed a procedure known as the *modified, modified free recall (MMFR) procedure,* in which subjects were given the "A" stimulus terms and then were asked to recall *both* A–B and A–C responses on the retention test. In this way, the experimenters hoped to determine whether responses from both lists were actually available to subjects at the time of testing.

The specifics of the Barnes and Underwood study were as follows. Subjects first learned an A–B paired associates list. Then, different groups of subjects were given various numbers of learning trials on an A–C list. Finally, all subjects were tested using the MMFR procedure. The results of this test are shown in Figure 11.8. When subjects were given only a single A–C learning trial, they recalled a number of A–B responses, but very few A–C responses. Subjects given greater numbers of A–C trials, however, showed a marked change in recall performance. As more A–C trials were given, subjects tended to give more and more A–C responses and fewer and fewer responses from the A–B list. This result is clearly consistent with the idea that A–C learning leads to extinction of the A–B associations. As more A–C trials occur, A–B responses tend to become less available for recall. This lack of availability strongly suggests that the A–B responses do, in fact, extinguish.

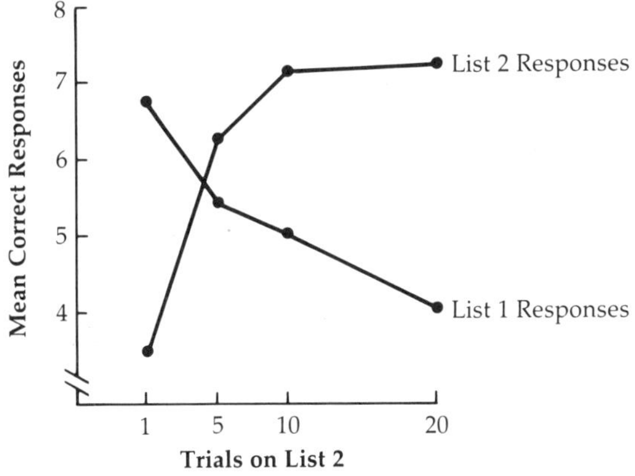

FIGURE 11.8 Results of the modified, modified free recall procedure. (From Barnes and Underwood, 1959.)

Despite these early triumphs for the two-factor theory, many later studies have raised doubts about the basic assumptions inherent in this approach. First, an experiment by Postman and Stark (1969) questioned whether the apparent unavailability of a target response proves that the response has been unlearned. In this experiment subjects learned an A–B list followed by an A–C list and later were given a retention test for the A–B responses. Instead of asking for recall of the responses, however, Postman and Stark gave their subjects a recognition test, consisting of the response terms that had appeared on the A–B list along with a number of distractor items. The subjects were asked to identify the test items that had previously been paired with the "A" stimuli when the A–B list was learned.

Postman and Stark found little evidence of RI using this type of recognition test. Subjects were clearly able to recognize the appropriate A–B responses when these were presented. Such a finding presents a problem for the two-factor approach. One must assume that if A–B responses are unlearned in an interference paradigm, these responses should be unavailable for either recall *or* recognition. This is obviously not the case.

Another problem that has arisen for the two-factor theory concerns the role of spontaneous recovery in interference studies. According to the two-factor approach, spontaneous recovery is almost entirely responsible for the increase in PI effects seen when retention intervals are long. Such recovery is also presumed to be the basis for the shrinkage of RI effects over time. Yet, several studies using the Barnes and Underwood MMFR procedure have failed to find the same kind of evidence for spontaneous recovery reported in that original experiment (see, for example, Ceraso & Henderson, 1965; Houston, 1966).

Although evidence for spontaneous recovery is still found in some studies, most researchers have noted that maximal recovery tends to occur within about 20 minutes after a second list is learned (Postman, Stark, & Fraser, 1968; Postman, Stark, & Henschel, 1969). Such a discovery suggests that spontaneous recovery may not be the mechanism by which PI effects increase over time. In most experiments, PI effects do not even begin to show up until an hour or more after second list learning. In addition, these PI effects usually continue to grow for hours or even days after learning the target list. Thus, the occurrences of spontaneous recovery and PI effects do not appear to coincide in time.

Response-set interference We have seen problems associated with both the extinction and the spontaneous recovery ideas that are inherent in the two-factor theory. In an effort to circumvent these problems, several researchers have suggested modifications to the two-factor approach. For example, Postman, Stark, and Fraser (1968) have proposed the *response-set interference hypothesis.*

Postman, Stark, and Fraser hypothesized that when a subject learns an initial A–B list, two processes are involved: formation of the appropriate A–B associations, followed by learning that the "B" responses in this list constitute a unique set that must be remembered as a set. In effect, subjects learn that when the "A" stimulus terms are presented, they must focus or concentrate on the set of "B" responses to find a correct answer for each "A" stimulus. It is hypothesized that subjects come to rely on a *response selector mechanism* to help them focus on one set of responses. This mechanism allows them to concentrate on one response set and inhibits all responses that are not a part of the appropriate set.

To illustrate how a response selector mechanism works, assume that a subject learns an A–B list followed by an A–C list. Postman, Stark, and Fraser propose that A–C learning will be difficult initially, because the subject's response selector mechanism is still "tuned" to the set of "B" responses. As trials progress, however, two things happen. First, subjects begin to switch the response selector mechanism to the "C" set of responses, causing the "B" set of responses to be inhibited. With set "B" thus inhibited, subjects can accomplish the second step in the learning process—the association of "A" stimuli with specific "C" responses.

Before looking at how the response-set hypothesis accounts for interference effects, it is important to emphasize that A–C learning does not result in the unlearning or extinction of the original A–B associations. A–C learning simply leads to the inhibition or suppression of a subject's tendency to focus on the set of "B" responses. Thus, after A–C learning has occurred, both A–B and A–C associations are still intact.

A second important feature of the response-set hypothesis concerns the nature of the selector mechanism. Once the selector has been switched to a given set of responses, it is thought to remain focused on that set for a period of time. During that time it is extremely difficult for a subject to switch the mechanism to another response set. In this sense, the selector is like a pendulum gathering momentum. Once it has started in one direction, it is difficult to change its movement until a period of time has passed and the pendulum is ready to move in the opposite direction. In much the same way, once the response selector has been switched to a given set of responses, it becomes difficult to switch it to another set until a period of time has passed.

To illustrate how the response-set hypothesis works, again consider the typical RI paradigm. According to this view, once the interfering A–C list has been learned, both the A–B and A–C associations are available, but the response selector is focused on the set of "C" responses. This means that for a short time after A–C learning, the "B" responses are being inhibited and subjects tend to give responses only from the A–C list. This explains why RI effects are so strong just after an interfering list has been learned. However, as time passes following A–C learning, it becomes easier for a subject to switch the response selector to the "B" set of responses, which he is being asked to recall. This means that RI effects should gradually diminish over time and this, of course, is what usually occurs.

The same kind of explanation is offered for the usual pattern of interference effects found in the PI paradigm. A subject learns the interfering A–C list first and then the target list, A–B. While the target list is being learned, the response selector focuses on the set of "B" responses and remains focused on this set for a period of time after A–B learning. Thus, shortly after A–B learning, a subject is unlikely to give any "C" responses and is, therefore, unlikely to show evidence of PI. As time passes, however, it becomes easier to focus the selector mechanism on either the "B" or "C" response set. This means that after longer retention intervals, there is an increased likelihood of A–C responses competing with A–B responses on a test. This increased response competition is presumed to result in increased PI effects.

Finally, the response-set hypothesis is capable of explaining why interference effects may occur using recall procedures but may be absent when recognition testing is used (see Postman & Stark, 1969). The response-set hypothesis states that a subject's inability to remember a target list is never due to "unlearning" of the target associations. Both interfering and target associations remain intact throughout an interference experiment. Recall difficulties result from a subject's inability to switch the response selector to the target response set at the time of testing. Postman, Stark, and Fraser suggest that simply by presenting the target responses, recognition testing exerts sufficient force on a subject's selector mechanism to refocus it on a given target set of items. Thus, recognition testing removes the inhibition temporarily attached to target responses, making these responses more likely when testing occurs.

In general, the response-set hypothesis does a better job of explaining interference phenomena than did the original two-factor theory. The principal advantage of the idea of Postman, Stark, and Fraser is that it does not rely on unlearning or extinction as a major factor in the production of forgetting. Instead, this approach views interference as resulting from a temporary inability to retrieve the appropriate response set at the time of testing. As we will see, this view fits easily with the more contemporary idea that much of our forgetting is due to retrieval difficulties.

Contemporary Views of Forgetting

In recent years there have been few attempts to elaborate on the early interference theories or even to formulate replacements. This decreased interest in interference theories of forgetting results from a variety of factors. First, most early theories of this type were proposed to account for PI and RI phenomena in traditional Verbal learning paradigms. As we have seen, however, the study of these traditional paradigms has waned rather dramatically in recent years. Most current research is aimed at elucidating complex cognitive processes rather than at exploring the rules that govern verbal associations.

A second reason for this diminution in interest in interference theories is that the applicability of these theories to forgetting as it occurs in the real world has been questioned. Doubts were first raised by Underwood, who was a major proponent of interference theories. Underwood noted that subjects will readily forget a single list of words learned in the laboratory even when no interfering list is presented. He reasoned that to explain such forgetting on the basis of interference, one must assume that verbal items learned and used outside the laboratory interfere with retention of a laboratory list.

To test this assumption of outside sources of interference, several researchers studied the issue of whether single-list forgetting is caused by "extra-experimental" sources of interference. For example, in some experiments some of the subjects were given lists of frequently used words, while others received lists of infrequently used words. It was assumed that the frequently used words, which were likely to have numerous associations in everyday life, would be subject to greater interference from outside the laboratory. Thus, according to interference theory, high frequency words should be forgotten more rapidly than words used less frequently. In general, the results of these experiments did not support the interference interpretation (see, for example, Ekstrand & Underwood, 1965; Postman, 1961; Underwood & Keppel, 1963b). Such studies suggest that although interference theories may be capable of explaining PI and RI effects in traditional Verbal learning paradigms, they may not fare as well in attempting to explain interference produced by experiences outside the laboratory.

A third factor that has led to a decline of interest in these traditional theories is the realization that forgetting often results from a combination of retrieval difficulties. In our discussion of the encoding specificity hypothesis in Chapter 10, we reviewed experimental data indicating that retrieval failures can occur whenever encoding and retention testing conditions are different. From such data it is now clear that forgetting need not involve either memory decay or specific interference effects. Forgetting can result simply from a failure to provide effective retrieval cues on a retention test.

This contemporary interest in retrieval failure as a cause of forgetting has led to an increasing desire to understand how memories are encoded and retrieved. Still, this current emphasis does not ignore interference as a source of forgetting. Just as Underwood originally stated, most researchers still believe that interference contributes to the forgetting process. Now, however, it is generally assumed that the forgetting produced by interference is really only one more example of retrieval failure at work. In effect, many view interference effects much as Postman, Stark, and Fraser (1968) did. That is, interference does not cause memories to be lost or unlearned. Instead, interfering items simply make it more difficult for target items to be retrieved without confusion.

This tendency to view interference as an instance of retrieval failure can be seen in the theorizing of Martin (1972). In an effort to explain interference effects, Martin proposed the *encoding variability hypothesis* (see Chapter 6). This hypothesis emphasizes the idea that in learning a simple association in a paired associates paradigm, a subject may view the stimulus terms in a variety of ways. For example, a subject may attend to the sound of a stimulus, its meaning, the characteristics of its letters, or even other words the stimulus term brings to mind. By the same token, a subject may encode a stimulus term in a number of different ways.

Since stimulus encoding tends to be variable, a subject who learns an A–B list followed by an A–C list may or may not encode these lists similarly. For instance, in learning list A–B the subject may attend to the sound of the "A" stimuli, perhaps associating the "B" responses with these sounds. Later, when list A–C is being learned, the subject may focus on the initial letters in each stimulus term and may associate each "C" response with one of these letters. If such were the case, one would expect little interference, since functionally the subject would be learning very dissimilar lists. We would expect interference effects to occur only when A–B and A–C lists were encoded similarly.

This kind of analysis illustrates how the study of interference has evolved over the years. Early researchers attempted to formulate general theories to account for interference effects of all types. These theories carried the assumptions that verbal associations are relatively simple and that forgetting could be understood simply by determining whether two lists contained similar stimulus terms. More recently, researchers have found that even the formation of a "simple association" involves rather complex encoding processes. Given this fact, a complete understanding of forgetting is probably not possible at present. Such a level of knowledge awaits additional research on the encoding process and on how encoding influences an individual's ability to retrieve.

Forgetting in Nonhuman Species

We have seen that studies of human forgetting can be divided into two distinct categories. Some deal with the forgetting of stimuli over short retention intervals, while others focus on the forgetting of learned associations over much longer periods. The same distinction can be found in studies of the forgetting processes in nonhuman, animal species. Likewise, different theories have been proposed to explain the forgetting of animals in these different paradigms.

Here we briefly examine the paradigms that have been used to study both short- and long-term forgetting in animals. We will note some of the major causes of forgetting in these paradigms, and we will describe some of the theories used to account for forgetting when it occurs. Our discussion will reveal striking parallels between the forgetting theories in this area and the kinds of theories used to explain forgetting in humans. We begin by looking at forgetting in short-term retention paradigms.

Short-Term Forgetting in Animals

Probably the most common paradigm used to study short-term forgetting in animals is the delayed matching-to-sample (DMTS) procedure. Recall that in this paradigm animals are presented with one stimulus (usually a visual stimulus) and seconds later are given two or more comparison stimuli, which include the original sample. The animal's task is to choose the comparison stimulus that matches the sample stimulus it originally saw.

Although the DMTS procedure is used extensively to study short-term forgetting in pigeons and monkeys, rats have been found to be particularly inept when it comes to performing this kind of task. For this reason, short-term forgetting in rats is most often studied using paradigms such as *the delayed alternation procedure.* In this task a rat is placed in a T maze and forced to enter one arm of the maze (in most cases the other arm is blocked). After a retention interval of several seconds, the rat is placed back in the start compartment of the maze and is given a choice of entering either arm. Reinforcement, however, occurs only when the rat chooses the arm that was blocked on the first trial. The assumption is that to choose the opposing arm consistently on the retention test, the rat must remember the arm it originally entered.

Although other paradigms have been used to study short-term retention in animals, the DMTS and delayed alternation paradigms are probably the most common. It is notable that in both these paradigms the same general forgetting curve is usually found. Animals normally perform very well when the retention interval is short, but performance declines steadily when the retention interval is lengthened. The actual rate of forgetting depends on the type of paradigm employed, on the species being tested, and on a number of other experimental factors. However, in virtually all cases, forgetting does increase steadily as the retention interval grows longer. Figure 11.9 shows some typical forgetting curves for pigeons in a DMTS paradigm and for rats in the delayed alternation procedure.

The forgetting curves in Figure 11.9 are plainly reminiscent of those found with human subjects. It is also clear that short-term forgetting in animals can be influenced by some of the same factors that affect human forgetting. For instance, we saw that human retention can be disrupted by presenting distractor items during a retention interval (RI effects). This manipulation also increases

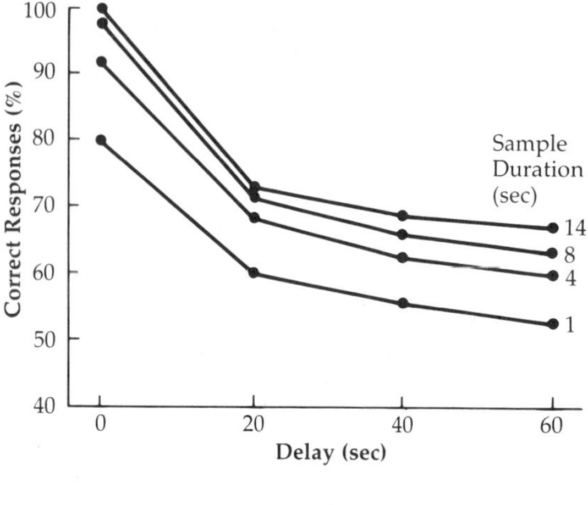

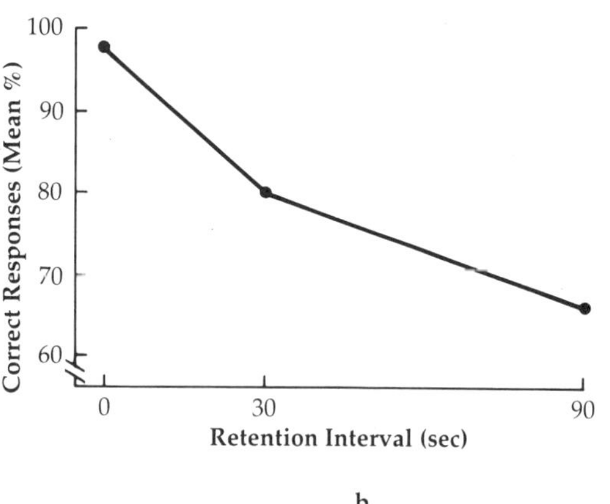

FIGURE 11.9 Examples of short-term retention performance in animals. **a.** Retention curves of pigeons given different durations of sample exposure in a DMTS paradigm. (From D. S. Grant, 1976.) **b.** Retention curve for rats in a delayed alternation paradigm. (From Feldman and Gordon, 1979.)

forgetting in the DMTS situation. Grant and Roberts (1976), for example, gave pigeons visual samples and then tested them for retention after 5 seconds. They found that forgetting could be enhanced significantly by presenting a white light to the pigeons during the retention interval. Similar results have been reported by a number of experimenters (see, for example, Tranberg & Rilling, 1980; Zentall, 1973). In a related finding, Etkin (1972) has demonstrated that monkeys remember much better in a DMTS paradigm when the retention interval is spent in total darkness (see also, D'Amato, 1973). One possibility is that such a manipulation may decrease an animal's distractions during the retention interval.

Not only are animals susceptible to distractions during a retention interval, they also are affected by stimulus presentations that precede a target stimulus (PI effects). To illustrate this point, consider an early experiment by Grant and Roberts (1973). In this study pigeons were confronted with DMTS trials of two types. On control trials, a color sample was presented and after a retention interval, two comparison stimuli were shown. On experimental trials, the pigeons received first one color stimulus (S_1) and then the sample color stimulus (S_2) shortly thereafter. After a retention interval, both S_1 and S_2 occurred as comparison stimuli and the pigeons were required to choose S_2. From the results of this study (Figure 11.10), you can see that forgetting of the sample was more pronounced when another visual stimulus preceded the sample presentation.

Results similar to those of Grant and Roberts have been reported when rats are tested in a delayed alternation paradigm. In one such study (Gordon, Brennan, & Schlesinger, 1976), rats received either a regular delayed alternation trial (forced to one arm, then given a free choice of arms) or a trial on which prior interfering information was given. The interfering trial consisted of forcing the rats to one arm of the maze (for example, the left) and then forcing them to the opposite arm (the right arm). After a retention interval, the rats were given a free choice test to determine whether they would respond by choosing the arm opposite the one they had most recently visited. This procedure led to pronounced forgetting of the most recently visited arm, in much the same way that prior color pre-

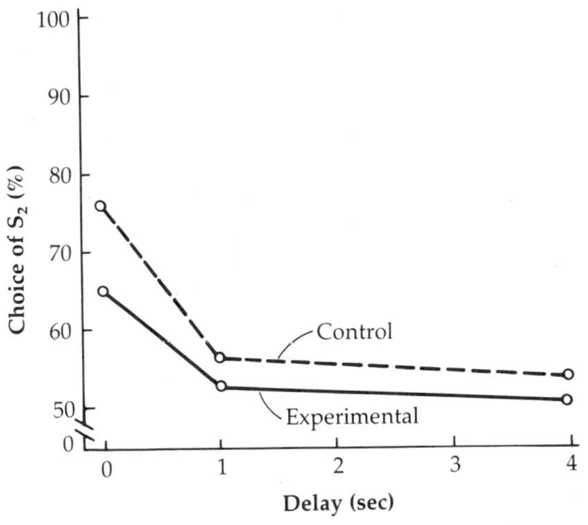

FIGURE 11.10 Example of PI in the pigeon's short-term memory. Control trials are regular DMTS trials, while experimental trials involve presenting an interfering stimulus before the sample (S_2). (From Grant and Roberts, 1973.)

sentations disrupted sample retention in the pigeon.

To this point, much of the work on short-term forgetting in animals has been rather empirical simply attempting to determine which variables influence the forgetting process. Probably the most influential theory of short-term forgetting has come from Roberts and Grant (1976). Although this approach, which has been called the *trace strength hypothesis*, was developed specifically to explain short-term forgetting in pigeons, the idea has served as a framework for the study of forgetting in other species.

Basically, the trace strength hypothesis states that when an organism perceives a stimulus such as a sample, the organism forms a memory trace of that stimulus in short-term or active memory. The strength of that trace or representation depends on factors such as the intensity and duration of the stimulus, as well as the number of stimulus exposures the organism receives. Once established, the trace begins to decay as a function of time. The animal's retention performance simply depends on the strength of the trace at the time of testing.

To explain interference effects, the trace strength model presents two ideas. The first is that when multiple stimuli are presented, an organism establishes independent traces representing each stimulus. The traces are called "independent" because it is assumed that the formation of one trace has no effect on the strength of another trace. Thus the notion that one trace can displace another from storage is rejected by this point of view. The second important idea is that an animal's test performance results from the competition of memory traces at the time of testing. If one trace is clearly stronger than the others, that trace will control test performance. However, if two traces are similar in strength, a nontarget trace may compete with a target trace and cause forgetting on a test.

In recent years Grant (1981) has modified his hypothesis to some degree. Based on studies of directed forgetting (reviewed in Chapter 8), he now assumes that animals can maintain the strength of a trace through active rehearsal. He also allows that animals may form representations that are more like instructions than actual stimulus traces. However, the hypothesis still places the burden of forgetting on a decay process, and this rather simple idea has proved to be very effective in explaining short-term forgetting in animals. Few other theories have been stated so explicitly or tested to the same degree.

Long-Term Forgetting in Animals

In studies of long-term forgetting, researchers have usually trained animals to perform a new response in a Classical or an Instrumental conditioning paradigm, under the assumption that the acquisition of a new response requires an animal to form some new association during training. After a retention interval, which may vary from minutes to days, the animal is tested to determine whether it will still respond in accord with its training.

In many of these long-term retention paradigms, animals exhibit forgetting curves of the very same kind observed with humans—that is, retention performance usually decreases steadily as the retention interval gets longer. In a number of circumstances, however, these normal forgetting curves fail to materialize. For example, it is quite common for rats to display nonmonotonic forgetting curves when they have learned an instrumental response based on negative reinforcement. The phenomenon was first demonstrated by Kamin (1957b) and has come to be known as the *Kamin effect.* Basically, Kamin found that if rats learn a shock avoidance response and are tested for retention after various intervals, they tend to show excellent retention on immediate tests and on tests conducted 24 hours after learning. However, if a rat is tested after some intermediate retention interval (for example, 1–6 hours), the animal shows substantial evidence of forgetting.

In a similar vein, some studies have reported that when rats have learned a new response, they tend to show cyclical forgetting curves for a number of days (Holloway & Wansley, 1973). That is, their test performance may cycle between excellent and very poor within a 24-hour postlearning period. Still others have found that after Classical fear conditioning, rats often show poorer performance shortly after learning than they do after longer retention intervals (see, for example, McAllister & McAllister, 1963). Such variations in forgetting curves have presented real challenges for theorists who attempt to explain long-term forgetting in animals.

One way to explain long-term forgetting in animals is to propose a simple decay hypothesis. We might assume that as soon as an animal has formed a new memory, that memory begins to decay or deteriorate as a function of time. This would, of course, explain why retention performance usually decreases steadily over time. Using this view, we might explain nonmonotonic forgetting curves as resulting from fluctuations in an animal's willingness to perform (for example, changes in motivation), not from any fluctuation in an animal's ability to remember. Although some theorists have suggested such a view (see, for example, Gleitman, 1971), we will find that most studies of animal retention give little support to the idea that memories actually decay over time.

A second plausible interpretation of long-term forgetting is an explanation based on interference effects. We should note in this context that several studies indicate that animals are susceptible to interference effects in long-term retention situations. For example, Spear (1971) reports experiments in which rats are trained on two conflicting responses in the same stimulus situation. Later they are tested to see whether they will perform the most recently acquired response. These rats exhibit much poorer retention than animals trained *only* on the most recent response. Similar interference effects have been observed by a number of experimenters (see Spear, 1978). Still, despite the occurrence of such interference effects, there have been few attempts to explain long-term forgetting in animals in terms of an interference theory.

Without doubt, the most influential theory of long-term forgetting is a retrieval failure hypothesis advanced by Spear (1973, 1978), who, as we have noted, has been a major proponent of the encoding specificity hypothesis in his work on animal retention. Spear has suggested that virtually all instances of long-term forgetting can be viewed as examples of retrieval failure. In other words, forgetting occurs not because a memory decays or becomes lost from storage but because animals often have problems in accessing the appropriate memory in a test situation. In some cases retrieval is difficult because the cues present at the time of testing are unlike the cues that were present during learning. In other cases, retention test cues may activate multiple memories, confusing the animal with respect to which memory is appropriate for that specific test.

To illustrate how this retrieval failure hypothesis has been applied, let's consider a few example situations. First, how might such a hypothesis explain the normal forgetting curve animals exhibit? At the time of learning, Spear believes that an animal encodes its memory in terms of the stimuli present in its internal and external environments. Shortly after learning, retention performance is good, because most of the cues that were present during learning are still present at the time of the test. However, as a retention interval lengthens, an animal's internal body state and its external context begin to change. Moreover, additional stimulus changes occur as time passes. Thus, after long retention intervals, retention test cues will tend to be very different from the cues present during learning. This mismatch of training and testing cues is thought to result in a retrieval failure and forgetting.

A second phenomenon that is amenable to the retrieval failure interpretation is the interference effect we find when an animal learns conflicting responses in the same situation. Spear asserts that when two such responses are learned close together in time, the memories of these responses will tend to be encoded using the same stimuli. Therefore, on a retention test the same cues that tend to activate one memory will also tend to activate the other. According to this view, interference results from an inability to retrieve one memory in isolation from another.

This interpretation implies that interference effects should be reduced dramatically if conflicting responses are learned at very different times or in very different contexts. Either of these circumstances should result in the two memories being encoded very differently, such that on a test, cues that activate the appropriate memory would not at the same time activate the memory of the conflicting response. In accord with this prediction, several studies have shown that interference effects can be almost eliminated if conflicting responses are learned far apart in time or in different environments (see, for example, Gordon & Spear, 1973; Gordon, Mowrer, McGinnis, & McDermott, 1985).

Finally, this hypothesis can account for most of the experimental results consisting of nonmonotonic forgetting curves. Spear states that most fluctuating forgetting curves result from predictable changes in an animal's internal body state after learning. Good retention is normally found whenever an organism's internal state is similar to the state that was present during learning. Poor retention results when internal fluctuations produce states different from the one present during learning.

Spear points out that the Kamin effect may be one example of a phenomenon that is based on fluctuations in an animal's internal state. At the time an avoidance response is learned, the hormonal state of an animal is very similar to its hormonal state 24 hours after learning. However, the hormonal state 1–6 hours after learning happens to be very different from the learning state. Thus, if the encoding specificity principle were accepted, one would clearly expect forgetting 1–6 hours after avoidance training. The same principle would predict improved retention 24 hours after avoidance learning. The results of several experiments tend to support this interpretation of the Kamin effect (see Spear, 1978).

Aside from being able to account for a variety of forgetting phenomena, the retrieval failure hypothesis draws further support from cueing or reminder experiments. Recall that a major implication of this view is that memories are not lost from storage, but are simply irretrievable at certain times. Studies have shown that numerous instances of forgetting in animals can be eradicated if the animals are exposed to reminder cues before retention testing. In most cases, reminder procedures involve briefly exposing animals to one or more of the stimuli that had been present at the time of learning. Animals given reminder cues before testing often do not show the same degree of forgetting exhibited by animals that had not been reminded (see Gordon, 1981; Lewis, 1979; Spear, 1978).

The mechanism by which reminder cues alleviate forgetting is not yet clear. What is clear, however, is that such cues could not be expected to work if an animal has forgotten because of memory decay or loss. For an animal to be reminded by a training cue, its memory of training must be assumed to be in storage. Thus, these studies indicate that most instances of forgetting in animals result from failure to retrieve a stored memory, not from a loss of memory from storage.

It is notable that the encoding specificity principle, which was developed to account for human retrieval phenomena, has such power in explaining the long-term forgetting of animals. At present, the retrieval failure hypothesis serves more as a research framework than as a bona fide forgetting theory. However, as more is learned about encoding and retrieval processes in animals, it should be possible to state this hypothesis in more explicit theoretical terms.

Summary Statements

The chapter dealt with theoretical explanations for forgetting. We began by looking at how theorists have viewed short-term forgetting in humans. We saw that one of the earliest views was that short-term memories decay over time unless those memories are rehearsed. In reviewing several tests of this hypothesis, we concluded that while some short-term forgetting may result from memory decay, most such forgetting is apparently caused by interference effects.

Next we looked at explanations for long-term forgetting in humans. Most of the discussion centered on the role of interference in long-term forgetting. We discussed McGeoch's response competition theory and found it unable to account for most interference effects. We also described the two-factor interference theory and looked at the various experiments done to test this view. We identified major problems in connection with the two-factor idea that unlearning or extinction occurs in interference paradigms. We ended this discussion by looking at certain modifications of the two-factor approach, such as the response-set interference hypothesis. During this discussion we noted how contemporary views of forgetting have evolved since the time of the classic interference studies.

The remainder of the chapter was devoted to a description of theories used to explain forgetting in animals. We noted that short-term forgetting in animals is most often attributed to some type of memory decay process. Long-term forgetting, however, seems to result from failures in the retrieval process, not from memory decay over time.

References

ADAMS, C. (1980). Postconditioning devaluation of an instrumental reinforcer has no effect on extinction performance. *Quarterly Journal of Experimental Psychology, 32,* 447–458.

ADAMS, C. (1982). Variations in the sensitivity of instrumental responding to reinforcer devaluation. *Quarterly Journal of Experimental Psychology, 34B,* 77–98.

ADAMS, C., & DICKINSON, A. (1981). Actions and habits: Variations in associative representations during instrumental learning. In N. E. Spear and R. R. Miller (Eds.), *Information processing in animals: Memory mechanisms.* Hillsdale, NJ: Erlbaum.

ALLEN, M. (1968). Rehearsal strategies and response cueing as determinants of organization in free recall. *Journal of Verbal Learning and Verbal Behavior, 7,* 58–63.

ALLISON, J. (1983). *Behavioral economics.* New York: Praeger.

AMSEL, A. (1958). The role of frustrative nonreward in noncontinuous reward situations. *Psychological Bulletin, 55,* 102–119.

AMSEL, A. (1967). Partial reinforcement effects on vigor and persistence. In K. W. Spence and J. T. Spence (Eds.), *The psychology of learning and motivation,* Vol. 1. New York: Academic Press, pp. 1–65.

AMSEL, A. (1972). Inhibition and mediation in Classical Pavlovian and Instrumental conditioning. In R. A. Boakes and M. S. Halliday (Eds.), *Inhibition and learning.* London: Academic Press, pp. 275–299.

AMSEL, A., & ROUSSEL, J. (1952). Motivational properties of frustration: Effect on a running response of the addition of frustration to the motivational complex. *Journal of Experimental Psychology, 43,* 363–368.

AMSEL, A., & WARD, J. S. (1965). Frustration and persistence: Resistance to discrimination following prior experience with the discriminanda. *Psychological Monographs, 79*(4, whole no. 597).

ANDERSON, J. R. (1976). *Language, memory, and thought.* Hillsdale, NJ: Erlbaum.

ANDERSON, J. R. (1978). Arguments concerning representations for mental imagery. *Psychological Review, 85,* 249–277.

ANDERSON, J. R. (1983). A spreading activation theory of memory. *Journal of Verbal Learning and Verbal Behavior, 22,* 261–295.

ANDERSON, J. R., & BOWER, G. H. (1973). *Human associative memory.* Washington, DC: Winston.

ANDERSON, J. R., & BOWER, G. H. (1974). A propositional theory of recognition memory. *Memory and Cognition, 2,* 406–412.

ARCHER, E. J. (1960). A re-evaluation of the meaningfulness of all possible CVC trigrams. *Psychological Monographs, 74*(10, whole no. 497).

ARDREY, R. (1966). *The territorial imperative.* New York: Dell.

ARMUS, H. L. (1959). Effect of magnitude of reinforcement on acquisition and extinction of a running response. *Journal of Experimental Psychology, 58,* 61–63.

ASRATYAN, E. A. (1965). *Conditioned reflex and compensatory mechanisms.* Oxford: Pergamon Press.

ATKINSON, R. C., & JUOLA, J. F. (1973). Factors influencing speed and accuracy of word recognition. In S. Kornblum (Ed.), *Attention and performance,* Vol. IV. New York: Academic Press.

ATKINSON, R. C., & SHIFFRIN, R. M. (1968). Human memory: A proposed system and its control processes. In K. W. Spence and J. T. Spence (Eds.), *The psychology of learning and motivation: Advances in research and theory,* Vol. 2. New York: Academic Press.

ATKINSON, R. C., & SHIFFRIN, R. M. (1971). The control of short-term memory. *Scientific American, 225,* 82–90.

AVERBACH, I., & CORIELL, A. S. (1961). Short-term memory in vision. *Bell System Technical Journal, 40,* 309–328.

AZRIN, N. H., & HAKE, D. F. (1969). Positive conditioned suppression: Conditioned suppression using positive reinforcers as the unconditioned stimuli. *Journal of Experimental Analysis of Behavior, 12,* 167–173.

BADDELEY, A. D. (1976). *The psychology of memory.* New York: Basic Books.

BADDELEY, A. D. (1978). The trouble with levels: A reexamination of Craik and Lockhart's framework for memory research. *Psychological Review, 85,* 139–152.

BADDELEY, A. D., GRANT, S., WIGHT, E., & THOMSON, N. (1975). Imagery and visual working memory. In P. M. Rabbit and S. Dornic (Eds.), *Attention and performance,* Vol. 5. New York: Academic Press.

BAKER, A. G. (1977). Conditioned inhibition arising from a between-sessions negative correlation. *Journal of Experimental Psychology: Animal Behavior Processes, 3,* 144–155.

BAKER, A. G., & MACKINTOSH, N. J. (1977). Excitatory and inhibitory conditioning following uncorrelated presentations of CS and US. *Animal Learning and Behavior, 5*(3), 315–319.

BAKER, A. G., & MERCIER, P. (1982). Manipulation of the apparatus and response context may reduce the US pre-exposure interference effect. *Quarterly Journal of Experimental Psychology, 34B,* 221–234.

BAKER, A. G., MERCIER, P., GABEL, J., & BAKER, P. A. (1981). Contextual conditioning and the US pre-exposure effect in conditioned fear. *Journal of Experimental Psychology: Animal Behavior Processes, 7,* 109–128.

BALAZ, M. A., CAPRA, S., HARTL, P., & MILLER, R. R. (1981). Contextual potentiation of acquired behavior after devaluing direct context–US associations. *Learning and Motivation, 12,* 383–397.

BALAZ, M. A., CAPRA, S., KASPROW, W. J., & MILLER, R. R. (1982). Latent inhibition of the conditioning context: Further evidence of contextual potentiation of retrieval in the absence of context–US associations. *Animal Learning and Behavior, 10,* 242–248.

BALDA, R. P., & TUREK, R. J. (1984). The cache-recovery system as an example of memory capabilities in Clark's nutcracker. In H. L. Roitblat, T. G. Bever, and H. S. Terrace (Eds.), *Animal cognition.* Hillsdale, NJ: Erlbaum.

BALSAM, P. D., & TOMIE, A. (1985). *Context and learning.* Hillsdale, NJ: Erlbaum.

BARNES, J. M., & UNDERWOOD, B. J. (1959). "Fate" of first-list associations in transfer theory. *Journal of Experimental Psychology, 58,* 97–105.

BARON, M. R. (1965). The stimulus, stimulus control, and stimulus generalization. In D. I. Mostofsky (Ed.), *Stimulus generalization.* Stanford: Stanford University Press.

Bartlett, F. C. (1932). *Remembering: A study in experimental and social psychology*. Cambridge: Cambridge University Press.

Bauermeister, J. J., & Schaeffer, R. W. (1974). Reinforcement relation: Reversibility within daily experimental sessions. *Bulletin of the Psychonomic Society, 3,* 206–208.

Baum, M. (1970). Extinction of avoidance responding through response prevention (flooding). *Psychological Bulletin, 74,* 276–284.

Baum, M., & Myran, D. D. (1971). Response prevention (flooding) in rats. The effects of restricting exploration during flooding and of massed vs. distributed flooding. *Canadian Journal of Psychology, 25,* 138–146.

Beecroft, R. S. (1956). Verbal learning and retention as a function of the number of competing associations. *Journal of Experimental Psychology, 51,* 216–221.

Beecroft, R. S. (1966). *Classical conditioning*. Goleta, CA: Psychonomic Press.

Beery, R. G. (1968). A negative contrast effect of reward delay in differential conditioning. *Journal of Experimental Psychology, 77,* 429–434.

Begg, I. (1971). Recognition memory for sentence meaning and wording. *Journal of Verbal Learning and Verbal Behavior, 10,* 176–181.

Bekerian, D. A., & Bowers, J. M. (1983). Eyewitness testimony: Were we misled? *Journal of Experimental Psychology: Learning, Memory and Cognition, 9,* 139–143.

Bellezza, F. S., Cheesman, F. L., & Reddy, B. G. (1977). Organization and semantic elaboration in free recall. *Journal of Experimental Psychology: Human Learning and Memory, 3,* 539–550.

Berlyne, D. E. (1963). Motivational problems raised by exploratory and epistemic behavior. In S. Koch (Ed.), *Psychology—A study of science,* Vol. 5. New York: McGraw-Hill, pp. 284–364.

Bersh, P. J., & Keltz, J. R. (1971). Pavlovian reconditioning and the recovery of avoidance behavior in rats after extinction with response prevention. *Journal of Comparative and Physiological Psychology, 76,* 262–266.

Bexton, W. H., Heron, W., & Scott, T. H. (1954). Effects of decreased variation in the sensory environment. *Canadian Journal of Psychology, 8,* 70–76.

Birch, D. (1965). Extended training extinction effect under massed and spaced extinction trials. *Journal of Experimental Psychology, 70,* 315–322.

Bitterman, M. E. (1964). Classical conditioning in goldfish as a function of the CS–US interval. *Journal of Comparative and Physiological Psychology, 58,* 359–366.

Bjork, R. A. (1972). Theoretical implications of directed forgetting. In A. W. Melton and E. Martin (Eds.), *Coding processes in human memory.* Washington, DC: Winston.

Bjork, R. A. (1975). Short-term storage: The ordered output of a central processor. In F. Restle, R. M. Shiffrin, N. J. Castellad, H. R. Lindman, and D. B. Pisoni (Eds.), *Cognitive theory,* Vol. 1. Hillsdale, NJ: Erlbaum.

Black, A. H. (1959). Heart rate changes during avoidance learning in dogs. *Canadian Journal of Psychology, 13,* 229–242.

Black, R. W. (1968). Shifts in magnitude of reward and contrast effects in instrumental selective learning: A reinterpretation. *Psychological Review, 75,* 114–126.

Blodgett, H. C. (1929). The effect of the introduction of reward upon the maze performance of rats. *University of California Publications in Psychology, 4,* 113–134.

Boe, E. E., & Church, R. M. (1967). Permanent effects of punishment during extinction. *Journal of Comparative and Physiological Psychology, 63,* 486–492.

Bolles, R. C. (1970). Species-specific defense reactions and avoidance learning. *Psychological Review, 77,* 32–48.

Bolles, R. C. (1975). *Theory of motivation,* 2nd ed. New York: Harper & Row.

Bomba, P. C., & Siqueland, E. R. (1983). The nature and structure of infant form categories. *Journal of Experimental Child Psychology, 35,* 294.

Bourne, L. E. (1982). Typicality effects in logically defined concepts. *Memory and Cognition, 10,* 3–9.

Bourne, L. E., & Restle, F. (1959). A mathematical theory of concept identification. *Psychological Review, 66,* 278–296.

Bousfield, W. A. (1953). The occurrence of clustering in the recall of randomly arranged associates. *Journal of General Psychology, 49,* 229–240.

Bouton, M. E., & King, D. A. (1983). Contextual control of the extinction of conditioned fear: Tests for the associative value of the context. *Journal of Experimental Psychology: Animal Behavior Processes, 9,* 248–265.

Bouton, M. E., & Swartzentruber, D. (1986). Analysis of the associative and occasion-setting properties of contexts participating in a Pavlovian discrimination. *Journal of Experimental Psychology: Animal Behavior Processes, 12,* 333–350.

Bower, G. H. (1961). A contrast effect in differential conditioning. *Journal of Experimental Psychology, 62,* 196–199.

Bower, G. H. (1972a). A selective review of organizational factors in memory. In E. Tulving and W.

Donaldson (Eds.), *Organization of memory.* New York: Academic Press.

Bower, G. H. (1972b). Mental imagery and associative learning. In L. Gregg (Ed.), *Cognition in learning and memory.* New York: Wiley.

Bower, G. H. (1981). Mood and memory. *American Psychologist, 36,* 129–148.

Bower, G. H., Clark, M. C., Lesgold, A. M., & Winzenz, D. (1969). Hierarchical retrieval schemes in recall of categorized word lists. *Journal of Verbal Learning and Verbal Behavior, 8,* 323–343.

Bradshaw, C. M., Szabadi, E., & Bevan, P. (1976). Behavior of humans in variable interval schedules of reinforcement. *Journal of Experimental Analysis of Behavior, 26*(2), 135–141.

Bradshaw, J. L. (1984). A guide to norms, ratings, and lists. *Memory and Cognition, 12*(2), 202–206.

Bransford, J. D., Barclay, J. R., & Franks, J. J. (1972). Sentence memory: A constructive versus interpretive approach. *Cognitive Psychology, 3,* 193–209.

Bransford, J. D., & Franks, J. J. (1971). The abstraction of linguistic ideas. *Cognitive Psychology, 2,* 331–350.

Bransford, J. D., Franks, J. J., Morris, C. D., & Stein, B. S. (1979). Some general constraints on learning and memory research. In L. S. Cermak and F. I. M. Craik (Eds.), *Levels of processing in human memory.* Hillsdale, NJ: Erlbaum.

Bransford, J. D., & Johnson, M. K. (1972). Contextual prerequisites for understanding: Some investigations of comprehension and recall. *Journal of Verbal Learning and Verbal Behavior, 11,* 717–726.

Breitmeyer, B. G., & Ganz, L. (1976). Implications of sustained and transient channels for theories of visual pattern masking, saccadic suppression, and information processing. *Psychological Review, 83,* 1–36.

Brennan, M. J., & Gordon, W. C. (1977). Selective facilitation of memory attributes by strychnine. *Pharmacology, Biochemistry & Behavior, 7,* 451–457.

Briggs, G. E. (1954). Acquisition, extinction, and recovery functions in retroactive inhibition. *Journal of Experimental Psychology, 47,* 285–293.

Briggs, G. E. (1957). Retroactive inhibition as a function of the degree of original and interpolated learning. *Journal of Experimental Psychology, 53,* 60–67.

Broadbent, D. E. (1958). *Perception and communication.* Oxford: Pergamon Press.

Brogden, W. J. (1939). Unconditioned stimulus-substitution in the conditioning process. *American Journal of Psychology, 52,* 46–55.

Brooks, L. R. (1968). Spatial and verbal components of the act of recall. *Canadian Journal of Psychology, 22,* 349–368.

Brown, A. S. (1976). Catalog of scaled verbal material. *Memory and Cognition, 4*(1B), 1S–45S.

Brown, B. L. (1970). Stimulus generalization in salivary conditioning. *Journal of Comparative and Physiological Psychology, 71,* 467–477.

Brown, J. A. (1958). Some tests of the decay theory of immediate memory. *Quarterly Journal of Experimental Psychology, 10,* 12–21.

Brown, J. S. (1942). The generalization of approach responses as a function of stimulus intensity and strength of motivation. *Journal of Comparative Psychology, 33,* 209–226.

Brown, P. L., & Jenkins, H. M. (1968). Autoshaping of the pigeon's key peck. *Journal of Experimental Analysis of Behavior, 11,* 1–8.

Brown, R. T., & Wagner, A. R. (1964). Resistance to punishment and extinction following training with shock or non-reinforcement. *Journal of Experimental Psychology, 68,* 503–507.

Brown, R. W., & McNeil, D. (1966). The "tip of the tongue" phenomenon. *Journal of Verbal Learning and Verbal Behavior, 5,* 325–337.

Bruner, A. (1965). UCS properties in Classical conditioning of the albino rabbit's nictitating membrane response. *Journal of Experimental Psychology, 69,* 186–192.

Bruner, A. (1969). Reinforcement strength in Classical conditioning of leg flexion, freezing, and heart rate in cats. *Conditional Reflex, 4,* 24–31.

Bruner, J. S., Goodnow, J. J., & Austin, G. A. (1956). *A study of thinking.* New York: Wiley.

Brush, F. R. (1957). The effects of shock intensity on the acquisition and extinction of an avoidance response in dogs. *Journal of Comparative and Physiological Psychology, 50,* 547–552.

Bugelski, B. R. (1938). Extinction with and without sub-goal reinforcement. *Journal of Comparative Psychology, 26,* 121–134.

Burkhardt, P. E., & Ayres, J. J. B. (1978). CS and US duration effects in one-trial simultaneous fear conditioning as assessed by conditioned suppression of licking in rats. *Animal Learning and Behavior, 6,* 225–230.

Burr, D. E. S., & Thomas, D. R. (1972). Effect of proactive inhibition upon the postdiscrimination generalization gradient. *Journal of Comparative and Physiological Psychology, 81,* 441–448.

Bush, R. R., & Mosteller, F. (1951). A mathematical model for simple learning. *Psychological Review, 58,* 313–323.

Butler, R. A. (1954). Incentive conditions that influence visual exploration. *Journal of Experimental Psychology, 48,* 19–23.

Calhoun, W. H. (1971). Central nervous system stimulants. In E. Furchtgott (Ed.), *Pharmacological and biophysical agents and behavior.* New York: Academic Press.

CAMP, D. S., RAYMOND, G. A., & CHURCH, R. M. (1967). Temporal relationship between response and punishment. *Journal of Experimental Psychology, 74,* 114–123.

CAMPBELL, P. E., BATSCHE, C. J., & BATSCHE, G. M. (1972). Spaced-trials reward magnitude effects in the rat: Single versus multiple food pellets. *Journal of Comparative and Physiological Psychology, 81,* 360–364.

CAMPBELL, B. A., & KRAELING, D. (1953). Response strength as a function of drive level and amount of drive reduction. *Journal of Experimental Psychology, 45,* 97–101.

CAPALDI, E. D. (1971). Simultaneous shifts in reward magnitude and the level of food deprivation. *Psychonomic Science, 23,* 357–359.

CAPALDI, E. J. (1967). A sequential hypothesis of instrumental learning. In K. W. Spence and J. T. Spence (Eds.), *The psychology of learning and motivation,* Vol. 1. New York: Academic Press, pp. 67–156.

CAPALDI, E. J. (1971). Memory and learning: A sequential viewpoint. In W. K. Honig and P. H. R. James (Eds.), *Animal memory.* New York: Academic Press, pp. 111–154.

CAPALDI, E. J. (1978). Effects of schedule and delay of reinforcement on acquisition speed. *Animal Learning and Behavior, 6,* 330–334.

CAPALDI, E. J., & BOWEN, J. N. (1964). Delay of reward and goal box confinement time in extinction. *Psychonomic Science, 1,* 141–142.

CAPALDI, E. J., & KASSOVER, K. (1970). Sequence, number of nonrewards, anticipation, and intertrial interval in extinction. *Journal of Experimental Psychology, 84,* 470–476.

CAPALDI, E. J., & STANLEY, L. R. (1965). Percentage of reward vs. *N*-length in the runway. *Psychonomic Science, 3,* 263–264.

CAVANAGH, J. P. (1972). Relation between the immediate memory and the memory search rate. *Psychological Review, 79,* 525–530.

CERASO, J., & HENDERSON, A. (1965). Unavailability and associative loss in RI and PI. *Journal of Experimental Psychology, 70,* 300–303.

CHERRY, E. C. (1953). Some experiments on the recognition of speech with one and with two ears. *Journal of the Acoustical Society of America, 25,* 975–979.

CHOMSKY, N. (1965). *Aspects of the theory of syntax.* Cambridge, MA: MIT Press.

CHURCH, R. M., RAYMOND, G. A., & BEAUCHAMP, R. D. (1967). Response suppression as a function of intensity and duration of a punishment. *Journal of Comparative and Physiological Psychology, 63,* 39–44.

CIEUTAT, V. J., STOCKWELL, F. E., & NOBLE, C. E. (1958). The interaction of ability and amount of practice with stimulus and response meaningfulness in paired-associated learning. *Journal of Experimental Psychology, 56,* 193–202.

COATE, W. B. (1964). Effect of deprivation on postdiscrimination stimulus generalization in the rat. *Journal of Comparative and Physiological Psychology, 57,* 134–138.

COFER, C. N., BRUCE, D. R., & REICHER, G. M. (1966). Clustering in free recall as a function of certain methodological variations. *Journal of Experimental Psychology, 71,* 858–866.

COLAVITA, F. B. (1965). Dual function of the US in Classical salivary conditioning. *Journal of Comparative and Physiological Psychology, 60,* 218–222.

COLLIER, G. (1969). Body weight loss as a measure of motivation in hunger and thirst. *Annals of the New York Academy of Science, 157,* 594–609.

COLLIER, G., KNARR, F. A., & MARX, M. H. (1961). Some relations between the intensive properties of the consummatory response and reinforcement. *Journal of Experimental Psychology, 62,* 484–495.

COLLINS, A. M., & LOFTUS, E. F. (1975). A spreading activation theory of semantic processing. *Psychological Review, 82,* 407–428.

COLLINS, A. M., & QUILLIAN, M. R. (1969). Retrieval time from semantic memory. *Journal of Verbal Learning and Verbal Behavior, 8,* 240–247.

COLLINS, A. M., & QUILLIAN, M. R. (1972). How to make a language user. In E. Tulving and W. Donaldson (Eds.), *Organization and memory.* New York: Academic Press.

COMMONS, M. L., HERRNSTEIN, R. J., & RACHLIN, H. (Eds.) (1982). *Quantitative analysis of behavior,* Vol. 2. *Matching and maximizing accounts.* Cambridge, MA: Ballinger.

CONRAD, C. (1972). Cognitive economy in semantic memory. *Journal of Experimental Psychology, 92,* 149–154.

CONRAD, R. (1964). Acoustic confusions in immediate memory. *British Journal of Psychology, 55,* 75–84.

CONRAD, R. (1972). Short-term memory in the deaf: A test for speech coding. *British Journal of Psychology, 63,* 173–180.

CONRAD, R., & HULL, A. J. (1964). Information, acoustic confusion and memory span. *British Journal of Psychology, 55,* 429–432.

CONRAD, R., & HULL, A. J. (1968). Input modality and the serial position curve in short-term memory. *Psychonomic Science, 10,* 135–136.

COOPER, L. A., & SHEPARD, R. N. (1973). Chronometric studies of the rotation of mental images. In W. G. Chase (Ed.), *Visual information processing*. New York: Academic Press.

COPPAGE, E. W., & HARCUM, E. R. (1967). Temporal vs. structural determinants of primacy in strategies of serial learning. *Journal of Verbal Learning and Verbal Behavior, 6,* 487–490.

COTTON, J. W. (1953). Running time as a function of amount of food deprivation. *Journal of Experimental Psychology, 46,* 188–198.

CRAIK, F. I. M. (1970). The fate of primary memory items in free recall. *Journal of Verbal Learning and Verbal Behavior, 9,* 143–148.

CRAIK, F. I. M., & KIRSNER, K. (1974). The effect of a speaker's voice on word recognition. *Quarterly Journal of Experimental Psychology, 26,* 274–284.

CRAIK, F. I. M., & LOCKHART, R. S. (1972). Levels of processing: A framework for memory research. *Journal of Verbal Learning and Verbal Behavior, 11,* 671–684.

CRAIK, F. I. M., & SIMON, E. (1980). Age differences in memory: The roles of attention and depth of processing. In L. W. Poon, J. L. Fozard, L. S. Cermak, D. Arenberg, and L. W. Thompson (Eds.), *New directions in memory and aging: Proceedings of the George Talland memorial conference.* Hillsdale, NJ: Erlbaum.

CRAIK, F. I. M., & TULVING, E. (1975). Depth of processing and the retention of words in episodic memory. *Journal of Experimental Psychology: General, 104,* 268–294.

CRAIK, F. I. M., & WATKINS, M. J. (1973). The role of rehearsal in short-term memory. *Journal of Verbal Learning and Verbal Behavior, 12,* 599–607.

CRESPI, L. P. (1942). Quantitative variation in incentive and performance in the white rat. *American Journal of Psychology, 55,* 467–517.

CROWDER, R. G. (1971). The sound of vowels and consonants in immediate memory. *Journal of Verbal Learning and Verbal Behavior, 10,* 587–596.

CROWDER, R. G. (1976). *Principles of learning and memory.* Hillsdale, NJ: Erlbaum.

CROWDER, R. G., & MORTON, J. (1969). Precategorical acoustic storage (PAS). *Perception and psychophysics, 5,* 365–373.

D'AGOSTINO, P. R., & DEREMER, P. (1973). Repetition effects as a function of rehearsal and encoding variability. *Journal of Verbal Learning and Verbal Behavior, 12,* 108–113.

DALLETT, K. M. (1962). The transfer surface reexamined. *Journal of Verbal Learning and Verbal Behavior, 1,* 91–94.

D'AMATO, M. R. (1973). Delayed matching and short-term memory in monkeys. In G. H. Bower (Ed.), *The psychology of learning and motivation: Advances in research and theory,* Vol. 7. New York: Academic Press.

D'AMATO, M. R., & FAZZARO, J. (1966). Discriminated lever-press avoidance learning as a function of type and intensity of shock. *Journal of Comparative and Physiological Psychology, 61,* 313–315.

D'AMATO, M. R., FAZZARO, J., & ETKIN, M. (1968). Anticipatory responding and avoidance discrimination as factors in avoidance conditioning. *Journal of Experimental Psychology, 77,* 41–47.

D'AMATO, M. R., SCHIFF, D., & JAGODA, H. (1962). Resistance to extinction after varying amounts of discriminative or nondiscriminative instrumental training. *Journal of Experimental Psychology, 64,* 526–532.

D'AMATO, M. R., & WORSHAM, R. W. (1974). Retrieval cues and short-term memory in Capuchin monkeys. *Journal of Comparative and Physiological Psychology, 86,* 274–282.

DARK, V. J., & LOFTUS, G. R. (1976). The role of rehearsal in long-term memory performance. *Journal of Verbal Learning and Verbal Behavior, 15,* 479–490.

DARWIN, C. J., TURVEY, M. T., & CROWDER, R. G. (1972). An auditory analogue of the Sperling partial report procedure. *Cognitive Psychology, 3,* 255–267.

DEAUX, E. B., & PATTEN, R. L. (1964). Measurement of the anticipatory goal response in instrumental runway conditioning. *Psychonomic Science, 1,* 357–358.

DEESE, J. (1959). Influence of inter-item associative strength upon immediate free recall. *Psychological Reports, 5,* 305–312.

DELIN, P. S. (1969). The learning to criterion of a serial list with and without mnemonic instructions. *Psychonomic Science, 16,* 169–170.

DENNY, M. R. (1971). Relaxation theory and experiments. In F. R. Brush (Ed.), *Aversive conditioning and learning.* New York: Academic Press, pp. 235–295.

DEUTSCH, J. A., & DEUTSCH, D. (1963). Attention: Some theoretical considerations. *Psychological Review, 70,* 80–90.

DEVILLIERS, P. A. (1974). The law of effect and avoidance: A quantitative relationship between response rate and shock frequency reduction. *Journal of Experimental Analysis of Behavior, 21,* 233–235.

DICKERSON, D. J. (1966). Performance of preschool children on three discrimination shifts. *Psychonomic Science, 4,* 417.

DIETER, S. E. (1976). Continuity and intensity of shock in one-way avoidance learning in the rat. *Animal Learning and Behavior, 4,* 303–307.

DOMJAN, M. (1983). Biological constraints on Instrumental and Classical conditioning: Implications for general process theory. In G. H. Bower (Ed.), *The psychology of learning and motivation*, Vol. 17. New York: Academic Press.

Donders, F. C. (1868). *Over de snelheid van psychische processen, Ondersoekingen gedaan in het Psysiologisch Laboratium der Utrechtsche Hoogeschool, 2,* 92–120. Translated by W. G. Koster, *Acta Psychologica*, 1969, *30,* 412–431.

Dore, L. R., & Hilgard, E. R. (1937). Spaced practice and the maturation hypothesis. *Journal of Psychology, 4,* 245–259.

Dougher, M. J. (1983). Clinical effects of response deprivation and response satiation procedures. *Behavior Therapy, 14,* 286–298.

Dougher, M. J., Crossen, J. R., & Garland, R. J. (1986). An experimental test of Cautella's operant explanation of covert conditioning procedures. *Behavioral Psychotherapy, 14,* 226–248.

Dunham, P. J. (1971). Punishment: Method and theory. *Psychological Review, 78,* 58–70.

Durlach, P. J., & Rescorla, R. A. (1980). Potentiation rather than overshadowing in flavor-aversion learning: An analysis in terms of within-compound associations. *Journal of Experimental Psychology: Animal Behavior Processes, 6,* 175–187.

Dyal, J. A., & Holland, T. A. (1963). Resistance to extinction as a function of number of reinforcements. *American Journal of Psychology, 76,* 332–333.

Ebbinghaus, H. (1885). *Über das Gedächtnis.* Leipzig: Dunker & Humbolt.

Efron, R. (1970a). The relationship between the duration of a stimulus and the duration of a perception. *Neuropsychologia, 8,* 37–55.

Efron, R. (1970b). Effect of stimulus duration on perceptual onset and offset latencies. *Perception and Psychophysics, 8,* 231–234.

Eich, J., Weingartner, H., Stillman, R., & Gillin, J. (1975). State-dependent accessibility of retrieval cues and retention of a categorized list. *Journal of Verbal Learning and Verbal Behavior, 14,* 408–417.

Eisenberger, R. (1972). Explanation of rewards that do not reduce tissue needs. *Psychological Bulletin, 77*(5), 319–339.

Eisenberger, R., Karpman, M., & Trattner, T. (1967). What is the necessary and sufficient condition for reinforcement in the contingency condition? *Journal of Experimental Psychology, 74,* 342–350.

Ekstrand, B. R., & Underwood, B. J. (1963). Paced versus unpaced recall in free learning. *Journal of Verbal Learning and Verbal Behavior, 2,* 288–290.

Ekstrand, B. R., & Underwood, B. J. (1965). Free learning and recall as a function of unit-sequence and letter-sequence interference. *Journal of Verbal Learning and Verbal Behavior, 4,* 390–396.

Elliot, M. H. (1928). The effect of change of reward on the maze performance of rats. *University of California Publications in Psychology, 4,* 19–30.

Ellis, H. C. (1969). Transfer and retention. In M. H. Marx (Ed.), *Learning: Processes.* New York: Macmillan.

Ellis, H. C., & Hunt, R. R. (1983). *Fundamentals of human memory and cognition.* Dubuque, IA: William C. Brown.

Ellis, H. C., Thomas, R. L., & Rodriguez, I. A. (1984). Emotional mood states and memory: Elaborative encoding, semantic processing, and cognitive effort. *Journal of Expermimental Psychology: Learning, Memory, and Cognition, 10,* 470–482.

Ellison, G. D. (1964). Differential salivary conditioning to traces. *Journal of Comparative and Physiological Psychology, 57,* 373–380.

Elmes, D. G., & Bjork, R. A. (1975). The interaction of encoding and rehearsal processes in the recall of repeated and nonrepeated items. *Journal of Verbal Learning and Verbal Behavior, 14,* 30–42.

Elmes, D. G., Dye, G. S., & Herdian, N. J. (1983). What is the role of affect in the spacing effect? *Memory and Cognition, 11,* 144–151.

Engle, R. W., & Bukstel, L. (1978). Memory processes among bridge players of differing expertise. *American Journal of Psychology, 91,* 673.

Estes, W. K. (1959). The statistical approach to learning theory. In S. Koch (Ed.), *Psychology: A study of a science,* Vol. 2. New York: McGraw-Hill.

Estes, W. K. (1960). Learning theory and the new "mental chemistry." *Psychological Review, 67,* 207–223.

Estes, W. K. (1973). Memory and conditioning. In F. J. McGuigan and D. B. Lumsden (Eds.), *Contemporary approaches to conditioning and learning.* Washington, DC: Winston.

Estes, W. K., & Skinner, B. F. (1941). Some quantitative properties of anxiety. *Journal of Experimental Psychology, 29,* 390–400.

Etkin, M. W. (1972). Light-produced interference in a delayed matching task with Capuchin monkeys. *Learning and Motivation, 3,* 313–324.

Eysenck, M. W., & Eysenck, M. C. (1979). Processing depth, elaboration of encoding, memory stores, and expended processing capacity. *Journal of Experimental Psychology: Human Learning and Memory, 5,* 472–484.

Fehrer, E. (1956). Effects of amount of reinforcement and pre- and postreinforcement delays on learning and extinction. *Journal of Experimental Psychology, 52,* 167–176.

Feigenbaum, E. A., & Simon, H. A. (1962). A theory of the serial position effect. *British Journal of Psychology, 53,* 307–320.

Feldman, D. T., & Gordon, W. C. (1979). The alleviation of short-term retention decrements with reactivation. *Learning and Motivation, 10,* 198–210.

Ferster, C. B., & Skinner, B. F. (1957). *Schedules of reinforcement.* New York: Appleton-Century-Crofts.

Finch, G. (1938). Salivary conditioning in atropinized dogs. *American Journal of Physiology, 124,* 136–141.

Fiske, D. W., & Maddi, S. R. (1961). *Functions of varied experience.* Homewood, IL: Dorsey.

Flaherty, C. F. (1982). Incentive contrast: A review of behavioral changes following shifts in reward. *Animal Learning and Behavior, 10,* 409–440.

Flaherty, C. F., & Caprio, M. (1976). Dissociation between instrumental and consummatory measures of incentive contrast. *American Journal of Psychology, 89,* 485–498.

Flaherty, C. F., Riley, E. P., & Spear, N. E. (1973). Effects of sucrose concentration and goal units on runway behavior in the rat. *Learning and Motivation, 4,* 163–175.

Flexser, A. J., & Tulving, E. (1978). Retrieval independence in recall and recognition. *Psychological Review, 85,* 153–171.

Fowler, H. (1965). *Curiosity and exploratory behavior.* New York: Macmillan.

Fowler, H., Blond, J., & Dember, W. N. (1959). Alternation behavior and learning: The influence of reinforcement magnitude, number, and contingency. *Journal of Comparative and Physiological Psychology, 52,* 609–614.

Fowler, H., & Miller, N. E. (1963). Facilitation and inhibition of runway performance by hind- and forepaw shock of various intensities. *Journal of Comparative and Physiological Psychology, 56,* 801–806.

Fowler, H., & Trapold, M. A. (1962). Escape performance as a function of delay of reinforcement. *Journal of Experimental Psychology, 63,* 464–467.

Frey, P. W., & Sears, R. J. (1978). Model of conditioning incorporating the Rescorla–Wagner associative axiom, a dynamic attention process, and a catastrophe rule. *Psychological Review, 85,* 321–340.

Friedman, H., & Guttman, N. (1965). Further analysis of the various effects of discrimination training on stimulus generalization gradients. In D. I. Mostofsky (Ed.), *Stimulus generalization.* Stanford: Stanford University Press.

Gallistel, C. R. (1980). *The organization of action: A new synthesis.* Hillsdale, NJ: Erlbaum.

Gammack, J. G., & Young, R. M. (1985). Psychological techniques for eliciting expert knowledge. In M. A. Bramer (Ed.), *Research and development in expert systems.* Cambridge: Cambridge University Press.

Gamzu, E., & Williams, D. R. (1971). Classical conditioning of a complex skeletal response. *Science, 171,* 923–925.

Ganz, L., & Riesen, A. H. (1962). Stimulus generalization to hue in the dark-reared Macaque. *Journal of Comparative and Physiological Psychology, 55,* 92–99.

Garcia, J., Ervin, F. R., & Koelling, R. A. (1966). Learning with prolonged delay of reinforcement. *Psychonomic Science, 5,* 121–122.

Garcia, J., & Koelling, R. A. (1966). Relation of cue to consequence in avoidance learning. *Psychonomic Science, 4,* 123–124.

Geiselman, R. E. (1975). Semantic positive forgetting: Another cocktail party problem. *Journal of Verbal Learning and Verbal Behavior, 14,* 73–81.

Gerall, A. A., & Obrist, P. A. (1962). Classical conditioning of the pupillary dilation response of normal and curarized cats. *Journal of Comparative and Physiological Psychology, 55,* 486–491.

Gibbs, M. E., & Mark, R. F. (1973). *Inhibition of memory formation.* New York: Plenum Press.

Gillund, G., & Shiffrin, R. M. (1984). A retrieval model for both recognition and recall. *Psychological Review, 91*(1), 1–67.

Glanzer, M., & Clark, W. H. (1962). Accuracy of perceptual recall: An analysis of organization. *Journal of Verbal Learning and Verbal Behavior, 1,* 289–299.

Glanzer, M., & Clark, W. H. (1963). The verbal loop hypothesis: Binary numbers. *Journal of Verbal Learning and Verbal Behavior, 2,* 301–309.

Glanzer, M., & Cunitz, A. R. (1966). Two storage mechanisms in free recall. *Journal of Verbal Learning and Verbal Behavior, 5,* 351–360.

Glanzer, M., & Dolinsky, R. (1965). The anchor for the serial position curve. *Journal of Verbal Learning and Verbal Behavior, 4,* 267–273.

Glass, A. L., & Holyoak, K. J. (1975). Alternative conceptions of semantic memory. *Cognition, 3,* 313–339.

Glaze, J. A. (1928). The association value of nonsense syllables. *Journal of Genetic Psychology, 35,* 255–269.

Gleitman, H. (1971). Forgetting of long-term memories in animals. In W. K. Honig and P. H. R. James (Eds.), *Animal memory.* New York: Academic Press.

Glickman, S. E., & Jensen, G. D. (1961). The effects of hunger and thirst on Y maze exploration. *Journal of Comparative and Physiological Psychology, 54,* 83–85.

Godden, D. R., & Baddeley, A. D. (1975). Context-dependent memory in two natural environments: On land and under water. *British Journal of Psychology, 66,* 325–331.

Gold, P. E., & King, R. P. (1974). Retrograde amnesia: Storage failure versus retrieval failure. *Psychological Review, 81,* 465–469.

Goldstein, A. G., & Chance, J. E. (1971). Visual recognition memory for complex configurations. *Perception and Psychophysics, 9,* 237–241.

Gonzalez, R. C., & Bitterman, M. E. (1964). Resistance to extinction in the rat as a function of percentage and distribution of reinforcement. *Journal of Comparative and Physiological Psychology, 58,* 258–263.

Goodrich, K. P. (1959). Performance in different segments of an instrumental response chain as a function of reinforcement schedule. *Journal of Experimental Psychology, 57,* 57–63.

Goodrich, K. P. (1960). Running speed and drinking rate as a function of sucrose concentration and amount of consummatory activity. *Journal of Comparative and Physiological Psychology, 53,* 245–250.

Gordon, W. C. (1981). Mechanisms of cue-induced retention enhancement. In N. E. Spear and R. R. Miller (Eds.), *Information processing in animals: Memory mechanisms.* Hillsdale, NJ: Erlbaum.

Gordon, W. C. (1983). The malleability of memory in animals. In R. L. Mellgren (Ed.), *Animal cognition and behavior.* New York: North Holland.

Gordon, W. C., Brennan, M. J., & Schlesinger, J. L. (1976). The interaction of memories in the rat: Effects on short-term retention performance. *Learning and Motivation, 7,* 406–417.

Gordon, W. C., Flaherty, C. F., & Riley, E. P. (1973). Negative contrast as a function of the interval between preshift and postshift training. *Bulletin of the Psychonomic Society, 1*(1a), 25–27.

Gordon, W. C., McCracken, K. M., Dess-Beech, N., & Mowrer, R. R. (1981). Mechanisms for the cueing phenomenon: The addition of the cueing context to the training memory. *Learning and Motivation, 12,* 196–211.

Gordon, W. C., McGinnis, C. M., & Weaver, M. S. (1985). The effect of cueing after backward conditioning trials. *Learning and Motivation, 16,* 444–463.

Gordon, W. C., & Mowrer, R. R. (1980). The use of an extinction trial as a reminder treatment following ECS. *Animal Learning and Behavior, 8*(3), 363–367.

Gordon, W. C., Mowrer, R. R., McGinnis, C. P., & McDermott, M. J. (1985). Cue-induced memory interference in the rat. *Bulletin of the Psychonomic Society, 23*(3), 233–236.

Gordon, W. C., Smith, G. J., & Katz, D. S. (1979). Dual effects of response blocking following avoidance learning. *Behavior Research and Therapy, 17,* 479–487.

Gordon, W. C., & Spear, N. E. (1973). The effect of reactivation of a previously acquired memory on the interaction between memories in the rat. *Journal of Experimental Psychology, 99,* 349–355.

Gormezano, I. (1965). Yoked comparisons of Classical and Instrumental conditioning of the eyelid response, and an addendum on "voluntary responders." In W. F. Prokasy (Ed.), *Classical conditioning: A symposium.* New York: Appleton-Century-Crofts.

Gormezano, I. (1966). Classical conditioning. In J. B. Sidowski (Ed.), *Experimental methods and instrumentation in psychology.* New York: McGraw-Hill.

Graf, P. (1982). The memorial consequences of generation and transformation. *Journal of Verbal Learning and Verbal Behavior, 21,* 539–548.

Grant, D. A. (1973). Cognitive factors in eyelid conditioning. *Psychophysiology, 10,* 75–81.

Grant, D. S. (1976). Effect of sample presentation time on long-delay matching in the pigeon. *Learning and Motivation, 7,* 580–590.

Grant, D. S. (1981). Short-term memory in the pigeon. In N. E. Spear and R. R. Miller (Eds.), *Information processing in animals: Memory mechanisms.* Hillsdale, NJ: Erlbaum.

Grant, D. S., & Roberts, W. A. (1973). Trace interaction in pigeon short-term memory. *Journal of Experimental Psychology, 101,* 21–29.

Grant, D. S., & Roberts, W. A. (1976). Sources of retroactive inhibition in pigeon short-term memory. *Journal of Experimental Psychology: Animal Behavior Processes, 2,* 1–16.

Greene, E., Flynn, M. S., & Loftus, E. F. (1982). Inducing resistance of misleading information. *Journal of Verbal Learning and Verbal Behavior, 21,* 207–219.

Greenspoon, J., & Ranyard, R. (1957). Stimulus conditions and retroactive inhibition. *Journal of Experimental Psychology, 53,* 55–59.

Grings, W. W., Lockhart, R. A., & Dameron, L. E. (1962). Conditioning autonomic responses of mentally subnormal individuals. *Psychological Monographs, 76,* No. 558.

Groninger, L. D. (1971). Mnemonic imagery and forgetting. *Psychonomic Science, 23,* 161–163.

Grossen, N. E., & Bolles, R. C. (1968). Effects of a Classically conditioned "fear signal" and "safety signal" on nondiscriminated avoidance behavior. *Psychonomic Science, 11,* 321–322.

Guttman, N., & Kalish, H. I. (1956). Discriminability and stimulus generalization. *Journal of Experimental Psychology, 51,* 79–88.

HABER, A., & KALISH, H. I. (1963). Prediction of discrimination from generalization after variation in schedule of reinforcement. *Science, 142,* 412–413.

HABER, R. N., & STANDING, L. G. (1969). Direct measures of short-term visual storage. *Quarterly Journal of Experimental Psychology, 21,* 43–54.

HAKE, D. F., & POWELL, T. (1970). Positive reinforcement and suppression from the same occurrence of the unconditioned stimulus in a positive conditioned suppression procedure. *Journal of Experimental Analysis of Behavior, 14,* 247–257.

HALL, J. F. (1954). Learning as a function of word frequency. *American Journal of Psychology, 67,* 138–140.

HALL, J. F. (1984). Backward conditioning in Pavlovian-type studies. *Pavlovian Journal of Biological Science, 19,* 163–170.

HAMMOND, L. J. (1967). A traditional demonstration of the active properties of Pavlovian inhibition using differential CER. *Psychonomic Science, 9,* 65–66.

HAMMOND, L. J. (1968). Retardation of fear acquisition by a previously inhibitory CS. *Journal of Comparative and Physiological Psychology, 66,* 756–759.

HANSON, H. M. (1959). Effects of discrimination training on stimulus generalization. *Journal of Experimental Psychology, 58,* 321–334.

HASHER, L., & ZACHS, R. T. (1979). Automatic and effortful processes in memory. *Journal of Experimental Psychology: General, 108,* 356–388.

HAYES, J. R. M. (1952). Memory span for several vocabularies as a function of vocabulary size. In *Quarterly Progress Report.* Cambridge, MA: Acoustics Laboratory, Massachusetts Institute of Technology.

HEARST, E. (1978). Stimulus relationships and feature selection in learning and behavior. In S. H. Hulse, H. Fowler, and W. K. Honig (Ed.), *Cognitive processes in animal behavior.* Hillsdale, NJ: Erlbaum.

HEARST, E., & JENKINS, H. M. (1974). *Sign-tracking: The stimulus-reinforcer relation and directed action.* Austin, TX: Psychonomic Society.

HEARST, E., & KORESKO, M. B. (1968). Stimulus generalization and amount of prior training on variable-interval reinforcement. *Journal of Comparative and Physiological Psychology, 66,* 133–138.

HEARST, E., KORESKO, M. B., & POPPER, R. (1964). Stimulus generalization and the response-reinforcer contingency. *Journal of Experimental Analysis of Behavior, 7,* 369–380.

HEBB, D. O. (1949). *The organization of behavior.* New York: Wiley.

HEBB, D. O. (1955). Drives and the CNS (conceptual nervous system). *Psychological Review, 62,* 243–254.

HERRNSTEIN, R. J. (1961). Relative and absolute strength of response as a function of frequency of reinforcement. *Journal of Experimental Analysis of Behavior, 4,* 267–272.

HERRNSTEIN, R. J. (1969). Method and theory in the study of avoidance. *Psychological Review, 76,* 49–69.

HERRNSTEIN, R. J. (1979). Acquisition, generalization, and discrimination reversal of a natural concept. *Journal of Experimental Psychology: Animal Behavior Processes, 5,* 116–129.

HERRNSTEIN, R. J., & DEVILLIERS, P. A. (1980). Fish as a natural category for people and pigeons. In G. H. Bower (Ed.), *The psychology of learning and motivation,* Vol. 14. New York: Academic Press.

HERRNSTEIN, R. J., & HINELINE, P. N. (1966). Negative reinforcement as shock frequency reduction. *Journal of Experimental Analysis of Behavior, 9,* 421–430.

HERRNSTEIN, R. J., LOVELAND, D. H., & CABLE, C. (1976). Natural concepts in pigeons. *Journals of Experimental Psychology: Animal Behavior Processes, 2,* 285–302.

HESS, E. N. (1965). Excerpt from: Ethology: An approach toward the complete analysis of behavior. In T. E. McGill (Ed.), *Readings in animal behavior.* New York: Holt, Rinehart & Winston.

HETH, D. C., & RESCORLA, R. A. (1973). Simultaneous and backward fear conditioning in the rat. *Journal of Comparative and Physiological Psychology, 82,* 434–443.

HILGARD, E. R., & MARQUIS, D. G. (1940). *Conditioning and learning.* New York: Appleton-Century-Crofts.

HILL, W. F., & SPEAR, N. E. (1962). Resistance to extinction as a joint function of reward magnitude and the spacing of extinction trials. *Journal of Experimental Psychology, 64,* 636–639.

HINSON, R. E. (1982). Effects of UCS pre-exposure on excitatory and inhibitory rabbit eyelid conditioning: An associative effect of conditioned contextual stimuli. *Journal of Experimental Psychology: Animal Behavior Processes, 8*(1), 49–61.

HINSON, R. E., & SIEGEL, S. (1980). Trace conditioning as an inhibitory procedure. *Animal Learning and Behavior, 8*(1), 60–66.

HINTZMAN, D. L. (1974). Theoretical implications of the spacing effect. In R. L. Solso (Ed.), *Theories in cognitive psychology: The Loyola Symposium.* Hillsdale, NJ: Erlbaum.

HINTZMAN, D. L. (1976). Repetition and memory. In G. H. Bower (Ed.), *The psychology of learning and motivation*, Vol. 10. New York: Academic Press.

HINTZMAN, D. L. (1986). "Schema abstraction" in a multiple-trace memory model. *Psychological Review, 93*(4), 411–428.

HINTZMAN, D. L., & BLOCK, R. A. (1971). Repetition and memory: Evidence for a multiple-trace hypothesis. *Journal of Experimental Psychology, 88*, 297–306.

HINTZMAN, D. L., BLOCK, R. A., & INSKEEP, N. R. (1972). Memory for mode of input. *Journal of Verbal Learning and Verbal Behavior, 11*, 741–749.

HINTZMAN, D. L., BLOCK, R. A., & SUMMERS, J. J. (1973). Modality tags and memory for repetitions: Locus of the spacing effect. *Journal of Verbal Learning and Verbal Behavior, 12*, 229–239.

HINTZMAN, D. L., SUMMERS, J. J., & BLOCK, R. A. (1975). Spacing judgments as an index of study-phase retrieval. *Journal of Experimental Psychology: Human Learning and Memory, 1*, 31–40.

HINTZMAN, D. L., SUMMERS, J. J., EKI, N. T., & MOORE, M. O. (1975). Voluntary attention and the spacing effect. *Memory and Cognition, 3*, 576–580.

HOFFELD, D. R., KENDALL, S. B., THOMPSON, R. F., & BROGDEN, W. J. (1960). Effect of amount of preconditioning training upon the magnitude of sensory preconditioning. *Journal of Experimental Psychology, 59*, 198–204.

HOFFMAN, J. W., & FITZGERALD, R. D. (1982). Bidirectional heart-rate response in rats associated with excitatory and inhibitory stimuli. *Animal Learning and Behavior, 10*, 77–82.

HOLLAND, P. C. (1977). Conditioned stimulus as a determinant of the form for the Pavlovian conditioned response. *Journal of Experimental Psychology: Animal Behavior Processes, 3*, 77–104.

HOLLAND, P. C. (1983). Occasion-setting in Pavlovian feature positive discriminations. In M. L. Commons, R. J. Herrnstein, and A. R. Wagner (Eds.), *Quantitative analyses of behavior: Discriminative processes*, Vol. 4. New York: Ballinger.

HOLLAND, P. C. (1985). The nature of conditioned inhibition in serial and simultaneous feature negative discriminations. In R. R. Miller and N. E. Spear (Eds.), *Information processing in animals: Conditioned inhibition*. Hillsdale, NJ: Erlbaum.

HOLLOWAY, F. A., & WANSLEY, R. (1973). Multiphasic retention deficits at periodic intervals after passive-avoidance learning. *Science, 180*, 208–210.

HOMME, L. E., DEBACA, P. C., DEVINE, J. V., STEINHORST, R., & RICKERT, E. J. (1963). Use of the Premack principle in controlling the behavior of nursery school children. *Journal of Experimental Analysis of Behavior, 6*, 544.

HONIG, W. K. (1970). Attention and the modulation of stimulus control. In D. I. Mostofsky (Ed.), *Attention: Contemporary theory and analysis*. New York: Appleton-Century-Crofts.

HONIG, W. K. (1978). Studies of working memory in the pigeon. In S. H. Hulse, H. Fowler, and W. K. Honig (Eds.), *Cognitive processes in animal behavior*. Hillsdale, NJ: Erlbaum.

HOROWITZ, L. M. (1961). Free recall and ordering of trigrams. *Journal of Experimental Psychology, 62*, 51–57.

HOUSTON, J. P. (1966). First-list retention and time and method of recall. *Journal of Experimental Psychology, 71*, 839–843.

HOWELL, W. C. (1973). Representation of frequency in memory. *Psychological Bulletin, 80*, 44–53.

HUG, J. J. (1970). Number of food pellets and the development of the frustration effect. *Psychonomic Science, 21*, 59–60.

HULL, C. L. (1920). Quantitative aspects of the evolution of concepts. *Psychological Monographs, 28* (whole no. 123).

HULL, C. L. (1929). A functional interpretation of the conditioned reflex. *Psychological Review, 36*, 495–511.

HULL, C. L. (1935). The conflicting psychologies of learning: A way out. *Psychological Review, 42*, 491–516.

HULL, C. L. (1943). *Principles of behavior*. New York: Appleton-Century-Crofts.

HULL, C. L. (1952). *A behavior system*. New Haven: Yale University Press.

HULL, C. L., HOVLAND, C. I., ROSS, R. T., HALL, M., PERKINS, D. T., & FITCH, F. B. (1940). *Mathematico-deductive theory of rote learning*. New Haven: Yale University Press.

HULL, C. L., LIVINGSTON, J. R., ROUSE, R. O., & BARKER, A. N. (1951). True, sham and esophageal feeding as reinforcements. *Journal of Comparative and Physiological Psychology, 44*, 236–245.

HULSE, S. H., JR. (1958). Amount and percentage of reinforcement and duration of goal confinement in conditioning and extinction. *Journal of Experimental Psychology, 56*, 48–57.

HYDE, T. S., & JENKINS, J. J. (1969). Differential effects of incidental tasks on the organization of recall of a list of highly associated words. *Journal of Experimental Psychology, 82*, 472–481.

INTRAUB, H. (1979). The role of implicit naming in pictorial encoding. *Journal of Experimental Psychology: Human Learning and Memory, 5*, 78–87.

ISON, J. R. (1962). Experimental extinction as a function of number of reinforcements. *Journal of Experimental Psychology, 64,* 314–317.

Jacoby, L. L. (1978). On interpreting the effects of repetition: Solving a problem versus remembering a solution. *Journal of Verbal Learning and Verbal Behavior, 17,* 649–667.

James, C. T., & Abrahamson, A. A. (1977). Recognition memory for active and passive sentences. *Journal of Psycholinguistic Research, 6,* 37–47.

Jenkins, H. M., & Harrison, R. H. (1962). Generalization gradients of inhibition following auditory discrimination learning. *Journal of Experimental Analysis of Behavior, 5,* 435–441.

Jenkins, J. J. (1963). Mediated associations: Paradigms and situations. In C. N. Cofer and B. S. Musgrave (Eds.), *Verbal behavior and learning.* New York: McGraw-Hill.

Jenkins, J. J., & Russell, W. A. (1952). Associative clustering during recall. *Journal of Abnormal and Social Psychology, 47,* 818–821.

Jenkins, W. O., Pascal, G. R., & Walker, R. W. (1958). Deprivation and generalization. *Journal of Experimental Psychology, 56,* 274–277.

Jensen, A. R. (1962). Transfer between paired-associate and serial learning. *Journal of Verbal Learning and Verbal Behavior, 1,* 269–280.

Jensen, A. R., & Rohwer, W. D., Jr. (1965). What is learned in serial learning? *Journal of Verbal Learning and Verbal Behavior, 4,* 62–72.

John, E. R. (1967). *Mechanisms of memory.* New York: Academic Press.

Joinson, P. A., & Runquist, W. N. (1968). Effects of intra-list similarity and degree of learning on forgetting. *Journal of Verbal Learning and Verbal Behavior, 7,* 554–559.

Jonides, J., Kahn, R., & Rozin, P. (1975). Imagery improves memory for blind subjects. *Bulletin of the Psychonomic Society, 5,* 424–426.

Jung, J. (1963). Effects of response meaningfulness (m) on transfer of training under two different paradigms. *Journal of Experimental Psychology, 65,* 377–384.

Kahneman, D. (1973). *Attention and effort.* Englewood Cliffs, NJ: Prentice-Hall.

Kalish, H. I., & Haber, A. (1965). Prediction of discrimination from generalization following variations in deprivation level. *Journal of Comparative and Physiological Psychology, 60,* 125–128.

Kamin, L. J. (1954). Traumatic avoidance learning: The effects of CS–US interval with a trace conditioning procedure. *Journal of Comparative and Physiological Psychology, 47,* 65–72.

Kamin, L. J. (1957a). The effects of termination of the CS and avoidance of the US on avoidance learning: An extension. *Canadian Journal of Psychology, 11,* 48–56.

Kamin, L. J. (1957b). The retention of an incompletely learned avoidance response. *Journal of Comparative and Physiological Psychology, 50,* 457–460.

Kamin, L. J. (1959). The delay-of-punishment gradient. *Journal of Comparative and Physiological Psychology, 52,* 434–437.

Kamin, L. J. (1965). Temporal and intensity characteristics of the conditioned stimulus. In W. F. Prokasy (Ed.), *Classical conditioning: A symposium.* New York: Appleton-Century-Crofts.

Kamin, L. J. (1968). "Attention-like" processes in Classical conditioning. In M. R. Jones (Ed.), *Miami symposium on the prediction of behavior: Aversive stimulation.* Oxford, OH: University of Miami Press.

Kamin, L. J. (1969). Predictability, surprise, attention, and conditioning. In B. A. Campbell and R. M. Church (Eds.), *Punishment and aversive behavior.* New York: Appleton-Century-Crofts.

Kamin, L. J., Brimer, C. J., & Black, A. H. (1963). Conditioned suppression as a monitor of fear of the CS in the course of avoidance training. *Journal of Comparative and Physiological Psychology, 56,* 497–501.

Kasprow, W. J., Cacheiro, H., Balaz, M. A., & Miller, R. R. (1982). Reminder-induced recovery of associations to an overshadowed stimulus. *Learning and Motivation, 13,* 155–166.

Kellogg, R. T. (1982). Hypothesis recognition failure in conjunctive and disjunctive concept identification tasks. *Memory and Cognition, 19,* 327–330.

Kellogg, R. T., Robbins, D. W., & Bourne, L. E. (1978). Memory for intratrial events in feature identification. *Journal of Experimental Psychology: Human Learning and Memory, 4,* 256–265.

Kendler, H. H., & Kendler, T. S. (1962). Vertical and horizontal processes in problem solving. *Psychological Review, 69,* 1–16.

Keppel, G., & Underwood, B. J. (1962). Proactive inhibition in short-term retention of single items. *Journal of Verbal Learning and Verbal Behavior, 1,* 153–161.

Kerr, N. H. (1983). The role of vision in "visual imagery" experiments: Evidence from the congenitally blind. *Journal of Experimental Psychology, 112,* 265–277.

Kimble, G. A. (1961). *Hilgard and Marquis' conditioning and learning,* 2nd ed. New York: Appleton-Century-Crofts.

King, D. L. (1979). *Conditioning: An image approach.* New York: Gardner Press.

KINCAID, J. P., & WICKENS, D. D. (1970). Temporal gradient of release from proactive inhibition. *Journal of Experimental Psychology, 86,* 313–316.

KINTSCH, W. (1962). Runway performance as a function of drive strength and magnitude of reinforcement. *Journal of Comparative and Physiological Psychology, 55,* 882–887.

KINTSCH, W. (1968). Recognition and free recall of organized lists. *Journal of Experimental Psychology, 78,* 481–487.

KINTSCH, W. (1970). Models for free recall and recognition. In D. A. Norman (Ed.), *Models of human memory.* New York: Academic Press.

KINTSCH, W. (1974). *The representation of meaning in memory.* Hillsdale, NJ: Erlbaum.

KINTSCH, W. (1976). Memory for prose. In C. N. Cofer (Ed.), *The structure of human memory.* San Francisco: Freeman.

KINTSCH, W., & GLASS, G. (1974). Effects of propositional structure upon sentence recall. In W. Kintsch (Ed.), *The representation of meaning in memory.* Hillsdale, NJ: Erlbaum.

KINTSCH, W., & KEENAN, J. M. (1973). Reading rate and retention as a function of the number of propositions in the base structure of sentences. *Cognitive Psychology, 5,* 257–274.

KINTSCH, W., & VAN DIJK, T. A. (1978). Toward a model of text comprehension and production. *Psychological Review, 85,* 363–394.

KINTSCH, W., & WITTE, R. S. (1962). Concurrent conditioning of bar press and salivation responses. *Journal of Comparative and Physiological Psychology, 55,* 963–968.

KISH, G. B. (1966). Studies of sensory reinforcement. In W. K. Honig (Ed.), *Operant behavior: Areas of research and application.* New York: Appleton-Century-Crofts.

KISH, G. B., & ANTONITIS, J. J. (1956). Unconditioned operant behavior in two homozygous strains of mice. *Journal of Genetic Psychology, 88,* 121–124.

KLEIN, M., & RILLING, M. (1974). Generalization of free operant avoidance behavior in pigeons. *Journal of Experimental Analysis of Behavior, 21,* 75–88.

KNOUSE, S. B., & CAMPBELL, P. E. (1971). Partially delayed reward in the rat: A parametric study of delay duration. *Journal of Comparative and Physiological Psychology, 75,* 116–119.

KOLERS, P. A. (1979). A pattern-analyzing basis of recognition. In L. S. Cermak and F. I. M. Craik (Eds.), *Levels of processing in human memory.* Hillsdale, NJ: Erlbaum.

KOLERS, P. A., & OSTRY, D. J. (1974). Time course of loss of information regarding pattern analyzing operations. *Journal of Verbal Learning and Verbal Behavior, 13,* 599–612.

KONORSKI, J., & SZWEJKOWSKA, G. (1950). Chronic extinction and restoration of conditioned reflexes. I. Extinction against the excitatory background. *Acta Biological Experimentation, 15,* 155–170.

KOSSLYN, S. M., BALL, T. M., & REISER, B. J. (1978). Visual images preserve metric spatial information: Evidence from studies of image scanning. *Journal of Experimental Psychology: Human Perception and Performance, 4,* 47–60.

KRANE, R. V., & ISON, J. R. (1971). Positive induction in differential instrumental conditioning: Effect of the interstimulus interval. *Journal of Comparative and Physiological Psychology, 75,* 129–135.

KRANE, R. V., & WAGNER, A. R. (1975). Taste aversion learning with a delayed shock US: Implications for the "generality of the laws of learning." *Journal of Comparative and Physiological Psychology, 88,* 882–889.

KRECHEVSKY, I. (1932). Hypotheses in rats. *Psychological Review, 39,* 516–532.

KREMER, E. F. (1971). Truly random and traditional control procedures in CER conditioning in the rat. *Journal of Comparative and Physiological Psychology, 76,* 441–448.

KUCHARSKI, D., & SPEAR, N. E. (1984). Potentiation of a conditioned taste aversion in pre-weanling and adult rats. *Behavioral and Neural Biology, 40,* 44–57.

KUO, Z. Y. (1932). Ontogeny of embryonic behavior in aves. *Journal of Experimental Biology, 61,* 395–430, 453–489.

LACEY, J. I., & SMITH, R. L. (1954). Conditioning and generalization of unconscious anxiety. *Science, 120,* 1045–1052.

LASHLEY, K. S. (1951). The problem of serial order in behavior. In L. A. Jeffries (Ed.), *Cerebral mechanisms in behavior.* New York: Wiley.

LASHLEY, K. S., & WADE, M. (1946). The Pavlovian theory of generalization. *Psychological Review, 53,* 72–87.

LAWRENCE, D. H. (1949). Acquired distinctiveness of cues. I. Transfer between discriminations on the basis of familiarity with the stimulus. *Journal of Experimental Psychology, 39,* 770–784.

LAWRENCE, D. H. (1950). Acquired distinctiveness of cues. II. Selective association in a constant stimulus situation. *Journal of Experimental Psychology, 40,* 175–188.

LAWRENCE, D. H. (1952). The transfer of a discrimination along a continuum. *Journal of Comparative and Physiological Psychology, 46,* 511–516.

LEPLEY, W. M. (1934). Serial reactions considered as

conditioned reactions. *Psychological Monographs, 46* (whole no. 205).

LEUBA, C. (1955). Toward some integration of learning theories: The concept of optimal stimulation. *Psychological Reports, 1,* 27–33.

LEVINE, M. (1966). Hypothesis behavior by humans during discrimination learning. *Journal of Experimental Psychology, 71,* 331–338.

LEVINE, M. (1975). *A cognitive theory of learning.* Hillsdale, NJ: Erlbaum.

LEWIS, D. J. (1979). Psychobiology of active and inactive memory. *Psychological Bulletin, 86,* 1054–1083.

LEWIS, D. J., MILLER, R. R., & MISANIN, J. R. (1968). Control of retrograde amnesia. *Journal of Comparative and Physiological Psychology, 66,* 48–52.

LIEBERMAN, D. A., MCINTOSH, D. C., & THOMAS, G. V. (1979). Learning when reward is delayed: A marking hypothesis. *Journal of Experimental Psychology: Animal Behavior Processes, 5,* 224–242.

LIGHT, J. S., & GANTT, W. H. (1936). Essential part of reflex arc for establishment of conditioned reflex. Formation of conditioned reflex after exclusion of motor peripheral end. *Journal of Comparative Psychology, 21,* 19–36.

LIKELY, D., & SCHNITZER, S. B. (1968). Dependence of the overtraining extinction effect on attention to runway cues. *Quarterly Journal of Experimental Psychology, 20,* 193–196.

LOCKHART, R. S., & CRAIK, F. I. M. (1978). Levels of processing: A reply to Eysenck. *British Journal of Psychology, 69,* 171–175.

LOESS, H. (1964). Proactive inhibition in short-term memory. *Journal of Verbal Learning and Verbal Behavior, 3,* 362–368.

LOFTUS, E. F. (1979). *Eyewitness testimony.* Cambridge, MA: Harvard University Press.

LOFTUS, E. F., MILLER, D. G., & BURNS, H. J. (1978). Semantic integration of verbal information into a visual memory. *Journal of Experimental Psychology: Human Learning and Memory, 4,* 19–31.

LOGAN, F. A. (1954). A note on stimulus intensity dynamism (V). *Psychological Review, 61,* 77–80.

LORENZ, K. Z. (1965). *Evolution and modification of behavior.* Chicago: University of Chicago Press.

LOVEJOY, E. (1968). *Attention in discrimination learning.* San Francisco: Holden-Day.

LOVIBOND, P. F., PRESTON, G. C., & MACKINTOSH, N. J. (1984). Context specificity of conditioning, extinction and latent inhibition. *Journal of Experimental Psychology: Animal Behavior Processes, 10,* 360–375.

LOW, L. A., & LOW, H. I. (1962). Effects of CS–US interval length upon avoidance responding. *Journal of Comparative and Physiological Psychology, 55,* 1059–1061.

LUBOW, R. E., & MOORE, A. U. (1959). Latent inhibition: The effect of nonreinforced exposure to the conditioned stimulus. *Journal of Comparative and Physiological Psychology, 52,* 415–419.

MACCORQUODALE, K., & MEEHL, P. E. (1951). On the elimination of cue entries without obvious reinforcement. *Journal of Comparative and Physiological Psychology, 44,* 367–371.

MACKINTOSH, N. J. (1971). An analysis of overshadowing and blocking. *Quarterly Journal of Experimental Psychology, 23,* 118–125.

MACKINTOSH, N. J. (1974). *The psychology of animal learning.* London: Academic Press.

MACKINTOSH, N. J. (1983). *Conditioning and associative learning.* Oxford: Oxford University Press.

MACKINTOSH, N. J., & HOLGATE, V. (1967). Effects of several pretraining procedures on brightness probability learning. *Perception & Motor Skills, 25,* 629–637.

MACKINTOSH, N. J., & HONIG, W. K. (1970). Blocking and attentional enhancement in pigeons. *Journal of Comparative and Physiological Psychology, 73,* 78–85.

MACKINTOSH, N. J., & LITTLE, L. (1969). Intradimensional and extradimensional shift learning by pigeons. *Psychonomic Science, 14,* 5–6.

MADISON, H. L. (1964). Experimental extinction as a function of number of reinforcements. *Psychological Reports, 14,* 647–650.

MAHONEY, W. J., & AYRES, J. J. B. (1976). One-trial simultaneous and backward fear conditioning as reflected in conditioned suppression of licking in rats. *Animal Learning and Behavior, 4,* 357–362.

MAIER, S. F., & JACKSON, R. L. (1979). Learned helplessness: All of us were right (and wrong): Inescapable shock has multiple effects. In G. H. Bower (Ed.), *The psychology of learning and motivation.* New York: Academic Press.

MAIER, S. F., & SELIGMAN, M. E. P. (1976). Learned helplessness: Theory and evidence. *Journal of Experimental Psychology: General, 105,* 3–46.

MAKI, W. S. (1981). Directed forgetting in animals. In N. E. Spear and R. R. Miller (Eds.), *Information processing in animals: Memory mechanisms.* Hillsdale, N.J.: Erlbaum.

MAKI, W. S., MOE, J. C., & BIERLEY, C. M. (1977). Short-term memory for stimuli, responses, and reinforcers. *Journal of Experimental Psychology: Animal Behavior Processes, 3,* 156–177.

MALTZMAN, I. (1977). Orienting in Classical conditioning and generalization of the galvanic skin response to words: An overview. *Journal of Experimental Psychology, 106,* 111–119.

MANDLER, G. (1972). Organization and recognition. In E. Tulving and W. Donaldson (Eds.), *Organization of memory.* New York: Academic Press.

MARGOLIUS, G. (1955). Stimulus generalization of an instrumental response as a function of the number of reinforced trials. *Journal of Experimental Psychology, 49,* 105–111.

MARLER, P., & MUNDINGER, P. (1971). Vocal learning in birds. In H. Moltz (Ed.), *The ontogeny of vertebrate behavior.* New York: Academic Press.

MARTIN, E. (1972). Stimulus encoding in learning and transfer. In A. W. Melton and E. Martin (Eds.), *Coding processes in human memory.* Washington, DC: Winston.

MARTIN, E. (1975). Generation-recognition theory and the encoding specificity principle. *Psychological Review, 82,* 150–153.

MAYHEW, A. J. (1967). Interlist changes in subjective organization during free recall learning. *Journal of Experimental Psychology, 74,* 425–430.

MCALLISTER, D. E., MCALLISTER, W. R., & DIETER, S. E. (1976). Reward magnitude and shock variables (continuity and intensity) in shuttlebox-avoidance learning. *Animal Learning and Behavior, 4,* 204–209.

MCALLISTER, W. R., & MCALLISTER, D. E. (1963). Increase over time in the stimulus generalization of acquired fear. *Journal of Experimental Psychology, 65,* 576–582.

MCCAIN, G. (1969). The partial reinforcement effect following a small number of acquisition trials. *Psychonomic Science, 15,* 146.

MCDOWELL, J. J. (1981). On the validity and utility of Herrnstein's hyperbola in applied behavioral analysis. In C. M. Bradshaw, E. Szabadi, and C. F. Lowe (Eds.), *Quantification of steady state operant behaviour.* Amsterdam: Elsevier/North-Holland.

MCDOWELL, J. J. (1982). The importance of Herrnstein's mathematical statement of the law of effect for behavior therapy. *American Psychologist, 37,* 771–779.

MCFARLAND, C. E., FREY, T. J., & RHODES, D. D. (1980). Retrieval of internally versus externally generated words in episodic memory. *Journal of Verbal Learning and Verbal Behavior, 19,* 210–225.

MCGAUGH, J. L. (1966). Time-dependent processes in memory storage. *Science, 153,* 1351–1358.

MCGAUGH, J. L., & DAWSON, R. G. (1971). Modification of memory storage processes. In W. K. Honig and P. H. R. James (Eds.), *Animal memory.* New York: Academic Press.

MCGEOCH, J. A. (1932). Forgetting and the law of disuse. *Psychological Review, 39,* 352–370.

MCHOSE, J. H. (1963). Effect of continued nonreinforcement on the frustration effect. *Journal of Experimental Psychology, 65,* 444–450.

MCHOSE, J. H., & TAUBER, L. (1972). Changes in delay of reinforcement in simple Instrumental conditioning. *Psychonomic Science, 27,* 291–292.

MCKAY, D. C. (1973). Aspects of the theory of comprehension, memory, and attention. *Quarterly Journal of Experimental Psychology, 25,* 22–40.

MCSWEENEY, F. K., MELVILLE, C. L., BUCK, M. A., & WHIPPLE, J. E. (1983). Local rates of responding and reinforcement during concurrent schedules. *Journal of Experimental Analysis of Behavior, 40,* 79–98.

MEDIN, D. L. (1975). A theory of context in discrimination learning. In G. H. Bower (Ed.), *The psychology of learning and motivation,* Vol. 9. New York: Academic Press.

MELTON, A. W. (1963). Implications of short-term memory for a general theory of memory. *Journal of Verbal Learning and Verbal Behavior, 2,* 1–21.

MELTON, A. W. (1970). The situation with respect to the spacing of repetitions and memory. *Journal of Verbal Learning and Verbal Behavior, 9,* 596–606.

MELTON, A. W., & IRWIN, J. M. (1940). The influence of degree of interpolated learning on retroactive inhibition and overt transfer of specific responses. *American Journal of Psychology, 53,* 173–203.

MERIKLE, P. M. (1968). Paired-associate transfer as a function of stimulus and response meaningfulness. *Psychological Reports, 22,* 131–138.

MERVIS, C. B. (1980). Category structure and the development of categorization. In R. J. Spiro, B. C. Bruce, and W. E. Brewer (Eds.), *Theoretical issues in reading comprehension: Pespectives from cognitive psychology, linguistics, artificial intelligence, and education.* Hillsdale, NJ: Erlbaum.

MEYER, D. E., & SCHVANEVELDT, R. W. (1971). Facilitation in recognizing pairs of words: Evidence of a dependence between retrieval operations. *Journal of Experimental Psychology, 90,* 227–234.

MICZEK, K. A., & GROSSMAN, S. (1971). Positive conditioned suppression: Effects of CS duration. *Journal of Experimental Analysis of Behavior, 15,* 243–247.

MIKULKA, P. J., & PAVLIK, W. B. (1966). Deprivation level, competing responses, and the PREE. *Psychological Reports, 18,* 95–102.

MILLER, G. A. (1956). The magical number seven, plus or minus two: Some limits on our capacity for processing information. *Psychological Review, 63,* 81–97.

MILLER, G. A., GALANTER, E., & PRIBRAM, K. (1960). *Plans and the structure of behavior.* New York: Holt, Rinehart & Winston.

MILLER, N. E. (1948). Studies of fear as an acquirable drive. *Journal of Experimental Psychology, 38,* 89–101.

MILLER, N. E., & DEBOLD, R. C. (1965). Classically conditioned tongue-licking and operant bar pressing recorded simultaneously in the rat. *Journal of Comparative and Physiological Psychology, 59,* 109–111.

MILLER, N. E., & KESSEN, M. C. (1952). Reward effects of food via stomach fistula compared with those of food via mouth. *Journal of Comparative and Physiological Psychology, 45,* 555–564.

MILLER, R. R. (1970). Effects of environmental complexity on amnesia induced by electroconvulsive shock in rats. *Journal of Comparative and Physiological Psychology, 71,* 267–275.

MILLER, R. R., & SCHACHTMAN, T. R. (1985a). The several roles of context at the time of retrieval. In P. D. Balsam and A. Tomie (Eds.), *Context and learning.* Hillsdale, NJ: Erlbaum.

MILLER, R. R., & SCHACHTMAN, T. R. (1985b). Conditioning context as an associative baseline: Implications for the content of associations and the epiphenomenal nature of conditioned inhibition. In R. R. Miller and N. E. Spear (Eds.), *Information processing in animals: Conditioned inhibition.* Hillsdale, NJ: Erlbaum.

MILLER, R. R., & SPEAR, N. E. (Eds.) (1985). *Information processing in animals: Conditioned inhibition.* Hillsdale, NJ: Erlbaum.

MILLER, R. R., & SPRINGER, A. D. (1972). Induced recovery of memory in rats following electroconvulsive shock. *Physiology and Behavior, 8,* 645–651.

MILNER, B. (1966). Amnesia following operation on the temporal lobes. In C. W. M. Whitty and O. L. Zangwill (Eds.), *Amnesia.* London: Butterworths.

MINEKA, S., & GINO, A. (1979). Dissociative effects of different types and amounts of nonreinforced CS exposure on avoidance extinction and the CER. *Learning and Motivation, 10,* 141–160.

MOESER, S. D. (1983). Levels of processing: Qualitative differences or task–demand differences. *Memory and Cognition, 11,* 316–323.

MONTAGUE, W. E., ADAMS, J. A., & KIESS, H. O. (1966). Forgetting and natural language mediation. *Journal of Experimental Psychology, 72,* 829–833.

MOON, L. E., & LODAHL, T. M. (1956). The reinforcing effect of changes in illumination on lever pressing in the monkey. *American Journal of Psychology, 69,* 288–290.

MOORE, B. R. (1973). The role of directed Pavlovian reactions in simple Instrumental learning in the pigeon. In R. A. Hinde and J. Stevenson (Eds.), *Constraints on learning.* New York: Academic Press.

MORAY, N. (1959). Attention in dichotic listening: Affective cues and the influence of instructions. *Quarterly Journal of Experimental Psychology, 11,* 56–60.

MORRIS, C. D. (1978). Acquisition–test interactions between different dimensions of encoding. *Memory and Cognition, 6*(4), 354–363.

MORTON, J., CROWDER, R. G., & PRUSSIN, H. A. (1971). Experiments with the stimulus suffix effect. *Journal of Experimental Psychology Monographs, 91,* 169–190.

MOSCOVITCH, A., & LOLORDO, V. M. (1968). Role of safety in the Pavlovian backward fear conditioning procedure. *Journal of Comparative and Physiological Psychology, 66,* 673–678.

MOWRER, O. H. (1947). On the dual nature of learning—A reinterpretation of "conditioning" and "problem-solving." *Harvard Educational Review, 17,* 102–148.

MUMMA, R., & WARREN, J. M. (1968). Two-cue discrimination learning by cats. *Journal of Comparative and Physiological Psychology, 66,* 116–122.

MURDOCK, B. B., JR. (1962). The serial position effect of free recall. *Journal of Experimental Psychology, 64,* 482–488.

MURDOCK, B. B., JR. (1971). A parallel-processing model for scanning. *Perception and Psychophysics, 10,* 289–291.

NADEL, L., & WILLNER, J. (1980). Context and conditioning. A place for space. *Journal of Comparative and Physiological Psychology, 8,* 218–228.

NAUS, M. J. (1974). Memory search for categorized lists: A consideration of alternative self-terminating search strategies. *Journal of Experimental Psychology, 102,* 992–1000.

NEISSER, U. (1967). *Cognitive psychology.* Englewood Cliffs, NJ: Prentice-Hall.

NEISSER, U. (1969). *Selective reading: A method for the study of visual attention.* Nineteenth International Congress of Psychology, London.

NELSON, D. L. (1979). Remembering pictures and words: Appearance, significance and name. In L. S. Cermak and F. I. M. Craik (Eds.), *Levels of processing in human memory.* Hillsdale, NJ: Erlbaum.

NELSON, T. O. (1977). Repetition and depth of processing. *Journal of Verbal Learning and Verbal Behavior, 16,* 151–171.

NEUMANN, P. G. (1974). An attribute frequency model for the abstraction of prototypes. *Memory and Cognition, 2,* 241–248.

NEWMAN, J. R., & GRICE, G. R. (1965). Stimulus generalization as a function of drive level, and the relationship between two measures of response strength. *Journal of Experimental Psychology, 69,* 357–362.

NICKERSON, R. S. (1965). Short-term memory for complex meaningful visual configurations: A demonstration of capacity. *Canadian Journal of Psychology, 19,* 155–160.

NOBLE, C. E. (1952). An analysis of meaning. *Psychological Review, 59,* 421–430.

NORMAN, D. A. (1968). Toward a theory of memory and attention. *Psychological Review, 75,* 522–536.

NORMAN, D. A. (1973). Memory, knowledge, and the answering of questions. In R. L. Solso (Ed.), *Contemporary issues in cognitive psychology: The Loyola Symposium.* Washington, DC: Winston.

NORMAN, D. A., RUMELHART, D. E., & THE LNR RESEARCH GROUP. (1975). *Explorations in cognition.* San Francisco: Freeman.

NORTH, A. J., & STIMMEL, D. T. (1960). Extinction of an instrumental response following a large number of reinforcements. *Psychological Reports, 6,* 227–234.

OLTON, D. S., & SAMUELSON, R. J. (1976). Remembrance of places passed: Spatial memory in rats. *Journal of Experimental Psychology: Animal Behavior Processes, 2,* 97–116.

OSGOOD, C. E. (1949). The similarity paradox in human learning: A resolution. *Psychological Review, 56,* 132–143.

OVERMEIR, J. B., & SELIGMAN, M. E. P. (1967). Effects of inescapable shock upon subsequent escape and avoidance learning. *Journal of Comparative and Physiological Psychology, 63,* 22–33.

OVERTON, D. A. (1966). State-dependent learning produced by depressant and atropine-like drugs. *Psychopharmacologia, 10,* 6–31.

OVERTON, D. A. (1972). State-dependent learning produced by alcohol and its relevance to alcoholism. In B. Kissin and H. Begleiter (Eds.), *The biology of alcoholism,* Vol. II, *Physiology and behavior.* New York: Plenum Press.

PACKMAN, J. L., & BATTIG, W. F. (1978). Effects of different kinds of semantic processing on memory for words. *Memory and Cognition, 6,* 502–508.

PAIVIO, A. (1969). Mental imagery in associative learning and memory. *Psychological Review, 76,* 241–263.

PAIVIO, A. (1971). *Imagery and verbal processes.* New York: Holt, Rinehart & Winston.

PAIVIO, A., SMYTHE, P. C., & YUILLE, J. C. (1968). Imagery versus meaningfulness of nouns in paired-associate learning. *Canadian Journal of Psychology, 22,* 427–441.

PALMERINO, C. C., RUSINIAK, K. W., & GARCIA, J. (1980). Flavor–illness aversions: The peculiar roles of odor and taste in memory for poison. *Science, 208,* 753–755.

PAUL, J. H. (1959). Studies in remembering: The reproduction of connected and extended verbal material. *Psychological Issues, 1,* 1–152.

PAVLOV, I. P. (1927). *Conditioned reflexes.* Oxford: Oxford University Press.

PEARCE, J. M., & HALL, G. (1978). Overshadowing the Instrumental condtioning of a lever-press response by a more valid predictor of the reinforcer. *Journal of Experimental Psychology: Animal Behavior Processes, 4,* 356–367.

PEARCE, J. M., & HALL, G. (1980). A model for Pavlovian learning: Variations in the effectiveness of conditioned but not unconditioned stimuli. *Psychological Review, 87,* 532–552.

PECKHAM, R. H., & AMSEL, A. (1967). Within-subject demonstration of a relationship between frustration and magnitude of reward in a differential magnitude of reward discrimination. *Journal of Experimental Psychology, 73,* 187–195.

PERIN, C. T. (1942). Behavior potentiality as a joint function of the amount of training and degree of hunger at the time of extinction. *Journal of Experimental Psychology, 30,* 93–113.

PERKINS, C. C., & WEYANT, R. G. (1958). The interval between training and test trials as a determiner of the slope of generalization gradients. *Journal of Comparative and Physiological Psychology, 51,* 596–600.

PETERSEN, R. (1974). Isolation of processes involved in state-dependent recall in man. Paper presented at Federation of American Society for Experimental Biology meetings, Atlantic City, NJ.

PETERSON, D. A., & LEVIS, D. J. (1985). The assessment of bodily injury fears via the Behavioral Avoidance Slide-Test. *Behavioral Assessment, 7*(2), 173–184.

PETERSON, L. R., & PETERSON, M. J. (1959). Short-term retention of individual verbal items. *Journal of Experimental Psychology, 58,* 193–198.

PETERSON, N. (1962). Effect of monochromatic rearing on the control of responding by wavelength. *Science, 136,* 774.

POLLACK, I. (1953). The information of elementary auditory displays. II. *Journal of the Acoustical Society of America, 25,* 765–769.

POLSON, M. C., RESTLE, F., & POLSON, P. G. (1965). Association and discrimination in paired-associates learning. *Journal of Experimental Psychology, 69,* 47–55.

POSNER, M. I. (1967). Characteristics of visual and kinesthetic memory codes. *Journal of Experimental Psychology, 75,* 103–107.

POSNER, M. I. (1969). Abstraction and the process of recognition. In J. T. Spence and G. H. Bower (Eds.), *Advances in learning and motivation,* Vol. 3. New York: Academic Press.

Posner, M. I., Boies, S. J., Eichelman, W. H., & Taylor, R. L. (1969). Retention of visual and name codes of single letters. *Journal of Experimental Psychology, 79*(1, pt. 2).

Posner, M. I., Goldsmith, R., & Welton, K. E., Jr. (1967). Perceived distance and the classification of distorted patterns. *Journal of Experimental Psychology, 73,* 28–38.

Posner, M. I., & Keele, S. (1968). On the genesis of abstract ideas. *Journal of Experimental Psychology, 77,* 353–363.

Posner, M. I., & Keele, S. W. (1970). Retention of abstract ideas. *Journal of Experimental Psychology, 83,* 304–308.

Posner, M. I., & Konick, A. F. (1966). Short-term retention of visual and kinesthetic information. *Organizational Behavior and Human Performance, 1,* 71–86.

Posner, M. I., & Mitchell, R. F. (1967). Chronometric analysis of classification. *Psychological Review, 74,* 392–409.

Postman, L. (1961). Extra-experimental interference and the retention of words. *Journal of Experimental Psychology, 61,* 97–110.

Postman, L. (1962a). Repetition and paired-associate learning. *American Journal of Psychology, 75,* 372–389.

Postman, L. (1962b). The effects of language habits on the acquisition and retention of verbal associations. *Journal of Experimental Psychology, 64,* 7–19.

Postman, L. (1962c). Transfer of training as a function of experimental paradigm and degree of first-list learning. *Journal of Verbal Learning and Verbal Behavior, 1,* 109–118.

Postman, L. (1972). Transfer, interference, and forgetting. In J. W. Kling and L. A. Riggs (Eds.), *Woodworth and Schlosberg's experimental psychology.* New York: Holt, Rinehart & Winston.

Postman, L., & Stark, K. (1969). Role of response availability in transfer and interference. *Journal of Experimental Psychology, 79,* 168–177.

Postman, L., Stark, K., & Fraser, J. (1968). Temporal changes in interference. *Journal of Verbal Learning and Verbal Behavior, 7,* 672–694.

Postman, L., Stark, K., & Henschel, D. (1969). Conditions of recovery after unlearning. *Journal of Experimental Psychology Monograph, 82*(1, pt. 2).

Premack, D. (1959). Toward empirical behavior laws: I. Positive reinforcement. *Psychological Review, 66,* 219–233.

Premack, D. (1963). Prediction of the comparative reinforcement values of running and drinking. *Science, 139,* 1062–1063.

Premack, D. (1965). Reinforcement theory. In D. Levine (Ed.), *Nebraska Symposium on motivation,* Vol 13. Lincoln: University of Nebraska Press.

Premack, D. (1971). Catching up with common sense, or two sides of generalization: Reinforcement and punishment. In R. Glaser (Ed.), *The nature of reinforcement.* New York: Academic Press.

Purtle, R. B. (1973). Peak shift: A review. *Psychological Bulletin, 80,* 408–421.

Pylyshyn, Z. W. (1973). What the mind's eye tells the mind's brain: A critique of mental imagery. *Psychological Bulletin, 80,* 1–24.

Quillian, M. R. (1967). A theory and simulation of some basic semantic capabilities. *Behavioral Science, 12,* 410–430.

Rand, G., & Wapner, S. (1967). Postural status as a factor in memory. *Journal of Verbal Learning and Verbal Behavior, 6,* 268–271.

Randall, P. K., & Riccio, D. C. (1969). Fear and punishment as determinants of passive-avoidance responding. *Journal of Comparative and Physiological Psychology, 69,* 550–553.

Randich, A. (1981). The US pre-exposure phenomenon in the conditioned suppression paradigm: A role for conditioned situational stimuli. *Learning and Motivation, 12,* 321–341.

Randich, A., & LoLordo, V. M. (1979). Preconditioning exposure to the unconditioned stimulus affects the acquisition of a conditioned emotional response. *Learning and Motivation, 10,* 245–277.

Randich, A., & Ross, R. T. (1985). The role of contextual stimuli in mediating the effects of pre- and postexposure to the unconditioned stimulus alone on acquisition and retention of conditioned suppression. In P. Balsam and A. Tomie (Eds.), *Context and learning.* Hillsdale, NJ: Erlbaum.

Reason, J., & Mycielska, K. (1982). *Absent-minded? The psychology of mental lapses and everyday errors.* Englewood Cliffs, NJ: Prentice-Hall.

Reber, A. A., & Allen, R. (1978). Analogical and abstraction strategies in synthetic grammar learning: A functionalist interpretation. *Cognition, 6,* 189–221.

Reed, S. K. (1972). Pattern recognition and categorization. *Cognitive Psychology, 3,* 383–407.

Reese, H. W. (1965). Imagery in paired-associate learning in children. *Journal of Experimental Child Psychology, 2,* 290–296.

Reiss, S., & Wagner, A. R. (1972). CS habituation produces a "latent inhibition effect" but no active "conditioned inhibition." *Learning and Motivation, 3,* 237–245.

Reitman, J. S. (1971). Mechanisms of forgetting in short-term memory. *Cognitive Psychology, 2,* 185–195.

Reitman, J. S. (1974). Without surreptitious rehearsal, information in short-term memory decays.

Journal of Verbal Learning and Verbal Behavior, 13, 365–377.

RENNER, K. E. (1963). Influence of deprivation and availability of goal box cues on the temporal gradient of reinforcement. *Journal of Comparative and Physiological Psychology, 56,* 101–104.

RESCORLA, R. A. (1966). Predictability and number of pairings in Pavlovian fear conditioning. *Psychonomic Science, 4,* 383–384.

RESCORLA, R. A. (1967a). Inhibition of delay in Pavlovian fear conditioning. *Journal of Comparative and Physiological Psychology, 64,* 114–120.

RESCORLA, R. A. (1967b). Pavlovian conditioning and its proper control procedures. *Psychological Review, 74,* 71–80.

RESCORLA, R. A. (1968). Probability of shock in the presence and absence of CS in fear conditioning. *Journal of Comparative and Physiological Psychology, 66,* 1–5.

RESCORLA, R. A. (1969a). Conditioned inhibition of fear resulting from negative CS–US contingencies. *Journal of Comparative and Physiological Psychology, 67,* 504–509.

RESCORLA, R. A. (1969b). Conditioned inhibition of fear. In W. K. Honig and N. J. Mackintosh (Eds.), *Fundamental issues in associative learning.* Halifax: Dalhousie University Press.

RESCORLA, R. A. (1974). Effect of inflation on the unconditioned stimulus value following conditioning. *Journal of Comparative and Physiological Psychology, 86,* 101–106.

RESCORLA, R. A. (1980). *Pavlovian second-order conditioning: Studies in associative learning.* Hillsdale, NJ: Erlbaum.

RESCORLA, R. A., DURLACH, P. J., & GRAU, J. W. (1985). Contextual learning in Pavlovian conditioning. In P. D. Balsam and A. Tomie (Eds.), *Context and learning.* Hillsdale, NJ: Erlbaum.

RESCORLA, R. A., & HOLLAND, P. C. (1977). Associations in Pavlovian conditioned inhibition. *Learning and Motivation, 8,* 429–447.

RESCORLA, R. A., & SKUCY, J. C. (1969). Effect of response-independent reinforcers during extinction. *Journal of Comparative and Physiological Psychology, 67,* 381–389.

RESCORLA, R. A., & SOLOMON, R. L. (1967). Two-process learning theory: Relationships between Pavlovian conditioning and instrumental learning. *Psychological Review, 74,* 151–182.

RESCORLA, R. A., & WAGNER, A. R. (1972). A theory of Pavlovian conditioning: Variations in the effectiveness of reinforcement and nonreinforcement. In A. H. Black and W. F. Prokasy (Eds.), *Classical conditioning,* Vol. II: *Current theory and research.* New York: Appleton-Century-Crofts.

REYNIERSE, J. H., & RIZLEY, R. C. (1970). Stimulus and response contingencies in extinction of avoidance by rats. *Journal of Comparative and Physiological Psychology, 73,* 86–92.

REYNOLDS, G. S. (1961). Behavioral contrast. *Journal of Experimental Analysis of Behavior, 4,* 57–71.

RICHARDS, W. J., & LESLIE, G. R. (1961). Food and water deprivation as influences on exploration. *Journal of Comparative and Physiological Psychology, 55,* 834–837.

RICHARDSON, J., & BROWN, B. L. (1966). Mediated transfer in paired-associative learning as a function of presentation rate and stimulus meaningfulness. *Journal of Experimental Psychology, 72,* 820–828.

RILEY, D. A., & LEVIN, T. C. (1971). Stimulus generalization gradients in chickens reared in monochromatic light and tested with a single wavelength value. *Journal of Comparative and Physiological Psychology, 75,* 399.

RIPS, L. J., SHOBEN, E. J., & SMITH, E. E. (1973). Semantic distance and the verification of semantic relations. *Journal of Verbal Learning and Verbal Behavior, 12,* 1–20.

ROBERTS, W. A. (1969). Resistance to extinction following partial and consistent reinforcement with varying magnitudes of reward. *Journal of Comparative and Physiological Psychology, 67,* 395–400.

ROBERTS, W. A., & GRANT, D. S. (1976). Studies in short-term memory in the pigeon using the delayed matching-to-sample procedure. In D. L. Medin, W. A. Roberts, and R. T. Davis (Eds.), *Processes of animal memory.* Hillsdale, NJ: Erlbaum.

ROCK, I. (1957). The role of repetition in associative learning. *American Journal of Psychology, 70,* 186–193.

ROITBLAT, H. L. (1980). Codes and coding processes in pigeon short-term memory. *Animal Learning and Behavior, 8,* 341–351.

ROSCH, E. H. (1973). Natural categories. *Cognitive Psychology, 4,* 328–350.

ROSCH, E. H. (1977). Human categorization. In N. Warren (Ed.), *Advances in cross-cultural psychology,* Vol. 1. London: Academic Press.

ROSCH, E. H., & MERVIS, C. B. (1975). Family resemblances: Studies in the internal structure of categories. *Cognitive Psychology, 7,* 573–605.

ROSE, R. J. (1980). Encoding variability, levels of processing, and the effects of spacing of repetitions upon judgments of frequency. *Memory and Cognition, 8*(1), 84–93.

ROSS, J., & LAWRENCE, K. A. (1968). Some observations on memory artifice. *Psychonomic Science, 13,* 107–108.

ROTH, E. M., & SHOBEN, E. E. (1983). The effect of

context on the structure of categories. *Cognitive Psychology, 15,* 346–379.

Rothkopf, E. Z. (1971). Incidental memory for location of information in text. *Journal of Verbal Learning and Verbal Behavior, 10,* 608–613.

Rowe, E. J., & Rose, R. J. (1974). Instructional and spacing effects in judgment of frequency. Paper presented at the annual meeting of the Canadian Psychological Association.

Royer, J. M., Hambleton, R. K., & Cadorette, L. (1978). Individual differences in memory: Theory, data, and educational implications. *Contemporary Educational Psychology, 3,* 182–203.

Rudolph, R. L., & Honig, W. K. (1972). Effects of monochromatic rearing on the spectral discrimination learning and the peak shift in chicks. *Journal of Experimental Analysis of Behavior, 17,* 107.

Rundus, D. (1971). Analysis of rehearsal processes in free recall. *Journal of Experimental Psychology, 89,* 63–77.

Rundus, D. (1977). Maintenance rehearsal and single-level processing. *Journal of Verbal Learning and Verbal Behavior, 16,* 665–681.

Rusiniak, K. W., Hankins, W. G., Garcia, J., & Brett, L. P. (1979). Flavor–illness aversions: Potentiation of odor by taste in rats. *Behavioral and Neural Biology, 25,* 1–17.

Sachs, J. S. (1967). Recognition memory for syntactic and semantic aspects of connected discourse. *Perception and Psychophysics, 2,* 437–442.

St. Claire-Smith, R. (1979). The overshadowing of instrumental conditioning by a stimulus that predicts reinforcement better than the response. *Animal Learning and Behavior, 7,* 224–228.

Saltzman, I. J. (1949). Maze learning in the absence of primary reinforcement: A study of secondary reinforcement. *Journal of Comparative and Physiological Psychology, 42,* 161–173.

Sanders, G. S., & Simmons, W. L. (1983). Use of hypnosis to enhance eyewitness accuracy: Does it work? *Journal of Applied Psychology, 68,* 70–77.

Santa, J. L., & Lamwers, L. L. (1976). Where does the confusion lie? Comments on the Wiseman and Tulving paper. *Journal of Verbal Learning and Verbal Behavior, 15,* 53–57.

Schiff, R., Smith, N., & Prochaska, J. (1972). Extinction of avoidance in rats as a function of duration and number of blocked trials. *Journal of Comparative and Physiological Psychology, 81,* 356–359.

Schneiderman, N. (1966). Interstimulus interval function of the nictitating membrane response of the rabbit under delay versus trace conditioning. *Journal of Comparative and Physiological Psychology, 62,* 397–402.

Schoenfeld, W. N. (1950). An experimental approach to anxiety, escape and avoidance behavior. In P. H. Hock and J. Zubin (Eds.), *Anxiety.* New York: Grune & Stratton.

Schvaneveldt, R. W., Durso, F. T., Goldsmith, T. E., Breen, T. J., Cooke, N. M., Tucker, R. G., & Demaio, J. C. (1985). Measuring the structure of expertise. *International Journal of Man–Machine Studies, 23,* 699.

Seligman, M. E. P. (1969). Control group and conditioning: A comment on operationism. *Psychological Review, 76,* 484–491.

Seligman, M. E. P. (1970). On the generality of the laws of learning. *Psychological Review, 77*(5), 406–418.

Seligman, M. E. P. (1975). *Helplessness: On depression, development, and death.* San Francisco: Freeman.

Seligman, M. E. P., & Campbell, B. A. (1965). Effect of intensity and duration of punishment on extinction of an avoidance response. *Journal of Comparative and Physiological Psychology, 59,* 295–297.

Seligman, M. E. P., & Johnston, J. C. (1973). A cognitive theory of avoidance learning. In F. J. McGuigan and D. B. Lumsden (Eds.), *Contemporary approaches to conditioning and learning.* Washington DC: Winston, pp. 69–110.

Seward, J. P. (1949). An experimental analysis of latent learning. *Journal of Experimental Psychology, 39,* 177–186.

Shallice, T., & Warrington, E. K. (1970). Independent functioning of verbal memory stores: A neuropsychological study. *Quarterly Journal of Experimental Psychology, 22,* 261–273.

Shaughnessy, J. J. (1976). Persistence of the spacing effect in free recall under varying incidental learning conditions. *Memory and Cognition, 4,* 369–377.

Sheffield, F. D. (1966). A drive-induction theory of reinforcement. In R. N. Haber (Ed.), *Current research and theory in motivation.* New York: Holt, Rinehart & Winston, pp. 98–111.

Sheffield, F. D., & Roby, T. B. (1950). Reward value of a nonnutritive sweet taste. *Journal of Comparative and Physiological Psychology, 43,* 471–481.

Sheffield, F. D., Roby, T. B., & Campbell, B. A. (1954). Drive-reduction versus consummatory behavior as determinants of reinforcement. *Journal of Comparative and Physiological Psychology, 47,* 349–354.

Sheffield, F. D., Wulff, J. J., & Backer, R. (1951). Reward value of copulation without sex-drive reduction. *Journal of Comparative and Physiological Psychology, 44,* 3–8.

SHEPARD, R. N. (1967). Recognition memory for words, sentences, and pictures. *Journal of Verbal Learning and Verbal Behavior, 6,* 156–163.

SHEPARD, R. N. (1978). The mental image. *American Psychologist, 33,* 125–137.

SHEPARD, R. N., & METZLER, J. (1971). Mental rotation of three-dimensional objects. *Science, 171,* 701–703.

SHEPP, B. E., & EIMAS, P. D. (1964). Intradimensional and extradimensional shifts in the rat. *Journal of Comparative and Physiological Psychology, 57,* 357.

SHEPP, B. E., & SCHRIER, A. M. (1969). Consecutive intradimensional and extradimensional shifts in monkeys. *Journal of Comparative and Physiological Psychology, 67,* 199.

SHERRY, D. F., KREBS, J. R., & COWIE, R. J. (1981). Memory for the location of stored food in marsh-tits. *Animal Behavior, 29,* 1260–1266.

SHIFFRIN, R. N. (1973). Information persistence in short-term memory. *Journal of Experimental Psychology, 100,* 39–49.

SHULMAN, H. G. (1972). Semantic confusion errors in short-term memory. *Journal of Verbal Learning and Verbal Behavior, 11,* 221–227.

SIDMAN, M. (1953). Avoidance conditioning with brief shock and no exteroceptive warning signal. *Science, N.Y., 118,* 157–158.

SIDMAN, M. (1962). Classical avoidance without a warning stimulus. *Journal of Experimental Analysis of Behavior, 5,* 97–104.

SIEGEL, S., & DOMJAN, M. (1971). Backward conditioning as an inhibitory procedure. *Learning and Motivation, 2,* 1–11.

SINGER, M., & ROSENBERG, S. T. (1973). The role of grammatical relations in the abstraction of linguistic ideas. *Journal of Verbal Learning and Verbal Behavior, 12,* 273–284.

SKINNER, B. F. (1948). Superstition in the pigeon. *Journal of Experimental Psychology, 38,* 168–172.

SLAMECKA, N. J. (1964). An inquiry into the doctrine of remote associations. *Psychological Review, 71,* 61–77.

SLAMECKA, N. J., & GRAF, P. (1978). The generation effect: Delineation of a phenomenon. *Journal of Experimental Psychology: Human Learning and Memory, 4,* 592–604.

SMITH, E. E., SHOBEN, E. J., & RIPS, L. J. (1974). Structure and process in semantic memory: A feature model for semantic decisions. *Psychological Review, 81,* 214–241.

SMITH, M. C., COLEMAN, S. R., & GORMEZANO, I. (1969). Classical conditioning of the rabbit's nictitating membrane response at backward, simultaneous and forward CS–US intervals. *Journal of Comparative and Physiological Psychology, 69,* 226–231.

SMITH, S. M., GLENBERG, A. M., & BJORK, R. A. (1978). Environmental context and human memory. *Memory and Cognition, 6,* 342–353.

SNYDER, H. L., & HULSE, S. H. (1961). Effects of volume of reinforcement and number of consummatory responses on licking and running behavior. *Journal of Experimental Psychology, 61,* 474–479.

SOLOMON, R. L., KAMIN, L. J., & WYNNE, L. C. (1953). Traumatic avoidance learning: The outcomes of several extinction procedures with dogs. *Journal of Abnormal and Social Psychology, 48,* 291–302.

SOLOMON, R. L., & TURNER, L. H. (1962). Discriminative Classical conditioning in dogs paralyzed by curare can later control discriminative avoidance responses in normal states. *Psychological Review, 69,* 202–219.

SOLOMON, R. L., & WYNNE, L. C. (1954). Traumatic avoidance learning: The principles of anxiety conservation and partial irreversibility. *Psychological Review, 61,* 353–385.

SOLTYSIK, S. (1971). The effect of satiation upon conditioned and unconditioned salivary responses. *Acta Biological Experimentation, 31,* 59–63.

SPEAR, N. E. (1970). Verbal learning and retention. In M. R. D'Amato (Ed.), *Experimental psychology: Methodology, psychophysics, and learning.* New York: McGraw-Hill.

SPEAR, N. E. (1971). Forgetting as retrieval failure. In W. K. Honig and P. N. R. James (Eds.), *Animal memory.* New York: Academic Press.

SPEAR, N. E. (1973). Retrieval of memory in animals. *Psychological Review, 80,* 163–194.

SPEAR, N. E. (1976). Retrieval of memories. In W. K. Estes (Ed.), *Handbook of learning and cognitive processes,* Vol. IV, *Attention and memory.* Hillsdale, NJ: Erlbaum.

SPEAR, N. E. (1978). *The processing of memories: Forgetting and retention.* Hillsdale, NJ: Erlbaum.

SPEAR, N. E. (1981). Extending the domain of memory retrieval. In N. E. Spear and R. R. Miller (Eds.), *Information processing in animals: Memory mechanisms.* Hillsdale, NJ: Erlbaum.

SPEAR, N. E., GORDON, W. C., & MARTIN, P. A. (1973). Warm-up decrement as failure in memory retrieval in the rat. *Journal of Comparative and Physiological Psychology, 85,* 601–614.

SPENCE, K. W. (1936). The nature of discrimination learning in animals. *Psychological Review, 43,* 427–449.

SPENCE, K. W. (1937). The differential response in

animals to stimuli varying within a single dimension. *Psychological Review, 44,* 430–444.

SPENCE, K. W. (1956). *Behavior theory and conditioning.* New Haven: Yale University Press.

SPENCE, K. W., & ROSS, L. E. (1959). A methodological study of the form and latency of eyelid responses in conditioning. *Journal of Experimental Psychology, 58,* 376–385.

SPERLING, G. (1960). The information available in brief visual presentations. *Psychological Monographs, 74* (whole no. 11).

SPERLING, G., & SPEELMAN, R. G. (1970). Acoustic similarity and auditory short-term memory: Experiments and a model. In D. A. Norman (Ed.), *Models of human memory.* New York: Academic Press.

SPETCH, M. L., WILKIE, D. M., & PINEL, P. J. P. (1981). Backward conditioning: A reevaluation of the empirical evidence. *Psychological Bulletin, 89,* 163–175.

SPIVEY, J. E., & HESS, D. T. (1968). Effect of partial reinforcement trial sequences on extinction performance. *Psychonomic Science, 10,* 375–376.

STAATS, A. W., STAATS, C. K., & HEARD, W. G. (1959). Language conditioning of meaning to meaning using semantic generalization paradigm. *Journal of Experimental Psychology, 57,* 187–192.

STABLER, J. R. (1962). Performance in Instrumental conditioning as a joint function of time of deprivation and sucrose concentration. *Journal of Experimental Psychology, 63,* 248–253.

STADDON, J. E. R. (1979). Operant behavior as adaptation to constraint. *Journal of Experimental Psychology: General, 108,* 48–67.

STANDING, L., CONEZIO, J., & HABER, R. N. (1970). Perception and memory for pictures: Single trial learning of 2560 visual stimuli. *Psychonomic Science, 19,* 73–74.

STEIN, B. S. (1978). Depth of processing reexamined: The effects of the precision of encoding and test appropriateness. *Journal of Verbal Learning and Verbal Behavior, 17,* 165–174.

STERNBERG, S. (1966). High speed scanning in human memory. *Science, 153,* 652–654.

STERNBERG, S. (1967). Retrieval of contextual information from memory. *Psychonomic Science, 8,* 55–56.

STERNBERG, S. (1969). Memory scanning: Mental processes revealed by reaction-time experiments. *American Scientist, 57,* 421–457.

STERNBERG, S. (1975). Memory scanning: New findings and current controversies. *Quarterly Journal of Experimental Psychology, 27,* 1–32.

STROEBEL, C. F. (1967). Behavioral aspects of circadian rhythms. In J. Zubin and H. F. Hunt (Eds.), *Comparative psychopathology.* New York: Grune & Stratton.

SUTHERLAND, N. S., & MACKINTOSH, N. J. (1971). *Mechanisms of animal discrimination learning.* New York: Academic Press.

SUZUKI, S., AUGERINOS, G., & BLACK, A. H. (1980). Stimulus control of spatial behavior on the eight-arm maze in rats. *Learning and Motivation, 11,* 1–18.

TEICHNER, W. H. (1952). Experimental extinction as a function of the intertrial intervals during conditioning and extinction. *Journal of Experimental Psychology, 44,* 170–178.

TERRACE, H. S. (1973). Classical conditioning. In J. A. Nevin and G. S. Reynolds (Eds.), *The study of behavior: Learning, motivation, emotion and instinct.* Glenview, IL: Scott Foresman.

TERRY, W. S., & WAGNER, A. R. (1975). Short-term memory for "surprising" versus "expected" unconditioned stimuli in Pavlovian conditioning. *Journal of Experimental Psychology: Animal Behavior Processes, 1,* 122–133.

THEIOS, J., SMITH, P. G., HAVILAND, S. E., TRAUPMANN, J., & MOY, M. C. (1973). Memory scanning as a serial self-terminating process. *Journal of Experimental Psychology, 97,* 323–336.

THOMAS, D. R. (1962). The effects of drive and discrimination training on stimulus generalization. *Journal of Experimental Psychology, 64,* 24–28.

THOMAS, D. R., FREEMAN, F., SVINICKI, J. G., BURR, D. E. S., & LYONS, J. (1970). Effects of extradimensional training on stimulus generalization. *Journal of Experimental Psychology Monograph, 83,* 1–21.

THOMAS, D. R., & KING, R. A. (1959). Stimulus generalization as function of level of motivation. *Journal of Experimental Psychology, 57,* 323–328.

THOMAS, D. R., & LOPEZ, L. J. (1962). The effects of delayed testing on generalization slope. *Journal of Comparative and Physiological Psychology, 55,* 541–544.

THOMAS, D. R., & SWITALSKI, R. W. (1966). Comparison of stimulus generalization following variable-ratio and variable-interval training. *Journal of Experimental Psychology, 71,* 236–240.

THOMAS, D. R., WINDELL, B. T., BAKKE, I., KREYE, J., KIMOSE, E., & APOSHYAN, H. (1985). Long-term memory in pigeons: I. The role of discrimination problem difficulty assessed by reacquisition measures. II. The role of stimulus modality assessed by generalization slope. *Learning and Motivation, 16,* 464–477.

THOMPSON, C. P., HAMLIN, V. J., & ROENKER, D. L. (1972). A comment on the role of clustering in free recall. *Journal of Experimental Psychology, 94,* 108–109.

Thompson, R. F., Hicks, L. H., & Shvyrok, U. B. (1980). *Neural mechanisms of goal directed behavior and learning.* New York: Academic Press.

Thomson, D. M., & Tulving, E. (1970). Associative encoding and retrieval: Weak and strong cues. *Journal of Experimental Psychology, 86,* 255–262.

Thorndike, E. L. (1913). *Educational psychology,* Vol. II: *The psychology of learning.* New York: Teachers College, Columbia University.

Thorndike, E. L., & Lorge, I. (1944). *The teacher's word book of 30,000 words.* New York: Columbia University Press.

Thune, L. E. (1950). The effect of different types of preliminary activities on subsequent learning of paired associates material. *Journal of Experimental Psychology, 40,* 423–438.

Timberlake, W. (1980). A molar equilibrium theory of learned performance. In G. H. Bower (Ed.), *The psychology of learning and motivation,* Vol. 14. New York: Academic Press.

Timberlake, W. (1984). Behavior regulation and learned performance: Some misapprehensions and disagreements. *Journal of Experimental Analysis of Behavior, 41,* 355–375.

Timberlake, W., & Allison, J. (1974). Response deprivation: An empirical approach to instrumental performance. *Psychological Review, 81,* 146–164.

Tinbergen, N. (1951). *The study of instinct.* Oxford: Clarendon Press.

Tinbergen, N. (1952). The curious behavior of the stickleback. *Scientific American, 187,* 22–60.

Tolman, E. C., & Honzik, C. H. (1930). Introduction and removal of reward, and maze performance in rats. *University of California Publications in Psychology, 4,* 257–275.

Tomback, D. F. (1983). Nutcrackers and pines: Coevolution or coadaptation? In H. Nitecki (Ed.), *Coevolution.* Chicago: University of Chicago Press.

Tombaugh, T. N. (1966). Resistance to extinction as a function of the interaction between training and extinction delays. *Psychological Reports, 19,* 791–798.

Tombaugh, T. N. (1970). A comparison of the effects of immediate reinforcement, constant delay of reinforcement, and partial delay of reinforcement on performance. *Canadian Journal of Psychology, 24,* 276–288.

Tomie, A. (1976). Interference with autoshaping by prior context conditioning. *Journal of Experimental Psychology: Animal Behavior Processes, 2,* 232–324.

Trabasso, T., Deutsch, J. A., & Gelman, R. (1966). Attention and discrimination learning of young children. *Journal of Experimental Child Psychology, 4,* 9.

Tracy, W. K. (1970). Wavelength generalization and preference in monochromatically reared ducklings. *Journal of Experimental Analysis of Behavior, 13,* 163.

Tranberg, D. K., & Rilling, M. (1980). Delay-interval illumination changes interfere with pigeon short-term memory. *Journal of Experimental Analysis of Behavior, 33,* 33–49.

Trapold, M. A., & Fowler, H. (1960). Instrumental escape performance as a function of the intensity of noxious stimulation. *Journal of Experimental Psychology, 60,* 323–326.

Trapold, M. A., & Spence, K. W. (1960). Performance changes in eyelid conditioning as related to the motivational and reinforcing properties of the UCS. *Journal of Experimental Psychology, 59,* 209–213.

Treisman, A. M. (1960). Contextual cues in selective listening. *Quarterly Journal of Experimental Psychology, 12,* 242–248.

Treisman, A. M. (1964). Verbal cues, language, and meaning in selective attention. *American Journal of Psychology, 77,* 206–219.

Treisman, A. M. (1969). Strategies and models for selective attention. *Psychological Review, 76,* 282–299.

Treisman, A. M., & Geffen, G. (1967). Selective attention: Perception or response? *Quarterly Journal of Experimental Psychology, 19,* 1–17.

Tulving, E. (1962). Subjective organization in free recall of "unrelated words." *Psychological Review, 69,* 344–354.

Tulving, E. (1968). When is recall higher than recognition? *Psychonomic Science, 10,* 53–54.

Tulving, E. (1972). Episodic and semantic memory. In E. Tulving and W. Donaldson (Eds.), *Organization and memory.* New York: Academic Press.

Tulving, E. (1983). *Elements of episodic memory.* Oxford: Clarendon Press/Oxford University Press.

Tulving, E., & Osler, S. (1968). Effectiveness of retrieval cues in memory for words. *Journal of Experimental Psychology, 77,* 593–601.

Tulving, E., & Pearlstone, Z. (1966). Availability versus accessibility of information in memory for words. *Journal of Verbal Learning and Verbal Behavior, 5,* 381–391.

Tulving, E., & Thomson, D. M. (1973). Encoding specificity and retrieval processes in episodic memory. *Psychological Review, 80,* 352–373.

Tulving, E., & Watkins, O. C. (1977). Recognition failure of words with a single meaning. *Memory and Cognition, 5,* 513–522.

Twedt, H. M., & Underwood, B. J. (1959). Mixed

vs. unmixed lists in transfer studies. *Journal of Experimental Psychology, 58,* 111–116.

Uhl, C. N., & Garcia, E. E. (1969). Comparison of omission with extinction in response elimination in rats. *Journal of Comparative and Physiological Psychology, 69,* 554–562.

Uhl, C. N., & Young, A. G. (1967). Resistance to extinction as a function of incentive, percentage of reinforcement, and number of reinforced trials. *Journal of Experimental Psychology, 73,* 556–564.

Uhl, N. P. (1966). Intradimensional and extradimensional shifts as a function of amount of training and similarity between training and shift stimuli. *Journal of Experimental Psychology, 72,* 429–433.

Underwood, B. J. (1945). The effect of successive interpolations on retroactive and proactive inhibition. *Psychological Monographs, 59* (whole no. 273).

Underwood, B. J. (1952). Studies of distributed practice. VII. Learning and retention of serial nonsense lists as a function of intralist similarity. *Journal of Experimental Psychology, 44,* 80–87.

Underwood, B. J. (1957). Interference and forgetting. *Psychological Review, 64*(1), 49–59.

Underwood, B. J. (1961). Ten years of massed practice on distributed practice. *Psychological Review, 68,* 229–247.

Underwood, B. J. (1964). The representativeness of rote Verbal learning. In A. W. Melton (Ed.), *Categories of human learning.* New York: Academic Press.

Underwood, B. J. (1966). Individual and group predictions of item difficulty for free learning. *Journal of Experimental Psychology, 71,* 673–679.

Underwood, B. J. (1969). Attributes of memory. *Psychological Review, 76,* 559–573.

Underwood, B. J., Ekstrand, B. R., & Keppel, G. (1964). Studies of distributed practice. XXIII. Variations in response-term interference. *Journal of Experimental Psychology, 68,* 201–212.

Underwood, B. J., Ekstrand, B. R., & Keppel, G. (1965). An analysis of intralist similarity in Verbal learning with experiments on conceptual similarity. *Journal of Verbal Learning and Verbal Behavior, 4,* 447–462.

Underwood, B. J., & Erlebacher, A. H. (1965). Studies of coding in Verbal learning. *Psychological Monographs, 79*(13, whole no. 606).

Underwood, B. J., & Goad, D. (1951). Studies of distributed practice. I. The influence of intralist similarity in serial learning. *Journal of Experimental Psychology, 42,* 125–134.

Underwood, B. J., & Keppel, G. (1962). One-trial learning? *Journal of Verbal Learning and Verbal Behavior, 1,* 1–13.

Underwood, B. J., & Keppel, G. (1963a). Coding processes in Verbal learning. *Journal of Verbal Learning and Verbal Behavior, 1,* 250–257.

Underwood, B. J., & Keppel, G. (1963b). Retention as a function of degree of learning and letter-sequence interference. *Psychological Monographs, 77* (4, whole no. 567).

Underwood, B. J., Runquist, W. N., & Schulz, R. W. (1959). Response learning in paired-associates lists as a function of intralist similarity. *Journal of Experimental Psychology, 58,* 70–78.

Underwood, B. J., & Schulz, R. W. (1960). *Meaningfulness and verbal learning.* Philadelphia: Lippincott.

van Dijk, T. A., & Kintsch, W. (1983). *Strategies of discourse comprehension.* New York: Academic Press.

von Wright, J. M. (1959). The effect of systematic changes of context stimuli on repeated recall. *Acta Psychologia, 16,* 59–68.

Wagner, A. R. (1959). The role of reinforcement and nonreinforcement in an "apparent frustration effect." *Journal of Experimental Psychology, 57,* 130–136.

Wagner, A. R. (1961). Effects of amount and percentage of reinforcement and number of acquisition trials on conditioning and extinction. *Journal of Experimental Psychology, 62,* 234–242.

Wagner, A. R. (1969). Stimulus validity and stimulus selection in associative learning. In W. K. Honig and N. J. MacKintosh (Eds.), *Fundamental issues in associative learning.* Halifax: Dalhousie University Press.

Wagner, A. R. (1976). Priming in STM: An information processing mechanism for self-generated or retrieval-generated depression in performance. In T. J. Tighe and R. N. Leaton (Eds.), *Habituation: Perspectives from child development, animal behavior, and neurophysiology.* Hillsdale, NJ: Erlbaum.

Wagner, A. R. (1978). Expectancies and priming in STM. In S. H. Hulse, H. Fowler, and W. K. Honig (Eds.), *Cognitive processes in animal behavior.* Hillsdale, NJ: Erlbaum.

Wagner, A. R. (1981). S.O.P.: A model of automatic memory processing in animal behavior. In N. E. Spear and R. R. Miller (Eds.), *Information processing in animals: Memory mechanisms.* Hillsdale, NJ: Erlbaum.

Wagner, A. R., Logan, F. A., Haberlandt, K., & Price, T. (1968). Stimulus selection in animal discrimination learning. *Journal of Experimental Psychology, 76,* 171–180.

Wagner, A. R., Rudy, J. W., & Whitlow, J. W. (1973). Rehearsal in animal conditioning.

Journal of Experimental Psychology, 97, 407–426 (monograph).

Wagner, A. R., & Terry, W. S. (1975). Backward conditioning to a CS following an expected vs. a surprising UCS. *Animal Learning and Behavior, 3,* 370–374.

Walk, R. D., & Walters, C. P. (1973). Effect of visual deprivation on depth discrimination of hooded rats. *Journal of Comparative and Physiological Psychology, 85,* 559.

Ward, L. B. (1937). Reminiscence and rote learning. *Psychological Monographs, 49,* no. 220.

Warner, L. H. (1932). The association span of the white rat. *Journal of Genetic Psychology, 41,* 57–90.

Watkins, M. J. (1974). When is recall spectacularly higher than recognition? *Journal of Experimental Psychology, 102,* 161–163.

Watkins, M. J., & Tulving, E. (1975). Episodic memory: When recognition fails. *Journal of Experimental Psychology: General, 1,* 5–29.

Waugh, N. C. (1970). On the effective duration of a repeated word. *Journal of Verbal Learning and Verbal Behavior, 9,* 587–595.

Waugh, N. C., & Norman, D. A. (1965). Primary memory. *Psychological Review, 72,* 89–104.

Weinberg, H. I., Wadsworth, J., & Baron, R. S. (1983). Demand and the impact of leading questions on eyewitness testimony. *Memory and Cognition, 11,* 101–104.

Weingartner, H., Miller, H., & Murphy, D. L. (1977). Mood–state-dependent retrieval of verbal associations. *Journal of Abnormal Psychology, 86*(3), 276–284.

Weisman, R. G., & Litner, J. S. (1969). Positive conditioned reinforcement of Sidman avoidance behavior in rats. *Journal of Comparative and Physiological Psychology, 68,* 597–603.

Weiss, R. F. (1960). Deprivation and reward magnitude effects on speed throughout the goal gradient. *Journal of Experimental Psychology, 60,* 384–390.

Whitlow, J. W. (1976). The dynamics of episodic processing in Pavlovian conditioning. In D. L. Medin, W. A. Roberts, and R. T. Davis (Eds.), *Processes of animal memory.* Hillsdale, NJ: Erlbaum.

Whitlow, J. W., & Estes, W. K. (1979). Judgments of relative frequency in relation to shifts of event frequencies: Evidence for a limited-capacity model. *Journal of Experimental Psychology: Human Learning and Memory, 5,* 395–408.

Whitlow, J. W., & Skaar, E. (1979). The role of numerosity in judgments of overall frequency. *Journal of Experimental Psychology: Human Learning and Memory, 5,* 409–421.

Wickelgren, W. A. (1966). Distinctive features and errors in short-term memory for English consonants. *Journal of the Acoustical Society of America, 39,* 388–398.

Wickelgren, W. A. (1977). *Learning and memory.* Englewood Cliffs, NJ: Prentice-Hall.

Wickelgren, W. A. (1979). *Cognitive psychology.* Englewood Cliffs, NJ: Prentice-Hall.

Wickens, D. D. (1970). Encoding categories of words: An empirical approach to meaning. *Psychological Review, 77,* 1–15.

Wickens, D. D. (1972). Characteristics of word encoding. In A. W. Melton and E. Martin (Eds.), *Coding processes in human memory.* Washington, DC: Winston.

Wiesel, T. N., & Hubel, D. H. (1965). Comparison of the effects of unilateral and bilateral eye closure on cortical unit responses in kittens. *Journal of Neurophysiology, 28,* 1029–1040.

Wike, E. L., Mellgren, R. L., & Wike, S. S. (1968). Runway performance as a function of delayed reinforcement and delayed box confinement. *Psychological Record, 18,* 9–18.

Williams, D. R. (1965). Classical conditioning and incentive motivation. In W. F. Prokasy (Ed.), *Classical conditioning: A symposium.* New York: Appleton-Century-Crofts, pp. 340–357.

Williams, S. B. (1938). Resistance to extinction as a function of the number of reinforcements. *Journal of Experimental Psychology, 23,* 506–521.

Wingfield, A. (1973). Effects of serial position and set size in auditory recognition memory. *Memory and Cognition, 1,* 53–55.

Wingfield, A., & Bolt, R. A. (1970). Memory search for multiple targets. *Journal of Experimental Psychology, 85,* 45–50.

Wiseman, S., & Tulving, E. (1976). Encoding specificity: Relation between recall superiority and recognition failure. *Journal of Experimental Psychology: Human Learning and Memory, 2,* 349–361.

Wittgenstein, L. (1953). *Philosophical investigations.* New York: Macmillan.

Wollen, K. A., Weber, A., & Lowry, D. (1972). Bizarreness versus interaction of mental images as determinants of learning. *Cognitive Psychology, 3,* 518–523.

Wynne, J. D., & Brogden, W. J. (1962). Effect upon sensory preconditioning of backward, forward, and trace preconditioning training. *Journal of Experimental Psychology, 64,* 422–423.

Yerkes, R. M., & Morgulis, S. (1909). The method of Pavlov in animal psychology. *Psychological Bulletin, 6,* 257–273.

Young, R. K. (1962). Tests of three hypotheses

about the effective stimulus in serial learning. *Journal of Experimental Psychology, 63,* 307–313.

YOUNG, R. K., & CASEY, M. (1964). Transfer from serial to paired-associate learning. *Journal of Experimental Psychology, 67,* 594–595.

ZEAMAN, D., & HOUSE, B. J. (1963). The role of attention in retardate discrimination learning. In N. R. Ellis (Ed.), *Handbook of mental deficiency: Psychological theory and research.* New York: McGraw-Hill.

ZELNIKER, T. (1971). Perceptual attenuation of an irrelevant auditory verbal input as measured by an involuntary verbal response in a selective attention task. *Journal of Experimental Psychology, 87,* 52–56.

ZENTALL, T. R. (1973). Memory in the pigeon: Retroactive inhibition in a delayed matching task. *Bulletin of the Psychonomic Society, 1,* 126–128.

ZENTALL, T. R., COLLINS, W., & HEARST, E. (1971). Generalization gradients around a formerly positive S–. *Psychonomic Science, 22,* 257–259.

ZIFF, D. R., & CAPALDI, E. J. (1971). Amytal and the small trial, partial reinforcement effect: Stimulus properties of early trial nonrewards. *Journal of Experimental Psychology, 87,* 263–269.

Source Notes

CHAPTER 2 **24,** Figure 2.4 from "Classical Conditioning of the Rabbit's Nictitating Membrane Response at Backward, Simultaneous, and Forward CS—US Intervals," by M. C. Smith, S. R. Coleman, and I. Gormezano, *Journal of Comparative and Physiological Psychology*, 1969, *69*, 226–231. Copyright 1969 by the American Psychological Association. Reprinted by permission. **26,** Figure 2.5 from "Probability of Shock in the Presence and Absence of CA in Fear Conditioning," by R. A. Rescorla, *Journal of Comparative and Physiological Psychology*, 1968, *66*, 1–5. Copyright 1968 by the American Psychological Association. Reprinted by permission. **27,** Figure 2.6a from "Performance Changes in Eyelid Conditioning as Related to the Motivational and Reinforcing Properties of the UCS," by M. A. Trapold and K. W. Spence, *Journal of Experimental Psychology*, 1960, *59*, 209–213. Copyright 1960 by the American Psychological Association. **27,** Figure 2.6b from "Yoked Comparisons of Classical and Instrumental Conditioning of the Eyelid Response, and an Addendum on Voluntary Responders," by I. Gormezan. In W. F. Prokasy (Ed.), *Classical Conditioning: A Symposium.* Copyright 1965 by Appleton & Lange. Reprinted by permission. **27,** Figure 2.6c from "Context Specificity of Conditioning, Extinction, and Latent Inhibition," by P. F. Lovibond, G. C. Preston, and N. J. Mackintosh, *Journal of Experimental Psychology: Animal Behavior Processes*, 1984, *10*, 360–375. Copyright 1984 by the American Psychological Association. Reprinted by permission. **31,** Figure 2.7 adapted from "Relation of Cue to Consequence in Avoidance Learning," by J. Garcia and R. A. Koelling, *Psychonomic Science*, 1966, *4*, 123–124. Reprinted by permission of Psychonomic Society, Inc. **41, 42,** Figures 2.10 and 2.11 from "Trace Conditioning as an Inhibitory Procedure," by R. E. Hinson and S. Siegel, *Animal Learning & Behavior*, 1980, *8*, 60–66. Reprinted by permission of Psychonomic Society, Inc.

CHAPTER 3 **60,** Figure 3.1 adapted from "Backward Conditioning to a CSA Following an Expected vs. a Surprising UCS," by A. R. Wagner and W. S. Terry, *Animal Learning and Behavior*, 1975, *3*, 370–374. Copyright 1974 by the American Psychological Association. Adapted by permission. **61,** Figure 3.2 adapted from "Taste Aversion Learning with a Delayed Shock US: Implications for the Generality of the Laws of Learning," by R. V. Krane and A. R. Wagner, *Journal of Comparative and Physiological Psychology*, 1975, *88*, 882–89. Copyright 1975 by the American Psychological Association. Adapted by permission. **65,** Figure 3.3 adapted from "Effect of Inflation on the Unconditioned Stimulus Value Following Conditioning," by R. A. Rescorla, *Journal of Comparative and Physiological Psychology*, 1974, *86*, 101–106. Copyright 1974 by the American Psychological Association. Adapted by permission. **67,** Figure 3.4 from "Contextual Learning in Pavlovian Conditioning," by R. A. Rescorla, P. J. Durlach, and J. W. Graw. In P. Balsam and A. Tomie (Eds.), *Context and Learning.* Copyright 1985 by Lawrence Erlbaum Associates, Inc. Reprinted by permission.

CHAPTER 4 **75, 76,** Figures 4.1 and 4.2 reprinted with permission from "Forgetting as Retrieval Failure," by N. E. Spear. In W. K. Honig and H. P. R. James (Eds.), *Animal Memory*. Copyright 1971 by Pergamon Press, Inc. **82,** Figure 4.4 from "Effects of Schedule and Delay of Reinforcement on Acquisition Speed," by E. J. Capaldi, *Animal Learning and Behavior*, 1978, *6*, 330–334. Copyright 1978 by the American Psychological Association. Reprinted by permission. **86,** Figure 4.6 from "Escape Performance as a Function of Delay of Reinforcement," by H. Fowler and M. A. Trapold, *Journal of Experimental Psychology*, 1962, *63*, 464–467. Copyright 1962 by the American Psychological Association. Reprinted by permission. **88,** Figure 4.7 from "The Gradient of Delay of Secondary Reward in Avoidance Learning," by L. J. Kamin, *Journal of Comparative and Physiological Psychology*, 1957, *50*, 457–460. Copyright 1957 by the American Psychological Association. **89,** Figure 4.8 from "Fear and Punishment as Determinants of Passive-Avoidance Responding," by P. K. Randall and D. C. Riccio, *Journal of Comparative and Physiological Psychology*, 1969, *69*, 550–53. Copyright 1969 by the American Psychological Association. Reprinted by permission. **97,** Figure 4.13 from "Resistance to Extinction Following Partial and Consistent Reinforcement with Varying Magnitudes of Reward," by W. A. Roberts, *Journal of Comparative and Physiological Psychology*, 1969, *67*, 395–400. Copyright 1969 by the American Psychological Association. Reprinted by permission. **98,** Figure 4.14 from "Amount and Percentage of Reinforcement and Duration of Goal Confinement in Conditioning and Extinction," by S. H. Hulse, *Journal of Experimental Psychology*, 1958, *56*, 48–57. Copyright 1958 by the American Psychological Association.

CHAPTER 5 **114,** Figure 5.2 from "Negative Contrast as a Function of the Interval between Preshift and Postshift Training," by W. C. Gordon, C. F. Flaherty, and E. P. Riley, *Bulletin of the Psychonomic Society*, 1973, 1(1a), 25–27. Reprinted by permission of the Psychonomic Society, Inc. **118,** Figure 5.4 adapted from "Classical Conditioning and Incentive Motivation," by D. R. Williams. In W. F. Prokasy (Ed.), *Classical Conditioning: A Symposium.* Copyright 1965 by Appleton-Century Crofts. Copyright 1965 by Appleton & Lange. Reprinted by permission. **125,** Figure 5.6 adapted from "Effect of Partial Reinforcement Trial Sequences on Extinction Performance," by J. E. Spivey and D. T. Hess, *Psychonomic Science*, 1968, *10*, 375–376. Copyright 1968 by the Psychonomic Society, Inc. Reprinted by permission. **128,** Figure 5.7 adapted from "The Effects of Termination of the CS and Avoidance of the US on Avoidance Learning: An Extension," by L. J. Kamin, *Canadian Journal of Psychology*, 1957, *11*, 48–56. Copyright 1957 by the Canadian Psychological Association. Reprinted by permission.

CHAPTER 6 **144,** Figure 6.2 from "The Serial Position Effect in Free Recall," by B. B. Murdock, Jr., *Journal of Experimental Psychology*, 1962, *64*, 482–488. Copyright 1962 by the American Psychological Association. Reprinted by permission. **145,** Figure 6.3 from "The Conflicting Psychologies of Learning—A Way Out," by C. L. Hull, *Psychological Review*, 1935, *42*, 491–516. Copyright 1935 by the American Psychological Association. **146,** Figure 6.4 from "The Interaction of Ability and Amount of Practice with Stimulus Meaningfulness (m,m') in Paired-Associate

Learning," by V. J. Cieutat, F. E. Stockwell, and C. E. Nobel, *Journal of Experimental Psychology*, 1958, *56*, 193–202. Copyright 1958 by the American Psychological Association. **153,** Figure 6.5 adapted from "Availability vs. Accessibility of Information in Memory for Words," by E. Tulving and Z. Pearlstone, *Journal of Verbal Learning and Verbal Behavior*, 1966, *5*, 381–391. Copyright 1966 by Academic Press. Reprinted by permission. **155,** Figure 6.6 adapted from "Imagery Versus Meaningfulness of Nouns in Paired-Associate Learning," by A. Paivio, P. C. Smyth, and J. C. Yuille, *Canadian Journal of Psychology*, 1968, *22*, 427–441. Copyright 1968 by the Canadian Psychological Association. Adapted by permission. **157,** Figure 6.7 from "Bizarreness versus Interaction of Mental Images as Determinants of Learning," by K. A. Wollen, A. Weber, and D. Lowry, *Cognitive Psychology*, 1972, *3*, 518–523. Copyright 1972 by Academic Press. Reprinted by permission. **160,** Figure 6.8 from "The Effect of Different Types of Preliminary Activities on Subsequent Learning of Paired-Associate Materials," by L. E. Thune, *Journal of Experimental Psychology*, 1950, *40*, 423–438. Copyright 1950 by the American Psychological Association. **162,** Figure 6.9 adapted from "Transfer of Training as a Function of Experimental Paradigm and Degree of First-List Learning," by L. Postman, *Journal of Verbal Learning and Verbal Behavior*, 1962, *1*, 109–118. Copyright 1962 by Academic Press. Reprinted by permission.

CHAPTER 7 169, Figure 7.1 from "Discriminability and Stimulus Generalization," by N. Guttman and H. I. Kalish, *Journal of Experimental Psychology*, 1956, *51*, 79–88. Copyright 1956 by the American Psychological Association. **171,** Figure 7.3 from "Comparison of Stimulus Generalization Following Variable Ratio and Variable Interval Training," by D. R. Thomas and R. W. Switalski, *Journal of Experimental Psychology*, 1966, *71*, 236–240. Copyright 1966 by the American Psychological Association. Reprinted by permission. **172,** Figure 7.4 adapted from "Generalization Gradients around a Formerly Positive S-," by T. Zentall, N. Collins, and E. Hearst, *Psychonomic Science*, 1971, *22*, 257–259. Reprinted by permission of Psychonomic Society, Inc. **172,** Figure 7.5 from "Stimulus Generalization and Amount of Prior Training on Variable Interval Reinforcement," by E. Hearst and M. B. Koresko, *Journal of Comparative and Physiological Psychology*, 1968, *66*, 133–139. Copyright 1968 by the American Psychological Association. Reprinted by permission. **174,** Figure 7.6 adapted from "Stimulus Generalization and the Response-Reinforcement Contingency," by E. Hearst, M. B. Koresko, and R. Poppen, *Journal of the Experimental Analysis of Behavior*," 1964, *7*, 369–380. Copyright 1964 by the Society for the Experimental Analysis of Behavior. Reprinted by permission. **174,** Figure 7.7 from "The Effect of Delayed Testing on Generalization Slope," by D. R. Thomas and L. J. Lopez, *Journal of Comparative and Physiological Psychology*, 1962, *44*, 541–544. Copyright 1962 by the American Psychological Association. Reprinted by permission. **175,** Figure 7.8 from "Effects of Discrimination Training on Stimulus Generalization," by H. M. Hanson, *Journal of Experimental Psychology*, 1959, *58*, 321–334. Copyright 1959 by the American Psychological Association. **186, 188,** Figures 7.9 and 7.10 from "Hypothesis Behavior by Humans During Discrimination Learning," by M. Levine, *Journal of Experimental Psychology*, 1966, *71*, 331–338. Copyright 1966 by the American Psychological Association. Reprinted by permission. **192,** Figure 7.11 adapted from "Perceived Distance and the Classification of Distorted Patterns," by M. I. Posner, R. Goldsmith, and K. E. Welton, *Journal of Experimental Psychology*, 1967, *73*, 28–38. Copyright 1967 by the American Psychological Association. Adapted by permission.

CHAPTER 8 199, Figure 8.1 from "The Control of Short-Term Memory," by R. C. Atkinson and R. M. Shiffrin, *Scientific American*, 1971, *225*(2), 82–90. Copyright 1971 by Scientific American. Reprinted by permission of W. H. Freeman, Inc. **205,** Figure 8.3 adapted from "Input Modality and the Serial Position Curve in Short-Term Memory," by R. Conrad and A. J. Hull, *Psychonomic Science*, 1968, *10*, 135–136. Reprinted by permission of Psychonomic Society, Inc. **206,** Figure 8.4 adapted from "Waiting for the Stimulus Suffix: Decay, Rhythm, and Readout in Immediate Memory," by R. G. Crowder, *Quarterly Journal of Experimental Psychology*, 1971, *23*, 324–340. Copyright 1971 by The Experimental Psychology Society. Adapted by permission. **210,** Figure 8.5 from "Toward a Theory of Memory and Attention," by D. A. Norman, *Psychological Review*, 1968, *75*, 522–536. Copyright 1968 by the American Psychological Association. Reprinted by permission. Also: Figure 8.5 from "Memory, Knowledge, and the Answering of Questions," by D. A. Norman. In R. L. Solso (Ed.), Contemporary Issues in Cognitive Psychology: The Loyola Symposium. Washington, D.C.: Winston. Reprinted by permission. **213,** Figure 8.6 adapted from "Short-Term Retention of Individual Verbal Items," by L. R. Peterson and M. J. Peterson, *Journal of Experimental Psychology*, 1959, *58*, 193–198. Copyright 1959 by the American Psychological Association. **219,** Figure 8.7 adapted from "Depth of Processing and the Retention of Words in Episodic Memory," by F. I. M. Craik and E. Tulving, *Journal of Experimental Psychology*, 1975, *104*, 268–294. Copyright 1975 by the American Psychological Association. Adapted by permission.

CHAPTER 9 232, 233, Figures 9.1 and 9.2 from "Chronometric Studies of the Visual Rotation of Mental Images," by L. A. Cooper and R. N. Shepard. In W. G. Chase (Ed.), *Visual Information Processing*. Copyright 1973 by Academic Press. Reprinted by permission. **233,** Figure 9.3 from "Mental Rotation of Three-Dimensional Objects," by R. N. Shepard and J. Metzler, *Science*, February 1971, Vol. 171, pp. 701–703. Copyright 1971 by the AAAS. Reprinted by permission. **234,** Figure 9.4 from "Visual Images Preserve Metric Spatial Information," by S. M. Kosslyn, T. M. Ball, and B. J. Reiser, *Journal of Experimental Psychology: Human Perception and Performance*, 1978, *4*, 47–60. Copyright 1978 by the American Psychological Association. Reprinted by permission. **234,** Figure 9.5 adapted from "Spatial and Verbal Components of the Act of Recall," by L. R. Brooks, *Canadian Journal of Psychology*, 1968, *22*, 349–368. Copyright 1968 by the Canadian Psychological Association. Reprinted by permission. **237,** Figure 9.6 from "Recognition Memory for Syntactic and Semantic Aspects of Connected Discourse," by J. D. S. Sachs, *Perception and Psychophysics*, *2*, 437–442. Copyright

1967 by Psychonomic Society, Inc. Reprinted by permission. **243, 244,** Quotes from *Remembering: A Study in Experimental and Social Psychology,* by F. C. Bartlett, 1932, Cambridge University Press. **245,** Figure 9.8 from "Contextual Prerequisites for Understanding: Some Investigations of Comprehension and Recall," by J. D. Bransford and M. K. Johnson, *Journal of Verbal Learning and Verbal Behavior,* 1971, *11,* 717–726. Copyright 1972 by Academic Press. Reprinted by permission. **251, 253,** Figures 9.10 and 9.11 from "Retrieval Time from Semantic Memory," by A. M. Collins and M. R. Quillian, *Journal of Verbal Learning and Verbal Behavior,* 1969, *8,* 240–247. Copyright 1969 by Academic Press. Reprinted by permission. **254,** Figure 9.12 from "A Spreading Activation Theory of Semantic Processing," by A. M. Collins and E. J. Loftus, *Psychological Review,* 1975, *87,* 407–428. Copyright 1975 by the American Psychological Association. Reprinted by permission.

CHAPTER 10 263, 265, Figures 10.1 and 10.2 from "High Speed Scanning in the Human Memory," by S. Sternberg, *Science,* 1966, *153,* pp. 652–654. Copyright 1966 by the AAAS. Reprinted by permission. **270,** Three stages of experiment from "Encoding Specificity and Retrieval Processes in Episodic Memory," by E. Tulving and D. M. Thomson, *Psychological Review,* 1973, *80,* 352–373. Copyright 1973 by the American Psychological Association. **272,** Figure 10.3 based on "A Propositional Theory of Recognition Memory," by J. R. Anderson and G. H. Bower, *Memory and Cognition,* 1974, *2,* 406–412. Copyright 1974, The Psychonomic Society, Inc. **277,** Figure 10.4 from "Acquisition-Test Interactions between Different Dimensions of Encoding," by D. C. Morris, *Memory and Cognition, 6,* 354–363. Reprinted by permission of Psychonomic Society, Inc. **280, 282,** Figures 10.5 and 10.6 from "Semantic Integration of Verbal Information into a Visual Memory," by E. F. Loftus, D. G. Miller, and H. J. Burns, *Journal of Experimental Psychology: Human Learning and Memory,* 1978, *4,* 19–31. Copyright 1978 by the American Psychological Association. Reprinted by permission **285, 287,** Figures 10.7 and 10.8 from "Mechanisms for the Cueing Phenomenon: The Addition of the Cueing Context to the Training Memory," by W. C. Gordon, K. M. McCracken, N. Dess-Beech, and R. R. Mowrer, *Learning and Motivation,* 1981, *12,* 196–211. Copyright 1981 by Academic Press. Reprinted by permission.

CHAPTER 11 297, Figure 11.3 adapted from "Proactive Inhibition in Short-Term Retention of Single Systems," by G. Keppel and B. J. Underwood, *Journal of Verbal Learning and Verbal Behavior,* 1962, *1,* 153–161. Copyright 1962 by Academic Press. Reprinted by permission. **297,** Figure 11.4 adapted from "Characteristics of Word Encoding," by D. D. Wickens. In A. W. Melton and E. Martin (Eds.), *Coding Processes in Human Memory.* Copyright 1972 by V. H. Winston & Sons. Reprinted by permission. **304,** Figure 11.7 adapted from "Acquisition, Extinction, and Recovery Functions in Retroactive Inhibition," by G. E. Briggs, *Journal of Experimental Psychology,* 1954, *47,* 285–293. Copyright 1954 by the American Psychological Association. **305,** Figure 11.8 adapted from "Fate of First-List Associations in Transfer Theory," by J. M. Barnes and B. J. Underwood, *Journal of Experimental Psychology,* 1959, *58,* 97–105. Copyright 1979 by the American Psychological Association. **310,** Figure 11.9a adapted from "Effect of Sample Presentation Time on Long Delay Matching in the Pigeon," by D. S. Grant, *Learning and Motivation,* 1976, *7,* 580–590. Copyright 1976 by Academic Press. Adapted by permission. **310,** Figure 11.9b adapted from "The Alleviation of Short-Term Retention Decrements with Reactivation," by D. T. Feldman and W. C. Gordon, *Learning and Motivation,* 1979, *10,* 198–210. Copyright 1979 by Academic Press. Adapted by permission. **311,** Figure 11.10 adapted from "Trace Interaction in Pigeon Short-Term Memory," by D. S. Grant and W. A. Roberts, *Journal of Experimental Psychology,* 1973, *101,* 21–29. Copyright 1973 by the American Psychological Association. Adapted by permission.

Author Index

Abrahamson, A. A., 238
Adams, C., 117, 120
Adams, J. A., 158
Allen, M., 152
Allen, R., 189
Allison, J., 111
Amsel, A., 121, 122, 124
Anderson, J. R., 142, 157, 238, 239, 247, 257, 272, 273
Antonitis, J. J., 107
Aposhyan, H., 173
Archer, E. J., 139, 146
Ardrey, R., 2
Armus, H. L., 97
Asratyan, E. A., 67
Atkinson, R. C., 198–201, 206, 207, 209, 211–216, 224, 227, 231, 274, 279, 293
Augerinos, G., 283
Austin, G. A., 187
Averbach, I., 203
Ayres, J. J. B., 24, 42, 51, 59
Azrin, N. H., 118
Backer, R., 107
Baddeley, A. D., 221, 235, 249, 278
Baker, A. G., 29, 42, 43
Baker, P. A., 29
Bakke, I., 173
Balaz, M. A., 33, 68, 69
Balda, R. P., 282, 284
Ball, T. M., 233–235
Balsam, P. D., 70
Barclay, J. R., 243
Barker, A. N., 110
Barnes, J. M., 304, 305
Baron, M. R., 89
Baron, R. S., 279
Bartlett, F. C., 243, 244
Batsche, C. J., 81
Batsche, G. M., 81
Battig, W. F., 220, 221
Bauermeister, J. J., 111
Baum, M., 100, 132
Beauchamp, R. D., 88

Beecroft, R. S., 19, 149
Beery, R. G., 83
Begg, I., 238
Bekerian, D. A., 281
Bellezza, F. S., 220
Berlyne, D. E., 108
Bersh, P. J., 100
Bevan, P., 79
Bexton, W. H., 107
Bierley, C. M., 258
Birch, D., 99
Bitterman, M. E., 23, 126
Bjork, R. A., 143, 213, 214, 218, 278
Black, A. H., 130, 283
Black, R. W., 83
Block, R. A., 142, 143, 215
Blodgett, H. C., 113
Blond, J., 109
Boe, E. E., 90
Boies, S. J., 231
Bolles, R. C., 30, 40, 117, 127
Bolt, R. A., 265
Bomba, P. C., 192
Bourne, L. E., 187, 189, 193
Bousfield, W. A., 151
Bouton, M. E., 68, 70
Bowen, J. N., 97
Bower, G. H., 83, 142, 152, 154, 157, 238, 239, 247, 249, 257, 272, 273, 278
Bowers, J. M., 281
Bradshaw, C. M., 79
Bradshaw, J. L., 139
Bransford, J. D., 223, 242–246
Breen, T. J., 257
Breitmeyer, B. G., 203
Brennan, M. J., 75, 310
Brett, L. P., 33
Briggs, G. E., 300, 301, 303, 304
Brimer, C. J., 130
Broadbent, D. E., 198, 207, 209, 211
Brogden, W. J., 38, 64
Brooks, L. R., 215, 234, 235
Brown, A. S., 139
Brown, B. L., 163, 172
Brown, J. A., 212, 292
Brown, J. S., 173
Brown, P. L., 21
Brown, R. T., 84
Brown, R. W., 274, 275
Bruce, D. R., 153
Bruner, A., 28, 50
Bruner, J. S., 187
Brush, F. R., 133
Buck, M. A., 96
Bugelski, B. R., 105
Bukstel, L., 257
Burkhardt, P. E., 24
Burns, H. J., 279, 280
Burr, D. E. S., 173, 176, 178
Bush, R. R., 38, 49
Butler, R. A., 107

Cable, C., 193
Cacheiro, H., 33
Cadorette, L., 246
Calhoun, W. H., 225
Camp, D. S., 89
Campbell, B. A., 85, 107, 109, 110, 133
Campbell, P. E., 81, 98
Capaldi, E. D., 84
Capaldi, E. J., 82, 97, 98, 122–126, 133
Capra, S., 68, 69
Caprio, M., 82
Casey, M., 144
Cavanagh, J. P., 211
Ceraso, J., 305
Chance, J. E., 247
Cheesman, F. L., 220
Cherry, E. C., 207
Chomsky, N., 239
Church, R. M., 88–90
Cieutat, V. J., 146
Clark, M. C., 273
Clark, W. H., 215, 231
Coate, W. B., 173
Cofer, C. N., 153
Colavita, F. B., 50
Coleman, S. R., 23, 24
Collier, G., 84, 110
Collins, A. M., 250–256
Collins, W., 172
Commons, M. L., 96
Conezio, J., 246
Conrad, C., 253
Conrad, R., 204, 205, 215, 231
Cooke, N. M., 257
Cooper, L. A., 232, 233
Coppage, E. W., 145
Coriell, A. S., 203
Cotton, J. W., 84
Cowie, R. J., 282
Craik, F. I. M., 145, 214–222, 225, 227, 279
Crespi, L. P., 81–83
Crossen, J. R., 79
Crowder, R. G., 204–206
Cunitz, A. R., 145

D'Agostino, P. R., 143
Dallett, K. M., 163
D'Amato, M. R., 86, 98, 129, 259, 310
Dameron, L. E., 19
Dark, V. J., 221
Darwin, C. J., 204
Dawson, R. G., 224, 225
Deaux, E. B., 118
DeBaca, P. C., 111
DeBold, R. C., 119
Deese, J., 147
Delin, P. S., 154
Demaio, J. C., 257
Dember, W. N., 109
Denny, M. R., 127
DeRemer, P., 143

Dess-Beech, N., 284–287
Deutsch, D., 209
Deutsch, J. A., 185, 209
deVilliers, P. A., 96, 193
Devine, J. V., 111
Dickerson, D. J., 185
Dickinson, A., 117, 120
Dieter, S. E., 86
Dolinsky, R., 145
Domjan, M., 24, 30, 40, 42, 43, 59
Donders, F. C., 266
Dore, L. R., 79
Dougher, M. J., 79, 111
Dunham, P. J., 90
Durlach, P. J., 33, 67, 69, 70
Durso, F. T., 257
Dyal, J. A., 98
Dye, G. S., 143

Ebbinghaus, H., 136, 138–144, 249
Efron, R., 204
Eich, J., 278
Eichelman, W. H., 231
Eimas, P. D., 185
Eisenberger, R., 107, 111
Eki, N. T., 143
Ekstrand, B. R., 148, 149, 308
Elliot, M. H., 83
Ellis, H. C., 161, 222
Ellison, G. D., 23
Elmes, D. G., 143
Engle, R. W., 257
Erlebacher, A. H., 151
Ervin, F. R., 25
Estes, W. K., 20, 69, 141, 142, 249
Etkin, M. W., 129, 310
Eysenck, M. C., 222
Eysenck, M. W., 222

Fazzaro, J., 86, 129
Fehrer, E., 97
Feigenbaum, E. A., 144
Feldman, D. T., 310
Ferster, C. B., 78, 93, 94
Finch, G., 63
Fiske, D. W., 108
Fitch, F., 144
Fitzgerald, R. D., 40
Flaherty, C. F., 82, 83, 114
Flexser, A. J., 275
Flynn, M. S., 279
Fowler, H., 85, 86, 91, 108, 109
Franks, J. J., 223, 242, 243
Fraser, J., 306–308
Freeman, F., 176, 178
Frey, P. W., 67
Frey, T. J., 222
Friedman, H., 175

Gabel, J., 29
Galanter, E., 156
Gallistel, C. R., 259
Gammack, J. G., 257
Gamzu, E., 26, 56
Gantt, W. H., 63
Ganz, L., 178, 203
Garcia, E. E., 126
Garcia, J., 25, 30, 31, 33, 51, 61
Garland, R. J., 79
Geffen, G., 207
Geiselman, R. E., 213
Gelman, R., 185
Gerall, A. A., 50
Gibbs, M. E., 224
Gillin, J., 278
Gillund, G., 274
Gino, A., 100
Glanzer, M., 145, 215, 231
Glass, A. L., 257
Glass, G., 238
Glaze, J. A., 139, 146
Gleitman, H., 312
Glenberg, A. M., 278
Glickman, S. E., 109
Goad, D., 149
Godden, D. R., 278
Gold, P. E., 226
Goldsmith, R., 192
Goldsmith, T. E., 257
Goldstein, A. G., 247
Gonzalez, R. C., 126
Goodnow, J. J., 187
Goodrich, K. P., 84, 110
Gordon, W. C., 42, 75, 77, 100, 114, 225, 226, 284–287, 310, 313, 314
Gormezano, I., 20, 23, 24, 27
Graf, P., 222
Grant, D. A., 19
Grant, D. S., 227, 258, 259, 310, 311
Grant, S., 235
Grau, J. W., 67, 69, 70
Greene, E., 279
Greenspoon, J., 278
Grice, G. R., 173
Grings, W. W., 19
Groninger, L. D., 155
Grossen, N. E., 40
Grossman, S., 118
Guttman, N., 169, 175

Haber, A., 173
Haber, R. N., 203, 204, 246
Haberlandt, K., 35, 51
Hake, D. F., 118
Hall, G., 52, 58, 119, 120
Hall, J. F., 24, 42, 147
Hall, M., 144
Hambleton, R. K., 246
Hamlin, V. J., 152
Hammond, L. J., 40
Hankins, W. G., 33
Hanson, H. M., 175

Harcum, E. R., 145
Harrison, R. H., 174, 175
Hartl, P., 68, 69
Hasher, L., 190
Haviland, S. E., 265
Hayes, J. R. M., 211
Heard, W. G., 170
Hearst, E., 21, 63, 171–174
Hebb, D. O., 108, 224
Henderson, A., 305
Henschel, D., 306
Herdian, N. J., 143
Heron, W., 107
Herrnstein, R. J., 96, 127, 129, 130, 193
Hess, D. T., 98, 125
Hess, E. N., 4
Heth, D. C., 24, 51
Hicks, L. H., 20
Hilgard, E. R., 79, 127
Hill, W. F., 99, 126
Hineline, P. N., 129
Hinson, R. E., 29, 40–43, 57
Hintzman, D. L., 142, 143, 215, 249
Hoffeld, D. R., 38
Hoffman, J. W., 40
Holgate, V., 183
Holland, P. C., 29, 40, 64, 70
Holland, T. A., 98
Holloway, F. A., 285, 312
Holyoak, K. J., 257
Homme, L. E., 111
Honig, W. K., 176, 178, 259
Honzik, C. H., 113
Horowitz, L. M., 148
House, B. J., 183
Houston, J. P., 305
Hovland, C. I., 144
Howell, W. C., 142
Hubel, D. H., 107
Hug, J. J., 121, 122
Hull, A. J., 204, 205, 231
Hull, C. L., 49, 62, 84, 105, 106, 108, 110, 112, 114, 115, 127, 140, 141, 144, 145, 177, 178, 186, 187, 190, 194
Hulse, S. H., Jr., 97, 98, 110
Hunt, R. R., 222
Hyde, T. S., 218

Inskeep, N. R., 215
Intraub, H., 157, 247
Irwin, J. M., 301, 302
Ison, J. R., 98, 99

Jackson, R. L., 90
Jacoby, L. L., 222, 223
Jagoda, H., 98
James, C. T., 238
Jenkins, H. M., 21, 174, 175
Jenkins, J. J., 151, 179, 218
Jenkins, W. O., 173
Jensen, A. R., 144, 161
Jensen, G. D., 109
John, E. R., 224
Johnson, M. K., 244–246
Johnston, J. C., 127, 131–133
Joinson, P. A., 149
Jonides, J., 157, 247
Jung, J., 163
Juola, J. F., 274

Kahn, R., 157, 247
Kahneman, D., 210, 222
Kalish, H. I., 169, 173
Kamin, L. J., 23, 28, 33–35, 50, 52, 56, 87–89, 99, 128–130, 312, 313
Karpman, M., 111
Kasprow, W. J., 33, 69
Kassover, K., 98
Katz, D. S., 100
Keele, S. W., 191, 192
Keenan, J. M., 238
Kellogg, R. T., 189, 190
Keltz, J. R., 100
Kendall, S. B., 38
Kendler, H. H., 187
Kendler, T. S., 187
Keppel, G., 141, 148–150, 296–298, 308
Kerr, N. H., 235
Kessen, M. C., 106, 110, 111
Kiess, H. O., 158
Kimble, G. A., 64
Kimose, E., 173
Kincaid, J. P., 297
King, D. A., 68
King, D. L., 62
King, R. A., 173
King, R. P., 226
Kintsch, W., 84, 119, 238–241, 250, 257, 262, 268–270, 275
Kirsner, K., 215, 221
Kish, G. B., 107
Klein, M., 176
Knarr, F. A., 110
Knouse, S. B., 98
Koelling, R. A., 25, 30, 31, 51, 61
Kolers, P. A., 221, 222
Konick, A. F., 235
Konorski, J., 44
Koresko, M. B., 171–174
Kosslyn, S. M., 233–235
Kraeling, D., 85
Krane, R. V., 31, 61, 99
Krebs, J. R., 282
Krechevsky, I., 182
Kremer, E. F., 58
Kreye, J., 173
Kucharsky, D., 33
Kuo, Z. Y., 3

Lacey, J. I., 179
Lamwers, L. L., 271
Lashley, K. S., 144, 177, 178, 182
Lawrence, D. H., 183

Lawrence, K. A., 155
Lepley, W. M., 140, 144
Lesgold, A. M., 273
Leslie, G. R., 109
Leuba, C., 108
Levin, T. C., 178
Levine, M., 187–190, 194
Levis, D. J., 78
Lewis, D. J., 225–227, 314
Lieberman, D. A., 82
Light, J. S., 63
Likely, D., 98
Litner, J. S., 26, 56, 129
Little, L., 184
Livingston, J. R., 110
Lockhart, R. A., 19
Lockhart, R. S., 214, 216–218, 220, 221, 225, 227, 279
Lodahl, T. M., 107
Loess, H., 297
Loftus, E. F., 10, 254–256, 279–281, 286
Loftus, G. R., 221
Logan, F. A., 28, 35, 51
LoLordo, V. M., 24, 28, 42, 57, 59
Lopez, L. J., 173, 174
Lorenz, K. G., 2
Lorge, I., 146
Lovejoy, E., 183
Loveland, D. H., 193
Lovibond, P. F., 27
Low, H. I., 87
Low, L. A., 87
Lowry, D., 156, 157
Lubow, R. E., 28
Lyons, J., 176, 178

MacCorquodale, K., 113
Mackintosh, N. J., 24, 27, 29, 33, 43, 51, 83, 117, 119, 125, 126, 176, 178, 179, 183, 184
Maddi, S. R., 108
Madison, H. L., 98
Mahoney, W. J., 24, 42, 51, 59
Maier, S. F., 90
Maki, W. S., 227, 258
Maltzman, I., 179
Mandler, G., 274
Margolius, G., 172
Mark, R. F., 224
Marler, P., 3
Marquis, D. G., 127
Martin, E., 141, 142, 271, 308
Martin, P. A., 77
Marx, M. H., 110
Mayhew, A. J., 152
McAllister, D. E., 86, 173, 312
McAllister, W. R., 86, 173, 312
McCain, G., 122
McCracken, K. M., 284–287
McDermott, M. J., 313
McDowell, J. J., 96
McFarland, C. E., 222
McGaugh, J. L., 224, 225
McGeoch, J. A., 300, 301, 314
McGinnis, C. M., 42, 313
McHose, J. H., 83, 122
McIntosh, D. C., 82
McKay, D. C., 208, 209
McNeill, D., 274, 275
McSweeney, F. K., 96
Medin, D. L., 69
Meehl, P. E., 113
Mellgren, R. L., 98
Melton, A. W., 142, 216, 301, 302
Melville, C. L., 96
Mercier, P., 29
Merikle, P. M., 163
Mervis, C. B., 190, 191
Metzler, J., 215, 232, 233
Meyer, D. E., 255
Miczek, K. A., 118
Mikulka, P. J., 84
Miller, D. G., 279, 280
Miller, G. A., 156, 211
Miller, H., 278
Miller, N. E., 91, 106, 110, 111, 119, 127
Miller, R. R., 33, 39, 68, 69, 226
Milner, B., 215
Mineka, S., 100
Misanin, J. R., 226
Mitchell, R. F., 231
Moe, J. C., 258
Moeser, S. D., 220
Montague, W. E., 158
Moon, L. E., 107
Moore, A. U., 28
Moore, B. R., 63
Moore, M. O., 143
Moray, N., 206, 208
Morgulis, S., 17
Morris, C. D., 223, 277
Morton, J., 204, 205
Moscovitch, A., 24, 42, 59
Mosteller, F., 38, 49
Mowrer, O. H., 127
Mowrer, R. R., 226, 284–287, 313
Moy, M. C., 265
Mumma, R., 183
Mundinger, P., 3
Murdock, B. B., Jr., 143, 144, 265
Murphy, D. L., 278
Mycielska, K., 275
Myran, D. D., 100

Nadel, L., 69
Naus, M. J., 265
Neisser, U., 203, 208
Nelson, D. L., 221
Nelson, T. O., 221
Neumann, P. G., 193
Newman, J. R., 173
Nickerson, R. S., 246
Noble, C. E., 146

Norman, D. A., 198, 209, 210, 239, 257, 294
North, A. J., 98

Obrist, P. A., 50
Olton, D. S., 282, 283
Osgood, C. E., 163
Osler, S., 276
Ostry, D. J., 222
Overmeir, J. B., 90
Overton, D. A., 285

Packman, J. L., 220, 221
Paivio, A., 147, 154–157, 246, 247
Palmerino, C. C., 33
Pascal, G. R., 173
Patten, R. L., 118
Paul, J. H., 244
Pavlik, W. B., 84
Pavlov, I. P., 16–18, 33, 40, 49, 169
Pearce, J. M., 52, 58, 119, 120
Pearlstone, Z., 153, 276
Peckham, R. H., 121
Perin, C. T., 98
Perkins, C. C., 173
Perkins, D. T., 144
Petersen, R., 278
Peterson, D. A., 78
Peterson, L. R., 212–214, 292–297
Peterson, M. J., 212–214, 292–297
Peterson, N., 178
Pinel, P. J. P., 24
Pollack, I., 211
Polson, M. C., 148
Polson, P. G., 148
Popper, R., 173, 174
Posner, M. I., 191, 192, 231, 232, 235
Postman, L., 140, 141, 147, 162, 164, 165, 305–308
Powell, T., 118
Premack, D., 110, 111
Preston, G. C., 27
Pribram, K., 156
Price, T., 35, 51
Prochaska, J., 100
Prussin, H. A., 204
Purtle, R. B., 175
Pylyshyn, Z. W., 157, 247

Quillian, M. R., 250–254, 256

Rachlin, H., 96
Rand, G., 278
Randall, P. K., 89
Randich, A., 28, 29, 56
Ranyard, R., 278
Raymond, G. A., 88, 89
Reason, J., 275
Reber, A. A., 189
Reddy, B. G., 220
Reed, S. K., 192
Reese, H. W., 156
Reicher, G. M., 159
Reiser, B. J., 233–235
Reiss, S., 43
Reitman, J. S., 213, 295, 296, 298
Renner, K. E., 98
Rescorla, R. A., 24, 26, 29, 33, 36, 37, 39, 40, 42, 44, 50–58, 63–67, 69, 70, 120, 126, 130, 178
Restle, F., 148, 187
Reynierse, J. H., 99
Reynolds, G. S., 176
Rhodes, D. D., 222
Riccio, D. C., 89
Richards, W. J., 109
Richardson, J., 163
Rickert, E., 111
Riesen, A. H., 178
Riley, D. A., 178
Riley, E. P., 83, 114
Rilling, M., 176, 310
Rips, L. J., 253, 256
Rizley, R. C., 99
Robbins, D. W., 189
Roberts, W. A., 97, 258, 310, 311
Roby, T. B., 106, 107, 109, 110
Rock, I., 140, 141
Rodriguez, I. A., 222
Roenker, D. L., 152
Rohwer, W. D., Jr., 144, 161
Roitblat, H. L., 259
Rosch, E. H., 190–193
Rose, R. J., 142, 143
Rosenberg, S. T., 243
Ross, J., 155
Ross, L. E., 19
Ross, R. T., 29, 144
Roth, E. M., 254
Rothkopf, E. Z., 221
Rouse, R. O., 110
Roussel, J., 121
Rowe, E. J., 142
Royer, J. M., 246
Rozin, P., 157, 247
Rudolph, R. L., 178
Rudy, J. W., 59
Rumelhart, D. E., 239, 257
Rundus, D., 142, 221
Runquist, W. N., 148, 149
Rusiniak, K. W., 33
Russell, W. A., 151

Sachs, J. S., 237
St. Claire-Smith, R., 119
Saltzman, I. J., 104, 105
Samuelson, R. J., 282, 283
Sanders, G. S., 281
Santa, J. L., 271
Schachtman, T. R., 69
Schaeffer, R. W., 111
Schiff, D., 98
Schiff, R., 100
Schlesinger, J. L., 310
Schneiderman, N., 23

Schnitzer, S. B., 98
Schoenfeld, W. N., 127
Schrier, A. M., 185
Schulz, R. W., 147–149
Schvaneveldt, R. W., 255, 257
Scott, T. H., 107
Sears, R. J., 67
Seligman, M. E. P., 30, 58, 90, 127, 131–133
Seward, J. P., 113
Shallice, T., 215
Shaughnessy, J. J., 142
Sheffield, F. D., 106, 107, 109, 110
Shepard, R. N., 215, 232, 233, 267
Shepp, B. E., 185
Sherry, D. F., 282
Shiffrin, R. N., 198–201, 206, 207, 209, 211–216, 224, 227, 231, 274, 279, 293, 295
Shoben, E. J., 253, 254, 256
Shulman, H. G., 236
Shvyrok, U. B., 20
Sidman, M., 77, 129
Siegel, S., 24, 40–43, 59
Simmons, W. L., 281
Simon, E., 222
Simon, H. A., 144
Singer, M., 243
Siqueland, E. R., 192
Skaar, E., 142
Skinner, B. F., 20, 78, 80, 93, 94
Skucy, J. C., 126
Slamecka, N. J., 144, 222
Smith, E. E., 253, 256
Smith, G. J., 100
Smith, M. C., 23, 24
Smith, N., 100
Smith, P. G., 265
Smith, R. L., 179
Smith, S. M., 278
Smythe, P. C., 147, 154, 155
Snyder, H. L., 110
Solomon, R. L., 63, 99, 130, 131
Soltysik, S., 28
Spear, N. E., 33, 39, 69, 76, 77, 83, 99, 126, 142, 225, 259, 284–286, 312–314
Speelman, R. G., 231
Spence, K. W., 19, 27, 115–119, 175, 181, 182, 184, 185
Sperling, G., 201–204, 231
Spetch, M. L., 24
Spivey, J. E., 98, 125
Springer, A. D., 226
Staats, A. W., 170
Staats, C. K., 170
Stabler, J. R., 84
Staddon, J. E. R., 111
Standing, L. G., 203, 204, 246
Stanley, L. R., 126
Stark, K., 305–308
Stein, B. S., 222, 223
Steinhorst, R., 111
Sternberg, S., 262–266
Stillman, R., 278
Stimmel, D. T., 98
Stockwell, F. E., 146
Stroebel, C. F., 285
Summers, J. J., 143
Sutherland, N. S., 183
Suzuki, S., 283
Svinicki, J. G., 176, 178
Swartzentruber, D., 70
Switalski, R. W., 171
Szabadi, E., 79
Szwejkowska, G., 44

Tauber, L., 83
Taylor, R. L., 231
Teichner, W. H., 99
Terrace, H. S., 24
Terry, W. S., 24, 51, 59, 60
Theios, J., 265
Thomas, D. R., 171, 173–176, 178
Thomas, G. V., 82
Thomas, R. L., 222
Thompson, C. P., 152
Thompson, R. F., 20, 38
Thomson, D. M., 268, 270–272, 275, 276
Thomson, N., 235
Thorndike, E. L., 112, 114, 115, 146
Thune, L. E., 160
Timberlake, W., 111
Tinbergen, N., 2
Tolman, E. C., 113
Tomback, D. F., 281, 282
Tombaugh, T. N., 97, 98
Tomie, A., 29, 57, 70
Trabasso, T., 185
Tracy, W. K., 178
Tranberg, D. K., 310
Trapold, M. A., 27, 85, 86
Trattner, T., 111
Traupmann, J., 265
Treisman, A. M., 207–209
Tucker, R. G., 257
Tulving, E., 151–153, 218–221, 223, 248, 249, 268, 270–272, 275–277
Turek, R. J., 282, 284
Turner, L. H., 63
Turvey, M. T., 204
Twedt, H. M., 163

Uhl, C. N., 98, 126
Uhl, N. P., 185
Underwood, B. J., 141, 142, 146–153, 163, 249, 250, 259, 296–298, 301, 302, 304, 305, 307, 308

van Dijk, T. A., 240
von Wright, J. M., 278

Wade, M., 177, 178, 182
Wadsworth, J., 279
Wagner, A. R., 24, 31, 35, 36, 39, 43, 44, 51–55, 58–62, 67, 84, 97, 121, 178, 259
Walk, R. D., 178

Walker, R. W., 173
Walters, C. P., 178
Wansley, R., 285, 312
Wapner, S., 278
Ward, J. S., 121
Ward, L. B., 160
Warner, L. H., 87
Warren, J. M., 183
Warrington, E. K., 215
Watkins, M. J., 214, 223, 267, 268, 271
Watkins, O. C., 271
Waugh, N. C., 142, 198, 294
Weaver, M. S., 42
Weber, A., 156, 157
Weinberg, H. I., 279
Weingartner, H., 278
Weisman, R. G., 26, 56, 129
Weiss, R. F., 84
Welton, K. E., Jr., 192
Weyant, R. G., 173
Whipple, J. E., 96
Whitlow, J. W., 59, 61, 142
Wickelgren, W. A., 231, 239, 249
Wickens, D. D., 249, 297
Wiesel, T. N., 107
Wight, E., 235
Wike, E. L., 98
Wike, S. S., 98
Wilkie, D. M., 24
Williams, D. R., 26, 56, 118
Williams, S. B., 98
Willner, J., 69
Windell, B. T., 173
Wingfield, A., 265
Winzenz, D., 273
Wiseman, S., 271
Witte, R. S., 119
Wittgenstein, L., 190, 191
Wollen, K. A., 156, 157
Worsham, R. W., 259
Wulff, J. J., 107
Wynne, J. D., 38, 64
Wynne, L. C., 99, 131

Yerkes, R. M., 17
Young, A. G., 98
Young, R. K., 144
Young, R. M., 257
Yuille, J. C., 147, 154, 155

Zachs, R. T., 190
Zeaman, D., 183
Zelniker, T., 211
Zentall, T. R., 172, 310
Ziff, D. R., 122

Subject Index

Acoustic codes, *see* Memory codes
Acquired distinctiveness of cues, 183–184
Acquisition curve, 27
Active memory, 225
Adaptive mechanisms, 2–8
Adjacent associations in serial learning, 143–145
All-or-none hypothesis, 141
Amsel's frustration theory of extinction, 121–122
Anchor point hypothesis of serial learning, 145
Anticipation method, 137
Atkinson–Shiffrin memory model:
  description of, 198–201
  evidence pertaining to, 201–216
Attention:
  in discrimination learning, 182–185
  as selective filter mechanism, 199, 206–211
Attributes, 249–250, 259
Autoshaping, 21
Avoidance learning (*see also* Instrumental/Operant conditioning; Negative reinforcement):
  cognitive theory of, 131–133
  intensity of aversive stimulus in, 86–87
Avoidance learning (*continued*)
  one-way form of, 77
  paradigm for studying, 76–77
  reinforcement in, 126–133
  signal-aversive stimulus interval in, 87
  termination of signal in, 87–88
  two-factor theory of, 127–131
  two-way form of, 77
  unsignaled form of, 77

Backward associations, 164
Backward conditioning, 23–24, 42, 59–60
Backward masking, 203
Bar press response, 78
Behavioral contrast, *see* Contrast effects
Behavioral tradition, 11–12
Blank trials procedure, 188
Blocking, 29, 33–34, 50–51, 56, 119–120
Broadbent's selective filter theory, 207–209 (*see also* Attention)
Buffer, 198, 200
Buffer circuits, 197

Caching, 281–284
Capacity models of attention, 210–211 (*see also* Attention)
Capaldi's sequential theory of extinction, 122–126
Characteristic features, 256–257
Chunks of information, 211–212
Classical conditioning, 13–70
  contiguity theory of, 49–51
  contingency theory of, 51–62
  excitatory conditioning type, 15
  excitatory conditioning variables in, 22–38
  extinction of, 43–44
  inhibitory conditioning type, 15–16, 38–39
  inhibitory conditioning variables in, 40–43
  measurement of CR in, 20–22, 39–40
  nature of association in, 62–66
  necessary and sufficient conditions for, 49–62
  paradigms of, 16–21
  Pavlov's demonstration of, 16–18
  role of contextual stimuli in, 66–70
  theoretical issues in, 47–70
  Wagner's priming theory of, 58–62
Classical excitatory conditioning, *see* Classical conditioning
Classical inhibitory conditioning, *see* Classical conditioning
Clustering, 151–154
CNS stimulants, 225
Coding, 150–151
Cognitive theory of avoidance, *see* Avoidance learning
Cognitive tradition, 11–12
Competing response hypothesis, *see* Amsel's frustration theory of extinction
Component analysis approach, 163–165
Computer analogy, *see* Information processing approach
Concept, *see* Concept learning)
Concept learning, 168, 185–193
  defined, 185
  in nonhuman species, 193
  theories of, 186–193
Conceptual similarity, 148–150
Concurrent schedules, *see* Schedules of reinforcement
Conditioned emotional response (CER), 20–21
Conditioned response (CR):
  defined, 17–18
  extinction of, 43–44
  measurement of, 20–22, 39–40
  relation to the UR, 64
Conditioned stimulus (CS):
  compounds, 32–36
  correlation with the US, 25–26
  defined, 17–18
  intensity of, 27–28
  number of pairings with the US, 27
  prior experience with, 28–29
  relatedness with the US, 29–32
  temporal arrangement with the US, 23–25
Consolidation theory, 224–225
Contextual stimuli:
  as CSs, 67–69
  as cues for a CS–US relationship, 69–70
Contextual stimuli (*continued*)
  defined, 66
  role in generalization, 178–179
Contiguity theory, 49–51
Contingency, 14–16
Contingency theory, 51–62
Contingent relationship, *see* Contingency
Continuous reinforcement, 84, 92, 98, 121–126
Contrast effects:
  behavioral form of, 176
  Crespi's demonstration of, 82–83
  implications for theories of reinforcement, 114–115
  negative form of, 83
  positive form of, 83
  simultaneous paradigm for studying, 83
  successive paradigm for studying, 83
Control processes, 199–200, 213–214
Craik and Lockhart's levels of processing approach:
  description of, 216–218
  evidence pertinent to, 218–223
CS–US interval, 24–25
CS–US relevance, 30
Cumulative record, 93–95

Decay theory, 292–293, 311–312
Defining features, 256–257
Delayed alternation procedure, 309–310
Delayed matching-to-sample (DMTS), 257–259, 309–311
Directed forgetting, 213–214, 227
Discrimination learning, 168, 174–185, 193
  defined, 168
  influence on generalization gradients, 174–177
  theories of, 181–185
Distinctiveness of memory codes, 222
Distractor item, 267
Distractor task, 292, 294–295
Distributed vs. massed practice, 142–143
Drive-reduction hypothesis (Hull's), 105–108
Dual-coding hypothesis, 156–158, 246–247

Echoic store, 203
Elaborative rehearsal, 214 (*see also* Rehearsal)
Electroconvulsive shock (ECS), 224–225
Emitted behaviors, 71
Encoding, 196–197, 200, 217–218, 225
Encoding specificity hypothesis, 223, 275–278, 284–286, 308, 312, 314
Encoding variability hypothesis, 141, 143, 308
Episodic memory:
  description of, 248–249
  organization of, 249–250
Escape learning (*see also* Instrumental/Operant conditioning; Negative reinforcement):
  amount of reinforcement in, 85
  delay of reinforcement in, 85
  paradigm for studying, 76
Exemplar theories of concept learning, *see* Prototype theories of concept learning
Expectancy, 131
Exteroceptive stimuli, 30

Extinction:
  in Classical conditioning, 43–44
  in Instrumental conditioning, 96–100
  response prevention in, 100, 132
  spontaneous recovery following, 44, 96
  theories of, 120–126
Extra-experimental sources of interference, 307–308
Extradimensional shift, 184–185
Eyelid conditioning, 18–19

Familiarization studies, 226
Family resemblance, 191
Feature comparison model, 256–257 (*see also* Semantic memory)
Finger withdrawal, 19
Fixed interval (FI) scallop, 94
Fixed interval schedule, *see* Schedules of reinforcement
Fixed ratio schedule, *see* Schedules of reinforcement
Flooding, 100
Forgetting:
  defined, 290–291
  in long-term retention paradigms, 298–309
  in nonhuman species, 309–314
  in short-term retention paradigms, 291–298
Formal similarity, 147–150
Forward associations, 164
Forward delayed conditioning, 23
Forward trace conditioning, 23
Fractional anticipatory goal response, 115–119
Free recall learning, 137–138

Galvanic skin response (GSR), 19
Generalization decrement hypothesis, *see* Capaldi's sequential theory of extinction
Generation effect, 222–223
Generation-recognition hypothesis, 269–272
Genetic preparedness, 30–32
Goal response (R_g), 115

Higher order conditioning, 36–37
Hippocampus, 215
Hoarding, *see* Caching
Hull's associative theory of concept learning, 186–187
Hull's drive-reduction hypothesis, 105–108
Hull's generalization theory, 177–178
Hypothesis-testing theory of concept learning, 187–190
Hypothesis-testing theory of discrimination, *see* Noncontinuity theories of discrimination

Icon, 201
Iconic storage, 201
Imagery value of verbal items, 147
Implosive therapy, 100
Inactive memory, 225
Incentive motivation, 115
Incidental learning paradigm, 142
Incidental stimuli, *see* Contextual stimuli
Incremental hypothesis, 141
Inference, 241–246
Information processing approach, 196
Instincts, 2–4
Instrumental/Operant conditioning, 71–133
  extinction of, 96–100, 120–126
  Instrumental conditioning paradigms, 74–78
  Instrumental conditioning variables, 81–91
  Instrumental/Operant distinction, 73–74
  nature of reinforcement in, 104–112, 126–132
  Operant conditioning paradigms, 78–79
  Operant conditioning variables, 91–96
  role of reinforcement in, 112–120
Interference theory:
  as an explanation of long-term forgetting, 298–307
  as an explanation of short-term forgetting, 292–293
Interoceptive stimuli, 30
Intradimensional shift, 184–185
Intrusion errors, 301

Kamin effect, 312–313
Key peck response, 78–79

Lag effect, 142
Lashley–Wade generalization theory, 177–178
Latent inhibition, 28, 43
Latent learning, 113–114
Learned helplessness, 90
Learning:
  defined, 5–6
  types commonly studied, 7–8
Learning curve, 27
Learning-to-learn, 160
Level of processing, *see* Craik and Lockhart's levels of processing approach
Lexical decision task, 255
Long-term memory store:
  codes used in, 236–247
  in consolidation theory, 224
  description of, 200
  differences from short-term memory, 211–216
  forgetting from, 298–309, 311–314
  organization of memories in, 247–257
  retrieval from, 266–287
Long-term retention paradigm, 291

Maintenance rehearsal, 214 (*see also* Rehearsal)
Matching law, 96
Maze tasks, 75–76
  complex maze, 75–76
  eight-arm radial maze, 282–283
  T-maze, 75–76
Meaning codes, *see* Memory codes
Meaningfulness of verbal items, 146–147
Meaningful similarity, 147–150
Memory:
  definition, 9
  topics commonly studied, 10–11
Memory codes:
  acoustic, 198–199, 215, 230–232, 246
  in long-term memory, 236–247
  meaning, 156–158, 214, 235–246
  motor, 235
  physical feature, 258–259
  rule, 258–259

Memory codes (*continued*)
  in sensory registers, 198–199, 202–203
  in short-term memory, 214–215, 230–236
  visual, 156–158, 198–199, 202–203, 231–235, 246–247
Memory construction, 278–281, 286–287
Memory processes, 196 (*see also* Control processes; Encoding; Rehearsal; Retrieval; Storage)
Memory structures, 197 (*see also* Long-term memory store; Sensory register; Short-term memory store)
Mental imagery, 154–158
Mental rotation, 232–233
Method of Loci, 155
Modified free recall (MFR), 303–304
Modified, modified free recall (MMFR), 304–305
Momentary response probability, 111
Motor codes, *see* Memory codes

Natural concepts:
  in humans, 190–193
  in nonhuman species, 193
Natural language mediation, 158
Negative contingency, *see* Contingency
Negative contrast (depression) effect, *see* Contrast effects
Negative punishment, *see* Punishment
Negative reinforcement:
  amount of, 85
  in avoidance learning, 76–78, 126–133
  defined, 72–73
  delay of, 85
  in escape learning, 76
Negative transfer, *see* Transfer
Nictitating membrane response, 20
N-length, 126
Noncontinuity theories of discrimination, 182–185
Nonsense syllables, 139
Nonspecific transfer, *see* Transfer
N–R transition, 124–126

One-way avoidance paradigm, *see* Avoidance learning
Operant chamber, 78
Optimal stimulation hypothesis, 108–109
Overshadowing, 32–33

Paired associates learning, 138
Paradigm, 17
Partial reinforcement, 84, 92–96, 98, 121–126
Partial reinforcement extinction effect (PREE), 98, 121–126
Partial report procedure, 201–202
Pavlovian conditioning, *see* Classical conditioning
Peak-shift phenomenon, 175–176
Pegword technique, 155–156
Permanent memory registration, *see* Storage
Permanent memory store, *see* Long-term memory store
Pertinence, 209
Poisoning paradigm, *see* Taste aversion paradigm
Positive contingency, *see* Contingency
Positive contrast (elation) effect, *see* Contrast effects
Positive punishment, *see* Punishment
Positive reinforcement:
  amount of, 81
  defined, 72
  delay of, 82
  effects of deprivation on effectiveness of, 84–85
  quality of, 81–82
  schedules of, 84, 92–96
  shifts in, 82–84
Positive transfer, *see* Transfer
Postreinforcement pause, 93
Potentiation, 33
Predictive relationships, 13–14
Preference, 131–132
Premack's reinforcement theory, 110–112
Primacy effect, 145
Primary memory, 217, 225
Primary reinforcement, *see* Reinforcement
Priming, 255 (*see also* Wagner's priming theory)
Proactive interference (PI), 296–299, 303, 305–308, 310
Probe-digit procedure, 294
Processing effort, 222
Proposition, 238–247 (*see also* Memory codes)
Prototype theories of concept learning, 191–193
Punishment:
  defined, 73
  delay of, 89–90
  duration of, 88–89
  intensity of, 88–89
  negative form of, 73
  noncontingent delivery of, 89–90
  positive form of, 73
  response produced by, 91
Pursuit rotor task, 79

Recall test, 139, 267–274
Recency effect, 145
Recognition test, 139, 267–274
Reflex arc, 2
Reflexes, 2
Rehearsal:
  in Classical conditioning, 58–62
  as a determinant of memory codes, 230–231
  as an explanation for distributed practice effects, 142
  as an explanation for the recency effect, 145
  prevention of, 212–213, 292–296
  in short-term memory, 199–200
  types of, 214
Reinforcement (*see also* Negative reinforcement; Positive reinforcement):
  in avoidance learning, 126–133
  categories of, 72–73, 104–105
  defined, 72
  nature of, 105–112
  role of, 112–120
Release from proactive interference (PI), 297–298
Reminder cues, 286–287, 313–314
Reminder paradigm, 226
Remote associations in serial learning, 144–145
Rescorla–Wagner conditioning model, 52–58
Response blocking, *see* Response prevention
Response competition hypothesis, 300–301

Response deprivation, 111
Response differentiation, 164
Response learning, 164
Response prevention, 100, 132–133
Response satiation, 111
Response selector mechanism, 306–307
Response-set interference hypothesis, 306–307
Response term, 138
Retardation test for conditioned inhibition, 39–43
Retention interval, 139
Retention test, 139–140, 267
Retrieval:
  in Atkinson–Shiffrin model, 200
  defined, 197
  from long-term memory, 266–278
  memory construction at time of, 278–281, 286–287
  in nonhuman species, 281–286
  from short-term memory, 262–266
Retrieval cues:
  defined, 275
  effectiveness of, 275–278, 284–286
  on recall tests, 267–268
  on recognition tests, 267–268
  for spatial memories in animals, 281–284
Retrieval failure, 308, 312–314
Retroactive interference (RI), 296, 299–300, 303, 305–310
Retrograde amnesia, 224–225
$R_{g}-S_{g}$ mechanism, 115–119

Savings measure of retention, 140
Schedules of reinforcement (*see also* Positive reinforcement)
  concurrent type, 95–96
  effects in instrumental paradigms, 84
  effects in operant paradigms, 92–96
  effects on extinction, 98, 121–126
  fixed interval type, 94–95
  fixed ratio type, 92–93
  variable interval type, 95
  variable ratio type, 93–94
Schema, 243–246
Secondary memory, 217, 225
Secondary reinforcement, *see* Reinforcement
Selective filter theory, *see* Broadbent's selective filter theory
Semantic generalization, 179–180
Semantic memory:
  description of, 248–249
  organization of, 250–257
Sensory memory store, *see* Sensory register
Sensory preconditioning, 37–38, 63–64
Sensory register, 198–199, 201–206
Serial exhaustive search, 264–266
Serial learning, 136–137
Serial position effect, 143–145
Serial self-terminating search, 264–266
Shadowing, 206
Shaping, 79–80
Sheffield's consummatory response hypothesis, 109–110
Short-term memory store:
  codes used in, 230–236
Short-term memory store (*continued*)
  in consolidation theory, 224
  description of, 198–200
  evidence for existence of, 211–216
  forgetting from, 292–298, 309–311
  in nonhuman species, 257–259
  retrieval from, 262–266
Short-term retention paradigm, 291
Signal, *see* Avoidance learning; Predictive relationships
Signal value, 35
Simultaneous conditioning, 23–24
Simultaneous contrast paradigm, *see* Contrast effects
Single process model of retrieval, 267–269
Skinner box, 78
Specific transfer, *see* Transfer
Spence's continuity theory of discrimination, 181–185
Spence's fractional anticipatory goal response hypothesis, 115–119
Spontaneous recovery, 44, 96, 302–306 (*see also* Extinction)
Spreading activation model, 254–256 (*see also* Semantic memory)
Stage model of memory formation, *see* Atkinson–Shiffrin memory model
State-dependent learning, 278, 285
Stimulus control, 180
Stimulus differentiation, 164
Stimulus dimension, 170
Stimulus generalization, 116, 122, 149, 167–180, 186
  in Capaldi's sequential theory of extinction, 122
  in concept learning, 186
  defined, 168
  measures of, 169–171
  in paired associates learning, 149
  in Spence's fractional anticipatory goal response hypothesis, 116
  theories of, 177–180
  variables that affect, 171–176
Stimulus generalization gradients:
  absolute, 170–171
  excitatory, 170
  inhibitory, 170–172
  relative, 170–171
  shallow, 169–170
  slope of, 169
  steep, 169–170
Stimulus term, 138
Storage, 197, 200, 216, 224–225
Straight runway, 74–75
Study–test procedure, 137
Subjective organization, 151–152
Successive contrast paradigm, *see* Contrast effects
Suffix effect, 205
Summation test for conditioned inhibition, 40–43
Superstitious behavior, 80
Suppression ratio, 20–22
Switching experiments, 67, 285
Symbolic matching-to-sample, 258–259

Taste aversion paradigm, 25, 30–33, 58, 60–62

Teachable language comprehender (TLC), 250–254 (*see also* Semantic memory)
Temporal lobe, 215
Text base, 240–241
Thorndike–Hull view of reinforcement, 112–115
Time-out period, 94
Tip-of-the-tongue (TOT) phenomenon, 274–275
Trace strength hypothesis, 311
Transfer, 139, 158–165
  defined, 139, 158
  explanations of, 163–165
  negative form of, 159
  nonspecific form of, 159–160
  paradigms for studying, 161–163
  positive form of, 159
  specific form of, 160–165
  zero form of, 159
Transfer paradigms, *see* Transfer
Trials-to-criterion score, 137
Trigrams, *see* Nonsense syllables
Truly random control procedure, 58
Two-factor theory of avoidance, *see* Avoidance learning
Two-factor theory of interference:
  description of, 301–303
  evidence pertaining to, 303–306
Two-way avoidance paradigm, *see* Avoidance learning

Unconditioned response (UR):
  conditioning in absence of, 63–64
  defined, 16–18
  as an element in the learned association, 62–66
  relation to the CR, 64
Unconditioned stimulus (US):
  conditioning in the absence of, 36–38
Unconditioned stimulus (US) (*continued*)
  correlation with the CS, 25–27
  defined, 16–18
  as an element in the learned association, 62–66
  intensity of, 27–28
  number of pairings with the CS, 27
  prior experience with, 28–29
  relatedness with the CS, 29–32
  surprisingness of, 52–57, 59–60
  temporal arrangement with the CS, 23–25
Unlearning, 301
Unsignaled avoidance situation, *see* Avoidance learning
US pre-exposure effect, 28–29, 56–57

Variable interval schedule, *see* Schedules of reinforcement
Variable ratio schedule, *see* Schedules of reinforcement
Verbal learning, 135–165
  effect of item characteristics on, 146–150
  effect of procedural variables on, 140–146
  effect of subject strategies on, 150–158
  paradigms for studying, 136–138
  retention of, 139–140
  transfer of, 139, 158–165
  types of items used in, 138–139
Visual codes, *see* Memory codes

Wagner's priming theory, 58–62
Warmup effect, 159–160
Working memory, 198–200

Zero transfer, *see* Transfer